**Cases in
Public Education
Leadership**

Managing
School Districts
for High Performance

**Cases in
Public Education
Leadership**

Managing School Districts
for High Performance

Editors

Stacey Childress

Richard F. Elmore

Allen S. Grossman

Susan Moore Johnson

Harvard Education Press
Cambridge, Massachusetts

Library of Congress Control Number 20079323116

Paperback ISBN 978-1-891792-49-6
Library Edition ISBN 978-1-891792-75-5

Published by Harvard Education Press,
an imprint of the Harvard Education Publishing Group

Harvard Education Press
8 Story Street
Cambridge, MA 02138

Cover: YayDesign

The typefaces used in this book are Bembo and Univers.

Contents

MODULE I
Making Coherence Concrete

MODULE II
Finding and Supporting Personnel

MODULE III
Building a High-Performing Organization

MODULE IV
Managing Schools across Differences

MODULE V
Sustaining High Performance over Time

Introduction

This course book is intended to be used by current and future public school district leaders. It addresses the challenges they face as they work to ensure that all students have rich learning opportunities and achieve at high levels throughout a system of schools. Pockets of excellence exist in all school districts—spectacular classes in otherwise dreary schools and stunning schools in mediocre districts. However, to truly serve all students and meet the demands of the new accountability environment, leaders at all levels of a school district must find a way for such pockets of excellence to become the norm, rather than the exception, throughout their organization.

The work of school and district leaders has changed dramatically and rapidly, due to the demands of external accountability, including standards-based reforms at the state level and the federal No Child Left Behind Act of 2001. In the past, public educators valued well-intentioned efforts and lauded heroic leaders who were visible, active, and worked tirelessly on behalf of students and schools. But new public expectations now require them to be responsible for results, not simply appearances or best efforts.

This shift of attention to the learning outcomes of all students means that responsibility for better teaching and learning must be shared widely. School districts are complicated organizations, and they rarely improve in response to simple mandates that call for uniform compliance. If reforms are to work, they must be carefully adapted for each community, school, and classroom. Because everyone has a role to play in improving the academic performance of all students, leadership must be distributed throughout the district.[1] However, for distributed leadership to be effective, teachers, principals, central office administrators, school board members, and teachers union leaders must understand the nested nature of school organizations.

The most important work in a district happens in classrooms, where teachers work with their students to master challenging academic content. However, the classroom does not stand alone. It is nested within a school, where teachers must collaborate and coordinate their curriculum and teaching so that students experience a coherent academic program over time. Schools, in turn, are nested within districts, which are uniquely positioned to ensure equity and to increase the capacity of all schools—not just some—to succeed. Educators in all roles need to understand how to work productively across the various levels of this nested system so that they can achieve excellent results for all students. They need to anticipate how their decisions will affect their colleagues' work and what their actions ultimately mean for student learning.

Just when requirements for high academic performance are increasing, large numbers of principals and superintendents have begun to retire, creating a demand for new, skilled, and committed leaders. This opens public education to the next generation of school and district leaders, who are eager to learn new strategies for achieving high-quality outcomes for all students. This book is designed to prepare them for these challenges.

The PELP Coherence Framework

The concept of organizational coherence is at the center of this book. Basically, organizational coherence means that the various parts of a school district are designed so that they work in sync with one another to achieve district goals. This concept grew out of our work with the Public Education Leadership Project at Harvard University (PELP), a collaboration among faculty members at Harvard's graduate schools of business and education in partnership with a network of urban school districts. Through this project, we identified five common managerial challenges that urban districts face as they seek to implement a strategy for improving performance:

1. Implementing the strategy effectively across schools with different characteristics

2. Redesigning the organization so that it supports the strategy

3. Developing and managing human capital to carry out the strategy

4. Allocating resources in alignment with the strategy

5. Using performance data for decision making, organizational learning, and accountability

The district leaders we talked with, however, tended to see each of the five challenges as a separate problem rather than as related parts of a larger problem or solution. For example, effectively developing teachers' skills involves using timely, detailed, student performance data to highlight areas where teachers need to change or improve their instructional techniques. Similarly, allocating resources in ways that are aligned with students' specific learning needs is essential to

ensure that a strategy can be implemented in meaningful ways in different sorts of schools.

Rather than focusing our research and case-writing on these separate challenges, we developed the PELP Coherence Framework (PCF) to help leaders recognize the interdependence of various aspects of their school district—its culture, systems and structures, resources, stakeholder relationships, and environment—and to understand how they reinforce one another to support the implementation of an improvement strategy. The framework helps leaders use organizational design, human capital management, resource allocation, and accountability and performance improvement systems in coherent ways so that they can implement their strategy. This book brings together more than twenty of the cases and readings we developed over four years to illustrate these ideas.

The framework has roots in what business has taught us about organizational alignment. However, that knowledge has been elaborated by what we know about reform in education. Throughout its development, the framework has been informed by our interactions with senior leaders of large urban districts who face unique managerial challenges because of the size and complexity of their school systems, and often because of the poverty of the communities they serve as well. Putting a districtwide strategy into practice requires building a coherent organization that connects to teachers' work in classrooms and enables people at all levels to carry out their part of the strategy. The framework identifies the organizational elements critical to high performance and poses a series of diagnostic questions about each element, all in an effort to bring them into coherence with the strategy and with each other. The elements of the framework are the instructional core, strategy, culture, structure, systems, resources, stakeholder relationships, and the environment.

Strategy and the Instructional Core: At the center of the framework is the instructional core,

PELP Coherence Framework

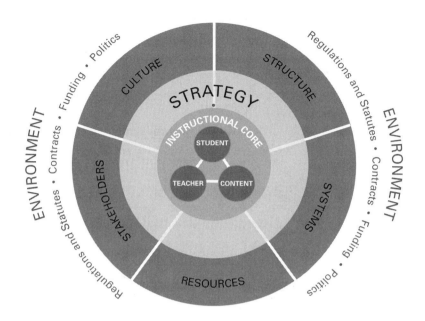

herence at the district, school, and classroom levels will make a district's chosen approach more effective and sustainable.

Most other organizational decisions, resources, and activities should be directed toward supporting the district's strategy to make the core more powerful and effective. The other elements of the framework are aspects of the organization that must be brought into coherence with the strategy and each other.

Culture: Culture consists of the norms and behaviors in an organization; in other words, everyone's shared understanding of "how things work around here." Culture, whether strong or weak, does not change readily in response to edicts or slogans. Rather, it is reshaped gradually by changes in many individuals' practices and beliefs. When district leaders take specific actions, such as redefining roles or relationships, altering performance expectations, or using job assignments in creative ways, they send signals about which behaviors they value and desire throughout the organization. Over time they can upend an entrenched counterproductive culture and see it replaced by a productive one.

The public education sector has long had a culture that valued effort—or the appearance of effort—more than results. As long as people seemed to be working hard, they could go about their business without being asked to work with colleagues or to be accountable for their students' performance. At its worst, this type of culture can lead to defeatism among teachers and administrators ("I taught it, but they didn't learn it"). In today's accountability environment, how-

which represents the critical work of teaching and learning that goes on in classrooms. The core includes three interdependent components: teachers' knowledge and skill, students' engagement in their own learning, and academically challenging content.[2] Surrounding the instructional core is strategy—the set of actions a district deliberately undertakes to strengthen the instructional core with the objective of increasing student learning and performance districtwide. In order to make teaching and learning more effective, a district's improvement strategy must articulate how it will strengthen and support the instructional core through integrated activities that increase teachers' knowledge and skill, change the students' role in the teaching and learning process, and ensure that curriculum is aligned with benchmarks for performance. However, *how* each district strengthens and supports the core may vary. In other words, two districts may design very different but equally effective strategies. The PELP Coherence Framework, rather than prescribing a particular strategy, asserts that organizational co-ever, successful districts must develop a culture of collaboration, high expectations, and accountability throughout their schools.

Structure: Structure includes how people are organized, who has responsibility and accountability for results, and who makes or influences decisions. Districts usually develop their organizational structures haphazardly to support generation after generation of reform efforts, and then leave them in place long after the reform fad they were built for has passed from the scene. As a result, a district's structure often constrains rather than enables high performance and must be reinvented to support the implementation of an improvement strategy.

Systems: School districts manage themselves through a variety of important systems. In the same way that circulatory and nervous systems perform vital processes inside the skeletal structure of living organisms, an organization's systems provide the means by which important work flows through its structure. Some systems are formally designed by the district, while others emerge informally through practice. Whether formal or informal, the purpose of systems is to increase the district's efficiency and effectiveness in implementing strategy.

Systems are built around such important functions as career development and promotion, compensation, student assignment, resource allocation, organizational learning, and measurement and accountability. Effective systems are even-handed and efficient, eliminating the need for individuals to "reinvent the wheel" or "know the right people" to get important things done.

Resources: Money is usually the first thing leaders think about when resources are mentioned, and money is obviously important. But organizational resources also include people, time, and other assets such as technology and data. District leaders must allocate the full range of resources in ways that are coherent with the district's strategy if it is to be implemented effec-

tively. This means being disciplined about which current and planned activities receive necessary resources and, just as importantly, which do not. Because district resources are usually quite constrained, freeing up the resources necessary to fully invest in activities that are crucial to and coherent with the strategy usually means cutting off the flow to others.

Stakeholder Relationships: Stakeholders are people and groups inside and outside the organization who have a legitimate interest in the schools and can influence the success of the district's strategy. These include teachers unions, parents, students, school boards, community and advocacy groups, and local politicians and policymakers. Conducting and managing stakeholder relationships in a way that is coherent with the strategy is especially challenging because stakeholders often disagree about what success looks like or how to achieve it. However, effective strategies are informed by the views and priorities of such groups. In moving ahead, district leaders must either persuade a majority of stakeholder groups about the wisdom of their strategy or build a sufficient alliance among some that will prevent the others from becoming a disruptive force.

Environment: A school district's environment includes all of the external factors that can have an impact on strategy, operations, and performance. The environment in which public school districts operate is especially complex and dynamic, including the various funding sources available (both public and private); the political and policy contexts at the city, state, and national levels; the collective bargaining arrangements that are in place; and the characteristics of the particular community.

While district leaders have little direct control over the environment, they must spend significant time trying to manage its effects in order to consistently implement a districtwide strategy. The environment can affect a school system by enforcing nonnegotiable demands, constraining decisionmaking, reducing resources, evaluating performance, and imposing sanctions. However, the environment can also serve as an enabler if district leaders can promote an understanding of the schools' needs and thus influence the regulatory and statutory, contractual, financial, and political forces that surround them.

Content and Organization of This Volume

This book is organized into five modules that contain cases about leaders in real organizations working on real performance problems. Most of the modules begin with a case about a private-sector company or nonprofit organization that introduces the ideas presented in the module. Our extensive use of these cases shows that introducing a new concept in a noneducation setting and then exploring the same ideas more deeply through relevant cases based in public school districts is a powerful learning combination.

Each module has its own set of learning objectives, and all five modules fit together to explore overall concepts of strategy and coherence, as well as more specific areas such as human resource management and accountability. Every module has a set of questions to consider as you read and discuss all of the pieces, and each case within a module has its own set of discussion questions to help guide your preparation. Your instructor will assign work in each module to support an overarching set of course goals.

- *Module I* introduces the concepts of strategy and coherence through a series of cases and a conceptual note. This content sets the stage for the remaining modules in the book.

- *Module II* addresses the importance of strategic human resource management in building a high-performing district. The cases in this module explore the elements of a sound human resource system, including ways of recruiting and hiring people and developing

their skills in order to support a district's strategy for improving student learning.

- *Module III* takes up the challenge of becoming a results-oriented organization through cases that illustrate using performance data for accountability and learning, creating a performance-based compensation system, and building and managing a strong organizational culture in order to enhance district performance.

- *Module IV* highlights the difficulty of implementing a strategy consistently across a number of schools that are different from one another. It also offers a set of cases that demonstrate some emerging approaches currently underway in organizations dealing with this challenge.

- *Module V* offers the opportunity to put together all of the ideas in the first four modules by exploring two districts that have had relative success over a number of years but are now faced with trying to sustain and accelerate their student learning outcomes.

Learning and the Case Method

For many, learning by the case method is a new experience. Rather than having participants encounter abstract theories or research findings, this approach immerses them in real-world situations. Each case has been chosen or written because it illustrates important problems, practices, or concepts. In reading and discussing a case in the context of these larger ideas, participants can see the relationship between theory and practice. Importantly, the participants who read and discuss a case are not asked to be interested bystanders but are challenged to diagnose the situation the case presents and propose a course of action as if they were the protagonist. Since many cases hinge on an important decision that must be made, participants have the opportunity to develop an approach that is consistent both with the facts of the case and with the larger concepts or theories it illustrates and to test out that approach with others.

Unlike the case studies that are included in many textbooks on school administration, these cases are not meant to be examples of either best or worst practice. Many include some promising practices, but none should be seen as a template to be taken and applied to another setting. Like the real world they come from, the cases often are messy, with irrational people and unexpected complications. Thus, thinking like a leader or manager in one of these cases requires coping with the limitations and realities of everyday life in organizations, diagnosing what works well, what does not, and what a real leader in a real district might do about it. As a group, the cases and readings are designed to help students build a habit of mind of thinking coherently about district strategy and organization.

It is important to leave yourself plenty of time to prepare for a case discussion. Each case includes discussion questions to serve as guides for your analysis. Good preparation typically requires reading the case several times. First, one might read to understand the central issue, the actors, and the chronology of events. One might then examine the materials in the appendix to see how they are relevant to the events of and decisions made in the case. Next it would be important to read the case again, focusing this time on the decision or action that is called for. You may find it helpful to discuss your ideas about the case with a small group of colleagues (a study group) before the in-class case discussion. This allows participants to verify their understanding of the facts of the case and to give their proposals for action a trial run in a small setting.

In class discussions, the participant is a member of a learning community that works together to examine the facts, consider the underlying concepts, and explore and assess alternative actions. Finding the "right" answer or "cracking the case" is not the goal of a good case discussion, since there is little to be learned through

such an approach. Rather, the goal is to practice informed diagnosis, thoughtful planning, and critical reflection on what works and why.

The piece that follows is a well-regarded introduction to learning by the case method that has been used for decades at the Harvard Business School to help orient new graduate students and executive education participants to the pedagogy. Rather than invent our own introduction, we adapted this classic slightly for use by current and future school system leaders and included it in this volume to help them get off to a good start. Our hope is that our readers will find it useful as they begin their journey into the case method.

Notes

1. J. P. Spillane, "State and Local Government Relations in the Era of Standards-Based Reform: Standards, State Policy Instruments, and Local Instructional Policy-making," *Educational Policy* 13 (1999); Richard F. Elmore, "Building a New Structure for School Leadership," Washington, DC: Albert Shanker Institute, 2000.

2. David K. Cohen and Deborah Loewenberg Ball, "Instruction, Capacity, and Improvement," CPRE Research Report Series RR-43, Philadelphia: University of Pennsylvania, Consortium for Policy Research in Education, 1999.

John S. Hammond

Learning by the Case Method:
A Note for Education Administrators

The case method is not only a relevant and practical way to learn leadership and managerial skills, it is also exciting and fun. But, it can also be confusing if you don't know much about it. This note is designed to remove the confusion by explaining how the case method works and then to suggest how you can get the most out of it.

Simply stated, the case method calls for discussion of real-life situations that leaders and managers have faced. Case writers, as good reporters, have written up these situations to present you with the information available to the executives involved. As you review the case, you will put yourself in the shoes of the managers, analyze the situations, decide what you would do, and come to class prepared to defend and support your conclusions.

How Cases Help You Learn

Cases will help you sharpen your analytical skills, since you must produce quantitative and qualitative evidence for your recommendations. In case discussions, instructors will challenge you and your fellow participants to defend your arguments and analysis. You will hone both your problem-solving and your ability to think and reason rigorously.

Because case studies cut across a range of organizations and situations, they provide you with an exposure far greater than you are likely to experience in your day-to-day routine. They also permit you to build knowledge in various management subjects by dealing selectively and intensively with problems in each field. You will quickly recognize that the problems you face as a manager are not unique to one organization or industry. From this you will develop a more professional sense of management.

In class discussions, participants bring to bear their expertise, experience, observations, analyses, and rules of thumb. What each class member brings to identifying the central problems in a case, analyzing them, and proposing solutions is as important as the content of the case itself. The lessons of experience are tested as different participants present and defend their analyses, each gained by different experiences and

Professor John S. Hammond prepared the original version of this note building on earlier notes by professors E. Raymond Corey and Martin Marshall of the Harvard Business School. Lecturer Stacey Childress made minor edits to this version to adapt it for education administrators for the Public Education Leadership Project at Harvard University.

attitudes gained by working in different jobs. Your classmates and you will differ significantly on what's important and how to deal with common problems, interdependencies, organizational needs, and the impact of decisions in one sector of the organization on other sectors. Perhaps the most important benefit of using cases is that they help leaders and managers determine what the real problem[1] is and to ask the right questions. An able organizational leader once said, "Ninety percent of the task of a top manager is to ask useful questions. Answers are relatively easy to find, but asking good questions is the most critical skill. The discussion questions suggested for each case are just to help you focus on certain aspects of the case. In presenting them the faculty is not preempting your task of identifying the problems in the case. You still must ask yourself: "What really are the problems that the manager has to resolve?" Too often in real-life situations managers manipulate facts and figures without the problems having been specifically defined.

A final benefit that the faculty seeks is to re-invigorate the sense of fun and excitement that comes with being a manager. You will once again sense that being a manager is a great challenge—intellectually, politically, and socially.

In short, the case method is really a focused form of learning by doing.

How to Prepare a Case

The use of the case method calls first for you, working individually, to carefully read and think about each case (two hours of preparation time for each case is a good rule of thumb). No single way of preparing a case works well for everyone. However, here are some general guidelines that you can adapt to create a method that works best for you.

1. *Read the first few paragraphs, then go through the case almost as fast as you can turn the pages,* asking yourself, "What, broadly, is the case about, and what types of information am I being given to analyze?" You will find that the text description at the beginning is almost always followed by a series of exhibits that contain added quantitative and qualitative information for your analysis.

2. *Read the case very carefully, underlining key facts and making marginal notes as you go.* Then ask yourself, "What are the basic problems these managers have to resolve?" Try hard to put yourself in the position of the managers in the case. Make the managers' *problems* your problems.

3. *Note the key problems or issues* on a pad of paper. Then go through the case again.

4. *Sort out the relevant considerations for each problem area.*

5. *Do appropriate qualitative and quantitative analysis.*

6. *Develop a set of recommendations, supported by your analysis of the case data.*

Until now, your best results will come if you have worked by yourself. However, if you have time, it is useful before class to engage in informal discussions with some of your fellow participants about the cases. This can be done at social hours, meals, or planned get-togethers. (Discussion groups are important enough to be mandatory scheduled activities in many executive education programs.) The purpose of these discussions is *not* to develop a consensus or "group" position; it is to help members refine, adjust and amplify their own thinking.

To maximize the benefit to you of this group process it is extremely important not to skip or skimp on the individual preparation beforehand. If you take the easy way out and just familiarize yourself with the facts, saving all preparation to be done with your discussion group, you will deprive yourself of the opportunity to practice the very skills that you wanted to obtain when you enrolled.

What Happens in Class

In class, usually your instructor will allow participants to discuss whatever aspects of the case they wish. The faculty's job is to facilitate the discussion, to pose questions, prod, draw out people's reasoning, play the devil's advocate, and highlight issues. A healthy debate and discussion will ensue. You will benefit most if you participate actively in this debate. Sometimes faculty will present conceptual frameworks and invite you to use them to organize your thoughts and to create new insights. Other times they'll generalize, summarize, or tell about relevant situations in other organizations.

They'll try to keep the discussion on track and moving forward. To do this, they'll usually organize and document the ongoing debate on the blackboard. While faculty may suggest the pros and cons of a particular action, only occasionally will they give their own views. Their job isn't to help the class reach a consensus; in fact, often the thought process will be far more important than the conclusions. Near the end, instructors will summarize the discussion and draw out the useful lessons and observations which are inherent in the case situation and which will emerge from the case discussion.

A typical request at the end of a case discussion is, "What's the answer?" The case method of learning does not provide *the* answer. Rather, various participants in the discussion will have developed and supported *several* viable "answers."

> [Management] is not, at least not yet, an exact science. There is no single demonstrably right answer to an organizational problem. For the student [of management], it cannot be a matter of peeking in the back of a book to see if he or she arrived at the right solution. In every situation, there is always a reasonable possibility that the best answer has not yet been found—even by teachers.[2]

Sometimes when the faculty knows the outcome of the case they will share it with you at the end of the discussion. While it is fascinating to know how things turned out, the outcome isn't the answer either. It is simply one more answer, which you may feel is better or worse than yours. What is important is that *you* know what you would do in that situation, and most importantly, *why,* and that your skill at arriving at such conclusions has been enhanced.

You can't acquire judgment or skill simply by reading books or listening to lectures any more than you can become a great swimmer simply by reading a book on swimming. While the knowledge obtained from books and lectures can be valuable, the real gains come from practice at analyzing real situations.

How You Can Get the Most Out of the Process

There are a number of things you can do to get the most out of the process.

1. *Prepare.* Not only is a thorough individual preparation of each case a great learning experience, it is key to being an active participant in the case discussion.

2. *Discuss the cases with others beforehand.* As mentioned earlier, this will refine your reasoning. It's not cheating, it's encouraged. However, you'll be cheating yourself if you don't prepare thoroughly before such discussions.

3. *Participate.* In class, actively express your views and challenge others. Learning by talking may seem contrary to how you learned in other settings. You may have been urged to be silent and learn from others, especially the faculty. In case discussions, when you express your views to others, you commit which, in turn, gets you involved. Talking forces you to decide; you can no longer hedge.

4. *Share your related experience.* During class if you are aware of situation that relates to the topic being discussed and it would enrich the discussion, tell about it. So-called war stories heighten the relevance of the topic.

5. *Constantly relate the topic and case at hand to your sector* no matter how remote the connection seems at first. Don't tune out because of a possible disconnect. You *can* learn *a lot* about human resources in public education by studying about human resources in the airline industry, and vice versa. It's not a matter of whether it relates, but how.

6. *Apply what you are learning to your own specific management situations, past and future.* This will greatly heighten relevance. Even better is to pick a situation that you know you will face in the future where you could productively use some good ideas. For example, how might I build an effective accountability system for a school or a district? Make note of each good idea from the discussion that helps. Not only will these ideas improve the outcome of your future endeavors, they will stick in your mind forever because they were learned in the context of something important to you.

7. *Note what clicks.* Different people with different backgrounds, skills, and styles will take different things out of the discussion. Your notes will appropriately be quite different from your neighbors'.

8. *Mix it up.* Use the discussion as an opportunity to get to know intriguing people with different points of view. Get to know them outside of class and continue your learning there.

9. *Try to better understand and enhance your own management style.* By hearing so many other approaches to a given management situation you will be exposed to many styles and thereby better understand your own. This understanding will put you in a better position to improve it.

You will learn from rigorous discussion and controversy. Each member of the class—and the instructor—assumes a responsibility for preparing the case and for contributing ideas to the case discussion. The rewards for these responsibilities are a series of highly exciting, practically oriented education experiences that bring out a wide range of topics and viewpoints.

Notes

1. See, for example, Hammond, Keeney, and Raiffa, *Smart Choices: A Practical Guide to Making Better Decisions,* Cambridge, MA: Harvard Business School Press, 1999, especially Chapter 2.

2. Charles I. Gragg, "Because Wisdom Can't Be Told," HBS Case No. 9–451–005.

Making Coherence Concrete

Today's accountability pressures require public school districts to meet ambitious performance improvement goals in all schools, regardless of their past performance or current capacity to improve. High-performing classrooms and schools exist in virtually every district, but no large urban district has figured out how to ensure that all of its schools—not just some—achieve high levels of learning for all students.

Why is this so? Reform efforts of the last three decades have primarily targeted classrooms and schools. Without question, the most difficult and important work in a district happens in classrooms as teachers work with their students to master challenging academic content. But in order to increase the effectiveness of teaching and learning in every classroom and school, the district office must become an architect of improvement—clearly a monumental task. Consider the sheer complexity of a large urban school district. They serve tens of thousands of students whose learning needs vary tremendously. Very strong—and vocal—stakeholders often disagree with one another about what success looks like. Elected officials often pursue policies that are disconnected from student perfor-

mance, are unrealistic given available resources, conflict with one another, or all of the above. Operating under these conditions, district leaders find it extremely difficult to improve student performance throughout their districts. They are tempted to pursue the latest hot ideas for transforming education and to make decisions that are politically expedient rather than managerially sound. As a result, districts often wind up with a slew of unrelated initiatives that collectively consume massive resources but end up accomplishing little.

As we explained in the introduction to this volume, leaders must develop a districtwide strategy for improving teaching and learning and then design and manage the entire organization in a coherent way that strengthens and supports the strategy. When leaders fail to achieve organizational coherence, the system does not work well for anyone—students, teachers, administrators, or parents.

If annual planning and resource allocation systems do not support shared goals across schools, teachers and principals will find ways to take care of their own classrooms and buildings. Principals who have longstanding relationships with central office administrators might succeed more often than their newer colleagues, thus creating or reinforcing inequities across the system. A principal who knows the right person in the central office will be able to have classroom computers networked quickly, while one who doesn't might wait a year.

If professional development is fragmented and uncoordinated, it will be disconnected from the district's instructional objectives and therefore irrelevant to the day-to-day work that people are expected to perform. When this happens, staff members do not receive the support they need to work effectively within the districtwide strategy, and they retreat to their schools and classrooms in relative isolation to do their best work independent of the districtwide strategy. The result is that while the performance problems remain widely shared, the knowledge and skill necessary to improve performance is widely dispersed. In the end, students bear the costs created by the lack of coherence. The fundamental task for leaders around the district is to create an organization in which people are supported and are held accountable for a common set of expectations and goals. Only then can a district become a system of high-performing schools that serve the learning needs of all students.

Leaders who have developed districtwide strategies for improving the achievement of all students know how daunting it is to implement them across an entire school district. In our work with district leadership teams over the last several years, we observed something striking about the way team members thought about their managerial challenges. They identified the challenges easily, but most viewed them as distinct issues to be solved one by one. For instance, Human Resources had sole responsibility for hiring new teachers, while a curriculum and instruction department was exclusively responsible for teacher professional development. Instead of this fragmented approach, district leaders must

design and manage their organizations as integrated systems in which challenges are interdependent parts of a whole that is directly linked to the work of teachers and students in classrooms. The PELP Coherence Framework (PCF) was designed to explain how the parts of a district should work together so that they are consistent with each other and support the implementation of the strategy.

The PCF consists of the organizational elements that a leader must consider when designing a districtwide strategy to improve performance. As mentioned in the introductory chapter, such a strategy must be focused on strengthening the instructional core. The instructional core includes teachers' knowledge and skill, students' engagement in their own learning, and academically challenging content. Once a strategy is developed, a district's culture, systems and structures, resources, stakeholders, and environment must be designed and managed in such a way that they are coherent with the strategy and with one another. Module I includes a number of cases that provide a foundation for you to think in new ways about accomplishing this task, as well as a reading that explains the framework in detail.

Learning Objectives

Because Module I introduces the concept of strategy and organizational coherence, we suggest the following learning objectives for this module:

- Understand the concepts of strategy and coherence and become familiar with the PELP Coherence Framework

- Use the PCF as a diagnostic tool to assess the strategy and coherence of a number of school districts that are pursuing different districtwide strategies and that are at various stages of their reform cycles

Cases

Module I begins by introducing the concepts of strategy and coherence in a private-sector company. "Taco Bell, Inc., 1983–1994" follows a company over a ten-year period as it evolves its strategy and attempts to design and manage its headquarters and field offices in ways that support each phase of the strategy. "Bristol City Schools" adapts the coherence concepts from Taco Bell to public education, allowing for the diagnosis of a large urban district struggling with the implementation of a districtwide strategy.

The "Note on the PELP Coherence Framework" provides an in-depth yet practical explanation of the PCF, illuminates the concepts introduced in Taco Bell and Bristol City, and provides a framework for diagnosis and action planning that will be useful throughout all of the modules in the book.

To wrap up the opening module, "Pursuing Educational Equity at San Francisco Unified School District" demonstrates a school superintendent's efforts to bring the district's stakeholders, culture, systems, structures, resources, and environment into coherence with a strategy to increase overall achievement levels around the district while narrowing the performance gap for minority and low-income students over several years.

Discussion Questions

The following questions will serve as a guide to identifying the common ideas embedded in the case series in this module:

1. Evaluate the degree to which each organization in Module I has achieved organizational coherence with its strategy. What are the factors contributing to their coherence or lack thereof?

2. Are some of the framework elements easier to change than others? For example, is it more difficult to create a culture of accountability or to implement a well-defined accountability system? Why? What are the managerial implications of your answer?

3. How are the managerial choices the case protagonists make about any one element of the framework interrelated with the strategy and the other framework elements?

Taco Bell Inc. (1983–1994)

When John Martin, President and CEO, joined Taco Bell in 1983, he found himself at the helm of a chain of Mexican fast-food restaurants with an appropriate logo—a man sleeping under a sombrero. Having made a career in the fast-food industry as president of La Petite Boulangerie, Hardee's Food Systems and Burger Chef, Martin believed he could wake the man under the sombrero. The question remained, however, as to whether Martin could make him dance to parent PepsiCo's demanding beat. John Martin reflected on those early days:

> Our biggest problem was that we didn't know what we were. We thought maybe we were in the Mexican food business . . . The reality was, we were in the fast-food business, and by not understanding who we were, who our potential customer was, we were just slightly missing the mark.

Company and Industry Background

The fast-food market, which had grown substantially during the 1960s and 1970s, was showing signs of maturing by the early 1980s (see Exhibit 1 for statistics on the fast-food industry in the early 1980s). Competition had become more intense as industry participants fought aggressively for every point of market share. In 1982, Taco Bell, a $700 million fast-food chain, had 1,489 restaurants, 60% of which were franchised units. The company had 40% of the Mexican fast-food market,[1] but a negligible market share of total fast-food. Martin knew that if his company was going to compete with its much larger, more established rivals, he would have to make significant changes.

In the early 1980s, production at Taco Bell was labor-intensive and used low levels of technology. Suppliers delivered fresh, raw food to each restaurant several times a week. Managers and crew members used their time before opening and during lulls in demand to clean and prepare ingredients for menu items. Assembly occurred when customers ordered. Because corporate headquarters stressed food control and customer demand was difficult to predict, there were often shortages of prepared raw ingredients (chopped tomatoes, shredded lettuce, etc.), which resulted in significant delays for customers.

Cooking was also done on-site. Variations in who was cooking and the sometimes frenetic pace often led to inconsistent spicing and stirring. As a result, taste and food quality could vary dramatically even within an individual restaurant. Areas dedicated to food preparation and cooking took up about 70% of the floor plan in a typical Taco Bell restaurant. Even though 50% of some competitors sales were delivered out of drive-through windows, Taco Bell had none in the early 1980s.

The food assembly line in the kitchen lay parallel to and directly behind the customer service area. As customers waited to place their orders and receive their food, they watched the backsides of crew members as they frenetically assembled each order. One Taco Bell executive referred to this sight as "the good, the bad, and the ugly."

Cashiers took orders and wrote them manually on a plastic board. As the production crew read and filled the orders, cashiers erased existing orders before moving on to the next customer. The system resulted in frequent fulfillment errors.

Within the restaurants, restaurant managers (RMs), assistant restaurant managers (ARMs), and shift supervisors were directly involved with receiving fresh food shipments each week, overseeing food preparation throughout the day, ensuring customer service, overseeing clean-up, and lending a hand when necessary—particularly during meal-time rush hours. RMs also faced the time-consuming task of manually developing work crew schedules in a business with an annual turnover rate of 220%. Taco Bell's manual systems, which were also used for placing orders and performing other administrative tasks, led to significant oversights and errors, provided no data for management analysis, and forced employees to spend a great deal of time in repetitive, paper-intensive, non-value-added tasks.

RMs reported directly to district managers (DMs), who often played the role of policeman, pointing out problems in restaurants and ensuring that corporate standards were maintained (see Exhibit 2 for a summary of Taco Bell's line organization in 1983). They regularly performed "white glove" inspections of the physical restaurants and audits of the financial books, often creating antagonistic relationships with their RMs, who they spent almost no time coaching or developing.

1983–1988: Establishing Direction and Implementing Incremental Change

Starting in 1983, John Martin began a series of changes in the Taco Bell organization designed to alter the company's mind-set, as well as its capabilities for pursuing a strategy to compete with the major fast-food chains. The first thing he did was to modernize Taco Bell's physical units. These changes included remodeling the restaurants, increasing seating capacity, adding drive-through windows, installing new signs, and outfitting employees in more contemporary uniforms. The company also added new menu items, including Nachos, Taco Salad, Mexican Pizza, Double Beef Burrito Supreme, Seafood Salad, and Soft-Shell Tacos.[2]

In addition, Martin accelerated the company's growth, averaging 249 new stores per year from 1983 to 1988, an increase from less than 100 units per year that had been added in the late 1970s. This expansion also extended Taco Bell's geographic presence into the Midwest, Southeast, and Northeast. In the process, the company replaced its old 1,600-square-foot mission-style restaurants with more modern 2,000-square-foot units.

During the same period, the parallel food assembly line was replaced by a double assembly line perpendicular to the customer service area. This improved product flow, increased capacity, and made serving easier in the drive-through windows that were being installed. The Plexiglas boards used for writing orders were also replaced by electronic point-of-sale systems (cash registers). These were tied to television monitors over the food assembly line, which indicated what had been ordered. The new electronic system allowed the company to track sales, product mix and inventory much more closely.

Training and development were also improved in the mid–1980s, although training for ARMs and RMs continued to reflect a human resource strategy predicated on very high turnover. Training for district managers, however, was not significantly changed. The head of operations training provided this overview:

> As to training, we were definitely a procedures, policies, and practices organization. We made sure each manager knew how to make every product, knew the appropriate weights for every product—by "knew" I mean had memorized. We were very operationally driven . . . there was a little work on staffing, but only at the crew level, dealing primarily with crew entry and exit.

1988–1991: Transforming the Business

The Mexican segment of upscale restaurants, fast-food, and supermarket food sales grew substantially during the 1980s. In the on-going battle for market share in the maturing fast-food industry, Taco Bell and its competitors began to introduce new products to attract customers. Some incremental business was generated by this strategy, but the new products also had a negative effect on kitchen efficiency, which influenced both costs and quality of service. The introduction of fajitas, for example, required new grills and exhaust systems costing Taco Bell $30 million. Reflecting on Taco Bell's market position in 1988,[3] Martin said:

> We were really a small player. One of the things that struck us was, perhaps we needed to figure out a different way to go about this—as opposed to trying to compete head-on with the big guys who had well-established, entrenched brands. Maybe instead of directly competing, maybe we ought to try to change the game a little bit . . .

> We're really not in the business of making food. We're in the business of feeding people.

Changing the Rules of the Game

Recognizing the industry's margin squeeze, Martin developed a new, more holistic business strategy focused on customer value. As part of the process of determining how to define value, in 1987, Martin commissioned a study to better understand what Taco Bell's best customers wanted from a fast-food restaurant. This was followed by another study in early 1989. The result of these two studies confirmed what Martin suspected from his years in the fast-food industry. Customers said they wanted FACT: fast-food Fast; fast-food orders Accurate;[4] fast-food served in a restaurant that was Clean; and fast-food at the appropriate Temperature.[5] FACT clarified that, at Taco Bell, a commitment to customer value required a fundamental change in management thinking; the organization needed to stop viewing quality and price as incompatible tradeoffs.

Armed with this information and in an effort to begin "changing the rules of the game," in early 1988, Taco Bell adopted a strategy of value pricing (see Exhibit 3) fully recognizing that, if the company was to dramatically lower prices while preserving quality, it would also have to dramatically reduce costs. To achieve these seemingly incompatible goals, Martin realized that incremental change would not work; a radical redefinition of the business was needed.

K-Minus and SOS

One of the most far-reaching changes implemented at Taco Bell during the late 1980s was an initiative called, K-Minus. With "K-Minus" (standing for kitchen minus), the restaurant kitchen became a heating and assembly unit. Virtually all chopping, cooking, and associated clean-up was transferred to corporate headquarters. Ground beef, chicken, and beans all arrived at the restaurant pre-cooked in plastic bags ready to be heated and served. Other food products, such as lettuce, tortillas, and even guacamole also arrived prepared, packaged and ready for use in assembling menu items. With this bold move, Taco Bell inverted the space configuration of their typical restaurant from a 70% kitchen/30% customer service ratio to 30% kitchen/70% customer service. In addition to enabling dramatic improvements in efficiency and much tighter control of the quality and consistency of its food, K-Minus also greatly expanded seating capacity within the restaurants and provided space to expand drive-through and other non–eat-in sales. A decrease in real estate expenses in proportion to sales and in aggregate labor costs resulted.

To meet customers' demand for speed and quality, Taco Bell also instituted its Speed of Service (SOS) program. This initiative redesigned processes still further and developed specific measures of performance. Recipes were reformulated and heated holding areas were developed. By 1990 Taco Bell restaurants could pre-assemble and hold 60% of their most popular menu items ready for immediate sale for up to 10 minutes. These additional changes increased peak hour transaction capacity by 54%, and reduced customer waiting times by 71%.

The Changing Role of the Restaurant Manager

While it was reconfiguring operations to cut costs and increase speed of delivery, Taco Bell also transformed the roles of its managers. A key point-person in implementing the strategy was the restaurant manager; this position was recast as restaurant general manager (RGM). Employees occupying this new role were expected to take on more decision making responsibility and accountability for their restaurant, developing staff and managing P&L. John Martin explained:

> The new role of the RGM was born in the notion of self-sufficiency. Restaurants can, in fact, operate by themselves. The bottom line is there's no rocket science in a fast-food

restaurant. . . . The difficulty is that you have 1,500 things all going on at once. . . . The typical top-down command and control can't deal with those things under any circumstances.

Taco Bell's senior vice president of human resources offered another view of the role changes:

> At the time we designed the new Taco Bell, in late 1989, we realized that we'd need a whole new people system. We were going to be asking people to do new things and we realized that we'd need new training, both in content and delivery. How we paid people would have to be different, and how we managed people would have to change. We'd go to more management by exception, more coaching, broadening spans, taking out layers. Communication would have to improve. The culture would have to change.
>
> There was a two- to three-year timeframe in which we significantly raised the bench on RGM skills. We went through an analysis of the caliber of the original RGMs, . . . and we determined that about one-third of our RGMs could grab the spirit of what we were trying to do at the restaurant level. Another third, with development and coaching could achieve the stated standard of performance. We thought that one-third could not make the mark.

To fill the new RGM role, Taco Bell began looking for people with skills and potential different than for the old restaurant manager's role. After a brief interview, an RGM candidate took a life-themes indicator test to identify the presence of traits necessary in RGMs. Individuals who were hired began a training program, which under the new strategy focused heavily on leadership and operating management skills. RGMs received training in operational policies and procedures, and five days of leadership training that covered topics such as situational leadership, coaching, managing conflict, restaurant communication systems, creative problem solving and decision making, and implementing change.

Transforming the District Manager's Role

The district manager's role at Taco Bell also changed under the new strategy. With a new title of "marketing manager," by 1990, district managers' spans of control had increased from 6 restaurants to 12. Despite the greatly increased responsibilities some marketing managers tried to retain their traditional "policeman approach" in dealing with RGMs. By 1991, however, the span of control for marketing managers was expanded to 20 restaurants, and they were virtually forced to begin managing by exception and to change from policeman to coach.

Many of the former district managers could not make the transition. To fill the vacancies, Taco Bell took the radical step of looking for talent outside the fast-food industry. They began recruiting sales and product managers with *Fortune* 500 company experience, and began to hire graduates from the top MBA programs in the country. Convinced they could teach these new general managers about the industry, senior management sought candidates with leadership and management skills who could coach and develop RGMs while also building the business in their area. On-going training for marketing managers was also enhanced. By 1990, six days of leadership training included a range of topics such as leadership practices, methods to create a shared vision, coaching, communication, adapting to change, technology/MIS, and finance.

Changing Incentives

Altering compensation and non-monetary reward systems was also critical to transforming middle management roles at Taco Bell. In 1989, the average base salary for restaurant managers was $28,700 with a $4,400 annual bonus, which was almost always paid. This compensation was standard in the fast-food industry, and unhappy

Taco Bell managers simply "walked across the street" to another fast-food chain. They had no commitment or sense of ownership to the company.

When the skill levels and responsibilities were increased in the new RGM's role, the average base salary was raised to $32,000 (with a range of $26,000 to $40,000). The target incentive bonus was increased to $12,000. Non-monetary compensation also played a key role in retaining managers, since monetary rewards peaked early in a successful RGM's career, Career paths, which traditionally had been very limited, were redesigned. For example, the RGM was no longer limited to managing a single restaurant. In the new organization, they were able to expand their job and increase their pay by opening new points of distribution[6] and building business through new channels.

Market manager compensation was also redesigned to attract more highly skilled individuals and to create incentives that would keep them challenged. In the late 1980s, the average district manager's salary had been $38,000 with an average bonus of $5,500. By 1991, the average base salary for marketing managers was $48,000. This excluded an expanding group of "hot shots" whose base averaged $60,000. The discrepancy was caused by the need to offer a higher base to more experienced managers recruited from outside the industry. Target bonuses for all marketing managers were $1,200 per unit supervised.

The leaner management organization created special concerns about career advancement for marketing managers. Instead of vertical advancement within the Taco Bell management hierarchy, success needed to be redefined. Potential career moves for market managers included either expanding their current job by growing the Taco Bell business in their area or assuming a new position within the expanding Taco Bell business. New positions included: becoming a manager at one of Taco Bell's larger restaurants (for example, Chevy's); assuming a position as an international market manager; or moving into product or business management in Taco Bell's new retail business.[7]

To support the job expansion career approach, Taco Bell created a very broad salary range for marketing managers. Movement through the range was determined by the strength of an individual's performance, the complexity of their market, and job tenure.

Creating Safety Nets

The new, lean Taco Bell had the potential for significant profit and growth if things ran smoothly, but it also had the potential for disaster if company standards were not maintained. With the removal of layers of management and frequent supervision of restaurants, new controls were implemented to ensure adherence to the company policies and value systems. There were three primary "safety nets."

- A toll-free telephone number was installed for customers to comment on Taco Bell's restaurants, food and service. Calls were answered by an external vendor that recorded comments and forwarded them to the relevant operations area.

- Mystery shopping was a second safety net. A mystery shopping service regularly sent individuals to rate restaurants on specific quality issues, and these reports were used in calculating bonuses for restaurant managers.

- Marketing surveys, also known as the customer intercept program, were conducted by teams of Taco Bell employees who would arrive unannounced at a restaurant and spend the day asking customers to fill out brief questionnaires about their Taco Bell experience. The data was used in determining the market manager's bonus and to better understand how the chain was viewed in a particular geographic market.

Developing the Information Infrastructure

Taco Bell's managers needed an information and communication system that would make it possible to perform in their new roles. In 1988, an MIS project was initiated that would provide a personal computer in every store linked to a local POS system, to the marketing managers and to corporate headquarters. Known as TACO (Total Automation of Company Operations), the new system provided the infrastructure, information and analytical tools needed to support new management roles.

TACO reduced operational paperwork for restaurant general managers by at least 10 hours a week. It also provided RGMs with reports on food costs, labor costs, inventory, perishable items, and period-to-date costs, all with variances. TACO also had functions that helped RGMs with labor scheduling and service operations planning; for example, TACO could provide an estimate of the sales volume to anticipate on Friday between 1 and 2 P.M. based on the previous six weeks' volume. The schedule could be adjusted by the RGM to account for holidays or special events, or it could be disregarded entirely at the manager's discretion. Commenting on the value of the computer system, John Martin said:

> The restaurant manager now has more information than the corporation ever gets. He or she has it immediately and has the tools to take care of problems without someone saying, "You've got a problem." Talking empowerment is one thing. Really living it is another.

The information needs of marketing managers were also supported by the system, which provided them with daily, weekly and monthly reports on store operations in their district. TACO also tracked sales for senior management by downloading the information from store registers to a central computer. This eliminated several accounting positions at corporate headquarters.

Finally, TACO had a communications function that was critical for coordinating interactions between marketing managers and store managers. Previously, marketing managers either had to mail information, visit or call store managers. TACO gave marketing managers an electronic mail system that provided another way to communicate with RGMs.

1991–1994: Continuous Transformation—Creating the Learning Organization

From 1988 to 1994 the fast-food industry was mired in a recession and achieved only single-digit growth. But with the changes John Martin had initiated, Taco Bell had grown from $700 million in revenues in 1983 to $1.6 billion in 1988. And at the end of 1993, Taco Bell's total system sales were almost $4 billion. Since the radical changes initiated by Martin in 1988, the company had more than doubled its sales and tripled its profits; in keeping with its value strategy, customer satisfaction had also increased (see Exhibit 4).

But Martin was not satisfied. His strategic vision was no longer limited to the fast-food segment. By late 1991, Martin had reformulated the firm's strategy yet again; to be successful in the future, Taco Bell would create and dominate the convenience food business—a business that reached out to customers any time and any place they were hungry.

John Martin's goal for Taco Bell was to evolve into a $25 billion food retailer with a worldwide distribution system of over 200,000 POAs by the year 2000. To reach this aggressive goal, Taco Bell would have to expand beyond fast-foods. The company began a string of acquisitions, and by 1994, Taco Bell had three restaurant brands: Taco Bell, Hot-n-Now, and Chevys Mexican Restaurants. In addition, the company had expanded its signature brand of retail products through Taco Bell New Concepts, Taco Bell Supermarket Retail, and Taco Bell International (see Appendix A for a summary of the Taco Bell brand in 1994).

Organizing to Manage Complexity

In anticipation of the expansion of the business, Martin used lessons learned in K-Minus to enable efficient management across multiple brands, channels, and markets. Rather than add multiple layers of infrastructure, the company developed a concept called *shared resources*. Managers were asked to identify the infrastructure requirements for the new lines of business; they then met together to identify how they could capitalize on the strengths of Taco Bell's existing infrastructure or infrastructure that was available elsewhere in PepsiCo. For example, the Frito-Lay marketing, sales and distribution infrastructure could be used to support the Taco Bell line of retail products.

While the shared resources concept was critical for the success of the new strategy, Martin recognized that the more critical threat to the company's future success was embedded within the very foundation of its current success. That threat was complacency.

Creating a Learning Organization

To ensure future success, Martin realized that Taco Bell would need to move beyond changing its structure, roles and processes; the company would also need to change its culture—the deeply embedded beliefs and values that framed how individuals made decisions and took actions. The new Taco Bell would need to embrace continuous, yet intelligent, change. Survival and success in the future would depend upon learning faster than the competition. Martin explained:

> [Learning organizations] are able to capture, share and take action on information better and faster than the competitor. A learning organiza-

tion isn't top-down and it isn't bottom-up. It works side to side. It's an organization that gobbles up information and experiences like a sponge and shares those learnings throughout the enterprise in minutes, hours, and days rather than weeks, months, and years.

Taco Bell believed the benefits of creating such an organization would include: increased individual awareness and collective organizational IQ; greater organizational flexibility and speed of response; institutionalization of employee self-sufficiency and innovation; and increased individual and team productivity. But moving to this self-sufficient learning model involved further refinement of the organizational design. Taco Bell pursued a number of initiatives to create and support a new learning culture.

Pushing Down Decision-Making

In the early 1990s, much of Taco Bell's growth was fueled by its greatly expanded use of carts, kiosks, vans, and Taco Bell Express units. Between 1991 and 1993, Points of Access (POAs) increased from 3,670 to 9,707 (see Exhibit 5). Taco Bell's carts and kiosks became a common sight at such varied locations as high school and college cafeterias, airports, malls, convenience stores, gas stations and even the Moscow subway system.

To support such rapid expansion, Taco Bell continued to increase its managers' spans of responsibility. This enabled further movement from the command and control culture of the past, and enabled the company to rapidly increase POAs while simultaneously reducing the traditional field management structure (see Exhibit 6). An integral part of increasing managers' spans of responsibility was the development of team-managed units (TMUs).

TMUs were teams of crew members sufficiently trained to manage a store without a full-time on-site manager. The intent was to create teams of crew members who were capable of performing all of the day-to-day tasks of a general manager (GM).[8] Senior management considered TMUs a natural evolution of Taco Bell's empowerment strategy, and by the end of 1993 there were TMUs in 90% of the company-owned restaurant locations stores. As Taco Bell broadened its business in the early 1990s, TMUs were a critical mechanism that permitted general managers (GMs) to manage multiple POAs. But the teaming concept had several other important impacts. It forced GMs to increasingly become coaches and trainers, working with their crews to help them broaden their jobs and accept new levels of responsibility. Implementing TMUs also helped create a culture of interdependence and information sharing among crews and management that would be essential to creating both self-sufficient crew-run stores and a learning organization, in general.

Just as crew members were compensated for assuming additional responsibilities, Taco Bell's compensation system for GMs was changed as well. GMs continued to have a variable pay system, but it was much more highly leveraged. Managers' base pay averaged $30,000, but they were able to earn another $30,000 in bonus pay. GMs were evaluated on three criteria: (1) performance at meeting profit targets, (2) customer service ratings, and (3) actual store sales.[9] To promote information sharing in the new environment, some marketing managers also experimented with a shared incentive system by contributing their bonuses to a pool that would be shared equally by all employees in the region. This initiative was designed to promote an environment of greater cooperation and communication among employees.

Expanding Information Access

To support the self-sufficient team-based organization and to facilitate the company's ability to learn and change, access to information changed dramatically at Taco Bell. Initial implementation of the TACO system had provided restaurant managers with information about store operations. But in the new environment, the focus expanded to getting that same information into the hands of crew members actually running the stores. There was wide agreement that the employees closest to the customer and daily operations were in the best position to make full use of this information.

To make information useful to TMUs, Taco Bell introduced TACO II. This new, more user friendly computer system was designed to provide crew members with the information they needed to make decisions and take action. For example, instead of reporting a ."05% meat variance" yesterday, the system would report that the variance was equal to 300 tacos, which was something crew members could both relate to and act on.

The team-based culture and the new technology system were essential for supporting an empowered organization. Said one marketing manager, "In the old system, the crews were afraid to make decisions because they were afraid they would get reprimanded by the AGM. Now, the crews make their own decisions. For example, our crew people order the food. This is much better because they know more about what we use daily than the AGMs and GMs. The managers don't make tacos and they don't go in back to get boxes of food."

Building an Intellectual Network

The development of an intellectual network was another initiative that Taco Bell saw as critical to its self-sufficiency and organizational learning paradigm. This was intended to be an on-line communications system that allowed every Taco Bell employee to disseminate information, ask questions, get answers and perform their jobs better. Shared data bases would be a key component of the network, incorporating "best practices" information on a wide variety of subjects. The network would also use expert systems such as the company's Contract Authoring System.

This PC-based set of real estate contracts had been written and cleared by Taco Bell's legal department, and simple rules were built into the system. Through the use of TACO II, senior management was able to delegate greater authority, while still maintaining necessary control in areas of high risk. In this way, TACO II extended the concept of safety nets from measurement of customer satisfaction to include control of operations.

Taco Bell expected the intellectual network to facilitate knowledge transfer and communication in ways that would allow the company to continue its rapid growth in POAs without a corresponding increase in bureaucracy. The intent was to use the network to maintain a sense of community within the burgeoning organization and to help retain the company's verbal culture. To further support this latter objective and to enhance communications, Taco Bell extended its e-mail systems and installed voice mail and computer conferencing. Managers noted that voice mail quickly became a key component of the communication infrastructure.

Ongoing Innovation

As Taco Bell managed for today, it also organized to ensure that the company would continue to innovate in the future. For example, the company developed a "restaurant of the future" testing site near its corporate headquarters. Here new innovations could be developed and tested. In 1994, there were several innovations being tested at the restaurant of the future. For example, an Automated Taco Assembler capable of making 900 tacos per hour without human assistance was expected to reduce waste, increase consistency and quality, and reduce kitchen labor by 16 hours per day. A Customer Activated Terminal (CAT)—a touch screen ordering system—would enable customers to place their orders from kiosks and roving sales crew to take orders outside the walls of the physical restaurant.

Can Taco Bell Get There from Here?

If you wait until something is broken to fix it . . . there may not be anything left to fix.
—*John Martin, September 1988*

John Martin had long been viewed a futuristic leader in the industry and the company—someone who was constantly willing to think "outside the box" and improve things before they were broken. In his pursuit of value, extraordinary convenience and accessibility, and unparalleled customer satisfaction, John Martin was an acknowledged champion of the consumer, and it appeared that the industry agreed when it awarded Martin the International Foodservice Manufacturers Association's 1993 Silver Plate Foodservice Operator of the Year award.

Martin, however, was proud of all that the employees in the company had accomplished (see Exhibit 7). He believed that with a clear vision and the capacity and willingness to change, Taco Bell had only begun to tap into available opportunities. In his words:

> In its more than three decades of operation, Taco Bell has accomplished much. But we know that the best still lies ahead. Today we feed 50 million people each and every week. But, our vision is to be broader than just a fast-food restaurant. In the United States, there are one billion feeding occasions every day. That present us with unlimited opportunities. What's exciting is that our people are on the forefront of the changes we are making in our business. By being empowered to take greater ownership, our people will drive even greater changes. In doing so, not only will we deliver value to our customers, but we will also provide greater value to our people by being an employer of choice. Together we're transforming the careers and jobs that people can have in this industry.

John Martin's vision was certain to bring about dramatic change and progress for Taco Bell and its people . . . and its customers. Yet the year 2000 was only six short years away. Was Taco Bell positioned to be able to achieve its vision of growing to $25 billion in sales and 200,000 POAs? Were the actions to date sufficient to take them there? Only time would tell.

Notes

1. Richard Martin, *Nations Restaurant News,* July 16, 1990

2. Dean Takahashi, "Taco Bell. . . ," *The Orange County Register,* August 13, 1989. The first four products mentioned are trademarked products of Taco Bell Corp.

3. During the 1980s, industry labor costs as a percentage of sales grew on average by 18%, but at Taco Bell those costs increased 50%, in part because of the ongoing high costs of turnover. And, with real estate prices and construction costs outstripping the rate of inflation, the industry's average cost to develop a restaurant site increased by almost 8%. Finally, food costs declined by an industry average of 15% during this period, but Taco Bell's costs actually increased slightly from 27% to 30%.

4. Taco Bell estimated that 60% of orders delivered in the fast-food industry (including at their chain) were delivered incorrectly.

5. Hot food hot, cold food cold.

6. Points of distribution outside a traditional Taco Bell restaurant were called "pods." Subsequently, they would come to be called Points of Access (POAs). Examples included taco carts in malls and supermarkets, being the vendor for a school lunch program, and operating a Taco Bell Express (miniature, or "sardine") store.

7. During the early 1990s, Taco Bell expanded their business concept beyond the fast-food business. As part of that expansion, they developed a consumer product line to be distributed through supermarkets, convenience stores and other retail outlets, and they purchased Chevy's, a casual dining Mexican restaurant chain. (See Appendix A for a summary of the Taco Bell brands in 1994.)

8. In 1992, the titles "Restaurant General Manager" and "Assistant Restaurant General Manager" were changed to "General Manager" and "Assistant General Manager." This change reflected the expansion of their responsibilities beyond the traditional restaurant.

9. Shari Caudron, "Master the Compensation Maze," *Personnel Journal,* 72, no. 6 (June 1993).

10. Peter Romeo, "Can Lightning Strike Twice?" *Restaurant Business,* August 10, 1993.

Exhibit 1
Early 1980s Fast-Food Industry Statistics

ROI (store level)	18.7%
Operating margin (store level)	15.3%
Sales per dollar of capital cost	$1.14
Hamburger chain, average sales per store	$618,028
Chicken chain, average sales per store	$381,160
Mexican chain, average sales per store	$411,263
Sales growth, 1970–1980 compound annual	16.6%
Labor as a percent of sales (industry average)	21.9%
Food cost as a percent of sales (industry average)	37.2%
McDonald's advertising cost as a percent of sales	5%
Capital necessary to commence operations, McDonald's	$650,000
Capital necessary to commence operations, Kentucky Fried Chicken	$475,000

Source: Robert Emerson, *The New Economics of Fast-food* (New York: Van Nostrand Reinhold, 1990).

Exhibit 2
Taco Bell Line Organization, 1983

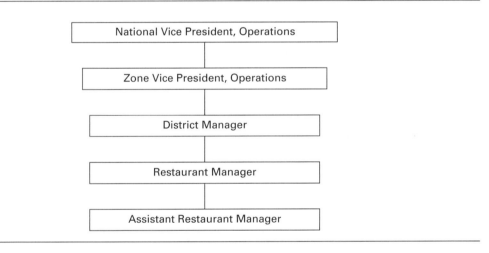

Exhibit 3
Taco Bell Menu Selections Price Comparisons

	1983	1988	1991
Taco	$.67	$.79	$.59
Burrito Supreme	1.32	1.65	1.49
Pintos and cheese	.59	.79	.59
Tostada	.63	.79	.59
Pepsi (largest)	.79	.99	.99

Note that the largest Pepsi increased in size during the late 1980s.

Exhibit 4
Company Performance

	1993	1992	1991	1990	1989	1988	1987	1986	1985	1984	1983
Financial Highlights ($ billions)											
Total System Sales	$3.9	$3.3	$2.8	$2.4	$2.1	$1.6	$1.5	$1.3	$1.1	$0.9	$0.7
Company Store Sales	2.91	1.95	1.61	1.40	1.17	0.9	0.8	0.7	0.5	0.5	0.4
Average Unit Sales Total System (in $000)	925	876	814	771	686	589	579	560	550	539	439
Net Worldwide Operating Profit (in millions)	253	215	181	150	113	76	85	78	68	59	43

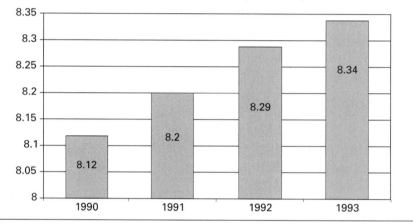

Customer Satisfaction (1990–1993)

Exhibit 5
Points of Access, 1989–1993

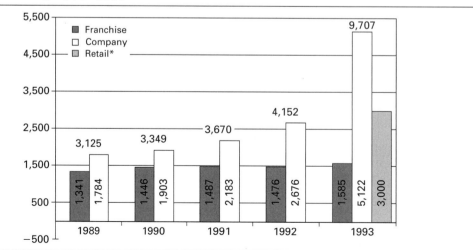

Exhibit 6
Span of Responsibility, 1989–1993

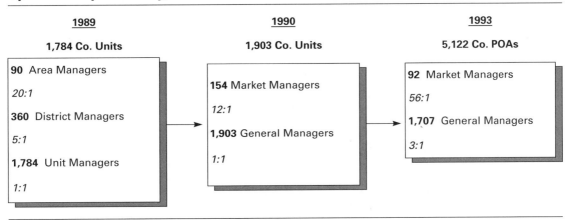

1989	1990	1993
1,784 Co. Units	**1,903 Co. Units**	**5,122 Co. POAs**

1989 — 1,784 Co. Units

90 Area Managers
20:1
360 District Managers
5:1
1,784 Unit Managers
1:1

1990 — 1,903 Co. Units

154 Market Managers
12:1
1,903 General Managers
1:1

1993 — 5,122 Co. POAs

92 Market Managers
56:1
1,707 General Managers
3:1

Exhibit 7

Summary of Changes at Taco Bell (1983–1994)

	Phase 1: 1983–1988	Phase 2: 1988–1991	Phase 3: 1991–1994
Context	Fast-food market maturing; New products; Operating costs increase, Mexican segment takes off	Margins squeezed; Battle for market share; Value pricing strategy becomes dominant	Recession in fast-food industry, single-digit growth; Market share falls as competitors respond
Vision	From regional Mexican restaurant to fast-food restaurant	From making food to feeding people	Dominate convenience food segment
Strategic Initiatives	Incremental process redesign; Product/geographical expansion; Infrastructure changes; Build fast-food brand image.	Information-enabled business transformation; Customer value orientation.	Create an empowered learning organization; Continuous improvement; Extend brand through acquisitions and retail
Process	Modernize facilities; Add drive-through windows; Add new menu items; Accelerate unit growth from 100 to 249 stores per year; Redesign food preparation process	FACT studies; K-Minus and SOS; Increased kitchen capacity enhances non-eat-in sales Expand into new POAs; Safety nets implemented around customer value.	Dramatically extend POAs; Team-based processes replace assembly line; Operational innovations, e.g., robotics, customer-activated terminals, process flow mapping
Power	No change	RGMs take on more decision making within restaurant and assume responsibility for multiple POAs; More management-by-exception; Increase span of responsibility.	Continue to increase span of responsibility; Team-managed units replace hierarchical operations at the restaurant level; Extend "empowerment" to crew level.
People	Improved operational training and development	Recruit more skilled RGMs; Hire outside industry; New training program for leadership skills; New compensation and non-monetary rewards; New career paths	Crew members trained to manage stores in teams; Variable pay system; Experiment with shared incentive systems; Career paths extended
Principles	No change in values	Focus on customer value as key principle driving decision making and action; Safety nets implemented to provide necessary boundary checks	Focus is on changing culture and values; Emphasize continuous innovation, empowerment, and learning; Safety nets extended to provide necessary boundary systems
Information and Communication	Install POS system	TACO system provides communication and information infrastructure	TACO II extends access to information and communication infrastructure to TMUs; Intellectual network; Voice mail and computer conferencing complement e-mail
Value Created	Total system sales grow from $700 million in 1983 to $1.6 billion in 1988; Net profit grows from $43 million to $76 million	Increased peak hour transaction capacity by over 54%; Reduced customer waiting times by over 71%; Total system sales grow to $2.8 billion; Net profit grows from $76 million to $181 million	Improved customer satisfaction from 8.12 to 8.34; Total system sales grow to almost $4 billion in 1993; Net profit grows to $253 million in 1993

Appendix A
Taco Bell's Three Brands

Brand Taco Bell

Brand Taco Bell was the company's core business and it included all of the points of access by which *Taco Bell* reached customers: (1) traditional restaurants, (2) new concepts, (3) international operations, and (4) retail.

Taco Bell Restaurants

Once the company's core distribution outlet, traditional restaurants became just one of many ways to reach new customers.

Taco Bell New Concepts

New concepts included non-traditional points of access such as school lunch programs, carts, Express units, kiosks, and joint ventures with sister companies Pizza Hut and KFC.

Taco Bell International

Taco Bell International operated over 100 non-U.S. POAs in 21 countries at the end of 1993.

Taco Bell Supermarket Retail

After reviewing marketing studies which indicated that Taco Bell had a higher brand awareness among shoppers than Doritos, the company decided to enter the supermarket retail business. The company worked with its sister company Frito Lay which provided the production and distribution infrastructure for the new Taco Bell products. In 1993, they began test marketing 18 products in 3,000 stores throughout Ohio, Georgia, Chicago, Michigan, and Indiana. The markets were chosen because they offered a diversity of customers, taste preferences, and Taco Bell brand awareness. Taco Bell entered the market with virtually no advertising, except for newspaper inserts and in-restaurant couponing. The success of the tests was immediately evident as Taco Bell quickly became the number one or two food brand in the supermarket Mexican retail food sections. Results were so positive that Taco Bell anticipated expanding to 10,000 supermarkets (POAs) in 1994. Taco Bell executives viewed the 150,000 U.S. supermarkets as 150,000 potential POAs and expected the retail business to be worth several hundred million dollars.

Retail was yet another way for Taco Bell to access a different eating occasion. Executives noted that the people who shopped in grocery stores were often very different from those that frequented Taco Bell restaurants. By entering retail, Taco Bell entered people's homes and went to another place where consumers ate.

Hot-n-Now

Taco Bell's first advance outside Mexican fast-food was their acquisition of the double drive-through hamburger chain Hot-n-Now. The Kalamazoo, Michigan chain was purchased in 1991 and consisted of 77 stores in 23 markets. The stores sold only hamburgers, French fries, and sodas. They had two drive-through windows and a walk-up window. Operations were designed to provide high-quality fast-food in a quick and inexpensive manner.

Taco Bell executives expected Hot-n-Now to become a significant part of their growth for the decade ahead. Industry-wide hamburger drive-through sales reached $25 billion in 1992, making the hamburger drive-through segment larger than the entire chicken and seafood segments.[10] Consistent with Taco Bell's expansionist tendencies, the company planned to increase the chain to 5,000 locations during the next decade.

Chevys

Taco Bell ventured into the casual-dining market with the May 1993 purchase of Chevys

Mexican Restaurant. The 37 store chain was a full-service restaurant/bar located primarily in Northern California. Taco Bell's market research indicated that as fast-food users aged and had more disposable income, they migrated towards casual dining.

Taco Bell executive saw the Chevys acquisition as a natural step in the creation of a superbrand as well as a natural progression for its broader set of consumers. By capturing an entirely different eating occasion (casual dining) it allowed Taco Bell to access new customers. Taco Bell planned rapid nationwide expansion for the Chevys chain, taking it to 300 restaurants with $1 billion in sales.

CASE 1.2

DISCUSSION QUESTIONS

1. What is Campbell's strategy? Is there an underlying theory of action about how to improve student outcomes that is driving the strategy?

2. What is your diagnosis of the degree to which the systems and culture at BCS are coherent with the strategy?

3. What advice would you give Campbell?

Richard F. Elmore ■ Allen S. Grossman ■ Modupe Akinola

Bristol City Schools (BCS)

Jean Campbell, superintendent of Bristol City Schools (BCS), could not believe what she had just read. Sitting at the head of the table in the BCS conference room, she stared in disbelief at her executive staff assembled around her. Campbell had been notified that one of BCS's five area superintendents, Lisa Craig, had tendered her resignation. The resignation letter given to her by Tom Hassler, deputy superintendent of BCS, cited "excessive stress" as the primary reason for Craig's resignation. "The excessive stress of the area superintendent position has become a serious health risk for me as a result of my abnormally high blood pressure," wrote Craig. "This, coupled with my desire to spend more time with my family, has left me no choice but to offer my resignation. I want to be able to give 110% to BCS. Unfortunately, I am not able to do so at this time."

Although Campbell's initial vision called for eight area superintendents to oversee the 147 BCS schools, budget constraints and turnover had left Campbell with only five area superintendents. With Craig's resignation, this number was now down to four. In fact, Craig was the

third BCS leadership team member to resign that year (see Exhibit 1 for BCS organizational chart). As Campbell exited the boardroom, she said to her executive staff, "This is unacceptable. We cannot support Lisa Craig's resignation."

Historical Background

BCS Demographics

Serving 85,692 students in SY04,[1] BCS was a rapidly growing school district in the United States (see Exhibit 2 for BCS facts and figures). Since 1993, the total enrollment of BCS grew by 20%, up from 71,410 students. This growth rate surpassed that of surrounding districts, many of which experienced enrollment increases ranging from 10% to 15% during the same period. BCS encompassed a diverse student body with more than 60 languages other than English spoken at home. Whites represented 31% of BCS students, African-Americans 38%, and Hispanics 16%, while Asians and other ethnicities accounted for 12% and 3%, respectively. At the start of SY04, 60% of BCS students were eligible for free or reduced-price meals, and 11% were learning English for the first time.

Bristol City Schools is a fictional district created using a composite of actual data, people, and events from a number of urban school districts.

BCS's increasing enrollment rate was primarily attributed to Bristol's growing minority population. Over the past 15 years, Bristol had experienced significant growth in its immigrant population as a result of the region's flourishing economy. This gradual influx of immigrants had created pockets of wealth and poverty within Bristol that were easily discernible by the railway lines. South of the Stutton/Greenburg railway line were affluent communities, while north of the railway line housed the majority of the poor neighborhoods.

Superintendent Jean Campbell

During the early 1990s, public dissatisfaction with stagnating student achievement, BCS financial crises, reports of impropriety among district staff, and growing tensions with the unions stimulated the first major reform wave for BCS, led by then-superintendent Eric Layne. Under Layne, BCS balanced the budget; improved school facilities; established accountability measures; ended social promotion; and expanded after-school, early-childhood, and summer school programs. In January 2001, Layne announced his intentions to retire at the end of the academic year, resulting in an aggressive search process for a successor.

In July 2001, the Bristol School Board in an 8–1 vote selected Dr. Jean Campbell as the next superintendent of BCS. A native of Albuquerque, New Mexico, Campbell had experience in education dating back to 1963. Campbell began her career as a math teacher at Sewanee High School in 1963 and culminated it in her most recent position as superintendent of Linden Public Schools. Campbell was renowned in Linden for improving student achievement in low-performing schools and decreasing achievement disparities among all groups of students. As a result of her impressive track record, Campbell was an obvious choice for Bristol City School Board members. "The board made it clear to me that my experience in Linden set me apart

from the other candidates," recalled Campbell. "I was charged by the board to demonstrate a laser-like focus on academic achievement, which was the focal point of my tenure in Linden."

Under Campbell's leadership, BCS had begun to make steady improvements in student achievement. Over Campbell's two-year tenure, test scores had risen, and some headway had been made on the troubling long-standing gap in test scores and grades between white and minority students (see Exhibit 3 for student achievement data). Campbell had worked with staff to develop clear expectations for students at each grade level and implemented standardized reading and math curricula across the district so that students frequently changing schools would be familiar with the curricula. Campbell had also led the effort to revamp early-childhood education and had put more teachers and resources in lower-performing schools.

In addition to making strides in student achievement, Campbell had made significant progress in building relationships with key BCS external stakeholders. Campbell had begun to reverse the decade-long inimical relationship between BCS and the local union, the Bristol Education Association (BEA), representing teachers and administrators. Campbell had also intensified efforts to involve parents in BCS and had challenged BCS and the community to mobilize around student achievement.

Despite these accomplishments, several issues remained at the core of BCS's continuing reform efforts. Among these were gaps in student achievement by race and ethnicity, rising teacher and principal turnover, slowing rates of student improvement, and high school reform. Additionally, Campbell faced several organizational challenges as a result of budget constraints. With budget cuts throughout the state, central-office staffing had been reduced, resulting in inefficiencies and gaps in communication at BCS.

Campbell's Philosophy

As articulated in its mission statement, BCS aimed to "ensure that each student achieve his or her potential by supporting high-quality teaching and learning and comprehensive academic programs, working in conjunction with the entire community." Campbell strongly believed that the way to achieve this mission was to focus on improving the quality of instruction in BCS. "My experience in Linden demonstrated that student learning will increase when the interaction between teachers and students is improved," noted Campbell. "You can have the best curriculum in the world, but if the teacher cannot teach it, student performance will not move one inch." As a result of this philosophy, Campbell had mobilized the district around deepening teacher practice.

From 2001 through 2002, BCS administration established an aggressive professional development program for its entire staff. Penelope Greene, associate superintendent for instruction, recalled this period: "We examined professional development programs of districts across the country and hired consultants to assist us in developing a comprehensive program that could be rolled out over two to three years." The professional development program ultimately created by BCS included individualized coaching and monthly training for teachers and principals. In addition, the professional development program trained area superintendents, those responsible for supervising teachers and principals, in areas such as performance management and instructional leadership. "This professional development program was especially attractive to schools as it was fully funded by the district," noted Greene. In general, resource allocation had been centralized at BCS since the early 1980s, and professional development at BCS had typically come from unrestricted general funds. Based on a standard staffing formula, BCS's Budget and Finance Department would use enroll-

ment numbers to determine the number of staff members required to sufficiently run each school in the district for the academic year. Once staff had been determined and salary and benefits estimated, schools could use any remaining allocated funds toward discretionary uses. "The fact that the newly developed professional development program did not take from schools' discretionary funds was extremely appealing to principals," Greene concluded.

Although budget constraints had drawn significant attention to the professional development program, Campbell was determined to test the program in 40 of the 147 schools during SY04. "The budgeting process for SY04 was a disaster," Campbell observed. "In January 2002, I was notified by our state representative that the BCS budget would be reduced by 7% as a result of state budget cuts. I was forced to make some tough decisions and opted to reduce administrative and support expenditures, decrease summer school sessions, institute both hiring and wage freezes, and lay off some teachers. These actions resulted in major backlash from the unions and the local community" (see Exhibit 4 for BCS budget). As a result of this budget scenario, many internal and external BCS stakeholders had urged Campbell to reduce professional development expenditures. Campbell and the Bristol City School Board had refused to acquiesce to these demands, keeping professional development at 3% of the BCS budget.

The Professional Development Program

Piloting the Professional Development Program

The professional development program developed by BCS provided teachers with specific blocks of time for professional development directed at improving teachers' skills and practices. Another hallmark of the program was the use of "walkthroughs" to assist principals and teachers with specific instructional support needs. At least once each semester, area superintendents, each of whom was assigned to eight pilot schools, would visit their assigned schools to analyze teacher practice and school and classroom environments with the school principal. Walkthroughs were not intended to be a mechanism for judging teacher performance, but rather to provide the principal and area superintendent with an opportunity to discuss classroom observations and agree upon areas of improvement and key next steps. These walkthroughs provided useful data on the integration of teaching tools and techniques introduced during the monthly professional development sessions that teachers were required to attend. Monthly professional development sessions focused in detail on curriculum and instructional practice in specific content areas.

In addition to walkthroughs, area superintendents were responsible for supervising principals and coaching them in the evaluation and supervision of teachers. The district also required principals to participate in monthly principal conferences by area. This professional development provided principals with informational knowledge on coaching models and walkthrough procedures. According to Associate Superintendent for Instruction Greene, principals responded very differently to the monthly principal conferences. "Area superintendents have reported that many principals are frustrated with the conferences," observed Greene. "Their biggest complaint is that the majority of principal conferences evolve into griping sessions. Many are skeptical as to the true value of attending these conferences."

As a result of the professional development program, the 40 pilot schools had begun to experience increased rates of improvement. One school that had boasted particularly impressive results was Ridgeway Middle School as demonstrated during walkthroughs and by its students' performance on the State Test of Basic Skills

(STBS), the annual statewide evaluation for certain grade levels.

Maria Fernandez, the area superintendent with oversight of Ridgeway Middle School, attributed most of the school's success to teacher coaching and adherence to the districtwide curriculum. Fernandez explained:

I have been an area superintendent in BCS for the past eight years and have never witnessed such dramatic results in a school. Each of my walkthroughs demonstrated that teachers at Ridgeway were diligently following the standardized Pearlman math and Sutton reading curricula adopted by BCS in 2001. This past summer, we instituted a one-week, 40 hour-long curriculum training program to train teachers on the new standardized curriculum. While the process was time intensive, the hours were well spent. The summer curriculum training has also been supplemented through monthly training sessions during the year. This curriculum training in addition to the mandatory teacher training from the professional development program has transformed teaching and learning in the classroom, particularly at Ridgeway.

However, Fernandez expressed concerns over the perception of walkthroughs. "Teachers are still very distrustful of walkthroughs," noted Fernandez. "I feel a negative sentiment each time I enter the school." Despite the attempts of BCS area administrators to model good instructional oversight for principals and to position walkthroughs as learning vehicles, teachers felt threatened by the presence of the area superintendent and principal in the classroom and had expressed this concern to both district and union representatives. Fernandez recalled her colleague Frank Roman's troubling story regarding this issue. "Following my walkthrough, I pulled aside a teacher to tell him he was doing a good job," said Roman. "I mentioned he should try using the chalkboard to explain especially difficult concepts. This teacher later complained to his principal about my comment. The teacher thought my comment was inappropriate." Fernandez wondered whether the teacher's reaction was indicative of poor instructional oversight on the part of Roman, or whether teachers were still unclear about the purpose and goal of walkthroughs.

Evaluating the Professional Development Program

The most recent weekly area superintendent meeting had surfaced a variety of challenges with the existing professional development program. Area superintendents had complained about the time constraints placed on them as a result of the numerous administrative issues on their plate. Many area superintendents found themselves mired in paperwork, particularly related to federal mandates. For instance, area superintendents with coverage over schools with largely immigrant populations spent a large percentage of their time completing English Language Acquisition (ELA) paperwork. Not only were these area superintendents constantly monitoring BCS's conformity to regulations surrounding ELA teacher certification, but they were also responsible for tracking student attendance in ELA programs. This task was especially complicated given the three-year ELA program participation limit per student. BCS's high mobility rate impeded area superintendents from effectively tracking this data. Area superintendents were also responsible for completing No Child Left Behind (NCLB) paperwork. This included notifying parents that their children were eligible for school choice if their children were in BCS schools identified as needing improvement, corrective action, or restructuring. Fifty BCS schools fell into this category, requiring area superintendents to send personalized parental letters no later than the first day of the school year following the year for which a par-

ticular school had been identified for improvement.

These responsibilities had hindered many area superintendents from following the established walkthrough schedule. Furthermore, many area superintendents had found themselves actively involved in strengthening community relations. For example, a recent altercation on the front steps of Merrywood High School had resulted in hours of meetings with parents and the community for the principal and area superintendent in charge of Merrywood High.

These demands had not only prevented area superintendents from performing walkthroughs but had also interfered with their own professional development. The professional development program was intended to give area superintendents greater clarity on their role as instructional leaders and involved specific training for area superintendents based on their individual developmental needs. All five area superintendents had extensive experience in education, as three were former principals and two had come from district administration. Greene believed many still needed training in areas such as performance management, coaching, instructional leadership, time management, and more technical matters such as budgeting and data collection and analysis.

According to Tom Hassler, deputy superintendent of BCS, area superintendents remained confused about their role in the organization. "Each area superintendent has gone off in a somewhat different direction," expressed Hassler. "Some spend significant time dealing with the community, others tend to micromanage teachers and principals. There is no shared understanding of the role of the area superintendent." Furthermore, Hassler was concerned about the numerous calls he received weekly from principals. Rather than going directly to area superintendents for questions and feedback, principals were communicating directly with Hassler and Greene. Hassler speculated that this was a vestige of site-based management and the former de-centralized management system at BCS. In addition, for the 40 schools in which the professional development program was being implemented, the level of best-practice sharing across the district was unclear. Teachers, principals, and area superintendents complained that there were too few opportunities for participants in the professional development program to meet and capture both the strengths and weaknesses of the program.

This feedback corroborated Campbell's greatest concern, that her vision for BCS had not filtered down throughout the organization. "We have clearly articulated a vision over the past few years," expressed Campbell. "All of our efforts are centered around improving teacher quality. Area superintendents should be focused on those activities that directly support this vision. I don't understand what the confusion is all about."

While the professional development pilot was at the forefront of Campbell's mind, several additional issues concerned her. Among these were BCS's recruitment process and its performance evaluation system.

Recruitment

Campbell and the BCS leadership team had grown increasingly frustrated about the way in which teacher recruitment was handled both at the school level and the district level. "A strong professional development program needs to be accompanied by a recruitment system which brings talented teachers to the district," noted Campbell. Teacher recruitment was of particular concern for BCS administrators, as 20% of new teachers left the district within three years and several teachers were approaching retirement.

Associate Superintendent of Human Resources Mary Richards had managed both recruitment and staffing for BCS since 1995.

Richards had been the head of human resources at Bevelis Corporation and at two nonprofit organizations, Year Corps and the American Red Cross, before transitioning to her role as head of HR at BCS. "I was looking for opportunities to share the expertise I had gained in human resources both in the private and nonprofit sectors. I was particularly interested in working at BCS, as my children had gone through the BCS system and my eldest daughter had been a teacher in the district for three years," Richards recalled. During her eight-year tenure, Richards had made sweeping changes in BCS's HR function. Richards had introduced electronic payroll and direct-deposit systems, led the task force in creating the new professional development program, and implemented an online teacher application system. Richards's goal was to make BCS a paperless organization by 2006. Richards could be heard saying, "If it's not online, it's not on time" and had this slogan plastered across the HR department.

Despite attempts to streamline the hiring process, Richards considered teacher recruitment to be the most challenging item on her agenda. "The recruiting process has become increasingly mismanaged," Richards remarked. "Schools continue to hire new teachers in a haphazard manner. It is no wonder why each July we are scrambling to fill the numerous teacher vacancies throughout the district." In order to gain better clarity on recruitment practices across the district, Richards would informally interview new teachers at randomly selected schools within BCS. Richards was greatly dismayed by her most recent interview as she had asked John Cowen, a ninth-grade history teacher at Jackson-Randolph High School, about his hiring process. Richards had received the following response from Cowen:

> I had told one of my ed school classmates, who at the time was a teacher in BCS, that I was

planning to relocate to Bristol City. This buddy of mine had seen me teach on several occasions and said he would recommend me to his school principal, as there were a few vacancies at his high school. After hounding his school administrators to interview me, I finally received an interview. You know, this friend of mine has a lot of clout, as he was a student member of the school board when he was a senior in high school. He is also very politically active in Bristol City, so he was very confident that he could get me an interview.

In April, I flew down to the school for an informational interview. I was told by my interviewers that they did not know if any positions would be available for the following school year. I knew this was not the case, as my friend had already told me about some vacancies, so I just sat tight. In the meantime, my friend continued to bother his school administrators about me because as he put it, "They were not hot on the recruiting trail." Well, two weeks after the interview, I was offered a job. I was elated.

The funny thing is, I had also applied to BCS via the online application system on the Web site. To this day, I haven't heard back from BCS, although I am now a teacher at Jackson-Randolph.

Richards had heard many stories similar to this one. In fact, in her last meeting with her boss, Chief Administrative Officer Larry Jordan, she had stated that "clearly some schools have managed the hiring process quite well. However, we need to find the best balance between a centralized and decentralized recruitment system." Jordan had mentioned this issue to Campbell during SY03. Campbell too was unclear about the most effective way to address BCS's recruitment inefficiencies and was looking to Jordan and Richards for some recommendations.

Performance Evaluation

Richards had also expressed concern to Jordan about whether performance evaluation needed to be subsumed under the Instruction Department. In some ways, Richards believed that the existing structure in which Richards managed the performance evaluation process while Greene and her team conducted performance evaluations was logical, as Richards and her team were responsible for all confidential employee files. However, over time, Richards had experienced increasing resistance from Greene's team in her attempts to manage the statewide performance evaluation process.

In 2000, Richards had worked with Greene to prepare her area superintendents to implement the state-mandated performance evaluation process across all BCS schools. The performance evaluation process required that each teacher undergo three formal observations during the year. Formal observations were utilized in addition to walkthroughs. The first formal observation was to occur at the beginning of the academic year, while the remaining two could occur at any point during the year. Formal observations were conducted by certified administrators with both teaching and administrative experience. Formal observations were preceded by pre-observation meetings between the certified observer and the teacher being observed. In these meetings, the observer would walk the teacher through the observation categories and the teacher would share the lesson plan for the week with the certified observer.

Once the pre-observation meeting had taken place, the observer would watch the teacher in the classroom for 30 minutes to one hour. A post-observation interview would then be scheduled between the observer and the teacher to discuss the classroom observation and review the completed formal observation form. The post-observation interview would also include discussion around any areas of improvement and other desired outcomes. The final step in the performance evaluation process was for the formal observation form to be signed and placed in the teacher's employee file.

Many teachers had complained about the shortcomings of this performance evaluation process. "In my five years as a teacher in the district, I have had six formal observations when I should have had 15. I even know some teachers who have never been observed. How are we supposed to improve if we are never evaluated?" noted one teacher. Furthermore, teachers criticized the effectiveness of the process. "Formal observations aren't random, so any teacher can dupe the system if they want to. We have some great actors in my school who teach in a completely different manner when they are being observed. When the observer is in the classroom, it's show time!" stated another BCS teacher. "Sometimes, observers don't conduct the pre-observation, and some have even asked us to complete our own formal evaluation forms."

This feedback infuriated Richards, who had met with Greene on several occasions to express her discontent with the execution of formal observations. During their last meeting, Greene was exasperated and asked Richards, "How do you expect us to coordinate walkthroughs, receive and recommend professional development, and execute formal observations? We need to take things one step at a time. There is no way my group can meet all the demands you are placing on them." Both Richards and Greene had complained to Jordan and Hassler, both of whom had voiced their concerns to Campbell. In particular, Hassler had begun to question the role of performance evaluation in driving student improvement at BCS. "We need to think about what we are trying to accomplish with performance evaluations," he told Campbell. Hassler was especially worried about pace and timing. "I think BCS is going to implode if we keep up this pace of change," he cautioned.

Campbell was well aware of the pressures

being placed on her management team. However, she also realized that this was the first stage in implementing BCS's strategy and knew this reaction did not bode well for the many additional changes that needed to take place at BCS. If Richards and Greene could not collaborate on the existing performance evaluation system, Campbell wondered, how would BCS pull off more challenging tasks, such as implementing an information system to capture teacher and student-specific data in an effort to track teacher performance on a student-by-student basis and meet the demands of No Child Left Behind?

Next Steps

As Campbell walked down the corridor to her office, she reflected on the executive staff meeting. SY04 had placed numerous demands on BCS staff, and Campbell was concerned that the effects were becoming increasingly noticeable, causing morale to falter.

Campbell reached her office and dialed her assistant's extension. "I'd like to meet with Lisa Craig this afternoon. Can you make that happen?" she asked and put down the receiver at her assistant's affirmative response. Campbell sat at her desk, looked out the window, and wondered how she would convince Craig to resume her position at BCS and slow the attrition of key personnel.

Notes

1. PELP cases use the convention "SY" to designate, in this instance, school year 2003–2004.

Exhibit 1
BCS Organizational Chart

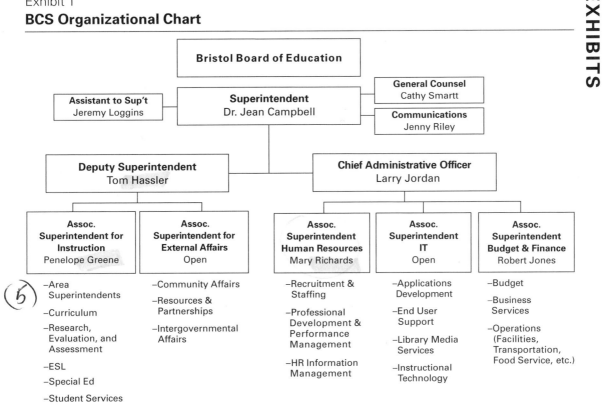

```
                    ┌─────────────────────────────┐
                    │  Bristol Board of Education  │
                    └─────────────────────────────┘
┌──────────────────┐    ┌─────────────────────────┐    ┌──────────────────────┐
│ Assistant to Sup't│───│      Superintendent      │────│   General Counsel    │
│  Jeremy Loggins   │    │    Dr. Jean Campbell     │    │    Cathy Smartt      │
└──────────────────┘    └─────────────────────────┘    ├──────────────────────┤
                                                         │   Communications     │
                                                         │     Jenny Riley      │
                                                         └──────────────────────┘
```

Deputy Superintendent Tom Hassler		Chief Administrative Officer Larry Jordan		
Assoc. Superintendent for Instruction Penelope Greene	**Assoc. Superintendent for External Affairs** Open	**Assoc. Superintendent Human Resources** Mary Richards	**Assoc. Superintendent IT** Open	**Assoc. Superintendent Budget & Finance** Robert Jones
–Area Superintendents –Curriculum –Research, Evaluation, and Assessment –ESL –Special Ed –Student Services	–Community Affairs –Resources & Partnerships –Intergovernmental Affairs	–Recruitment & Staffing –Professional Development & Performance Management –HR Information Management	–Applications Development –End User Support –Library Media Services –Instructional Technology	–Budget –Business Services –Operations (Facilities, Transportation, Food Service, etc.)

Source: Bristol City Schools.

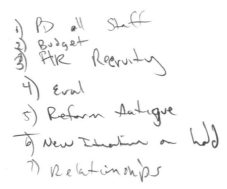

Exhibit 2

Bristol City Schools (BCS) Facts and Figures

	SY04
District Area Demographics:	
Total population	897,122
Per capita income (in 1999)	$23,951
Household income in 1999 below poverty level	15.6%
Student Demographics:	
Number of students (K–12)	85,692
African-American	38.4%
White	30.8%
Hispanic	15.6%
Asian	12.2%
Other	3.0%
Free and reduced-price lunch	60.3%
Students with IEPs	13.6%
English language learners	11.2%
Dropout rate	15.3%
Mobility rate	30.0%
Schools:	
Number of schools	147
Elementary (K–5 or K–6)	100
Middle	27
High (9–12 or 10–12)	20

Source: Bristol City Schools.

What is the cross-over data re. ELL & SPEC ED ELL & Mobility RACE & Mobility

Exhibit 3

State Test of Basic Skills (STBS) Results by Ethnicity and Race, 2001 and 2003 (Grades 3–8 Combined)

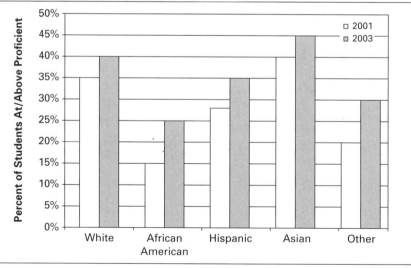

Source: Bristol City Schools.

Note: STBS is graded at four levels: below basic, basic, proficient, and advanced.

Exhibit 4

BCS Budget SY04 (US$ millions)

	SY04	% of Total
Total Budget	752.0	100%
Income		
Revenue from local sources	345.9	46%
Revenue from state sources	308.3	41%
Revenue from federal sources	67.7	9%
Revenue from other sources	30.1	4%
Total Income	752.0	100%
Expenses		
Salaries & Benefits	571.5	76%
Staff Development	22.6	3%
Books & Supplies		
Curriculum	37.6	5%
Other Supplies	22.6	3%
Services	45.1	6%
Other	52.6	7%
Total Expenses	752.0	100%

Source: Bristol City Schools.

Stacey Childress ■ Richard F. Elmore ■ Allen S. Grossman ■ Caroline King

Note on the PELP Coherence Framework

In today's accountability environment, public school districts face an imperative to achieve concrete performance goals related to student achievement. In order to accomplish these goals in all schools, not just some schools, the organizational elements of a district—its culture, structure and systems, resources, stakeholders, and environment—must be managed in a way that is coherent with an explicit strategy to improve teaching and learning in every classroom, in every school. Leaders who have tried to implement a district-wide strategy for improving the achievement of all students know how difficult it is to achieve this coherence.

The PELP Coherence Framework[1] is designed to help district leaders identify the key elements that support a district-wide improvement strategy, bring those elements into a coherent relationship with the strategy and each other, and guide the actions of people throughout the district in the pursuit of high levels of achievement for all students.

Overview

Webster's Dictionary defines coherence as "the quality of being logically integrated." Coherence, for the purpose of this note, means that the elements of a school district work together in an integrated way to implement an articulated strategy. The PELP Coherence Framework is designed to help leaders effectively implement an improvement strategy by strengthening coherence among actions at the district, school and classroom level. The framework emerged out of interactions with hundreds of U.S. public school leaders eager to identify ways to better organize and manage their complex organizations. Although it resembles models used in the business and nonprofit sectors, the framework was designed to fit the unique context and challenges of managing in public education.

The framework assists with achieving coherence by:

1. Connecting the instructional core with a district-wide strategy for improvement

2. Highlighting district elements that can support or hinder effective implementation

3. Identifying interdependencies among district elements

4. Recognizing forces in the environment that have an impact on the implementation of strategy

The PELP Coherence Framework is displayed on page 45.

At the center of the framework is the instructional core, which represents the critical work of teaching and learning that goes on in classrooms.[2] The core includes three interdependent components: *teachers'* knowledge and skill, *students'* engagement in their own learning, and academically challenging *content*.

Surrounding the instructional core is strategy—the set of actions a district deliberately undertakes to strengthen the instructional core with the objective of raising student performance district-wide. In order to make teaching and learning more effective, a district must develop a strategy that enhances all three components of the instructional core and their interaction. However, *how* each district provides this capacity and support to the core may vary. In other words, two districts may design two very different, but equally effective, strategies. The PELP Coherence Framework, rather than prescribing a particular strategy, asserts that gaining coherence among actions at the district, school, and classroom levels will make a district's chosen strategy more scalable and sustainable.

The framework includes five organizational elements critical to the successful implementation of a district-wide improvement strategy: culture, structures and systems, resources, and stakeholders. The effectiveness of each of these elements is directly influenced by the actions of district leadership. The outermost layer of the framework represents the environment in which districts operate and includes regulations and statutes, contracts, funding, and politics. These factors are primarily outside of the direct control of district leaders, but have the potential to greatly influence district strategy and operations.

The remainder of this note is divided into three sections. First, we share some brief thoughts on the importance of creating a mission, setting objectives, and developing a theory of action about how to create improvement in student outcomes. These three steps facilitate strategy formulation; in turn, strategy drives decisions about each of the organizational elements. In the second section, we discuss the role

and characteristics of an effective strategy. Finally, we define and describe each of the framework elements, and provide a set of critical questions that district leaders can use to diagnose their strengths and weaknesses and design action plans in their own pursuit of coherence.

Focusing on What Matters

Mission, Objectives, and Milestones

In public school districts, setting performance objectives can be difficult. Districts face competing priorities and demands from multiple constituencies at the local, state, and federal levels. In addition, unlike private sector organizations, school districts are designated producers of a public good in a particular geographic area and cannot choose to serve some customers and not others. Within these constraints however, districts are developing mission statements that target increased performance for *all* students (regardless of race, class, or prior academic performance) as their primary objective. A concrete performance objective for such a mission might be: *By 2012, 80% of students in the district will score in the proficient category or above on state reading and math tests, and there will be no gap between the performance of students of different ethnicities and/or socio-economic status.*

An ambitious long-term objective such as the one above can be made more manageable by setting intermediate milestones between the current performance and the desired performance. Milestones for the one, three, and five year marks allow a district to monitor its progress toward the larger objective, communicate success along the way, and respond to new information as it becomes available. Districts are increasingly breaking annual goals into more granular milestones at the school and classroom level. For example, in one large urban district, leaders underscore "the power of two," meaning if every teacher helps two additional students score proficient on the state reading assessment, the district will meet its annual performance goals for reading.

School districts must design and implement a district-wide strategy in order to fully achieve their objectives and the associated milestones at scale. A theory of action can facilitate effective strategy development.

Theory of Action and the Instructional Core[3]

Articulating an explicit theory of action[4] to link strategy to mission is a useful step in strategy formulation.[5] In this context, a theory of action represents the organization's collective belief about the causal relationships between certain actions and desired outcomes. Some find it useful to think of a theory of action as an "if . . . then . . ." statement, or a series of such statements.

In order to achieve their mission of increased performance for all students regardless of race, class, or prior academic performance, leaders in public schools districts should develop theories of action about how to strengthen the instructional core. For example, a number of districts believe deeply that high quality professional development for teachers is the most highly-leveraged way to improve student performance. They articulate their theory of action as: *"The most direct way to increase student learning is to improve teachers' instructional practice. Therefore, if we help all teachers improve their instructional practice, then we will accomplish high levels of achievement for all students."*

This theory of action focuses strategy development by narrowing the range of choices to those actions that people in the district believe

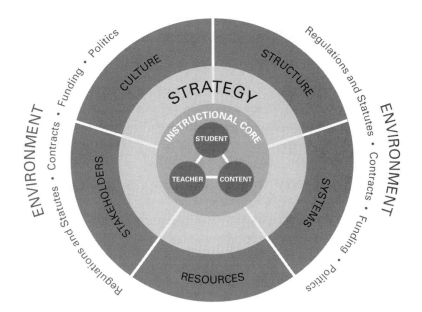

PELP Coherence Framework

have the highest likelihood of increasing achievement levels for all students; namely, decisions that focus resources on those activities aimed at improving the instructional practice of all teachers throughout the district. The above is intended as one example of a prevalent theory of action; a district's own theory of action might be different from this example and be quite effective. Once a leadership team has agreed on a theory of action, they can develop a strategy to put the theory into practice.

Strategy[6]

Strategy is the set of actions a district deliberately takes to provide capacity and support to the instructional core with the objective of raising student performance district-wide. Strategy informs how the people, activities, and resources of a district work together to accomplish a collective purpose. A district must begin at the nucleus of its organization—teaching and learning—and develop strategy from the inside-out. A district's improvement strategy should be grounded in providing capacity and support to the three components of the instructional core—teachers' knowledge and skill, student engagement, and academically challenging content.

Having a well articulated strategy helps leaders choose what to do, and just as importantly, what *not* to do. As a result, the district can put its scarce resources to use more effectively. Without a clear strategy, projects tend to be started one after the other, often moving on related, yet disconnected tracks. Programs are launched with fanfare and enthusiasm, and layered on top of existing programs that might not be effective and should have been stopped long ago. Often when district leaders do develop a strategy, they fail to engage others in its formulation or to communicate it effectively. As a result, the strategy remains largely in the heads of the senior managers, and is never fully embraced by the people on the front lines of the organization who are accountable for implementation.

Once a strategy is developed, district leaders must create an organization that supports rather than constrains its implementation. If the strategy is communicated clearly and the organization is designed to support it, the people doing the work are much more likely to understand how their efforts contribute to the overall mission of the district.

At the school level, it is important to understand that *how* a district supports individual schools to implement the strategy and improve student performance may look different from school to school. Districts are increasingly moving away from a "one-size-fits-all" approach to managing schools in favor of differentiating treatment in response to unique school needs and characteristics. For example, one large urban district grants increased autonomy to schools that accept four-year performance contracts; if student achievement and other indicators of school quality fail to improve, the district can re-

move the principal or close the school. Many districts limit the choices that low-performing schools can make, while others invest additional targeted resources in these schools to build their capacity.

For school districts engaging in differentiated treatment, achieving coherence gains added complexity. It is vital for leaders to define which aspects of the strategy should remain consistent across all schools and which aspects should be adapted for or by individual schools and under what conditions. At the same time, these districts may find they need more explicit integrating mechanisms, such as cultural norms or a consistent accountability system, to ensure that schools with different decision rights or varying levels of district support maintain a shared commitment to the strategy.

The following critical questions can help district leaders reflect critically on the effectiveness of their strategy to improve student performance.

Critical questions:

- In our district, what do we believe is the most powerful way to drive increased academic performance in every school? In other words, what is the most effective way to strengthen the instructional core—teachers' knowledge and skill, student engagement and academically challenging content? Where do we believe we can achieve the most leverage? (This is our "theory of action.")

- Given the above, what is our strategy for improving student performance throughout the district? Is our strategy consistent with our theory of action? If not, do we need to revise our strategy?

- Based on our strategy, what activities should be consuming our time and resources? What activities and programs currently consume our time and our resources? Are these aligned with our strategy, or are they diverting our focus?

Based on our strategy, which activities should we grow, drop or modify?

- Is our strategy clearly communicated and well understood? Do people working in the district office (education and operations departments) understand their role in supporting the strategy? Do principals and teachers from every school understand and embrace the strategy? How do we know? How can we do a better job of communicating our strategy and inspiring people to be committed to implementing it?

- Are there aspects of the strategy that should be common across all schools? Are there aspects of the strategy that should be adapted for or by individual schools? Under what conditions? What criteria will be used to identify different schools' needs and their different decision rights? Do we currently treat some schools differently from other schools—either formally or informally? If so, are we behaving in ways that are consistent with our strategy and the conditions we articulated? Do we have adequate integrating mechanisms?

Framework Elements

Five organizational elements are critical to the successful implementation of a district-wide improvement strategy: culture, structures and systems, resources, and stakeholders. The outermost layer of the framework is the district's operating environment. Definitions and descriptions for each element follow, as well as critical questions that help district leaders conceptualize how each element would look if it were coherent with the strategy and diagnose any discrepancies in their current state. District leaders should walk away with a better understanding of how their organization is presently supporting (or hindering) strategy execution and with concrete ideas that can be translated into action steps for moving the organization towards greater coherence with the strategy.

Culture[7]

Culture consists of the norms and behaviors in the organization; in other words, everyone's shared understanding of "how things work around here." The public education sector has long had a culture that valued effort more than results. As long as people seemed to be working hard, they could go about their business without being asked to work with colleagues or to be accountable for the performance of their students. At its worse, this type of culture can lead to defeatism among teachers and administrators ("I taught it, but they didn't learn it"). In today's accountability environment, this way of operating is no longer acceptable. As a result, districts must establish a culture of collaboration, high expectations, and accountability.

District leaders often view culture as something amorphous that defies management. However, by taking specific actions such as redefining roles or relationships, altering performance expectations, and using job assignments in creative ways, leaders can upend an entrenched counterproductive culture.

Leaders must engage people in specific behaviors that will reshape their individual beliefs about their own practice and student learning. Substantial empirical research on schools has indicated that "the effectiveness of districts, in terms of student learning and development, is significantly influenced by the quality and characteristics of district culture."[8] Some examples of norms and beliefs to consider are: attitudes about accountability, orientation towards students and staff, conflict resolution methods, the reciprocity between the district office and schools, and the approach to stakeholders.

Critical questions:

- What does our strategy say about our district; in other words, "What do we believe"? As an organization, do we behave in ways that are consistent with these beliefs, or in contradictory ways?

- What behaviors are needed from people throughout the district to implement our strategy (e.g. risk-taking, collaboration, problem-solving, etc.)? How can we model these desired behaviors for our people? And give them opportunities to apply these behaviors in their daily work?

- What norms should be established to support the desired behaviors (e.g. tolerance for mistakes that further organizational learning, an attitude of service for schools, etc.)? What actions can we take to embed these norms in the way we work and interact? What do our current norms and behaviors suggest about our existing culture? Does our existing culture support or hinder our ability to implement our strategy?

Structures and Systems

Although structures and systems are separate components of our framework, we learned through extensive work in school districts that they are so interdependent that is most effective to discuss them together. They include things such as roles and responsibilities, reporting relationships, teams, accountability mechanisms, compensation arrangements, resource allocation methods, organizational learning processes, and training programs. Districts have usually developed systems and structures haphazardly to support generation after generation of reform efforts. These systems and structures tend to stay in place long after the fad they were built for has passed from the scene. As a result, systems and structures do not reinforce each other and often constrain rather than enable high performance. To effectively support a strategy, the structures and systems often have to be reinvented.

Structure: Structure helps define how the work of the district gets done. It includes how people are organized, who has responsibility and accountability for results, and who makes or influences decisions. Structures can be both formal and informal.

Formal Structures: Formal structures are deliberately established organizational forms that can be either relatively permanent or temporary. Examples of permanent structures are departments reflected on an organizational chart or standing groups such as the superintendent's cabinet. Temporary structures are time-limited, as is often the case with task forces or cross-functional teams established to plan or implement a new project or program.

Structural decisions can often hinder rather than support effective implementation of strategy. For example, many districts separate the organizational units that deliver professional development from the line management of schools. This arrangement makes it difficult to hold principals accountable for the professional development activities in their own schools, and for principals to hold professional developers accountable for school level objectives.

A word of caution is in order. Historically, the public education sector has relied too heavily on formal structural changes alone to drive improvement. A classic example is the debate over how "tightly" a district office should manage its relationship with schools, usually seen as a dichotomy between centralization and decentralization. Advocates tend to decry whatever default structure exists as the primary reason for poor performance. If districts are heavily decentralized and underperforming, then leaders (especially newly arrived ones) blame the structure for a lack of focus and discipline and move quickly to centralize authority and control to the central office. The reverse is true when leaders find a highly centralized structure and a poor performing district—they push decisions about resources and programs out to principals, ostensibly freeing them from the burdens imposed by a centralized bureaucracy that is out of touch with the needs of schools.

Both arguments have merit, but neither is "the answer." Organizational structure should be designed to support the effective implementation of a strategy for improvement, and framing structural design questions as a debate over centralized or decentralized power is too simplistic and usually misses the point—people at all levels of the district have a role to play in improving performance. Decisions about structure should put *performance* at the center of the debate, rather than power, politics, or ideology.

Informal Structures and Power: Informal structures—the way decisions get made or the way people work and interact outside of formal channels—can be as (or even more) powerful than formal structures. Informal structures can be either positive—principals calling each other to share ideas—or negative—decisions get made by people "in the know" instead of through established working groups. While formal power is primarily based on rank or position, informal power is garnered and reinforced through social networks. Informal power can be difficult to manage because it is usually earned or developed through tenure, expertise or competence.[9] District leadership can have some influence over informal power by creating developmental committee assignments and job rotations, which allow individuals to gain informal power.

Since those who possess informal power have considerable influence over the behavior of others in the district, it is important for the leadership team to assess how this power can either be leveraged or needs to be mitigated in order to accomplish the strategy.[10] For example, individuals with strong informal power can help champion organizational values (e.g. collaboration) or potentially controversial initiatives; by the same token, they can be powerful roadblocks. The same holds true for informal structures; some can be leveraged while others may need to be disrupted. Asking questions such as, "Who do you go to when you really need to get something done?" or "How do things *really* work around here?" can help reveal informal structures and sources of power.

Systems: School districts manage themselves through a variety of systems, which are the processes and procedures through which work gets done. Some systems are formally designed by the district, while others emerge informally in practice. Whether formal or informal, the purpose of systems is to increase the district's efficiency and effectiveness in implementing strategy.

Systems are built around such important functions as career development and promotion, compensation, student assignment, resource allocation, organizational learning, and measurement and accountability. Most practically, systems help people feel like they do not have to "reinvent the wheel" when they need to get an important, and often multi-step, task done.

For example, in the wake of unprecedented amounts of student performance data, many districts talk about the desire to increase "data-driven decision making," yet many schools lack the expertise or capacity to do this well. One large urban district recently unveiled a year-long "school quality review" process that trains school staff how to form hypotheses to explain the root causes of poor performance, put interventions in place and evaluate their progress. The school quality reviews represent an important system for strengthening organizational learning and the capacity to drive improvement among those closest to the students.

School districts also must develop systems to comply with myriad external requirements even if these systems do not drive strategy implementation. For instance, federal regulations such as the No Child Left Behind Act of 2001 (NCLB) and desegregation legislation have required that school districts develop systems and processes to address these external demands. The emphasis on accountability has also put pressure on districts to develop complex systems to better track and manage student performance data.

Critical questions:

- Which roles are critical to implementing our strategy? How do these roles and responsibilities need to be defined? What skills and knowledge do people in these roles need to be successful?

- Which reporting relationships would be most beneficial for implementing our strategy? How can these relationships be made clear to everyone? How are we currently organized? Who reports to whom and why? What is the span of control of our key middle managers?

- What informal structures or sources of power are influential in the district? Are they helping or hindering strategy implementation? How do we make decisions, particularly ones that impact schools? Who is involved? How do we solicit input from others? How do we communicate our decisions? How can decision-making be more transparent and coherent?

- When will we need cross-functional collaboration? How can we effectively structure this (e.g. ongoing teams, short-term task forces, updates, etc.)? What existing structures or practices need to be modified to facilitate this?

- How can we recruit and select people aligned with our strategy? How can we design and deliver professional development programs that are in line with our strategy and that provide value to teachers and administrators?

- Do we have a rigorous process in place to facilitate continuous learning among our educators and administrators? How might we create a system that enables people to analyze student data in order to improve performance? If we had such a system, do our people have the capacity to make effective decisions based on the results of their analysis? What is our plan for ensuring that this capacity exists at every school in the district?

- What types of accountability mechanisms are needed to help everyone feel responsible for driving improved student outcomes? How will we measure our performance? Over the long-term? On an interim basis? Have we defined what success looks like (or "what we're trying to accomplish") at the district, school and classroom level? Are we measuring and communicating our progress?

- How can performance evaluation be used to help people focus on the work required to implement our strategy? Can compensation be used as an incentive to meet performance goals? Should these incentives target individuals, groups or both?

- What systems do we need to help people get their work done more effectively and efficiently? Are any of our systems overly cumbersome and/or outdated given our strategy?

Resources

Money is usually the first thing leaders think about when resources are mentioned. Money is obviously important, but organizational resources also include people and physical assets such as technology and data. District leaders must allocate the full range of resources in ways that are coherent with the district's strategy in order to implement it effectively. This means being disciplined about which current and planned activities receive necessary resources, and just as importantly, which ones do not. Because district resources are usually quite constrained, freeing up the resources necessary to fully invest in activities that are coherent with the strategy usually means cutting off the flow to others.

People: District budgets typically allocate nearly 80% of their expenses to the salaries and benefits of the people in the organization. At the school level, the average is closer to 90%. Given this, district and school leaders must think rigorously about how to deploy the organization's most valuable asset: its people. This includes a serious look at the skills and knowledge that people need in order to successfully implement the strategy, and an analysis that reveals any gaps between what people know how to do and what the strategy requires of them.

For example, if the knowledge and skill of teachers is believed to be the most highly-leveraged component in the instructional core, the district must invest heavily in achieving coherence in this area. In addition to investing directly in professional development, some districts are more actively influencing personnel assignments. For example, some innovative leaders are finding ways to encourage and support highly-skilled educators in taking on challenging assignments such as leading or teaching in a chronically low-performing school. Often this requires changes to collective bargaining agreements that use seniority as the primary factor in allocating people to jobs—this can be difficult, but worth the effort.

Financial Resources: Districts are also re-thinking how financial resources flow throughout the organization so that they are more coherent with the strategy and more likely to produce desired outcomes. This can take a variety of forms, such as setting benchmarks for what percentage of total funds must be spent in schools versus at the central office or establishing ratios for instructional to non-instructional expenses. In some cases, leaders are challenging fundamental assumptions, such as the notion that every child costs the same to educate. In a number of districts, this thinking has led to the implementation of a "weighted student formula" that attaches a dollar amount to each individual student based on a set of characteristics (i.e. prior academic performance, family income, and grade-level). The money then follows the student to his or her school, and schools receive their annual resources based on their unique student enrollments. Whether or not such a formula makes sense should be considered in light of a district-wide strategy for improvement. However, thinking creatively about how money

flows around the organization is critical to implementing strategy.

Technology: Building the technology infrastructure necessary to support annual reporting demands from external accountability mechanisms is important. It is also critical to invest in technology to manage student performance data on a more frequent basis in order to support organizational processes that require teachers and administrators to use data to make better instructional decisions. Many districts are requiring every school to administer benchmark assessments three to four times per year and to use the data for continuous improvement. To support this, strategic investments in data warehouses, assessment and analysis tools, and knowledge management applications are necessary. They can save teachers an enormous amount of time required for administrative tasks, and help them make more effective instructional decisions that are directly responsive to their students' learning needs.

Critical questions:

- How can we allocate our resources to be more coherent with our strategy? What assumptions about students and their learning needs are reflected in the way we manage and allocate resources? Do we continue to financially support activities, departments, or programs that are inconsistent with our strategy? Do we need to modify contracts or agreements with bargaining units in order to more effectively allocate personnel?

- What knowledge and skill do district and school staff need to implement our strategy? What is the gap between what they know and what we are asking them to do now? What will it take to close this gap?

- How can we think more strategically about matching people's experience and knowledge with roles and assignments that are critical to the strategy? Do we have a full enough understanding of what are people know and can do so that we could make sound matches of experience and opportunity? If not, how can we develop this?

- Do we have the technology infrastructure we need to not only meet external reporting demands, but to capture and analyze data in a way that allows people at all levels of the organization to make better decisions about improving the teaching and learning that happens in classrooms? Do we have a clear understanding of who needs what data to be more effective in their roles? If not, how can we develop this?

- Do we have a clear framework for deciding when we should build technology tools ourselves and when we should buy them from a capable vendor?

Stakeholders

Stakeholders are people and groups inside and outside the organization who have a legitimate interest in the system and can influence the effectiveness of the strategy. These include teachers' unions, parents, students, school boards, community and advocacy groups, and local politicians and policymakers. Managing stakeholder relationships in a way that is coherent with the strategy is especially challenging because stakeholders rarely agree on what success looks like. District leaders must either persuade a majority of stakeholder groups to back the strategy or, at the very least, secure the backing of one or two with enough power to prevent the others from becoming a disruptive force.

Stakeholder Categories

- *District and school staff*—all paid employee groups throughout the organization

- *Governing bodies*—boards, committees, and/or political figures that set and administer district policies, e.g., board of education, mayor, local school site councils

- *Unions and associations*—local, state, and national collective bargaining units, e.g., teacher unions, administrator professional associations, custodial unions

- *Parents and parent organizations*—Parent Teacher Association (PTA), Parents for Public Schools, individual parents, parent volunteers

- *Students*—formal student leaders or groups, temporary coalitions formed around a specific cause or individual students

- *Civic and community leaders and organizations*—chambers of commerce, National Association for the Advancement of Colored People (NAACP), politicians, local business leaders, local and national foundations, nonprofits, churches

Critical questions:

- Who are our stakeholders? Which stakeholders will be affected by the strategy and how? Which stakeholders can have an impact (positive or negative) on the implementation of the strategy? How can we think about prioritizing and/or sequencing our stakeholder relationships? Who are our most natural allies? Our most influential ones?

- Is our strategy well understood by all stakeholders? How can we help them better understand their role in supporting our strategy? Are any stakeholders causing us to pursue activities that are incoherent with (or not central to) our strategy?

- How might we best communicate our progress to our stakeholders in a way that garners their support and their willingness to influence other stakeholders and the environment that are coherent with our strategy? How can we proactively manage our relationships with stakeholders so that they will want to contribute to our success?

Environment

A district's environment includes all of the external factors that can have an impact on strategy, operations and performance. The environment in which public school districts operate includes the various funding sources available (both public and private), the political and policy context at the city, state, and national levels, the collective bargaining arrangements in place, and the characteristics of their particular community.

District leaders have little direct control over the environment, but must spend significant time trying to manage its effects in order to consistently implement a district-wide strategy. The environment can have an impact on districts by enforcing nonnegotiable demands, constraining decision making, limiting resources, evaluating performance, and imposing sanctions. However, the environment can also serve as an enabler if district leadership can influence these regulatory and statutory, contractual, financial, and political forces that surround them.

District leaders must consider the factors in the environment and determine how those factors, singly or collectively, create demands, constraints, or opportunities that have an impact on their ability to implement their strategy.[11] The categories of the environment in the PELP Coherence Framework are:[12]

1. *Regulations and statutes*—legal and regulatory influences on the district, e.g., board election policies, mandates from state departments of education, No Child Left Behind legislation

2. *Contracts*—agreements between the district and various bargaining units that have an impact on strategy and operations

3. *Funding*—all sources of revenue available to the district, both public and private, including local and state tax levies, categorical funds for state and federal programs, and grants from individuals and foundations

4. *Politics*—the political landscape in which the district operates, including local governance dynamics, the relative power of special interest groups, state-wide debates regarding issues such as choice and accountability, and electoral politics at the local, state and federal levels

Critical questions:

• How can we effectively align external actors (e.g. foundations, community leaders) in support of our strategy? Do we need to realign (or pull back from) the efforts of any external actors to better support our strategy?

• What funding sources (public and private) are available to us? How can the terms of these sources be made most beneficial? What would it take to achieve this?

• What federal, state and local policies would be most beneficial to implementing our strategy? What is the most effective approach to advocating for these? Are there any regulations or statutes that are constraining our ability to implement our strategy that we can advocate to change? Are there any ways we could better leverage existing regulations or statutes?

• What contractual arrangement with our bargaining units would be most beneficial? What would it take to achieve this? Are there any levers for change that we are not currently exercising?

• How would we like our community to perceive us; what is our "brand" (e.g. best district in the city, affordable with quality, etc.)? What is the gap between how we would like to be perceived and how we are perceived? How can we improve our image?

• What are the key political influences on the district? How do these impact our strategy? Ideally, how can we leverage these influences to our advantage?

Conclusion

The PELP Coherence Framework is designed to focus the attention of public school district leaders on the central problem of increasing the achievement levels of all students by making all the parts of a large district work in concert with its strategy. The framework can be useful when evaluating or changing an existing strategy, as well as when developing a new one. By providing a common language and consistent way to address the challenge of creating (and sustaining) coherence, the PELP Coherence Framework can help leaders build high-performing school districts that improve educational outcomes for every student, in every school. This mission is no longer lofty or optional given today's heightened accountability environment; it is simply the job public school districts are expected to perform.

Notes

1. The PELP Coherence Framework draws on organizational alignment frameworks such as The Congruence Model developed by Professor Michael Tushman of Harvard Business School and Professor Charles O'Reilly of the Graduate School of Business at Stanford University. For an explanation of the Congruence Model, see their book, *Winning Through Innovation,* Harvard Business School Publishing Corporation, 1997.

2. David K. Cohen and Deborah Loewenberg Ball, "Instruction, Capacity, and Improvement," CPRE Research Report Series RR-43, Philadelphia: University of Pennsylvania, Consortium for Policy Research in Education, 1999.

3. This section is adapted from "Note on Strategy in Public Education," PEL-011, by Stacey Childress.

4. The term "theory of action" in this note is adapted from the work of Professor Chris Argyris of the Harvard Graduate School of Education, and is similar to the concept of "theory of change" currently popular in non-profit strategy and management.

5. Other methods of strategy formulation exist; therefore, "theory of action" does not appear explicitly on the framework graphic. For the purposes of this note, the authors use theory of action as one way to develop strategy.

6. This section is adapted from "Note on Strategy in Public Education," PEL-011. Please refer to this note for a fuller discussion of the characteristics of effective strategy and its role in the public education sector.

7. The sections on culture, structure and systems draw from M. L. Tushman and C. A. O'Reilly, *Winning Through Innovation,* Boston: HBS Press, 2002, M. L. Tushman and D. A. Nadler "A Model for Diagnosing Organizational Behavior," *Organizational Dynamics,* Autumn 1980, and "Organizational Alignment: The 7S model," Jeff Bradach, HBS No. 497–045.

8. Robert G. Owens, *Organizational Behavior in Education,* Needham Heights, MA: Prentice Hall, 2001, p. 175

9. See Linda A. Hill, "Influence as Exchange," HBS No. 497–049 for a discussion of networks and sources of informal power.

10. See W. E. Baker, *Networking Smart: How to Build Relationships for Personal and Organizational Success,* New York: McGraw Hill, Inc., 1994 for examples of proactive and explicit strategies used to manage informal networks.

11. Adapted from M. L. Tushman and D. L. Nadler, "A Model for Diagnosing Organizational Behavior," *Organizational Dynamics,* Autumn 1980, p. 41.

12. Please note that the examples are not intended to be exhaustive, but rather to clarify some of the categories of environmental factors that exist in public education.

DISCUSSION QUESTIONS

1. How would you articulate SFUSD's strategy to improve student outcomes?

2. What activities must SFUSD be good at in order to execute this strategy across the district? At the central office? At schools?

3. What criteria seem to drive the reallocation of decision-making authority? What are the organizational implications of moving from a mostly centralized control to one where individual schools are allocated responsibilities for creating budgets? Please use Exhibit 6 in your analysis.

4. How are the weighted student formula and the academic planning process linked? How do they work? Be prepared to explain each in detail in class.

5. What are the biggest barriers to the effectiveness of the weighted student formula and site-based budgeting system? What advice would you give to Ackerman and her team for addressing these barriers?

Stacey Childress ■ Robert Peterkin

Pursuing Educational Equity at San Francisco Unified School District

On an afternoon in April 2004, Superintendent Arlene Ackerman hung up the phone with California Secretary of Education Richard Riordan feeling both excited and challenged. The state was considering mandating that school districts implement a weighted student formula (WSF) to allocate financial resources to individual schools, and move decision-making about those resources from central offices to schools. Knowing that Ackerman had implemented a system at San Francisco Unified School District (SFUSD) that accomplished both of those objectives, Riordan had asked her to brief his staff on what SFUSD had learned through three years of implementation.

Ackerman and her staff had already begun asking themselves the same questions. Was the WSF aligned with SFUSD's strategy to achieve educational equity? What capacity had the district developed, or did it still need to develop, to successfully shift to site-based decision making? How should SFUSD resolve the challenges and tensions that had emerged in the first three years of implementation? And perhaps most intriguing of all, could SFUSD connect the implementation of the WSF to improved student achievement data? Ackerman thought quietly for a few moments, and then walked out of her office to find key members of her team to tell them about Riordan's request.

Background and Context

Demographics, Finances, and Student Achievement

Founded in 1851 as the first public school district in California, San Francisco Unified School District (SFUSD) was the fifth largest in the state, serving 57,805 students in 116 schools with 3292 classroom teachers by SY03[1]. The diverse student body was 31% Chinese, 21% Latino, 15% African-American, 10% White, 7% Filipino, and 16% other non-white minorities. Thirty percent of total students were English language learners, and 56% were eligible for free or reduced price lunch. Special education (SPED) students represented 11% and gifted and talented students accounted for 12% of total students.

The certificated teacher force was 55% White, 14% Chinese, 10% Latino, 8% African-American, and 13% other non-white minorities. The United Educators of San Francisco (UESF) historically played a collaborative role with district management, but with the election of new leadership in June 2003, shifted to a stance that union leadership described as "cooperative rather than collaborative."

SFUSD's $660 million budget was independent from the city of San Francisco's budget. In California, districts operated under a state revenue limit, which attempted to equalize per student spending across districts. If funding through the local tax base went up, the state's contribution was reduced to offset the increase and preserve the limit. Local sources accounted for 93% of SFUSD's revenue limit funding. From 2001–2003, expenses increased 11%, while revenues grew only 4% (Exhibit 1 contains district financial information).

In aggregate, SFUSD students performed better in absolute terms than their counterparts in other urban districts in California on the California Standards Test, but African American and Latino students were overrepresented in the bottom two quartiles. Additionally, as in other urban districts in the U.S., the total number of students scoring in the bottom two quartiles in reading and math on the SAT-9, a national norm-referenced test, was considered too high by district stakeholders[2] (Exhibit 2 contains student achievement data).

Governance

A seven-member elected board of education was responsible for district-level governance. Members, called commissioners, were elected at-large to serve four-year terms, with no term limits. The board elected a chair from among themselves. A well-regarded middle school principal noted that the board was subject to the same "interest-based politics" as other elected bodies in San Francisco. Commissioners often saw themselves as representatives of specific community groups or special interests that had supported their candidacy, rather than as at-large members with a citywide perspective. One commissioner observed that some candidates for the board of education saw the body as a stepping-stone to the board of supervisors, San Francisco's powerful city council.

The board was responsible for establishing educational goals and standards, approving curriculum, and approving the overall budget and expenditures. They also approved all union contracts. The board appointed a superintendent of schools to manage the day-to-day administration of all district functions, including the hiring of all personnel. Between 2000 and 2004, the board shifted from nearly unanimous support for Ackerman's proposals, to a 4–3 split in favor of most resolutions proposed by the superintendent and district staff.

Each school had a locally elected school site council (SSC) that shared decision-making with the principal regarding the use of state and federal grants. Elections were held every two years. SSCs at the elementary school level included the principal and elected parents, teachers, and school staff. Middle and high school SSCs also included elected students. These groups ranged from 12 to 25 members, depending on the size of the school, and state law and district policy mandated their composition and responsibilities.[3] The engagement and capacity of SSCs varied across the district.

SSC–school site council

Superintendent Arlene Ackerman and "Excellence for All"

In summer 2000, the board of education appointed Dr. Arlene Ackerman superintendent of schools following a nation-wide search. With over 30 years of experience in public education as a teacher, principal and deputy superintendent in numerous districts, Ackerman had most recently been the superintendent of the public school system in Washington, D.C. A graduate of Harvard's doctoral program for urban superintendents, Ackerman quickly articulated five core beliefs intended to guide the work of all stakeholders on behalf of SFUSD students: (1) Children come first; (2) Parents are our partners; (3) Victory is in the classroom; (4) Leadership and accountability are the keys to our success; and (5) It takes the entire community to ensure the success of all students.

Ackerman immediately faced a volatile issue regarding a series of desegregation suits and countersuits that had begun in 1983 with *San Francisco NAACP v. SFUSD,* and continued in 1990 with *Ho v. SFUSD.* As a result, the district operated under a consent decree, managed by a federal judge, which required SFUSD to meet educational equity targets for all students in the district. In 1999, before Ackerman's arrival, a consent decree advisory committee issued a report highlighting severe deficiencies in the district's progress regarding these targets. After her arrival, Ackerman appointed four committees, including an educational equity committee, to explore the findings of the report and make recommendations. The committees included members from SFUSD central and school staff, parents, board members, community leaders, and union leadership.

The educational equity committee found that by 2000, the achievement gap between African-American and Latino students and their white and Chinese counterparts was widening. After controlling for student and school characteristics in 10 years of standardized test data, the committee discovered that African-American and Latino students as a group scored lower than other SFUSD ethnic groups, regardless of poverty or other factors. For African-American students, the achievement gap widened in the upper grades, indicating that these students did comparatively worse the longer they remained in school. In the early grades, non-poor African-American and Latino students scored higher than poor white and Chinese students in some years, but by seventh grade, poor and non-poor African-American and Latino students dropped below poor white and Chinese students. Many stakeholders connected these findings to the consent decree advisory committee's 1999 assertion that substantial numbers of SFUSD teachers and administrators had lower expectations for African-American and Latino students, and that some schools used a "dumbed-down" curriculum for these students. The committee put forth recommendations to address these findings, which were incorporated into a district-wide strategy for improvement.

Historically, district leadership had viewed the consent decree as a constraint, but Ackerman and her team decided to align their district-wide improvement strategy with the decree's requirements, and developed a five-year plan dubbed "Excellence for All." Over 3000 teachers, parents and other community members attended public input sessions and school meetings to discuss the plan, and 2500 people completed an open-ended form requesting feedback on the plan. The input was incorporated into the final version of "Excellence for All."

"Excellence for All" had three main elements: a focus on academic achievement for all students; the equitable allocation of district resources; and accountability for results. The academic achievement element included professional development for teachers and principals in instructional strategies and the use of data, a focus on literacy in all grades, and increased expectations for all learners. The plan included timetables for implementation of the various components. As one K-8 principal described, "Excellence for All" is goal oriented. Kids enter the system at a variety of performance levels, but the plan's clear targets help us focus attention on underperforming students."

After obtaining unanimous board approval in April 2001, Ackerman submitted "Excellence for All" to the federal judge monitoring the consent decree. The judge approved the 231-page document as SFUSD's plan to meet the desegregation requirements of the consent decree, and implementation of "Excellence for All" became a legal requirement (Exhibit 3 includes "Excellence for All" goals).

Executing a Strategy to Achieve Equity

In order to execute "Excellence for All," Ackerman and her team pursued a set of actions to meet the objectives of improving achievement for all students, allocating resources equitably, and instilling accountability for results. These actions included: giving parents a choice about where their children attended school; creating classrooms all over the city that represented the diversity of the entire student population and in which teachers had high expectations for all learners; and placing decisions about and accountability for instructional programs and the resources to support them in the hands of school communities.

Student Assignment and the Diversity Index

Historically, geographic boundaries around each of the city's schools dictated student assignment. In 2001, SFUSD data suggested middle class and affluent neighborhood schools had challenging curriculum programs, and that the number of seats available in these schools was greater than the number of children who lived in the surrounding neighborhoods. By contrast, schools in low-income neighborhoods had fewer seats

available than students, dramatically lowered teacher expectations for African-American and Latino students, and a dearth of honors and advanced placement courses. "Excellence for All" committed the district to providing equitable access to schools with academically challenging programs, as well as improving the quality of deficient schools.

In order to meet the requirements of the consent decree, SFUSD could not use race as a factor in assigning students to schools. A local business leader framed the issue as "a broader question for the city. San Francisco's diversity is a great asset. But we're at a crucial time in defining what a truly great diverse American city can be, and how we educate our kids is an important component of that definition." In early 2001, Ackerman convened a task force comprised of representatives of various stakeholder groups in SFUSD and the city to develop a method to give parents choice and to balance the diversity of the city's schools. Over the course of several months, the task force created a new "educational placement" process. The process was implemented in SY02 to place kindergarteners in elementary schools, 6th graders in middle schools, and 9th graders in high schools.

The process allowed parents to rank up to five of the district's schools as assignment preferences for their children.[4] As mandated by state law, SFUSD posted on its website an annual school accountability report card (SARC) for every district school. SARCs included information about the academic program, student and teacher demographics, and test score data by grade for each school. Parents were encouraged to use SARCs to inform their preferences. Additionally, SFUSD ran an annual fair at which principals and their teams set up booths displaying the distinctive characteristics of their schools, and interacted with parents seeking information. Parental preference and student residency were then used as key factors in the assignment process. The task force also created a diversity index for use in creating schools with balanced profiles. Based on research regarding social predictors of academic performance, the diversity index included six non-race factors to describe students: socioeconomic status, academic achievement status, mother's educational background, language proficiency status, home language, and academic performance rank of the sending school.

SFUSD partnered with WestEd, a nonprofit research and service agency, to develop a software program that used parental preference, student residency, and the diversity index to place students in schools. The system included a parameter that allowed siblings in the same grade range to be placed in the same school. The educational placement process was not without critics. Some parents in the Chinese community believed their children disproportionately experienced the negative effects of the new system by being forced to attend schools outside of their neighborhoods. Other detractors claimed that schools largely remained homogenous reflections of the surrounding neighborhoods, whether Chinese, Latino, or African-American. However, the system provided an element of choice to parents and achieved a more balanced diversity profile in many of the district's schools. In SY03, 63% of all students received their first choice, and 83% were placed in one of their preferred schools (Exhibit 4 provides more detail on the diversity index and assignment process).

Rethinking Resources

Historically, SFUSD schools received resources through a staffing ratios model. In this method, the central office allocated resources to schools in the form of teachers, counselors, librarians, and administrators based on the number of students enrolled at each site. Additionally, the schools received a small budget for supplies. As a result, the central office controlled the vast majority of spending at the school level. With the implementation of Excellence for All and the new educational placement system, Ackerman and her team re-evaluated the existing resource allocation model. Having been involved in the implementation of WSFs in two of her previous districts, Seattle and Washington, D.C., she decided to explore the method for SFUSD. Ackerman explained:

> As an educator, my first concern was to connect resource allocation to academic issues—resources should support increased student achievement. Next, we needed to address equity and transparency in the distribution of resources. Often, adults in high performing schools are more adept at navigating the system than adults in low performing schools. This can lead to resource disparities between schools. And finally, more money doesn't necessarily lead to higher achievement levels. We needed to introduce some accountability for producing results at all levels of the district. With a weighted student formula, the dollars follow the students and adults at the school level decide how to spend those dollars based on what's best for that particular group of kids. The central office provides data, supports schools, and monitors outcomes, so everyone is involved, and everyone is accountable.

Myong Leigh, chief of policy and planning, chaired a committee created to make recommendations to Ackerman for implementing a WSF. Committee members visited Seattle and Sacramento to learn from their WSF implementations. They also studied the District of Columbia's WSF—Leigh had been on Ackerman's staff in D.C. and understood some of the advantages and challenges. These districts each varied in the mechanics of their WSF, but all gave schools the responsibility for managing their own budgets.

Nancy Waymack, who had played a key role with Ackerman and Leigh in implementing the WSF in D.C., later joined SFUSD's policy and planning division. She observed, "We started out looking at WSF as a resource allocation tool, but it quickly took on implications that were much more ambitious, including involving school communities more actively in the academic planning process." Leigh pointed out that previously "the school site academic plans had been seen primarily as compliance documents required for receiving state and federal funds. By linking resource allocation decisions through the WSF to site level decision making about the academic plans, the district could transform these into living documents, created by school site councils using student data to make decisions about instructional programs and resources."

Along with Leigh and Waymack, the WSF committee involved over 40 people between 2000 and 2004, including teachers, parents, union leadership, principals, and central office staff. They met twice each week over four months beginning in late 2000 and weekly over another four months in the following year, to synthesize information about previous WSF implementations and design a system that fit SFUSD. The committee developed a set of weights for various student characteristics and developed recommendations about which resource decisions should remain at the central office and which should be moved to schools (see Exhibit 5 for allocation of decision rights).

In the spring of 2001, SFUSD launched a WSF pilot with 27 volunteer schools, and then incorporated lessons learned from that experiment into a revised mechanism. In spring 2002, with unanimous approval from the board of education, SFUSD rolled out the WSF as the primary resource allocation mechanism for all schools. During this process, schools linked their budgets to their academic plans for SY03. By SY04, the second full year of implementation, approximately 60% of the district's unrestricted general funds were allocated to schools through the WSF.

Implementing the Weighted Student Formula and Site-Based Budgeting

The new WSF system included a complex process to calculate school revenues, as well as a new academic planning process that required principals to work with their SSCs to link resources to specific elements of their academic plans. The state mandated that the SSCs be involved in shared decision-making, but only with respect to state and federal grant funds. Because of this significant shift in the responsibilities of school staff and SSCs, the central office created and delivered professional development to prepare them for their new duties.

Strengthening Capacity

SFUSD's department of research, planning, and evaluation developed and delivered training in a "data-planning model" to strengthen the ability of SSCs, principals, and teachers to use data to develop academic plans that addressed the specific needs of their students. The data-planning model included analyzing current performance and student learning gaps at the school level; developing a plan that included specific actions to address the gaps and the alignment of resources to those gaps; implementing the plan throughout the school year; monitoring the implementation; and evaluating progress on site specific goals and student achievement at the end of each year. Principals and SSC members also received training from the central office on the WSF mechanism and on the budgeting process and software. Training for new and returning SSC members took place for half a day at the beginning of each school year, and again in January.

Five assistant superintendents for instructional support and operations (ISOs) supported the schools. Each ISO was accountable for a group of schools, and ensured that principals received ongoing professional development, and any technical assistance they might require in managing their SSC relationships or facilitating the academic planning and budgeting process. A former principal who was now an ISO pointed out, "The WSF brings new challenges to principals as instructional leaders. We need to figure out how to support them not only with training, but with systems." One middle school principal noted, "With the WSF and site-based budgeting, my role has changed dramatically, and the skills I need to manage my SSC and make resource decisions are new for me. I'm excited, but also a bit overwhelmed. Part of the difficulty is that it's not clear which of my old duties I should let go of in order to make room for the new ones."

School Revenues: WSF and other allocation pools

The central office determined revenue levels by forecasting student enrollment for each school. The WSF allocation was based on these forecasts and had a number of components: a foundation amount for each school; a specific dollar amount for each enrolled student called the base funding factor; an additional dollar amount for students with specific characteristics; and a loss or gain limit. Additionally, schools received lump sum allocations for restricted and categorical funds.

Forecasting Enrollment: Each January, using demographic and enrollment trend data, the central office developed a headcount projection for each school, which included specific counts for the types of students that were expected to enroll in the following academic year. The central office made adjustments in its forecasting procedures each year in order to increase the accuracy of projections. Ten days after the beginning of school, the actual enrollment at each school determined whether the revenue allocations would be adjusted. If the adjustment based on actual enrollment was less than $15,000 in either direction, no change to the budget was made.

Foundation Amount: The foundation amount was designed to ensure that every school

had the minimum funding necessary to pay the average salary and benefits of a principal and a clerk at the elementary, middle, or secondary school level. A school site could choose to spend more to upgrade the clerk position to a senior clerk or secretary with funds allocated through other parts of the weighted student formula.

Base Funding Factor: The base funding factor specified a uniform dollar amount to be allocated to schools for every enrolled student. Base funding was premised on the notion that it cost a specific dollar amount to educate each child in the district before accounting for grade level, socioeconomic status, or special learning needs. In SY04, the base funding factor was $2518.78 per student.

Weights: Additional amounts, determined by a multiplier to the base funding factor, were calculated to determine the total WSF for each student. Students in grades K–3 and 6–12, English language learners, students of low socioeconomic status, and those requiring special education services qualified for additional weights. Students in the early grades were weighted due to state- mandated class size requirements. In the upper grades, the weights represented the increased cost of delivering instruction across a number of subject areas. For English language learners (ELL), the weights varied depending on proficiency and grade-level. The weights for special education (SPED) students varied based on the severity of the student's need and were intended to cover materials and professional development for teachers. Special education teachers were still funded and allocated to schools by the central office based on SPED enrollment. The weight for socio-economic status was intended to provide for the additional services required to educate children in poverty, and was determined by a student's eligibility for free or reduced price lunch. Table 1 on page 63 displays the WSF factors for SY04 (see Exhibit 6 for WSF allocations for sample student profiles).

Loss/Gain Limit: SFUSD established a loss limit of $25 per student and a gain limit of $300 per student so that no school was disproportionately affected by the WSF. If a school's total allocation in SY03 was decreased by more than $25 per student from SY02, the district made up the difference in the funding allocation. If the school's total allocation in SY03 was increased by more than $300 per student over the SY02 level, those funds were re-allocated to the pool available to other schools.

Other Allocation Pools: Additional dollar-denominated allocations to schools came from federal funds such as Title I[5], restricted funds from the state to carry out certain programs, and money allocated to SFUSD to meet the conditions of the consent decree to end desegregation. These allocations were added to a school's revenue number on top of the funding level determined by the weighted student formula (see Exhibit 7 for representative school revenue allocations for SY04)

STAR Schools Program: The STAR (Students and Teachers Achieving Results) program was developed to provide additional resources to underperforming schools, as defined by specific state or local criteria. Resources came in the form of a central allocation of additional school personnel, district support, and instructional resources, rather than dollar allocations to school budgets. In SY03, 43 sites were designated as STAR schools and received resources as part of the program.

School Expenses: The Planning and Budgeting Process

In January of each year principals and their school site councils began developing academic plans and budgets for the next year using the central office revenue projections. As one SSC parent described, "Our academic plan used to be a laundry list of every program and activity we had ever done, including ones we probably wouldn't do again. There was something for everyone. With the WSF process, we had to develop a new discipline to prioritize and explain only those activities we would actually pursue, because we had to link funding to everything mentioned in the plan."

SSCs were encouraged to examine disaggregated student performance data provided by the central office to evaluate what was working from the previous year and to identify gaps that needed attention going forward[6]. The SSC then set the school's priorities for the coming year, in line with district-level priorities. Each priority had a narrow objective statement that set forth the guidelines against which performance would be evaluated. The SSC then worked collaboratively with the principal and faculty to select programs and activities to meet these objectives by addressing the needs of students. The central office provided guidance on research-based approaches for improving student achievement. One elementary school principal observed, "We always had to interact with our staffs, our SSCs and the central office, but the WSF and academic planning process provide a focal point for those conversations that has been useful. Now we are focused on what our kids need and how to give it to them. The academic plan wasn't all that useful before, now it's a real guide for running the school, and it involves more people in the accountability for our results."

After developing the academic plan, the SSC and principal determined the staffing level necessary to implement the plan. Although the SSC did not have hiring authority (principals hired school staff, and the central office hired principals), they did influence the staffing level and mix through the budgeting process. After requirements for teacher/student ratios and other contractual obligations were met, principals and the SSCs had discretion about how many and what types of teachers were best for implementing the instructional program. Schools used average teacher salaries set by the

Table 1
SFUSD Weighted Student Formula Factors, SY04

Grade Level	Base Weight	ELL Long-Term Non-Redesignated	ELL Beginning/ Intermediate	ELL Advanced/ Transitional	Socio-Economic Status	SPED Resource Specialist	SPED Non-Severe	SPED Severe
K	1.3300	–	0.0794	0.0615	0.0900	0.0097	0.0179	0.0315
1–3	1.3300	–	0.0794	0.0615	0.0900	0.0097	0.0179	0.0315
4–5	1.0000	–	0.0794	0.0615	0.0900	0.0097	0.0179	0.0315
6–8	1.1402	0.0953	0.0953	0.0615	0.0900	0.0097	0.0189	0.0328
9–12	1.1900	0.0953	0.2104	0.0615	0.0900	0.0097	0.0189	0.0328

central office to develop their salary and benefits budgets. Other non-personnel expenses were forecast based on historical costs of items such as materials and supplies using the districts buying power with approved vendors. (See Exhibit 8 for school budgets)

Principals submitted their academic plans and budgets to their ISOs in early March. The ISO checked the plans for basic elements, and distributed them to a cross-functional central office review team. These teams included the ISO and staff members from human resources, the budget office, research, planning and evaluation, and the chief academic officer's staff. In late March and early April, principals met with these teams to discuss their plans and receive guidance on any changes required. Waymack remembered, "Principals were initially anxious about the academic plan review, but found it helpful. The conversations were about data and how their resources were aligned with their plans. The process also elevated the understanding and awareness of central office staff about what goes on in schools, particularly those not directly involved in teaching and learning."

Accountability System

Prior to rolling out the WSF, SFUSD implemented an accountability system designed to measure progress against the district's annual priorities (also called The Superintendent's Priorities). The primary objective of the system was to support data-driven decision making by principals and SSCs to improve teaching and learning throughout the district.

Data Collection and Analysis

The district's research, planning, and evaluation department maintained multiple measures of student achievement, including the SAT-9 and CAT-6, student GPAs, SABE and the Brigance Screen[7], and other proficiency tests in various subjects. They also tracked attendance, suspensions, expulsions, retentions, and dropouts. Data was disaggregated by demographic parameters such as gender, ethnicity, socio-economic and English-learner status. Along with longitudinal reports highlighting two- and three-year trends, the department tracked the academic progress of individual students for whom there were multiple years of data. The department analyzed student data by grade-level and by school, but not by classroom or teacher. Schools received annual data for the purposes of developing the academic plan each year, and could also request "data-on-demand" any time during the year in order to inform instructional decisions.

Principal Evaluation System

A principal evaluation system was introduced in SY02. At the beginning of each school year, principals received their site's academic achievement targets and school leadership criteria. Among other things, the school leadership criteria included aligning resources with student learning needs in accordance with the WSF and ensuring a functioning SSC. Each principal was responsible for writing an individual management/leadership (M/L) plan to meet the academic targets and the priorities and activities in the school's academic plan.

Principals submitted these plans, which included requests for specific support necessary from central office departments to accomplish each element, to their ISO by mid-October of each school year. After discussing them with principals, ISOs responded to the M/L plans in writing by the first week of November. By the first week of December, each principal had a conference with their ISO to discuss ongoing progress. Between early January and the end of February the ISO conducted a mid-year evaluation based on the plan's school leadership components and provided feedback.

By April 1st, principals were required to provide a progress report on reaching the academic targets and meeting the leadership components. By mid-August the ISO conducted the final evaluation of each principal's performance on the student achievement targets and school leadership components, and met with the principal to discuss the final evaluation. At all evaluation points, student achievement and other school performance data was analyzed and discussed in the context of the school's academic plan and the principal's M/L plan. After two successive one-year contracts, principal contracts were renewable three years at a time. Principals who underperformed after receiving feedback through the principal evaluation process faced the possibility of non-renewal at the end of their contract periods.

One high school principal observed that the evaluation system seemed to be applied with varying quality across the district, both because of the differing abilities of individual principals to create management/leadership plans that were useful, and differences in the rigor applied to the evaluation by the ISOs. Even so, one board member lamented the fact that the community was largely unaware of the significant step SFUSD had taken with the principal evaluation system, and therefore didn't give district leadership the credit they deserved for instilling accountability.

Reflections: Stakeholder Perspectives on Implementation

Entering the academic planning and budgeting process for SY05, SFUSD had made a number of process improvements, student achievement was increasing overall, and the achievement gap had narrowed slightly. However, many stakeholders and district leaders articulated a number of challenges that remained.

Decision Rights: An elementary school principal who had been with SFUSD for four years explained, "My first year in the district we had the staffing ratios model, so I didn't have to think much about how resources linked to my academic plan. Then I participated in the WSF pilot, which was a real eye-opener. I worked hard at building trust with my staff and the community, and helping them understand how the process worked. The first full year of WSF we had more money than ever before, so it was terrific to engage our community in decisions about how to spend it. In the second and third years, we experienced significant decreases in funding and had to make cuts, but at least the district wasn't doing the cuts. We were."

A middle school teacher on her school's SSC framed it differently: "SSCs are really a way to take the heat off the district and push it to the school people. One central office person said to us last year, 'This is really tough; I'm glad it's you making the cuts and not me.' That really sums up the problem. The SSCs get to decide, but decide what? Which colleagues to cut?"

A senior union leader observed, "We need clarity about the roles of the SSC and the central office. On many issues, the SSC can decide, but the central office can overrule the decision. It's not clear what SSCs are really responsible for and what is just window dressing."

Ackerman agreed that more work was needed. "It's a different kind of central office when schools are making the decisions. We have to move from a compliance and 'no' orientation, to a support and 'how can I help?' orientation. Most departments have changed, but we still have work to do. We are holding people at central accountable for old-style behavior, and calling it when we see it."

A senior teacher described a different situation: "Our building had a very teacher-centric culture; the faculty had much more power than the principal. It's been hard for our faculty to adjust to the idea of an elected SSC that includes parents and non-teaching staff, along with a few teachers and the principal, making important decisions about instructional issues."

Matthew Kelemen, special assistant to the superintendent, was responsible for supporting the SSCs. He acknowledged that difficult decisions could cause significant tensions at schools. District policy provided for a resolution process if school level parties were unable to reach consensus—the chief academic officer, Elois Brooks, could convene a dispute resolution committee to make the decision. Kelemen noted, however, that quickly enforcing the formal district policy could have longer-term negative consequences for the academic planning and budgeting process. When site decision-makers faced difficulty, rather than abandoning the process and imposing a top-down decision, Kelemen and the appropriate ISO worked with them to reach agreement. As of spring 2004, schools had been able to reach decisions without intervention from the chief academic officer.

School Site Councils: An elementary school principal who served on the WSF committee identified a viable, functioning, school site council as the key to making the WSF work

as it was intended. A central office employee expressed concern about a complex system like the WSF being so reliant on the effectiveness of a complex structure like the SSC.

One parent noted that in schools with high numbers of "heavily weighted" kids, the parents of the students with the most resources "attached" to them seldom served on SSCs, adding that "principals need significant professional development on how to build and nurture an SSC, and how to build true participation and consensus among members."

A teachers' union leader expressed concern about faculty department chairs serving on school site councils, noting that in situations like this, "the formal decision makers are also taking on a role in a process that is supposed to increase democratic participation in decision making at schools." A middle school teacher observed that because of budget cuts, teachers in his building were running for SSC positions as a defensive move to protect their own programs. "The resource constraints sometimes pit people against people and program against program in our building. It's probably better overall that we make the decision at the school rather than having it come down from central, but nevertheless, it has caused real tension in our school."

A high school parent suggested that parents could be effective in resolving tensions between school employees, but thought "parents need serious training about how to bring up issues in SSC meetings that principals or teachers might disagree with. Many parents feel at a disadvantage because they aren't educators, so they'll defer to the principal or teachers even if they disagree with them." A teacher noted that detailed conversations of his SSC about instructional strategies to close the achievement gap were "a bit heady" for most parents, and wondered how feasible it was to expect them to fully understand issues that professional teachers spent their careers trying to master.

Another parent observed that it seemed wildly inefficient for each SSC to be dealing with similar issues in isolation, noting "we have over 100 groups in the district reinventing the wheel in a very tough budget environment. There must be common solutions that would work at many schools."

Average v. Actual Teacher Salaries: Using average teacher salaries for budgeting had benefits and drawbacks. The WSF committee explained, "Using average costs eliminates incentives to hire less expensive, less experienced teachers by allowing schools to hire and retain veteran teachers without suffering a financial penalty. Using actual costs would create incentives for schools to hire inexperienced teachers and staff members. Principals and SSCs are responsible for hiring individuals based on the needs of students, not based on budgetary implications."[8]

Supporters of using actual salaries felt that low-performing schools suffered under the policy because they had a bulk of less expensive teachers. By using actual salaries for budgeting, these schools could allocate the reclaimed money to additional staff or materials. Waymack performed an analysis in March 2004 to better understand teacher experience and average salary by school site. The analysis revealed that average salaries in STAR K-8 and middle schools were actually $1000 to $1500 higher than those in non-STAR schools. However, the average salary in STAR elementary schools was $2200 less than in non-STAR elementary schools, and $4100 less in STAR high schools than in their non-STAR counterparts.

Waymack described the dilemma, "We know that some schools have higher proportions of less expensive teachers, but using actual instead of average salaries in these schools usually wouldn't free up enough money to pay for additional staff. The WSF highlights the problem of

high concentrations of less experienced teachers in our low-performing schools. In the old staffing ratios model, the problem was the same but less transparent. The solution doesn't necessarily lie with changed WSF policies."

Resource Constraints: As one principal recalled, "In the first year of WSF, there was more money to decide about. In the last two years, because of the state funding crisis, we've had less money to work with each year." Salaries and benefits represented approximately 97% of school level budgets, both before and after the implementation of the WSF. However with rising health care costs, benefits expenses increased from 16% to 22% of school spending from SY02 to SY04, without a requisite increase in revenue. Reductions were required in other areas to make up the difference. In some schools, SSCs "consolidated" teachers in order to stay within their budget targets. Consolidation meant reducing the school's headcount, and selecting which teacher(s) would be removed in light of the academic plan priorities and seniority as dictated by the collective bargaining agreement. For example, in planning for SY05, a middle school SSC faced with cutting one teaching position had a protracted debate about whether to consolidate a popular science teacher or a computer teacher. In the end, they agreed that because the computer teacher worked across multiple subject areas, the position was more critical to the academic plan, even though the science teacher was highly capable and well regarded by students, parents, and teachers. Consolidated teachers were available for assignment to other schools.

In a few under-enrolled schools, the foundation amount combined with a WSF allocation based on so few students was barely enough to run the school. The WSF committee was revisiting the policy of funding these small schools, but an option also existed to close schools that were unable to attract enough students through the educational placement system to be financially viable.

Culture of Accountability: Acknowledging that the site-based budgeting movement had a mixed track record in public education, Ackerman described the kind of culture necessary at the central office and schools to make the WSF more than simply a decentralized budgeting mechanism. "Our version of the WSF doesn't simply give principals more autonomy. That's certainly an important element of it, but it's much more than that. The money is tied to a plan that is tied to goals that are measured by outcomes for which *everybody* is accountable, because *everybody* is involved: teachers, parents, principals, students, central office staff, and board members."

At the school level, moving to a shared accountability culture required new behaviors for principals, SSC members, and teachers. One principal described his SSC: "For years our SSC was largely perfunctory—I needed them to sign off on things, but they didn't make the calls, so they didn't feel responsible for my decisions. We're making progress, but it's difficult. "One district supporter observed, "My sense is that teachers remain resistant to the idea of being individually accountable for the performance of their students; until we figure out how to change this, I'm not sure we can ever fully build a culture of accountability. How can you hold the principal accountable for the results of a group of school staff who aren't accountable for their own piece of the problem?"

A middle school principal felt that while progress had been made in changing the old control and compliance culture at the central office, more work needed to be done in holding central staff accountable for supporting schools. "I wish there was more consistency across all the headquarters departments—some are much more responsive and supportive than others. I can always go to my ISO if I have a request that disappears into the system, or if I receive conflicting messages or competing demands from central folks, but I'd rather spend my time with my ISO on more productive conversations about teaching and learning."

Looking Forward

As Ackerman and her team considered the questions they needed to answer to brief Secretary Riordan's staff, they realized they had accomplished much and could add to the statewide conversation about a WSF and site-based budgeting. But they also realized they still had significant work ahead to build the organizational capacity required to execute at all levels in ways that would contribute to increased achievement for all SFUSD students. Ackerman knew one thing for certain: "The WSF isn't a silver bullet—the solution is much more complex than that."

Notes

1. SY denotes "school year." For example, SY03 indicates the school year spanning fall 2002 through spring 2003.

2. The California Standards Test measures student performance against CA content standards in language arts, mathematics, science, and history/social science. Until SY 02, SFUSD students in grades 2–11 took the SAT-9 in reading and math, a norm referenced exam. In SY 03, California replaced the SAT-9 with the CAT-6, a customized version of the SAT-9.

3. For more information on composition and responsibilities of SFUSD School Site Councils, see "The SFUSD School Site Handbook," revised September 2002. http://portal.sfusd.edu/template/de - fault.cfm?page=school_info.councils.resources

4. Lowell High School and School of the Arts were exempt from the assignment process. Students applied for admission to Lowell and acceptance was based on prior academic achievement, performance on standardized tests, and in some cases qualitative factors such as overcoming hardships. For admission to School of the Arts,

students were required to audition for space in their specific area of interest.

5. Title I is a federal program authorized under title I, part A, of the Elementary and Secondary Education Act of 1965 (as amended by the No Child Left Behind Act of 2001) targeted to underperforming students at high-poverty schools.

6. Data included individual, group and school level data such as SAT-9 scores, state Academic Performance Index information, and standards-based assessments. Schools were encouraged to develop their own tools for tracking progress in the classroom.

7. SABE is a norm-referenced Spanish language achievement test, and the Brigance Screen is a criterion-referenced assessment instrument for Kindergarten and Grade 1 to assess student development in key areas identified as indictors for success.

8. Excerpted from WSF committee meeting handout dated December 12, 2002, internal SFUSD document.

Exhibit 1
SFUSD Financial Statements, SY01–SY03

	SY03	SY02	SY01
REVENUES			
Revenue Limit Sources (1)	276,754,268	276,410,133	261,350,108
Federal Sources	76,352,578	73,293,413	45,200,857
Other State Sources (categorical)	182,142,791	178,520,965	197,459,348
Other Local Sources (categorical)	83,606,036	89,934,369	88,609,431
Total Revenues	618,855,673	618,158,880	592,619,744
EXPENDITURES (2)			
Current			
Instruction	327,087,582	328,234,715	303,868,564
Instruction related activities:			
Supervision of instruction	35,831,336	33,080,004	30,624,346
Instructional library, media, technology	5,853,040	4,664,772	4,318,488
School site administration	38,500,312	34,738,432	32,159,662
Pupil Services:			
Transportation	19,531,111	19,148,102	17,726,663
Food services	17,410,306	18,071,309	16,729,805
Other	25,919,750	22,150,171	20,505,877
General Administration			
Data processing	8,152,244	4,795,947	4,439,925
All other G&A	57,523,882	52,297,465	48,415,219
Plant services	43,799,772	36,464,847	33,757,918
Facility acquisition and construction	34,419,948	19,241,307	26,674,763
Ancilliary services	1,950,728	16,841,880	15,591,641
Community services	14,164	37,768	34,964
Other (outgo)	35,245,061	22,182,869	27,982,010
Debt Service			
Principal	3,863,206	3,762,721	3,912,337
Interest and other	4,587,272	5,097,066	3,605,233
Total Expenditures	659,689,714	620,809,375	590,347,415
Deficiency of revenues over expenditures	(40,834,041)	(2,650,495)	2,272,329
OTHER FINANCING SOURCES (USES)			
Transfers in	27,886,693	16,805,060	9,451,062
Other sources	248,844	3,672,907	2,600,000
Transfers out	(26,652,585)	(16,805,060)	(14,345,453)
Other uses	—	(104,410)	—
NET FINANCING SOURCES (USES)	1,482,952	3,568,497	(2,294,391)
NET CHANGE IN FUND BALANCES	(39,351,089)	918,002	(22,062)
Fund Balance—Beginning	87,457,745	86,607,925	93,392,844
Prior Period Adjustments	(689,958)	(68,182)	(840,803)
Equity Transfers	3,714,731	—	—
Fund Balance—Ending	51,131,429	87,457,745	92,529,979

Source: SFUSD Annual Financial Reports (June 30, 2003, June 30, 2002, and June 30, 2001), and case writer analysis.

Notes: (1) The California Legislature sets revenue limits for each CA district in an effort to equalize funding per pupil across districts. If local property tax revenues rise within a district, the increase goes toward the district's revenue limit. The state's share is then reduced by the same amount. Local sources account for 93% of SFUSD's revenue limit total. Categorical aid is granted in addition to the revenue limit funds.
(2) In SY01, expenditures were categorized differently in SFUSD annual report than subsequent years. Except for Facility acquisition and construction, Debt service, and Transfers, all costs are estimated across line items by using the same percent to total allocation of these costs from SY02.

Exhibit 2

Students Scoring At or Above Basic on the California Standards Test, SY01–SY03

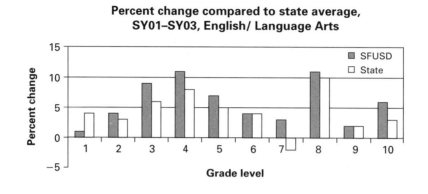

Percent change compared to state average, SY01–SY03, English/ Language Arts

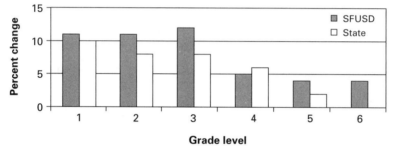

Percent change compared to state average, SY02–SY03, Mathematics

Percentage of students scoring at or above basic

Grades 2–11 English/Lang Arts	2001	2006	% change	Grades 2–7 Mathematics	2002	2006	% change
District	66%	74%	8%	District	64%	76%	12%
African American	41%	51%	10%	African American	35%	50%	15%
Hispanic	45%	58%	13%	Hispanic	43%	61%	18%

Source: California Department of Education website CST results, http://star.cde.ca.gov/, accessed August 15, 2006; and SFUSD Office of Research, Data, and Accountability; by phone August 16, 2006.

Exhibit 3
Excerpted Goals from "Excellence for All" Five-Year Plan

OVERVIEW OF EDUCATIONAL EQUITY GOALS

1. Increase the academic achievement of students of all races and ethnicities, and of English Language Learner and non-English Language Learner status, District-wide and for each school, and narrow the existing academic achievement gap between students of different races, ethnicities, and English Language Learner status, with this goal to be realized through the establishment of specific growth targets for improved academic achievement at each school, as measured by standardized tests and performance assessments.

2. Increase the enrollment and success of students of all races and ethnicities, and of English Language Learner and non-English Language Learner status, in honors courses, District-wide and for each school, at the middle and high school levels.

3. Increase the number and percentage of students of all races and ethnicities, and of English Language Learner and non-English Language Learner status, taking and completing Advanced Placement (AP) courses, District-wide and at each high school.

4. Increase the number and percentage of students of all races and ethnicities, and of English Language Learner and non-English Language Learner status, taking and earning a 3 or better on AP exams, District-wide and at each high school.

5. Decrease the overrepresentation of students from specific racial/ethnic groups and English Language Learner status in special education programs to the extent practicable by eliminating inappropriate referrals to and placements in such programs, District-wide and at each school.

6. Increase the exit rates for students of all races and ethnicities, and of English Language Learner and non-English Language Learner status, from special education programs, District-wide and at each school.

7. Increase the attendance rates for students of all races and ethnicities, and English Language Learner and non-English Language Learner status, District-wide and at each school, so that the attendance rate for students of each race, ethnicity, and English Language Learner status at every school is at least 98 percent.

8. Decrease the suspension rates for non-expulsionable offenses for students of all races and ethnicities, and of English Language Learner and non-English Language Learner status, District-wide and for each school.

9. Enhance early childhood education so that all children entering kindergarten in SFUSD, regardless of race or ethnicity or of English Language Learner or non-English Language Learner status, will possess the tools and skills necessary to be successful in school.

10. Increase the number and percentage of qualified, diverse teachers, Districtwide and at each school, particularly at targeted schools. Targeted schools are those with a high number or percentage of low-performing students. A qualified, diverse teacher is defined as one who is credentialed and has:

    - classroom experience (3–5 years);
    - content-area expertise;
    - pedagogical expertise; and
    - cultural competencies.

Exhibit 4
Diversity Index and Educational Placement Process

Six Diversity Index Factors used to create a student's profile: (answers to these questions are gathered from information provided on the application form and from test score data supplied by the California Department of Education).

- **Socioeconomic Status:** Does the student and/or the student's family participate in any of the following programs: free/reduced lunch, CalWORKS, and/or public housing?

- **Academic Achievement Status:** Incoming Kindergarteners: Did the Student attend pre-school? Students entering grades 1–12: Did the student score above or below the thirtieth (30th) percentile on the most recent standardized test of record'?

- **Mother's Educational Background:** Did the student's mother graduate from high school?

- **Language Status:** Is the student fully proficient in English?

- **Home Language:** Is English the student's home language? This is determined by the answers to the language survey questions on the application form.

- **Academic Performance Rank of Sending School:** Is the Academic Performance Index ranking of the student's current school 4 or above? The California Department of Education ranks every public school in California by academic performance, and assigns each school an Academic Performance Index (API). Note: this factor is excluded for Kindergarteners.

How the Diversity Index Works

1. After placement of younger siblings and students with program needs, the index looks at all grades/programs where there are more requests than seats available and counts how many seats are available.

2. The index averages the "profiles" of all the pre-assigned students to create a "base profile" for the program/grade.

3. The index divides the students who have requested the program into two groups: students who live in the schools' attendance area and students who live outside the schools' attendance area.

4. The index selects students living in the attendance area and assigns the student whose profile is the most different from the base profile in the grade/program.

5. The base profile is recalculated, to include the profile of the student just assigned.

6. The index recalculates how many seats remain for assignment, and the process is repeated until students from the attendance area no longer contribute diversity to the base profile or no more seats remain for additional placements.

7. When students from the attendance area no longer contributed to the diversity of the base profile, all students who requested the grade/program are considered for assignment.

8. The index recalculates the base profile by including the profile of the last student assigned and assigns a student whose profile is the most different from the base profile.

9. This process continues until there are no more seats available.

Source: Internal SFUSD document.

Exhibit 5

Allocation of Budget Decision Rights

Site Budget Responsibility	Central Office Budget Responsibility
General education teachers	Itinerant staff
Paraprofessionals	Boiler plant engineers salary and overtime
Librarians	Transportation
Counselors	Business services (Accounting, Purchasing)
Building administration—Leadership	Human resources
Building administration—Office Support	Legal services
Parent Liaisons	Athletic coaches
Noontime supervisors (elementary)	Food and nutrition services
Elementary advisors	Telecommunications / telephones
Substitutes—staff development absences	Substitutes—non-staff dev. absences
Extra-duty pay for student activities	Professional development*
ELL school-based teachers and paraprofessionals	Special education school-based teachers and paraprofessionals (except 1-on-1);Special education related service providers
School supplies	Furniture (Purchase, Repair and Maintenance)*
Library books	Equipment (Purchase, Repair and Maintenance)*
Instructional materials and technology utilized by Special Ed, ELL teachers (excluding assistive technology)	Utilities
Extended learning opportunities (after-school and Saturday school programs)	Assistive technology for Special Education
Optional test preparation or other assessment-related activities	Maintenance and grounds-keeping staff and supplies*
Custodial supplies	District-wide assessment
Replacement texts	Custodial staff salaries and overtime* Basic texts (new adoptions) Language interpreters and translations* Capital Outlay—parts and materials* Information technology and hardware* Security personnel STAR schools staff (except Parent Liaisons)

Source: Internal SFUSD document.

*These items are provided centrally but sites may supplement these through their WSF funds.

Exhibit 6

Sample WSF Allocations by Student Type, Using SY04 WSF Guidelines

Base Funding factor	$2518.78

Example A: Second grader, free lunch, beginner English language learner

Second grade weight	1.33
ELL beginning weight	.0794
Socio-economic status weight	.090
Total weight factor =	1.4994 × $2518.78 = $ 3776.99 – Total WSF allocation

Example B: Fifth grader, designated as non-severe special education

Fifth grade weight	1.00
SPED non-severe weight	.0179
Total weight factor =	1.0179 × $2518.78 = $ 2563.87 – Total WSF allocation

Example C: Seventh grader, long-term English language learner, reduced price lunch

Seventh grade weight	1.1402
ELL long-term weight	.0953
Socio-economic status weight	.090
Total weight factor =	1.3255 × $2518.78 = $ 3338.64 – Total WSF allocation

Example D: Eleventh grader, no weights

Eleventh grade weight	1.190
Total weight factor =	1.190 × $2518.78 = $ 2997.35 – Total WSF allocation

Source: Case writer analysis using SFUSD weights from page 8.

Exhibit 7

SFUSD Sample School Revenue Allocations, SY05

SCHOOL YEAR 2004–2005
HORACE MANN MIDDLE SCHOOL

Salary Total

SBCP	SI	SCE	LEP	Title I TAS	Title I SWP	Consent Decree	WSF	WSF SPED	TOTAL
0		0	0	0	92,674	244,928	1,657,572	0	1,995,174

Benefits Total

SBCP	SI	SCE	LEP	Title I TAS	Title I SWP	Consent Decree	WSF	WSF SPED	TOTAL
0	0	0	0	0	31,976	84,544	560,459		676,979

Extended Service Total

SBCP	SI	SCE	LEP	Title I TAS	Title I SWP	Consent Decree	WSF	WSF SPED	TOTAL
14,367	0	0	0	0	0	6,809	0	0	21,176

Non-Personnel Total

SBCP	SI	SCE	LEP	Title I TAS	Title I SWP	Consent Decree	WSF	WSF SPED	TOTAL
42,282	0	0	0	0	17,038		24,197	3,724	87,241

Proposed Budget Total

SBCP	SI	SCE	LEP	Title I TAS	Title I SWP	Consent Decree	WSF	WSF SPED	GRAND TOTAL
56,649	0	0	0	0	141,688	336,281	2,242,228	3,724	2,780,570

Amount Allocated

SBCP	SI	SCE	LEP	Title I TAS	Title I SWP	Consent Decree	WSF	WSF SPED	GRAND TOTAL
56,649	0	0	0	0	141,688	336,281	2,242,228	3,724	2,780,570

SCHOOL YEAR 2004–2005
CESAR CHAVEZ ELEMENTARY

Salary Total

SBCP	SI	SCE	LEP	Title I TAS	Title I SWP	Consent Decree	WSF	WSF SPED	TOTAL
40,002		0	0	0	61,369	95,026	1,005,887	0	1,202,284

Benefits Total

SBCP	SI	SCE	LEP	Title I TAS	Title I SWP	Consent Decree	WSF	WSF SPED	TOTAL
14,428	0	0	0	0	21,652	33,704	341,220		411,004

Extended Service Total

SBCP	SI	SCE	LEP	Title I TAS	Title I SWP	Consent Decree	WSF	WSF SPED	TOTAL
0	0	0	0	0	0	5,613	4,771	0	10,384

Non-Personnel Total

SBCP	SI	SCE	LEP	Title I TAS	Title I SWP	Consent Decree	WSF	WSF SPED	TOTAL
17,476	0	0	0	0	7,169	23,113	26,370	2,340	76,468

Proposed Budget Total

SBCP	SI	SCE	LEP	Title TAS	Title I SWP	Consent Decree	WSF	WSF SPED	GRAND TOTAL
71,907	0	0	0	0	90,190	157,455	1,378,248	2,340	1,700,140

Amount Allocated

SBCP	SI	SCE	LEP	Title I TAS	Title I SWP	Consent Decree	WSF	WSF SPED	GRAND TOTAL
71,907	0	0	0	0	90,190	157,455	1,378,248	2,340	1,700,140

LEGEND: Categorical funds

SBCP–School Based Coordinated Programs (state); **SI**–School Improvement (state); **SCE**–State Compensary Education; **LEP**–Limited English Proficiency (state); **TAS**–Targeted Assistance School (Federal Titlel); **SWP**–School Wide Program (Federal Title I); **Consent Decree**–court-ordered desegregation funds (state)

Source: SFUSD internal documents.

Exhibit 8

SFUSD Sample School Site Budgets, SY05

618, HORACE MANN MIDDLE SCHOOL, 2004–05 Budget, Summary Report

Total Allocation 2,780,570	Count	FTE	Salaries	Benefits	Non Personnel	Extended Hours
1101 Classroom Teacher	30	28.8	1,559,894	534,787		
1102 Substitute Teachers Salary	0					4,771
1102 Substitute Teachers Salary	1				3,724	1,870
1105 Certified Extended Hourly	0					4,939
1201 Librarians Salaries	1		0	0		
1202 Counselor	2	1.5	81,245	27,854		
1202 Head Counselor	1	1	67,297	21,679		
1301 Assistant Principal Middle Sch	1	1	79,785	24,642		
1301 Principal Middle School	1	1	96,238	28,912		
2101 Instructional Aides Salaries	3	.75	22,859	8,245		
2402 Senior Clerk Typist	3	2	87,856	30,860		
4310 Instructional Materials and Supplies	6				49,038	
4313 Supplies	3				5,197	
5622 Rental/Lease of Equipment	1				18,000	
5803 Consultants	1				2,000	
5811 Field Trips	1				2,000	
5890 Other Services	2				4,282	
5912 Postage	1				3,000	
Totals	58	36.05	1,995,173	676,978	87,241	21,176
Percent of Allocation			72.30%	24.53%	3.16%	0.77%

603, CESAR CHAVEZ ELEMENTARY, 2004–05 Budget, Summary Report

Total Allocation 1,700,140	Count	FTE	Salaries	Benefits	Non Personnel	Extended Hours
	0	2.25	0	0		
1101 Classroom Teacher	17	17	920,771	315,673		
1102 Substitute Teachers Salary	0					7,577
1105 Certified Extended Hourly	0					2,806
1301 Principal Elementary	1	1	89,105	27,390		
2101 Instructional Aides Salaries	7	4.375	133,341	48,094		
2402 Secretary II	1	1	50,174	16,726		
2901 Community Relations Specialist	1	.25	8,893	3,120		
4211 Library Books	1				2,500	
4313 Supplies	1				29,968	
5642 Repair & Maintenance Equipment	1				2,000	
5803 Consultants	4				40,000	
5811 Field Trips	1				2,000	
Totals	35	25.87	1,202,284	411,004	76,468	10,383
Percent of Allocation			71.15%	24.32%	4.53%	.61%

Source: SFUSD internal documents.

Finding and Supporting Personnel

The public schools spend huge sums—well over 80 percent of their budgets—to pay teachers and principals. This large investment makes good sense, given that education is fundamentally a people business: Success depends on what those teachers and principals do every day. Ironically, however, many school districts—especially large urban ones—do little to guarantee that their investment pays off. Decisions about who is hired, where they work, what they do, and how they are compensated often are defined by past practice, delayed by red tape, driven by organizational politics, and decided by happenstance rather than a well-reasoned, efficient process. As a result, school districts squander the opportunity to substantially improve teaching and learning. An effective approach would involve systematically recruiting the right people for these crucial jobs, assigning them to the positions where their skills are most needed, preparing them to be effective in their work, and compensating them in ways that promote both good work and loyalty.

School districts' lack of attention to the recruitment, assignment, support, and compensation of teachers and principals stems from a number of factors. It is due in part to the very size of the educational enterprise. A large school district typically employs thousands of teachers and principals—numbers that discourage district officials from paying close attention to the characteristics of individuals or the needs of particular schools. Large-batch processing of personnel is simply more efficient, even if it is ultimately ineffective. Moreover, public education has historically adopted factory-like policies and practices that, in the name of efficiency, encourage centralized and standardized approaches to managing personnel. They feature generic rather than specialized positions and settings. State-issued professional licenses and teachers union contracts, both of which tend to treat all teachers or principals alike, have further reinforced the use of standardized approaches. As districts grew over time and routines rather than reason shaped practice, those in the personnel office came to know less and less about their people—both those they might hire and those they already employed. They processed more and more paper, yet could do little from their bureaucratic perch downtown to support and improve education in the schools.

Schools within a district are not uniform

organizations. They offer specialized programs, serve distinct communities, rely on different curricula, and develop unique cultures. A teacher or principal who succeeds in one setting cannot simply be transferred from place to place and be expected to achieve the same results. Teaching English-language learners in one community calls for different skills than teaching English-speaking students in another. Teaching math at a school that prepares students for entry-level jobs in the health-care field requires a different curriculum than does teaching math in a school that prepares all students for college. Candidates holding the same professional license vary as well, offering different strengths, training, and life experience. Thus, in hiring, careful matches must be made between a person and a school if the teachers and principals are to contribute their best to students' learning. And if districts discover that the candidates they need are not immediately available, they must consider how to recruit them or, if need be, to prepare them.

Accountability in public education has increased the pressure on school districts to have the best possible teachers and administrators. Research confirms that teachers are the most important school-level factor in students' success. At the same time, principals repeatedly are shown to make the difference between the success or failure of any school-improvement effort. However, just when it has become clear that public education cannot succeed without skilled, committed, and well-placed teachers and principals, it is becoming harder and harder to prepare, recruit, and support them.

Large numbers of veteran teachers and principals who began their careers in the late 1960s and early 1970s have begun to retire, creating an increasing number of openings each year. In addition, there is evidence that attrition rates among new teachers and principals are rising, especially in high-need urban schools. It has been forty years since school districts have had to recruit, hire, and place so many new teachers and administrators and, for the most part, they are not up to the task. During the 1980s and 1990s, when enrollments did not expand, personnel administrators became accustomed to having a surplus of applicants. In the 1960s, schools could count on recruiting large numbers of individuals who had limited access to other professions—in particular, well-educated men of color and women. Today, however, the labor market has changed, and the very individuals who were once excluded from other fields are now actively recruited by them. For the first time in history, school districts must compete for talented candidates. This is especially true for positions in subjects that have a shortage of teachers (math, science, special education, foreign languages) and for assignments in low-income, low-performing schools.

Learning Objectives

The cases in this module illustrate some of the challenges school districts face today in developing a systematic and effective approach to human resources (HR) management. We have chosen two cases that focus on teachers, recognizing that the challenges and lessons of these cases also are relevant to principals. Closely considering these two urban districts' approaches reveals similarities and differences in the challenges they face and the strategies they employ. We suggest the following learning objectives for this module:

- Understand the tensions that exist between the needs of the system and the needs of the schools

- Recognize the role that various factors—union contracts, HR organization, budget approval, and principals' initiative—play in timely hiring and effective assignment

- Recognize the importance of coordinating services within the district office so that principals and teachers can find assistance and clarity rather than confusion or obstruction

- Understand the potential of technology to provide information that will attract new candidates and facilitate their hiring and placement

- Consider alternative approaches to the preparation of principals and compensation of teachers

Cases

The opening case in Module II introduces the challenges of human capital management with a case drawn from a highly regulated segment of the private sector. "Southwest Airlines: Using Human Resources for Competitive Advantage" focuses on a company's successful strategy of relying on productive approaches in human resources.

The following two cases focus on teachers as part of a human resources system in public education. "Reinventing Human Resources at the School District of Philadelphia," examines a school system's effort to transform its human resources department from a marginal, bureaucratic office into a far more agile and coherent department that serves the needs of its schools. It features the work of the key HR administrator as he moves the district toward site-based hiring for all teachers. "Staffing the Boston Public Schools," examines factors that lead to late, ineffectual hiring throughout the district and create special hardships in low-performing, low-income schools. It tracks changes in the teachers contract and the HR office and shows how they combine to give schools a more streamlined staffing schedule and better information about prospective candidates.

Discussion Questions

The following questions will serve as a guide to identifying the common ideas embedded in the case series in this module:

1. What are the components of an effective human resources system and how do they relate to one another?

2. How can a school district provide well-aligned and coherent HR services (including recruitment, hiring, support, and compensation) to ensure that it has a stable, skilled cohort of teachers and school administrators?

3. How can a large school district simultaneously attend to the staffing needs of individual schools and to the administrative and contractual demands of the district?

DISCUSSION QUESTIONS

1. What is Southwest's strategy? How would it answer the question, "What business are we in?" Why has it been successful for so long? Can its success be replicated by a competitor?

2. Why or why not?

3. Analyze Southwest's human capital management system. How does this system link to the execution of its strategy?

4. How would you describe the culture of the organization?

5. What could cause Southwest to fail?

Southwest Airlines: Using Human Resources for Competitive Advantage (A)

The work force is dedicated to the company. They're Moonies basically. That's the way they operate.[1]

—*Edward J. Starkman, Airline Analyst PaineWebber*

Ann Rhoades, VP People for Southwest Airlines, was packing her briefcase at the end of a 17 hour day. Tomorrow was an off-site meeting with the top nine executives of Southwest Airlines. The agenda for the meeting was to review Southwest's competitive position in light of recent actions by United and Continental, both of whom had entered Southwest's low fare market. That day's *New York Times* (September 16, 1994) had an article which characterized the situation as a major showdown in the airline industry:

"This is a battle royal that has implications for the industry," said Kevin C. Murphy, an airline stock analyst at Morgan Stanley. The battle will, after all, be as much a test of strategy as a contest between two airlines. United and other big carriers like USAir and Continental have decided that they can lower their costs by creating a so-called airline-within-an-airline that offers low fares, few frills, and frequent service. The new operations are unabashedly modeled after Southwest, the pioneer of this strategy and keeper of the healthiest balance sheet in the industry.[2]

The reasons for this competition were easy to understand. Over 45 percent of United's revenues came from passengers who flew through their California hubs. As a market, the California corridor was the most heavily traveled in the , with 80 percent more traffic than the Boston–New York–Washington corridor. Yet, United's share in this market had fallen from 38 percent in 1991 to 30 percent in 1993.

During the same period, Southwest's had

increased from 26 percent to 45 percent. Other airlines, like Continental, had also been hurt by Southwest's competition. Southwest's success spawned a number of imitators, including new airlines like Kiwi and Reno Air as well as major airlines like United and Continental. Concerned with this new competition, the market had driven down Southwest's stock price and analysts were raising questions about how sustainable Southwest's advantage really was.

Rhoades, a former marketing executive with an MBA from the University of New Mexico and a background in banking, had joined Southwest in 1989 to help transform the so-called People Department (Human Resources in most organizations). Southwest had always believed that an important part of their competitive advantage rested with their people and how they were managed. Ann's job was to help leverage this advantage. At tomorrow's meeting she would be asked to review Southwest's current position in light of the new competition. She had prepared a brief overview of what she saw as the major threats and opportunities of the competition and an assessment of Southwest's strengths and weaknesses in light of these changes. However, she wanted to reflect one last time on these issues to be sure she was not missing anything. Her major concerns were whether Southwest was getting the most in competitive advantage from their own people, and whether the competition could imitate their successful human resource practices.

Background

History

On June 18, 1971 Southwest Airlines, headquartered at Love Field in Dallas, began flying with three Boeing 737 aircraft serving the Texas cities of Dallas, Houston, and San Antonio. Southwest's competition was Texas International and Braniff, and, to a lesser extent, Continental. Continental used every political and regulatory

means to ensure that Southwest would not get off the ground, including keeping Southwest out of the recently built Dallas-Fort Worth airport and waging a four year legal battle that left Southwest almost bankrupt at the time of its first flight. One outcome of the legal battle was the so-called Wright Amendment, named after James Wright, then Speaker of the House of Representatives. The Wright Amendment prohibited any air carrier from offering direct service into Love Field from any place beyond Texas and the four contiguous states of Oklahoma, Louisiana, Arkansas, and New Mexico. This law meant that passengers flying into Southwest's central location at Love Field from destinations beyond these four states would have to purchase separate tickets for each leg of the trip and could not check baggage through to their final destination. Furthermore, neither airlines nor travel agents were permitted to advertise connections through Love Field. Ostensibly, this law was intended to encourage traffic through the new Dallas-Fort Worth hub. In fact, it was aimed at stopping Southwest.

Herb Kelleher, CEO and one of the airline's founders and then Southwest's corporate counsel, said, "You know, anger can be a great motivator. For me, this became a cause. I was a crusader freeing Jerusalem from the Saracens."[3] More recently, he was quoted as saying, I have told people that I would retaliate if I became very angry, but now I think I would revise that. Let's just say that if I become peckish, I will attack."[4] This aggressive, underdog spirit still pervades the company, especially among longer serving employees. Many see the goal of keeping this spirit alive as one of the firm's great challenges. Delise Zachry, an instructor from the People Training Department, noted, "In 1971, 198 people got together and did something that was impossible. Now we need to update the culture to today's problems."

In the early days, Southwest gained attention by putting its flight attendants in hot pants and using its location at Love Field to launch an advertising campaign ("Make Love, Not War"), a theme that is still used today when Southwest refers to itself as the "Love" (LUV) airline. This designator is Southwest's stock ticker symbol. All aircraft have a small heart emblazoned on their sides and hearts are used prominently on corporate communications and advertising. From its inception, Southwest has encouraged its employees to identify with others at the company, deliver great customer service and have fun. They have also pursued a low fare strategy.

In the mid-80s USAir and American, attempting to increase their share of the valuable California market, purchased Air California and Pacific Southwest Airlines (PSA), two successful regional carriers. However, American soon withdrew from some cities and routes when they could not be served profitably. USAir made a number of marketing and service mistakes and also cut back service in the region. Southwest seized the opportunity to expand in California. From basically a zero market share in California in 1989, Southwest moved to the leading airline in passenger boardings in 1993 and now serve 10 cities in the state with more than a 70 percent average market share for city-pairs served.

The Current Situation

From the beginning, Southwest has maintained the same strategy and operating style that it maintains to the present. It concentrates on flying to airports that are underutilized and close-in to a metropolitan area—e.g., Love Field in Dallas, Hobby in Houston, San Jose and Oakland in the Bay Area, Midway in Chicago—although it does fly to major airports like LAX and SFO. The company also began flying fuel-efficient 737s, and now has over 200 of them, the only type of aircraft it flies. Southwest service involves frequent on-time departures as well as low cost fares. They emphasize point-to-point routes, with no central hub and an average flight time of 65 minutes. According to its 1993 an-

nual report, 80 percent of their customers fly non-stop to their final destination. By avoiding a hub and spoke system, they are able to avoid the delays often associated with connecting flights. This makes short-haul trips more attractive to travellers who might otherwise consider driving. It also pays off in shorter turnaround times (70% of their flights had a 15 minute ground time in 1991) and higher equipment utilization. For example, Southwest aircraft spent an average of 11 hours in the air daily compared to an industry average of 8, and they averaged 10.5 flights per gate versus 4.5 for the industry.

Following this strategy, Southwest has always seen themselves as competing not so much with other airlines as with surface transportation. For instance, in 1993 the average passenger fare was roughly $60 for a trip of 500 miles. In 1984 the comparable numbers were $49 and 436 miles. For example, in August of 1994 the roundtrip fare from Oakland to San Diego, a distance of over 1,000 miles, was $135. Southwest uses these low fares and frequent flights to increase passenger volume two to three times. For example, somewhere around 8,000 people used to fly between Louisville and Chicago weekly; after Southwest entered the market that number climbed to 26,000. They dramatically lower the fares and increase the frequency of flights. For instance, in August of 1994 they flew 39 times roundtrip daily between Dallas and Houston, 25 times between Phoenix and Los Angeles, and 20 times between Sacramento and Los Angeles. When American moved out their San Jose hub because they were losing money, Southwest moved in and were profitable from the first day of service. In 1992, they were the leading carrier in passenger boardings in 27 of the 34 airports served. They dominate most of their major markets with almost 70 percent of the intra-Texas and over 50 percent of the intra-California markets in 1994.

Consistent with their strategy of low costs, low fares and frequent flights, Southwest also keeps their fares simple. Unlike other airlines that rely heavily on computers and artificial intelligence programs to maximize flight revenue, Southwest typically offers only two fares on a route, a regular coach fare (there is no first- or business-class) and an off-peak fare. It also tries to price all fares the same within a state (for instance, currently $69 to fly anywhere within California). Southwest has never sold interline connections to other carriers and has been unwilling to pay to be part of other airlines' reservations systems. As a result, only 55 percent of Southwest's seats were booked by travel agents compared to 90 percent of tickets for major airlines. In 1994, United announced that their Apollo System would no longer carry Southwest's schedules or issue its tickets. This makes issuing tickets more difficult for travel agents who often have to call the airline rather than working through a computer as they do with other airlines—a clear incentive to travel agents not to book Southwest flights.

To further simplify their operations, Southwest has never offered meal service on its flights. Meals can add $40 per passenger to the cost of a flight. Instead, passengers on Southwest are served beverages, peanuts (referred to as "frills"), and on longer flights, crackers or other light snacks such as cookies. There is no assigned seating. Upon arrival at a Southwest gate, each passenger holding a reservation is given a reusable plastic boarding pass with numbers from 1 to 137, the maximum load of their 737 aircraft. Passengers are loaded in groups of 30 and the boarding passes are collected for use on the next flight. Standby passengers are boarded if seats are available in the order in which they sign up at the departure gate.

Although they are not connected to other airlines' reservation systems or affiliated with other frequent flyer programs, Southwest does have its own frequent flyer club ("The Company Club"), also a model of simplicity. It is based on the number of trips flown, not the mileage. Members keep a card that is stamped every time a plane is boarded. After accumulating 16 segments, a free ticket is awarded and a Company Club card is issued. The card is then read into the computer system for each trip. This approach economizes on operating costs since it requires no effort to keep track of mileage. Based on some negative advertising by United about Southwest's frequent flyer program, Herb Kelleher recently sent a letter to all Company Club members detailing how awards from Southwest took less mileage to obtain and were more widely available than other airlines. Kelleher argues that their program is the greatest value because it gives you free travel faster, for much less money, without giving up great service." For instance, after 50 roundtrips within a 12-month period, a companion flies free with a Company Club member, even if you're travelling on an award ticket.

Overall, Southwest Airlines has been profitable in every one of the last 21 years, a record achieved by no other major airline. It was consistently profitable even during the 1991–1992 period, during which some 40 percent of the total capacity of the airline industry was seeking bankruptcy protection or ceased operation completely. Exhibit 1 presents selected financial and operating data for last ten years. According to *Money* magazine, for the twenty-year period 1972–1992, Southwest's stock earned the highest returns of any publicly traded stock—a compounded return of over 21,000%. Only Wal-Mart comes close to being as good as an investment over this period.

Competitive Advantage

Although the reasons for Southwest's success were many, one highly visible advantage could be seen in their cost structure. Kelleher recognized that short-haul flying was inherently more costly than longer flights (the plane is taking off and landing more often and has to be handled at every gate). He understood that the lowest-cost provider could leverage that cost advantage most where costs are highest. Exhibit 2 shows the costs per available seat mile for two comparable quarters in 1993 and 1994. Southwest's costs averaged roughly 7.1 cents while the larger airlines had costs up to 10 cents or more per mile, 20–30 percent higher. This achievement is even more striking when noting that Southwest's costs in 1984 were 5.86 cents. So, over a decade its costs had increased by only about 20 percent.

Part of this cost advantage derives from the remarkable productivity Southwest gets from their work force. For example, they routinely turnaround an aircraft in 15 minutes from the time it arrives at the gate until it leaves (see Exhibit 3 for the anatomy of a 15 minute turnaround). United and Continental average 35 minutes. Southwest's gates are typically manned by a single agent and with a ground crew of six or fewer, rather than the three agents and twelve ground crew common at other airlines.

These low costs also come from other sources. Southwest pilots, for example, spend more time in the air than pilots at other airlines. While pilots at United, American, and Delta earn up to $200,000 a year for flying an average of 50 hours a month, Southwest's pilots average $100,000 a year flying 70 hours a month. Flight attendants and pilots help clean the aircraft or check passengers in at the gate. Harold Sirkin, an airline specialist with BCG said, "Southwest works because people pull together to do what they need to get a plane turned around. That is a part of the Southwest culture. And if it means the pilots need to load bags, they'll do it."[5]

Southwest's employees also routinely volunteer to help customers in need. Once a customer arrived at the airport for a vacation trip with his dog in tow, only to learn that he couldn't bring the dog with him. Rather than have him cancel the trip, the gate agent took care of the dog for two weeks so the fellow could enjoy his holiday. Another employee accompanied an elderly passenger to the next stop to insure that she was

able to change planes. Stories of this sort abound.

These efforts pay off in employee productivity. In 1993, for example, Southwest had an average of 81 employees per aircraft while United and American had 157 and 152, respectively. The industry average was in excess of 130. Southwest served an average of 2,443 passengers per employee while United and American served 795 and 840, about the industry average. This means that Southwest needs a smaller load factor to break even than the other carriers (usually around 55 percent). Second, the point-to-point strategy and the use of less congested airports improves the efficiency of flight operations and helps insure high levels of aircraft utilization. Finally, by using a single type of aircraft, Southwest was able to save on maintenance and training costs.

But Southwest is not just a low fare/low cost carrier. It also emphasizes customer service. In fact, the word "Customer" is always capitalized in all Southwest corporate communications, whether it is the Annual Report or an internal newsletter. Colleen Barrett, Executive Vice President—Customers and highest ranking woman executive in the airline industry, insists on this. She is also adamant about treating employees as internal customers and tries to make sure that Southwest is a comfortable and fun place to work. "If you're comfortable, you're smiling more and you give better service," Barrett says. "It doesn't take a rocket scientist to figure that out."[6] The results are undeniable. In the airline industry service is measured by on-time performance, having the fewest lost bags, and having the fewest number of customer complaints. If an airline is the best in all three categories in a single month, it wins the so-called "Triple Crown." Southwest has won the monthly Triple Crown 24 times. In 1992, the Department of Transportation began giving an annual Triple Crown. Southwest won the award in 1992, 1993, and 1994.

Leadership at Southwest

While a number of industry experts attribute Southwest's accomplishments to its unwavering adherence to its low cost niche strategy, others disagreed and argued that its real competitive advantage lay its leadership. A recent *Fortune* article, for instance, was entitled "Is Herb Kelleher America's Best CEO?"[7] The piece cites a Department of Transportation report as noting that Southwest was the "principal driving force for changes occurring in the airline industry," and credits Kelleher with much of this. The author quotes Michael Derchin, a veteran airline analyst who has been monitoring Southwest almost from its beginning, says, "I think Herb is brilliant, charming, cunning, and tough. He is the sort of manager who will stay out with a mechanic in some bar until four o'clock in the morning to find out what is going on. And then he will fix whatever is wrong." In his view, the difference between Southwest and other carriers is in the effort Herb gets out of the people who work for him." The *Fortune* writer, Ken Labich, concluded his article by noting that, "The greatest obstacle to long-term prosperity at Southwest may be Kelleher's mortality."

Although Southwest is headquartered in Dallas, Herb Kelleher isn't a native Texan. He is not a pilot either. He's a lawyer who grew up on the East Coast, majored in philosophy and literature, graduated from NYU Law School, clerked for a New Jersey Supreme Court justice, and practiced law in Newark, New Jersey. After visiting his wife's parents in San Antonio, he announced that he wanted to move to Texas. By the mid-1960s he was happily practicing law in San Antonio. One day in 1966 a client named Rollin King described his experience in California on PSA, a short-haul commuter airline, and suggested that Texas could benefit from a similar operation. The two sketched out some plans, borrowed money, and started Southwest.

From the beginning, Herb has adopted a visible, hands on, slightly over-the-top style—al-

ways ready to promote a party and have fun. He appeared one Halloween at a Southwest maintenance hanger dressed in drag with a feathered boa imitating Corporal Klinger from the television program, *M*A*S*H*. He's also appeared in print advertisements and at company parties dressed as Elvis Presley. (Ann Rhoades suggested that this was fine, but they try not to encourage him to dress like Ethel Merman.) He's renowned for his love of Wild Turkey bourbon. When Herb met the president of the company that produces it, he told him that he may be just a man to most people, but to me he is a god."[8] While recovering from minor surgery, he received over 3,000 cards and gifts from employees, including an intravenous drip set-up—but with Wild Turkey rather than saline solution. He also smokes five packs of cigarettes a day. He says, "I've always felt that there's no reason that work has to be suffused with seriousness, that professionalism can't be worn lightly. Fun is a stimulant to people. They enjoy their work more and work more productively." He believes that, "You don't have to surrender your individuality to work for Southwest Airlines." This is seen in the phrase sometimes heard at Southwest, "work is important don't spoil it with seriousness."[9]

And Kelleher does have fun. He constantly interacts with customers and Southwest employees. He routinely visits maintenance facilities in the early morning hours. Tom Burnett, the Teamster leader who represents Southwest mechanics and cleaners, says, "Let me put it this way. How many CEOs do you know who come into a cleaners' break room at 3 on a Sunday passing out doughnuts or putting on a pair of overalls to clean a plane?"[10] Once while rushing to catch a flight at Love Field he stopped his car in the loading zone and began talking with a Southwest employee. After an animated few minutes, he realized he was late and rushed off to make his plane. When he arrived in Houston, a Southwest employee asked him if he knew where his car was? He'd left it idling at curbside.

Kelleher has also appeared in television ads for American Express—not because he's such a big user, but because he has lost more cards during a year than any other AMEX customer. Colleen Barrett, an EVP of the company, is always sticking money in his pockets since he routinely forgets his wallet. Reflecting on Herb's propensity to engage people in conversation, she says, "I could add four hours to Herb's day if I could get him to walk and talk at the same time." One friend says, "There is an unwritten rule that, if you don't want to stay up all night drinking and talking, then you stay the hell away from Herb."[11]

This philosophy pervades the entire company. Serious attention is paid to parties and celebrations. Every year, for instance, each station (city) is given a budget for parties for the employees and their families. Most stations supplement this by doing their own fund raising. Up until several years ago, all Southwest employees used to fly to Dallas for the annual company party. Now that the company has grown too large for that, they hold a rolling party in several cities with Herb and the senior managers moving from one location to another. Celebrations and contests occur continually, including chili cookoffs and Christmas parties. The Love Field corporate headquarters in Dallas is filled with pictures of Southwest employees at parties, awards, trips, celebrations, and banners. In fact, there is no corporate art in the headquarters. All paintings and sculptures, and there are many, are those donated by employees.

Colleen Barrett also reflects the relaxed management style. Officially, she is responsible for communication, marketing, public relations, people (human resources), governmental affairs, and scheduling (see Exhibit 4 for an organization chart). She is also heading the merger efforts with Southwest's recent acquisition of Morris Air. Unofficially, she has been described as a combination of den mother, management guru, and customer ombudsman. She is a stickler for detail and provides the organizational counterweight to Kelleher's sometimes chaotic style. "She's the backbone of the airline," said one employee. Colleen claims that "The company is only as good as its people," and constantly reinforces that theme. "We'll never jump on an employee for leaning too far toward the customer, but we come down on them hard for not using common sense."

For instance, about four years ago she became concerned with the size and geographic dispersion of the company and set up a culture committee consisting of 65 people from all levels and regions of the company. This committee meets with Colleen four times a year for a full day to preserve and enhance the Southwest spirit. After determining that some distant locations were operating functionally but without the teamwork that Southwest values, they decided to try to reduce this tendency. One outcome was a systematic effort for groups of employees to express their appreciation to others for their contributions. So, for instance, the pilots held a barbecue for the mechanics on the flight line at 3:00 Other groups, including pilots, decided to thank the reservations agents by coming in and spending a shift with them. Even the officers and directors of the company have a program, called "Day in the Field," that requires them to spend one day per quarter working in a front line job. Colleen is adamant that this means really work, not stand around and drink coffee.

The People Department

About five years ago the human resources function at Southwest was renamed "The People Department." This reflected a concern that the old human resources group was, in the words of John Turnipseed, manager of People Services, "a police department." To counteract this, Ann Rhoades first threw away the 300 page corporate handbook and brought in new people with marketing backgrounds. Currently, to join the department an employee must first have line experience. She sees the role of the People Department as saying "yes" rather than "no" and wants them to "Do what it takes to make the Customer happy." Employees are the customers of her group. Although they deal with approximately 18,000 employees, the People Department has a staff of about 100. All members of the department sign the department's mission statement, which is prominently displayed in a very large poster on the wall of their headquarters' office. It reads:

> Recognizing that our people are the competitive advantage, we deliver the resources and services to prepare our people to be winners, to support the growth and profitability of the company, while preserving the values and special culture of Southwest Airlines.

Ann takes this charge seriously and believes in what she calls the two Cs; compassion and common sense. She worries about maintaining the culture and tells people to break the rules if they need to. While in many companies human resources is considered a backwater, the People Department at Southwest is "like the keeper of the flame," says Treasurer John Owen.[12] Ann notes that, "Most HR people have no courage. They never take a chance. No guts. No capability of making a decision. They're so afraid of being fired We need to have confidence in people doing the right thing." To do this, she believes that it is imperative that you get the right people into HR to begin with. This also underlies the Southwest policy of hiring and firing for attitude. Her department is also continually feeding back information to employees such as on-time performance, turnaround times, number of customers boarded or the cost of a day's health care for the airline in terms of the number of bags of peanuts served on their flights. The intent is to keep people focused and make them aware of how their actions affect costs.

Recruiting

To insure that they get the right people, Southwest is extraordinarily selective in their recruiting. In 1993, they had 98,000 job applicants. Of these, roughly 16,000 were interviewed, and 2,700 hired—including one aspiring employee who submitted her resume on the icing of a large sheet cake, demonstrating the creative spirit that Southwest looks for. To insure fit, there is an emphasis on peer recruiting. For example, pilots hire other pilots, often coming in on their day off to do background checks. As Ann noted, "They can get far more information in a phone call to the chief pilot of another airline than anyone else." They even turned down a top pilot who worked for another major airline and did stunt work for movie studios. Even though he was a great pilot, he made the mistake of being rude to a Southwest receptionist. Teamwork is critical. As Ann noted, "If they say 'I' too much in the interview, they don't get hired." She described how one group of eight applicant pilots were being kidded about how seriously they were dressed (dark suits and black shoes and socks). They were encouraged to loosen up. Six of them accepted the invitation to wear the standard Southwest Bermuda shorts and interviewed for the rest of the day in suit coats, ties, Bermuda shorts and dress shoes and socks. They were the six hired.

To further screen for the Southwest Spirit, customers are sometimes involved in the interviewing for new flight attendants. The process consists of an application, a phone screening interview, a group interview, three additional interviews (two with line employees), and a consensus assessment and a vote. During the interview process, the applicant will come into contact with other Southwest employees. These people are also invited to give their assessments of whether the person would fit in at the company. The entire process focuses on a positive attitude and teamwork. For example, applicants are given crayons to draw a picture that tells the story of their life. They look for people who are willing to draw outside the lines. Even their advertisements emphasize the Southwest spirit. One ad for people with computer skills showed a picture of a techno-nerd, with tape holding his glasses together, and emphasized that "We're not looking for your average computer geek." Others convey a sense for the type of employee Southwest wants to attract (see Exhibit 5 for several illustrations).

As befits a company where selection is important, Southwest has spent a lot of time identifying the key components comprising effective performance and behavior. For instance, the People Department identified their to5 pilots and systematically interviewed them to identify common characteristics. One key trait identified was the ability to work as a part of the team. This is now used as a part of their pilot selection process. The company believes that most skills can be learned and doesn't screen heavily on these except for certain specialist jobs, like pilots and mechanics. Attitudes are what count. Kelleher says, "We draft great attitudes. If you don't have a good attitude, we don't want you, no matter how skilled you are. We can change skill levels through training. We can't change attitude."[13] For example, John Turnipseed described an EEO complaint for not hiring a person for a position who had 15 years of experience while selecting a person who had no experience. Southwest successfully made the case that the culture was critical and had to be considered in selection.

An important awareness on the part of the People Department is that the company rejects more than 95,000 applicants each year. These are all potential customers. Therefore, the recruiting process is designed to not make applicants feel inferior or rejected. Ann claims that some people have told her they had a better experience being rejected by Southwest than they did being hired by other companies. Rita Bailey, a corporate employment manager, always tries to call

any internal or managerial applicants that are turned down. She uses this as a chance to counsel them, trying to be honest but not damaging their self esteem. She invites them to call again if they want to talk more. She is concerned not only how well a person will do at the job they are applying for, but also how they'll do in the next job. She says, "It's important to do it this way or you're setting people up to fail when they get promoted."

The company hires very few people with MBAs, and even those that do get hired are selected for their fit not for their credentials. In fact, they prefer people without extensive industry experience. For example, 40 percent of their pilots come directly from the military, 20–30 percent from small commuter airlines, and the rest from the major airlines. To encourage employees to help in the recruitment effort, Southwest offers a free space-available pass (which permits a person to travel free when the plane isn't full) to any employee who recommends someone who is hired to fill a position that is difficult to fill, such as in finance or information systems. Southwest doesn't have a nepotism policy (except for officers) and has 481 couples who work for the company. When these people describe the firm as "family," a common reference throughout the airline, they really mean it.

Training

Given the emphasis on selecting for attitudes and fit and the importance of culture, it follows that training is an important part of Southwest. In 1993 alone, 6,500 employees went through Southwest's University for People. Headed by Liz Simmons and with a staff of eight, the training group offers a variety of courses ranging from the "New Hire Celebration" (it's not called orientation) designed to get new employees enthused and excited, to senior management courses. Delise Zachry believes that, "Our level of external service is only as good as our internal service." She worries that the success of the company may induce a sense of complacency and noted that all the positive press accounts don't help.

New flight attendants go through four weeks of classes, typically with less than five percent attrition. Much of this training is oriented towards customer servicethe care and feeding of customers." Customer expectations about service are quite high, and these are communicated to both new and experienced employees. All new hires are exposed to the history, principles, values, mission, and culture of the company. They are also told how the company views leadership and management. In all training, there is an emphasis on teamwork and team building, all in good humor. For instance, new hires often do a celebratory skit at the conclusion of their training. One new pilot class donned dark sunglasses and white canes and stumbled into Kelleher's office.

For managers, there is a three and a half day course on leadership, pricing, revenue management, and on how the business works. A member of senior management always attends a two hour session and talks openly with the participants. Training is virtually 100 percent internal. "If it ain't born and bred here, they don't want any part of it," says Delise, a training instructor. Front-line leadership gets a specially designed two-day course each year. These programs are designed to address particular needs, like cross-functional teamwork, and are heavily experiential. They involve managers from different levels and different parts of the organization, but never have a superior and a subordinate in the same session. Each year as the new program begins, the senior team is always the first to go through it. In addition to this special program, supervisors receive 80 hours of training per year. Courses include the usual offerings of communication, time management, and career planning, as well as others emphasizing the employee's role in creat-

ing legendary customer service and more interpersonal explorations around accepting responsibility and developing trust.

For the past 18 months, training has offered a course called "The Climb;" a two and a half day ropes and outward bound course. This course is open to the entire company, but is attended by intact work teams. Delise notes that it's hard to get people to change in their normal work setting. To generate the emotional contact necessary to foster change, the entire team lives for the time together, completely cut-off from phones, cars, and contact with other outside issues. At the end of the program, each team develops an action plan to insure that their new behaviors are transferred to the work setting. The senior executive team attended this course during 1994.

The other highlighted training is "The Front-Line Forum," in which 12–15 individuals with 10–15 years experience in the company are brought together to discuss how the company is doing and how it has changed. They meet with top nine officers and explore questions like, "We promised you something around the culture and spirit of the company. Have we delivered?" Although the selection is done randomly, the idea is to assemble some people in the group who may be a bit beaten down to see what needs to be done to keep the culture alive.

Southwest does not have any tuition reimbursement program for taking outside courses. It also tends not to sponsor people to attend outside training.

Overall, it is clear that training is an important form of two-way communication. Not only are the values of hard work, fun, and cost consciousness inculcated, but the training is used to get internal customer feedback. For Delise the issue is "To figure out how we can get better everyday, not worry about American Airlines or Delta."

The Southwest Work Force

The company is 89 percent unionized with nine separate unions, but has had only one six-day walkout by the machinists over a decade ago. Mike Levine, former dean of Yale's School of Organization and Management and current vice president for marketing at Northwest Airlines notes that, "Herb really is an extremely gifted labor-relations talent, especially when you consider he has somehow managed to get union people to identify personally with this company."[14] Obviously, those covered by a contract are paid on the basis of seniority. Kelleher insists that there be few work rules in union contracts. Exhibit 5 displays rates of progression over time for a number of different job classifications. These data are from recent contracts and illustrate the general relationship between pay and seniority for those covered by collective bargaining agreements. Part of this includes a system whereby employees can bid for shift and work hours. In almost every job class there are people earning between $40,000 and $60,000 a year. Everyone receives a raise on the anniversary of their employment. Libby Sartain, Director of Benefits and Compensation, notes, "There's no miracle compensation program here. The story is low pay at the beginning and high pay after you get seniority." Below market wages are offered to clericals and management positions. Most people take a salary cut to join Southwest. One former manager at EDS who left to join Southwest was offered two and a half times his starting salary to stay with EDS.

The only big difference is that at Southwest pilots and flight attendants are paid by the trip. As Kelleher says, "Those airplanes aren't making any money while they're sitting on the ground."[15] While comparisons are a bit tricky, *Fortune* reported that for 1992 the average wage at Southwest was $44,305 compared to $45,801 at American and $54,380 at United. Derek Deck of the Air Conference (a trade group that gathers comparable wage data across airlines) believes that Southwest employees may earn less per hour than at other airlines, although they do have the flexibility to work more hours and earn more. Controlling for seniority, he estimates that a flight attendant at Southwest would earn about $18 an hour, compared to $20 an hour at Continental and $23 at USAir. Deck also believes that Southwest personnel can, and often do, fly more trips giving them 10–15 hours more per month.

Executive compensation is modest by some firm's standards. In 1992, Kelleher earned a salary of $393,042 and a bonus of $ 120,000. In 1994, he was named one of the five lowest-paid CEOs in Dallas, and the lowest-paid on a performance-adjusted basis; an award he is particularly proud of. He does holds stock worth around $90 million, a paltry sum besides the likes of Larry Ellison at Oracle or Bill Gates at Microsoft. In fact, there was no executive stock option plan until a few years ago. There are no country club memberships, no company cars, and officers stay in the same hotels as the flight crews.

However, profit-sharing covers all employees who have been with the firm for over a year, and they are required to invest 25 percent of their profit sharing money in Southwest stock in a retirement account. In 1993, those eligible received eight percent of their salary as a bonus. Employees can also take advantage of a discounted stock purchase program. This has produced several millionaires. Approximately 85–90 percent of the employees own stock in the company, with about 11 percent of Southwest's outstanding shares owned by employees. However, Libby Sartain notes that she tries to encourage employees to diversify and not hold too much of the company's stock.

Because of its conservative hiring policies and growth, Southwest has a young work force; the average age is 34. Twenty-three percent of the employees are minorities, with 10–12 percent at the managerial level. Women are widely represented, also at the highest levels of the company. John Turnipseed described how when an EEO audit team arrived in Dallas, he simply gave them an office and pointed out where the files were. In most companies, auditors have to request specific documents, which are then retrieved and brought to the auditors. He acknowledges that they aren't perfect, but intended to correct any problems. He described how apologetic the auditors were at having to write up several violations.

As might be expected, turnover is low, running four and a half percent in 1993, less than half that of other major airlines. The company has never had a furlough or layoff. Because of limitations in their labor contracts, they use few temporary or part-time employees. They do have a pool of ex-employees (e.g., retirees, people who want to stay at home) that they can call on in case of emergencies. All temporary workers are paid benefits on a pro-rata basis. There is little cross-training although they encourage "days in the field" so employees can try front-line jobs. Only in the marketing and reservations departments are there formal teams. The culture, however, promotes informal teamwork and employees routinely help each other out.

The Southwest Spirit

Southwest tries hard to manage and maintain its culture. Wander around the halls at the Dallas headquarters and you hear several themes over and over: customer service, hard work, equality, cost consciousness, dedication, fun, and, most frequently of all, family. Of course, this invites the cynic in all of us. One employee who had worked at several other large companies said, "I was pretty dubious at first, having been at places where everyone but the top two or three people were considered commodities. But I have come to appreciate a place where kindness and the human spirit are nurtured."[16] Aside from the efforts

of Colleen Barrett and the culture committee (and its 35 local subcommittees), there are continual efforts to preserve the values that brought Southwest to its current position. John Turnipseed says that trust is built by constantly sharing information. "The level of trust has never been broken. In many organizations, everybody's against someone—union versus management, head office versus the field, etc. Not here."

The family spirit can be seen in many ways. For instance, there is the catastrophe fund, which in the last two years raised $500,000 in voluntary contributions for distribution to other Southwest employees who needed help. During the last oil crisis, unbeknownst to management the employees raised $130,000 to help defray fuel costs. When a former employee developed a drug problem, the company arranged to pay for his medical care so long as he stayed in the rehabilitation program.

Kelleher and his management team seem acutely aware of the potential problems as they continue to grow. He says, "The bigger we get, the smaller I want our employees to think and act." Ann Rhoades says, "You have to work at the culture. It doesn't just happen." Rita Bailey described how there is plenty of peer pressure "not to 'bad mouth' the family. Employees don't put up with a lot of complaining." Colleen Barrett describes how when she talks to people, they are always skeptical and want to know the "real" story. She says, "There are no deep, dark secrets here. It's so simple. It's a cult. It's a religion with us." Kelleher echoes this view when describing the spirit of Southwest employees, "The people who work here don't think of Southwest as a business. They think of it as a crusade."[17] This doesn't mean that people are unrealistic. A pilot indicated, "It's not a Mary Kay-type atmosphere where we're all starry-eyed. It's mutual respect."[18] A longtime observer of the airline industry says, "At other places, managers say that people are their most important resource, but nobody acts on it. At Southwest, they have never lost sight of the fact."

The Competitive Threat

As she finished gathering up papers for tomorrow's meeting, Ann reflected on the airline industry in general and Southwest's position in particular. The industry overall, with few exceptions had been characterized by notoriously poor labor relations and authoritarian management. In 1983, Frank Lorenzo led Continental Airlines into bankruptcy so he could rid the airline of its union. Carl Icahn faced numerous strikes during the time he controlled Trans World Airlines, hiring replacement workers during some of them. Eastern Airlines ultimately failed because of the conflict between Lorenzo and the unions. Robert Crandall of American Airlines pioneered the two-tiered wage structure in which newly hired employees would be brought in at lower wages than the currently-employed workers. During the 1993 Thanksgiving Season, American's flight attendants struck in an attempt to roll back wages. In this light, Southwest's policies stood out—labor peace, trust, non-adversarial relations, open sharing of information, and high productivity.

More recently, several other airlines were undergoing employee buyouts. By 1994, TWA was largely employee owned. Northwest narrowly avoided bankruptcy when its unions agreed to an eleventh hour swap of wage concessions for an ownership stake. United has followed suit. USAir was offering stock and board seats in return for employee wage concessions. Continental Airlines had also emerged from Chapter 11 with what the press claimed was a more employee-oriented management. Executives at Delta said they would announce their plans for a new low-fare strategy in the coming months. The pilots at American suggested a similar strategy to management.

But it wasn't these general trends that con-

cerned Ann as much as two direct threats. Both United and Continental had begun low cost airlines-within-an-airline to challenge Southwest directly. They were not only directly imitating the Southwest strategy, they were also using their policies and procedures. An old adage at Southwest was not to provoke their major competitors. Obviously, they had done more than provoke them; they had challenged them directly.

Continental Lite

Under the guidance of CEO Bob Ferguson, Continental Airlines emerged from its second bankruptcy in April, 1993. In May, Ferguson announced his plan to split the company into two operations; one that would concentrate on short-haul, low fare flights (named Continental Lite or CALite), and the other featuring first-class service at business class prices. He believes that because of their low cost structure, lower even than Southwest, Continental would be able to compete successfully. While imitating many of Southwest's practices, including the use of humor by flight attendants, Ferguson believes that he can attract the business traveler. By concentrating primarily on the East Coast market, he can take advantage of greater density, shorter flights, and avoid competing directly with Southwest, at least in the short-term.

Continental Lite was rolled out in October, 1993, with 173 daily departures from 14 cities. By summer, it had expanded to 28 percent of Continental's capacity, with plans to ultimately grow to 40 percent. Fares were cut dramatically. For example, the Newark-Greensboro went from $273 to $99 and the Greensboro-Greenville from $226 to $59. The early results, however, are mixed. CALite currently is flying with about 59 percent of their seats filled. Customer reaction is not always positive. Some frequent flyers were miffed that there was no priority boarding or meal service. Flight attendants are concerned about the increased workloads

(Like Southwest, they clean cabins between flight segments) and lack of breaks between flights. Ground crews are trying hard, but turn-arounds are still taking over 30 minutes rather than the hoped for 20. Even the pilots were up-set until the company began providing meals for them during their busy schedules. (In one instance, a flight was delayed while the pilots ate in the airport terminal.) In March of 1994, Conti nental had the worst marks of any domestic air-line in terms of customer complaints, on-time performance, and mishandled baggage.

Financial results are also not yet up to ex-pectations. Continental lost $38.5 million on revenues of $3.9 billion from April, 1993, when they emerged from bankruptcy protection, through the end of 1993. Management expects to break even in the second half of 1994 and doesn't see these results as a disaster. Chief Fi-nancial Officer Daniel Garton says that only 20 percent of CALite's routes are losing money and notes that because USAir and Delta responded aggressively to Continental's fare cuts, profits have been weaker than expected.[19] Some airline industry observers believe that Continental's costs may still be too high.

This is also complicated because CALite still relies more heavily on one-stop and connecting passengers than does Southwest. The clear trend in the industry has also been for fewer business travelers. In 1982, over 50 percent of travelers paid full-economy fare or higher (e.g., business-class). Currently, that figure is less than 40 per-cent. Gordon Bethune, Continental's COO, says, "Up to a two-hour flight, it's already a commod-ity business. A $10 difference will grab anybody's passenger these days."[20] Flights of up to two hours represent over 60 percent of domestic traffic.

Ferguson, whose style has been described as "harsh and uncommunicative," is undeterred. A 1972 graduate of Lehigh University with a de-gree in finance, he began his career at Bankers Trust making loans to the airline industry. He left Banker's to move to one of his clients, Braniff International, and subsequently left them to join Frank Lorenzo at Texas Air. While there, he helped Lorenzo buy People Express, a suc-cessful low-fare carrier in the early 80s that failed in 1986 after overexpanding. A harsh task-master, Ferguson has been known to drive exec-utives away. Since taking over in 1991, at least a dozen top managers have left. One commented on his management style by noting that, "It's very pointed, even nasty. If he doesn't like an idea, he seems to go out of his way to ridicule it."[21] Another said, "He can't resist reverting to Lorenzo-style management." Ferguson admits to not suffering fools easily and says, "I will not tol-erate not doing a good job. I will tell you in front of yourself, 20 people, 100 people." A per-son familiar with his style claims that "Ferguson has to become more people-oriented and de-pend more on the recommendations of his man-agement team."[22] He denies that he has people-skill problems and has plans to give as much as four percent of the stock to employees. He has also hired Donald Valentine as marketing chief for CALite; Valentine was previously head of marketing for Southwest. Ferguson concedes that CALite has had some start-up pains and hasn't operated very efficiently so far but sees this as just the usual problems of changing the organization.

United's Shuttle

On July 28, 1994 United announced what had been the year's worst-kept secret: On October 1st they would begin their own airline-within-an-airline on the West Coast. The goal of this operation, named "The Shuttle," was to cut costs by 30 percent on these routes and regain the market share that Southwest had captured. To do this, United aimed at reducing their costs per available seat mile to 7.4 cents. The Shuttle was scheduled to begin with 184 daily flights on 13 routes, expanding to almost 300 flights by yearend. United announced that they would match the going price on all routes on which they went head-to-head with Southwest. Their service would include advance seat assignments, a first-class cabin, and United's frequent flyer mileage program. "People want to fly us because they can consolidate their frequent flier miles and get better service," said United's Senior Vice President for planning.[23]

Herb Kelleher referred to United's announcement as a "declaration of war" and intimated that Southwest might begin flying other United routes to drain revenue. He also talked about raising fares on longer routes to generate revenue to lower the bar without hurting their own profits. On August 30, Kelleher sent a memo, entitled "Commencement of Hostilities," to all Southwest employees detailing Southwest's response to United's challenge. This memo concludes:

> Southwest's essential difference is not machines and "things." Our essential difference is minds, hearts, spirits, and souls. Winston Churchill stated: "Success is never final." Indeed, "success" must be earned over and over again or it disappears. I am betting on your minds, your hearts, your souls, and your spirits to continue our success. Let's win this one and make aviation history—again!

The President of America West, a Phoenix-based low-fare airline that had been bloodied by Southwest, said, "Taking on Southwest head-to-head is unwise for anyone."[24]

On July 12, United had completed negotiations for an employee buyout. In return for 55 percent of the company, employees, excluding the 17,000 flight attendants who voted not to participate in or agree to work rule changes, promised $4.9 billion in wage cuts and productivity gains. As a part of this agreement, Steve Wolf, the former CEO, was required to step down and was replaced by a Chrysler executive, Gerald Greenwald, with no previous airline in-

dustry experience, but who was reputed to be a good people-person. Wolf claimed that he left United in good financial shape with great success on their overseas' routes and a fleet that averaged only nine years old. Wolf estimated that the $1 billion in losses in 1992 would have been a $700 million profit if they hadn't been competing with Southwest. "We just need to come up with a strategy that will offset their competitive advantage," he said.[25]

Unfortunately, not everyone is sure that The Shuttle can succeed. The culture at United is almost the opposite that of Southwest. One pilot claimed, "We live by the letter of the law, in every way." Another noted that, "Mechanics and pilots have always had a rift between them That's a conflict as old as aviation history." Another worried, "As for management, I don't know if they can change their culture. There's a lot of dinosaurs over there at headquarters. There are a lot of power struggles over there, and they worry more about those than they do running the airline." One cynic claimed that, "Most of the expansion we've done over the past few years a blind man could have accomplished. I wouldn't really credit Steve Wolf with any of that." These sentiments were not restricted solely to the pilots. Based on interviews around the airline, Ken Labich at *Fortune*, reported mixed opinions about the future among United employees:[26]

> "You've also got to hope that the way we do things will change. [United] is the kind of place where management usually thinks they are way up there, and the rest of us are way down here. They want to make sure the shareholders get what they want, but they don't care much about the employees. All that's got to change."
>
> —*Mechanic*

> "I'm afraid a lot of people are still looking at the situation as us versus them—management versus labor, union versus non-union there are clearly union people out there who are saying,

'Wait till we take over.' I don't know how we will ever get out of that."

—Planner

"We've always been treated like angry children who don't deserve what they get. Upper management has been adversarial and confrontational with us for over 10 years now; I don't think Mr. Wolf liked the flight attendants at all. We are managed differently from the other groups. We're disciplined if we're sick more than 3 days per month or if we arrive late for a flight We're the only group that has to hop on a scale every month. Pilots certainly aren't held to those standards. When it comes to the boys in the cockpit, things are different. The pilots stay in downtown hotels, and we're stuck out at the airport. When we have to deadhead, they fly in first class and we're in the back of the plane. That says it all The irony, of course, is that the bosses ought to think a lot harder about how we feel if they want to keep their customers happy. We're the people who spend all the time with the passengers. To the public, we are United."

—Flight Attendant and Union Representative

"People think a reservation job is easy, but it's actually very difficult. Customers aren't nice on the phones any longer, like they were when I came here 15 years ago they're rude to us. Then we get so busy, with so many calls on hold, that we can't spend time with people and provide the good service."

—Reservation Agent

"I'd say there has been an intense lack of trust toward management among the people I work with. We feel that they haven't been dealing straight with us for a long time. They wanted to satisfy shareholders and if people lost their jobs—well, that's business these days There's

been turmoil since 1985, when people on Wall Street started looking at us like we were some cash cow they could milk."

—Ramp Agent

Although the head of the new airline had not yet been announced, the betting was on Alan "Sky" Magary. Magary, a veteran with 24 years in the industry, was an innovator, credited with ideas such as foot rests and smoke-free flights. A former Northwest Executive described how when Magary was there, he came up with the idea of using patterned fabrics for the seats to disguise coffee stains. Magary had spoken publicly about the potential for The Shuttle and United's plans to reduce costs to 7.4 cents a seat mile. There was some skepticism about this goal among industry analysts, one of whom commented that, "Only a deranged MBA could have thought this up."[27]

The Off-Site Meeting

As Ann pondered the situation, she wondered if this competitive threat could seriously damage Southwest, and what actions, if any, Southwest's senior management should take? Could United and Continental really imitate the Southwest approach? Of course, the threat was made more complicated because of the size and growth of Southwest. With 14,000 employees, it was no longer the small firm it had been. She worried that this could affect the family feeling. She also worried about the overconfidence their success could breed. Herb had been quoted in a recent interview as saying, "We have to be the world's first company to refute the old law that companies die from excessive prosperity."[28] How could they avoid these attitudes? There was also the tricky problem of succession. Herb had been at the head of the company since 1963. How would the organization deal with this problem if it became necessary? It was clear to her that the success of the company really did rest with the human resources, and her job was to insure that these were managed effectively. But what should they be doing to deal with these problems? Well, she had seven hours before tomorrow's 7 a.m. meeting to reflect on her options.

Notes

1. Peter Elsworth, "Southwest Air's new push west," *New York Times,* June 16, 1991.

2. Adam Bryant, "United's bid to rule western skies," *New York Times,* September 16, 1994.

3. Edward Welles,) "Captain Marvel," *Inc.,* January, 1992.

4. Kenneth Labich, "Is Herb Kelleher America's best CEO?" *Fortune,* May 2, 1994.

5. E. Scott Reckard, "Shuttle dogfight good news for air travelers," *San Francisco Chronicle,* October 2, 1994.

6. Jeff Pelline, "Southwest Air's driving force," *San Francisco Chronicle,* June 10, 1993.

7. Labich, "Is Herb Kelleher America's best CEO?"

8. Labich, "Is Herb Kelleher America's best CEO?"

9. Evan Ramstad, "Cattle call carrier lassos riders, profits," *San Francisco Chronicle,* April 7, 1991.

10. Bridget O'Brian, "Southwest Airlines is a rare carrier: It still makes money," *Wall Street Journal,* October 26, 1992.

11. Labich, "Is Herb Kelleher America's best CEO?"

12. Wendy Zellner, "Go-go goliaths," *Business Week,* February 13, 1995.

13. Subrata Chakravaty, "Hit 'em hardest with the mostest," *Forbes,* September 16, 1991.

14. Labich, "Is Herb Kelleher America's best CEO?"

15. O'Brian, "Southwest Airlines is a rare carrier."

16. Labich, "Is Herb Kelleher America's best CEO?"

17. Richard Teitelbaum, "Where service flies right," *Fortune,* August 24, 1992.

18. Frank Gibney, *Newsweek,* May 30, 1988

19. Wendy Zellner, "Why Continental's CEO fell to earth," *Business Week,* November 7, 1994.

20. Howard Banks, "A sixties industry in a nineties economy," *Forbes,* May 9, 1994.

21. Wendy Zellner, "This is Captain Ferguson, please hang on to your hats," *Business Week,* May 23, 1994.

22. Zellner, "This is Captain Ferguson."

23. Wendy Zellner, "Dogfight over California," *Business Week,* August 15, 1994.

24. Zellner, "Dogfight over California."

25. Kenneth Labich, "Will United fly?" *Fortune,* August 22, 1994.

26. Labich, "Will United fly?"

27. Susan Chandler, "'Sky' Magary picks a dogfight," *Business Week,* September 19, 1994.

28. Banks, "A sixties industry."

Exhibit 1

Ten-Year Financial Summary

Selected Consolidated Financial Data
(in thousands except per share amounts)

	1993	1992	1991	1990	1989	1988	1987	1986	1985	1984
Total operating revenues	$2,296,673	$1,802,979	$1,379,286	$1,237,276	1,057,729	860,434	778,328	768,790	679,672	535,948
Operating income	291,973	193,804	72,611	87,261	102,040	85,890	30,447	88,963	78,524	68,497
Net income	**$154,284**	**$97,385**	**$33,148**	**$50,605**	**74,505**	**57,952**	**20,155**	**50,035**	**47,278**	**49,724**
Net income per common and common equivalent share	$1.05	$.68	$.25	$.39	$.54	$.41	$.14	$.34	$.34	$.38
Cash dividends per common share	$.03867	$.03533	$.03333	$.03223	$.03110	$.02943	$.02890	$.02890	$.02890	$.02890
Total assets	$2,576,037	$2,368,856	$1,854,331	$1,480,813	$1,423,298	$1,308.389	$1,042,640	$1,061.419	$1,002,403	$646,244
Long-term debt	$639,136	$735,754	$617,434	$327,553	354,150	369,541	251,130	339,069	381,308	153,314
Stockholders' equity	$1,054,019	$879,536	$635,793	$607,294	591,794	567,375	514,278	511,850	466,004	361,768

Consolidated Financial Ratios

	1993	1992	1991	1990	1989	1988	1987	1986	1985	1984
Return on average total assets	6.2%	4.6%	2.0%	3.5%	5.5%	5.1%	1.9%	4.8%	5.6%	8.1%
Return on average stockholders' equity	16.0%	12.9%	5.3%	8.4%	12.9%	10.8%	4.0%	10.3%	11.4%	14.7%
Debt as a percentage of invested capital	37.7%	45.5%	49.3%	35.0%	37.4%	39.4%	32.8%	39.8%	45.0%	29.8%

Consolidated Operating Statistics

	1993	1992	1991	1990	1989	1988	1987	1986	1985	1984
Revenue passengers carried	36,955,221	27,839,284	22,669,942	19,830,941	17,958,263	14,876,582	13,503,242	13,637,515	12,651,239	10,697,544
Load factor	68.4%	64.5%	61.1%	60.7%	62.7%	57.7%	58.4%	58.8%	60.4%	58.5%
Average length of passenger haul	509	495	498	502	517	516	577	542	472	436
Trips flown	546,297	438,184	382,752	338,108	304,673	274,859	270,559	262,082	230,227	200,124
Average passenger fare	$59.97	$58.33	$55.93	$57.71	$54.21	$55.68	$55.66	$54.43	$51.91	$48.53
Passenger revenue yield per RPM	11.77¢	11.78¢	11.22¢	11.49¢	10.49¢	10.79¢	9.65¢	10.050	11.000	11.12¢
Operating revenue yield per ASM	8.35¢	7.89¢	7.10¢	7.23¢	6.86¢	6.47¢	5.84¢	6.11¢	6.88¢	6.71¢
Operating expenses per ASM	7.25¢	7.03¢	6.76¢	6.73¢	6.20¢	5.82¢	5.61¢	5.41¢	6.08¢	5.86¢
Fuel cost per gallon (average)	59.15¢	60.82¢	65.69¢	77.89¢	59.46¢	51.37¢	54.31¢	51.42¢	78.17¢	82.44¢
Number of employees at year end	15,175	11,397	9,778	8,620	7,760	6,467	5,765	5,819	5,271	3,934
Size of fleet at year end	178	141	124	106	94	85	75	79	70	54

Exhibit 2

Airline Costs per Available Seat Mile

	3rd Quarter 1993	3rd Quarter 1994
Southwest	7.13	7.03
Continental	7.64	7.56
United	8.11	8.32
American	8.06	8.08
TWA	9.23	8.66
Delta	8.66	8.95
Northwest	9.36	9.79
USAir	10.94	10.74

Source: The Economist, November 5, 1994.

Exhibit 3

Anatomy of a 15-Minute Turnaround

7:55	Ground crew chat around gate position
8:03.30	Ground crew alerted and move to positions
8:04	Plane begins to pull into gate; crew moves toward plane
8:04.30	Plane stops; jetway telescopes out; baggage door opens
8:06.30	Baggage unloaded; refueling and other servicing underway
8:07	Passengers off plane
8:08	Boarding call; baggage reloading, refueling complete
8:10	Boarding complete; most of ground crew leave
8:15	Jetway retracts
8:15.30	Pushback from gate
8:18	Pushback tractor disengages; plane leaves for runway

Source: Subrata Chakravaty, *Forbes,* 1991.

Exhibit 4
Southwest Airlines Organizational Chart

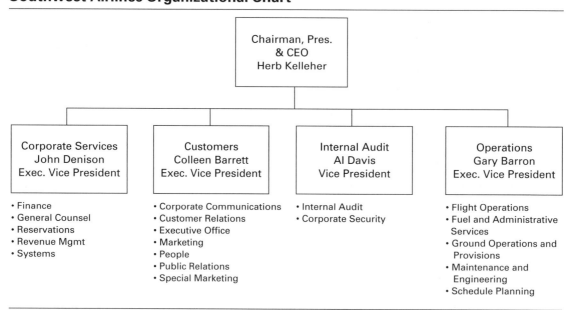

	Corporate Services John Denison Exec. Vice President	Customers Colleen Barrett Exec. Vice President	Internal Audit Al Davis Vice President	Operations Gary Barron Exec. Vice President

- Chairman, Pres. & CEO — Herb Kelleher

Corporate Services — John Denison, Exec. Vice President
- Finance
- General Counsel
- Reservations
- Revenue Mgmt
- Systems

Customers — Colleen Barrett, Exec. Vice President
- Corporate Communications
- Customer Relations
- Executive Office
- Marketing
- People
- Public Relations
- Special Marketing

Internal Audit — Al Davis, Vice President
- Internal Audit
- Corporate Security

Operations — Gary Barron, Exec. Vice President
- Flight Operations
- Fuel and Administrative Services
- Ground Operations and Provisions
- Maintenance and Engineering
- Schedule Planning

Exhibit 5

Pay Scales for Three Selected Jobs

Period	Flight Attendant	Reservation Agent	Customer Service Agent
1st 3 months	$13.37	$5.75	$6.00
2nd 3 months	13.37	6.25	6.50
2nd 6 months	14.99	6.75	7.00
2nd year	16.06	7.50	7.79
3rd year	17.13	8.15	8.41
4th year	18.20	8.68	8.82
5th year	19.27	9.12	9.27
6th year	26.20	9.57	9.73
7th year	28.17	10.05	10.22
8th year	33.06	10.56	10.73
9th year	34.03	11.09	11.26
10th year	34.96	11.64	11.83
11th year	35.88	12.22	12.42

Flight attendant pay progression ends after the 13th year. Customer service and reservation agent salary increases stop after the 18th year of employment, although after that time they are eligible for a bonus based on the cost of living index and a profitability factor for the company.

DISCUSSION QUESTIONS

1. What explains the problems that existed in the School District of Philadelphia's department of human resources (HR) prior to January 2005?

2. What is Tomás Hanna's vision for HR?

3. Evaluate the actions that Tomás Hanna has taken to date.

4. What should Hanna do to address the core challenges that remain?

David A. Thomas ■ Caroline King

Reinventing Human Resources at the School District of Philadelphia

Promising wholesale change in its hiring process and employee relations, the Philadelphia School District has ousted the top four managers in its human resources department . . . In a school system that has been hard up for teachers and can little afford to alienate its applicants and workforce, chief executive Paul Vallas said yesterday that complaints rolled in about the department, which oversees 25,000 employees. He described it as "insensitive" and "unresponsive." "We've got to put the *human* back in *human resources,*" Vallas said . . .

The District also announced yesterday the promotion of Tomás Hanna, who had been director of teacher recruitment and retention since August 2002, as the senior vice president of human resources.

The Philadelphia Inquirer[1]

On a sunny spring day in mid–April 2005, Tomás Hanna glanced at the now infamous January 11 newspaper clip. The article captured Hanna's greatest professional challenge of his 14-year career with the School District of Philadelphia and he kept it taped to his computer as a daily reminder of his charge, which was nothing less than leading a full-scale transformation of the District's human resources (HR) department. The scores of photos and drawings decorating his office reminded him why he had accepted the daunting task—the over 217,000 Philadelphia students who deserved a high-quality, committed teacher in their classrooms every day.

As Hanna reflected on his first 90 days in office, he felt positive about the changes underway. He had recruited four new directors to help him drive change in the 120-member department. Plans to implement site-based selection—a new process that allowed all schools to interview and hire teacher candidates for the first time—beginning May 1, 2005 were on schedule. Following CEO Paul Vallas's lead, Hanna was reaching out to the Philadelphia Federation of Teachers (PFT) in hopes of restoring a severed relationship.

However, Hanna remained cognizant of the formidable challenges ahead. Most immediately, Hanna knew that for many internal and external observers, site-based selection was a "make or break" test of his ability to lead change in HR. A 2003 blue-ribbon task force, known as the "Campaign for Human Capital," (the Campaign) specifically cited the District's centralized hiring process as a key obstacle for recruiting and retaining high-quality teachers, and in response, District leadership had pushed hard to win school-based hiring in the new 2004–2008 PFT contract. Hanna worried about the capacity of the District's 274 schools and HR to effectively enact site-based selection.

Looking ahead, Hanna had to find ways to institutionalize other important Campaign goals, such as diversifying teacher recruitment, supporting new teachers, and strengthening leadership development for principals. Hanna also remained deeply troubled by the District's inability to place the best teachers in the lowest performing schools. Hanna recognized that a lot of this work depended upon his team's ability to develop strategic relationships with other internal District departments and the unions—not an easy task given HR's historical isolation, transactional culture, and acrimonious labor relations.

The School District of Philadelphia

In SY05, the School District of Philadelphia (the "District") was the eighth-largest public school system in the country and the largest in the Commonwealth of Pennsylvania.[2] The District had a $1.9 billion annual budget and enrolled approximately 217,405 PK-12 students in 274 schools. Similar to its urban counterparts across the U.S., the District served an increasingly diverse and low-income student body. African-Americans comprised 66% of district enrollment, Hispanics 15%, whites 14%, and Asians 5%. Eighty percent qualified for free or reduced-price meals, up from 55% in 1997, and 7% were learning English for the first time (see Exhibit 1 for district facts and figures).

The District was emerging from a period of turmoil and rapid change. SY05 marked the District's third year operating under the joint oversight of the state and city of Philadelphia.[3] In December 2001, as the District faced a hostile state takeover due to chronically low academic achievement and a $200 million operating deficit, then Republican Governor Mark Schweiker and Democratic Philadelphia Mayor John Street brokered the shared agreement. Schweiker and Street created a new five-member governing board, the School Reform Commission (SRC), with the governor appointing three members and the mayor two. The SRC selected the District's CEO, assumed fiduciary responsibility for the District, and gained some extraordinary powers under Act 46 of the Pennsylvania School Code (see Exhibit 2).

The SRC appointed its first CEO, Paul Vallas, in July 2002. The head of Chicago Public Schools from 1995–2001, Vallas enacted a series of large-scale reforms aimed in improving academic achievement throughout the District. Under Vallas's strategic plan, "Students Succeeding 2002–2008," the District standardized the K-9 curriculum, increased instructional time for literacy and mathematics, implemented six-week benchmark assessments, strengthened professional development, reduced class sizes in grades K-3, and earmarked $1.5 billion for capital improvements.

Vallas also worked to repair badly damaged relationships with the District's five collective bargaining units, most notably with the 20,000-member PFT. Evidence of the acrimony from the highly contentious 2000 contract negotiations lingered. The union and District maintained different versions of some contract language,[4] grievances skyrocketed, and PFT relations with HR had reached a stalemate.

By SY05, Vallas's efforts appeared to be gaining traction. Student performance on the Pennsylvania System of School Assessment (PSSA) tests had improved steadily since 2002, with the District's annual achievement gains outpacing state averages (see Exhibit 3). The number of schools demonstrating adequate yearly progress under the federal No Child Left Behind Act surged from 22 in SY02 to 160 in SY04. Vallas also restored the District's financial health, and in May 2004, he submitted the District's first balanced budget in seven years. The SRC credited Vallas and his leadership team with ameliorating union relationships; building bridges to the business, philanthropic, and university committees; and restoring public confidence in the school system. Strengthening human capital management in the District, however, remained an intractable problem and Vallas hoped that Hanna's leadership and a new 2004–2008 PFT contract had finally created the conditions for change.

Efforts to Reform Human Resources

The Office of Human Resources

The 120-person HR office was responsible for developing and implementing all personnel and employment policies, including recruiting and hiring staff, interpreting and enforcing labor contracts, and managing payroll and benefits. An executive director (ED) reported to the District's chief operating officer (COO) (see the District's organizational chart in Exhibit 4). Four directors reported to the ED and oversaw four major HR divisions: (1) recruitment and selection, (2) employee operations, (3) classification and compensation, and (4) labor relations.

Multiple indicators suggested entrenched problems hampered HR's effectiveness, ranging from hard data showing that over 50% of teachers left the District within three years[5] to anecdotal comments relating the department's appalling lack of customer service. The department also experienced a revolving door of leadership with three different executive directors serving between July 2002 and November 2004. A number of initiatives were designed to "workaround" the deficiencies of HR, such as the Campaign for Human Capital (see below) and the transfer of benefits from HR to the finance office in late 2002.

As SY05 began, HR was led by a former private industry executive with experience on a suburban school board who had been appointed as the department's ED in November 2003. Despite directing his new hire to "shake things up in HR," Vallas grew impatient with the slow pace of change in the department. Vallas emphasized the need for a radically different approach to HR:

> Our HR department was still working under the assumptions of the old economy when we were flooded with applications and teachers spent their careers with the District. HR did not respond, or see a need to change, to meet the needs of a new economy. We have to be ready to compete on multiple levels now. Teachers come to us from all walks of life with different professional expectations; we are not their only employment option. Also, we have to hire the most innovative principals and talented teachers we can to ensure our students develop the complex, critical thinking skills they need to be successful in college and the workforce.

External and Internal Reviews

Vallas commissioned two external reviews of HR in the fall of 2004.[6] Concurrently, District leadership completed an internal assessment of the department. These reviews identified three primary challenges for improving HR's effectiveness: strategic and operational issues, the relationship with the teachers' union, and the highly centralized teacher hiring process.

Strategic and Operational Issues: While District and external evaluators alike critiqued HR's transactional orientation, one external group suggested that leadership's attitude toward HR and the absence of a direct reporting relationship between the CEO and HR exacerbated the problem. A former senior manager shed light on the situation:

> HR was viewed, internally and externally, as the people who processed new employees. We were not invited to the table when District lead-

ership made strategic decisions, many of which had considerable HR implications, such as the opening of 28 small high schools by 2008. Often, we were not asked to give our input on the recruitment and staffing issues, but rather, were expected to 'just make it happen.' This pattern further reinforced the perception of HR as not strategic and left many HR employees feeling unmotivated and unaware of the big picture.

The department's four divisions—and smaller task-oriented units—operated as silos, in which people rarely shared information or interacted with staff in other areas. A recruitment manager recalled contacting a colleague in placement and being denied new teachers' starting salary information because "that was not part of my job." District employees outside of HR also complained that HR was stubbornly unresponsive. While some HR employees perceived themselves as the "gatekeepers" who protected the District by ensuring personnel policies and procedures were followed, other HR staff suggested that they would have liked to have been more helpful, but were purposefully cut-off from the rest of the organization. A 12-year HR employee who wrote job descriptions for vacant positions explained, "Writing classifications takes a lot of back and forth with the hiring department in order to clarify the role, responsibilities, and qualifications. But my director wouldn't allow me to call managers above my level within HR or in other departments. "

Due to the District's financial constraints, HR had been passed over for major technology upgrades. For example, the three functional groups involved in hiring new teachers—recruitment, selection, and placement—did not collect data in a standard format or centralized database. As a result, data was either lost, tracked on paper, or stored in stand-alone databases. Capacity constraints also reduced the effectiveness of the District's AMS Advantage technology system which had been implemented in 1999 to manage "back office" transactions, such as entering employees in the payroll system. After receiving numerous, and constant, complaints from employees with missing paychecks or delayed benefits, the PFT began calling the HR tool the "disadvantage" system. Employee records were also in complete disarray as each HR unit, such as benefits or certification, kept separate paper files on the same employee. Compiling a comprehensive employee file could take up to a week.

Relationship with the Teachers' Union: Vallas also grew increasingly frustrated that HR leadership had not fostered more collaborative relationships with the District's unions, particularly the PFT. Ted Kirsch, who had served as the PFT President since 1990, characterized the attitude in HR towards the union from the late 1990s to 2004 as "highly contentious and lacking any semblance of trust, respect, and dialogue." Arlene Kempin, the PFT's chief personnel officer who had occupied an office within HR since 1983, experienced the impact of what she described as a "complete communication breakdown between HR and the PFT" firsthand. "HR sent out employee directives, and even though I was just down the hall, my first introduction to a memo was usually a flood of calls from our members asking me if they had to comply," recalled Kempin.

Highly Centralized and Cumbersome Teacher Hiring Process: Historically, and in accordance with the PFT contract, HR interviewed, hired, and assigned all new teachers centrally. (The only exception was teacher hiring in schools that had voted for full site-based selection.[7]) Teams from the recruitment and selection division interviewed applicants, ranked successful candidates according to their interview score and application date, and then turned over the list to a placement team in the employee operations division. As vacancies occurred during the year, the placement group contacted the highest scoring and earliest applicant on the list of selected candidates and took responsibility for "on-boarding" new teachers. One external study determined that in addition to the inefficiencies created by the multiple hand-offs, many qualified applicants actually found other jobs while waiting for HR to work through its historical list.

To fill the average 1,250 vacancies that occurred at the end of each school year, the placement team compiled a list of open positions by school by April 15 and invited candidates to rank their preferences. Many newly hired teachers ranked their school choices based on little more than anecdotal information from HR staff. External evaluators concluded that new teachers experienced an information-poor hiring process in which they felt detached from the schools they were selecting. In contrast, site selected teachers appeared more knowledgeable about their schools (see Exhibit 5).

Further compounding the process was a PFT contract stipulation prohibiting the District from hiring any new teachers until vacancies had first been filled by more senior teachers bidding for transfers.[8] Not only did the provision prolong the District's hiring timeline, but as veteran teachers typically transferred to increasingly higher-performing schools, newer teachers were often assigned to the neediest schools.[9] Principals, who had no input in the centralized new teacher hiring process and could not refuse seniority-based transfers, complained that they were unable to build their own staffs at the same time that they were being held increasingly accountable for improving academic achievement. Indeed, a 2004 study of 13 large urban school systems' hiring and assignment practices determined that Philadelphia was the only district in which schools never had the opportunity to interview teacher candidates.[10]

The Campaign for Human Capital and Tomás Hanna

High teacher turnover rates plagued the District, mirroring a trend evidenced in major metropolitan school systems around the country. An analysis of the 919 teachers hired in SY00 demonstrated that only 43% remained in the District four years later, and of those, only 29% had stayed in the same school all four years. High-poverty schools were disproportionately impacted (see Exhibit 6). In August 2002, Vallas appointed Tomás Hanna as his special assistant for recruitment and retention, a newly created position independent of the HR office. Hanna brought to the task a proven track record in the District—12-years of service, including teaching and three successful principalships in struggling schools—and was known for his energy, creativity, and commitment to ensuring every student achieved high academic standards.

Hanna's Charge: From August 2002 to December 2004, Hanna designed and led the "Campaign for Human Capital" (the Campaign).[11] The Campaign's goal was to position the District as "the employer of choice for prospective and experienced teachers." Hanna recruited nearly 100 representatives from the central office, schools, SRC, employee unions, business community, and local universities to serve on the Campaign's steering committee and ad hoc task forces.

Between November 2002 and May 2003, these groups diagnosed the major challenges and opportunities for strengthening teacher recruitment and retention in the District. The Campaign issued recommendations in five areas: 1) defining teacher competencies, 2) marketing the District's competitive advantages, 3) collaborating strategically with external stakeholders, 4) enhancing the professional environment, which among other things, called for replacing the District's centralized teacher hiring process and seniority-based transfer process with site-based selection, and 5) maximizing communication and engagement with teachers (see Exhibit 7 for a summary of the recommendations). The Campaign officially disbanded in May 2003.

Hanna secured $11.2 million to fund key recommendations, and retained a coordinating and oversight role as the Campaign moved into an implementation phase. Hanna managed some projects, while turning other initiatives over to specific central offices. For example, Hanna worked with the chief academic officer's staff and regional superintendents to revamp leadership development programs for principals. The finance office successfully accelerated the budgeting process to accommodate earlier teacher hiring, while HR was to tackle key recommendations related to teacher recruitment and retention.

While Hanna enjoyed his more operational duties, he met considerable reluctance within HR to enact Campaign proposals and, with Vallas's blessing, Hanna exerted greater leadership. Hanna acknowledged that his role within HR became increasingly ambiguous and stirred-up deep-seated tensions. "A lot of people in HR, especially the leadership, felt purposefully shut-out of the Campaign and didn't feel inclined to move quickly to execute the recommendations," noted Hanna.

Results: In SY05, however, the Campaign's work showed signs of real progress.[12] The number of teacher applications rose 44% between 2002 and 2004. Ninety-one percent of new teachers hired in SY04 completed their first year in the classroom, as compared with 73% in SY03. The percentage of first-year teachers returning to teach in the District for a second year had steadily increased from an all-time low of 73% in 2000 to 77% in 2003, rising again to 85% in 2004.

The District's vacancy rate also showed promising trends. School opened in September 2003 with 95 unfilled teaching positions, down from 138 in September 2002. In September 2004, vacancies increased temporarily to 143, primarily resulting from the fact that the District had to hire 400 more positions than prior years due to a K–3 class size reduction initiative and one-time $25,000 early retirement incentive. By January 2005, however, the District boasted one of its lowest vacancy rates in over three years (0.5%) with only 40 unfilled teaching slots.

Meanwhile, District leadership grew increasingly concerned about HR's ability to play the leadership role necessary to institutionalize and deepen the Campaign's work. SRC Commissioner and Campaign co-chair Sandra Dungee Glenn remarked, "The Campaign demonstrated that the District's ability to improve student achievement hinged upon a attracting, developing, and retaining a highly-qualified workforce, but it also exposed the brokenness of the HR department. We realized we didn't have the leadership or capacity in HR to drive a human capital management strategy."

Impetus for Change: The 2004 PFT Contract and Partial Site-Based Selection

Building upon the Campaign's success and the constraints identified in the District's centralized HR practices, the SRC and District leadership vowed to radically redefine the teacher hiring and assignment process through the 2004–2008 PFT contract. Initial SRC proposals included moving the most senior teachers to the lowest-performing schools and opening up every teaching position to site-based selection—both of which inspired a backlash among teachers and PFT leadership.

Vallas, however, was committed to securing a contract supported by both labor and management stating that "our students' success depends on everyone working together, not against each other." The District and PFT eventually softened their positions and signed a watershed contract on October 14, 2004. For the first time, principals and their school-based selection committees in all 273 District schools gained the ability to screen, interview, and hire candidates for 50% of their teaching vacancies under a new partial site-based selection process starting May 1, 2005.[13] Transferring senior teachers would fill the remaining 50% of vacancies. Principals designated which positions to fill via site based selection or the traditional transfer process.

After an initial HR screening, all new teachers would have to apply for positions directly at schools and could only be hired into the District through site-based selection. Concurrently, senior teachers desiring to change schools could either apply for site-based selection positions or transfer through the traditional seniority process. Any vacancies unfilled by August 1 would automatically be turned over to HR and be filled by either seniority-based transfers or new teachers placed on one-year "special assignments" (see Exhibit 8 for the PFT contract timeline).

The 2004 PFT contract also designated that any new District school and 10 low-performing/ historically hard-to-staff middle schools would fill all positions through full site-based selection, in addition to any school that had voted for full site-based selection. For the SY06 hiring season, 50 schools would fill 100% of their vacancies through site-based selection.[14] The remaining 224 District schools would fill positions through partial site-based selection. The District estimated that nearly 80% of open positions for SY06 would be filled through site-based selection. As veteran teachers retired, more small high schools opened, and more schools supported the process, the District hoped site-based selection would be used for 100% of teaching vacancies by 2015.

As the negotiations ended, Vallas knew he needed the right person to implement the PFT contract and move HR forward more broadly. After the executive director of HR quietly left the District in November 2004, Vallas approached Hanna. "Tomás was a clear first choice," Vallas explained. "He knew HR in and out, he's an excellent communicator, and he showed he could deliver results with the Campaign." Hanna recalled, "Vallas had offered me the head of HR before, but I turned it down because I didn't want to leave the 'education side of the house,'" adding, "Now, I saw the opportunity to join the education and operations sides under one roof. Plus, we had won site-based selection, and while I knew it would be a huge managerial challenge, it was exciting and I felt ready."

Hanna's First 90 Days

While Vallas officially announced Hanna's appointment as senior vice president for HR on January 11, 2005, Hanna had been preparing for the transition since October 2004 and had actually assumed the role in mid-December 2004. During those three months, Hanna scoured the external reviews of HR, consulted key Campaign advisors, and surveyed the District. Hanna remarked:

> I view my HR assignment as my fourth principalship. It's really about getting everyone on the same page and working together towards one goal, except now it involves the entire District. When I was a principal, I walked the halls and talked to everybody—the union's building reps, the new teachers, the veterans, the custodians, and most importantly, the students. So, now, I walk around all of the nooks and crannies of the HR office, other central office departments, the unions, and as much as I can, I get into schools.

A Fresh Start

Hanna's first move was to assemble a new leadership team. During his transition period, Hanna met frequently with Vallas and COO Natalye Paquin to discuss their vision for HR. The three reached consensus that Hanna would have the latitude to replace the four long-serving HR directors with his own executive team. Hanna also made an unprecedented call to PFT President Ted Kirsch soliciting suggestions.

On January 6, 2005, Hanna dismissed his four direct reports. "Letting those four people go and not giving them 'soft landings' to other positions in the District was the most difficult thing I've ever done," Hanna commented. "But I wanted to send a clear message, both internally and externally, that change was finally coming to HR and I wanted to model the behavior we're looking for. If you're not here for the kids, then you shouldn't be here."

The public outcry Hanna expected in reaction to the firings never happened. In particular, PFT leadership welcomed the change. Kirsch commented, "You can cut off the head, but until all of the organs learn to work differently, the body will behave in the same old ways." Hanna acknowledged, however, that within HR, the move was highly controversial and unsettling. "These four directors had been here a long time and had close relationships with many staff," noted Hanna. "I knew people were scared for their own jobs, but also wondering if I had a plan."

Building a New Team

On January 10, 2005, Hanna reorganized the department into three new areas—(1) employee entry, (2) employee service operations, and (3) employee relations—purposefully renaming the offices with "employee" to signal customer service as a priority. Hanna's most significant structural change was to join the recruitment, selection, and placement functions within employee entry. That same day, Hanna installed three new directors:

Shawn Crowder, Executive Director of Employee Entry: As director of the new 65-member employee entry division, Shawn Crowder oversaw the recruitment, selection, and placement of all instructional and non-

instructional employees in the District. For teachers alone, that meant hiring approximately 1,250 new teachers and transferring 3,000 veterans per year.

Prior to joining Hanna's team, Crowder spent 14 years with CIGNA Insurance Company. After working her way up through CIGNA's investment and group insurance divisions, she transitioned to the company's HR department, where she became director of staffing operations and managed the hiring of 5,000–7,000 employees annually. Crowder met Hanna in early 2004 and became intrigued by the Campaign. "I wanted to make a career switch and find somewhere I could really make a difference. Hiring the best people to staff our schools and teach our kids is the most important job in the world," explained Crowder.

Upon joining the District and Hanna's team, Crowder met individually with each of her 65 employee entry staff members, seeking to both understand their roles and responsibilities and to "find the talent buried below the surface." Encountering a flat division in which each employee reported directly to her predecessor, Crowder quickly assigned approximately a half dozen team leaders. Crowder also began tackling the "entrenched silos" of her division by piloting cross-training and cross-functional teams. However, Crowder's biggest priorities were overseeing the new site-based selection process and ensuring all teacher vacancies were filled by the first day of school on September 1, 2006.

Susan Gilbert, Executive Director of Employee Support Operations: Susan Gilbert joined HR in January 2005. Hanna tapped Gilbert to lead employee support operations, a 50-member team responsible for all of the back-office HR functions, including benefits, personnel records, health services, classification and compensation, unemployment, retirement and the teacher helpline.

Gilbert came to HR from the Districts finance office, which she had joined in 2000 following a 25-year career in financial services with three Philadelphia banks. As the payroll director, Gilbert encountered a complete mess where current employees were routinely not getting paid on time or correctly, but most of the problems stemmed from inaccurate input into the Advantage system. After cleaning up payroll, the Districts CFO asked Gilbert to take over employee benefits from HR in late 2002. Again, it was a nightmare, nothing was systematized or monitored, recalled Gilbert. We recovered $8 million simply by going through our bills and discovering we had been paying medical coverage for over 1,000 people who had long since left the District.

During the first 90 days, Gilbert concentrated on streamlining employee support operations. "My staff has a wealth of system-specific knowledge, but many of the processes are disjointed, outdated, and inefficient," she explained. Gilbert had interviewed her 50 direct reports, and with their help, was documenting current business processes, identifying bottlenecks, and outlining plans for new systems. Acknowledging the importance of reducing employee complaints and union grievances, Gilbert transferred benefits back under HR in order to improve customer service and better coordinate the information flow.

Andy Rosen, Executive Director of Employee Relations:

Hanna appointed Andy Rosen as executive director of employee relations, a six-member team that interpreted union contracts for principals and other administrators around issues such as work rules, teacher performance, and the new site-based selection provisions. A lawyer and member of the Districts General Counsels office for 26 years, Rosen had worked closely with the bargaining units and the HR labor relations office. Rosen transferred to HR in July 2004, helping to renegotiate the Districts five employee contracts.

Rosen, who had previously worked with all six members of his team, kept the division stable.

His team focused on helping administrators to understand the new labor contracts and navigate site-based selection. Echoing an issue also raised by Crowder and Gilbert, Rosen aimed to strengthen employee confidence, initiative, and ownership.

Deputy Director and Other Executive Team Members:

In January 2005, Hanna created a new deputy director position, but after a failed recruitment attempt, the position remained vacant through April. Acknowledging that he was "getting too mired in the day-to-day operations," Hanna hoped that a deputy would help free up his own time to focus more on strategic planning. Hanna also brought back Herb Kaufman, a former senior manager with over 35 years of experience in the department who had retired in 2003, as an internal consultant. Debra Weiner, a key member of the Campaign's work team, and Zoraida Olmo, Hanna's confidential secretary during the Campaign, rounded out Hanna's executive team.

Implementing Site-Based Selection

Hanna recognized that site-based selection was a high-stakes endeavor, not only for his credibility as a leader, but for the entire organization. Many District leaders hoped that if the 225 schools new to this process had a positive experience with partial site-based selection, they would voluntarily vote for full site-based selection in subsequent years. Key internal and external Campaign advisors would also be watching to see if site-based selection helped improve teacher recruitment and retention. Given HR's outdated technology and notorious inefficiency, however, Hanna knew he had skeptics. Indeed, Hanna often wondered if "the PFT finally agreed to partial site-based selection because they knew we couldn't walk and chew gum at the same time."

Designing the Roll Out:

Upon assuming the helm of HR in mid-December 2004, Hanna charged ahead to plan for the May 1, 2005 site-based selection roll out. Between December

2004 and April 2005, Hanna estimated that he dedicated 90% of his time to overseeing the new process. He assembled a cross-functional work group comprised of representatives from HR, information technology (IT), and the PFT that began meeting weekly to design and lead implementation. He said:

> I knew HR could not do this alone. We needed to draw out resources from across the District, and I felt it was important to have the PFT at the table every step of the way. The work group has been essential in mapping out this complex new process and developing solutions. Arlene Kempin from the PFT and her colleagues have been critical in pinpointing potential landmines out in the trenches. And since we know we won't get it perfect the first time, the work group will continue to meet weekly after we "go live," and we've agreed to have two to three "step back" meetings with PFT leadership so we can identify problems and tweak the process as we go along.

An IT manager who served on the committee reflected, "As we laid out the various steps and 'owners' involved in implementing partial site-based selection, I sensed that many HR staff did not have a clear picture of the current teacher hiring process from start to finish. It seemed like the first time people from recruiting, selection, and placement had talked to each other about what they did."

Training School Selection Committees:
After outlining critical steps and deadlines, the workgroup first designed information and training sessions for principals and their selection committees. Beginning on January 11, 2005, Hanna deployed small teams of employee relations staff, members of the chief academic officer's unit, and PFT representatives to deliver the training in the 225 schools. Kempin commented on the usefulness of the team approach.

"It is really powerful for teachers to see the District and the PFT explaining this new process together. They see that for the first time in a long time, we are in agreement and working together to make this a success."

Attracting and Tracking Applicants: When Shawn Crowder came on board, she and her division began to take the lead on site-based selection within HR. Crowder's team worked with principals to ensure that each school Web site posted basic demographic data and the positions open to either site-based selection or seniority transfer by May 1, 2005.

Working with IT, Crowder's team developed an online tool to track site-based selection applicants across all schools. Starting May 1, teachers would be able to indicate their intent to apply for a site-based selection position through a school's website; however, the applicant had to mail in hard copies of their resume and application materials to the school in order to be officially considered for the position. Crowder hoped to transition to a web-based application in spring 2007.

Using the applicant tracking tool, principals could print out an updated report of the intended applicants every day, match the list with incoming resumes, and begin to review resumes with their selection committees. Meanwhile, Crowder's team could track the applicants systemwide. She explained, "Applicant tracking will allow us to see which positions are getting flooded with applicants, and more importantly, which positions are not, at which point my team will have to think about how to give that school additional support, such as helping them intensify their marketing efforts or adding additional information to their Web site."

Indeed, some principals, regional superintendents, and the PFT were concerned that site-based selection would exacerbate the challenge of filling vacancies in historically hard-to-staff schools. A regional superintendent observed:

My schools are in a high-poverty high-crime area with one-third of the District's English language learners and special education students. Teacher turnover soars to 40% in some schools. Four of my schools have voted for full site-based selection, and it has been successful in two because there is strong leadership and staff buy-in. I predict partial site-based selection will roll out unevenly this year. Some principals who will do whatever it takes to sell their schools and see partial site-based selection as a real opportunity. But, I know other principals who are very nervous about how to guide their selection committees and attract great teachers.

Districtwide, in schools with poverty rates of 90% or above, almost half of teachers (49%) had five years or less of teaching experience. In comparison, only 23% of teachers in schools with poverty rates below 80% had been in the classroom 0–5 years (see Exhibit 9). PFT President Kirsch commented, "I fear that with site-based selection, the rich will keep getting richer, and the poor will keep getting poorer." Another regional superintendent also feared that one of the District's "dirty secrets"—principals had often encouraged low-performing teachers to voluntarily transfer to other schools under the seniority process rather than be written up—could likely continue under partial site-based selection.

Interviewing and Hiring Applicants: In mid–April 2005, the implementation work group was still debating how to structure the interview process and hiring timeline. Each principal appointed a selection committee—comprised of the principal, and three to five school staff, parents, or community members—to interview and hire candidates for site-based selection positions.

Initially, it was assumed that each committee would conduct interviews in their respective buildings. This approach gave applicants an opportunity to visit the school and allowed the se-

lection committee the flexibility to set their own interview dates. However, some members of the work group worried that such an independent process was fraught with potential confusion.

Applicants might encounter financial and time challenges trying to interview at schools across the city, and might be forced to accept or reject an offer while their application was still under review at another school. Each school also had to maintain a racial balance among its staff, meaning that site-based selection committees had to keep careful tabs on the offers it made and implications of acceptances.[15] Since the applicant tracking tool did not allow principals to report which candidates had been interviewed or hired, site-based selection committees with late interview dates might spend unnecessary time pouring through resumes of applicants that had already been hired by other schools. Another concern was that site-based selection committees who had been unable to fill vacancies by the end of the current school year might not meet during the summer to conduct interviews because they were not getting paid. Thus, the PFT and some HR staff lobbied for a limited number of regional- or content area- job fairs in May and June 2005 so that applicants could interview with multiple schools at the same place and time.

Institutionalizing Other Campaign Recommendations

While site-based selection was Hanna's flagship initiative in the short-term, he and his team continued to spearhead efforts to institutionalize other important aspects of the Campaign.

Recruitment: With support from PECO Energy, the District had sponsored 10 "Rolling out the Red Carpet" events since 2003 to attract talented juniors and seniors from local universities into teaching. Crowder aimed to diversify the participant pool by targeting freshman and sophomores, non-education majors, and historically black colleges and schools with high Latino populations. "We've been focusing so intently on universities, so I'm trying to figure out where the 'diamonds in the rough' might be for other sources of applicant flow, especially for people of color" explained Crowder, who aimed to increase the percentage of new teachers of color from 27% to 35%.

At the same time, Crowder hoped to build upon successful efforts such as the $1100 student teacher stipends, literacy intern, and alternative teaching programs for career changers. "We're already strengthening external partnerships with groups like Teach for America and the New Teacher Project, but we're wondering if we can tap into professional organizations or develop rotational programs with urban or suburban districts," she added. Crowder recruited a Temple University employee to manage recruitment and external partnerships who joined the District in March 2005.

Crowder hoped that her new hire would allow her to focus more on other recruitment activities. "Believe it or not, we hire more non-instructional positions than teachers every year," observed Crowder. "While the classroom teachers are my most important customers, they cannot do their jobs if we don't have the right other people in place, like budget and IT directors, even bus drivers." Crowder tapped a former member of Hanna's Campaign team, Arasi Swamickannu, to oversee non-instructional staff recruitment. "Arasi can translate the Campaign perspective—a proactive, customer-service oriented approach to hiring—to non-instructional hiring," suggested Crowder.

Retention: The District launched a number of initiatives to help increase teacher satisfaction and retention.[16] Beginning in SY04, the District instituted a paid, mandatory two-week summer orientation for all teachers new to the District and revamped its state-mandated induction program for new teachers. The District strengthened its incentive package in SY05, offering a $4500 hiring bonus paid in two installments over a three-year period ($1500 after five months, $3000 after 37 months) and an annual $1000 tuition reimbursement. Teachers serving in hard-to-staff schools received up to $2400 for tuition expenses.

The District deployed 61 teacher coaches in SY04 and SY05, master teachers released from the classroom to help new teachers deepen their skills, at a cost of $5.3 million per year. Each teacher mentor was typically assigned 20 teachers in up to as many as eight different schools. In a sample survey of new middle school teachers, over 80% responded that their coaches had helped them with instructional strategies, classroom management, materials, and content knowledge. New teachers also reported increased support from principals (see Exhibit 10).

Despite these efforts, however, the District would continue to face ongoing retention challenges. A 2003 Research for Action survey of new teachers found that 51% planned to stay in the District three years or less. Younger teachers intended to leave at an accelerated rate, as 70% of teachers age 25 or younger planned to leave within three years. Research for Action suggested that a range of factors contributed to teacher flight, including an inclination to try multiple professions within the span of a career, "out of control" working conditions, and enforcement of NCLB certification requirements. The District did not conduct exit interviews, a process Hanna intended to quickly introduce.

Leadership Development: The District responded to the Campaign's finding that strong principals were key instruments for improving teacher retention by revamping professional development for both current and aspiring principals. Beginning in 2003, Hanna carved out three days of the District's one week summer academy for sitting principals to focus on improving support for "rookie, novice, and veteran teachers." Regional superintendents and principals helped Hanna create and deliver the content. While principals developed teacher retention plans during the sessions, PFT leadership complained that regional superintendents did not sufficiently monitor or evaluate the plans, which in the union's view, had become "another piece of meaningless paper."

In the spring of 2003, Hanna launched a monthly leadership academy for aspiring principals that covered four topics: leadership, diversity, school climate, teaching to proficiency, and parent/community and civic engagement. Of the 20 assistant principals, teacher leaders, and other certificated staff selected to participate in a year-long pilot in SY04, 19 were appointed principals in SY05. In February 2005, the Broad Foundation awarded the District $4.3 million to further strengthen its training for aspiring principals and add a paid, full-time internship under a mentor principal. Hanna turned over responsibility for delivering the content for the new academy, which planned to sponsor 15 aspiring principals, in SY06 to Judith Lewis, the District's first assistant superintendent for staff development who joined the chief academic officer's team in November 2003.

Building Bridges across the District

Hanna and his team set out to build bridges across internal District departments. He explained:

> Historically, district leadership often made decisions very late in the teacher hiring process which made HR have to scramble to fill classrooms. For example, the District did not announce how many teachers it would accept into an early retirement incentive program until late May of last year, well after the transfer and hiring process had already started. When over 1,000 teachers applied for early retirement, the District accepted 320 applicants, but many more of the remaining teachers decided to retire anyways without the incentive. So, in June, HR was faced with the prospect of needing to hire

many more new teachers than originally projected.

> While I recognize that HR has a long way to go, we also need to stop shooting ourselves in the foot as a district. Our fundamental problem is that HR is placed in operations, reporting to the COO, and divorced from the education side of the house, where all the action is happening in terms of principal appointments and moving teachers around. So, I'm working hard to get my team to infiltrate the organization and ensure that we are at the table when executive-level issues are being discussed—from day one.

Hanna, who had previously reported directly to Vallas during the Campaign, continued to attend Vallas's weekly meeting with his three direct reports, the chief academic officer (CAO), chief financial officer (CFO), and chief operating officer (COO). At Hanna's request, he and CAO Gregory Thornton also met weekly to discuss issues coming down the pipeline, such as the planned opening of 10 small high schools in September 2006. Assistant Superintendent for Staff Development Lewis's staff also helped Hanna's team deliver the site-based selection to training to schools in January and February 2005. "Tomás called me in because he wanted something more engaging than the usual 'stand and deliver' information session," explained Lewis. "Initially, my staff was a little reluctant about working with HR given their reputation, and there are still communication and technology issues to be sorted out, but we made a huge step forward." Hanna had also convened standing meetings with the COO and CFO.

Hanna regularly brought his new directors to many executive level meetings. He shared an example: "Last week, Shawn Crowder and Andy Rosen took the lead on explaining how we are going to roll out site-based selection to the SRC. Vallas called me later to say he and the SRC were very impressed and pleased." Hanna also encouraged his staff to develop their own relationships. In an effort to improve customer service to schools, Crowder began meeting regularly with the District's school management officer, the position in the CAO's office to which the District's 10 regional superintendents reported.

Engaging External Actors

Hanna, himself a former building representative from his teaching days and member of the PFT executive board, maintained frequent communication with PFT leadership and staff. He had also made concerted efforts to involve Arlene Kempin and other PFT staff who sat in the HR office in site-based selection planning and other decisions.

In April 2005, PFT President Ted Kirsch commented, "Our relationship with HR is like night and day since Tomás arrived. Before, HR had a war mentality, and we were the enemy. Tomás understands that we want to work together to do whatever is best for our students. Tomás calls to ask for our input, and we know we can call him whenever we have an issue to discuss." In March 2005, the PFT extended an unprecedented invitation to Hanna and his leadership team to attend a PFT staff meeting. Hanna recalled, "It gave my new team and the PFT folks a great opportunity to meet each other. And for me, it was refreshing to look around the room and see so many people I had personal relationships with as a teacher. I think they could finally take it seriously when I said 'The District is here to help; we're here to help, and we're going to fix HR.'"

Hanna continued to cultivate and deepen external relationships. The Broad Foundation's $4.3 million grant for the principals' academy was the District's largest private donation since 2001. PECO Energy's $500,000 pledge in December 2004 extended the company's involvement beyond teacher recruiting into leadership

development and math skills development programs. Since SY04, 200 Teach for America volunteers, 61 New Teacher Project interns, and 25 math and science professionals trained by Drexel University and the Philadelphia Education Fund had served in District schools.[17]

Hanna also formed an informal "kitchen cabinet" of external advisors, including Campaign co-chair and business executive Rosemarie Greco and Robert Croner, a Campaign committee member and senior vice president for human resources at Radian Group, Inc. Croner commended Hanna's performance to date:

> Tomás has the three keys that I believe are necessary to successfully lead any HR department: organizational credibility, a belief system that human capital is the driver of organizational value, and a deep passion for his work. He also recognizes where his own professional gaps are and filling them. He calls me about once a month to ask my opinion and has even asked to come shadow me for a day to see how I handle certain issues. The only thing that concerns me is Tomás's reporting relationship. Tomás certainly has the personal credibility to get Vallas's ear. But given the bureaucratic culture of the District, I think it would send a powerful message to the organization to have HR report directly to the CEO. Then, everyone would know that HR is a strategic concern, not an operational activity, and that when the District says "people are our most important asset," it is not just lip service.

Customer Service Is Number One

"From day one, I've always said 'customer service' is number one," shared Hanna. "HR had an abysmal reputation for being unhelpful and unresponsive. From the outside, it seemed like HR always had 20 different ways to say 'no,' and I've told my department that needs to change by 180 degrees." Hanna knew he also had to address unsatisfactory employee performance, an issue that had long been tolerated in the department. "While the general perception of HR was one of incompetence, everyone found someone in HR they could trust and always went to that person, even if the issue was completely outside their responsibilities," he explained. "I met with principals and regional superintendents and they told me 'HR is broken, fix it, but please don't change the people.'"

Hanna instituted weekly HR staff meetings in January 2005, at which he made a point to share both commendations and complaints. In April, he commented, "We're finally starting to get more 'thank yous' and it feels good. Even Vallas told me he's starting to hear good things about HR." Hanna and his team also made the rounds, connecting with groups like IT and finance, and asking, "How can HR help you? How can we work together better?" As a measure of progress, Hanna recounted how the chief of staff asked Hanna to help think through the timing of bringing in a new CFO, a vacant position recently filled with the assistance of a search firm. "In the old days, HR only would have been called in to process the person's paperwork," explained Hanna. "My goal is that we'll soon be seen as professional enough to manage executive level succession planning and hiring."

A regional superintendent suggested, however, that Hanna's new team still had to do some work to earn their credibility in the field:

> People in schools are not sure what to make of the shake-up in HR. All they know is that the people at the top they used to rely on is no longer there, and at the same time, HR is coming along with site-based selection, which is a new and complex process for most schools. Most principals are just doing their jobs, and are hanging back to wait and see and if HR delivers by helping fill all their vacancies by the first day of school in September.

While staff morale suffered after the dismissal of the four former directors, Hanna and his leadership team were working to improve employees' satisfaction and service. Multiple staff members commented that they were pleased with Hanna's "open door policy" and their increased autonomy. "Before, we always had to ask permission. Now, if I see something that can be improved, I feel like I can do it," shared a HR senior analyst. She added, "And Tomás respects us. He's always coming by to say, 'Here's our issue, what do you think we should do?' That never happened before."

Looking Ahead

Ultimately, Hanna's goal was to reposition HR in the District from the "headache that needs to be fixed to a strategic partner." CAO Gregory Thornton stressed the sense of urgency around Hanna's charge. "Paul Vallas inherited a broken district; the past three years have been a period of triage," observed Thornton. "Now that we've stopped the bleeding, we can begin to think more strategically. We need a systemwide human capital management plan that enables us to build, retain, and support a quality workforce at every level of the organization."

Once Hanna had been able to successfully hire a deputy director for HR, Hanna planned to immerse himself in long-term strategic planning. To that end, he and his leadership team had outlined new performance goals and metrics for the department (see Exhibit 11). Hanna planned to task his new deputy with driving the performance goals throughout the department and developing personnel appraisal and performance management systems for HR. "Everyone needs to understand HR's role in accelerating student achievement and each individual should be able to see their part in moving the District forward," explained Hanna.

COO Natalye Paquin reflected on Hanna's efforts to date:

Tomas is an extremely talented person, but he still has some growing to do as he transitions from being the Campaigns project manager to leading and managing the HR department of a $2 billion organization with over 27,000 employees. I firmly believe that Tomas was the right person to take over HR. However, it takes a much different skill set to conduct the symphony orchestra versus tune and play all of the instruments yourself.

Tomás must be careful not to revert back into the role he played during the Campaign where he assumed the responsibility of getting everything done himself. He has taken a lot of important, and good, first steps. There is a lot more to be done. We need to streamline and automate many of our processes. And, we need greater consistency in implementing policy to really turn things around in HR. Also, ninety-nine percent of the staff are the same and may approach problem solving from the same perspective. The District needs to build a critical mass of leaders who represent a diversity of thought and experience, and who will help strengthen the professional expertise of the District.

That day in mid-April 2005, however Hanna was well aware of the rocky road ahead. His team's next 90 days would be consumed with implementing site-based selection and managing the teacher transfer process to ensure that every student would have a classroom teacher come September 1, 2006. Hanna knew he would be defined by how successfully site-based selection rolled out, and he knew he could be out of a job if things did not go well.

Beyond that, Hanna knew HR also had to think creatively about how the District was going to meet the *No Child Left Behind* requirement to have a "highly qualified" teaching staff by June 2006. Only 89% of the District's teaching force met the federal requirement in 2005,

and the gap would be hard to close in only one academic year.[18] The department also needed serious technology upgrades in order to modernize business processes. More broadly, Hanna knew he had to work doggedly to reinforce his message for change inside the department and across the District.

Hanna also worried about what the District should do to get the best teachers in front of the most academically at-risk students—an issue that often kept Hanna awake at night. As Hanna wondered if the District would need a second Campaign for Human Campaign to specifically address this challenge, he knew that this time around, he would manage any new Campaign from within, not apart from, HR.

Notes

1. "School district ousts four managers," *The Philadelphia Inquirer,* January 11, 2005

2. SY is a PELP convention that denotes "school year." For example, SY05 refers to the 2004–2005 school year.

3. See "Finding a CEO for the School District of Philadelphia: Searching for a Savior?" HBS Case No. 803–72, Boston: Harvard Business School Publishing, 2003, for additional background on the District.

4. Specifically, the PFT and District maintained different contract language around high school teaching loads and an enhanced compensation system. Case writer interview with PFT vice president Jerry Jordan, June 1, 2005.

5. R. Neild, E. Useem, and E. Farley, *Quest for Quality: Recruiting and Retaining Teachers in Philadelphia,* Philadelphia: Research for Action, April 2005, p. 16.

6. This section includes findings from two internal district documents: The Council of Great City Schools, *Restructuring, Reengineering and Rebuilding Human Resource Management in the School District of Philadelphia,* October 2004, and the Bronner Group, *The School District of Philadelphia: Analysis of Current Teacher Hiring Process,* January 2005.

7. Under the 2000 PFT contract, schools could elect to hire all open positions through site-based selection if two-thirds of the faculty voted in favor by December 31 of each year. A school's union representatives decided whether or not to hold such a vote. In fall 2003, 12% of district schools voted for full site-based selection; 16% approved site-based selection in fall 2004.

8. There were two types of transferring teachers: voluntary and forced. *Voluntary* transfers were teachers who wanted to leave their school. *Forced* transfers—or "excessed teachers"—were those whose current positions had been eliminated due to declining enrollment, course cancellation, or some other reason and were forced to leave their school.

9. M. D. Chester, R. Offenberg, and M. D. Xu, *Urban Teacher Transfer: A Four-Year Cohort Study Of the School District of Philadelphia Faculty,* as cited in Neild, Useem, and Farley, *Quest for Quality,* April, 2001, p. 21.

10. E. Useem and E. Farley, *Philadelphia's Teacher Hiring and School Assignment Practices: Comparisons with Other Districts,* Philadelphia: Research for Action, April 2004, N.B. The study cited site-based selection schools as the only exception.

11. See "The Campaign for Human Capital at the School District of Philadelphia," PELP Case No. 009, Boston: Harvard Business School Publishing, 2004, for additional background on the Campaign.

12. Teacher statistics in this section from Neild, Useem, and Farley, *Quest for Quality,* pp. 15-25, and district files.

13. Schools that voted for full site-based selection in the fall of 2004 would continue to fill every position through site-based selection.

14. The 50 schools comprised 42 schools that had voted for full site-based selection, which included two of the hard-to-staff middle schools, plus the other eight hard-to-staff middle schools.

15. Under the 2004–2008 contract, "the faculty in a school shall be deemed to be racially balanced if the percentage of African American teachers is between 75% and 125% of the city-wide percentage of such minority teachers at that organizational level (i.e., elementary, middle or high school)."

16. Information in this section is summarized from Neild, Useem, and Farley, *Quest for Quality,* pp. 27–39.

17. Neild, Useem, and Farley, *Quest for Quality,* pp. 28–30.

18. Neild, Useem, and Farley, *Quest for Quality,* p. 9

Exhibit 1

The School District of Philadelphia Facts and Figures

Overview	SY04
District Area Demographics	
Total Population[a]	1,517,550
Median household income (in 1999)	$16,509
Families below poverty level (in 1999)	18.4%
Percent of county residents holding bachelor degree or higher	10.3%
Unemployment (2004)[b]	4.7%
Student Demographics	
Number of students (PK–12)	217,405
African-American	65.5%
Hispanic	14.5%
White	14.2%
Asian	5.3%
Native American	0.2%
Economically Disadvantaged	80.0%
Limited English Proficient[c]	6.6%
Special education students[d]	11.9%
Graduation rate[e]	60.5%
Dropout rate[f]	9.8%
Schools and Staff (Largest district in PA)	
Number of schools	274
Elementary	176
Middle or Intermediate	43
Ninth grade	43
Senior high	5
Alternative	7
Total headcount	~27,000
Teachers	~12,000
Average teacher salary[g]	$50,971
Student/teacher staffing ratio (Elem, Middle, High)	~30:1

Source: Data from http://www.philsch.k12.pa.us unless cited otherwise.

[a] "School District Demographics," Census 2000 Web site, http://www.nces.ed.gov/surveys/sdds/singledemoprofile.asp? county1=4218990&state1=42, accessed June 15, 2004.

[b] "Philadelphia Area Unemployment Rate Falls to 4.7 Percent in December; Job Count Rises by 15,500 From a Year Ago, " Bureau of Labor Statistics Web site, http://stats.bls.gov/ro3/cesqphl.pdf, accessed June 15, 2004.

[c] "Philadelphia School Profile," Pennsylvania Department of Education Web site, http://www.paprofiles.org/profiles / district. Asp, accessed June 18, 2004.

[d] Ibid.

[e] "Philadelphia School Profile," Pennsylvania Department of Education Web site, http://www.paprofiles.org/ profiles/ PrintDistrictProfile1.asp, accessed June 18, 2004. Data is from SY02.

[f] Standard & Poor's School Evaluation Services Web site, http://www.ses.standardandpoors.com/, accessed June 17, 2004. Data is from SY02. Dropout rate is a one-year snapshot of all students who drop out of school during one year. This rate considers all students in grades 9–12.

[g] Standard & Poor's School Evaluation Services Web site, http://www.ses.standardandpoors.com/, accessed June 17, 2004. Data is from SY02.

Exhibit 2
School Reform Commission (SRC) Powers under Act 46

The SRC was created under Act 46 of the Pennsylvania School Code. The SRC acts in place of the Philadelphia Board of Education and has complete control of every aspect of Philadelphia Public Schools. Under the Act 46, the SRC can:

- Suspend the Pennsylvania School Code
- Suspend the State Board of Education regulations
- Hire, or delegate its power to, for-profit corporations to manage the school district
- Turn over public schools to private groups and corporations
- Hire noncertified teachers and managers
- Reassign, suspend, or dismiss professional employees
- Terminate collective bargaining agreements
- Levy taxes and incur debts

Source: The General Assembly of Philadelphia Senate Bill No. 640 Web site, http://www2.legis.state.pa.us/WU01/LI/BI/BT/2001/0/SB0640P1473.pdf, and http://www.savephillyschools.org/schoolboard/, accessed July 27, 2004.

Exhibit 3

PSSA Results, Philadelphia and State, 2001–2004 (% scoring Proficient or Advanced)

Philadelphia
Pennsylvania System of School Assessment
Percent Scoring Proficient and Advanced

	Grade	2001	2002	2003	2004	Annualized Change
Reading						
Philadelphia	5	18.3	20.8	23.4	31.6	4.3
Pennsylvania	5	56.1	57.0	58.0	62.7	2.2
Philadelphia	8	23.0	24.1	30.4	41.2	6.1
Pennsylvania	8	60.1	58.8	63.4	68.9	2.9
Philadelphia	11	34.0	28.7	30.1	27.0	−2.3
Pennsylvania	11	58.1	59.0	59.2	60.8	0.9
Math						
Philadelphia	5	17.5	18.7	23.1	30.7	4.4
Pennsylvania	5	53.0	53.1	56.3	61.8	2.9
Philadelphia	8	16.2	17.9	19.7	30.9	4.9
Pennsylvania	8	51.0	51.7	51.3	57.9	2.3
Philadelphia	11	23.8	23.6	21.6	22.9	−0.3
Pennsylvania	11	47.9	49.6	49.1	49.1	0.4

Source: The Council of Great City Schools, *Beating the Odds V: A City-by-City Analysis of Student Performance and Achievement Gaps on State Assessments,* March 2005.

Note: PSSA results are reported in four performance levels: 1) Advanced, 2) Proficient, 3) Basic, and 4) Below Basic. Students scoring Proficient or Advanced are considered to have met Pennsylvania state standards. Under the federal *No Child Left Behind Act* (NCLB), schools and districts receive an accountability rating based on the percentage of students demonstrating proficiency on standards-based state assessments, such as the PSSA. All students are expected to demonstrate proficiency in reading and mathematics by 2014 under NCLB.

Exhibit 4

School District of Philadelphia Organizational Chart (2004)

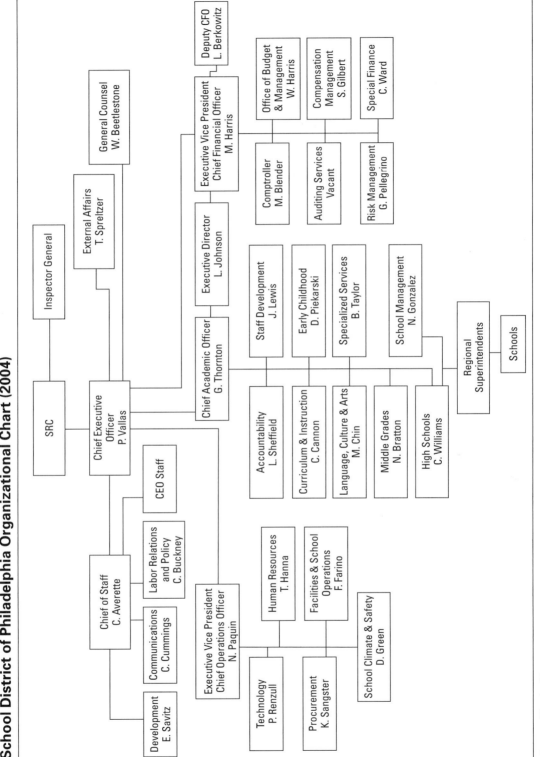

Source: District files.

Exhibit 5

Teachers' Prior Knowledge of Their Schools

Percentage of 2003–04 new teachers reporting prior knowledge of their school: site-selected teachers vs. centrally assigned teachers

New teachers' knowledge of:	Site-selected	Centrally assigned
Student demographics	83%	59%
Principal's reputation	66%	21%
Special programs/projects	61%	16%
Staff collegiality	53%	14%
Educational approach	53%	14%
N = 454		

Source: Neild, R., Useem, E. and Farley, E. (April 2005). *Quest for Quality: Recruiting and Retaining Teachers in Philadelphia.* Philadelphia, PA: Research for Action, p. 32.

Note: Data from a December 2003 Research for Action survey of new teachers. 454 new teachers, about 45% of those hired by December 2003, responded.

Exhibit 6

Analysis of Teacher Turnover Rates in the School District of Philadelphia

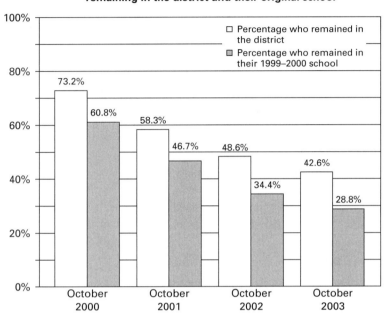

Percentage of 1999–2000 new teachers remaining in the district and their original school

Legend:
- ☐ Percentage who remained in the district
- ▨ Percentage who remained in their 1999–2000 school

	October 2000	October 2001	October 2002	October 2003
Remained in district	73.2%	58.3%	48.6%	42.6%
Remained in school	60.8%	46.7%	34.4%	28.8%

Table 3

One- Two- and Three-Year Teacher Retention Rates by School Poverty Level

Poverty Level of School	N	1999–00	99–00 to 00–01	99–00 to 01–02	99–00 to 02–03
0% to 80% poverty	6315	100%	85%	77%	66%
80% to 90% poverty	4570	100%	81%	71%	57%
90% + poverty	1996	100%	78%	67%	51%
Missing	294	100%	83%	71%	50%
Total	13175	100%	83%	74%	60%

Sources: Neild, R., Useem, E. and Farley, E. (April 2005). *Quest for Quality: Recruiting and Retaining Teachers in Philadelphia.* Philadelphia, PA: Research for Action, p. 16, and Neild, R. C. (February 2003). *Teachers in the School District of Philadelphia.* Philadelphia, PA: Research for Action, p. 3.

Exhibit 7
Summary of the Campaign for Human Capital Recommendations

Theme 1: Defining Teacher Competencies
Recommendations:

- The District should identify teacher characteristics that are correlated with successful urban teaching.

- The District should pinpoint the 20 regional institutions that have historically produced the most successful teachers with the greatest longevity and identify the urban historically black colleges and universities with teacher education programs.

- The District should track teacher performance against the tools used to select teachers in order to ensure that selection processes are valid and effective.

Theme 2: Marketing the District's Competitive Advantages
Recommendations:

- The District should undertake an aggressive print, electronic, and in-person marketing campaign.

- The District should aim for a salary scale at the 50th percentile of districts in the surrounding four counties in preparation for the next PFT contract.

- The District should immediately implement a $1,000 per teacher annual reimbursement for certification/ recertification courses.

Theme 3: Collaborating Strategically with External Stakeholders
Recommendations:

- The District should work more closely with teacher education institutions to 1) enhance classroom preparation for incoming teachers, 2) encourage local institutions to require at least one semester of student teaching in District schools, 3) market teacher programs to outstanding teachers and administrators, and 4) provide preservice training for teachers.

- The District should work more closely with civic, corporate, and cultural organizations so that these institutions can provide training to District staff and cosponsor recognition events for teachers.

Theme 4: Enhancing the Professional Environment
Recommendations:

- The District should recruit retirees to fill vacancies in hard-to-staff schools and hard-to-fill disciplines and should utilize retirees as coaches for inexperienced and uncertified teachers.

- The District should institute the following human resources practices: 1) move up the hiring timetable, 2) use scores on the general knowledge portion of the PRAXIS teachers exam to screen teacher applicants, 3) give priority to teacher applicants who have been student teachers in Philadelphia and who elect to teach in a hard-to-staff school and a hard-to-fill discipline, and 4) implement an online application system.

- The District should modify the way in which it allocates teachers to each school to prevent over hiring in schools with high absenteeism, high turnover, and large numbers of new teachers.

- The District should revise the current site-selection process in the PFT contract.

Exhibit 7 (continued)

- The District should provide preservice training to every new teacher, and each new teacher should have a new-teacher coach from either school or regional staff and a mentor from school staff. New teachers should also receive in-service training throughout the year provided by regional staff.

- The District should create an Office of Alternative Certification within Human Resources to support teachers entering the system without having completed certification requirements. The District should continue to expand opportunities for paraprofessionals to become teachers.

Theme 5: Maximizing Communication and Engagement with Teachers
Recommendations:

- The District should alter its top-down communication style by regularly communicating essential information, expectations, and policies to all staff.

- The District should implement strategies to ensure teacher input in key decisions through annual surveys, focus groups, and online discussion forums on the District Web site.

Source: Adapted from *The Three Rs Retention, Recruitment, and Renewal: A Blueprint for Action* (February 2003).

Exhibit 8

PFT Contract Assignment and Selection Process Timeline

The Parties agree that the dates set forth will govern the assignment and selection procedure as set forth in Art. XVIII, Sec. C(11).

Timeline for Assignment and Selection Process

April 15	Allotments completed.
April 15-May 1	Human Resources organizes the schools and determines where the vacancies exist.
May 1	The School District designates which vacancies are "traditional" and which are "site selected" on a one-to-one basis. In a school with an even number of vacancies, the number is equally divided between "traditional" and "site selected."[a] The School District will honor all Right-to-Return requests.
May 1-May 31	"Traditional" transfer process (open to forced transfers and voluntary transfers) is run by Human Resources. All timely filed voluntary transfer requests will be honored during this time.
May 1-Aug.1	Site-based selection process open to veteran teachers, new hires and unassigned forced transfers takes place in schools. All timely filed voluntary transfer requests will be honored during this time.
Aug. 2	All vacancies turned over to Human Resources.
Aug. 8	The School District will honor all timely filled voluntary transfer requests and Right-to-Return requests.
Aug. 16	Remaining vacancies will be filled by Human Resources in conformity with the seniority provisions in the Agreement. All such placements will be by special assignment. If both the teacher and the Principal agree in writing, prior to April 1st, the teacher will be assigned to the school.

[a] "In the 2005/2006 school year and 2007/2008 school year, if there is an odd number of vacancies in a school, the "odd" vacancy shall be filled through the traditional process. In the 2006/2007 school year and 2008/2009 school year, if there are an odd number of vacancies in a school, the "odd" vacancy shall be filled through site-based selection."

Source: PFT Contract with the School District of Philadelphia. September 1, 2004–August 31, 2008.

Exhibit 9

Teacher Experience by School Poverty Level

Table 12
Teacher Experience by School Poverty Level: 2002–03

Poverty Level	N	Avg. exp.	New	1–5 yrs	6–10 yrs	11–20 yrs	21–30 yrs	30+ yrs
0% to 80% poverty	6161	15.7	4%	19%	14%	23%	28%	11%
80% to 90% poverty	4099	11.1	7%	32%	17%	22%	17%	5%
90% + poverty	1773	8.8	8%	41%	15%	20%	12%	3%
Missing	349	13.4	5%	31%	13%	18%	27%	7%
Total	12382	13.1	6%	30%	15%	21%	21%	7%

Source: Neild, R. C. (February 2003). *Teachers in the School District of Philadelphia.* Philadelphia, PA: Research for Action, p. 6.

Exhibit 10

New Teachers' Assessments of Support from Principals

Percentage of new teachers who said they were given basic supports during their first week on the job: 2002–03 and 2003–04

	Percentage 2002–03	Percentage 2003–04
During your first week on the job, were you:	N=366*	N=454
Given curriculum scope and sequence?	32%	67%
Given student forms?	28%	58%
Given staff handbook?	64%	80%
Told name of PFT building representative?	50%	70%
Given a mailbox?	73%	97%

*366 out of 598 new teachers (61%) filled out the survey in October 2002 at a district induction session.

New teachers' assessments of support from principals: 2003–04

Did your principal:	Percentage "yes"
Seem generally welcoming?	82%
Seem genuinely interested in what you were doing in the classroom?	66%
Offer to make time to meet about your concerns?	64%
Seem sensitive to the added pressures of being a new teacher in the district?	61%
Act helpful in introducing you to fellow teachers?	56%
Help you in locating supplies?	52%

N=454

Source: Neild, R., Useem, E. and Farley, E. (April 2005). *Quest for Quality: Recruiting and Retaining Teachers in Philadelphia.* Philadelphia, PA: Research for Action, pp. 34–35.

Exhibit 11
HR Performance Goals and Metrics (draft April 2005)

The Human Resources department mission is to transform The School District of Philadelphia into the employer of choice for experienced and aspiring educators committed to urban education.

Department goals and objectives (all deliverables by June 30, 2005)

Goal 1: Hire quality staff to fill all instructional and non-instructional positions

- 99.04% of teaching positions will be filled as of April 1, 2005 (vacancies below 45)

- 75% of October 2004 vacancies will be filled as of April 1, 2005

- 80% of site-based selection positions will be filled

- 87% of 2004–05 teachers will be certified or enrolled in the PA intern program

- A survey of principals and regional superintendents will be created to document satisfaction with HR support in site-based selection (to be administered in October 2005)

- A teacher diversity workteam will be convened to develop strategies for hiring teachers of color to work toward the goal that 35% of new teachers will be of color

- % of non-instructional positions will be filled

- 75% of affected non-instructional employees will meet NCLB requirements (60% now)

- 95% of participants in the principals' academy will be available for appointments

- 95% of participants in assistant principals' academy will be available for appointments

- An initial automated applicant and teacher tracking system developed in collaboration with IT will be in place

- A RFQ for a fully applicant and teacher tracking system will be issued in partnership with IT

- Roll Out the Red Carpet will provide opportunities for 400 prospective teachers, including 150 (38%) prospective teachers of color, to visit schools, meet district leadership and experience cultural attractions of the city

Goal 2: Support instructional staff to increase retention

- 90% of new teachers will complete school year

- 87% of new teachers will indicate an intention to return for 2005–06 school year (85% last year)

- Qualitative data on reasons teachers and principals leaving will be collected an analyzed

- A professional development module on strategies for teacher support will be prepared in consultation with CAO staff for summer principal professional development (Retention Plans)

- A series of HR/CAO work sessions will identify strategies for enhancing teacher retention, more equitable distribution of teachers, and principal support which will be incorporated into pre-service teacher training and on-going staff development, aspiring principals' academy, the performance appraisal process, and more collegial PFT and CASA [Commonwealth Association of School Administrators, a non-bargaining unit] relationships

Goal 3: Improve customer satisfaction for all district employees

- A comprehensive HR directory will be available to all District employees online

- A single point of contact for all inquiries will be identified

Exhibit 11 (continued)

- The teacher helpline and welcome center will be upgraded

- A screening test will be administered to all customer service employees to determine a baseline of customer service skills

- A monitoring process will be implemented and rewards and sanctions instituted to address exemplary and unsatisfactory customer service performance

- A customer service survey of district employees and 2005 job applicants will be administered and improvement goals established for 2005–06

Goal 4: Create an organizational culture within HR that is a model for the district

- Two issues of a bimonthly newsletter, the Human Capital Bulletin, will be published featuring data on our progress in filling positions with qualified employees, introductions of new staff, information about district priorities and programs that affect our work, and a showcase of best practices from other big city school systems and corporations

- Employee goals and objectives and performance appraisals will be completed for all staff

- The entire organization will be aware of the performance appraisal process via communication and ongoing training

- An internal professional development program will be created to strengthen staff skills in customer service, technology, writing, presentations, data management and analysis, team-building, collaborative decision-making, and employee motivation

- A feasibility study will be completed regarding HR certification courses provided through a university partner, or other agency

- A Human Capital Advisory Committee will host worksite visits to corporate HR depts. and assess the feasibility of HR staff participation in corporate HR staff development programs

- Visits to high vacancy and low vacancy schools will enable staff to understand the connections between their responsibilities and students' opportunities to succeed in school

Goal 5: Improve business processes

- Cost per hire will be computed for teachers and other positions in partnership with the office of management and budget

- Time to fill will be calculated for teachers, principals and other positions

- Comparative data on the above measures will be gathered from other big city school districts

- Goals will be set for reducing cost per hire, time to fill, and HR expenses factors

Goal 6: Implement all contracts with enhanced collegiality

- Training will delivered with PFT and cabinet members and school administrators in work rules, teacher performance, site-based selection, and recruiting and interviewing prospective teachers

- 75% of participants in training for contract implementation will report satisfaction

- A satisfaction survey will be administered to labor partners to identify strengths and needs in collegiality

Source: District files.

DISCUSSION QUESTIONS

1. What factors and forces currently shape the assignment and hiring process in the BPS?

2. How do the key players in the case (Payzant, Contompasis, Harvey-Jackson, McGann, and Stutman) define the problem that the BPS faces in effectively staffing the schools? What constraints and opportunities does each face?

3. How would you assess the progress that has been made so far?

4. Consider the challenge of ensuring that every hard-to-staff school has a stable teaching staff of well-qualified teachers. What are the components of a comprehensive solution? What specific steps would you recommend to Superintendent Payzant and President Stutman?

Susan Moore Johnson ■ Jennifer M. Suesse

Staffing the Boston Public Schools

After leading the Boston Public Schools (BPS) for nearly 10 years, Superintendent Thomas W. Payzant remained focused on improving instruction to raise student achievement. Since his appointment in 1995, Payzant had led the district to adopt a standards-based approach to instruction by insisting that high expectations, ongoing assessment, and data-driven reform were needed in every classroom of every school. He had worked to improve relations with key stakeholders including elected and appointed officials, union leadership, district employees, and community leaders. By adopting challenging curricula and working with staff to define clear goals and establish a system of professional development, Payzant and his team sought to create a culture of continuous improvement and high performance at BPS. Overall, the district's progress had been recognized by education experts and Payzant's peers.

Like many superintendents across the nation, however, Payzant wrestled with the ongoing challenge of recruiting and retaining a workforce of teachers who were qualified and committed to do the work necessary to raise all students' achievement. Staffing low-performing schools was especially critical. Nationwide, observers and scholars generally offered four explanations for the persistent staffing problems experienced by large urban districts. First, some argued that seniority-based transfer rules in the union contract encouraged good teachers to move out of low-performing schools and delayed the hiring and assignment of their replacements. Second, delays in approving state or local budgets meant that districts could not finalize staffing allocations and offer contracts to new teachers until late July or August, by which time many applicants had taken jobs in other districts and schools. Third, the human resource departments of local school districts were often very bureaucratic, dysfunctional, and unable to manage the hiring and transfer process efficiently. Fourth, many analysts contended that low-performing schools failed to recruit and retain strong teachers because they suffered from poor leadership and inadequate working conditions at the school site.[1] Payzant knew that each of these factors had affected Boston in the past, and he and his leadership team were working to address them.

BPS Background

Serving 58,600 students in 139 schools in 2004–2005,[2] BPS was the largest school district in Massachusetts and the 55th largest in the United States.[3] Founded in 1647, BPS was the nation's oldest school district. After 1993, it operated as part of the Boston city government, headed by Mayor Thomas M. Menino. The district's downtown Court Street headquarters were located directly across the street from the mayor's office, and he was an active supporter of the schools. BPS was the city's largest department, and in 2004–2005, its $656 million annual expenditures accounted for 35% of the city's total budget. Mayor Menino appointed the seven members of the governing School Committee, which in turn appointed the superintendent. This system for appointing School Committee members, established in 1989, replaced a district-based election process that many observers felt had hindered the modernization of district management at BPS. Even in 2005, vestiges of the old political bureaucracy lingered at Court Street, and district officials were still working to articulate, update, or eliminate antiquated processes and procedures.

Ten-Year Reform Strategy: Focus on Children

Payzant came to Boston in 1995 fresh from serving two years as the assistant secretary for elementary and secondary education under President Clinton. He had also headed four other school districts, including the San Diego Unified School District from 1982 to 1993. With the support of Mayor Menino and the School Committee, Payzant led efforts to improve the quality of instruction across BPS. In concert with other influential stakeholders, Payzant developed a

five-year plan for reform called "Focus on Children," which was expanded and renewed in 2000. Payzant explained:

> Our theory of change was that BPS needed to shift its focus to the primary goal of improving teaching and learning to enable all students to achieve high standards of performance. In conjunction with statewide education reforms including the development of a comprehensive assessment system, we established an aggressive emphasis on high standards, an instructional focus on literacy and mathematics, and targeted professional development for principals, headmasters, and teachers.[4]

Both Focus on Children I and II aimed to institutionalize instructional improvement. The strategy revolved around the "Six Essentials of Whole-School Improvement." These were:

1. *The core essential—effective instruction:* Use effective instructional practices and create a collaborative school climate to improve student learning.

2. *Student work and data:* Examine student work and data to drive instruction and professional development.

3. *Professional development:* Invest in professional development to improve instruction.

4. *Shared leadership:* Share leadership to sustain instructional improvement.

5. *Resources:* Focus resources to support instructional improvement and improved student learning.

6. *Families and community:* Partner with families and community to support student learning.[5]

One integral element of the 10-year reform plan was developing systemwide instructional capacity. Both the literacy and mathematics curricula—BPS used the Readers and Writers "workshop" format in literacy and TERC *Investigations* program in mathematics—required sophisticated teaching strategies. When the programs were first introduced, these teaching strategies were unfamiliar to many new and veteran BPS teachers, who often found the new expectations for standards-based, student-centered, and constructivist pedagogy to be very challenging. In order to support teachers and principals as they learned to use the new instructional materials and strategies, BPS introduced a collaborative coaching and learning system in 2002. Effective practice schools were designated across the system as models for professional development and continuous improvement. Anticipating his retirement in June 2006, Payzant reflected on the progress at BPS:

> Over the last nine years, I have focused my energy on improving instruction and leadership at BPS. Conversations about schooling have shifted to focus on *how* to accelerate the continuous improvement of teaching and learning to enable all students to meet high standards, and nearly 70% of the BPS principal corps has turned over during my tenure. The centerpiece of our school improvement strategy has been to appoint principals who are strong instructional leaders and provide coaches in literacy and math to assist with school-based professional development for teachers at each site. Our results suggest that we are on the right track. Now, our challenge is to move forward and remain focused despite budget constraints at the state level, which may slow the pace of continuous improvement. We are working to identify the supports schools need to function effectively, to find ways of working within the contract for developing people, to develop a broader diversity of teaching strategies across the faculty, and to figure out how to improve principals' ability to evaluate teachers.

The Policy and Regulatory Context

The need to develop teachers' and principals' capacity for improved instruction had significant implications for staffing across the BPS system. As was the case for most urban school districts, many aspects of the district's organization, including staffing procedures, were subject to state and federal policies, as well as to a local collective bargaining agreement with the Boston Teacher's Union (BTU). Established in 1945, the BTU represented more than 8,000 members, including more than 4,000 teachers, working across the BPS system.

The Contract: In Boston, BPS and BTU representatives negotiated a collective bargaining agreement, or contract, every three years. The contract's preamble stated that, although BPS had been recognized as one of the "best urban schools in the nation," there were great challenges facing the school system. In signing the contract, both parties affirmed their commitment to transforming the traditional "litigious and suspicious" labor-management culture in order to meet the needs and expectations of the Boston community. They wrote:

> In absolute terms, dropout rates are high, graduation standards and college matriculation rates are low, and the skills and prospects of many students in the system are well below their potential. This contract is dedicated to doing better. A commitment to change, however, is not enough. Our 1989–1992 contract was also intended to promote change, and it accomplished less than was hoped. There are lessons in that experience, and they are reflected in this agreement. Change will not come of its own accord; it requires intensive, carefully planned, and skillfully executed implementation. Strong, consistent leadership and widespread training is needed to transform the traditional labor management culture. To achieve real educational im-

provement, the parties and the community will have to work together collaboratively.[6]

The 231-page agreement included articles detailing rules and rights regarding effective working relationships, staffing, professional development, working conditions, compensation and benefits, and dispute resolution for BTU members. The contract had evolved gradually, though there were occasional watersheds. Following contract negotiations in the mid-1980s, for example, the use of seniority as a criterion for staffing decisions had diminished as principals gained a greater say in hiring and placing teachers in their schools.

Transfer Rights (mid-1980s): Seniority was a powerful force in both BPS culture and practice. When new teachers entered BPS, they were granted "provisional" employment and offered one-year renewable contracts. According to state law, after three years of satisfactory service, "provisional" teachers earned "permanent" status—the equivalent of tenure (see Exhibit 1 for 2003–2006 definitions of seniority and certification). Barring dismissal or a budget-induced layoff, permanent teachers were guaranteed ongoing employment within the BPS system.[7]

Historically, seniority rights enabled permanent teachers to select their assignments for the following school year from any of the positions available within the system. Veteran teachers who wanted to transfer between schools were ranked in order of seniority within BPS and then could select their next assignment from the list of posted vacancies. Since provisional teachers had only annual appointments, permanent teachers could "bump" into any open position, which included any position held by a provisional teacher. At one time, veteran teachers could also place a "blind bid" on a school, even if there were *no* openings. If a position became vacant, the most senior qualified teacher with a bid on file would be assigned the position without review by the principal. Neither principals nor the human resources (HR) office could interfere with the transfer process, and new teachers were often moved from school to school, rarely retaining desirable assignments. Veteran teachers, on the other hand, accumulated greater privileges and opportunities for choice assignments with each passing year of service.

In the mid-1980s, BPS and the BTU agreed to modify the impact of seniority on transfers and increase principals' role in the process by allowing up to three permanent teachers to apply to any open position within any school. Once all permanent teachers had listed their preferences, principals could interview the three most senior applicants and select among them. HR then reviewed all the preferences and made the final assignments. This new process gave principals more choices and authority in staffing, although seniority still determined the pool of candidates. This also led BPS principals to negotiate informally among themselves about various staffing arrangements. During conversations regarding the 1997–2000 contract, the practice of blind bidding was discussed and eliminated.

New Rights for Provisional Teachers and a Compressed Hiring Timeline (2000): Another significant breakthrough occurred in 2000 when, under the leadership of Payzant and BTU President Edward J. Doherty, the parties attempted to address barriers to successfully recruiting and retaining well-qualified teachers including "bumping" and late-hiring timelines. After vigorous community debate and a near strike, BPS and BTU negotiators agreed that permanent teachers would no longer have the right to bump first-year provisional teachers out of their positions. The parties recognized that talented prospective teachers might never take a job in BPS without such assurance. Thus, BPS principals gained the ability for the first time to protect promising provisional teachers on their staff by issuing "letters of reasonable assurance," thereby indicating that their positions were not available to permanent teachers seeking new assignments. The change also enabled schools to achieve greater stability in staffing as they engaged in school improvement efforts.

In addition to these changes in teacher assignment provisions, the 2000 contract included provisions aimed at compressing the overall hiring timeline.[8] Prior to the 2000 contract agreement, voluntary transfers began in March. Then, the process for reassigning permanent teachers without assignments followed in April, through a process BPS called the "excess pool." Unassigned teachers (those who were returning from leave or whose positions had been cut because of changes in program or enrollment) selected open positions in order of seniority.[9] The transfer and excess-pool processes were conducted in person and administered by hand, which was time consuming and cumbersome, resulting in delays that prevented BPS from posting any remaining positions or interviewing external candidates before June 1.

After successfully negotiating the 2000 contract, BPS expected to begin the transfer process in February rather than March, so that new positions could be posted openly and external candidates interviewed much earlier in the hiring season. In theory, the expedited hiring timeline allowed BPS to compete for candidates with suburban districts. BPS principals welcomed this change, since many felt that timelines extending until July or August prevented them from ever interviewing some of the most qualified candidates, many of whom seemed unable or unwilling to wait that long for the possibility of an interview.

HR Operations at Court Street (2000–2004)

Following the tense 2000 negotiations, all eyes were focused on Court Street to see whether or not the BPS HR department would meet the new deadlines for transferring teachers internally, posting open teaching positions, and hiring new teachers from outside the system. Concur-

rently, many observers wondered whether the BPS HR system would succeed in recruiting and retaining new teachers.

A Complicated Political Legacy: Like HR department staff in many bureaucratic organizations, BPS HR staff worked in what some officials called a "silo structure." Their isolation from other parts of the school system, poor infrastructure for data collection, and lack of technology was the unfortunate legacy of decades of unstable funding and intermittent mismanagement. This situation left HR department employees ill equipped to manage the staffing demands of BPS schools. Although entrepreneurial principals were able to "work the system," most administrators acknowledged that the old staffing structure was outdated and ineffective. For as long as most BPS officials could remember, the HR system had been paper based, compliance focused, and relationship driven. Chief Operating Officer Michael Contompasis recalled:

> When I was the headmaster at Boston Latin School [an exam school] in the 1980s, I would be here at BPS Court Street headquarters nearly every day in July and August, just walking between the floors and departments to get my teachers hired or arrange transfers. But, it wasn't just for arranging personnel issues. You had to be here in person for everything: facilities, budgets, textbooks, etc. That's the only way I could build the relationships I needed to get things done.

Implementing Concessions Earned in the 2000 Contract: In preparing for staffing in early 2001, Contompasis and the HR director met biweekly with a management "SWAT team" of senior personnel and technology and budget staff. Stakeholders were pleased when job openings were announced on schedule. The SWAT team had compressed the teacher-transfer process from three months to four weeks and created an interim computerized system for the annual staffing forecast (called "probable org"), which had previously been a purely paper-based activity. Before school began in September 2001, HR processed over 35,000 resumes for 1,181 positions, and new hires filled slightly more than half (54.8%) of the vacancies.[10] Overall, outside evaluators felt that BPS made important gains in the first year of implementation but identified a number of areas in which the process could be improved.

Although district officials were eager to build on success, the new staffing calendar stalled in early 2003 when the city encountered unexpectedly severe reductions in proposed state aid. This forced BPS officials to recalculate staffing allocations, in addition to cutting 10% from each school's overall budget. Although the mayor and the City Council eventually reinstated some BPS funding for 2003–2004, BPS ultimately lost 400 teaching positions. In the aftermath of this process, the BPS budget director said, "Asking principals to consider their staffing three separate times—twice to reduce staff and then once to restore certain resources—was extremely difficult and disruptive. It pushed the completion of the staffing process well into the early summer."

Thus, though the HR department made some headway in implementing new procedures from 2001 to 2003, efforts to address the underlying technological and cultural barriers stalled due to a lack of financial resources and internal support. District officials estimated that many vacancies remained when school opened in September 2003.

A New HR Director: In late 2003, during the city's fiscal retrenchment, Payzant hired Barbara McGann to take over HR operations. Like her predecessor, McGann reported to the chief operating officer, but Payzant added her to his leadership team, with which he met regularly (Exhibit 2 includes the 2004–2005 BPS organization chart). McGann was fresh from attending a program for prospective urban superintendents sponsored by the Broad Foundation. Prior to coming to BPS, she had worked with the Red Cross and also served as the provost of the Naval War College and commander of naval recruiting.

When McGann arrived at BPS in January 2004, Court Street was buzzing to complete "probable org," the annual staffing forecast. HR staff worked closely with BPS principals and the budget office to determine which positions would be vacant for the following year. Once probable org finished, the transfer, assignment, and hiring processes could begin. The city's 2004–2005 budget for BPS did not include funds to reinstate positions or services cut in prior years, so conversations around the office were heated. McGann recalled:

> I arrived during probable org, which is a very complicated process involving all the schools and most of the HR staff. During my first few weeks on the job, I was very aware of my status as a newcomer to both the education sector and BPS. As I watched the staffing team at work, I was astounded to see that they did not work together. Also, the planning process was undertaken without the use of computers or comprehensive checklists. There was also some debate about whether or not we would keep or terminate the remaining teachers in our system who were unlicensed, and the discussion was taking place without any data about who those people were or what they were doing. Having come from helping one large bureaucracy—the Navy—to adopt computerized technology, the situation at BPS was still unbelievable. There wasn't even a basic database for all of our teachers. I knew that there had been turnover in my position, but the animosity and isolation within the department was greater than I had anticipated.

As McGann settled in, she began reviewing some of the facts at hand. Though the hiring timeline had been compressed following the landmark 2000 contract negotiations, many deadlines were still being missed. McGann was not sure whether or not the district would be ready to begin the transfer process in March, but she was very worried about hiring new teachers for the fall. So, she created a New Teacher Support Team/Recruitment Center to focus on recruiting new teachers. This team issued early letters of commitment to highly sought-after candidates, including teachers of color and certified math, science, special education, and English as a second language (ESL) specialists. The recruiting team then sought to match these candidates with vacancies across the system. McGann also hired a technology consultant who helped her to develop and implement an online application system that spring. In addition to her focus on recruiting, McGann began a massive reorganization of the HR department. In a mid-year interview with *The Boston Globe,* McGann commented, "We're missing the best and the brightest, but we think we have a plan."[11]

BPS Staffing 2004–2005: Spotlight on Principal Teresa Harvey-Jackson and the John Marshall Elementary School

As they were for McGann, recruiting and retaining talented teachers was one of Principal Teresa Harvey-Jackson's biggest priorities. After 11 years as the principal of the John Marshall Elementary School (the "Marshall"), Jackson was convinced that finding new and experienced teachers who could work successfully with her 673 students in Dorchester, the low-income Boston neighborhood where her school was located, was one of the most important aspects of her job.

Despite her convictions and experience, however, Jackson had faced a number of challenges in hiring the Marshall's staff for 2004–

2005 (see Exhibit 3 for the Marshall's profile). Although she had anticipated some turnover, her options for recruiting new staff were limited by the district's hiring policies and internal transfer procedures, as well as McGann's HR reorganization. Jackson had hired and fired many teachers during her tenure as a principal, so despite these regulations and uncertainties, she sought to find the best possible staff prior to the start of school in September. As she reflected at midyear on the problems she had encountered in filling 14 vacancies, Jackson said:

I think the number of staffing challenges we had this year has been extraordinary. While some years are harder than others, this year has proven to be one of the most difficult I have experienced during my tenure at BPS. In one second-grade class, we have seen four different teachers. We were unable to find a credible certified librarian candidate until December. Then, two permanent teachers were out sick for the 2003–2004 school year, and their positions were filled by substitute teachers. Although neither teacher planned to return for the 2004–2005 school year, their positions were permanent and could not be posted. Had the superintendent not intervened, those slots would have been filled again by substitutes. Staffing our bilingual fourth-grade class has also been problematic. The first teacher quit, and I terminated the second due to poor performance. Neither teacher was certified. We are comfortable with the current substitute teacher, but as of March, we still have not hired a qualified or certified bilingual teacher. This is upsetting, given that fourth graders are held accountable for mastering a fourth-grade curriculum which is assessed by the state. These students need consistent, high-quality instruction, and having four teachers in a four-month period does not meet their needs.

Jackson knew that her students' performance on state exams (the Massachusetts Comprehensive Assessment System, or MCAS, pronounced "EM-cass") was monitored closely. Although the district had recognized the school as an "effective practice school" earlier in the year, the students' MCAS scores remained unacceptably low (see Exhibit 4 for a comparison of the Marshall's and district's MCAS performance). In January 2004, the Massachusetts Department of Education sent a state-appointed panel of experts to visit the Marshall to determine if the school was underperforming and if intervention was necessary. Although the commissioner concluded that the school was not underperforming and that Jackson and BPS had "a sound school improvement plan for improving student achievement, [and that] conditions appear[ed] to be in place at the school to support successful implementation of the plan," the evaluators noted that the number of relatively new teachers in the building (14 of 54) and the number of teachers working outside their areas of certification were among a number of obstacles to success.[12]

Thus, for Jackson, as well as McGann and Payzant, effective staffing at the Marshall was critical. Preparations for hiring teachers began months in advance. The formal staffing process started with school budgeting in December. Four additional steps including probable org, systemwide transfers and excess pools, open postings, and general applications spanned the winter, spring, and summer months. Hiring often continued even after school began. For Jackson, the 2004–2005 school-based staffing process began with the budgeting process in December 2003.

Step 1: Budgeting and Internal Review

In a system as large and as complex as BPS, the allocation of teaching positions changed from year to year in response to budget constraints, program modifications, shifting demographics,

and policies regarding class size. Some vacancies could be predicted, but there were always unexpected changes. Retiring teachers were not required to give advanced notice of their retirements, and some teachers waited until after the school year ended to decide whether or not to return the following year. Plus, there was always the possibility of unplanned openings due to maternity leaves. Jackson, however, was confident that she could cope with unexpected vacancies, noting that "anything is easier than trying to fill 23 vacancies as I did in my first year as principal of the Marshall."

School Budgeting: Jackson was expected to submit her preliminary school budget to the budget office when she returned from winter recess in early January 2004. After reviewing her budget and projected enrollment, Jackson anticipated she would lose one class in each of the first, third, and fourth grades and need to add a second-grade class. She expected a few other shifts as well after the school-site council decided to replace one ESL class with a program designed to accommodate immigrant students in grades three, four, and five who had no previous formal education.[13]

Reviewing Provisional Staff: Next, Jackson decided who among her provisional teaching staff would receive a letter of reasonable assurance, guaranteeing them a position for the following year. Responsibility for supervision and evaluation of her staff was divided among the Marshall's three-member administrative team, and Jackson consulted with her colleagues in making these decisions. First- and second-year provisional teachers could either receive a permanent position or a renewed one-year appointment (hence retaining provisional status for another year). Third-year provisional teachers were either made permanent or terminated. Jackson noted:

> After budgeting, I always begin the staffing
> process by deciding which of my provisional

teachers I want to keep. When we gained the ability to protect our provisional teachers in 2000, I could make provisional teachers permanent even during their first year. Prior to that, any permanent teacher could transfer into their position without my having any say about it whatsoever. Although granting permanent status to first-year teachers would save me from having to go to the excess pools or outside to hire new teachers, I tend to do so rarely. Since we can rehire provisional teachers as long as their current positions remain available for the next school year, I prefer to wait. I don't think watching somebody teach from September to January has proven to be a reliable way to predict future performance.

Permanent Teachers' Preferences: Once Jackson had identified the provisional teachers she intended to keep, she made a list of likely vacancies. Jackson circulated this list among the Marshall's permanent teaching staff in early January, with a sheet asking them to list their assignment preferences for the following year. They could rank their interest in potential vacancies at the Marshall or elect to keep their current position. Some teachers selected different assignments from openings within the building, and a handful of others indicated that they would transfer elsewhere in the BPS system.

Step 2: Probable Org

Once she had received teachers' preference sheets, Jackson sat down to review the 25-page probable org summary from the HR office, which included all the Marshall's budgeted dollars and positions as well as a list of individual staff members. With pencil in hand, Jackson went line by line through the Marshall's seven-page roster, which listed all teachers including their position code and seniority status. Overall, she expected that her teaching staff would be reduced by 4.2 full-time equivalencies (FTEs) (see

Exhibit 5 for a summary of the Marshall's 2004–2005 allocation).

After analyzing the permanent teachers' preferences and BPS enrollment projections, Jackson identified nine vacancies for 2004–2005. She needed to hire three special-education teachers, as well as a fifth-grade teacher, a fourth-grade sheltered English instructor, a resource room teacher, a Spanish-language-based bilingual teacher, an English-language-based bilingual teacher, and a librarian. Between transfer requests and some expected retirements, all of the Marshall's permanent teachers retained assignments within the building, and none entered the excess pool. Jackson then submitted her entire worksheet to the HR department.

Step 3: Systemwide Transfers

Since the majority of BPS teachers were guaranteed a job starting each September, a period for transfers—both voluntary and involuntary—preceded each hiring season (see Exhibit 6 for excerpts from sections I and J from the 2003–2006 BPS-BTU contract). New openings could not be posted for external applicants before internal staff—in this case, other permanent teachers across the BPS system—had an opportunity to apply unless 60% of the faculty voted to approve an exception.[14] Jackson elected not to ask the faculty to vote on posting any vacancies for outside hiring prior to the transfer process, although some other BPS principals did seek and receive the faculty votes necessary for open postings.

Once HR received probable org worksheets from all the principals, the staff generated a comprehensive list of vacant positions across BPS. Although the HR staff worked to meet the strict deadlines, due to the complexity of the task and some tardy submissions by principals, the list of transfer postings was not available until March 3, 2004. At that time, any permanent teacher in the system was eligible to apply for these openings.[15] No veteran teachers applied for a transfer to the Marshall.

Step 4: Excess Pools

Once the window for voluntary transfers was closed, BPS began the "excess" process. In addition to having agreed to concessions on the timing of transfers, BPS and BTU had agreed in 2000 that principals would be prohibited from using the excess pool to force the involuntary transfer of unwanted teachers. In an attempt to reduce unnecessary internal shuffling among veteran teachers, permanent teachers were prohibited from entering the excess pool voluntarily. BTU President Richard Stutman explained, "The new excess and hiring protocols continue to balance the needs and choices of both unassigned teachers and administrators while streamlining both."

This change in policy aimed to address an unspoken issue within BPS. Some district employees, including Jackson, felt that some principals and teachers abused the excess process. Since principals had the power to shift assignments within their buildings, they could eliminate unwanted teachers' positions, forcing those teachers into the excess pool in lieu of completing the evaluations required for dismissal, which could take years to complete. Jackson remarked, "Nobody really talks about it openly, but we all know of cases when a colleague closed out a position instead of evaluating out an ineffective teacher." Some teachers were also known to put themselves into the excess pool in an effort to avoid negative evaluations from their principals. Thus, although the excess pool existed to serve legitimate needs within the system, the perception that some administrators and teachers had "worked the system" harmed the overall perception of the process, and some officials described the misuse of the excess pool as a "dance of the lemons."

In late April, Jackson went downtown to Court Street to meet with several excess-pool groups, armed with her list of nine vacancies. Prior to this meeting, she had spoken with some of her fellow principals about various candidates who might be available, and Jackson hoped to recruit a few individuals in particular. She stood in front of a room of "excessed" permanent elementary teachers and briefly described her school and available positions. Teachers had the opportunity to hear presentations from any of the 66 elementary principals who sought elementary staff and then selected their top three choices in order of their seniority. The contract guaranteed that permanent teachers would be placed in one of the three positions they selected.

When the pools were finished, seven candidates indicated interest in filling three of the Marshall's nine vacancies. Jackson interviewed all seven candidates with the Marshall's personnel sub-committee and then submitted her list of candidates in order of preference to HR.[16] A few weeks later, she received the results of the transfer and excess process. When reviewing the final assignments, Jackson saw that three permanent teachers had been added to her roster. She had interviewed two, but one name was unfamiliar. When she called the HR office for details, Jackson recalled:

> It turns out that if teachers are eligible for a disability-related 504 accommodation, HR will place their preferences at the top of the list, and they don't even have to show up at the excess pool. I asked HR for some information about her disability in order to make the necessary arrangements in my building, but they told me they were not legally able to provide specifics. So, I called another office to learn how to accommodate her disability. This was helpful since I did not have a chance to meet this teacher until the first day of school. Unfortunately, she was unfamiliar with our curriculum and lacked the summer training that most of our teachers had completed.

Step 5: Open Postings and General Applications

In late May, the transfer and excess process was finally complete. The Marshall's remaining six vacancies could be viewed by external candidates via the BPS website, and hiring from outside BPS could begin. Some principals maintained a waiting list of candidates—former interns, favorite substitutes, or paraprofessionals who had become certified teachers—and were prepared to extend offers to these individuals as soon as possible. However, by this point in the year, many suburban districts had already completed their hiring, and there were fewer candidates than there had been earlier in the spring. McGann reminisced, "Throughout the spring, my staffing team was missing deadlines. It took time for me to make necessary personnel changes, and it was incredibly frustrating for me to watch the weeks slip away in the meantime."

Deluge of Résumés: Unlike that in prior years, the 2004–2005 application process was handled entirely online due to the first round of technology upgrades introduced by McGann and the HR team. Jackson was deluged with more than 200 résumés, which disrupted some of her staffing systems at the Marshall. She noted:

> Every other year I got a stack of résumés from the HR office, and I distributed them evenly among the five members of our personnel committee. We each skimmed through our allotted applications to see which candidates should be reviewed by the whole group and then handed those files to the school secretary for xeroxing and distribution. This was time consuming, but not arduous, and we had it down to a system. This year, however, I had to access hundreds of applications online myself, none of which had been screened by HR. Since I was looking for at least two people with dual bilingual/special-education certifications and a librarian with a mas-

ter's in library science, the pickings were slim. Many applicants were totally unqualified for my vacancies. Some people applied for more than one position, so there were some duplicates. I couldn't tell which candidates were viable without printing them all out, which took forever. Overall, the process was a nightmare.

After struggling with the online application procedure and the departure of several HR staffing coordinators downtown on whom she had relied to get things done, Jackson and the four other members of her personnel committee began interviewing external candidates in August. During the summer, Jackson discovered that in addition to the six remaining vacancies identified in probable org, she needed to hire an extended-day kindergarten teacher, another special-education teacher, as well as a part-time teacher for the Literacy Through Art program. This brought her total vacancies to nine. Moreover, one second-grade teacher and one kindergarten teacher were out on extended sick leave, and she was determined to hire teachers, not substitutes, for those positions this year. Fortunately, the superintendent's office agreed with her that the students should not have to have substitutes for another year and permitted Jackson to seek two provisionals just before school opened. Thus, Jackson needed to hire 11 new staff in August before school began.

Summer Hiring: Two Paths to the Marshall: Two teachers Jackson interviewed during August were new to BPS. One was a young graduate of Lesley University who had been looking for a position at BPS since before she started graduate school. While working toward her master's degree and dual certification in elementary and special education, she did internships in BPS schools. Early in her graduate program, she approached the principal of a BPS school that specialized in special education about possible openings. The principal was impressed with her credentials, but he had no vacancy. They kept in touch, and at some point he forwarded her résumé to a special-education coordinator who had once worked with Jackson. The teacher said:

> I think Teresa ended up with my résumé because of the special-education coordinator, because I got a call in mid-August, long after submitting my applications. I think I sent BPS my résumé more than 100 times between January and whenever they put up the online application system. I only got two calls from principals, both of whom were looking for resource room help, not for a teacher dealing with behavioral difficulties. Having worked as an intern and tutor at BPS in college, I knew that this was how the system worked, but it was very stressful. I could never get any information from anyone. But, once I discovered that nobody could get any information, I didn't feel so alone anymore. At least I knew that BPS hires late. So, when Teresa finally called me about the lab cluster position in the second week of August, I was thrilled. I came in for my interview and had an offer before I left the building. It is a shame that BPS hires so late, because some good people really can't wait. Knowing how hard it is to break into this system, I would have taken whatever job I was offered. But, sometimes things just work out, because I can see myself in this job for at least 10 years.

Another new candidate that Jackson hired in August was a career changer who had a bachelor's in fine arts and had also earned her master's from Lesley University in 2004. She applied for art and classroom teaching positions at many districts in the Greater Boston area, including BPS and some wealthier suburbs like Lexington. She never applied, however, for any position at the Marshall. The teacher explained:

> I applied online three or four times but never got anything other than an automated e-mail response. Originally, I wanted to work in the suburbs and was recruited by some of the suburban districts. But, when a friend of mine who taught at the Marshall told me in late August about their search for a part-time teacher of "literature through art," I had to find out more. This was my dream job—an opportunity to integrate my love of art and children's literature, with hours that suited my situation as a single mom perfectly. I never saw my job advertised, however, even though I was checking the BPS website regularly. I immediately gave my friend my résumé, and a week later I was interviewing with the principal and two other teachers about the position. Unlike my interviews with other districts that felt frantic or rushed, the Marshall group was thorough and welcoming. I could tell that, while they needed to fill the position, Teresa was being particular about whom she hired. I got a tour of the school, and a week later Teresa called me with an offer. After a few months in the classroom, I can honestly say I love this job working with kids in an urban setting. Even though the work can be difficult, I just cannot see myself working in the 'burbs.

School Begins

By the time school began in September 2004, Jackson had filled 13 of the 14 total vacancies at the Marshall. The librarian's position remained stubbornly empty. Jackson was pleased with the two new teachers she had hired in August, but unfortunately some of the other new staff members were less successful. For example, within the first three weeks of school, two permanent BPS teachers new to the Marshall left the district rather than risk unsatisfactory evaluations. A third told Jackson that she was "overwhelmed by the needs of the children" and resigned. Jackson filled two of these positions with incoming permanent teachers, who were forced to transfer out of other BPS positions and into the Marshall following the systemwide enrollment review in October.[17] While Jackson felt that one of these last-minute transfers was a good match for the school, she was frustrated that she was forced to take the second teacher as well.

Jackson continued to search for a certified librarian with a master's in library science, since she had lobbied extensively to gain BPS funding for reestablishing the Marshall's library program. She said, "I needed a certified librarian in order to use my allocation for library materials and technology. It was a substantial amount, and while I saw many good candidates, they were not qualified. It was frustrating not to have someone, and I worried we would lose our funding." Then, in December, Jackson heard about a librarian who was finishing her degree at Simmons College later that month. Jackson met her and hired her instantly.

Reflections

"I know what skills I am looking for in new staff in order to ensure that we can deliver meaning-ful and appropriate instruction here at Marshall," Jackson said in reflecting on the staffing process. "Most days I wish I had more authority over staffing in my school. Even though Massachu-setts grants principals the right to hire and fire, BPS principals do not have this responsibility. This is problematic." Chief Operating Officer Contompasis echoed Jackson's concerns. He noted:

> When I came into this system in the 1960s, I was a teacher and a BTU member. My goal was to give teachers a voice within their working en-vironment. I felt that principals [and the district] had too much authority. Too many decisions at that time were being made because of politics, and adults did not always consider our students' best interests. The relationship between the dis-trict and the union was sometimes adversarial,

and we had a lot of difficult issues to resolve. But, things have changed. We have site-based decision making and relaxed seniority rules, but we still need to move forward in eliminating im-pediments that principals have to manage. The goal continues to be finding common ground that allows principals to include teachers in an advisory capacity around key decisions but also ensures that principals have the authority to get things done.

Ongoing Efforts

Altogether 505 new teachers joined BPS by the end of September 2004. Of this group, 116 were selected in June, 300 were selected by the end of August, and 89 were hired after school began. While reviewing the 2004–2005 staffing process, Payzant and his team could see signs of progress as well as problems that still required attention. Reform efforts in the HR department were on-going, and the district's relationship with the BTU continued to evolve.

HR Reorganization Continues

McGann continued her reorganization of assign-ments within her department, and officials from across the district remarked upon the rapid changes happening in HR. Instead of having in-dividual specialists (e.g., one person handled all HR requests for paraprofessionals), she decided that HR needed cross-trained teams that could answer questions from principals and prospective teachers according to level (e.g., elementary or secondary). She also asked veteran BPS principal Joseph Shea to become the director of staffing. Through the Broad Foundation's fellowship pro-gram, McGann also hired an MBA graduate as her deputy director.

By the end of 2004, the cubby barriers in HR offices on the third floor at Court Street had been totally removed. Approximately six people had retired or left the department, which now included about 30 members, and employees' desks were spread across the open-concept space. McGann noted, "Change is underway, but it is slow. People still tend to gravitate toward old patterns. Rather than giving answers on the spot, they pass questions along to specific individuals—which can be frustrating for principals. But, Shea sits right in the middle of the floor, which is by design, and he can overhear and address issues as they arise." To signal the importance of the HR work, Payzant elevated McGann's position from director to assistant superintendent.

Evolving Union Relationship

In addition to instituting changes within the system, McGann and other district officials (including Contompasis, who headed the BPS negotiating team) were slowly building relationships with the new BTU president, Stutman. Stutman, elected following Doherty's retirement in 2003, had previously been the BTU's secondary schools' field representative. Although some district officials had been concerned that Stutman's reputation for independence would threaten ongoing efforts to collaborate, observers felt that the relationship between BPS and the BTU was relatively steady. As the school year progressed, district and union officials continued to build relationships as they worked through ongoing issues including some thorny staffing questions associated with the BPS high school reform strategy.[18] Near the end of January 2005, Stutman reflected on his role, the staffing process, and the challenges ahead:

> Staffing our schools is an exceedingly complex project, and one I have always found fascinating. When we look at the hiring calendar, the BTU supports completing the transfer process as soon as possible. It can't be run too early, however, without the risk of missing real vacancies that haven't yet surfaced in the accompanying budget process. So, the timing is a balancing act. There has never been anything in the con-

tract that prevented principals from hiring once the transfer process has finished, but some principals just are not ready to take the initiative and hire as early as May. Too often, these same principals end up with more than their share of new teachers. In the ideal world, BPS would place new or struggling teachers in the best schools to give them assistance and a boost in the best, most suitable, environment, but there aren't any incentives at the moment to do this.

> On another note, Barbara McGann is helping HR move into this century technology-wise. She is fairly reasonable and has 100 ideas a minute. HR has made progress, but the staffing process continues to lag in part because some principals just don't submit information in a timely manner. To me, the issue of staffing low-performing schools is all about principals. Teachers don't avoid low-performing schools. They avoid miserable or inept principals. The state designations of low-performing schools change from year to year; that standard is arbitrary. When choosing a school, teachers do not worry about whether it's been designated a low-performing school. Instead, they calculate the nature of a principal's relationship with the staff, as well as the quality of the building, its location, and sometimes, even parking spaces.

Next Steps

As Payzant considered these challenges and looked ahead to the future, he commented:

> The issue of deciding who has the right to teach where is complicated, and staffing our low-performing schools is a perennial puzzle. Leaders in every sector struggle to convince talented and experienced individuals to take on the toughest assignments. We face tough questions. How can we continue to improve our relationship

with the BTU? How can we support HR as it works to become more effective when we have deferred needed improvements in central office infrastructure in trying to minimize the impact of $85 million in cuts made in 2003 and 2004 on schools? How will principals, our instructional leaders, be in classrooms every day, participate in common planning time with teachers, and attend to many operational tasks and also find the time necessary to document the performance of ineffective teachers and remove them from the profession? We must answer these questions and figure out how to build a system that supports teachers and principals in closing the achievement gap and getting all students to the standard of proficiency.

Notes

1. While public sentiment often cited undesirable neighborhoods or resource constraints as the primary cause of urban teacher shortages, a report issued by the New Teacher Project in 2003 (available at http://www.tntp.org/report.html) found that districts with ambitious recruiting strategies and timely hiring could attract five or more applicants for every opening.

2. The BPS system included six early-learning centers (K–1), 66 elementary schools (K–5), 12 K–8 schools, 18 middle schools, one 6–12 school, 25 high schools, three "exam" schools (7–12), six special education schools (K–12), and two alternative (at-risk) programs. Of these 139 schools, 17 were pilot schools and two were charter schools approved and funded by BPS.

3. U.S. Department of Education rankings were based on 2000–2001 enrollment.

4. BPS school leaders are called both principals and headmasters. For simplicity, subsequent references to principals imply both groups.

5. The six essentials were refined over time. A detailed description and history of Focus on Children I and II was published by BPS online at http://boston.k12.ma.us/teach/foc.asp.

6. The full text of this agreement is available at http://www.btu.org/leftnavbar/contractdownload.html.

7. In the event of a layoff, the contract and state law stipulated that BPS teachers would be released in reverse seniority order.

8. "Toward an Open Teacher Hiring Process: How the Boston Public Schools and the Boston Teachers Union Can Empower Teachers to Hire and Keep the Best Teams," an issue paper published by the Boston Plan for Excellence in March 2000, provided detailed examples in its description and analysis of these barriers. *The Boston Globe* carried full coverage of the final agreement on October 21, 2000.

9. Prior to 2000, teachers in the excess pool included those whose positions had been eliminated, those returning from extended leaves, and any permanent teachers who were voluntarily giving up their previous assignments.

10. Implementation results for key hiring and transfer contract provisions are explained in greater detail in Special Report 02–1, "Implementing the Boston Teachers' Contract: Process Is Generally Successful But Key Opportunities Missed," published in March 2002 by the Boston Municipal Research Bureau, Inc., in collaboration with the Massachusetts Advocacy Center.

11. Kevin Rothstein, "By cutting application red tape, Hub public schools' aim: Hire," *The Boston Globe,* May 14, 2004.

12. The Winter '04 School Panel Review Report was published by the Massachusetts Department of Education on February 17, 2004, and posted online at http://www.doe.mass.edu/sda/review/cohorts/?FilterYear=2004&orderBy=.

13. In the 1980s, BPS adopted a site-based management system called the "school-site council." The contract outlined the council's membership, role, and responsibilities in Article III (http://btu.org/leftnavbar/contractdownload.html). At Marshall, this governing group included Jackson, seven elected BTU members, and seven parent representatives.

14. See contract Section I 1 (b) in Exhibit 6.

15. According to contract Section I 1 (c), schools could reject transfer applications from any teacher who had "received two interim overall unsatisfactory evaluations between September and February of that year" (see Exhibit 6).

16. Each BPS school-site council had a personnel subcommittee, which included two teachers (elected by union members in their school) and one parent in addition to the principal. Overall, teachers, parents, and administrators spoke highly of this arrangement. Although the contract granted principals the authority to veto personnel subcommittee recommendations, this right was exercised rarely.

17. These permanent teachers had filled positions in other BPS schools when unexpectedly low class sizes resulted in staff reduction. In these cases, teachers were moved according to seniority. Newest teachers were moved first.

18. BPS was in the process of converting some of its large, comprehensive high schools into "small schools" as part of a nationwide high school reform experiment funded by the Gates Foundation. Historically, permanent teachers were "attached" to positions in specific buildings, which insiders called "building" or "attachment rights." Before BPS could break up schools and reassign secondary school teachers, these building-attachment rights needed to be addressed.

Exhibit 1

Seniority and Certification: Excerpts from 2003–2006 BPS-BTU Collective Bargaining Agreement Sections G & H

G. Seniority

Seniority in the teachers' unit is defined as total years of professional service in the Boston Public School system for which salary credit is given for step advancement, including years on maximum whether or not such teaching experience (120 days) results in a provisional contract in any year.

Time spent in authorized leave of absence granted for any reasons prior to September 1, 1980 will continue to count as seniority in the teachers unit. Paid leave of absence granted on or after September 1, 1980 including leave covered by workmen's compensation, will continue to count as seniority in the teachers' unit. Unpaid leave of absence granted on or after September 1, 1980 for any reason other than for union business under Section VIII(Q)(1) will not count as seniority in the teachers' unit. Any time spent on an involuntary layoff prior to an offer of recall shall be counted as seniority in the teachers' unit; however, such time shall not count towards career awards or other salary advancement. The Union will indemnify the Committee against any cost or damages arising out of any dispute or proceeding connected with the prior sentence.

The Union shall be supplied with a current seniority list of all members of the bargaining unit.

The settlement agreement contained in Appendix B shall apply to all similar situations where the Superintendent breaks a larger school into smaller schools or small learning communities. The seniority provisions referenced in Paragraph 3 of the appendix will continue in each circumstance for 16 full years commencing from the beginning of the September following the year this provision is implemented in a given school.

H. Certification/Program Areas

1. Program Areas

Employees shall be assigned to program areas in which they are qualified. Program areas are listed in Appendix A. The School Committee reserves the right to establish additional program areas, subject to any collective bargaining obligation as may be required by law.

2. Qualifications

Employees shall be deemed qualified in a program area by holding a valid state certificate or approval for such area and by meeting one of the following criteria:

(a) A state certificate not more than five (5) years old.

(b) A mean score on the National Teachers Examination, not more than ten (10) years old.

(c) Fifteen (15) course credits, graduate or undergraduate, approved as relevant to qualification, all of which are not more than five (5) years old.

(d) Two (2) years of teaching experience within ten (10) years. A creditable year is one in which at least 50% of the weekly schedule is in the subject area.

Exhibit 1 (continued)

3. Ranking

Teachers shall be ranked by seniority (as defined in Section V(H) above) within each program area, including teachers on recall lists.

4. Schedule and Procedures

For the purposes of determining qualifications and placement in a program area, all valid credentials must be filed with the Personnel Department on or before January 15th of any year, unless the results of the NTE or PRAXIS exam are not available by January 15th, in which case, the application will be due by 2/15.

Employees must respond to alleged erroneous placement or non-placement in a program area or to an error in their seniority date within thirty (30) days of the receipt of such information from the School Department.

5. Leave of Absence; Promotion

Teachers on leave of absence for more than ten (10) years or who were promoted out of the bargaining unit shall be considered qualified in the program area in which they have taught immediately prior to such leave of absence or promotion in addition to any program area in which they are qualified under Section (2) above.

6. Recall

Teachers on recall shall be placed in program areas in which they are qualified under Section 2 above.

Source: District files.

Exhibit 2
BPS Organizational Chart

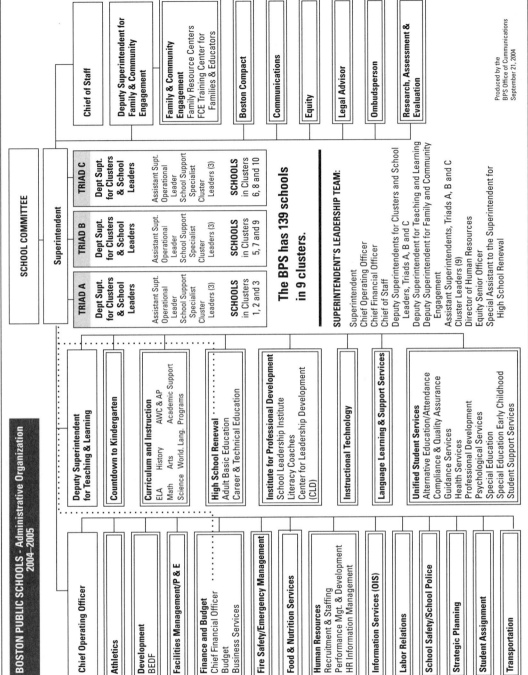

Source: District files.

Exhibit 3

Marshall School Profile

	Marshall School	BPS[a]
Students		
Total 2003–2004 enrollment[b]	681	60,164
% special education	17.3%	19.5%
% bilingual education	15.7%	19.0%
% African-American	61.8%	46.4%
% Hispanic	34.5%	30.4%
% Asian	1.6%	8.8%
% White	1.0%	14.0%
% American Indian	n/a	0.4%
% Low-income	86.6%	73.4%
Average attendance	93%	91.4%
Staff		
Total teachers (FY04)[c]	50	4,385
Tenure at the Marshall less than 5 years	19	n/a
Tenure at the Marshall 5–10 years	13	n/a
Tenure at the Marshall more than 10 years	18	n/a
% licensed[d]	98%	85.6%
Total administrators	3	520
Total support staff[e]	3	435

Source: District files and Marshall School analysis.

[a] District figures cited from "2004 BPS District Report Card," downloaded from http://boston.k12.ma.us/bps/facts.asp on March 3, 2005.

[b] Enrollment figures calculated at the end of the 2003–2004 school year.

[c] For the purposes of clarity, this figure includes only classroom teachers, including two teachers who share a job.

[d] License figures tally teachers holding at least one Massachusetts state teaching license.

[e] Figure includes the student support coordinator, the clinical coordinator, and the evaluation team facilitator.

Exhibit 4

Marshall and District Performance Data Comparison: Grade 4 MCAS Results 2002–2004

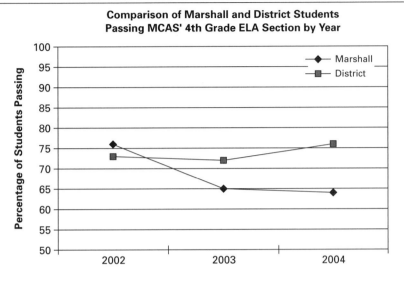

Comparison of Marshall and District Students Passing MCAS' 4th Grade ELA Section by Year

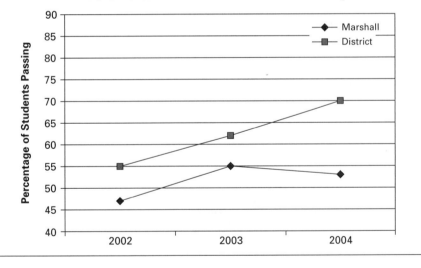

Comparison of Marshall and District Student Performance on MCAS' 4th Grade Math Section by Year

Exhibit 5

"Probable Org" Summary of Teaching Positions Available at the Marshall for the 2003–2004 and 2004–2005 School Years (as of January 2004)

Teaching Positions[a]	FTE		Change
	03–04	04–05	
General Fund			
Kindergarten	4.0	4.0	
Bilingual Kindergarten (Spanish)	1.0	1.0	
Grade 1	5.0	4.0	−1.0
Grade 2	4.0	4.0	
Grade 3	4.0	3.0	−1.0
Grade 4	4.0	3.0	−1.0
Grade 5	4.0	4.0	
Reading Specialist		0.5	+0.5
Literacy Specialist		0.5	+0.5
SPED Resource	5.0	4.0	−1.0
SPED Speech & Language	2.0	2.0	
SPED Primary Transition	1.0	1.0	
SPED Lab Cluster	4.0	4.0	
Bilingual Teacher (Spanish, 1/grade)	5.0	5.0	
Elementary Specialist	0.6		−0.6
Science Specialist	2.0	2.0	
Arts Specialist	1.0	0.4	−0.6
Arts/Literacy Specialist	1.0	1.0	
Music Specialist	1.0	1.0	
Physical Education Specialist	1.0	1.0	
Librarian		1.0	+1.0
Swimming Instructor	1.0	1.0	
Special Revenues, Grants			
Kindergarten Teacher (Math)	0.5	0.5	
Grade 1 Reading Recovery		0.5	+0.5
Bilingual ESL	1.0		−1.0
Native Literacy Teacher		1.0	+1.0
Elementary Specialist	0.5		−0.5
Reading Specialist	1.0		−1.0
Total	**53.6**	**49.4**	**−4.2**

Source: Casewriter and Marshall School staff analysis of BPS documents.

[a] This list does not include the principal or other administrators, teacher aides, custodial and food service staff, the special-education compliance officer, or the school nurse.

Exhibit 6

Transfer Procedures: Excerpts from 2003–2006 BPS-BTU Agreement Sections I & J

I. Transfers

1. General Procedures

These general procedures are subject to the provisions of Article III(C)(4)(c).

The Committee shall not be required to post for transfer any position held by a "provisional" teacher whom the Committee has made "permanent." Any position which is posted for transfer may be filled by a provisional teacher whom the Committee has made "permanent." Except as specified in the prior two sentences or elsewhere in this Agreement, all vacancies which under prior collective bargaining agreements were to be filled by transfer shall be filled in the manner set forth below:

(a) All vacancies shall be posted on the School Department website (www.boston.k12.ma.us) no later than April 15th. All applications for vacant positions must be submitted no later than 10 school days after posting on the website. The website shall be the only medium for posting vacancies.

Internal candidates must use the MYBPS intranet system for submission of applications, including data information form and resume. Human Resources will not accept paper applications.

Positions held by provisional teachers with a letter of reasonable assurance will not be posted provided that one BTU Building Rep. has granted written approval. The Department of Human Resources will send out letters of reasonable assurance to provisional teachers no later than April 15th. The School Department will provide a list of such positions to the union prior to initiating the posting process. BTU members will have in-school access to a computer with internet capability and a printer.

(b) *Open Postings:*

The current practice regarding open postings will continue. Any school that wishes to open post a position must obtain a 60% vote of the faculty before February 15th.

(c) *Transfer Eligibility:*

All permanent teachers, including those on leave of absence, are eligible to apply for transfers during the month of March. Provisional teachers with a letter of reasonable assurance shall be eligible to apply for transfers to their own positions under the transfer process. However, any permanent teacher who seeks a position to which a provisional teacher has applied under this section will be granted an interview by the School Site Council Personnel Subcommittee.

Teachers may be considered for transfer in any subject area in which they recertify under the 1993 Massachusetts Educational Reform Act, even if they do not hold an active Boston program area; however, a school's Personnel Subcommittee shall not be required to select any such individual.

Any teacher who has received two interim overall unsatisfactory evaluations between September and February of that year may be rejected for transfer by the School Site Council Personnel Subcommittee.

(d) If no permanent teacher applies for a position that appears in the April 15th posting, the personnel subcommittee may consider and select any qualified applicant who applies to the posting, so long as there is no permanent excessed teacher in that subject area.

In cases where there is only one applicant for a vacancy on the transfer posting, the personnel subcommittee will not be required to hire that single applicant, and the vacancy will go into the ex-

Exhibit 6 (continued)

cess pool. If there is no permanent excessed teacher in that subject area, the personnel subcommittee may consider and select any qualified applicant who applies for the position.

(e) The BTU may challenge the omission of a vacancy from the April 15th posting. The challenge must occur within 10 days of the posting. The challenge may be overridden by a 60% vote of the faculty of the school where the vacancy is challenged. Should the challenge not be overridden, the vacancy shall be posted on the BPS web page prior to the running of the excess pools for 5 school days. Permanent teachers only are eligible to apply.

(f) Transfers will take effect the following September, unless the posting otherwise provides.

(g) Members of the bargaining unit shall have ten (10) school days to apply for transfer.

(h) In the event that a position sought through transfer no longer exists on the effective date of transfer, the person seeking the transfer shall remain in his/her former position as if the vacancy had not been posted.

(i) Upon rehiring after three (3) consecutive years of provisional service, provisional nurses shall attain the same rights and benefits relative to transfer as nurses who have been permanently appointed.

J. Excessing Procedure

1. This excessing procedure will not apply to "provisional" teachers, but will apply to "permanent" teachers and nurses with more than three (3) consecutive years of service. All permanent teachers who are unassigned after the March Transfers shall be invited to a mid-April Excess (reassignment) Pool. These pools shall not be held during the April school vacation week. No teacher shall be involuntarily excessed from her/his school or assignment after the running of these pools.

The above paragraph is not intended to prohibit the School Department from excessing teachers in the fall to correct class size problems.

2. Excessing from a school building shall be first by volunteers within a program area, then by reverse seniority within a program area. An employee who holds seniority in a program area other than the one from which he/she has been excessed shall be offered a vacancy in the building in such other program area. If there is no such vacancy he/she will be placed directly onto a system-wide excess list.

3. In the event of excessing during the school year on or after November 1, in cases of class consolidation, the Department may elect to excess and reassign the junior teacher in one of the classes being consolidated rather than the least senior teacher in the program area within the building.

4. Not more than five (5) days notice shall be required for excessing during a school year.

5. Permanent or temporary vacancies within a program area will be filled from the system-wide excess list periodically by matching the aggregate number of such vacancies against an equal number of persons on the excess list by seniority within such program area, in accordance with the following procedure:

Teachers will bid on listed vacancies in order of seniority. Each teacher must make three (3) bids, except that the next-to-last teacher must make two (2) bids and the most junior teacher must make one (1) bid. When a vacancy has received three (3) bids, bidding will be closed on that vacancy. Teachers will be assigned to one (1) of their bids.

Exhibit 6 (continued)

Teachers in the excess pool shall be limited on one (1) bid per school.

6. Vacancies will continue to be filled until late August, at which time teachers who are not matched against vacancies will be assigned in a suitable professional capacity, including substitute service, and will remain eligible to fill vacancies as they occur up to November 1. There shall be no bumping from the system-wide excess list.

The Committee shall not be required to post in the teachers reassignment pool any position held by a non-tenured teacher who has been made "permanent" by the Committee.

7. An employee exercising a right to return to the teacher bargaining unit after layoff or demotion shall be carried on the system-wide excess list in the applicable program area.

8. An excessed employee who is excessed from his building and who is qualified in more than one (1) program area may elect annually to bid for assignment in one (1) program area other than the one from which he was excessed, in which case he will bid only within the newly elected program area; provided, however, such election may not be made into a program area in which there is an active recall list.

9. No teacher may voluntarily excess him/herself without the approval of the director of the Office of Human Resources.

10. All excessed teachers and nurses will by notified by April 15th.

11. No teacher receiving an overall annual performance evaluation of unsatisfactory will have bidding rights through the excess pools. Such teachers will be assigned to a teaching position by the Superintendent.

12. Any teacher who has received two or more overall interim unsatisfactory evaluations between September 1st and the date of the excess pool will not be allowed to participate in the excess pool. Such teachers may appeal (for purposes of participating in the excess pool only) his or her interim evaluations to a three member panel. One member of the panel will be selected by the Superintendent, one by the President of the BTU, and the third member will be selected by both the Superintendent and the BTU President. The teacher must appeal the decision to deny him/her access to the excess pool within five school days of such denial. The panel will hold a hearing within five working days from the day after the date the appeal is filed. The decision will be rendered at least two days before the running of the pool. No briefs will be submitted. The decision of the panel with regard to the teacher's right to participate in the excess pool will be final and not subject to grievance and arbitration.

13. Any teacher who receives his or her third bid in an excess pool may exercise a one-time option of returning to the excess pool in the following year.

14. Subsequent to the running of the excess pools the School Department shall post on the BPS web page all remaining and new vacancies. Such postings will be updated every two weeks through the close of school and at least weekly during the summer through August 31st. The Boston Teachers Union shall be notified of all postings.

15. Disputes concerning the interpretation or application of this excessing policy will be processed as grievances under the contractual grievance and arbitration procedure as modified herein:

Exhibit 6 (continued)

(a) all intermediate steps are hereby waived;

(b) counsel for the B.T.U. and the Committee shall cooperate in obtaining the services of a referee who shall be available to arbitrate the dispute within one week after a grievance is communicated by the Union;

(c) arbitration will be conducted on an expedited bases without written briefs and with oral or written awards to be rendered not later than three days following the date of hearing not to exceed one day.

It is the intent of the parties that wherever possible remedial relief of any violation shall not delay implementation of an excessing procedure nor require the undoing of sequentially filled vacancies made in good faith.

16. These excessing procedures are subject to all applicable state and federal laws and lawful orders pursuant thereto.

17. The parties will cooperate in addressing any special problems that may exist in any school in relation to this policy.

18. Rule of one will apply if pools not completed prior to July 1st. Rule of two will apply if excess pools completed by workday prior to July 1st. Rule of three will apply if excess pools completed by the 4th work day before the end of school year.

Rule of One: The selection of assignments is conducted by strict seniority.

Rule of Two: The teacher will make two selections and will receive one.

Rule of Three: The teacher will make three selections and will receive one.

19. Reassignment pool vacancies will be listed on the BPS website five school days before each pool. BTU members will have in-school access to a computer with internet capability and a printer.

20. All seniority lists will be placed on the BPS website, and the BTU will be provided access to them. The School Department shall provide a copy of the seniority list to the BTU before conducting the mock pool. BTU members will have in-school access to a computer with internet capability and a printer.

21. No personnel subcommittee shall be required after completion of the first teacher posting.

22. The excessing procedure shall apply to Student Support Coordinators. Wherever the word "teacher" appears in this Article V(J), it shall be interpreted to include Student Support Coordinators.

Source: District files.

Building a High-Performing Organization

In today's high-stakes environment, school administrators across the country face the challenge of shaping public school districts that are organized and managed for high performance, in which everyone in the district, whether in the schools or the district office, works toward the continuous improvement of learning for all students. The district's important systems and structures should be designed to support and reward behaviors that will lead to excellent outcomes. The organizational culture must be deliberately created and nurtured so that it values results, not just well-intentioned efforts. High-performing organizations are exceptionally difficult to create in any sector. To succeed, leaders and managers must first understand that their decisions and actions are the key determinants of success and then focus unrelentingly on building and sustaining a high-performing organization. While many districts throughout the country are diligently working to build such organizations, few have succeeded to date. Part of the reason is that the performance imperative in public education is a relatively new phenomenon.

The broad-based emphasis on performance originated with a powerful combination of federal, state, and local forces. Together they created pressure to achieve measurable results that is now relentless and by all predictions will be enduring. Beginning in the late 1990s, virtually every state passed some form of performance-based accountability policy—introducing statewide comprehensive testing, establishing targets for improved student achievement, and putting in place rewards and sanctions for school performance. In 2001, performance-based accountability became the centerpiece of the federal No Child Left Behind Act (NCLB), which took the fifty state accountability policies and embedded their intent and content into a single legal framework. By setting clear parameters for the design of state accountability systems, the law in effect created a state-administered national accountability system for U.S. education. NCLB set ambitious targets for school performance and introduced federal sanctions for failure to meet these targets.

This focus on performance has dramatically changed public educators' work environments. In the past, teachers worked in relative isolation from one another. Performance goals for teachers and principals, if they existed, were often ambiguous. Today, people at all levels of a school district are measured and evaluated based on concrete data that is widely available. Expectations for student achievement have also changed. Today, there is a widely accepted norm that all students, regardless of race, ethnicity, or family background, can and must improve academically. As one superintendent stated, "We have a no-excuses policy when it comes to academic results." But how does a district respond to these new dynamics?

Public education has a history of looking for silver-bullet solutions. In reality, to achieve continuous improvement, districts must implement a host of systems and structures that are coherent with an articulated districtwide improvement strategy, and with one another. These include well-constructed and conscientiously implemented accountability systems, compensation systems that are aligned with performance expectations, and organizational learning processes that enable teachers, principals, and district office personnel to meet their performance objectives. Leaders must understand that achieving success is not a destination but a dynamic, ongoing process that requires leaders to modify their organizations as conditions change. But, most importantly, leaders must realize that the core of success is the ability to transform the culture of their organizations.

Cultural change does not take place because of proclamations from the district office or by widely disseminating catchy slogans. Leaders must use a range of available managerial levers to build new organizational systems and structures that require and prompt people throughout a district to behave in new ways. These new behaviors must then be purposefully encouraged and rewarded. A district's systems and structures must support a culture that stimulates creativity, raises every individual's expectation of his or her own performance and that of others, and increases the capacity of everyone in the district to adapt to and assimilate new practices. If all schools within a district are to improve steadily,

everyone in the district has to assume responsibility for doing his or her part. An organizational culture that values collaboration, high expectations, trust, learning, and individual and group accountability for results is essential to building a high-performing organization.

Learning Objectives

The cases in this module introduce the challenges of putting into place the culture, systems, and structures required for building high-performing public school districts. We suggest the following learning objectives for this module:

- Recognize that building a complex school system into a high-performing organization is not achieved through any single set of actions, e.g., instituting an accountability system or pay-for-performance for teachers, but requires changes in all aspects of the organization that are coherent with an improvement strategy and one another

- Understand that while structures and systems are necessary components of building a high-performing organization, the most powerful element for establishing and sustaining performance is an organization's culture

- Realize that building and sustaining a culture of performance requires specific managerial actions that are deliberate and strategic

- Recognize that having the right data is a prerequisite for building accountability, but that using data as an effective tool for learning about the causes of poor performance and the actions needed to improve is by far the greatest challenge

Cases

Module III begins with a case outside the education sector. "NYPD New" explores how the new chief of the New York City Police Department, William Bratton, uses deliberate managerial actions and data to change an entrenched culture, moving its focus away from measuring and rewarding efforts to an almost single-minded emphasis on results. The case highlights both the uncertainty and excitement of people at all levels of the organization when demands are made to change behaviors and long-held core beliefs.

The module then moves to the education sector with "Learning to Manage with Data in the Duval County Public Schools." This case explores the processes being tried to select and use the burgeoning amount of achievement data collected by Duval County Public Schools. Even with an abundance of data, the principal and teachers of Lake Shore Middle School are not improving student performance; in fact, performance is declining. The case raises the questions of what kind of data are most useful for informing instructional practice and how you effectively use them. The third case, "The Mason School: Using Data to Improve Instruction," contrasts with the previous one. At Mason, teachers and the principal understand how to use the data to address students' individual learning needs. The case explores how everyone in a school uses data to guide and evaluate their actions to improve student performance.

The next case is "Compensation Reform at Denver Public Schools," which follows a lengthy labor-management initiative to develop and launch a performance-based pay system. ProComp, a comprehensive compensation system for Denver public school teachers, is designed to gradually move the district from a standardized salary scale that rewards advanced degrees and longevity to a more varied and flexible approach that includes a menu of incentives and rewards. This case addresses the role a compensation system can play in driving the implementation of a districtwide improvement strategy.

Module III concludes with "Managing at Scale in the Long Beach Unified School District (LBUSD)." This case highlights the challenges of building a culture that has the students at the center of all the work done by the adults in the district. What does it take for LBUSD to develop a commonly held belief that the academic performance of every child in every school must continuously improve every year? The case examines what actions district leaders might consider to build and sustain a culture across time and changes in leadership.

Discussion Questions

The following questions will serve as a guide to identifying the common ideas embedded in the case series in this module:

1. What systems and structures are available to help leaders and managers build a high-performing organization? What are the key challenges in creating and maintaining their effectiveness?

2. How do leaders and managers move from thinking about culture as an abstract, fuzzy concept to a concrete element of an organization that is instrumental in building a high-performing school district?

3. How does the district office culture relate to and impact a school's culture? What are the desired characteristics of a performance culture in both the schools and the district office?

4. What are the key success factors in first transforming and then sustaining the beliefs and behaviors in a culture of performance?

DISCUSSION QUESTIONS

1. What were the most critical challenges Bratton faced when he took the job at NYPD?

2. What were Bratton's most important decisions and/or actions to address those challenges and achieve results?

3. What were the most important management processes that Bratton established at NYPD? What were they designed to do?

NYPD New

Commissioner William Bratton and his executive staff could take satisfaction in the progress made by the New York Police Department (NYPD) toward goals they had set at the outset of 1994 to reduce major crimes in the City. Their efforts had produced better results than even some of them had expected, better even than portrayed in the popular television drama carrying the Department's name. So much better, in fact, that the Commissioner recently had trumpeted the City's rapidly improving crime record to a bond rating agency responsible for rating New York City's debt, pointing out that improvements in quality of life would have an eventual favorable impact on the City's desirability as a place to do business, further strengthening its credit-worthiness.

Although the Department was in the process of delivering results desired by the City's residents, many questioned whether and how the highly-publicized, results-oriented emphasis of Bratton's first twenty-four months as Commissioner could be sustained. (Exhibit 1 contains a report of New York's crime statistics compared with other major U.S. cities.)

As Bratton's team of deputy commissioners (civilians) and chiefs (uniformed personnel) gathered in his office on a morning in late January, 1996, he pondered the appropriate strategy that would enable his organization to continue to produce results with the budget shortfalls that the City was experiencing. The Thursday, January 25 copy of the *New York Times* on his desk, the very same desk used by Teddy Roosevelt when he was Police Commissioner 100 years earlier, carried a front page article headlined, "Giuliani (Rudolph Giuliani, the Mayor of New York) Weighing Cuts to Police to Help Decrease Budget Deficit." It was no surprise, in that it reflected his recent discussions with Mayor Giuliani, whose administration faced a $2 billion (6%) deficit in fiscal 1995 in spite of significant efforts to reduce the budget.

Bratton opened his weekly Executive Staff meeting by pointing out that achieving a further 10% reduction in major crimes during 1996 was beginning to pale in difficulty and complexity to several other challenges facing the Department. These included reduction in funding from the City, restrictions on ways the Department could deploy its resources and reward performance, and the difficulty of sustaining the momentum that had produced greatly improved results in the past two years. After pointing out that the department was "going into a very stressful year," Bratton challenged his deputies to be as creative in responding to these new challenges as they had in reducing crime.

History

Founded in 1845, the New York Police Department was the largest municipal police organization in the U.S. At various times in its history, it had been a model for big city policing. However, like other large municipal police organizations, its work was measured in terms of effort, such as the speed with which 911 (emergency) calls were answered and the number of patrols dispatched. From time to time, it had experienced periodic claims of corruption and police brutality.

As Bratton described it:

> We, as an organization, like many police departments in America during the 1970s and 1980s, became very reactive in our approach to crime . . . the traditional or professional policing model that was made up of rapid response: Dial 911 and we'll come very quickly . . . We focused on random patrol as the chief preventive measure—the idea that all these cars riding around would scare the criminals into submission. (Additionally), there was reactive investigation, something we always had done-after-the-fact investigation. And it was often controlled by a strong, centralized organization; in the case of the NYPD, you had to go up to the top of the organization to make even the most basic decisions.[1]

The concept of community policing began to sweep police departments in the U.S. in the late 1980s. Under this concept, individual of-

ficers, often the youngest members of the force, were encouraged to spend more time in the neighborhoods, maintain more visibility, gain the confidence of the citizens of a neighborhood, and collect information that would lead to efforts to deter crime. Nevertheless, specialized units trained to handle particular types of crimes, especially those that were drug-related, continued to exist. This reflected a fear that some patrol officers might be tempted to become involved in corrupt activities, such as drug dealing, themselves. In general, community policing initiatives had created a tension between personnel deployment strategies designed to provide maximum visibility of officers and those designed to deal with high-crime areas.

Safe Streets, Safe City Program

In response to increases in crime of near-epidemic proportions, Mayor David Dinkins and the New York City Council had won approval from the State Legislature in 1991 to hire 6,000 officers and pay for them through increased property taxes and a 12.5% surcharge to the City's income tax. The bill specified the total head count of all police in the city to be achieved on August 1 of each year (38,310 for August 1, 1995).

The program, called Safe Streets, Safe City, was due to expire on June 20, 1996. It had been initiated under extensive potential pressures to take a tougher stance on crime. A proposal had been put forth by the Speaker of the City Council to maintain the surcharge, but to use it in the future to finance the repair of increasingly dilapidated schools.

Giuliani Assumes Office

The election of Mayor Rudolph Giuliani in November, 1993 opened a new era for the Department. Giuliani, a former U.S. Attorney for the Southern District of New York who had built his reputation as a tough fighter against corruption and organized crime, campaigned and won largely on a campaign that emphasized reductions in New York City's budget deficits and improved crime control. These were to be achieved largely by exempting the Police Department from cuts in budgets for uniformed personnel, cuts that were implemented for nearly every other function of the City's government. However, Giuliani inherited a Police Department that was badly in need of new technology and methods. Work was done by hand that could otherwise be computerized. Communication systems were badly outdated. Often police officers were more poorly armed than the criminals they confronted.

There was a very low level of trust among senior officers as well as between the leadership and the rank-and-file in the Department. One graphic example of this was the denial of access codes to automated criminal history files. Because of this policy, designed to limit misuse of information, officers in one precinct could not gain access to information about crimes committed outside the precinct. As a result, it was nearly impossible for an arresting officer to check a suspect's criminal record. Focus group meetings with frontline patrol people yielded responses such as "this place is not on the level" and "our bosses don't want to fight crime." John Linder, a communications consultant who, as part of an ongoing organization change effort, conducted a survey of what patrol officers believed the Department wanted from them, cited as most important: write summonses, hold down overtime, stay out of trouble, and clear the 911 backlog, in that order. Fighting crime was seventh on the list.

One of Giuliani's first actions was to appoint William Bratton, Police Commissioner of Boston, to a similar post in New York. He was sworn in on January 10, 1994.

Giuliani's New Police Commissioner

A product of a working class family in Dorchester, Massachusetts whose father held full-time jobs in a metal-plating shop by day and the post office at night, William Bratton credited his first police job as a patrolman in Mattapan, a tough neighborhood of Boston, with giving him the self-assurance that some of his detractors tended to regard as bravado. The experience led him, according to one account, to develop

> . . . a particularly powerful distaste for precinct bosses who stayed away from volatile situations and weighed in afterward with criticism of their subordinates. "When I was working District Fourteen, in Boston, we had a major broo-ha in one of the public parks, and every cop in the district was there . . . There were two sergeants, old-school guys, back in the station, and we were calling for P.S."—patrol supervisors—"and neither one of those bastards would come out. They were two cowards hiding in the station house. We had a lot of them like that in Boston. They didn't want to see anything."[2]

Bratton came to the job of Commissioner with a clear understanding of the problems of police administration in New York City. Before assuming the job that quickly led to his being named Commissioner of Boston's Police Department, he had served as the chief of the New York City Transit Police Department between 1990 and 1992. During that time, he had helped transform a somewhat demoralized force policing a transit system confronting increased robbery, fare beating, and a homeless population of about 5,000 living in transit facilities into an effective deterrent to these problems.

Bratton was an avid reader of management literature and fan of war movies. He occasionally referred to citizens as "customers," criminals as "competition," police officers as "sales representatives," and reduced crime as "profit." He and his wife, Cheryl Fiandaca, a former criminal-defense lawyer who was teaching at the John Jay College of Criminal Justice, lived with five cats and a dog in a two-bedroom apartment on Central Park South and were frequently seen at cultural events as well as some of the City's better restaurants.

At about the time Bratton was appointed to head up the transit police, Jack Maple, a lieutenant in the transit police, came to the attention of the Commissioner through a plan for reducing crime that he had drafted. Maple, given to drinking espresso and wearing bow ties, blazers, and two-tone wing-tip spectator shoes (with a homburg hat in winter), was a sartorial opposite of Bratton (who tended toward Hermes animal ties) and a somewhat distinctive sight even on the streets of New York. (According to Maple, he adopted the dress because, as a short, stocky person, he attracted no attention in his youth as a conventional dresser.) The two hit if off immediately, with Maple, labeled by one journalist as "the Police Department's secret crime-fighting weapon," becoming a co-architect of a plan to turn the Transit Police Department around. As Bratton said more than once to those curious about his attraction to Maple, "Jack grows on you."

The program to transform the transit police was focused on two main thrusts. The first involved an effort to deter petty as well as major crimes committed on the system by attacking "quality of life" misdemeanors. For example, "sweeps" by officers in plain clothes were organized to arrest those avoiding fares ("fare beaters"). The search that was done routinely after arrest often yielded weapons which served to deter more serious crime. In Bratton's words, "A search or the threat of one is, in itself, a deterrent to crime because it encourages people to stop carrying guns." In fact, searches of fare beaters alone had turned up more than 400 concealed weapons in the first year.

The second thrust involved equipping the police with 9 mm. weapons with larger magazines, new autos, and new uniforms to improve their image in their own eyes as well as the public's.

Challenges and Responses: First Steps

Challenges facing the Department in early 1994 included a restive public that had swept Giuliani into office in part for his promises of safer streets; a somewhat demoralized police force whose "business was to stay out of trouble, not to police the city," according to John Linder; and a prior administrative focus on effort (number of patrols dispatched) vs. results (crime reduction).

According to one member of Bratton's executive staff, "there was widespread backbiting, fear of failure, and low performance. The structure of the organization was completely top-down. The Department lacked focus, and without focus a police department can end up being a municipal yo-yo." A former Precinct Commander said that the attitude of the senior staff had been, "You people in the precincts just make work for us."

Upon assuming office, Bratton quickly replaced a number of senior staff members, the largest organization shake-up in some time. Having decided that primary responsibility for day-to-day operations would reside with the 76 precinct commanders, a systematic effort was instituted to determine which of them could adapt to a strategy focused on results. Eventually, three-fourths of all precinct commanders Bratton inherited were moved out of their jobs. In his first 24 months on the job, the average age of the Commissioner's senior staff had fallen from the low 60s to the mid 40s. Bratton took great satisfaction in the result, saying "I would pit my command staff against any *Fortune* 500 company."

Bratton's reputation among police officers as a "cop's commissioner" was reinforced during his first week on the job as he began pushing for weapons with larger 15-round magazines that he had secured for his transit police several years earlier. These had become the envy of, and a source of resentment among, members of the main force required to use non-automatic weapons. Improved bullet-proof vests were ordered along with darker uniforms that conveyed a more authoritative image.

Word got around rapidly among police that this was a commissioner who "backed you up" but who would not hesitate to take disciplinary action if necessary. He was quick to obtain reliable information and, where appropriate, defend officers accused of excessive force. But in the situation involving the disclosure of widespread police corruption in the 30th Precinct just three months into his administration, Bratton accompanied the arresting force, personally removing the badges of offending officers. Later, he called all precinct commanders to headquarters, threw the badges on the table, and announced to the assembled group that he was retiring the badges so that no other police officer would ever have to wear them. A short time later, however, he emphasized to a reporter that he had "no intention of becoming an anticorruption zealot."

The public saw in Bratton an articulate spokesman capable of relating to their concerns. Shortly after taking office, he began making frequent references, both inside and outside the Department, to "taking the City back from criminals one block, one street, and one neighborhood at a time." In contrast to Bratton's popularity with the public, reporters used adjectives like "mouthy" and "cocksure" to describe him. One commented that he had a "consuming interest in media relations." Bratton was so effective in these encounters that some reporters sensed a growing rivalry between him and the Mayor, something that both denied.

"Quality-of-Life" Legislation

Mayor Giuliani, prompted by polls showing that New Yorkers were concerned about a declining "quality of life," characterized by more graffiti and vagrancy, promised to enforce existing laws against those committing what were termed "quality of life" misdemeanors, including urinating in public, spraying graffiti, and disorderly conduct. Much as had been done at the Transit Police Department, police were marshaled to reduce "quality of life" misdemeanors thought to be most important by the citizenry. In the first quarter of 1994, for example, arrests of peddlers, public drinkers, and squeegee cleaners increased 38%, summonses increased 40%, and sales tax violation citations increased 49% over the previous year. The effort achieved its greatest notoriety when it was used to go after what came to be known as "squeegee pests," people who approached stopped autos, cleaned their windshields, and demanded money from their occupants. Squeegee pests were warned then arrested. By increasing efforts begun in mid-1993, squeegee pests practically vanished from the streets by spring of 1994.

In addition, existing laws were used, for example, to arrest graffiti "artists" who spray-painted municipal and other property as well as slum landlords who had allowed their properties to fall into a state of disarray. The theory behind these efforts had two different rationales. The first was the "broken windows" theory that if a broken window is not fixed in a building, soon all windows will be broken. It held that people engaging in one kind of misdemeanor might be inclined to commit others as well, especially that of carrying a concealed or unlicensed gun. Heightened enforcement of these laws resulted in an increased number of searches and increased questioning in a process that turned up several hundred weapons in the first six months of the initiative. Commissioner Bratton referred to these practices as the "linchpin" in his crime-fighting strategies. The idea was not new; when it had been proposed by a consultant to Bratton's predecessor, he had responded, "Give me 50 guys, suspend the Constitution, and we can do that."

Process and Organization Reengineering

Commissioner Bratton often referred to the work of his team as "reengineering an underperforming organization." The fame of the Department and pride of its police officers made this particularly difficult. According to Bratton, "Two years ago, the NYPD, like the emperor, had no clothes. This was an organization that was living on reputation."[3] To help, Bratton hired a consultant, John Linder, who had assisted him previously in Boston.

Linder's "Cultural Diagnostic"

Linder set about to collect data, change perceptions, and provide the basis for action through a detailed questionnaire, called a "cultural diagnostic," that encouraged members of the Department to disclose their feelings about their jobs in return for a promise of anonymity. Based on the returns from this "diagnostic," focus groups were organized in which respondents were promised anonymity in exchange for uncensored opinions. According to this report:

> John Miller, NYPD spokesman . . . says that cops, trained to defend the Department's image, detested Linder's therapy. "They hated the idea that they had to say it out loud. Linder put these guys through a bureaucratic AA meeting. You had to admit you had a problem, and you had to recount for everyone else in the group how long you'd had the problem and how serious it was."[4]

Reengineering Teams

Based on the results of Linder's effort, Bratton organized 300 members of the Department into 12 teams asked to address the following themes: building community partnerships, geographical vs. functional organizational structure, precinct organization, supervisory training, in-service training, productivity, paperwork, integrity, rewards and career paths, discipline, equipment

and uniforms, and technology. Management thought leaders such as Jack Welch and Michael Hammer were brought in to address the teams. The process produced more than 600 recommendations, 80% of which were implemented.

Resulting changes ranged from the obvious to the complex. For example, one early finding from the paperwork team was that there were at least 4,000 forms in active use within the Department. John Linder commented that the forms played a very distinctive role in the personnel strategies of previous administrations:

> These forms were used to hang people down the food chain. As an officer, you had two choices. Either you filled out the form wrong and got flogged for it. Or you filled it out properly and accurately and were asked, "Why didn't you do something about this?" Either way, you couldn't win.

Bratton himself cited several obvious problems with what he termed "bankers' hours":

> The auto-theft squad was working nine to five, and the drug units were mostly working ten to six, with a few going two to ten . . . The warrant unit was getting started at 7:30 a.m., and by the time they read the papers and had their coffee, it was ten before they'd start knocking on doors. The department was not really minding the store.[5]

Another study found that the average amount of police officer overtime associated with an arrest was 12 hours. It resulted from the fact that much of an officer's involvement in the preparation and presentation of a complaint by a district attorney had to be done in person, although it was solely within the discretion of a D.A. to alter the process. Because overtime was an important source of income for many officers, they did not complain about the waste of their time in the arrest and complaint process.

In the process of reengineering the organization, a reporting level was eliminated. This meant that precinct commanders, who formally reported to one of 17 division commanders, now reported directly to eight bureau commanders.

Because the incidence of drugs and guns often occurred in overlapping geographic patterns, specialized drug units were replaced with Strategic Narcotics and Gun teams who investigated situations involving both. In addition, new crime control strategies purposely required the formation of teams designed to break down the barriers that had separated the Patrol, Detective, and Organized Crime Control Bureaus.

Development of the Strategies

Many of the ideas developed by the reengineering teams made their way into seven strategies, written by Linder, each of which were published in separate booklets designed for wide distribution under seven titles: (1) Getting Guns off the Streets of New York, (2) Curbing Youth Violence in the Schools and on the Streets, (3) Driving Drug Dealers out of New York, (4) Breaking the Cycle of Domestic Violence, (5) Reclaiming the Public Spaces of New York, and (6) Reducing Auto-Related Crime in New York. In response to continuing concerns about police corruption, a seventh strategy was added in mid-1995 titled, "Police Strategy No. 7: Rooting out Corruption; Building Organizational Integrity in the New York Police Department."

Each strategy statement contained a statement of the problem, current practice, specific conditions warranting the strategy, the strategy itself, and changes in laws as well as departmental policies and procedures that would be necessary to facilitate the strategy.

Excerpts from Strategy No. 5 are shown in Exhibit 2. When first developed, the strategies were labeled "bullshit" by many frontline police officers. Attitudes had begun to change with their implementation.

Organization

Police work in New York City traditionally had been carried out in three separate organizations. One force was entrusted with general public safety. Another dealt with police work associated with housing issues. The third concerned itself with crime on the city's transit system. One of the new Commissioner's first objectives was to implement the merger of these three departments, a high priority of the new mayor. The three forces were consolidated in April 1995. The job structure and headcounts for the consolidated department are described in Exhibit 3. Exhibit 4 contains an organization chart for the Department.

Management by the Numbers

Among the more important initiatives of the new administration were a new emphasis on results vs. effort, reinforced by efforts to computerize statistics and graphics formerly organized by hand, as well as the institution of twice-weekly "CompStat" (computerized crime comparison statistics) crime-strategy meetings based on the more-current information. In addition to introducing new performance measures based on this information, other initiatives involved giving more authority to the 76 precinct commanders, redefining the role of the officers policing neighborhoods, reengineering processes, and introducing new technology. All of this effort, and the results it would produce, was a topic of some debate among those knowledgeable about police work and crime control.

New Performance Measures

New performance measures were instituted for precinct commanders. Instead of being measured on the amount of effort put forth by their units, they would now be held accountable for the quality of their plans for dealing with crime problems. Increased emphasis was placed on efforts thought to lead to crime reduction. These included the proportion of people arrested and searched in connection with misdemeanors and the frequency with which those arrested had their past police records checked at the time they were identified and searched. According to Deputy Commissioner Maple: "You don't get into trouble for increased crime, but for not having a strategy to deal with it."

Performance was monitored daily by the NYPD's leadership. As Bratton put it, "Can you imagine running a bank if you couldn't look at your bottom line every day?"

Results vs. Effort: Reducing Crime

Whether or not crime could be reduced was a matter of some debate among criminologists and sociologists. Since a study commissioned by the Johnson Administration, "The Challenge of Crime in a Free Society," was published in 1967, it had become conventional wisdom to assume that most inner-city crime was the inevitable product of poverty and racism. Among the theories used to explain a widespread decline in major crime in large cities between 1991 and 1995 were an improved economy, a smaller number of young males (representing an especially high crime risk in the population), increased numbers of drug dealers either dead or in jail, a switch from crack cocaine (a violence-inducing drug) to heroin (a depressant) as the drug of choice in cities, the settlement of many gang "turf wars," and reduced racism.[6] Rarely was credit given to police ability to control the rate of crime. All of this was perceived by members of the Department as devaluing its recent achievements. One newspaper columnist suggested that the reason for the striking results achieved by the Department was that New Yorkers were not reporting crime as frequently as in the past. One of Bratton's predecessors even suggested that the trends were the result of a conscious decision on the part of drug dealers that crime (other than drug dealing) was bad for business.

In response, Bratton pointed to the dramatic results achieved in New York in contrast to other major cities. He argued that most of the theories that discounted the NYPD's recent accomplishments essentially assumed that all police departments were equally effective, a thesis that would be hard to defend. Instead of measuring and rewarding effort, their approach involved identifying the causes of major crime and deploying resources to reduce the likelihood that crime would occur, effectively utilizing information and technology

For example, statistics suggested that there were three major circumstances associated with many murders: drugs, guns, and people with police records. Locations where drugs were dealt were well-known. People carrying licensed guns were known to the police; unlicensed guns were often found during police searches. With improved technology, such as cellular phones, quick checks could be run on the police records of individuals stopped for various offenses. By reallocating resources to places where drugs, guns, and people with prior records were found, dramatic reductions in murder could be achieved, according to this philosophy. This was accomplished by giving more authority to precinct commanders and holding them accountable for their performance numbers.

Precinct-Level Authority and Accountability

Prior to Bratton's administration, an emphasis on neighborhood policing had resulted in more police being placed "on the beat" in neighborhoods and more authority being given to them to deal with anti-crime initiatives at the grassroots level, calling in specialized experts from headquarters when necessary. Problems associated with this approach were that some neighborhoods were so crime-ridden that the young officers placed in them couldn't cope with the challenge. Novice police (most likely to be assigned foot patrol in the neighborhood police initiative) were less likely to use good judgment in threatening situations and often were lacking the human relations skills needed by neighborhood police. Precinct commanders had too little real control over the neighborhood police working for them, and resources were more difficult to allocate intelligently than under a plan that would place authority and accountability at a higher level. To correct the situation, Bratton's team decided to focus authority and accountability at the level of the precinct commanders.

The rationale for this action was that individuals at this level could bring sufficient deterrents to bear on difficult crime areas, resources could be reallocated from one "hot spot" to another within the precinct, results could be measured with greater consistency and reliability, and the precinct was a large enough unit to support its own specialized forces. Precinct commanders had been denied greater authority and accountability because it was feared that there was a risk of corruption if headquarters oversight could no longer be achieved through specialized services provided to the precincts.

As a result of this action, officers on neighborhood patrols were freed to concentrate their efforts on relating to neighborhood needs while obtaining leads on possible criminal activity.

The CompStat Meetings

If the precinct commander became the focal point for carrying out crime-reduction strategies, the CompStat meetings and associated activities became the engine for the effort. They were a product of Deputy Commissioner Jack Maple's favorite four-step philosophy for action, a philosophy that had become a mantra in the Department: (1) accurate, timely information, (2) rapid, focused deployment, (3) effective tactics, and (4) relentless follow-up and assessment. Prior to the initiation of the meetings, according to one senior staff member, "crime statistics were a way of keeping score at the end of the year, not a means for managing for results."

What became known as the "Louie and Jack Show," twice-weekly CompStat (computerized statistics) meetings, required precinct commanders to be ready to review their up-to-date computer-generated crime statistics and relate what they were going to be doing to achieve crime reduction. They were led by Chief of Department Louis Anemone and Deputy Commissioner Jack Maple and were held in the Department's "War Room," containing a number of large computer-fed screens and other devices for displaying statistics, at Headquarters in Lower Manhattan. A reporter sitting in on one meeting described it as follows:

> Maple called the precinct commanders to the front of the room in turn, questioning, prodding, cajoling, and occasionally teasing information out of them. They discussed ongoing investigations, special operations, and any unusual criminal activity. When the men and women from the 81st Precinct got their call, they were asked to explain a recent spate of shootings.
>
> "What's going on?" Maple wanted to know. "Why are these shootings happening? Is it a turf war? No? Well, somebody's not happy. Maybe they're cranky 'cause it's hot, but something's happening." When the shooting locations were put up on the huge map projected on the wall, along with those of drug complaints in the precinct, there was a clear overlap. Maple asked what was being done about the drug spots, and one of the narcotics officers said it was a tough area because the business was done inside and there were lots of lookouts. "That's fine," Maple said. "That's why we're detectives. Tell me what tactics we can employ to penetrate these locations." The detective said they would try some buy-and-bust operations and maybe get a couple of the guys behind the Plexiglas to rat when an arrest was hanging over their heads. Maple wasn't satisfied.

"I want you back here next week with a plan," he said to the precinct captain (normally each precinct comes in once every five weeks).[7]

In order to respond to the kinds of questions posed at CompStat meetings, precinct commanders began bringing with them to the meetings representatives from other bureaus (such as detectives) who were assigned to their precincts. The meetings thus encouraged inter-bureau coordination.

CompStat meetings had become well-known throughout the police world. Given the growing success of the Department, they were visited by police administrators and journalists from other parts of the U.S. and other countries. According to one precinct commander, "If your numbers don't look good, these meetings are not fun." Data displayed at a typical CompStat meeting is presented in Exhibit 5.

In addition to organizing CompStat meetings, Chief Anemone and Deputy Commissioner Maple toured the precinct commands, covering as many as 15 in a weekend. During these visits they checked to see, among other things, whether crime strategy maps were up-to-date, proper instructions were being given to patrol officers at roll-call, and communications from headquarters were displayed prominently.

Introduction of New Technology

Efforts to collect, organize, and display crime information by computer, part of a larger effort to modernize the Department's information systems, had required an investment of $500,000. They had become a cornerstone of the Department's strategy, and were thought to have a high return.

New uses of video conferencing technology allowed officers to interact with district attorneys in precincts in order to reduce the average time, much of it overtime, associated with the arrest-to-arraignment process from 14 to a goal of 2 hours. This was critically important in a po-lice force with wages averaging $24 per hour. (At least one district attorney, when advised of the costs incurred by current procedures, had even approved the use of the telephone for an officer's involvement in the arrest process).

Other technology-based initiatives, supported by a newly passed Federal Crime Bill and private sector donations, included the purchase of precinct-based computers and mapping software to develop crime analysis capabilities at the precinct level. Over $14 million of Federal Crime Bill funding also enabled the department to fully implement a larger decentralized arrest processing system project which would be critical to cutting arrest-to-arraignment time through the implementation of videoconferencing, Livescan computerized fingerprinting, photo imaging and enhancing the LAN network.

Continuing Challenges

New York City, according to FBI statistics, accounted for 61% of the total reduction in serious crimes for the entire U.S. during the first six months of 1995. Although Commissioner Bratton and his team could take satisfaction from this, it was clear that the job ahead would be made even more challenging by budgetary limitations, possible changes in the process for arbitrating labor wage disputes, restrictions on the deployment of resources, and the inability to reward good performance, all combined with the need to achieve higher productivity. Corruption within the Department was an issue that had to be given continuing attention. There was a persistent belief by some that the price of crime reduction, in terms of reduced civil rights, was high. And finally, it had become apparent that it would take much longer than two years to effect the attitude changes in the police force that were sought. As consultant Linder commented, "It's clear that the message hasn't filtered down into the ranks." But it would be difficult to sustain the high-intensity effort that had characterized Bratton's first two years in office.

All of this had to be achieved in an organization that had to be operated within constraints imposed by its public-sector nature. Exhibit 6 represents one view of basic differences between management in the NYPD and private-sector organizations.

Budgetary Limitations

Non-discretionary accounts dominated the Department's annual budget of about $2.3 billion, as shown in Exhibit 7. They covered salaries, overtime, shift differentials, uniform allowances, annuity payments and holiday pay for employees, and resulted largely from head counts that were mandated by Safe Streets, Safe City and other legislation as well as wage policies that were determined in large part by linkages between 81 labor contracts that the City had with various labor unions, including the police officers' union.

In discussions with the Mayor, it was clear that City Hall expected savings from payroll and other sources of at least $20 to $30 million in 1996. This was on top of budgetary constraints that had been placed on the Department's OTPS (other than personal services) accounts in 1994 and 1995. In an effort to maintain the size of the police force in service, as promised by the Mayor in his election campaign, the OTPS budget had been cut by 30% (down to $95 million) for fiscal 1996. This had to cover expenditures for such items as supplies, equipment, telephones, fuel, and rent. Some of the results were almost laughable. Jack Maple, for example, pointed out that his unit couldn't afford the supplies needed to display crime information in his office.

Perhaps the most significant cuts in discretionary budgets had come from overtime reduction. This account had been reduced from $113 million in 1993 to $79 million in 1995. While this had helped the Department meet its budget goals, it had hurt morale among frontline officers in the Department who could no longer

count on overtime income to help with such things as mortgage payments.

It was quite possible that the Mayor was ready to consider reductions in the size of the police force, although it would be politically difficult for him to allow any of those reductions in the number of police on patrol. His attitude toward head count had begun to change with the possible expiration of the Safe Streets, Safe City initiative, and a significant change in the arbitration process for the City's negotiations with its police and firefighters unions which could increase pay levels significantly. When queried about whether he was ready to abandon the staffing level of 38,310 mandated by legislation, the Mayor had pointed out that, because of attrition, the Department typically operated for most of the year at levels up to 1,800 persons fewer than those mandated.

Labor Contract Dispute Arbitration

Led by the Patrolmen's Benevolent Association of New York City, the State Legislature had passed and sent to the Governor for signature legislation shifting responsibility for contract dispute arbitration from the City's Office of Collective Bargaining to the State Public Employment Relations Board. It was thought that this action would result in larger salary increases from future arbitration. In its deliberations, the City's agency was required to consider such things as the City's ability to pay awards. In contrast, the State agency was required to take into consideration pay levels of communities surrounding New York City, which were as much as 35% higher than those in the City.

The bill, although vetoed previously by the Governor, had passed with only 8 legislators out of 200 opposing it. Previously, union officials had said they would make passage of the bill a litmus test for lawmakers when they allocated their much-coveted political campaign contributions.

The Mayor publicly had expressed his opposition to the bill and had asked the Governor not to sign it, weathering the criticism of the unions that had supported his political campaign. Privately, he had discussed with Commissioner Bratton whether or not deeper budget cuts would be required if the legislation were to be enacted. On January 25, alongside the report of the progress of the legislation, the *New York Times* reported that:

> Preliminarily, the Mayor has ordered each of his agencies to cut their budgets for the next fiscal year by 7.5 percent, although he has not said that each would have to cut that much. For the Police Department, a cut that size would total $170 million, from a $2.3 billion budget. It remained unclear yesterday what other cuts, if any, (other than 1,000 personnel from the Department yielding estimated savings of $20 to $30 million) would be considered for the Police Department.[8]

Possible Sources of Staffing Reductions

If staffing reductions were required, the Commissioner could achieve them through attrition, which occurred at the rate of about 1,600 police officers and 500 civilians annually, and a postponement of the starting date for the Police Academy class that graduated about 1,800 new recruits each year. The latter would, however, slow down Bratton's efforts to improve the overall quality of Department personnel by imposing tougher entry standards and an improved training program.

This might also require combining positions and moving more officers from "desk jobs" to patrols. In 1995 alone, 500 officers were freed for patrol work who had previously staffed public affairs, personnel, and payroll units prior to the merger of New York City's three police forces.

Restrictions on Resource Deployment

The Safe Streets, Safe City initiative, which established staffing targets for each precinct of the City, was a reflection of a general feeling on the part of residents that each precinct should have its "fair share" of police protection. These targets, which reflected conditions in the City in 1989, influenced the assignment of Police Academy graduates. As a result, precinct staffing levels were difficult to adjust to reflect changing police needs. (See Exhibit 8 for demographic and crime statistics as well as staffing levels for four precincts and Exhibit 9 for a precinct map of the City.) Most people still had not accepted the argument that crime reduction in heavily impacted crime areas would lead to less crime in low-crime neighborhoods, just as many had trouble believing that searches of those committing minor misdemeanors would eventually lead to reductions in serious crimes.

According to Jack Maple, while specialized units, such as Street Crime (plain clothes), Narcotics, and Vice, could be moved from one precinct to another for 30 days at a time, fully 18,000 frontline patrol personnel "couldn't be moved at a whim."

Nevertheless, he cited the 9th Precinct experience as evidence that moving specialized units worked. He pointed out that the Precinct had started out the first four months of 1995 with major crimes 50% over the previous year. By the end of the year, with the redeployment of specialized units to the Precinct, such crimes were down 4%. Drawing on his extensive reading of military history, Maple cited British use of radar in WWII in defending against enemy aircraft as a model for what the Department should strive for. It provided the RAF with a way of deploying its personnel and equipment quickly.

While attempting to maintain adequate headcount in personnel assigned to precincts, Commissioner Bratton was contemplating assigning 750 of the 1,800 March, 1996 graduates of the Police Academy class to replace more-experienced officers reassigned to the Mayor's announced effort to wage an all-out war against drugs in Brooklyn North. The resulting specialized units would be assigned to ten precincts in which drug-dealing was especially high. This, of course, would make it more difficult to replace frontline personnel in the remaining precincts.

The Brooklyn North initiative would involve the temporary reassignment of 1,200 officers from elsewhere in the Department to the shaded area outlined in Exhibit 9. Reassignments would be made from all bureaus. The initiative had created an air of anticipation and excitement in the Department. It was also thought to be a test of conventional thinking regarding restrictions on the deployment of resources.

Rewarding Performance

Jack Maple pointed out that police officers hadn't had a raise in spite of their increasing levels of effectiveness. The situation had been made more tense by the fact that the City Council had voted senior City officials, including a small number of Police Department officials, pay raises up to 20% as of July, 1995. These officials hadn't received pay raises for eight years.

Union labor contracts and civil service statutes made it very difficult to reward outstanding performance. The primary form of monetary incentives was provided by overtime, which had been reduced significantly through the application of stricter management accountability as well as the increased use of technology.

Other forms of recognition commonly employed within the Department were the temporary assignment of patrol officers to work with detective squads for 30 days and other preferred assignments. More often, a simple letter of recognition was written.

Increased Productivity

A declining budget would require increased productivity if the Department was to meet its goal for 1996. Staffing data for major U.S. cities is presented in Exhibit 10.

Along with the increased use of information and technology, more controversial means could

be attempted to improve productivity. For example, officers could be freed up for other tasks by replacing two-person patrols with one officer. But the outcry from officers, who had fought hard for two-person patrols on the grounds of increased safety, would be great.

Addressing Rising Complaints

With increased enforcement activities and personnel, there had been a 32% increase in 1994 in the number of complaints about police brutality, unfair treatment of citizens by police, and police corruption over the past two years. The Department's analysis of its information disclosed that

> . . . in 1994 . . . 4 million calls for service were answered in person by officers, 227,453 arrests were made, 5.4 million summonses were written—with a total of 9,922 complaints made by the public for police misconduct. Of the 2,152 cases reviewed in 1994 by the Civilian Complaint Review Board, an independent arm of city government, 5.1% (or 111 cases) were determined by CCRB to be worthy of prosecution in the Department's disciplinary process.

In February 1995, the Mayor created an independent citizens monitor, the Commission to Combat Police Corruption. At the time, plans already were underway in the Department to take steps to correct a situation disclosed in an early-1994 survey of Department personnel that found that "a long-standing, high-level concern about avoiding scandal and criticism had created within the NYPD a culture of organizational fear, self-protection, secrecy, and exclusion— which existed alongside continuing, everyday heroic action by individual members of the service."

Rooting Out Corruption

On June 14, 1995 Police Strategy No. 7: Rooting Out Corruption; Building Organizational Integrity in the New York Policy Department, was published. One of the biggest challenges of this initiative was described in the Strategy as follows:

> . . . Contemporary corruption in the NYPD occurs in pockets which, despite universal disapproval among honest officers, are protected by the "blue wall of silence." The tradition of not "ratting" on colleagues is common in most professions, but it is even more pronounced in police and military organizations where members sometimes rely on each other for physical survival. Mutual protection under violent circumstances becomes mutual protection under all . . . The "us versus them" attitude often called the "blue cocoon" can seem to condone disrespect of the public and even abuse of force in these same police and military organizations.

To counteract these tendencies, efforts were initiated to energize the Department's own investigative group, the Internal Affairs Bureau (IAB). This was to be done by changing the entire dynamic by which the IAB interacted with Department personnel. In the past, the relationship had been one of distrust, involving obsessive secrecy on the part of the IAB and an unwillingness to cooperate on the part of police officers. To change it, efforts were underway by the IAB to: (1) involve every command level in reducing corruption and brutality, (2) make available within the department monthly reports for each command on complaints broken down to the level of the precinct and even tour of duty, (3) computerize master profiles of individual officers that cross-referenced data on corruption, brutality, and discourtesy complaints with that regarding record of sick leave, emergency excusal, arrest activity, commendations, and disciplinary actions, (4) provide training to those in command positions about the detection of patterns leading to corruption. As part of a more proactive approach to deterrence, the IAB was encouraged to observe officers as they interacted

with IAB officers posing as civilians who might provide opportunities to commit crimes. In addition, the IAB would continue to initiate parallel investigations of complaints brought before the Civilian Complaint Review Board and implement Commissioner Bratton's order to stop giving one day's notice for random drug tests, which had enabled those tested to prepare.

To support the new policy of inclusion concerning issues of corruption, Strategy No. 7 set forth a new policy advocating consideration of a commander's entire record of performance rather than the career-ending loss of command that previously often had resulted when corruption was discovered in any of their units.

Sustaining the Effort

There was some question about whether the efforts of the first two years could be sustained, especially by a Department whose personnel had not received pay raises. As Jack Maple put it: "Armies like to fight short wars. We're slowin' down."

Notes

1. Marie Simonetti Rosen, "Moving the Biggest Mountain," *Law Enforcement News,* June 30, 1995, pp. 8–10. The word in parentheses is the author's.

2. James Lardner, "The C.E.O. Cop," *The New Yorker,* February 6, 1995, pp. 45–57, at p. 53.

3. Chris Smith, "The NYPD Guru," *New York,* April 1, 1996, pp. 28–34, at p. 31.

4. Smith, "The NYPD Guru," p. 31.

5. Craig Horowitz, "The Suddenly Safer City," *New York,* August 14, 1995, p. 25.

6. Most of these trends were not true for New York City.

7. Horowitz, "The Suddenly Safer City," pp. 21–25.

8. Steven Lee Meyers, "Giuliani Weighing Cuts to Police To Help Decrease Budget Deficit," *The New York Times,* January 25, 1996, pp. Al and B3.

Exhibit 1

Report of Crime Trends in Major U.S. Cities

The percentage decrease in crime for New York City for 1995 vs. 1993 was 25.9%. This compared with a percentage decrease for the 27 of the 29 largest cities (excluding New York and Chicago) of 5.4%.

Total Crime Index for 29 Largest Cities,
Listed in Order of Population

City	1993	1995	+ − %
New York	600,346	444,758	−25.9%
Los Angeles	312,790	266,204	−14.9%
Chicago	*	*	*
Houston	141,179	131,602	−6.8%
Philadelphia	97,659	108,278	+10.9%
San Diego	85,227	64,235	−24.6%
Phoenix	96,476	118,126	+22.4%
Dallas	110,803	98,624	−11.0%
Detroit	122,329	119,065	v2.7%
San Antonio	97,671	79,931	−18.2%
San Jose	36,743	36,096	−1.8%
Indianapolis	33,530	30,775	−8.2%
Las Vegas	48,367	60,178	+24.4%
San Francisco	67,345	60,474	−10.2%
Baltimore	91,920	94,855	+3.2%
Jacksonville	67,494	61,129	−9.4%
Columbus	58,604	58,715	+1.9%
Milwaukee	50,435	52,679	+4.4%
Memphis	62,150	65,597	+5.5%
Washington, D.C.	66,758	67,402	+1.0%
El Paso	46,738	41,692	−10.8%
Boston	55,555	52,278	−6.0%
Seattle	62,679	55,507	−11.4%
Nashville	55,500	56,090	+1.0%
Austin	51,468	42,586	−17.6%
Denver	39,796	34,769	−12.6%
Cleveland	40,006	38,665	−3.4%
New Orleans	52,773	53,399	+1.2%
Fort Worth	*49,801*	*39,667*	*−20.3%*
TOTAL	2,101,796	1,988,408	−5.4%

*Data for Chicago is not included because of reporting differences.

Exhibit 2

Excerpts from the Communication to Police Describing Police Strategy 5: Reclaiming the Public Spaces of New York

NEW YORK CITY POLICE DEPARTMENT
WILLIAM J. BRATTON, POLICE COMMISSIONER

FYI

July 8, 1994   Vol. 2 No. 11

"Reclaiming the Public Spaces of New York"

Police Strategy No. 5

On Wednesday, July 6th, Mayor Giuliani and I made public this Department's ambitious agenda for combating the wide range of criminal behavior we commonly refer to as quality-of-life offenses: street prostitution, aggressive panhandlers, sales of alcohol to minors, graffiti vandalism, public urination, unlicensed peddlers, reckless bicyclists and ear-splitting noise churned out by "boombox" cars, loud motorcycles, clubs and spontaneous street parties.

Legally, these crime and disorder problems are classified as misdemeanors and petty offenses. But in the hearts and minds of many New Yorkers, they carry felony weight. No one knows this better than you - the police officers, supervisors and precinct commanders who often hear local residents and merchants register their frustration at community meetings and on the beat.

Linchpin Strategy

Police Strategy No. 5, "Reclaiming the Public Spaces of New York," will serve as a linchpin, holding fast our overall efforts to significantly reduce crime and fear. Like our previous strategies, this plan builds on past successes and seeks to empower precinct commanders.

Tall Order

Clearly, the mayor and the Department's top leadership understand that we are asking a lot of you. Reversing what amounts to decades of declining standards for acceptable behavior on the city's streets is, after all, a tall order. It will take years of hard work. But we will make sure you have the training, the equipment and the support you need to get the job done.

Independence

First, the 75 precinct commanders will have more latitude and direct control over resources to meaningfully address specific quality of life conditions in their respective precincts. They will be relying less on other city agencies and the Department's specialized units, such as PMD, and more on the police officers and supervisors in their commands. For example, precincts battling chronic street prostitution were formerly dependent on fewer than 200 officers from Public Morals to run decoy operations. Now, commanders will be able to routinely deploy precinct personnel, trained by PMD, as undercovers to arrest individuals who patronize prostitutes (Operation John) or arrest "johns" and seize their cars (Operation Losing Proposition) - both formidable proven deterrents.

Similarly precincts with persistent "boombox" car conditions will be given sound meters and the training to conduct Operation Soundtrap to summons motorists and seize their cars.

Limiting Summonses

We are going to be more careful about who gets summonses

Additionally, we are compiling a computerized list of about 10,000 misdemeanor recidivists. Individuals with a history of five or more misdemeanor arrests within the last five years will not be eligible for DATs. Quite simply, we want summonses and DATs to be worth the paper they are written on. The time you spend issuing them is too valuable to waste.

Learning Civil-ity

The Department will continue to make the most of civil laws to put smoke shops, crack houses, illegal massage parlors and other criminal enterprises out of business. We have doubled the Police Department's Civil Enforcement Initiative to make a total of 34 attorneys available to assist precincts.

PRIDE, COMMITMENT, RESPECT

Exhibit 2 (continued)

Chronic EDPs

On June 1st, we kicked off a 90-day pilot program regarding emotionally disturbed people who pose a danger to themselves or others. Our goals are twofold: provide doctors, judges and prosecutors with information they need to make decisions and reduce the amount of time you spend guarding EDPs in hospital emergency rooms. We're partners in this program with Bellevue and Elmhurst Hospitals, the city Health and Hospitals Corporation, the state and city Offices of Mental Health and John Jay. We will closely evaluate its progress.

Moreover, we are developing a computer database of emotionally disturbed persons repeatedly taken into police custody so behavior that is either criminal or otherwise dangerous can be brought to the immediate attention of judges, prosecutors and psychiatrists.

Under-age Drinking

Precinct commanders who have identified bars, delis and clubs that persistently sell alcohol to minors will set up meetings with proprietors and representatives of the State Liquor Authority. Precinct captains and inspectors will explain the law, issue warnings and advise bar and deli owners that specially trained uniformed supervisors will be making regular inspections. Violators risk having their licenses revoked by the SLA. We will also expand our use of police cadets in sting operations.

Graffiti Vandalism

We will be making more use of night scopes to catch criminal mischief makers in the act. Additionally, Deputy Commissioner for Community Affairs Walter Alicea is organizing a conference to brainstorm ideas and duplicate successful programs (like one in the 104th Precinct) which combine education, vigorous enforcement and community service sentences for vandals.

Legislative Boost

Too often, police officers who earnestly try to address quality of life conditions are frustrated by a criminal justice system that fails to support your efforts. We have put together a legislative agenda to lobby for local laws against aggressive panhandling and reckless bicyclists, as well as state legislation allowing police to fingerprint unlicensed peddlers and motorists who drive with suspended licenses.

Meanwhile, we will assertively enforce existing statutes - harassment, assault, menacing, disorderly conduct and criminal mischief - to arrest aggressive panhandlers and others engaging in criminal behavior.

We know the most effective solutions to quality of life offenses combine sustained enforcement action, community involvement and a well coordinated effort by police, prosecutors, judges and other government agencies.

Finally, as the mayor and I stressed to reporters, this initiative will not take away from our strategies to get guns off the street, curb drug sales and reduce violent crime. It will, in fact, help.

As Chief of Department John F. Timoney puts it:

"If you take care of the little things, the big things will follow."

William J. Bratton

Exhibit 3

NYPD Structure and "Head Counts," by Position, January, 1996; and Staffing Levels, August, 1990 to March, 1996

Management Structure

The top management responsibilities in the NYPD were divided among uniformed managers called chiefs and civilian managers called deputy commissioners. Although there were important exceptions, the uniformed chiefs were primarily responsible for police operations and the civilian deputy commissioners oversaw various support functions such as budget, planning, community affairs and technology development.

The Police Commissioner, a civilian appointed by the mayor, was the chief executive officer of the police department with a wide range of responsibilities outside and inside the organization.

The Chief of Department was a four-star chief, the highest uniformed rank in the NYPD. He ran the day-to-day policing business. Reporting directly to the Chief of Department were five three-star bureau chiefs, also known as superchiefs, responsible for the Patrol Services Bureau, the Transit Bureau, and the Housing Bureau.

The Patrol Services Bureau (PSB) managed the 76 precinct commands which were overseen by eight borough commands. (Staffing: 20,838 uniformed personnel and 2,045 civilian personnel).

The Detective Bureau was the investigative arm of the department. There were detective squads in each of the precincts (usually commanded by a lieutenant) and reporting to detective borough commands. The borough commands also oversaw homicide and major crime squads. A traditional problem in the department had been a lack of coordination between detective and patrol operations because they had separate reporting structures in separate bureaus. (Staffing: 3,385 uniformed personnel and 305 civilian personnel).

The Organized Crime Control Bureau (OCCB) was established in 1971 on the heels of the Knapp Commission scandals to place all corruption-prone enforcement functions under a single, centralized command. Like the detective bureau, OCCB had a separate command structure, including divisions for Narcotics, Vice Enforcement, Auto Crime, and Organized Crime Investigations. (Staffing: 2,141 uniformed police and 108 civilians).

The Transit Bureau policed the city's vast subway system. The Transit patrol force worked out of 12 district commands supervised by four borough commands. The Transit Bureau also maintained a Homeless Outreach Unit, a Canine Unit and a Vandals Squad. (Staffing: 3,270 uniformed police and 181 civilians).

The Housing Bureau maintained nine police service areas (PSAs) to police the 330 public housing developments operated by the New York City Public Housing Authority. (Staffing: 2,155 uniformed police and 178 civilians).

Also reporting to the Chief of Department were the Operations Division, which managed major events and disaster response, and the Support Services Bureau, headed by a civilian director and responsible for the auto fleet, the property clerk, and other support services.

The reporting relationships described above were the formal ones. In practice, the Police Commissioner met with many managers besides his direct reports, and the deputy commissioners, bureau chiefs, and borough chiefs gathered for weekly executive staff meetings with the Police Commissioner, First Deputy Commissioner, and Chief of Department.

Exhibit 3 (continued)

Uniform Rank Structure

Police officers had a defined civil service career path. Up to the rank of captain, promotion was controlled by civil service exams for each rank. The entry rank was police officer and the successive ranks were sergeant, lieutenant, and captain. The department's 37,171 uniformed personnel, as of January, 1996 included 25,909 police officers, 4,229 sergeants, 1,365 lieutenants, and 391 captains. The ranks above captain were discretionary, but no one who had not attained the rank of captain could serve in them. There were 120 deputy inspectors, 65 inspectors, 27 deputy chiefs (one-star), 17 assistant chiefs (two-star), eight bureau chiefs (three-star) and one chief of department (four-star).

The title of detective was not a rank but a discretionary designation. Detectives were paid more than police officers of comparable rank and served in three grades, with Detective Third Grade being the lowest and Detective First Grade being the highest. Detectives retained their underlying civil service title (i.e. police officer). Most detectives served in the Detective Bureau, although there were numerous exceptions serving in other investigative and specialist assignments. There were about 5,000 detectives in the NYPD.

Most of the department's personnel were represented by unions, including all uniformed personnel up to and including the rank of deputy chief. Police officers were represented by the Patrolmen's Benevolent Association (LBA) and captains and all higher unionized ranks by the Captains Endowment Association (CEA). Among 37,171 uniformed personnel there were only 25 positions that are not unionized.

About 85 percent of the department's 6,800 civilian employees, including most clerical workers and the 911 operators, were represented by various locals of District Council 37, the union which represented the largest share of New York City municipal workers. About 10 percent were represented by the Teamsters Union, with the balance represented by the Communication Workers Union and other unions. Only 83 civilian managers were not unionized.

Staffing Levels, August, 1990 to March, 1996

Personnel Pool	August 22, 1990 (Pre-Safe Streets)	February 28, 1994 (Post-Safe Streets)	March 31, 1995 (Pre-Merger)	March 4, 1996 (Post-Merger)[a]
NYPD	25,465	31,532	29,985	32,134
Transit	4,288	4,216	4,280	3,139
Housing	2,200	2,565	2,804	2,038
Total uniform	31,953	38,311	37,069	37,311
Civilian	7,722	7,746	7,137	7,183
Total department	39,675	46,057	44,206	44,494

[a] Transit merged April 1, 1995; Housing merged May 1, 1995.

Exhibit 4

Organization Chart, New York Police Department, 1995

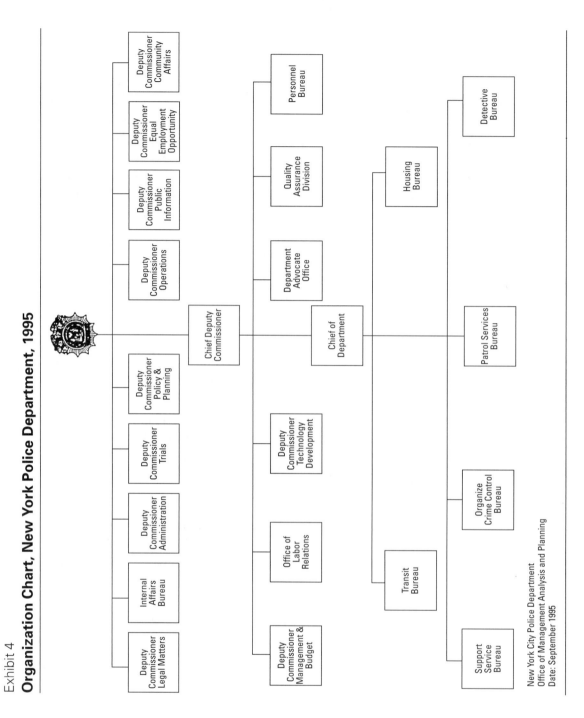

New York City Police Department
Office of Management Analysis and Planning
Date: September 1995

Exhibit 5
Example of Precinct-Level Data Displayed at CompStat Meetings

PRECINCT COMMANDER PROFILE

JOANNE JAFFE   033   PRECINCT   JOHN FREISEN

Rank: DEPUTY INSPECTOR   C.O. Prev Commands: 001 PCT

Years in Rank: 0yrs 6mos   Current Eval: 06/94-AS   Date Assigned C.O.: 12/04/95

Appointment Date: 11/07/79   Date of Promotion: 08/04/95

Education: BA,MA   Resident Pct:

Other Training: FBI TRAINING CONF

City Council Members: State Senator(s):
S.MICHAEL(D.7); G.LINARES(D.10)   F.LEICHTER, D.PATTERSON
                                                O.MENDEZ

COMMANDING OFFICER   Transit   Housing   Executive Officer
                            District: 03   PSA: 6
                            C.O.: DEP. INSP. JACKSON C.O.: CAPTAIN DUNNE
Precinct Demographics   Facilities: 174TH ST. YARD Facilities
Total: 0
White: 0.00 %
Black: 0.00 %
Hispanic: 0.00 %
Asian: 0.00 %
Amer Ind.:   0.00 %
Other: 0.00 %

Precinct Personnel

	pre-safe	1995	1996	%Change
Uniform	0	215	212	-1.40%
Civilian	0	17	15	-11.76%
RIP	No	***	***	***
Dom Viol	***	0	1	******%
Youth Off	***	0	3	******%
SNEU	***	0	7	******%

Unfounded Radio Runs

1994	1995	%Change	%CW95	%boro95
2758	11619	221.28	-9.94	-11.74

Domestic Violence (1995)

Radio Runs	DIR's	%Compliance
2198	1904	86.62

Uniform Absence (Avg. Days YTD)

1994	cw94	1995	cw95	LOD94	cwLOD94	LOD95	cwLOD95
0.00	5.76	4.95	6.31	0.00	3.93	1.92	2.96

Precinct Non-Crime

	1995	1996	%Change	%CW
RMP Acc	3	1	-66.67	14.59
Arr O/T	$0	$17179	....	-57.36
Oper O/T	$0	$10793	....	-27.93
Total O/T	$0	$44077	....	-26.69
Park Sum.	7395	6108	17.40	-10.09
Mov Sum.	1937	909	53.07	-31.38
Qual Life	830	632	23.86	-20.79

Integrity Monitoring

	1994	1995	%Change	%C/W	94ratio	95ratio
Bribe Arr	1	8	700.00	-21.7	1: 215.0	1:26.50
Tot CCIB	16	41	156.25	-7.70	1: 13.44	1: 5.17
Force	0	28	......	***	***	***
Abuse	0	12	....	***	***	***
Discourtesy	0	18		***	***	***
Off. Lang.	0	1	....	***	***	***

Legend: All Data through 01/31/96 except: Overtime, paid thru 02/02/96
Uniform Absence thru 12/31/95, Integrity Monitoring through 12/31/95,
Unfounded Radio Runs through 12/31/95, and Domestic Violence through 12/31/95.

Exhibit 5 (continued)

WEEKLY CRIME/COMPLAINT COMPARISON REPORT
REPORT COVERING THE WEEK OF 02/05/96 THROUGH 02/11/96

033 PRECINCT   Date Prepared: 02/13/96

CRIME COMPLAINTS

	1996 YTD	1995 YTD	%CHANGE	1996 MTD	1995 MTD	%CHANGE	1996 YTD	1995 YTD	CURRENT %CHANGE	1994 YTD	2 YEAR %CHANGE	1993 YTD	3 YEAR %CHANGE
MURDER	0	0	****%	0	0	****%	3	2	50.00%	5	****%	0	****%
RAPE	6	11	-45.45%	1	0	****%	8	6	33.33%	5	60.00%	0	****%
ROBBERY	8	12	-33.33%	13	17	-23.53%	73	65	12.31%	66	10.61%	0	****%
FEL. ASSLT	4	7	-42.85%	11	16	-31.25%	40	52	-23.08%	42	-4.76%	0	****%
BURGLARY	3	5	-40.00%	8	12	-33.33%	50	70	-28.57%	77	-35.06%	0	****%
GR. LARCENY	8	7	14.29%	7	9	-22.22%	26	48	-45.83%	31	-16.13%	0	****%
G.L.A.				11	11	0.00%	45	49	-8.16%	74	-39.19%	0	****%
TOTAL	30	42	-28.57%	51	65	-21.54%	245	292	-16.10%	295	-16.95%	0	****%
SHOOT VIC.	2	2	0.00%	2	2	0.00%	7	7	0.00%	6	16.67%	0	****%
SHOOT INC.	2	1	100.00%	2	1	100.00%	7	5	40.00%	6	16.67%	0	****%
RAPE 1*	0	0	****%	0	0	****%	6	3	100.00%	0	****%	0	****%

ARREST STATISTICS

	1996 YTD	1995 YTD	%CHANGE	1996 MTD	1995 MTD	%CHANGE	1996 YTD	1995 YTD	CURRENT %CHANGE	1994 YTD	2 YEAR %CHANGE	1993 YTD	3 YEAR %CHANGE
MURDER	0	0	****%	0	0	****%	1	2	-50.00%	0	****%	0	****%
RAPE	0	0	-100.0%	0	3	****%	3	2	50.00%	0	****%	0	****%
ROBBERY	9	9	0.00%	3	12	0.00%	20	13	53.85%	0	****%	0	****%
FEL. ASSLT	9		-50.00%	11	2	-8.33%	28	39	-28.21%	0	****%	0	****%
BURGLARY	2		****%	2	1	0.00%	8	13	-38.46%	0	****%	0	****%
GR. LARCENY				4	2	300.00%	12	11	9.09%	0	****%	0	****%
G.L.A.	1	3	-66.67%	1	4	-75.00%	8	16	-50.00%	0	****%	0	****%
TOTAL	13	17	-23.53%	21	22	-4.55%	80	96	-16.67%	0	****%	0	****%
GUN ARRESTS	1	2	-50.00%	2	4	-50.00%	6	21	-71.43%	0	****%	0	****%
NARC ARREST	51	72	-29.17%	71	124	-42.74%	265	442	-40.05%	0	****%	0	****%
PSB ARRESTS	79	105	-24.76%	106	180	-41.11%	438	689	-36.43%	0	****%	0	****%
OCCB ARR.	15	11	36.36%	30	24	25.00%	132	81	62.96%	0	****%	0	****%
D.B. ARR.	3	5	-40.00%	4	5	-20.00%	16	21	-23.81%	0	****%	0	****%
H.B. ARR.	0	0	-100.0%	0	14	-100.0%	4	20	-80.00%	0	****%	0	****%
T.B. ARR.	5	2	150.00%	6	3	100.00%	48	64	-25.00%	0	****%	0	****%
ALL ARRESTS	111	140	-20.71%	159	234	-32.05%	668	916	-27.07%	0	****%	0	****%

SUMMONS ACTIVITY

	1996 YTD	1995 YTD	%CHANGE	1996 MTD	1995 MTD	%CHANGE	1996 YTD	1995 YTD	CURRENT %CHANGE	1994 YTD	2 YEAR %CHANGE	1993 YTD	3 YEAR %CHANGE
PARKING	1308	1460	-10.41%	1676	2654	-36.85%	5752	8895	-35.33%				PARKING
MOVING	380	345	10.14%	455	699	-34.91%	1236	2555	-51.62%				MOVING
CRIMINAL	211	80	163.75%	252	177	42.37%	536	687	-21.98%				CRIMINAL
ECB	79	0	****%	97	2	4750.0%	204	14	1357.1%				ECB

FIGURES ARE PRELIMINARY AND SUBJECT TO FURTHER ANALYSIS AND REVISION

Exhibit 6

A Comparison of NYPD Operations and Private Sector Operations

Budget

As a city agency, the Police Department did not control either its operating or capital budget. Especially in difficult fiscal times, the Mayor's Office of Management and Budget, in negotiation with the department, set the budget goals and timetables. Budget cutting was a special challenge in the NYPD because 96 percent of the $2.3 billion budget went for salaries, including 87 percent for uniformed salaries. In recent years the cuts had come from either civilian attrition or from other than personnel services (OTPS).

Press

The NYPD received more press scrutiny than any private business and all but a few public agencies. Seven reporters worked full time in police headquarters. The tabloids and the local TV stations filled from a quarter to half their space with crime stories. What police did was news, what police didn't do was news, what police did wrong was big news. Business was conducted in a fishbowl, and it was easy to be distracted from the primary missions of the organization by the heavily covered issue of the day.

Civil Service

The civil service rules constrained management from many practices common in private business. In the lower ranks, people who did good work couldn't be rewarded with promotions. People who were good at exams were offered were the most likely to advance to the captain's rank. On the other hand, some high performers in the field might spend their entire careers as police officers or detectives. Because their titles were discretionary, detectives were an exception to this rule. A first grade detective might be paid as much as lieutenant without passing any exams.

Union

The police unions has considerable political power especially at the state level. In response to union prompting, the New York State legislature had passed a number of laws enhancing the privileges of police officers and restricting the power of the police commissioner and other police managers.

The Public

The NYPD was accountable to the public at every level. The Police Commissioner, as a mayoral appointee, and the NYPD, as a department of the city government, were directly accountable to the Mayor. The department personnel also interacted with many other elected officials from the state and city governments. Precinct commanders attended community board meetings and regularly met with a variety of community representatives. And of course, police officers on patrol interacted with millions of civilians each year. There was an independent Civilian Complaint Review Board which made recommendations to the Police Commissioner in cases where civilians had complained of police misconduct.

Exhibit 7

New York Police Department Budgets, Fiscal 1994–1996

	Budgets (in thousands)		
	FISCAL 1994	**FISCAL 1995**	**FISCAL 1996**
Personal Service	1,656,371	1,930,906	2,167,000
Other Than Personal Service	89,026	120,454	95,228
TOTAL	1,745,397	2,051,360	2,262,228

Exhibit 8

Demographic and Crime Statistics for Four Police Precincts, New York City, 1995 vs. 1993

| | 1995 Demographic Data | | | |
	Precinct 014	Precinct 046	Precinct 075	Precinct 103
Population	17162	118435	161387	92559
Total Households	7814	37369	49183	27445
- with persons < 18 yrs	6.68%	55.02%	52.10%	46.73%
same house > 5yrs (%)	44.81%	54.77%	62.10%	60.50%
median household income	$31,860	$14,605	$20,682	$30,092
per capita	$23,804	$6,428	$8,013	$10,860
households with public assist (%)	5.52%	36.53%	25.03%	13.96%
persons below poverty	25.52%	44.08%	30.79%	17.10%
families below poverty	10.07%	42.62%	29.00%	13.93%
persons over 3 yrs	17226	110276	152095	88289
pre-primary %	0.59%	1.60%	1.60%	1.27%
elem or HS %	3.99%	26.33	24.55%	20.50%
college %	12.55%	7.49%	6.88%	9.24%
males less than 16	8774	34670	49399	32494
males unemp %	7.07%	12.26%	9.91%	8.08%
females less than 16	7813	45319	64848	37910
female unemp %	5.82%	7.22%	6.49%	6.69%
persons 16–19	505	8086	11378	5417

	1995			
Seven Crimes:				
Murder	4	43	44	16
Rape	39	100	144	69
Robbery	1329	1591	2397	1488
Assault	470	1085	1280	787
Burglary	1893	1857	1531	1055
Gr. Larceny	6315	646	918	985
Gr. Larc. Auto	*253*	*588*	*1717*	*1088*
TOTAL	10303	5910	8031	5488
Year—End Personnel				
Head Count: Uniform	433	346	403	286
Civilian	38	27	26	27

	1993			
Seven Crimes:				
Murder	11	64	126	28
Rape	41	82	122	74
Robbery	2520	2132	3152	1742
Assault	670	1086	1474	853
Burglary	2687	2365	1854	1166
Gr. Larceny	9365	961	965	1214
Gr. Larc. Auto	*356*	*875*	*2665*	*1591*
TOTAL	15650	7515	10355	6668
Year—End Personnel				
Head Count: Uniform	395	293	348	256
Civilian	51	27	30	35

Exhibit 9
A Map of New York City Police Precincts

Shaded portion = area of offensive against drugs

Exhibit 10
Police Staff Ratios for Major U.S. Cities, 1995

City	Population	# Uniform Employees	Employees Per 100,000 Population
Washington, D.C.	570,000	4,106	720
New York	7,336,224	36,606a	499
Chicago	2,802,494	12,971	463
Philadelphia	1,560,576	6,101	391
Houston	1,758,016	4,935	281
Dallas	1,062,677	2,777	261
San Francisco	741,568	1,823	246
Los Angeles	3,50,381	7,869	222
Phoenix	1,076,108	2,088	194
San Antonio	999,900	1,969	170
San Diego	1,168,785	1,972	169
San Jose	815,235	1,209	148

Allen S. Grossman ■ James P. Honan ■ Caroline King

Learning to Manage with Data in Duval County Public Schools: Lake Shore Middle School (A)

As Lake Shore Middle School Principal Iranetta Wright drove toward Region III Superintendent Mary Brown's office in early June 2004, she felt both nervous and confident. As part of Wright's personnel evaluation, Brown had called a meeting with Wright to discuss Lake Shore's academic performance in SY04.[1] A lot was riding on the meeting for Wright, a first-year principal in the Duval County Public School (DCPS) district.

Wright knew that Brown would ask her to explain the school's 2004 Florida Comprehensive Assessment Test (FCAT) results. Nearly 70% of Lake Shore students had not met the state's rigorous standards in reading and math. Sixth and seventh graders' scores on the FCAT had declined substantially from SY03, while eighth graders made modest gains. At the end of SY04, the school's grade had dropped from a C to a D under Florida's high-stakes accountability system. Lake Shore was clearly falling further behind the district and state (see Exhibit 1 for student achievement trends).

The SY04 results were far from what Wright had envisioned when she was appointed Lake Shore's principal. During her first staff meeting, Wright had announced her goal of making Lake Shore the first A school in Region III of DCPS. Wright recalled how much time and effort she, her leadership team, and teachers had invested in using data to identify students' needs and implementing strategies to increase achievement for every student. Clearly, the school had experienced some major challenges in SY04—a new and inexperienced principal, an influx of low-performing students, and one-third of the staff being first-year teachers. But Wright was not one to look for excuses, and she knew Brown would not accept any. Wright was confident that she had made the best managerial and instructional decisions possible based on the available data, her staff's capacity, and the school's resources.

Wright also anticipated Brown asking her to evaluate her own effectiveness as an instructional leader and her ability to raise student achievement in SY05. DCPS had developed a strong culture of accountability for results, and Wright knew she was not guaranteed a second chance. Wright felt that she and her staff had learned a lot that would help the school improve next year. And Wright remained committed to seeing Lake Shore earn Region III's first A. As she pulled into the parking lot, Wright prepared to present her reflections and determination to Brown.

Duval County Public Schools

History and Demographics

Following the consolidation of the City of Jacksonville and Duval County governments in 1968, DCPS served the largest city in land area in the contiguous United States. In 2004, Duval County's 800,000 residents were 74% white, 22% African-American, and 4% other minority groups. Approximately 47% of adults in the county were functionally illiterate.[2] At 18.16%, the county had the highest percentage of students attending private schools in Florida.[3]

In SY04, approximately 130,000 students attended the district's 166 schools, making DCPS the sixth-largest school system in Florida. DCPS was divided into five administrative regions. The district's coastal areas (Regions IV and V) were more affluent and higher performing academically than the inland communities to the north and west (Regions I, II, and III). Whites comprised 46% of the student body, African-Americans 43%, Hispanics 5%, Asians 3%, and other ethnic/racial groups 3%. Fifty-nine percent of DCPS students attended "racially diverse schools."[4] Nearly 50% of students were eligible for free or reduced-price meals, and 3,000 students were learning English for the first time (see Exhibit 2 for DCPS demographics).

Governance

The DCPS School Board (the Board) was the policymaking body for the district. County residents elected seven members to serve four-year terms. Prior to the late 1990s, the relationship between the Board and DCPS leadership was strained. According to a local reporter in 2003, "One of the biggest slashes to the school system's reputation over the past years has not even focused on the academic achievement of students, but rather on the once-dubbed dysfunctional relationship between the School Board and the superintendent."[5] Indeed, the Board had ousted two superintendents, Herb Sang (1976–1989) and Larry Zenke (1989–1996), prior to their contracts' expiration.

Beginning in 1991, the Florida legislature required a school advisory council (SAC) comprised of the principal and elected parents, students, faculty, staff, and community members in every school. SACs assisted in the preparation, evaluation, and implementation of an annual state-mandated school improvement plan (SIP) designed to improve student achievement. SACs also helped prepare and approve a school's budget.

Superintendent John C. Fryer's Strategy: Aim High and Fryer's High Five

Background: By a 6–1 vote, the Board appointed John C. Fryer, Jr., a retired two-star U.S. Air Force general, superintendent in June 1998. Fryer sought out the new position, which he often referred to as "a calling," because he felt that he could contribute his leadership and management skills to the district.[6] When Fryer assumed the helm in August 1998, he observed, "What I see now is a lot of individual programs and efforts. But I don't see a system, and I don't see a coherence to it all."[7] Fryer recalled, "People warned me that I wouldn't find high-caliber employees in DCPS, but I found very hard-working and committed people. They just needed help thinking strategically."

Strategy—Fryer's High Five: Having spent nearly a year reading about education reform efforts nationwide, Fryer walked into DCPS with a strategy and a vision. Fryer unveiled five strategic priorities that quickly came to be known as "Fryer's High Five":

1. Academic achievement
2. Safety and discipline
3. High-performance management
4. Learning communities
5. Accountability

Fryer described academic achievement as the overarching aim. In 1999, the Board formally adopted "Fryer's High Five," and in 2002, enacted a five-year strategic plan with action strategies and performance metrics. Fryer's team aligned the metrics with Florida's Sunshine State Standards (SSS)[8] and internally developed student performance standards.

Stakeholder Relationships: Under Fryer's leadership, the Board-superintendent relationship transformed from adversarial to productive and focused on improving academic achievement. This shift occurred despite the fact that Fryer served under 13 different Board members from 1998 to 2004. In 2003, the Board awarded Fryer with his highest performance marks ever and a new three-year contract.[9]

Fryer also improved relations with the local collective bargaining unit, Duval Teachers United (DTU). By SY04, both DTU leadership and Fryer described their organizations' relationship as "productive and collaborative." Fryer also mobilized the Jacksonville business community. In January 1999, area CEOs established the World Class Alliance for Education to coordinate financial and volunteer efforts with High Five goals.

High-Stakes Accountability: External and Internal Demands for Data

Beginning around 2000, DCPS had to respond to mounting external pressures to report student-achievement data. Concurrently, Fryer's commitments to standards-based education and developing a results-oriented system created an internal demand for data.

Federal and State Regulations: In January 2002, President George W. Bush signed into law the No Child Left Behind Act of 2001 (NCLB), a framework for improving the country's public schools driven by rigorous standards and high-stakes accountability. NCLB set a nationwide goal for all public school students to achieve proficiency in reading and mathematics by 2014 and established annual adequate yearly progress (AYP) targets to benchmark schools' progress. For the first time, states, districts, and schools were required to report a wide range of achievement data, and schools were rewarded or sanctioned based on their students' performance (see Exhibit 3 for key NCLB provisions).

Concurrently, Florida boasted a rigorous standards-based state accountability system. The Florida A+ Accountability Plan (A+ Plan) rated each Florida public school annually with a letter grade, ranging from A to F, based on students' participation, performance, and growth on the Florida Comprehensive Achievement Test (FCAT).[10] School and district rankings became front-page news and carried serious consequences. While high-performing schools earned monetary and other incentives, D and F schools, labeled "challenged schools," received school improvement funds and frequent state monitoring. If a school received two F grades in four years, districts had to provide students with an "opportunity scholarship"—the ability to transfer into a higher-performing public school or a voucher to attend a private school. In SY03, the Florida Department of Education aligned the A+ Plan with NCLB requirements.

Fryer's Drive for Data: Fryer quickly realized that the district lacked the information systems to track student, school, and district progress toward the High Five goals and state standards. Fryer often said, "I could not have survived in air-to-air battle in my F-16 if my radar had only swept once a year. I need an instrument panel or a dashboard if I'm going to fly this plane at DCPS. We need real-time data about how our students, schools, and staff are doing if we're going to learn and continuously improve over time."

The nameplate outside Fryer's office, "Chief Learner," revealed his approach toward data as a resource for learning rather than for punitive purposes. Signaling his commitment, Fryer moved Director of Research and Evaluation Tim Ballentine and his team next door to the superintendent's office. When Fryer arrived, the district did not have its own infrastructure to house historical student data; instead, DCPS paid to use the City of Jacksonville's computer mainframe. Fryer charged Ballentine with creating a data warehouse in SY00, enabling the district to store, update, and retrieve data daily. Fryer also directed staff to establish a mission control room (MCR) to graphically display the district's annual performance and progress toward the High Five goals (see Exhibit 4 for MCR indicators). As a result of the district's new data investments, DCPS officials estimated that spending on research, evaluation, and technology increased from 1.3% to 2.1% of the annual budget between SY98 and SY04 (see Exhibit 5).

Developing the Data-Driven Principal: Fryer's own priority was to support the principals, and specifically, to strengthen their ability to use data to improve teaching and learning in the classroom. Fryer and his five regional superintendents revamped the recruitment, training, and evaluation procedures for principals to focus on instructional leadership and data-driven decision making. Principals visited the MCR during monthly principal conferences instituted in SY99, and many constructed similar rooms in their own schools. Starting in SY01, Ballentine's team created "research data affects change" (RESDAC) reports to provide every principal with student data; however, many principals viewed the 500-plus page RESDAC spreadsheets as more cumbersome than helpful.

Introducing the AIDE Data System: As DCPS struggled to provide actionable data to principals, the district drew upon the expertise of some data-savvy staff. Jill Budd, principal of Duncan Fletcher Middle School, and Patrick Barr, a district information technology staff member, began designing templates that Budd could re-create throughout the year. As news of Barr and Budd's innovations spread, Fryer asked Barr to build a user-friendly and interactive Web-based tool so that all principals could run similar reports. In response, Barr developed and piloted the Academic Interpretation and Data Evaluation (AIDE) system in SY03.[11]

AIDE allowed principals to view and analyze the RESDAC student data from their desktop computers. Similar to RESDAC, AIDE student records contained demographic information (e.g., age, ethnicity) and achievement data (e.g., FCAT scores and course grades for the previous year). AIDE disaggregated students' FCAT scores by the subject tests' skill sets, called "strands." AIDE also identified academically at-risk students by assigning one of five additional AIDE variables based on the student's FCAT performance. For example, AIDE assigned the variable "lowest 25%" to any student whose FCAT scale score fell in the school's bottom quartile.

Principals received AIDE datasets five times during the school year, one prior to the first day of class and updated versions at the end of each quarter, which included course grades and benchmark test results. Principals were able to create color-coded reports that sorted and presented student data for the entire school or by grade, subject, teacher, individual student, or FCAT achievement level, which ranged from a low of one to a high of five with three considered "proficient." The colors reflected students' FCAT levels: red identified Level 1s and 2s; green Level 3s, 4s, and 5s; and yellow flagged students to monitor.

In SY04, all principals and their administrative leadership teams had access to and were expected to use AIDE. At the end of SY04, the district launched Managing Academic Progress

(MAP), a management tool developed that contained 81 suggested AIDE tasks for principals to complete during the school year (see Exhibit 6). Barr also designed AIDE Express, a wizard-based report program that answered the 10 most frequently asked data questions in AIDE.

Reactions to AIDE: Principals voiced various opinions about how the RESDAC and AIDE data had changed their role and use of time. One middle school principal welcomed the ability to "see where my students are, where we want them to be, and key areas we need to improve in to get there." Others, felt overwhelmed: "My education did not prepare me to be a data analyst. And if I cannot understand the data or figure out next steps, how can I expect that of my teachers?" Most principals agreed, however, that the availability of data was helpful, and one high school principal praised AIDE:

> The data is very friendly now, and now that it's color coded, you can pull it up and people see exactly what the data is saying. It's like a traffic light. Anything that shows up in red means that you're in trouble and you really need to look in those areas. If it has yellow, it means that you're cautious, and green means you're OK. It's really useful when you have conferences with teachers, parents, and students.

A challenged-school elementary principal noted the impact of data on her teachers:

> Data has been a powerful tool for changing teachers' beliefs. The data showed that some teachers who always believed they were the best in the school actually weren't making the highest gains, which devastated some of the teachers but also motivated them to learn new techniques. The data also dispelled the belief that some students just cannot learn at high levels—they can improve, they just need effective and differentiated instruction.

Managing with Data at Lake Shore Middle School

Principal Iranetta Wright

A graduate of DCPS, Wright joined the district in 1993 as a mathematics teacher. After four years in the classroom, she left DCPS to become a successful senior salesperson for Mary Kay Cosmetics. After winning the pink Cadillac for her record sales, Wright decided to return to her self-described "passion," teaching, and was hired as a special education teacher at Lake Shore Middle School in SY98. During the year, Wright assumed various leadership positions and earned her administrative credential. She served as assistant principal at Fletcher Middle School from SY99 to SY02 and was appointed vice principal in SY03. Wright flourished under Principal Jill Budd's leadership in learning how to mine the RESDAC and AIDE data files. She recalled:

> When we piloted the AIDE program in SY03, our data-mining work became much less time consuming and tedious, which really allowed us to focus on being diagnostic and prescriptive as instructional leaders. In other words—what specifically were we going to do differently to help every student achieve at high levels. AIDE also made it easier to draw our coaches and teachers into the conversations about student performance. Finally, when everyone in the school had the data, we all had to take ownership of it and teachers started analyzing the data themselves. As our superintendent likes to say, "There's nowhere to hide."

In July 2003, Wright returned to Lake Shore, this time as a first-year principal. Region III Superintendent Mary Brown commented on Wright's selection, "We thought that Iranetta had the energy and experience—particularly the skills she developed using the AIDE data at Fletcher—to be a guiding light at Lake Shore and help move that school forward." Wright also considered her appointment "a perfect match" given her prior experience in the school, expertise with the school's large special needs student population, and commitment to high performance.

Lake Shore Demographics and Achievement

In SY04, Lake Shore enrolled 1,293 students in grades 6–8. Fifty-two percent of the students were African-American, 38% white, 5% Hispanic, and 4% Asian. Nearly 60% received free or reduced-price meals, 20% participated in special education, and less than 1% were limited English proficient.

Lake Shore had enjoyed stable leadership, as Wright's predecessor served as the school's principal from SY95 through SY03. In concert with Fryer's district-wide reform efforts, Lake Shore had implemented standards-based reforms school-wide, used mathematics and literacy coaches to help improve teachers' practice, and enrolled many veteran teachers in data analysis training workshops. Lake Shore students performed below district and state averages (see Exhibit 1), and the DCPS individual school profile demonstrated that a wide achievement gap divided white and minority students (see Exhibit 7). At the end of SY03, Lake Shore's state letter grade improved from a D to a C.

Lake Shore's Action Plan

Strategic Planning

Needs Assessment: Wright remembered her first days as the new Lake Shore principal. The first thing she did was call Lake Shore's leadership team—comprised of her vice principal, three grade-level administrators, mathematics and literacy coaches, department chairs, and lead teachers—together to start planning for SY04. Wright and her team assessed the overall needs of their sixth, seventh, and eighth graders by running the AIDE FCAT executive summary

reports for reading and math. Red dominated the color-coded reports, as about 70% of Lake Shore's students were performing below grade level as reflected by their Level 1 or 2 FCAT scores.

Next, the team generated the FCAT reading and math content score A+ reports to show how individual students scored on the different FCAT strands (see Exhibit 8). From these, Wright and her colleagues identified two major areas of weakness across all grade levels: words and phrases on the reading exam, and number sense in mathematics. Using the A+ report's real-time calculator, the team calculated that at least 50 students would need to move up to a Level 3 on both the FCAT reading and math exams in order to improve Lake Shore's letter grade to a B. The companion FCAT reading and math content score NCLB reports showed that Lake Shore's African-American, Hispanic, and limited English-proficient students did not meet NCLB adequate yearly progress (AYP) goals in SY03. An NCLB calculator enabled the team to see the percentage of students in each ethnic or ability group that would need to make gains on the FCAT to meet AYP targets for SY04.

The team also looked at reports to see how students of different teachers in the same grade level and subject performed on the FCAT (see Exhibit 9). A teacher demonstrated "gains" if an average of his students' FCAT achievement level increased; a teacher showed "losses" if her students' achievement level declined. Wright also pulled student data from Lake Shore's eight elementary feeder schools to get a sense of the incoming sixth graders. While seven of the feeders were A schools, sixth graders' performance often dropped once they came to Lake Shore.

The school faced additional challenges. In order to comply with Florida's new class-size reduction amendment and fill vacant positions due to attrition, Wright had to hire 23 teachers (about a quarter of the teaching staff) before the first day of school.[12] Lake Shore was also scheduled to receive 112 opportunity scholarship students transferring out of low-performing schools.

Designing a School Improvement Plan: As required by state law, Wright met with her school advisory council (SAC) in August to design Lake Shore's school improvement plan (SIP). As with all schools in DCPS, the SIP articulated the school's targets and strategies to meet Fryer's High Five goals. The district set the school's annual academic achievement targets based on the long-range goal of having every student score a 3 or above on the FCAT and demonstrate at least one year's growth on the test. Based on their needs assessment and data analysis, Wright, her team, and the SAC established targets for the other four High Five goals and outlined strategies, timelines, and responsibilities for all five goals.

Organizing to Meet Students' Needs

Class Scheduling: Lake Shore's 85 teachers worked in teams of four (math, reading, social studies, and science teachers), with each team assigned between 85 and 100 students. Teachers "looped" or remained with the same students in seventh and eighth grades. Wright selected specific teachers to work with some of the more at-risk students in remedial math and reading classes, which enrolled approximately 450 students with Level 1 FCAT scores. She then distributed students by FCAT level proportionately across the other teams. When teachers arrived for their in-service planning day before the first day of school, they received AIDE data profiles on every student in their class and on their team, often referred to within the district as "the hand you've been dealt." A first-year sixth-grade math teacher recalled feeling "overwhelmed by the data at first. My class report was almost entirely red with every student scoring a Level 1 or 2. I was new, and they were deficient

in almost every area; we were starting at ground zero together."

Schoolwide Interventions: Recognizing that nearly 70% of Lake Shore students were performing below grade level, Wright instituted a number of school-wide interventions. Wright asked every student to read 25 books per year, a campaign originally introduced by Fryer in SY99, and continued the "Principal's Book of the Month" initiative, which began under her predecessor. During monthly department meetings, teachers and coaches selected a "reading strategy of the month" to reinforce literacy skills in the classroom.

Safety Nets: Wright and her colleagues designed "safety net" programs to provide extra support to low-performing students. Safety nets were targeted at students scoring Level 1 or Level 2 on the FCAT, students performing in Lake Shore's lowest 25%, and bubble students, those scoring 10 points above or below a Level 3. Year-round safety nets included new remedial mathematics and reading classes and before- and after-school tutoring sessions. With the FCAT approaching in mid-February, Wright sent student profile reports (Exhibit 10) to the parents and family members of the Level 1 and 2 students in January with a cover note identifying the student's weakest strands and inviting the student to attend a two-week after-school "ramp-up" session focused on his or her specific weakness.

Supporting Teachers to Use Data: Given the high percentage of new teachers, Wright and her leadership team provided biweekly training sessions on FCAT strands, standards, and instructional strategies. Additional training was provided in mandatory grade-level meetings that took place monthly during teachers' free planning period and in quarterly "vertical breakouts," required meetings for teachers of the same subject across grade levels that occurred on paid professional development days. Teachers were also encouraged to attend monthly department meetings before school and to maintain and update data notebooks to track students' progress over the year.

In addition, Wright tried to change teachers' attitudes, commenting, "I want our teachers and staff to understand that the data is here to help us learn how we can be more effective for our students. It's not an 'I got you.' We're all in this together because Lake Shore's test scores are public, everyone knows our business. We have to know why our students are struggling in order to improve."

Monitoring Performance

Student Assessments: Lake Shore staff evaluated students' progress during the school year through two school-wide assessments. In October, Lake Shore administered a prewriting assessment to all students in anticipation of the eighth graders' first FCAT writing exam in February. In early January, all students took an FCAT reading and mathematics practice exam prepared by Lake Shore's math and literacy coaches.

While teachers frequently asked for benchmark data, literacy coach Katrina Short observed that the practice exam had limited impact: "The students scored very low on the practice exams, but we didn't believe that those results adequately reflected their performance or all the work we had done in the fall to prepare them for the FCAT. Instead, we thought we had designed the test poorly. In retrospect, we know that what the test was telling us was more right than wrong." Wright shared the results of the practice exam with teachers and students, arguing that "I learned during my time at Fletcher that comparing teachers and classrooms fosters a healthy competition in the school, especially among the students. They start saying, 'We have to beat Ms. Green's class on this test or the FCAT.'"

Concurrently, individual teachers designed their own tests and projects to evaluate students, and departments administered assessments at the end of each nine-week quarter. Teachers discussed student progress in weekly team meetings, their department and grade-level meetings, and informally during breaks or after school. Using an AIDE quarterly tracking chart, administrators and teachers monitored students' course grades, compared student achievement across teacher teams, and identified students earning below a 2.0 grade point average (GPA).

However, the most intensive and anticipated student assessment was the FCAT 2004. All Lake Shore students took the FCAT reading and math exams over four days in mid-February. Eighth graders also took the FCAT science and writing tests.

Teachers' Performance: Wright and her administrative team developed the "quick peek" process to evaluate teaching and learning at Lake Shore. During a quick peek, Wright or another administrator observed a classroom for 15 to 20 minutes and evaluated the teacher's implementation of the Sunshine State Standards and use of effective instructional strategies using a checklist aligned with the teachers' formal evaluation rubric. The administrator left a copy of the checklist with the teacher, and either party could ask for a follow-up meeting to discuss the feedback. Administrators conducted about one quick peek per month for every teacher.

When needed, Wright and her administrators scheduled conferences with teachers performing below expectations. Wright met with every teaching team at the end of each quarter to discuss its students' performance. If any of the team's students were earning below a 2.0 GPA, Wright handed out a student profile report (see Exhibit 10) to each team member and asked the team to design a comprehensive strategy to help the student improve. Wright also used the opportunity to compare student achievement across teaching teams.

School Performance: Wright shared Lake Shore's challenges and current issues with other principals, Regional Superintendent Brown, and the regional director during the Region III monthly principal conferences. The SAC reviewed the school improvement plan twice during the school year. Two small teams of visiting principals and central office staff conducted a "snapshot"—a district-wide process used to observe the implementation of standards in schools—at Lake Shore. At the beginning of the year, a data-driven decision-making snapshot team met with Wright, observed classrooms, and evaluated Lake Shore using a district-wide rubric (see Exhibit 11). The snapshot team found Lake Shore to be in the lowest implementation level, or preparing stage. In March, a second snapshot team observed Lake Shore's implementation of reading standards and again found the school in the preparing stage. Wright remarked:

> Even with all the teacher training and observations we've done, we learned that our teachers were not connecting all of the dots—the standards, our students' areas of deficit on the FCAT, the instructional strategies our coaches try to model, etc. After the snapshot, I gave every teacher the implementation rubric and the observers' feedback. We met as a school and discussed teachers' questions, what each level on the rubric meant, and shared ideas about how to improve.

Measuring Results

Principal and Teacher Evaluations: In September, Wright entered her school improvement plan targets for each of the High Five goals into the online Appraisal Plus system, the district's performance-evaluation tool for school administrators implemented in SY03. Administrators received points based on how many targets were achieved. The targets were weighted: academic performance (40%), safety and discipline (10%), high-performance management (25%), learning communities (10%), and accountability (15%). Based on the total score, administrators were recommended for *incentive, annual reappointment, probationary annual*

reappointment, or *no reappointment.* During Wright's midyear review in January, she and Brown discussed Lake Shore's progress toward the school's academic targets established by the central office. Wright recalled that "In January, I still felt very optimistic that we would meet our academic performance targets."

Wright frequently discussed student-achievement data with teachers during quick peeks, conferences, quarterly meetings, and the district-wide teachers' evaluations that took place every March. She explained the role of student-achievement data in teachers' evaluations:

> I make reference to how students performed on the previous year's FCAT—if they made gains or losses—and how students are performing during the current school year, but we're not at the point yet where we use FCAT data alone to dismiss or reward someone. There are just too many other variables that impact how a student scored and other reasons why a teacher may not be effective for Lake Shore students.

School Climate Survey: Administered in every DCPS school each spring, the SY04 school climate survey asked parents, employees, and students to rate their school's quality of instruction, staff, and safety. Compared to the SY03 survey results, Lake Shore students and staff gave higher marks for the principal's leadership, implementation of standards, and quality of instruction; however, parents' satisfaction declined slightly in these same areas.

FCAT 2004: In mid-May 2004, the Florida Department of Education released the 2004 FCAT results (see Exhibit 1). Wright was disappointed that the school had not met its academic performance targets. The percentage of Lake Shore's sixth and seventh graders scoring a Level 3 or above in reading had dropped between eight and 10 percentage points, while eighth graders made small gains. In math, sixth graders' performance also declined by five percentage points, while seventh and eighth graders' scores remained stagnant.

Wright also analyzed the data by teacher. Since the new FCAT data would not be uploaded into the AIDE program for a few more weeks, Wright created her own chart that showed students' gains and losses by teacher and distributed the chart to every teacher (see Exhibit 12). Wright explained her rationale for the transparency:

> Reporting the gains and losses by teacher helps us start very specific conversations. I expect teachers who are teaching the same subject, grade, and level kids to have gains within 5% of each other. If one doesn't, we need to explore if there is an issue with that teacher's instructional strategies. On the other hand, if all the teachers have very low gains or losses, it may signal a curriculum issue—either something is getting taught out of sequence or not at all.

By Wright's calculations, Lake Shore's letter grade would drop to a D and would not demonstrate adequate yearly progress under NCLB. Wright shared her reaction:

> At first, I was deflated because we had put in so much time and hard work, and we felt we had been very strategic in our efforts. Then, I started looking at the results by grade level and strands, and the performance of specific students. I want our school to first celebrate what worked well. Then, we need to talk about what the data is telling us in order to start learning what we can do differently to improve next year.

Challenges for Continuous Improvement

Professional Development: Translating Data Analysis to Instructional Strategies

Teachers: Lake Shore's staff observed that teachers needed additional professional development to make their instruction more data driven. A veteran math teacher said, "We really

needed more training up front about what content areas and skills are going to be tested in each FCAT strand." A remedial math teacher commented, "Over 75% of my Level 1 sixth graders made gains on the 2004 FCAT math exam. Some of my students went from a Level 1 to a Level 4 in one year! It is amazing, but I need help trying to figure out which instructional strategies had the most impact so that we can share them with other teachers and schools."

Wright observed that the "reading strategy of the month" professional development sessions had not been as effective as she had hoped. Wright also noted that she could have done a better job of sharing student data with teachers: "This year, we only gave teachers the student profile reports for students identified as at risk for failing at the end of each quarter. Otherwise, teachers never saw how their students performed in other subjects or content areas of the FCAT."

Administrators: Wright acknowledged: "Our coaches, department chairs, house administrators, even my vice principal and I, all need more training. We're all trying to learn how to learn from the data together." Fryer conceded: "Learning how to support our new and experienced principals to use data more effectively is a constant training need.

Training and Supporting New Teachers

Wright and others described the difficulty with providing adequate training and support to Lake Shore's high number of new teachers. By the end of SY04, Lake Shore had 35 first-year teachers—almost a third of its teaching force—who either started at the beginning of the school year or due to attrition came midyear and the school expected to have about 20 new teachers in SY05. The impact on students was tangible, as one parent and member of Lake Shore's SAC commented: "My daughter had three different seventh-grade science teachers this year and a substitute for half the year."

Wright observed, "We need to figure out a

way to help our new teachers develop a sense of community here at Lake Shore, connect with other teachers and administrators, and get the mentoring and ongoing support that they need. I know that some of our first-year teachers just felt lost in the shuffle, isolated, and sometimes, overwhelmed." Nevertheless, Wright also was quick to defend the performance of her first-year teachers:

> Our FCAT scores declined the most in the sixth grade, which was also the grade with most of our new teachers and transfer students from low-performing schools. However, when I compared students' gains and losses across teachers, I was surprised to find that some of the first-year teachers had even higher percentages of students that improved their FCAT achievement level compared to the veterans.

Wright had company, as principals throughout DCPS struggled to train and support the massive influx of new teachers required to comply with the state's new class-size reduction (CSR) amendment. The district estimated that the new hires would increase the district's teaching force from 6,000 in SY03 to over 8,500 by SY05. "The CSR requirements have stretched the district's training capacity far beyond what we could have ever programmed in advance," noted Fryer.

Curriculum, Assessment, and Alignment

Curriculum: During the year, the Lake Shore staff identified areas of misalignment among their curriculum, the state standards, and the FCAT. For example, a first-year sixth-grade math teacher recalled, "The FCAT practice exam pushed hard on fractions, but we had just started covering fractions in class. We switched gears and taught our students everything we could about fractions, but we really only had a few weeks before the FCAT."

Assessment: Almost every Lake Shore teacher and administrator talked about the need

for more frequent benchmark data. A veteran math teacher commented:

> I really wish we administered a baseline test at the beginning of the year to capture what students learned between when they took the FCAT in February and again in May. The FCAT AIDE data is useful, but it misses four months of learning. We need quarterly or end-of-unit assessments to evaluate if our curriculum and lesson plans are aligned with the state standards and the FCAT. That way we can pinpoint students' areas of weaknesses on an ongoing basis.

Assistant Superintendent for Curriculum and Instruction Ed Pratt-Dannals described the district-wide challenge of aligning standards, curriculum, instruction, assessments, professional development, and performance evaluation as "a constant work in progress in which data plays an integral role. We used data to set our High Five targets and develop a strategic plan to reach them, but we are also constantly collecting data on our students to measure our progress, learn, and fine-tune our work." Pratt-Dannals also noted that "Our principals and teachers are constantly asking for district-wide formative assessments and benchmark tests so that they can assess students' progress in real time and not have to wait for the FCAT scores to come back at the end of the year."

Sharing Best Practices across Classrooms and Schools

The eighth graders' FCAT gains confirmed for Wright, her team, and teachers that "looping" was having a positive impact on student achievement. Wright commented, "By the time students reach eighth grade, their teachers already know their individual strengths and weaknesses and feel more ownership for their success. Unfortunately, we cannot start looping in the sixth grade because most of our sixth-grade teachers are only certified as elementary teachers and cannot teach seventh and eighth graders."

The availability of data could also galvanize discussions among teachers. A first-year math teacher said, "This year, 25% of my students improved on the FCAT. Next year, my goal is for 50% to make gains. I want to work with my team and other math teachers so I can learn from my mistakes and know what questions to ask next year to make that goal a reality." A veteran math teacher observed:

> Two years ago, my students didn't improve and I was really embarrassed, but then I realized that I had to get over my pride and figure out my weak areas. We're professionals, and we have to adopt the mind-set that we're all capable of learning how to learn from each other and improve. When I got Mrs. Wright's chart that showed the percentage of students who improved an FCAT level by teacher, I saw that 62% of my students made gains this year, but others teachers had over 80%, so I decided to ask those teachers what they did. We're all in this together, and it benefits me as much as another teacher to help each other.

However, a veteran social studies teacher observed, "We have a lot of support and training on data use this year, and we talk a lot about it as a team, but it's hard to find the time to analyze data in an in-depth way with other colleagues in an ongoing and meaningful way."

Creating a High-Performance Culture with Accountability

Cultural changes at Lake Shore proved difficult and were often met with skepticism. Literacy coach Short noted, "One of our greatest challenges is getting buy-in about the importance of data use and then to train teachers how to analyze data. Most of our new teachers are basically teaching the way they were taught and do not

know what to do differently. Some of our veteran teachers resist change." A social studies teacher commented that the administration's attitude toward data use and teacher practice had gone from "benign neglect under the previous principal to micromanagement at times under Mrs. Wright." A mathematics teacher added, "Wright was very up front about wanting Lake Shore to be the first A school in Region III, and her management style has been very aggressive. Administrators had never visited our classrooms so often; we started calling this the 'year of observation.'"

Communicating Performance to Students, Parents, and the Public

Lake Shore and the district struggled to clearly communicate performance results to students, parents, and the community. A veteran science teacher noted, "The data is a real blur for students and parents. The terminology and format are in a language only spoken by teachers and administrators." One veteran math teacher commented, "We need to do a better job helping parents understand their children's data so they can support our work at home and send them to the extra tutoring sessions we offer." Superintendent Fryer concurred but remained committed to analyzing and reporting data:

> One of our greatest challenges is figuring out how to communicate our progress and our ongoing work to the public. . . . We want people to look at our results, at what we've accomplished over the past five years. I feel comfortable showing the warts and all because I can explain the data. We should be proud of where we've come, and it is OK to say we've still got a long way to go. My goal is the same as when I arrived in 1998, to make DCPS the highest-achieving urban school district in the country. Our data shows we're on our way.

Iranetta Wright Looks Ahead

Wright was aware of her leadership challenges and the district's expectations for results. She reflected, "We've done a lot at Lake Shore this year to promote rigorous standards, accountability for results, and high expectations for every student, I think we'll be in a much better position to move forward next year, but I do feel like the pressure is on to make sure we show improvements." Wright entered the Region III office determined to communicate her vision, determination and optimism to Regional Superintendent Brown.

Notes

1. SY is a PELP convention that denotes "school year." For example, SY04 refers to the 2003–2004 school year.

2. *Improving Adult Literacy,* Jacksonville, FL: Jacksonville Community Council, Inc., Spring 1999, p. 3.

3. Beth Kormanik, "How well has Duval really desegregated?" *The Florida Times-Union,* May 17, 2004.

4. "An agreement between the NAACP and DCPS defined 'racially diverse schools' as having between 20% and 55% black student enrollment," cited in Kormanik, "How well has Duval really desegregated?"

5. Cynthia L. Garza, "5 years of Fryer," *The Florida Times-Union,* April 20, 2003.

6. Nancy Mitchell, "Fryer says yes to schools post," *The Florida Times-Union,* June 17, 1998.

7. Nancy Mitchell, "I just don't quit," *The Florida Times-Union,* August 2, 1998.

8. Adopted in 1996, the Sunshine State Standards (SSS) specified the knowledge and skills students were expected to master in seven subjects in grades pre-K through 12.

9. Cynthia L. Garza, "Questions and answers: John Fryer," *The Florida Times-Union,* April 20, 2003.

10. The FCAT measured students' progress toward meeting the Sunshine State Standards (SSS). The A+ Plan required annual FCAT testing in reading and math for every grade 3–10 student; writing in grades 4, 8, and 10; and science in grades 5, 8, and 10. See "A+ Plan for Education," Governor Jeb Bush's official Web site, http://www.myflorida.com/myflorida/ government/governorinitiatives/aplusplan/index.html, and "FCAT,"

Florida Department of Education Web site, http://fcat.fldoe.org/, accessed May 6, 2004.

11. Barr issued DCPS an unlimited free license to use AIDE from his private software company, Academic Performance Series.

12. In November 2002, Florida voters approved a constitutional amendment limiting class sizes to 18 students in grades K-3, 22 students in grades 4–8, and 25 students in grades 9–12 by SY11. Implementation began in SY04. See "Class Size Reduction Amendment," Florida Dept. of Education Web site, http://www.firn.edu/doe/arm/class-size.htm, accessed July 2, 2004.

Exhibit 1

Student Achievement Trends, SY01–SY04

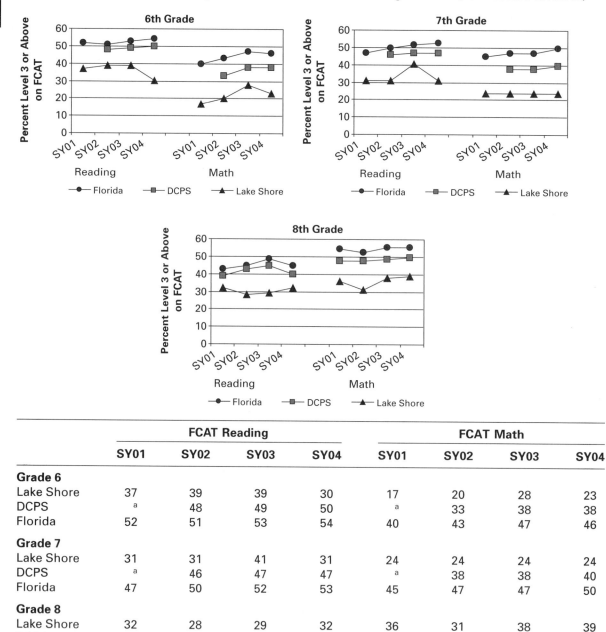

Percentage of Students Meeting Florida State Standards in Reading and Math (FCAT Level 3 or Above)

	FCAT Reading				FCAT Math			
	SY01	SY02	SY03	SY04	SY01	SY02	SY03	SY04
Grade 6								
Lake Shore	37	39	39	30	17	20	28	23
DCPS	a	48	49	50	a	33	38	38
Florida	52	51	53	54	40	43	47	46
Grade 7								
Lake Shore	31	31	41	31	24	24	24	24
DCPS	a	46	47	47	a	38	38	40
Florida	47	50	52	53	45	47	47	50
Grade 8								
Lake Shore	32	28	29	32	36	31	38	39
DCPS	39	43	45	40	48	48	49	50
Florida	43	45	49	45	53	53	56	56

Source: "Reading Scores Statewide Comparison for 2001 to 2004," "Mathematics Scores Statewide Comparison for 2001 to 2004," "Duval District (16) FCAT 2004 District Report," "Duval District (16) Lake Shore Middle School FCAT 2004 Report," Florida Department of Education Web site, http://fcat.fldoe.org, accessed May 24, 2004.

[a] Not available. DCPS was not required to test the sixth and seventh grade in every school until SY02.

Exhibit 2

DCPS Demographics

SY04 DCPS Overview

District Area Demographics (2000)

Total population	778,879
Per capita income	$20,753
Families below poverty level	203,225
Median household income	$40,539
Percent of county residents holding college degrees	21.9%
Unemployment (2004)[a]	4.9%

Student Demographics

Number of students (K–12)	129,553
White	46.2%
African-American	43.0%
Hispanic	4.8%
Asian/Pacific Islander	3.1%
Other	2.9%
Eligible for free and reduced-price lunch	49.2%
English-language learners	2.7%
Exceptional-education students	18.3%
Graduation rate (SY03)	63.7%
Dropout rate (SY03)	4.6%

Schools and Staff (sixth-largest district in Florida)

Number of schools	166
Elementary	106
Middle/Junior High	26
Senior High	19
Alternative	8
Charter	7
Total full-time employees (FTEs)	12,125
Average teacher salary	$40,335
Student/teacher ratio[b]	
PK–3	19.7 : 1
Gr. 4–8	21.4 : 1
Gr. 9–12	22.5 : 1

Source: District area demographics cited in "Duval County Public Schools," School District Demographics System, National Center for Education Statistics (NCES), U.S. Department of Education, Bureau of the Census, U.S. Department of Commerce. NCES Web site, http://www.nces.ed.gov/surveys/sdds/singledemoprofile.asp?county1=1200480 &state1=12, accessed June 2, 2004. Student, schools, and staff data from district files and "Duval County School District," Florida Department of Education Web site, http://www.firn.edu/doe/eias/flmove/duval.htm, accessed June 15, 2004.

[a] Data for January 2004. "Metropolitan Area at a Glance: Jacksonville, FL," U.S. Department of Labor, Bureau of Labor Statistics Web site, http://www.bls.gov.eag.fl_jacksonville.htm, accessed June 16, 2004.

[b] District files.

Exhibit 3

Key Provisions of the No Child Left Behind Act of 2001 (NCLB)

The No Child Left Behind Act of 2001 (NCLB) replaced the Elementary and Secondary Education Act first authorized in 1965 and dramatically expanded the federal government's role in public education. Key provisions of NCLB required:

- Approval of state accountability plans by the U.S. Department of Education

- Annual testing of at least 95% of all students in grades 3–8 on state reading and math exams aligned with state academic standards by SY06

- All students and student ethnic/racial and ability subgroups to score proficient or above on state tests by SY14, all schools to meet state adequate yearly progress (AYP) targets toward the 2014 goal beginning in SY03, and districts to allow students to transfer out of schools receiving federal Title I funds that failed to meet AYP goals

- States and school districts to issue report cards on district and school performance disaggregated by student ethnic/racial and ability subgroups by SY03

- All schools to have "highly qualified" teachers in all core content areas by SY06

Source: Information summarized from "No Child Left Behind," *Education Week* Web site, http://www.edweek. com/ context/topics/issuespage.cfm?id=59, accessed May 12, 2004.

Exhibit 4

Mission Control Room Indicators

Goal 1: Academic Performance	Goal 2: Safety and Discipline	Goal 3: High-Performance Management	Goal 4: Learning Communities	Goal 5: Accountability
1. FCAT performance by grade level, subject, and ethnicity	1. Parent perception of safety	1. School employee turnover rate	1. School volunteerism	1. Individual school profiles
2. FCAT performance vs. satisfactory grades	2. Student perception of safety	2. Employee satisfaction	2. Business partnerships	2. School improvement plans
3. Parent satisfaction with quality of instruction	3. Employee perception of safety	3. Teacher training	3. Kindergarten readiness	3. School department profiles
4. Student satisfaction with quality of instruction	4. Student conduct	4. School technology deployment and training	4. % of teachers with advanced degrees	4. Central office department improvement plans
5. Scholastic Aptitude Test (SAT) scores		5. Business services and purchasing	% of National Board-certified teachers	5. RESDAC/AIDE data
6. American College Test (ACT) scores		6. Facilities and maintenance	5. Student attendance	6. Learner profiles
7. Promotion rate		7. Transportation	6. Staff diversity	7. FCAT five-year performance
8. Four-year graduation rate		8. Instructional materials		8. A+ school grades
9. College readiness		9. Research, evaluation, and assessment		9. NCLB adequate yearly progress
10. Exceptional student education		10. Information technology		
11. Title I		11. K-12 educational administration costs		
12. Community education		12. Media services		
13. Applied technology and career development				
14. Magnet programs/school choice				
15. Academic and special programs				
16. Student services				
17. Jacksonville Urban Systemic Initiative				

Source: District files.

Exhibit 5

DCPS Financials, SY98–SY04

Table a Revenues and Expenditures SY98–SY04

	1997/98	1998/99	1999/2000	2000/01	2001/02	2002/03	2003/04
Revenues							
Federal	$ 1,721,281	$ 1,619,099	$ 4,287,934	$ 1,541,684	$ 1,640,600	$ 1,743,019	$ 1,597,309
State	405,778,561	412,743,414	409,843,999	423,450,174	409,067,682	417,428,037	429,206,973
Local	187,160,106	196,592,494	197,071,118	216,142,053	217,155,008	234,176,776	257,345,909
Private and/or Other	3,478,322	13,908,446	13,108,764	15,544,242	2,867,611	20,590,997	3,679,152
Total	$ 598,138,271	$ 624,863,452	$ 624,311,816	$ 656,678,153	$ 630,730,901	$ 673,938,829	$ 691,829,343
Expenditures							
Direct Instruction	363,552,785	372,711,276	363,641,381	380,952,747	395,325,301	413,925,275	434,618,373
Instructional Support[a]	59,973,787	62,576,686	64,771,606	70,116,037	70,319,321	76,658,127	73,757,071
General Admin[b]	27,084,187	35,776,189	38,162,097	44,482,311	38,675,947	42,701,352	39,799,010
School Admin	27,569,944	28,724,260	29,774,026	31,019,725	32,386,035	34,184,716	35,077,253
Facilities & Constr	2,452,295	3,209,306	4,458,630	6,099,265	1,467,344	895,049	937,633
Transportation	34,881,420	35,187,650	38,117,798	38,379,368	37,377,704	36,442,825	30,599,691
Plant Op/Maintenance	66,175,995	66,160,831	68,585,174	69,912,426	60,192,888	74,995,358	60,990,820
Community Services	6,828,555	7,463,490	7,829,456	8,017,213	544,311	657,150	641,617
Debt Service	531,160	547,267	489,982	479,277	1,394,863	1,392,447	942,700
Transfers	57,729	813,393	778,971	1,026,606	2,138,689	170,187	1,392,312
Total	$ 589,107,857	$ 613,170,348	$ 616,609,120	$ 650,484,976	$ 639,822,403	$ 682,022,487	$ 678,756,480
Surplus/Deficit	$ 9,030,414	$ 11,693,105	$ 7,702,695	$ 6,193,177	$ (9,091,503)	$ (8,083,658)	$ 13,072,863

[a] Includes pupil personnel, media services, curriculum, and instructional staff training.

[b] Includes central and board administration, fiscal services, and central services.

Table b Research, Evaluation and Technology Expenditures as a Percent of Total Budget

	1997/98	1998/99	1999/2000	2000/01	2001/02	2002/03	2003/04
Total Expenditures	$ 589,107,857	$ 613,170,348	$ 616,609,120	$ 650,484,976	$ 639,822,403	$ 682,022,487	$ 678,756,480
Research, Evaluation & Technology	$ 7,399,351	$ 11,503,959	$ 13,586,960	$ 14,353,852	$ 13,609,341	$ 14,762,472	$ 14,047,334
Research, Eval & Tech as a % of Total	1.3%	1.9%	2.2%	2.2%	2.1%	2.2%	2.1%

Source: District files.

Note: SY98–SY03 revenues and expenditures are audited, SY04's are unaudited.

Exhibit 6
Managing Academic Progress (MAP) Management Tool

Lake Shore Middle Map Profile							
			MAP Corridor				
All MAP Tasks		C and I	Scheduling		Safety Net		Accountability
		Pre-School	Pre-Plan		Instruction	Summative	
Print		Task		Component	Cycle	Report	Analyze
Task Report	1	Create cover sheet for MAP Profile		Accountability	Pre-School		NA
Task Report	2	Create school MAP Profile check list		Accountability	Pre-School		NA
Task Report	3	Create a demographic profile of your school		Scheduling	Pre-School		
Task Report	4	Print and complete the Curriculum and Instructional Gaps planning sheet		C and I	Pre-School		NA
Task Report	5	Determine the number of students in the five AIDE variable categories for reading and math		Scheduling	Pre-School		
Task Report	6	Develop an overview of student performance on FCAT A+		C and I	Pre-School		
Task Report	7	Present NCLB overview to Leadership Team for discussion and input		C and I	Pre-School		
Print					Close		
Record:	◄ ◄	1	► ►I ►* of 81				

The MAP corridor interfaced the MAP program with the Academic Interpretation and Data Evaluation (AIDE) system.

MAP tasks were divided into four instructional components: (1) *Curriculum and Instruction* (C and I), (2) *Scheduling,* (3) *Safety Net,* and (4) *Accountability.*

MAP tasks were also divided into four sequential cycles: (1) *Pre-School:* prior to the beginning of school, (2) *Pre-Plan:* began the first day teachers return to work and continued to the 10th instructional day, (3) *Instructional:* each 45-day instructional cycle, and (4) *Summative:* end of the school year.

Exhibit 7
Lake Shore Middle School Individual School Profile

2002-2003 School Profile
LAKE SHORE MIDDLE SCHOOL # 69
Region 3

Legend

N:	Number of students evaluated.
Pct:	Percentage of students achieving the standard for this criterion, by ethnicity. (N/S if N < 6 for a single grade or N < 10 for multiple grades.)
Gray bars:	Performance of all schools on this criterion, ranked from low to high.
Heavy dark vertical segment:	Performance of all students at this school.
Heavy dashed vertical line	Performance of all students in the district at specified grade level.

FCAT Sunshine State Standards (Percent of students at Student Achievement Level 3 or higher)

	Ethnicity	N	Pct
Reading Grade 06	White	140	48
	Afr-Amer.	139	30
	Hispanic	9	22
	Asian	9	33
	All	303	39
Reading Grade 07	White	178	58
	Afr-Amer.	170	24
	Hispanic	20	20
	Asian	17	47
	All	391	40
Reading Grade 08	White	149	40
	Afr-Amer.	150	21
	Hispanic	13	8
	Asian	10	40
	All	328	29
Math Grade 06	White	139	37
	Afr-Amer.	138	20
	Hispanic	8	12
	Asian	10	40
	All	301	28
Math Grade 07	White	178	37
	Afr-Amer.	171	9
	Hispanic	20	20
	Asian	17	35
	All	391	24
Math Grade 08	White	143	55
	Afr-Amer.	148	22
	Hispanic	13	15
	Asian	10	40
	All	320	37

Source: District files.

Exhibit 8

FCAT Sunshine State Math (SSM) Content Score A+ Report for Lake Shore Middle School

Lake Shore Middle Students

FCAT SSM Math Content Scores – A+

Sch	Stu Numb	Last Name	First Name	GPA	2003 FCAT Gr	SSM Level	SSM Scale	SSM Dev	Num ber #	%	Mea sure #	%	Geo metry #	%	Alge bra #	%	Data Anal #	%	NRM %ile	S	E	Gr	HR	L	E S E	C	PR SC H	B U B	25 + 2	L O S S	C O N
69	6779146	BEAL	GERARD	2.57	6	1	274	1519	2	33	2	22	5	56	3	38	4	44	20	M	B	6	609	F			T 143	X			
69	8007817	BUCKMAN	SAMMIE	2.62	6	1	100	770	3	33	0	0	1	11	0	0	2	22	10	M	H	6	615	H	K	251	R	Y	0	X			
69	7850303	BROOKBAN	RODOLFO	2.62	6	1	209	1239	1	11	0	0	3	33	2	25	3	33	23	M	B	6	612	R			92	X	X		
69	6715357	ATWOOD	DANNI	2.62	7	1	267	1631	2	22	2	22	6	67	6	38	4	44	31	M	W	7	701				J 216	X	X		
69	8125777	BURRELL	TALIB	2.62	6	1	239	1368	1	11	1	11	3	33	1	25	4	44	6	M	H	6	615	F			305		X		
69	6780071	BEALE	GERMAN	2.58	7	1	232	1490	2	22	1	11	2	25	3	38	2	22	21	M	B	7	701	F			T 169	X	X		
69	6495283	MERRY	LESLI	2.58	6	1	274	1519	5	56	3	33	4	44	3	38	4	44	36	F	W	6	620	N	V	251	207	X	X		
69	7436787	BOX	MYRICK	2.58	6	1	267	1488	2	22	5	56	2	22	5	56	5	56	44	M	W	6	604	F	K	251	256		X		
69	6834997	BILOTTA	JONATHAN	2.58	6	1	278	1536	3	33	4	44	2	22	2	25	6	67	61	M	W	6	608	F			18	X	X		
69	6748110	BANKS	ELIJAH	2.58	7	1	249	1559	1	11	0	0	3	33	4	44	4	44	16	M	B	7	705	F			21	X	X		
69	6775220	BAWLI	GALE	2.58	6	1	243	1386	2	22	3	33	2	22	1	12	3	33	44	M	B	6	611	F			31	X	X		
69	7616762	BRATCHER	PETER	2.12	7	1	100	958	1	11	1	11	1	11	0	0	2	22	1	M	W	7	730	H	J	252	149		X		

SSS Math Content Possible Points

	Minimum	0.00	1	100	770												1
	Average	2.46		268	1557	41		34		49		36		48		48
	Maximum	4.00	5	401	2172	100		89		100		100		100		99
	Standard Dev	0.83		57	250	20		22		21		20		23		26

Students in School: 1232
Students on Screen: 728
% on Screen: 59%

SSM 3 – 5	178	24%
SSM 1 – 2	550	76%
SSM Tested	728	100%

Biographical Data

Bubble		103
Lowest 25%		142
Levels 1 and 2		550
Level Loss		174
Conflict		106
Potential SSM Calculator	
SSM 3 – 5		24%
SSM 1 – 2		76%
Enter Number		0

Source: Management of Academic Progress (MAP) and Academic Interpretation and Data Evaluation (AIDE). Copyright Accelerated Data Solutions 2002–2004. All Rights Reserved.

Note: Page 1 of a 728-page report. Student names have been changed. Data could be sorted by all students, FCAT eligible students, or by FCAT level (3–5, 1 and 2, or lowest 25%).

Legend

GPA	Grade point average	#	# of points correct	
2003 FCAT Gr	Grade tested	%	% correct	
SSM Level	FCAT Math Level	NRM%ile	Norm Reference %	
SSM Scale	Scale score	S	Sex	
SSM Dev	Development score	E	Ethnicity	
Gr	Grade	R	Retained	BUB	Bubble
HR	Homeroom	ESOL	English Learner	25%	Lowest 25%
L	Lunch status	DDP	Dropout Prevention	1 + 2	Level 1 or 2
ESE	Special Ed	CHO	Choice (voucher)	LOSS	Loss
C	Cost	PRSCH	Prior School	CON	Conflict

Exhibit 9

FCAT Sunshine State Reading (SSR) Gain and Loss Report for Language Arts 3 by Teacher

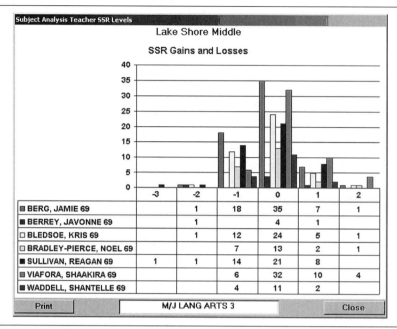

	-3	-2	-1	0	1	2
▨ BERG, JAMIE 69		1	18	35	7	1
▪ BERREY, JAVONNE 69		1		4	1	
▢ BLEDSOE, KRIS 69		1	12	24	5	1
▢ BRADLEY-PIERCE, NOEL 69			7	13	2	1
▪ SULLIVAN, REAGAN 69	1	1	14	21	8	
▨ VIAFORA, SHAAKIRA 69			6	32	10	4
▪ WADDELL, SHANTELLE 69			4	11	2	

Print   M/J LANG ARTS 3   Close

Source: Management of Academic Progress (MAP) and Academic Interpretation and Data Evaluation (AIDE). Copyright Accelerated Data Solutions 2002–2004. All Rights Reserved.

Note: Teachers' names have been changed.

Gain/Loss	Students' Change in FCAT Level from Prior Year
−3	# of students who dropped 3 FCAT levels
−2	# of students who dropped 2 FCAT levels
−1	# of students who dropped 1 FCAT level
0	# of students who maintained same FCAT level
1	# of students who increased 1 FCAT level
2	# of students who increased 2 FCAT levels

Exhibit 10
Student Profile Report

Lake Shore Middle Student Profile
CHRISTOPHER ARCHEVAL

Grade	Homeroom	GPA
7	704	2.41

Course Title	Qtr 1				Qtr 2				Qtr 3				Qtr 4				Exam	Final		
	Gr	A	T	C	Gr	A	T	C	Gr	A	T	C	Gr	A	T	C		Gr	A	T
M7 LANG ARTS 2	B-	0	0	10	B	1	0	HM	B	0	0	M	A-	1	0	OM	87	B	2	0
M7 WORLD GEOG	F	0	0	OP	B-	1	0	OM	C-	0	0	HN	B	1	0	FN	72	C	2	0
M7 HEALTH 3		0	0			0	0		C-	0	0	O		0	0		65	C-	0	0
M7 COMP PHYS ED 2		0	0			0	0			0	0		A	1	0	M	100	A	1	0
M7 COMP PHYS ED 2	A	0	0	N	A	0	0	N	O	0	0	N		1	0				1	0
M7 MATH 2	D	0	0	N	C-	1	0	N	B	0	0	N	B-	1	0	N	100	C	2	0
M7 RESEARCH 3		2	0			1	0			2	0			3	0				8	0
M7 COMP SCI 2	D	2	0	NPT	C	1	0	N	C	2	0	N	C-	3	0	N	100	C	8	0
M7 READ 1	B	1	0	N	B-	1	0	N	C	2	0	N	C-	3	0	N	70	C	4	0
M7 RESEARCH 4		2	0			1	0			2	0			3	0				8	0
Average	2.00				2.33				2.33				3.00					2.43		

Sunshine State Reading Scores

2003 FCAT Grade	7	2002 FCAT Grade	6	Gained/Lose	
2003 SSR Level	2	2002 SSR Level	3	-1	

Sunshine State Reading Content Scores

2003 Writing	Words and Phrases	Main Idea and Purpose	Comparisons	Reference and Research
2003 Content Score	50	50	58	71
Bench Mark 1				
Bench Mark 2				
Bench Mark 3				

SSR AIDE Variables

Scored 10% since Over or Below Level 3 Cut Score	Scored in the lowest 25% of the class	Scored in SSR Level 1 or 2	Lost at least 1 SSR Level	GPA of 3.0 but scored SSR Level 1 or 2
		X	X	

Sunshine State Mathematics Scores

2003 FCAT Grade	7	2002 FCAT Grade	6	Gained/Lose	
2003 SSM Level	2	2002 SSM Level	2	0	

Sunshine State Mathematics Content Scores

	Number Sense	Measurement	Geometry	Algebraic Thinking	Data Analysis
2003 Content Score	78	33	50	33	44
Bench Mark 1					
Bench Mark 2					
Bench Mark 3					

SSM AIDE Variables

Scored 10% since Over or Below Level 3 Cut Score	Scored in the lowest 25% of the class	Scored in SSM Level 1 or 2	Lost at least 1 SSM Level	GPA of 3.0 but scored SSM Level 1 or 2
		X		

Source: Management of Academic Progress (MAP) and Academic Interpretation and Data Evaluation (AIDE). Copyright Accelerated Data Solutions 2002–2004. All Rights Reserved.

Note: Sample data, fictional student name.

Exhibit 11

DCPS School Observation Rubric: Data-driven Decision-making Snapshot

Host Principal Rating

| 1. Preparing ☐ | 2. Getting Started ☐ | 3. Moving Along ☐ | 4. In Place ☐ |

Your Ratings (mark all that apply, and then assess the overall phase of implementation)

Preparing	Getting Started	Moving Along	In Place
☐ The School improvement plan (SIP) contains measurable objectives that are based on data-driven needs.	☐ School leaders conduct a yearly review of SIP objectives to determine adequate progress.	☐ School leaders conduct both midyear and end-of-year review of SIP objectives to determine adequate progress.	☐ School leaders regularly revise their SIP as a result of data collection and analysis. Frequent measures of student achievement are used to set and refine a course of action and to improve instruction and student learning.
☐ School leaders use aggregated school-level data to make decisions.	☐ School leaders use data disaggregated by subgroup to determine the current status of teaching and learning.	☐ Disaggregated data are distributed at least quarterly to all faculty to highlight patterns, in order to inform practices.	☐ The school has developed a climate of inquiry, supported by the allocation of time and resources, for individuals and teams of teachers to conduct ongoing explorations of student performance data in order to inform instructional decision making.
☐ At least some teachers use classroom tests at the end of an instructional unit to measure what students have learned.	☐ At least some teachers use a variety of data sources to keep track of the standards their students have mastered.	☐ Most teachers use a variety of data sources to keep on-going track of the standards their students have mastered in order to individualize and focus instruction.	
☐ School leaders use state test results to identify professional development needs for faculty.	☐ School leaders use a variety of disaggregated student performance data to plan professional development activities for faculty.	☐ School leaders use a variety of data (i.e. disaggregated student achievement data, annual performance appraisal data for teachers and administrators, etc.) in order to plan schoolwide and individual professional development.	☐ All teachers regularly use a variety of data sources to keep ongoing track of the standards their students have mastered and use this information to provide differentiated instruction.
☐ School staff process some data in-house (either manually or electronically).	☐ At least one person in the school is able to use computer technology for effective data processing.	☐ School leaders demonstrate competency in the use of computer technology to manipulate data.	☐ Ongoing collection and analysis of student achievement data are used to adjust and refine schoolwide professional development based on current student needs and staff competencies.
☐ The school provides parents with basic student achievement data such as quarterly report cards, standards mastery levels, and state assessment scores.	☐ Parents are provided with data concerning individual standards mastery, student achievement levels, and the means by which the levels are assessed.	☐ Most teachers document individual student achievement by collecting and maintaining performance and standards mastery data from a variety of sources for use in communicating with parents.	☐ Teachers and administrators routinely use technology to gather, disaggregate, and analyze different achievement indicators from a variety of sources.
			☐ All teachers regularly communicate with parents to ensure their understanding of their child's progress.

Source: District files.

Exhibit 12

Lake Shore FCAT 2004 Student Gains and Losses by Teacher

Grade and Level	Total No. of FCAT Eligible Students	Math Teacher	No. of Students with Math Gains	% of Students with Math Gains	English/ Language Arts Teacher	No. of Students with Reading Gains	% of Students with Reading Gains
6th Grade							
Standard	47	Wick	23	49%	Bushnell	30	64%
Standard	51	*Freund*[b]	12	24%	McDonald	19	37%
Standard	55	First	13	25%	*Cook*[b]	17	31%
Standard	76	*O'Hare*[b]	23	30%	*Kelly*[b]	19	25%
Standard	1	[c]			Hauser	1	100%
Standard[a]	30	*Magoon*[b]	7	23%	*Arroyo*[b]	8	27%
Advanced	30	Wick	20	67%	Bushnell	24	80%
7th Grade							
Standard	43	Sheffield	24	55%	Smith	17	40%
Standard	54	Quinn	20	37%	Jacobs	24	44%
Standard	81	Woodsome	50	62%	Bird	34	42%
Standard	62	*Upton*[b]	39	63%	*Richards*[b]	31	50%
Standard	13	[c]			Henry	8	62%
Advanced	15	Sheffield	11	73%	Smith	9	60%
8th Grade							
Standard	34	*Rupley*[b]	25	71%	Burnett	20	59%
Standard	51	Wigren	29	56%	*Joyce*[b]	21	41%
Standard	47	Ciampi	42	89%	Morrison	23	49%
Standard	50	Nicholas	40	80%	*Nelson*[b]	38	76%
Advanced	27	Nicholas	22	82%	*Nelson*[b]	16	59%
Advanced	34	*Rupley*[b]	30	89%	Burnett	22	65%

Source: Lake Shore Middle School files.

Note: "Gains" signified an increase of at least one achievement level on the FCAT math or reading test. Teacher names have been changed.

[a]Students in this homeroom were performing more than two years behind grade level.

[b]Denotes first-year teacher.

[c]Student(s) included in another class.

Susan Moore Johnson ■ Tiffany K. Cheng

Using Data to Improve Instruction at the Mason School

At a principals' meeting the day before, Janet Palmer Owens had listened as her deputy superintendent announced that Michael Contompasis, the superintendent of the Boston Public Schools (BPS), would arrange to meet individually with a few principals. He was especially interested in talking with those in schools where high proportions of low-income, minority students performed well on the state's standardized tests. Contompasis hoped to learn about their strategies for success so that the district could help more schools make significant gains in student performance. Owens realized that she might well be asked to meet with Contompasis. Her school—the Samuel Mason Elementary School ("the Mason")—had once been one of the lowest-performing schools in the district, but now was among the top-performing BPS elementary schools on the state assessment. Meanwhile, schools nearby struggled to educate students of similar backgrounds.

Owens was deeply committed to all students' academic success. As a school leader, she

believed that she had to "instill a sense of urgency in everyone" and insisted that "our focus on results is non-negotiable. You must do it. That's all I know! Results, results, results. This is about our children and we must get results." She thought her consistent focus on results had been essential to the Mason's impressive progress, but she also realized that improving performance across the school had required much more than sheer determination. As she thought about discussing her school's success with the superintendent, Owens realized that many changes both in her school and in the district had contributed to the Mason's steady improvement (see Exhibit 1). This was not a simple story with an obvious lesson.

Educating in a Context of Accountability

As the oldest public school system in the nation, BPS served 57,279 students in 145 schools in SY07.[1] Its diverse student body was 42% Black, 14% White, 9% Asian American, and 35% Hispanic/Latino. Among these students, 20% were in special education and 11% were enrolled in programs for English language learners. Seventy-three percent of BPS students qualified for free lunch.

District Background

BPS, like other urban districts, faced intense pressure to ensure that all students were learning at high levels. Since the 1970s, the district had utilized a Controlled Choice Plan in order to carry out a desegregation court order. Under the Controlled Choice Plan, BPS divided the city into three geographic zones and asked parents to rank their choices from among the 20–30 elementary schools in their community's zone. Some parents relied solely on test scores to choose schools, whereas others referred to a combination of measures that would often include test score rankings. Schools with low enrollments could be closed. A second approach to accountability was introduced in 1993 when Massachusetts passed an education reform law, which provided increased funding for public schools in exchange for more external scrutiny of results. The Massachusetts Comprehensive Assessment System (MCAS) became the state's tool for measuring educational performance. Developed in conjunction with Massachusetts' curriculum frameworks, the MCAS was a rigorous set of tests, containing both multiple-choice and open-response questions in reading, math, and science.

When the federal government passed the No Child Left Behind Act (NCLB) in 2002, Massachusetts began using the MCAS to meet federal requirements. Whereas initially it was administered in only three grades, federal law now required that students be tested annually in grades three through eight, and once in high school. In order to meet "adequate yearly progress" (AYP) standards, schools would have to achieve proficiency performance targets with all

subgroups having 40 or more students.[2] Schools that failed to meet AYP for two consecutive years were placed in the "needs improvement" category. Those that remained in that category were subject to corrective action, restructuring, or takeover by the state.

Still, these approaches had not transformed schools or eliminated inequity districtwide. In fact, publicly released test data revealed substantial and persistent discrepancies in student achievement across the district. Like many school districts, BPS had an achievement gap between subgroups of students from different ethnic and racial groups. For example, third-grade Black and Latino students scored in the "Very Low" and "Low" categories of the 2006 MCAS English Language Arts (ELA) and Math tests. Their Asian and White counterparts scored in the "Moderate" to "High" categories (see Exhibit 2 for BPS' 2006 MCAS performance figures).

Superintendent Thomas Payzant, who headed the district from 1995–2006, was a strong proponent of standards-based accountability and relied on a whole-school approach to promote improvement. When Payzant introduced new curricula in all subjects, coaches and additional instructional resources were deployed to support implementation in the schools. Within BPS district offices, Payzant's plan for reform created momentum to develop tools that schools and classroom teachers could use to assess and improve student performance.

Sustained Leadership Inside and Outside the District

During Payzant's tenure, BPS worked closely with the Boston Plan for Excellence (BPE), a local education foundation committed to enhancing professional development and literacy instruction in city schools. As the district's primary external partner, the BPE used two approaches to improving schools:[3] 1) testing new ideas that hold promise for accelerating improvement in schools and 2) pressing the district to look at its own policies and practices that slow reform.

The BPE provided critical support to the schools and central office, often creating, testing, refining, and implementing initiatives central to Payzant's reforms. The BPE was both a catalyst and agent for change in school practices through its professional development model of school-based coaching, tools for analyzing student performance data, professional networks for teachers and principals, and other important, research-driven innovations in education. In 2003, the BPE (in partnership with the district and Strategic Grant Partners) instituted and housed the Boston Teacher Residency Program (BTR), the district's homegrown teacher preparation and licensure program.

Providing Schools with Information, Tools, and Resources

Schools were under immense pressure to collect and analyze student performance data through a wide range of district assessments. Each year, they were expected to provide summary reports that detailed each major subgroup's performance against the district's standards. Many of the schools lacked the capacity and resources to manage such a large volume of data. At the request of school change coaches, the BPE began to explore ways to provide assistance.

The BPE created FAST Track, a technology tool that gave schools the ability to depict overall student performance with charts and graphs. However, FAST Track was not a "live" system—it did not keep pace with student mobility within the district. Moreover, teachers were not targeted as the main users and training focused on principals. The system faced barriers to implementation and was thus not widely adopted.

Responding to MCAS

When the state introduced MCAS in 1998, district officials realized that they needed to pro-

vide schools with information and technical tools to assist teachers and principals with data analysis. Maryellen Donahue, BPS Director of Research, Assessment, and Evaluation (RAE), developed the MCAS Toolkit for teachers, which included protocols for examining test results, identifying common student errors, and discussing alternative teaching strategies. Instructional leadership teams, composed of teachers and administrators within schools, used these protocols to analyze data reports provided by the Massachusetts Department of Education (DOE). Donahue recalled, "The focus was to start a conversation of, 'If kids are responding this way, what does it mean for my instruction? What does this mean for my classroom and for other classrooms across the school?'"

The MCAS Toolkit laid a strong foundation for analyzing student data, but teachers and principals found themselves overwhelmed by the paper-based process. The reports from the DOE were not organized by classes or subgroups. Although a few schools were able to input all the data into an electronic spreadsheet program, most lacked the skills and resources for this work and had to disaggregate the data by hand. Donahue noted, "As I look back on it, it was a big step. But, tedious doesn't even begin to describe the process." Without an electronic component to sort and organize the data for meaningful patterns and comparisons, most schools could learn little from their MCAS results.

Creating MyBPS Assessment: For Oversight or Instructional Improvement?

District personnel agreed that they needed assessment tools that would give teachers timely diagnostic information about their students' academic skills. During the 2001–2002 school year, Harvard Graduate School of Education professor Richard Murnane worked with the district to help guide and coordinate a data governance group, which included various administrators in BPS' district office and the BPE. Each month, they not only met to discuss progress made by each department office but also to promote task accountability among leaders, who often felt distracted by what one insider called "the need to put out fires."

Together, members of the governance group discussed what teachers and principals had told them about schools' assessment needs and decided to add assessment tools to an existing data system—MyBPS—which had functioned primarily as an HR portal to inform individual employees about payroll and budgets. Ultimately, the new tool became known as MyBPS Assessment.

MyBPS Assessment provided teachers and data teams with information in response to a series of questions a teacher might ask about MCAS data. For example, a teacher could start with a high-level look at her class' overall performance in reading. She could then decide to examine her students' performance on specific multiple choice questions in order to see if certain concepts proved particularly difficult for them as a group. She could also click through additional screens to view information about individual students and their responses to specific questions (see Exhibit 3 for sample screen shots of MyBPS Assessment).

By linking test items to state standards, MyBPS Assessment encouraged teachers to consider students' performance in relation to standards. Donahue said her mental model for MyBPS was an ATM: "It's almost as easy to use as an ATM. At least, that was my goal." MyBPS was available to teachers with a personal logon from any computer, including those at home. From the perspective of teachers, who had little time during the school day to study their data, this was especially important. BPE's Singleton stressed the value of making the system user-friendly: "There were too many instances where use of data at a school was entirely dependent on the professional development that teachers got

on how to use things like Excel. We said, 'Let's level the playing field so that everybody has the benefit of data analyses.'"

The data governance group confronted the important question of who, in addition to classroom teachers, would have access to the data. Some thought that central office administrators should be able to easily compare performance within classes and across schools in order to have better oversight of how each school and classroom was doing on different parts of the test. Others disagreed, arguing that a design focusing on the needs of central office administrators to monitor compliance would lessen its value for teachers and principals. In the end, the HR portal they had chosen to use as the basis for My BPS Assessment limited their options.

Donahue noted, "In the interest of focusing on teachers' needs, we've moved away—inadvertently, in a way—from the accountability function of the MCAS. The central office wanted to use MyBPS Assessment to see where and who the teachers were, and what they were doing." However, given the portal they were using, this was not possible. Those involved believed that the district would eventually build "a companion set of tools that would satisfy their oversight needs." Therefore, although several central office administrators currently had access to MyBPS Assessment, deputy superintendents and other central office administrators could not view or compare MCAS performance by school clusters, zones, or even the entire district.

The data group also had to decide who within schools would have access to student-level and classroom-level data. After much deliberation, they decided to provide access to student-level and classroom-level data to those in schools with responsibility for instruction and data analysis. Each school principal had the ability to then designate access to support staff as appropriate. Singleton commented, "If we started with the teachers, you could say you were at least opening up the MCAS to some sort of disaggregation for teaching and AYP purposes."

At schools, the use of MyBPS Assessment was self-governed by teachers and principals. Individual teachers could review information about their students and analyze performance by ethnicity, gender, year, and question type. Principals and school data-team members could customize data reports for currently enrolled students by designating codes such as bilingual or after-school program participation; they could also compare whole-class, whole-grade, or whole-school performance to district and state results.

FAST-R: A First Step in Formative Assessments

Although MyBPS Assessment provided teachers with information about their students' performance on the MCAS, these results were not available until August. Since most teachers began with a new class of students each September, they tended to be less interested in the data from the prior year. Without a mechanism to identify learning needs in a timely manner, teachers could not modify instruction to teach their current students the skills they needed.

Recognizing that delay, the BPE began to create a new set of interim assessments that focusing on a narrow range of reading skills—finding evidence in text and making inferences—which had been shown to greatly affect a student's overall performance on the MCAS. The system, Formative Assessment of Student Thinking in Reading (FAST-R), was designed for use in third, fourth, seventh, and tenth grades and consisted of ten multiple choice questions (see Exhibit 4 for more information about FAST-R.) In practice, teachers often gave FAST-R as a pre-test to assess a student's baseline understanding before teaching a unit. Teachers looked upon FAST-R favorably because it was designed to inform their teaching, rather than report to others about their students' success or

failure. Of great importance was the fact that the BPE and BPS returned the results within a week. Singleton said, "we wanted teachers to have the ability to administer frequently. There are always trade-offs in assessment, and we made that knowingly." Donahue's office was working on creating additional formative assessments that would measure students' understanding of key concepts through multiple measures—open-response and short-answer test items. Donahue hoped these assessments would complement FAST-R's use in the classroom.

Training and Support for Schools: The BPE was deeply involved in providing training for schools about how to interpret data and use these tools for instructional improvement. Before the FAST-R initiative, BPE staff had served as the primary source for support and implementation of FAST Track. Selected schools that had begun making substantial improvements on MCAS participated in BPE's training modules on using data for instructional improvement. Other BPS schools could also attend these trainings, as long as they were committed to using data to inform instructional practice.

When MyBPS Assessment was introduced, the BPE and BPS' department of RAE (Research, Assessment, and Evaluation) trained school principals, coaches, and key members of the schools' data teams. Teachers who were unfamiliar with the system received on-site support from coaches, who helped them understand how to use the information on MyBPS Assessment to become more effective teachers. The BPE and BPS had learned from previous initiatives that training had to be provided for school-based educators, but not necessarily the principals. The BPE's Singleton recalled: "When we first started doing work with data, we thought that the principals were the ones you needed to train on how to use systems. The principals were the wrong people, not because they don't have interest or expertise—they're too busy. They just can't do enough to lead a teaching effort that's responsive to data on their own."

Singleton went on to explain how they discovered the most effective way to ingrain the use of data and technology in schools:

We said to the school, "You tell us what it takes to get this into the lifeblood of your school committee." That turned out to be the most fruitful route to go. We still think it works best when there's somebody who knows more about instruction, who plays that role, because the farther the data manager is from [instruction], the less likely they'll know what they're missing. There [needs to be] somebody else who can take on the heavy lifting in the building without [the BPE] having to be there every day.

The principal and teachers at the Mason School had taken advantage of all these tools and resources.

The Mason School

The Mason School, located in a traditional, three-story brick building, was built in 1905. Situated in a densely populated area of Roxbury, Massachusetts, the school was relatively small compared with other BPS elementary schools, serving 215 students in 14 classes, pre-kindergarten through fifth grade. The student population, mirroring the surrounding neighborhood, was 63.7% African American, 25.6% Latino, 7.9% White, and 2.3% Multi-racial. Overall, the proportion of special education students at the Mason reflected districtwide proportions: 20.5% of the students at the school had been diagnosed with one or more disabilities; 77.7% of the students were designated low-income; and 10.2% were classified as English language learners.

A Look Back: 1990–1998

When the Controlled Choice Plan was implemented in 1990, the Mason was the least chosen elementary school in the entire city. Parents were reluctant to send their children to what some thought was a dangerous neighborhood for a sub-par schooling experience. That same year, the new principal, Mary Russo, began to work with teachers and parents to improve the school. With intense effort over the next several years, the Mason raised its performance and reputation. By 1997, the Mason's scores on the MCAS pilot exam were among the highest in the district. Of all the schools in its Controlled Choice zone, the Mason became one of the most frequently chosen by parents. That same year, President Clinton awarded the Blue Ribbon School Award to the Mason in recognition of its achievements.

Janet Palmer Owens' Arrival

In early 1998, Russo left the Mason to head a districtwide reform initiative and Janet Palmer Owens, then a guidance counselor at a BPS high school, was appointed principal. She had a long, rich, and varied career in BPS, having worked in numerous roles at elementary, middle, and high schools. "I had a lot of experience," she acknowledged, "but the challenge that I found was coming into a school that was very, very high-performing."

Taking over a successful school with a first-rate reputation might seem a plum assignment, but Owens immediately faced several obstacles. For years, the Mason had depended on a number of outside grants to augment funds from the district. These extra resources supported some of the personnel and programs that had been instrumental to the school's successful turnaround. In addition, the Mason housed a bilingual program that increased the school's baseline budget. Many of these outside grants were due to expire, and the bilingual program was slated to end in June, thus threatening the continuation of key programs.

Moreover, Owens realized that there was a possibility some students who had disabilities or were English language learners had not been tested. However, once MCAS testing was expanded to require test participation from all students regardless of English language proficiency or disability status, scores at the Mason dropped dramatically. Owens made certain that students in every subgroup were tested:

> When they were getting all those different awards as a result of gains in student achievement, the data was collected in a different type of way. Then, as things evolved with MCAS, it became a whole different way of collecting data and making sure that every single subgroup was included. It became the real thing because of MCAS. I made sure that every single person was tested, so I could have a baseline. Scores on everything dropped, in all the subgroups.

That year, the Mason went from being one of the top-scoring schools on the MCAS to being, once again, a low-performing school in the district (see Exhibit 5 for historical data on the Mason's MCAS performance).

Adding to these challenges were personnel issues that emerged as a result of the school's relentless pursuit of high performance and the change in leadership. After working tirelessly for seven years, some of the teachers moved on in search of new roles or careers. According to Owens, less than one-fourth of the teachers from the previous year remained at the Mason when she arrived.

Under the previous administration, the Mason had become a full-inclusion school, where students with disabilities were educated in classrooms alongside their peers in regular education. All teachers were required to hold dual-certification in regular and special education, thus making it possible for the Mason to use special education funds to reduce class size throughout the school. The typical class had 17 students. With Owens' commitment to educating all students, the established inclusion model increased her confidence that every student would be well served.

Through various partnerships with local universities and strategic use of funding for paraprofessionals, Russo had arranged to have two skilled adults in each classroom (the teacher and a fulltime intern or paraprofessional), thus providing more support for students and flexibility in the schedule. This arrangement, Owens knew, would accommodate the professional development needs of the teachers, especially the many new ones she would hire.

Owens also had the benefit of building on the school's experience with the Literacy Collaborative, a model for professional development aimed at improving literacy instruction schoolwide. Housed at Ohio State University, the Literacy Collaborative had engaged the Mason's teachers since the mid-1990s in systematic assessments, data collection, and analysis. Through that experience, teachers had come to see the value of reflecting together about their students' assessments. Such recognition was an essential element of a strong professional culture that valued the analysis of data. One teacher described the school's involvement with the Literacy Collaborative as a "huge advantage, because it created the push for data even before NCLB."

Moving Ahead at the Mason

With these varied challenges and opportunities, Owens intended to reestablish the preeminence of the Mason, while ensuring that it served all students. She believed in the value of analyzing and using data and aimed to expand the school's capacity in that regard.

In 2003, Hilary Shea, who had several years of experience as a teacher, was considering becoming a principal. She worked for a year as Owens' assistant to learn more about the principal's role. Owens recalled, "[Hilary] accompanied me to all the principal meetings, so I really gave her intense training that year in what it meant to be a principal." The two also attended the district's professional development sessions on data use and enrolled in a yearlong graduate course at the Harvard Graduate School of Education. The course, "Data Wise: Using Assessment Data to Improve Instruction," taught first by Murnane and subsequently by Kathryn Boudett, was designed to help school-based teams of educators analyze student assessment data to improve teaching and learning. Over time, teams from 36 schools in Boston had taken the course. Deputy superintendents recommended schools for participation. Owens recalled that her deputy superintendent "strongly urged us to go to Kathryn's class. Hilary had been on the data team with me . . . so we took Kathryn's course together and Hilary really got better and better in it."

Teacher Collaboration and Common Planning Time: Although Owens and Shea were developing expertise in analyzing data, both realized that this effort had to involve teachers if it were to really effect change. Given the nonstop schedule in most elementary schools, Owens knew that they would have to find protected time for groups of teachers to work together. Owens and Shea made creative use of interns and specialists to provide groups of teachers with 90-minute blocks of uninterrupted common planning time each week. Owen explained the difficulty of making such arrangements:

> To be able to get a group of teachers during the day that can meet uninterrupted for 90 minutes is a challenge. I make it happen by writing many grants to get additional funding. This pays for additional staff, who can then work with children to give teachers that uninterrupted time. The bottom line is that the paraprofessional is still in the classroom—they can cover the curriculum, but the teacher's out in the hall if there's any emergency. The system's in place—and that's my role as the administrator. It's very, very expensive, but that's the secret.

Common planning time was vitally important to the school's teachers because it allowed them to meet in grade-level teams, discuss student performance, and identify students who needed more support. For example, at one meeting, teachers worked together to create a data reporting form that the teachers would use with students to discuss strengths and concerns based on MCAS standards by subject area. Teachers then spent time in grade-level teams discussing their students' responses on a recent FAST-R administration. Shea said, "we want to make sure we flag questions that seem to give our students a great deal of trouble and also note whether certain students are performing poorly overall." Common planning time helped teachers at every grade level recognize common challenges and receive support from their colleagues. One teacher said, "We're quite thankful for it."

Although Owens could require that the teachers work together during these 90-minute blocks, she insisted that they decide how best to use the time. Teachers took turns facilitating the meeting, developing a detailed agenda and using protocols to ensure that scarce time would be well used. As they worked intently with their colleagues, their classes were taught by specialists in science, music, and art, fulltime interns from the Boston Teacher Residency Program or a local university, or by fulltime paraprofessionals who were prepared to continue instruction just as if the teacher were in the room.

Becoming a Pilot School: Risks and Rewards
In 1994, BPS and the Boston Teachers Union (BTU) jointly instituted within-district charter schools, called "pilot" schools, which were granted autonomy over curriculum and assessment, governance, staffing, schedule, and budget decisions in exchange for greater accountability. Importantly for the Mason, pilot schools could use their budget to staff a complicated schedule

that allowed for common planning time (see Exhibit 6 for a comparison of BPS and pilot schools). They could also decide what curriculum and assessments, in addition to MCAS, they would administer.

The Mason's teachers voted to become a pilot school in 2003. One teacher recalled, "We were already doing such great work with data before we obtained pilot status—but we really wanted to operate under true shared leadership." Another remarked, "We didn't want to ever have a time like we had years ago where there were budget cuts and somebody downtown said, 'You need to cut teachers.'" To Owens, having pilot status became critical to reallocating the school's resources in the service of instructional quality. She said: "When we became pilot, we were able to creatively use our additional funding to buy services. We could hire parents and get waivers for hiring BTR interns as paraprofessionals to reduce our class size that other schools wouldn't have been able to do." With these flexibilities, the school could focus even more on its use of data during common planning time and put into place processes that enabled stronger collaborations among teachers.

Most pilot schools did not work according to the provisions of the BTU collective bargaining agreement. Teachers at the Mason, however, chose to remain under the BTU contract, thus retaining the same rights and privileges of other teachers at regular district schools. Each pilot school was required to write and approve a "work agreement," explaining the ground rules for the teachers' employment. The Mason's work agreement explained that, while teachers were going to work under the contract, they would commit to additional responsibilities. One teacher said, "The way we wrote our proposal made it safe, that we were still governed under the union. That was the big piece that made a lot of teachers feel safe, and we didn't want to do it unless the whole staff had buy-in. It's beyond

what the union says, but it's what we've agreed to do" (see Exhibit 7 for the Mason's work agreement). Owens supported this decision: "There was no reason for us to change the BTU contract because we were doing really well. I don't believe in teachers working so many hours a day, becoming exhausted and never having the chance to lead a balanced life. After 2:30, I want [teachers] to plan for their classrooms." She realized that creative use of the pilot school autonomies of budget, staffing, and schedule would allow her to provide professional development within the regular school day.

As a pilot school with autonomy over curriculum and assessments, the Mason could decide which tests to use. Mason's math facilitator and fourth-grade teacher Aadina Balti explained: "Since we became a pilot school, we've used data more because we feel like we have more control over what we're doing with our curriculum. We have a little bit more leeway on how we're delivering our instruction or what we're using to assess it. We've also been better about creating more formal and informal assessments."

A School of Teacher Leaders

Often, schools have one or two outstanding teachers who become formal or informal leaders in the school. At the Mason, though, teachers repeatedly said that many of their colleagues assumed responsibility for leadership. Most were compensated with small stipends for their extra work, but extra pay was not why teachers assumed these roles. According to Owens: "Every single teacher has a leadership role. When I first came, we would talk about teacher leadership but the only teacher leaders in that building in 1998 were the two literacy coordinators and myself. I was running everything. And now every single teacher is a teacher leader." She described the teachers' roles in facilitating meetings of the Mason's Instructional Leadership Team. "It's just amazing to watch how they've grown.

They'll come to me and they'll have their agendas. We go over the agenda before the meeting. Then I come into the meeting with my notebook like everyone else, and they run it. It's all about teacher quality, and that's what translates into success."

In addition to her teaching responsibilities as one of the Mason's kindergarten/first-grade teachers, Caitlin McArdle worked as the Literacy Coordinator in the primary grades. She described her schoolwide role: "My job is to coach teachers on implementation of the Literacy Collaborative model. I'm also part of the school-based leadership team in terms of looking more globally at the implementation of responsibilities of collecting data, doing an annual school report, and talking about what the data shows."

In her role as the school's math facilitator, Balti supported teachers who needed help in math instruction. She said, "I'm not a formal coach—we ended up getting an actual math coach from the math department this year, so I'm working with her. I meet with teachers outside of the classroom time who need support or questions answered."

Notably, strong leadership among teachers required wise leadership by the principal. Owens was highly respected by her teachers, colleagues, and partners. The BPE's Singleton praised her for strategically engaging teachers throughout the school in responsibilities that mattered: "Janet is Janet. She's very strong, encouraging, and direct about what she wants people to be doing. There's a cascading effect of people in the right place at the right time that help out at the Mason."

Owens also hired teachers very deliberately. She made sure that candidates understood the Mason's expectations for commitment and performance. By recruiting interns through local universities and teacher certification programs, Owens was able to subsequently offer fulltime teaching positions to the best among them. According to Owens, more than half of the Ma-

son's teaching force initially came to the school as interns or support staff. By the time they became official faculty members, they were already very familiar with the school's strong professional culture and thus well-positioned to assume responsibility beyond their classroom. Owens said, "We hire from within—they learned as former interns. They continue to learn, as we all learn as a team."

To continue that learning, Owens took advantage of training offered by BPS. She reflected, "We're successful because we've accessed all the training and professional development from BPS and BPE." This development, she said, was instrumental in changing the ways in which the Mason collected, analyzed, and made decisions from data. Owens remarked:

> When I first came to the school, the only data I would see would be the Literacy Collaborative data. You'd see the results of all the different components of the literacy model, but that's all you'd see—there was no other data. Now, you have huge, thick binders around every single possible thing to see results with kids so that teachers are able to articulate and actually do it all on the computer.

She also learned from her deputy superintendents: "My deputies—I've been lucky. They are in the buildings, walking through—and they know what to look for. If the school's not doing it, the deputies are in there talking to principals. Every year, we have our principal's binder and we sit down with our deputy and talk through the data." Owens adapted this approach in supervising her own teachers. McArdle described Owens' data management with teachers: "In the beginning of the year, everyone wrote goals for themselves, and when Mrs. Owens had meetings with people on their goals, she had the data binder in front of her."

Ultimately, Owens believed in empowering her teachers to become fully engaged with the use of data. "It's all there so teachers can really and truthfully get the data themselves." She added, "Teacher leadership is huge. Teachers have to own it. They have to feel respected. They have to feel that they're a part of the process. They're professionals and being treated like professionals is critical, too."

The Data Queen

After a year as Owens' assistant, Shea realized that she wanted to remain a classroom teacher, rather than becoming a principal. "I definitely had my own passions," she said. "A lot of that has to do with instructional improvement and working with teachers around how to use data to move the school forward. But I love working with kids and wanted to retain that part of my job." Shea became a fourth/fifth-grade teacher while assuming various responsibilities that provided release time during part of the school day for her to work with teachers.

In her three years at the Mason, Shea worked to help teachers understand how to use data. Her colleague Balti commented, "Having worked with Hilary last year, I was able to see how she was doing it. That helped me figure out better ways to do it in my own classroom. We have opportunities to share our own practices so that people can figure out what works for them. I think it's just a matter of time before everyone develops a comfort level with how to use data." McArdle added, "Hilary is infatuated with data. She picks apart the MCAS data and does a lot of presentations for the staff so we're able to look at the big picture. I do have to say, she is our data queen."

Culture Change and the Use of Data

Traditionally, most teachers are accustomed to working independently and often know little about their colleagues' instructional practice or effectiveness. At the Mason, an established norm of teacher collaboration meant identifying and discussing each other's strengths and shortcom-

ings. Doing this effectively, said Owens, required strong professional standards and a school culture that supported such work.

For the opening faculty meeting in September, Shea prepared a student-by-student summary of MCAS data and the teachers discussed it together, reflecting on how each student was doing over time. Also, they examined their students' performance in sub-groups. McArdle described the process: "Every year, we will pick apart how our kids did in all the grades and down to 'Okay, question number 14; 80% of our kids got it wrong. This percentage answered [it this way] and this percentage answered it that way. Why? Why do we think this?'"

Shea explained how she worked with teachers:

> I've continued to break down the data in ways that make it very accessible to the staff. I lead the instructional leadership team in discussions about MCAS data to start those difficult conversations of cross-comparison data. For example, if a kid's scores on the MCAS are low but we have them reading on grade level according to his benchmark assessment, and he has a three on his report card, we ask, "Why is there a discrepancy?"

Throughout the year, teachers at the Mason tracked students' skill mastery. McArdle insisted, "The kids belong to all of us. Even though a student might be in third grade, he's everybody's child. We look globally at our kids and keep track of their reading levels together to see how we can all help them succeed." Balti added, "We're all pretty vocal about what we think we need to work on. Everyone wants to move forward and improve instruction so that our kids achieve proficiency. One of our key strengths is that we are trying to better ourselves as teachers." Shea agreed that everyone was invested in this effort: "There's a healthy level of competition—we care. We care about our kids, how they do, and their scores. [But also], you want to look good. You want to look like what you're doing is having an impact."

When children at the Mason were struggling, teachers created what McArdle referred to as the "safety net." Shea elaborated:

> It's very difficult for kids to get lost here. There's a lot of ways to flag the kids. Around this time of year, we create a list of what we call high-risk kids and indicate different content areas they need help. Our specialists will use any of their open blocks to pull individual or small groups, and it could be kids who are really high or kids who are really low, depending on the students' needs. We also have after-school tutoring.

McArdle emphasized that teachers have a common understanding in examining data at the Mason:

> The data is part of everything we do. There is always a purpose behind our professional development. It's data-driven—it's never arbitrary. When we're trying to think through something, we take out our data binders and ask, "What is the data telling you about what our kids' need?" Every classroom has a place where they're keeping information and data in relation to guided reading. We report every fall, winter, and spring—they're living binders and not just put in and put away. It's just embedded in everything that we do.

Shea said this process would never work if it were a top-down mandate. "Janet's really good about this sort of thing—she's supportive of us. It has to be organic and led by teachers. Otherwise, this type of work just wouldn't hold." She was clear, though, that Owens was no laissez-faire leader: "Holding people accountable is another piece. When the data is due, Janet holds everybody accountable. She will go after people if they don't hand it in on time." For her own part, Owens credited the teachers' resolve and

readiness to do the hard work: "Sometimes, you have to change your ways, and this group has always been that way. They want to learn and get to the next level. This is how they've grown up."

Using Data to Revise Curriculum and Instruction

The teachers in the school began to use MCAS data to make curricular changes across classrooms and grade levels. Shea offered one example from science:

> We felt that our students—in fact, all students across the city of Boston—were not doing as well on the MCAS as their actual knowledge of science would indicate. So we came to the conclusion that a big part was somewhat the vocabulary, and how the questions were phrased. We started to talk about it in common planning time and decided that the kids would take a pre-and post-test. These are made up of previous MCAS questions. In fourth and fifth grade, they take it as is. In third grade, it's slightly modified—sometimes it's read to them because they may not have the reading skills to be able to do some of the questions. In second grade, teachers make their own appropriate determination on how the assessment should go. That forced the kids to show their knowledge in more than one way.

Based on what they learned, the teachers specified topics that the science teacher should cover in certain grades and classes. Such efforts illustrated how the expertise needed for teachers to use data to improve instruction went well beyond technical competence. Although Shea's work with teachers about data changed instructional practice throughout the Mason, Shea was quick to point out that the technical skills of data analysis were not enough to make a difference:

> There are a lot of schools that I've worked with in BPS, and they have this data analysis techie. [The techies] make the most gorgeous graphs,

but they have no idea about instruction. The person couldn't go the next level. I talk to principals a lot and tell them that pretty graphs alone mean absolutely nothing if you don't have someone pushing the envelope on the ground floor. I could not do this job with the school if I did not teach part-time. Part of that has to do with credibility. But the other part is, how would I get the data and figure out what to do if I didn't have my own class?

Moreover, Shea insisted, using data to improve instruction takes time and requires focus:

You can't have a million initiatives. Last fall, we started to talk about our kids and their reading response letters. Students write a letter to their teacher (or whoever) about the book they're reading. The point of it is to teach your kids how to be reflective learners, to develop literary analysis, and summary skills. The letters weren't very good. They weren't changing for grades three through five, even though they do these from second grade on. Our kids weren't doing well in open response on the MCAS even though we put more time than most people into writing about reading. We had a whole professional development cycle around this and came to the conclusion that kids don't realize that the stakes and expectations are getting higher. It took almost a full year. Now, the quality of the letters is much higher. We have exemplars, rubrics for each grade. A lot of people would say, "One year on one little thing like that?" But that's actually using data to try to inform instruction.

Although the school initially relied on the BPE and BPS to help them progress, they became more self-reliant over time and counted on one another for feedback and leadership. They attended the district's professional development sessions selectively, often sending a representative who then reported back to others with new information or skills. While they continued to use MyBPS Assessment, teachers at the Mason often retrieved information about MCAS and state standards directly from the DOE website. They also began creating their own formative assessments based on the Fast-R model. At the central office, Donahue was exploring the possibility of creating a data bank of test items that teachers might draw from in creating their own assessments—a resource the Mason teachers would certainly welcome.

Excellence at Scale

Owens wondered how best to explain these developments to the interim superintendent. In her view, success resulted from many factors—technical support and training from the BPE and BPS, clear expectations by the deputy superintendent, flexible funding and staffing as a pilot school, having teachers who assumed leadership and took risks with colleagues, and a strong professional culture that supported their day-to-day efforts to change. The Mason and its accomplishments were not typical of other Boston schools (see Exhibits 8a and 8b for a comparison of demographic and performance data between the Mason and a neighboring school). Whatever the superintendent's approach, Owens believed that it was essential he recognize the need of individual schools to define their own approach and work toward their goals relatively unfettered by additional rules and requirements.

However, some in the district worried that there was not enough centralized oversight and control of student performance. Although schools that were already strong could make good use of autonomy, those that were failing might need firm advice about how to improve. One teacher said, "What we're doing at the Mason is great, but who knows what they're doing down the street?" Owens reported that several principals were now asking her to explain the Mason's success. However, most schools did not have teacher leaders with Shea's expertise, or groups of teachers who could candidly and con-fidently review student data together.

Much like the district's schools, central of-fice administrators remained relatively isolated, working together intermittently on specific tasks regarding data use. Even then, these efforts were sometimes at cross purposes. Further, several ad-ministrators began to express concern that the different departments themselves were not suf-ficiently aligned with one another to provide consistent answers and support to the schools. Certain offices—curriculum, research, and IT—were critical to these schools' progress since their decisions and requirements could either advance or block new approaches to instructional im-provement. However, this would require big changes in the BPS organizational culture. Noting how slowly the district changes direc-tion—"it's like turning the Titanic, to be quite honest with you"—Singleton emphasized the benefits of working closely with outside partners such as Murnane (who had integrated the efforts of various departments in order to create MyBPS Assessment). Singleton said, "the ability to have somebody who doesn't have a dog in the fight is really, really valuable. There's still a big role for having a third party serving as a broker or a mediator of stalled efforts."

As superintendent, Contompasis had to move the entire system to much higher levels of performance. One approach would be to en-courage innovation and exchange of informa-tion among principals and central administrators so that the schools would better serve all stu-dents. As she pulled together her data binders and school improvement plans, Owens began to reflect on what she would say if Contompasis asked to meet with her.

Notes

1. SY is a PELP convention that denotes "school year." For example, SY07 refers to the 2006–2007 school year.

2. Students were assigned to AYP subgroups based on their language proficiency, race, socioeconomic status, and disability status.

3. http://bpe.org/, accessed January 15, 2007.

Exhibit 1

Timeline: Key Events and Decisions at BPS and the Mason

1970s	**Controlled Choice in BPS**
1990	*Mason least chosen elementary school* *Russo appointed principal of Mason*
1995	Payzant appointed as superintendent "Focus on Children"
1997	*Mason among highest scoring, most chosen elementary schools* *National Blue Ribbon School award*
1998	MCAS administered in grades 4, 8, and 10 *Owens becomes principal of the Mason* *Mason MCAS scores drop*
2001	HGSE Data Wise
2002	NCLB requires testing in all elementary grades
2003	My BPS Assessment *Pilot school status for Mason*
2006	BPS wins Broad Prize *Mason among top performing elementary schools*

Source: Case writer.

Exhibit 2

BPS' 2006 MCAS Performance Figures

	2006 MCAS Performance Results for BPS Third Grade Students Percent of Students at Each Performance Level									
	English Language Arts					**Mathematics**				
AYP Subgroup	**A**	**P**	**NI**	**W**	**CPI**[a]	**A**	**P**	**NI**	**W**	**CPI**[a]
African-American/ Black	3	24	50	22	65	1	24	37	39	57.9
Hispanic/Latino	3	17	52	28	59.5	1	23	37	39	57.9
Asian American	13	33	40	14	75.8	4	58	25	13	83
White	17	36	36	11	80.1	5	50	29	15	79
Students with Disabilities	2	9	44	45	51.1	1	14	30	55	50.6
English Language Learners	5	20	49	26	61.8	1	29	35	35	62.3
Low Income	4	21	51	24	63.2	1	27	36	36	60.6
Non-Low Income	15	35	36	15	77.9	4	41	30	25	72.2

Source: Casewriter analysis from Massachusetts Department of Education.

A=Advanced; P=Proficient; NI=Needs Improvement; W=Warning/Failing

[a] The Composite Performance Index (CPI) is a measure of the extent to which students are progressing toward proficiency in English language arts (ELA) and mathematics. A CPI of 100 in a given content area means that all students have reached proficiency. CPI scores correspond to one of six performance rating categories: Very High (90–100); High (80–89.9); Moderate (70–79.9); Low (60–69.9); Very Low (40–59.9); and Critically Low (0–39.9).

Exhibit 3
MyBPS Assessment Screen Shots

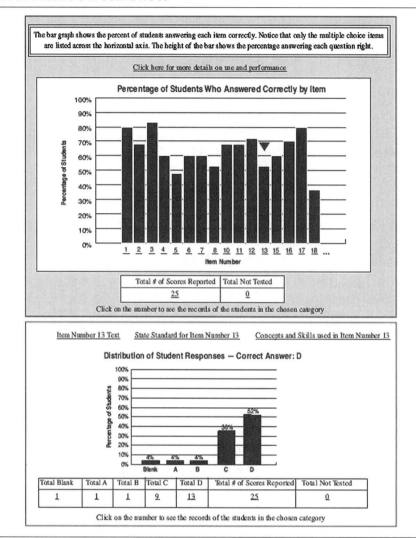

Source: Focus Newsletter for Boston Teachers, SY2004–2005, Issue #2. Boston Plan for Excellence, http://www.bpe.org/ documents/FocusMyBPS.pdf, accessed January 15, 2007.

Exhibit 3 (continued)

EXCERPT of Table: Students' Compositions, Scores, & Scorers' Comments

Total Students Proficient Category: 7

Student No.	First Name	Last Name	CC	CT	Over-all	SC1	SC2	SC3	SC4	WP Text Link
123456	Student	Name	6	6	12	OX	SW	SX	TL	Show Student Work
234567	Student	Name	6	7	13	LW	SW	GW	DL	Show Student Work
345678	Student	Name	6	8	14	TX	SW			Show Student Work
456789	Student	Name	7	7	14	TX	SW	SX	DL	Show Student Work
567890	Student	Name	6	8	14	OX	SW	GX		Show Student Work
678901	Student	Name	7	8	15	TX	SW			Show Student Work ◄
789012	Student	Name	7	9	16	TX	OX	SX	GX	Show Student Work

If you click here, you will get a PDF of this student's actual composition. ▼

Total Students Advanced Category: 2

Student No.	First Name	Last Name	CC	CT	Over-all	SC1	SC2	SC3	SC4	WP Text Link
654321	Student	Name	7	8	15	TX	DW	SW	MW	Show Student Work
543210	Student	Name	8	11	19	LW	LY	SX	MW	Show Student Work

Grade 4 Writing Prompt

Think about a friend who has been an important part of your life. How did you become friends with this person? Think about when you met, what you did, and how your friendship grew.

Write a story about this friendship. Give enough details to tell the reader about this friendship.

You have a total of four pages on which to write your final composition. Please begin here.

Have you ever had a best friend? I know I have her name is ... Deanna.
When I saw Deanna she was shy. I went up to her and said Hi what is your name. She said my name is Deanna. Then I said my name is Melissa. She said nice name. You got a nice name to. Then I ask her Do you want to be my friend She said yes I was happy when she said yes Then I said I sit right here.
Me and Deanna friendship grew by sharing. We love to share with each other and we like to tell each other stuff. When I told her that miss mason is nice ...

This is just the first of four pages Melissa wrote. When you click on "Show Student Work," you will get your student's entire composition.

Source: Focus Newsletter for Boston Teachers, SY2004–2005, Issue #2. Boston Plan for Excellence, http://www.bpe.org/ documents/FocusMyBPS.pdf, accessed January 15, 2007.

Exhibit 4
FAST-R

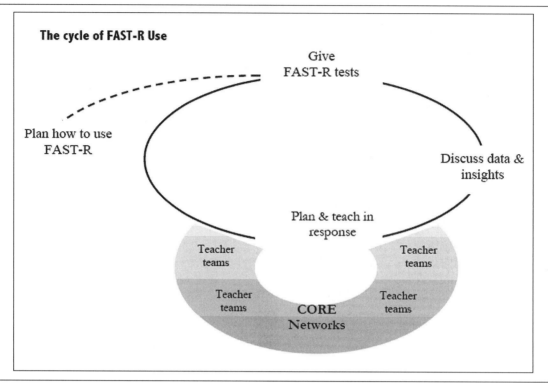

The cycle of FAST-R Use

Give
FAST-R tests

Plan how to use
FAST-R

Discuss data &
insights

Plan & teach in
response

Teacher
teams

Teacher
teams

Teacher
teams

Teacher
teams

CORE
Networks

Source: Chrismer, Sarah S., FAST-R Year II Evaluation, August 2005, p. 2. Boston Plan for Excellence, http://www.bpe.org/ documents/FAST-R_YearIIEvalFINAL.pdf, accessed January 15, 2007.

Exhibit 4 (continued)

FAST-R Student Performance Summary

These graphs show how many students selected each answer choice, while the annotated answer key highlights types of wrong answers, where answers were found in the text, and what thinking may have led to that answer choice.

The data can help you hypothesize about your students' reading and thinking, but talking with your students will confirm or contradict your hypotheses and help you plan mini-lessons, conferring, and guided reading instruction in response to your students' strengths and needs.

Key

- Correct answer
- OOP1 "near miss" answer; true based on text, but irrelevant
- OOP2 "mis-read" answer; based on misunderstanding of the text
- OOB answer; not based on text; plausible from prior knowledge
- No answer

This analysis represents the performance of:

School **Sample MS**   Grade: **07**   Class/Sec: **211**   Question Set: **G7NF2**

---

1. At the end of the passage, how does the author describe Arthur Ashe?

A. quiet — (OOP2 ¶ 3) Ashe's mother is described as "quiet" 3)

B. cool — (OOP1 ¶4)

C. tragic — (OOP1 ¶2) "tragedy" mentioned in paragraph 2

✓ D. unpredictable — found four sentences from the end of the passage

1. Finding Evidence

A - OOP2	0
B - OOP1	1
C - OOP1	1
D - Correct	13
No Answer	0

---

2. Why were other players frustrated while playing against Arthur Ashe?

A. He would brag about beating them. (OOB) students may be frustrated when others brag about winning

B. He never argued. — (OOP1 ¶3-4) true, but not what frustrated others

C. He was out of control when he played. — (OOP2 ¶4-5) students may confuse being "unpredictable" with being out of control

✓ D. He always appeared cool and in control. (¶4)

2. Finding Evidence

A - OOB	0
B - OOP1	4
C - OOP2	0
D - Correct	11
No Answer	0

---

3. According to this passage, Arthur Ashe and his mother were similar in that

A. they both argued a lot. — (OOP2 ¶3-4) neither argued

✓ B. they both died when their children were six years old. (¶2)

C. they both played volleyball very well. — (OOB) students who skipped the italicized intro may not know he was a tennis player and see "crosscourt half-volley" as a volleyball term

D. they both had long soft hair. — (OOP1 ¶3) she did, but there are no details about Arthur's hair

3. Finding Evidence

A - OOP2	0
B - Correct	9
C - OOB	3
D - OOP1	3
No Answer	0

Page
1 of 3

Source: Boston Plan for Excellence (2005). "Sample Data Packet (middle school)," http://www.bpe.org/documents/ SampleMSFAST-RDataPacket.pdf, accessed January 16, 2007.

Exhibit 4 (continued)

This analysis represents the performance of:

School **Sample MS**   Grade: **07**   Class/Sec: **211**   Question Set: **G7NF2**

---

4. At approximately what age did Arthur Ashe die?

A. six — (OOP2) Ashe was six when his mother died

B. twenty-seven — (OOP2) his mother died when she was twenty-seven

✓ C. in his forties or fifties — must be inferred from the second and third sentences of the passage

D. in his sixties or seventies — (OOB)

4. Making Inferences

A - OOP2	0
B - OOP2	13
C - Correct	2
D - OOB	0
No Answer	0

---

5. In paragraph 2, the author says that "death would come to him prematurely, as it had to his mother." What does prematurely mean?

A. painfully — (OOB) students may associate "pain" with death

✓ B. earlier than expected

C. suddenly and unexpectedly — (OOP1) plausible for students using a "plug in other words that make sense" strategy

D. peacefully — (OOB) this word looks like "prematurely"

5. Making Inferences
(word-in-context)

A - OOB	2
B - Correct	6
C - OOP1	5
D - OOB	2
No Answer	0

---

6. In paragraph 4, Arthur Ashe said "what he liked best about himself on a tennis court was his demeanor." What does demeanor mean?

A. bad attitude — (OOP2) plausible for students using a "plug in other words that make sense" strategy, but a misread of the description of Ashe

B. drive to win — (OOB) associated with athletes, but a misread of the description of Ashe

✓ C. conduct

D. gracefulness — (OOP1 ¶5) suggested by description of his playing

6. Making Inferences
(word-in-context)

A - OOP2	0
B - OOB	4
C - Correct	6
D - OOP1	5
No Answer	0

---

7. The author uses paragraph 4 to describe

✓ A. Ashe's self-control.

B. how Ashe learned to play tennis. — (OOB)

C. the influence Ashe's father had on him. — (OOP2 ¶3-4) his mother's "legacy" was "not-arguing," but his dad's influence is not discussed

D. how Ashe felt about tennis. — (OOP1) ¶4 is about how Ashe felt about himself on the court; his feelings for the sport are unexplored

7. Finding Evidence
()

A - Correct	14
B - OOB	0
C - OOP2	0
D - OOP1	1
No Answer	0

Source: Boston Plan for Excellence (2005). "Sample Data Packet (middle school)," http://www.bpe.org/documents/SampleMSFAST-RDataPacket.pdf, accessed January 16, 2007.

Exhibit 4 (continued)

This analysis represents the performance of:

School **Sample MS**   Grade: **07**   Class/Sec: **211**   Question Set: **G7NF2**

---

8. In paragraph 5, the phrase "a braid of cables" describes Arthur Ashe's

A. very long legs. — (OOP1) students may picture "cables" as an image for long, thin legs

✓ B. muscular body.

C. tennis racquet. — (OOB) students may associate "a braid of cables" with the strings of a tennis racquet

D. high energy. — (OOP2) mentioned in clause right after "a braid of cables"; students may know of electrical cables carrying energy

8. Making Inferences
(word-in-context)

A - OOP1	2
B - Correct	3
C - OOB	6
D - OOP2	4
No Answer	0

---

9. In paragraph 5, the author focuses on Arthur Ashe's

A. private life off the court. — (OOB) the text is entirely about Ashe on the court

B. physical appearance. — (OOP1) only in beginning of ¶ 5; too specific

✓ C. skills that made him a winning tennis player.

D. sad childhood that shaped the way he played. — (OOP2) while he "inherited" his mother's easygoing ways, her death in itself is not described as a cause of his self-control

9. Making Inferences
(main idea)

A - OOB	2
B - OOP1	2
C - Correct	11
D - OOP2	0
No Answer	0

---

10. The author's main purpose in writing this essay was to

A. warn the reader about the dangers of playing tennis. — (OOB) students choosing this answer may not have read or understood the passage

B. persuade the reader to start playing tennis at an early age. — (OOP2) Ashe started playing at an early age, but this essay is not designed to persuade others to do the same

C. entertain the reader with an amusing story about a tennis player. — (OOB)

✓ D. inform the reader about the qualities of a great tennis player.

10. Making Inferences
(author craft)

A - OOB	1
B - OOP2	1
C - OOB	2
D - Correct	11
No Answer	0

Source: Boston Plan for Excellence (2005). "Sample Data Packet (middle school)," http://www.bpe.org/documents/ SampleMSFAST-RDataPacket.pdf, accessed January 16, 2007.

Exhibit 5

The Mason's Historical MCAS Performance Data

	The Mason's MCAS Performance Data (Grade 4) Percent of Students at Each Performance Level							
	English Language Arts				Mathematics			
Year	A	P	NI	W	A	P	NI	W
1998	0	0	70	30	0	4	52	44
1999	0	4	93	4	7	15	67	11
2000	0	4	81	15	4	11	52	33
2001	0	45	52	3	10	37	53	0
2002	0	31	63	6	3	41	53	3
2003	0	36	50	14	0	14	64	21
2004	3	52	39	6	39	19	35	6
2005	0	48	44	7	11	19	56	15
2006	0	41	59	0	14	45	38	3

Source: Casewriter analysis from Massachusetts Department of Education.

A=Advanced; P=Proficient; NI=Needs Improvement; W=Warning/Failing

Exhibit 6

BPS and Pilot School Characteristics

Elementary School Characteristics	Pilot Schools	Boston Public Schools
Average number of students seen by core academic teachers each day	20	24
Length of student school day (minutes)	370	360
Length of teacher school day, including after-school contracted faculty meeting time (minutes)	409	386
Minutes per week of professional collaboration time	216	48 (minimum)
Number of full professional development days	8	3

Source: Center for Collaborative Education, 2006. "Progress and Promise: Results from the Boston Pilot Schools" http://www.ccebos.org/Progress_and_Promise.pdf, accessed January 15, 2007.

Exhibit 7
The Mason School Work Agreement

Teacher Agreement between
The Samuel Mason Pilot K-5 School
And

_____

(name of teacher)

Academic Year 2006–2007

I, _____, am voluntarily electing to work at the Samuel Mason Pilot Elementary School. I am signing this Agreement to indicate I understand and agree to the following terms and conditions of my employment.

The Mason is a Pilot School, under the Pilot Schools program described in the Collective Bargaining Agreement between the School Committee of the City of Boston and Boston Teachers Union (the "BTU Contract") and in the Pilot Schools Request for Proposals. Employees of Pilot Schools are to receive wages and benefits as they would at any other Boston Public School, as specified in Article VIII, Compensation and Benefits, of the BTU Contract for teachers. The Mason and the BTU Contract, as specified in this teacher agreement, will determine other terms and conditions of employment. While not attempting to be exhaustive, this Agreement states the more important terms and conditions of employment at the Mason. These terms and conditions may be subject to change from time to time by the governing body of the Mason Pilot School in consultation with the faculty and 66 2/3% vote as specified in Article IIIE.

a. Salary, benefits, seniority and membership in bargaining unit.

I will continue to accrue seniority as I would if I were working elsewhere in the Boston Public School ("BPS"). If hired as a teacher, I will receive the salary and benefits established in the BTU Contract, Article VIII and Article IIIE. I will be a member of the appropriate Boston Teachers Union ("BTU") bargaining unit.

b. Terms of employment.

My term of employment will be the 2006–2007 Mason Pilot School year, which includes no more than 2 working days preceding the beginning of the school year, as specified in the BTU contract. New teachers to the school may be required to attend an additional three days of orientation. If school days are cancelled during the school year, the Mason's school year will be subject to extension in the same amount as the regular BPS school year is extended. Holidays will be the same as those specified in the BTU contract. Regularly scheduled working hours for full-time teachers will be Monday through Friday, 8:20 A.M. to 2:35 P.M., with an extended day, 2:45–4:45pm, one day a week during which staff will be participate in contracted professional development / sub-committee meetings; including but not limited to faculty meetings, ILT, literacy training, math training, Achievement Gap/race and culture study group, and data team (all additional hours are voluntary, although staff are highly recommended to attend.) Please reference professional development schedule for the 2006–07 school year.

Exhibit 7 (continued)

b. Excessing

The excessing policy of the Mason School will follow the conditions of the BTU contract.

c. Dismissal

I will be subject to dismissal from BPS in accordance with the BTU contract and existing law. Additionally, the contract for provisional teachers is limited to one school year of employment.

d. Responsibilities

All Mason Pilot School Teachers agree to put Mason children in the forefront of planning, teaching and professional development. Teachers will provide multiple educational experiences for every learner to develop his or her best academically, socially, emotionally, and physically. Teachers will support and believe in the importance of an inclusive education by providing challenging curricula and instruction, which meets the individual needs of each child in reading, writing, mathematics, social studies, science and technology. Teachers will hold high expectations for achievement, behavior, and positive social interactions for everyone and will create a positive and respectful school culture that is nurturing, supportive, honors diversity; that celebrates one another's achievements and accomplishments.

- All teachers at the Mason Pilot School agree to be, or actively pursuing, dual certification in elementary **and** special education.

- All teachers at the Mason Pilot School must be a member of at least one subcommittee (ILT, SST, MLT, etc) to take place during our extended day.

- Each year all teachers at the Mason Pilot School will be working towards their own personal goals for PDP's towards recertification.

- All teachers at the Mason Pilot School agree to participate in CCL.

- All teachers at the Mason Pilot School will implement Literacy Collaborative model in grades K-5 and the CLI model in early childhood.

- All teachers at the Mason Pilot School will implement the TERC mathematics curriculum and Ten Minute Math.

- All teachers at the Mason Pilot School agree to open up their classrooms to learning site visits.

- All teachers will administer internal and district/state assessments according to proper test administration guidelines. Teachers will also turn in assessment results in accordance with pre-determined deadlines. Teachers will use data to inform their instruction as well as keep accurate and up-to-date information, including cumulative records, on students in an easy to find location.

- All Mason Pilot School Teachers will create opportunities for parents and families to be active partners in their children's education and in our educational community, including monthly communication, parent conference during the day, and curriculum-related activities that are open to families such as: publishing parties, performances, etc. (*Parent conferences will occur during the day and teachers will be provided with coverage.*)

Exhibit 7 (continued)

e. Dispute Resolution. **(Follows the BTU Contract, pp. 27–29)**

f. Performance Evaluation

The Mason Pilot School will use the performance evaluation system, described in Part V. G of the BTU contract. The teacher will maintain a copy of the Performance Evaluation Portfolio and the school will maintain another copy.

By signing this Agreement, I acknowledge that I have read all of the provisions of this Agreement and agree to all of its terms.

Date:

Name: _____

Accepted:

The Samuel Mason Pilot Elementary School

By: _____

Source: School files.

Exhibit 8a

Demographic Data of the Mason and Neighboring School Enrollment—SY06

SY06 Demographic Data		
	Mason	**Sequoiah**[a]
Total Enrollment	215	197
African American/Black	63.7%	75.6%
Hispanic/Latino	25.6%	15.2%
White	7.9%	3.6%
Asian American	0.0%	1.5%
Multi-racial	2.3%	2.5%
Students with Disabilities	20.5%	8.1%
Low-income students	77.7%	95.9%

[a] Sequoiah School is a pseudonym for a BPS elementary school located near the Mason School.

Source: Massachusetts Department of Education and casewriter analysis.

Exhibit 8b

Performance Comparison of the Mason and Neighboring School

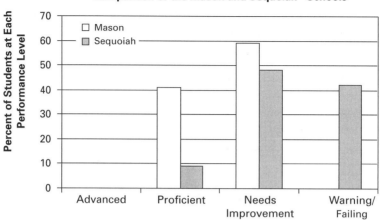

2006 MCAS English Language Arts Performance Comparison of the Mason and Sequoiah* Schools

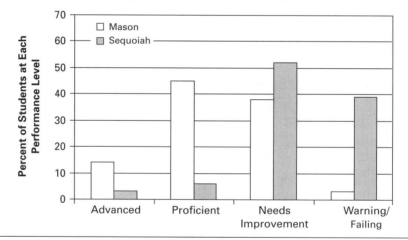

2006 MCAS Math Performance Comparison of the Mason and Sequoiah* Schools

*Sequoiah School is a pseudonym for a BPS elementary school located near the Mason School.

Source: Massachusetts Department of Education and casewriter analysis.

DISCUSSION QUESTIONS

1. What key factors sustained Denver's compensation reform initiative over 5 years and 5 superintendents?

2. In your estimation, which of ProComp's components (detailed in Exhibit 11) are the most effective? The least effective? Why?

3. Assuming DPS can raise $25 million from Denver voters, what are the biggest challenges for successful implementation? What advice would you give Wartgow for overcoming these challenges?

4. Would you suggest redesigning your district's compensation plan? Why or why not? If yes, is it possible to develop and implement? Why or why not? *(This final question is recommended only if the case is taught to practitioners.)*

Allen S. Grossman ■ Nancy Dean Beaulieu ■ Susan Moore Johnson ■
Jennifer M. Suesse

Compensation Reform at Denver Public Schools

On March 19, 2004, 59% of the Denver Classroom Teacher's Association (DCTA) approved a professional compensation system called "ProComp," a new comprehensive teacher compensation plan developed with Denver Public Schools (DPS). ProComp differed fundamentally from the typical model used to compensate public school teachers. Rather than automatic seniority-based raises, ProComp salaries were based on 10 elements, including teachers' contributions to student growth.[1] The plan also compensated teachers for receiving successful performance evaluations, serving in the most academically needy roles and schools, and improving their skills and knowledge. According to the DPS/DCTA agreement, ProComp would phase in beginning in January 2006, pending voters' approval in November 2005 of a property tax increase. The proposed mill-levy override would generate an additional $25 million—an annual tax increase of about $50 for the average Denver homeowner—to increase teachers' salaries by approximately 12% (individual raises would vary, and participation in ProComp would be optional for current DPS teachers).[2]

Debate was ongoing regarding teacher compensation reform, historically a contentious issue. Leaders from across the United States continued to watch Denver closely, since many felt teacher compensation reform was a key component of twenty-first century public school improvement efforts. Educators, lawmakers, and labor leaders acknowledged the imperfections of the traditional single-salary schedule—a model based on 1921 reforms that sought to equalize pay for women and minority teachers, as well as provide incentives for teachers' further education—but there was little agreement about fair, sustainable, and effective alternatives. Many observers saw ProComp's implementation as a massive undertaking for DPS, as well as a controversial experiment. Leaders from DPS and DCTA were amazed that they had come this far, given tensions lingering from unrest in the

1990s, including a strike in 1994, and repeated superintendent turnover. As they celebrated the March 19 victory and prepared to finalize the details of ProComp, both groups reflected on all that had happened since 1999, when a collective bargaining agreement launched a four-year pay-for-performance pilot, a forerunner of ProComp.

Background

DPS was the 44th-largest public school district in the U.S. and the second largest in Colorado, serving 72,489 students in 148 schools in 2003–2004. Fifty-two percent of the city's population was white, while 79% of DPS students were nonwhite. Sixty-six percent of DPS students were eligible for free or reduced-price meals, and one-fifth were learning English for the first time (Exhibit 1 profiles DPS demographics). A seven-member Board of Education, which included five members elected by neighborhood districts and two selected by the city at-large, governed DPS and set district policy. DPS was fiscally independent (not under city or county jurisdiction) and average spending per pupil was $6,397 in the 2003–2004 school year.

Colorado's legislature was focused on school accountability, and pressure for results was intense. The Colorado Student Assessment Program, or CSAP, a statewide set of exams, was implemented in 1997 and upgraded in 2002. Since 1997, DPS students' CSAP scores had made modest but steady gains (Exhibit 2 compares DPS scores with state averages). DPS was Colorado's only urban school district, and, as in many other large districts, districtwide achievement averages did not reveal the higher gains concentrated in the early grades as well as significant differences between white and nonwhite students' performance. In 2002 and 2003, Governor Bill Owens awarded DPS the state's Distinguished Improvement Award. DPS welcomed this recognition as affirmation of progress in achieving its mission of "providing all students

the opportunity to achieve the knowledge and skills necessary to become contributing citizens in our diverse society."

From 1973 to 2003, DPS had 12 different superintendents. Some observers said this turnover was responsible for poor communication and coordination between DPS departments and felt that it also contributed to the Board's "micromanaging" the central office from the late 1980s to the mid-1990s. After desegregation mandates were dismantled in 1995, DPS ended mandatory busing and phased in districtwide school choice for K–12 students. These political challenges, especially when combined with budget constraints and uneven growth throughout the system, took their toll on the central-office infrastructure and also strained relations and trust between DPS and DCTA.

In June 2001, Dr. Jerome "Jerry" Wartgow (pronounced Wart-GO) became DPS superintendent. His three goals for DPS were:

- Setting high expectations for students, parents, teachers, principals, and all other staff of DPS and the community it served

- Improving the performance of all students

- Closing the gap between better- and poorer-performing students

From all reports, Wartgow was a well-liked and respected community leader, with a reputation as a skilled fund-raiser. While not everyone in Denver supported Wartgow's initiatives, most felt that he brought a new level of professionalism and energy to reforming instructional practices and refining administrative processes. Shortly after arriving at DPS, Wartgow broke the district into quadrants and installed four area superintendents in an effort to integrate a highly decentralized network of schools. His financial and administrative teams worked to realign the DPS budget, merged the district's $2.5 billion retirement plan with the state's $25 billion program, and introduced universal e-mail use to the central office. Wartgow also resolved ongoing union negotiations, so all employees started 2001–2002 with contracts in place.

DPS-DCTA Relations

Neither before nor during Wartgow's tenure, were there smooth relations between DPS and DCTA. Collaboration ebbed and flowed, but both insiders and outsiders acknowledged that the relationship was relatively productive, "not a situation of entrenchment like in some cities." DCTA's leadership saw the union as a leader in professional teaching associations with the duty to "advocate for the rights and responsibilities of all educators and for an ethical system of quality public education for all students." DCTA was affiliated with the Colorado Education Association, as well as the National Education Association and the Teacher Union Reform Network. Its 3,200-person membership included 80% of DPS teachers, 45% of whom had been teaching five years or fewer.

Teacher Compensation: The Single-Salary Schedule

Historically, DPS's 4,076 teachers were paid according to a typical single-salary schedule, called a "steps and lanes" matrix. Thirteen "steps" were based on an individual's years of service at DPS while six "lanes" awarded salary increases for the acquisition of graduate credit and degrees (Exhibit 3 outlines the 2003–2004 salary schedule). For example, the starting salary for a teacher with a bachelor's degree and no teaching experience was $31,200 while a teacher with a Ph.D. and 12 years of teaching experience in DPS earned $64,919. Teachers who took on additional responsibilities, like coaching or extracurricular supervision, were eligible to earn additional compensation.

Experimenting with Compensation: The PFP Pilot

The political climate in the 1990s, both in Colorado and beyond, sought increased teacher accountability and student achievement in schools. Negotiated agreements between DPS and DCTA from 1982 to 1996 established committees to investigate means for connecting compensation to student achievement. On many occasions, groups composed variously of teachers, administrators, and union leaders met to discuss ideas, read reports, raise concerns, and make formal recommendations. Moreover, attempts to reform compensation for principals and administrators had been unsuccessful. Compensation experiments across the state, including one in neighboring Douglas County, increased the pressure for DPS to act.

Pay-for-performance (PFP) advocates argued that PFP was one way to attract and retain high-quality teachers, as well to provide a means for accountability. But, many educators worried that politicians perceived PFP as a "silver bullet." National union leaders and scholars cited three common challenges in a legacy of unsuccessful attempts to connect teacher compensation to student achievement. First, they highlighted the difficulty of developing assessments that could effectively demonstrate teachers' contributions while accounting for student population, mobility, or other factors outside teachers' control. Second, they pointed to the challenge of evaluating teachers fairly, without favoritism. Finally, some felt compensation programs that differentiated among individuals countered current efforts to foster collaboration among teachers. Bill Slotnik, executive director of the Community Training and Assistance Center (CTAC), a Boston-based not-for-profit that worked with DPS, observed that poor implementation and misunderstandings only added to these challenges:

> Three central themes characterize the track record of failed PFP efforts in school systems. First, many assumed that PFP was purely a question of incentives for teachers, when the reality is that much more is involved than just providing compensation. Second, many PFP plans

were punitive, created to weed out "bad teach-ers." Experience shows that any compensation system needs to be designed for all teachers and that poor performance is handled most ef-fectively through good management, not pun-ishment. Finally, most PFP attempts failed be-cause districts tried to implement them without making fundamental changes in the rest of the system.

Defining the PFP Pilot

1999–2000 Negotiations: Given these concerns, there was an outcry when Superinten-dent Irving Moskowitz first proposed paying teachers for their performance during bargain-ing in 1999 (see Exhibit 4 for a timeline of key events). Moskowitz and other Board members wanted to abolish the single-salary schedule, raise starting teacher salaries, and pay teachers according to their ability to meet student achievement objectives. Many DCTA members opposed this idea, but Betty Wissink, who was then DCTA vice president, recalled, "With the way the political winds were blowing, we knew Colorado would probably mandate some kind of performance pay for teachers if we didn't come up with our own solution. So, we said we would be willing to experiment, if we had time to do it right." DCTA wanted to study PFP to ensure that DPS knew how to implement it and could fund any proposed changes. No agreement was reached, however, and negotiations reached an impasse.

In August 1999, Superintendent Sidney "Chip" Zullinger negotiated the eventual settle-ment, which kept the existing salary schedule in place, and established a two-year PFP pilot. Jointly sponsored by DPS and DCTA, the PFP pilot was to explore means for developing a di-rect link between student achievement and teacher compensation. DPS and DCTA agreed that the pilot would be managed by a four-person "Design Team" composed of two DCTA

members and two DPS administrators who were released from other duties in order to devote their full time to planning, piloting, revising, im-plementing, and evaluating a performance pay plan for DPS elementary, middle, and high school teachers.

The agreement stated that a school could participate in the pilot if 85% or more of its fac-ulty volunteered. While the pilot ran, the exist-ing salary schedule remained in place. Participa-tion in the pilot required that teachers establish two performance objectives, and participating teachers received bonuses according to their progress in achieving their objectives. Three ap-proaches were used to measure teachers' progress in achieving their objectives. One approach measured improved student achievement ac-cording to the norm-referenced Iowa Test of Basic Skills. Another used a range of teacher-developed assessments, including the Colorado Student Assessment Program. The third ap-proach was based on teachers' acquisition of skills and knowledge, and teachers measured stu-dent achievement in a variety of ways.[3]

In the first year, teachers received $500 per objective met, as determined by the teacher and his or her principal, and an additional $500 sti-pend for participation. In subsequent years, par-ticipating teachers received $750 for each objec-tive met. Both parties agreed that the Design Team would report results of the PFP pilot and make recommendations no later than June 1, 2001.

The Heart of the Pilot: Objectives

Setting objectives was at the heart of the PFP pi-lot, but when the pilot began even those on the Design Team had only a vague sense of what high-quality objectives entailed or what systems were required for implementing a performance-based, objective-setting process across the dis-trict. Looking back, one school official recalled, "When we entered into this, I didn't see the dif-ficulty in a fairly simplistic objective-setting process. I can't get over that objectives are so hard to write."[4] Indeed, few teachers succeeded in writing sufficiently detailed objectives early on during the pilot (see Exhibit 5 for three exemplary objectives). However, 95% met their first objective, and 88% met their second objective. Over the pilot's four years, objective setting evolved. Teachers learned to identify the following for each objective: a specific student population, an interval during which progress would be made, a formal assessment, an expected growth expressed in objective terms, learning content and explicit strategies for makeup progress.

Pilot Extension

By early 2000, the Design Team realized that two years was not enough time to accomplish their goals, which included piloting PFP in secondary schools. Thus, DPS/DCTA raised additional funding and created a March 2000 DPS/DCTA memorandum of understanding to extend the pilot through 2003. In June 2000, the Design Team presented a report to the Board of Education outlining their progress and identifying major challenges for subsequent work. Brad Jupp, a former middle school teacher and negotiator who represented DCTA on the design team, described the value of ongoing communication between the Design Team and DPS, DCTA, and external parties:

> While having so many parties involved might at first seem like a headache, we were surprised to discover that it created a kind of check and balance system. Everyone made outrageous demands at times, but nobody—not DPS, nor DCTA, nor CTAC, nor the foundations—could go too far without the others. Even at the toughest times, there was a tone of reason that ensured a balanced perspective on key decisions and enabled us to move to the next level.

In 2000–2001, the Design Team developed a more comprehensive school support system and facilitated a series of workshops for pilot schools focused on objective setting, establishing baselines, and using academic achievement data to make instructional decisions. Midyear training highlighted means for conducting midpoint checks and adjusting instructional strategies. Finally, spring workshops addressed gathering final data and presenting evidence of meeting objectives. The Design Team also launched an online objective-setting tool for teachers, which helped teachers clarify objectives and provided DPS with a way to track them.

Improving Data Infrastructure: Creating OASIS

From the pilot's inception, the Design Team knew that success required substantial improvements to DPS's data infrastructure. For example, for teachers to show evidence of their students' growth, they needed baseline data from previous assessments. DPS did not link student and teacher records when the pilot began, so classroom teachers could not easily access aggregated records. DPS did assign student ID numbers upon enrollment, but teachers did not have unique ID numbers. Thus, tracking or aggregating student records had to be done by hand. Moreover, few DPS assessments were linked to districtwide curriculum standards, so teachers struggled to find acceptable means of measuring students' progress.

The Online Assessment Scores Information System (OASIS), developed by the DPS assessment and testing department at the urging of the Design Team, debuted in the spring of 2001. It provided pilot teachers with online access to students' assessment records. OASIS was designed to allow teachers to customize reports, and it included data for multiple years. Data could be grouped by teacher (so a teacher could track one class of children), and information could also be disaggregated by some demographic characteristics. One DPS administrator commented, "Working on the data aspect met a need and gave us momentum. We started with an idea and then created a system that means something to *both* teachers and administrators." At first, only pilot schools used the OASIS program, but soon some principals at nonpilot schools requested access for their teachers. OASIS highlighted a significant "technology gap" at DPS, exposing considerable variation in teachers' comfort with using computers and achievement data. While reactions to the PFP pilot across the district varied widely, there was nearly universal appreciation for OASIS.

One School's Story: PFP at Thomas Jefferson High School

Recruiting and retaining pilot schools was an ongoing challenge for the Design Team, and motivations for participation ranged greatly. Some schools were excited about the PFP idea and were glad to participate. Some teachers saw the money as a "bonus" for "preexisting practices." Some donated the money back to their schools, and a few opened savings accounts in anticipation of possible protest strikes. At least one school joined hoping to prove that PFP would fail.

In the pilot's third year (2001–2002), the Design Team finally overcame resistance from wary secondary school teachers and convinced two high schools to join. High schools varied considerably from K-8 settings, reflecting significant differences both in school culture and in size. Average enrollments were nearly three times greater than those of participating elementary schools.) Introducing the objective-setting process posed a major challenge in this environment, as high school principals managed a greater diversity of departments and programs. Many teachers remained skeptical, and opponents argued, "PFP would just create more bureaucracy, without improving performance." One Thomas Jefferson High School (TJ) teacher, who had been transferred out of a former DPS teaching assignment after publicly dis-

agreeing with his principal, welcomed PFP. He commented:

> If we'd had PFP in place then, I could have proven that I'd met my objectives regardless of how I felt about the principal and how she felt about me. One of the main criticisms of PFP is that principals can't be trusted to evaluate teachers fairly. To me, that's exactly the point. You don't have to trust them. You can write a standards-based objective based on numerical data. And then, what's there to argue about? This system treats teachers like professionals.

TJ's principal reflected, "I felt that the teachers who were marginal worked as hard or harder, and everyone brought a better quality to their objectives. A teacher who used to say that some of her kids were lazy now talks with me about the need for differentiated instruction." DCTA's representative at TJ, who taught advanced placement government and constitutional law, added:

> The objective-setting process did not go well in the first year. The "experts" who came in to assist were no help at all. They did not seem to understand that high schools are more complex than elementary schools and often provided confusing or contradictory advice. So, in the second year, we trained our own people to assist TJ teachers. The process was more successful because we were able to educate each other and our administrators about what constituted adequate progress in our respective areas. Another reason it worked is that we trust our principal; she really encourages and supports us when we try things.

Reflections on the PFP Pilot

Support and Criticism: By the pilot's conclusion, 13% of DPS schools—including thirteen elementary, two middle, and two high schools—had participated, and five different DPS superintendents had been involved. In addition to CTAC's findings about improved student achievement, advocates contended that PFP sharpened their focus on instruction, rewarded innovation, and increased potential lifetime earnings. Some participants also felt that the pilot had helped to boost morale and enabled them to receive more money, more often for good work. Advocates also saw PFP as the first step toward clarifying performance expectations for teachers at both the classroom and school levels and establishing agreement about what constituted adequate progress. PFP supporters across the district also saw DPS's efforts to establish objective setting and track student growth as a first step toward being able to truly differentiate instruction. Scott and others on the Design Team hoped that OASIS (or a next-generation product) could be used to compare results from different instructional strategies and approaches across classrooms and schools. Moreover, DPS board members continued their ongoing, adamant support for teacher compensation reform.

Critics, on the other hand, felt that tying teacher pay to student performance was undesirable and unfair. They argued that available means for assessing student achievement and teacher performance were unsophisticated and too subjective and they worried that paying for performance could overcompensate some at the expense of others. Detractors also felt that linking student achievement to individual teachers' paychecks was unmanageable and unsustainable given existing resource constraints. Those who had not participated in the pilot wondered, would PFP create more competition, cheating, gaming, or jealousy? With high student mobility rates across Denver and numerous children living in poverty, some teachers worried about being judged when so many factors with huge impact on their performance were completely outside their control.

Challenges of Scale: Many teachers and administrators were concerned with the ongoing question about whether any new compensation system could be integrated into existing management structures. DPS payroll and HR systems remained antiquated and, even as late as 2003, there were errors in paycheck processing. One official who worked with a PFP foundation partner remarked:

> To really make progress, we need to make sure that engagement in and accountability for the project stretches from the classroom, to the principalship, to area superintendent offices, to central administration. Over the life of the pilot, we haven't always had that, and it's made making progress tough. But I'm not sure we really know how to engage and keep everyone engaged and accountable.

Teachers also worried that principals did not have the skills or training to manage the objective-setting process properly, and even those who did might find the paperwork too burdensome. Wartgow himself noted that bringing the objective-setting process to scale across the district was "a monumental professional development undertaking for teachers, principals, and administrators alike." District insiders also worried that PFP did not address deeper systemic rifts between departments. A longtime DPS assessment specialist noted, "Like so many of our initiatives, PFP has been totally isolated, even from our literacy curriculum work, as well as from larger questions of assessment. I sense that someone in the district has an idea of where they are going with these projects, but it is a mystery to me." One DPS administrator commented:

> In a symbolic way, this is a means for us to say to teachers, what you do matters and we want to compensate you for doing a good job. We are

trying to pay you for what the district cares about. But, the systems aren't as strong as they could be. If we can bring focus and connection between compensation and what we are doing in other areas, this is a real opportunity on a substantive level as well.

The challenge of assessing student achievement in meaningful ways was another major concern. CTAC's Slotnik observed, "A core problem is that many of the existing assessments are flawed and used for purposes other than those for which they were intended. The entire PFP effort needs to be valid in three ways: statistically, so that accurate inferences may be drawn from the data; educationally, to ensure teacher buy-in; and politically, to obtain community support." One administrator noted, "Even state CSAP scores can only be used for about 30% of DPS teachers, since those tests do not really apply to specialists or anyone teaching K-3, 11th, or 12th grades." In the fourth year of the pilot, 166 unique assessments were used by teachers to measure student achievement.

The lack of integrated or coordinated professional development was also a worry. Many teachers were nervous about being held increasingly accountable for targets without systemic ways of providing them the support needed to ensure that they had the skills or tools necessary to achieve those goals. In mid-December 2003, a veteran DPS administrator asked: "What is the real bottom line for DPS? Will they have targeted expectations for teachers? Is it more valuable to write attainable objectives or stretch goals? How does this include a sense of rigor? Furthermore, while I know money is important, it's not what I have seen sustain extraordinary work."

Results: By the end of the objective-setting pilot, DPS had paid out approximately $2.8 million in stipends and bonuses to 644 teachers. In its evaluation report published in December 2001, CTAC focused on the impact of objectives on student achievement and perceptions of the pilot. Results showed that students whose teachers developed the highest-quality objectives—*regardless of whether or not those objectives were met*—made greater-than-average gains on two different standardized measures.

Structuring excellent objectives evolved over the life of the pilot. By the conclusion, CTAC had developed a rubric that outlined four levels of performance and the criteria upon which teachers' objectives should be judged (Exhibit 6 illustrates objective-setting performance, 1999–2003). The objectives that met the standards held high expectations for students and stated (1) what students would learn, taking into account the exact population, (2) the assessments and teaching strategies to be used during the year, (3) the teacher's rationale for selecting the objective, (4) what baseline data would be used to show prior knowledge and/or skills, and finally (5) what evidence would show that the objective had or had not been met.

A majority of participating teachers reported that they were not doing anything differently as a result of the PFP pilot, although nearly half also said that PFP had led to a greater focus on student achievement. CTAC and the Design Team found sporadic evidence of cheating or manipulation of data by teachers or principals, but it was not widespread. They also found that measures of cooperation among teachers at pilot schools stayed the same or increased slightly.

CTAC's final report also explored institutional factors as well as perceptions of participants and other parties before offering recommendations around four major areas: alignment, assessment, professional development, and leadership.[5] A DCTA official observed, "While our relationship with DPS had experienced ups and downs, overall, we built credibility as an organization. Moreover, many of our teachers learned that student growth is something that they understand and could accept as legitimate expectation for compensation." Some teachers felt that the study had provided them an unusual channel for sharing their concerns and suggestions, which they welcomed. Finally, nearly everyone across DPS who had worked with the individual members of the Design Team felt that their work had been of the highest quality and wondered how their efforts could be integrated into the system.

From Pilot to ProComp

Leading up to 2001, DPS administrators and those closest to the Design Team had recognized that the PFP pilot was disconnected from key operations in the central office. As the pilot unfolded, DPS and DCTA realized that its focus on objectives, while a valuable experiment, was too narrow to be expanded across DPS into a comprehensive compensation system.

To address this concern, Wartgow's administration collaborated with DCTA officials to convene the DPS/DCTA Joint Task Force on Teacher Compensation (JTF) in November 2001. Wartgow charged the JTF with developing an equitable and affordable salary system for teachers based, in part, on improved student achievement. Co-chaired by Richard "Rich" Allen, DPS assistant superintendent of Budget and Finance, and Gary Justus, a math teacher at Abraham Lincoln High School and an active leader within DCTA, the JTF had 10 other members including teachers, principals, central-office administrators, and community members jointly selected by DPS and DCTA (see Exhibit 7 for a list of JTF members).

No Design Team members were on the JTF, as technically their work was separate. Jupp commented:

> The JTF has taken on a board-like role; the Design Team works as support staff. The Design Team was too immersed in the pilot to create a credible, comprehensive compensation plan on our own. We needed to detach the development

for what became ProComp from the PFP pilot. It was critical to create a collaborative group that could take what we had learned from the pilot and integrate that with national research and their own experiences.

Wartgow recalled, "Magic started to happen when Brad and Rich put their heads together. Rich had worked with me for 12 years, and I never expected he'd take to the project like this, but those two led the group to invent this balanced compensation system."

DCTA and DPS developed a list of principles to guide the JTF's work. They agreed that any new compensation plan would continue to involve collective bargaining, include specialists, and provide for annual cost-of-living adjustments. Implementation of new compensation elements would phase in only when the system was ready to support and fund them; participation would be voluntary. Lastly, any proposal would aim to assure greater career earnings for all teachers, and teachers with advanced degrees would continue to receive higher starting salaries.

Joint Task Force

Once the JTF was assembled, they arrived at a few decisions that co-chair Allen described as "key drivers of all subsequent collaboration." First, they agreed that the JTF would not design "add-ons" to the existing salary schedule but rather work to create a comprehensive new system. "We also decided," Allen recalled, "that fundamental reform could not be achieved in a zero-sum environment. We agreed we would go for a mill-levy override." Third, the JTF established four common objectives for the new compensation system including motivational, career, professional, and system goals (see Exhibit 8 for a summary of these goals) against which progress was measured. Finally, the group agreed not to rush the research and development process in an effort to take full advantage of existing innovations and to avoid common pitfalls.

In November 2002, the JTF moved into its "design phase" and broke into subgroups to work on the four individual components of ProComp agreed upon by the group: knowledge and skills, professional evaluation, market incentives, and student growth. Members of the group described a huge breakthrough in February 2003, when a teacher representative to the JTF convinced the group to abandon the traditional matrix-salary schedule. He said, 'These grids don't help anybody. All they do is pigeonhole people, and we have the capacity to go beyond that in the twenty-first century.'" Some members also began building a financial model projecting salaries 50 years ahead in response to one of the main pitfalls of alternative compensation systems: that many districts created financially unsustainable plans.

The JTF unveiled the first "conceptual recommendation" in April 2003, kicking off a year of heated debate and discussion across Denver about how teachers should be compensated. A DCTA poll conducted that month suggested that 40% of those surveyed supported ProComp (although that name had not yet been developed), 25% opposed the idea, and the rest were undecided. There was ongoing confusion about exactly what the proposal was.

During this period, the JTF struggled to complete its work while also maintaining active communications across DPS. Communication materials highlighting the evolving proposal, which changed significantly from February 2003 to March 2004, were released every few months. Principals and DCTA site representatives were briefed again in November 2003 when the JTF released a detailed economic proposal summarizing the plan's four components, with complex charts detailing career earnings. The JTF presented its final ProComp proposal in February 2004 (see Exhibit 9).

ProComp's Four Components

Knowledge and Skills: Focusing on job-embedded staff development, this component built on one theory underlying the old salary schedule: the belief that students' achievement increases when their teachers have more education. The JTF wanted to focus on the relationship between increasing teachers' knowledge and skills and student growth, so ProComp included raises for demonstrated acquisition of knowledge and skills related to a teacher's instructional discipline. Prior to ProComp, salary increases were awarded only after individuals completed 30 graduate credits. Awards were capped after 60 hours of accumulated credit. ProComp's three-part model included incremental salary increases for completing approved courses, participating in action research or other projects, or demonstrating skills and reflecting on their use with students. Details of individual professional development units (or PDUs) were still undefined at the time of the March 2004 vote. ProComp continued the DPS practice of increasing salaries for teachers holding national board certification and replaced hourly compensation for district professional development with a $1,000 lifetime account to reimburse teachers for completing approved courses.[6]

Professional Evaluation: This two-part component sought to address the thorny issue of evaluation, and Allen acknowledged that it remained the "most undeveloped component." Existing protocols responded to rare instances of unsatisfactory evaluations by freezing a teacher's salary (preventing step or lane increases, as well as negotiated cost-of-living adjustments). ProComp aimed to recognize and reward teachers who demonstrated proficient and distinguished practice through triennial evaluations, and the March 2004 agreement acknowledged that existing evaluation tools would remain in place until DPS and DCTA could develop a mutually acceptable new instrument. In preliminary conversations about a new evaluation tool, both organizations focused on the question of evaluating instructional behavior, not contractual issues (e.g., tardiness, attire, or extra duty assignments). ProComp evaluations included corresponding increases for satisfactory performance. Salary increases for teachers who received unsatisfactory performance ratings were delayed for at least one year, until a satisfactory or better rating was received. Larger salary increases for distinguished teachers remained a topic for further exploration, as the JTF's initial proposal to reward extraordinary individual performance was dropped due to anxiety across the DPS community.

Market Incentives: This two-part component focused on the question of attracting and retaining teachers of demonstrated accomplishment to designated assignments and schools. The JTF worked to integrate the previous practice of awarding bilingual teachers' stipends for one year of service (which increased slightly for continuing service) and the DPS Teacher Incentive Program (which provided site-based incentives for teachers recruited and retained in designated assignments at low-performing schools) into the overall compensation model. ProComp included bonuses for teachers who worked in positions considered difficult to fill or in schools considered hard to serve. Distinguished teachers serving in those roles received higher bonuses. ProComp extended the existing practice of offering extra pay for teachers who completed extra duties.

Student Growth: This three-part component was most closely based on the work of the PFP pilot, although it included significant modifications. ProComp included salary increases for teachers who met two annual student growth objectives and bonuses for teachers who met at least one objective. Sustainable increases were available for teachers whose students exceeded a range of expected performance on CSAP scores.

Finally, bonuses were also included for teachers and staff at schools recognized as distinguished based on academic gains.[7] Jupp recalled long debates about how to reconcile individual teacher objectives with large-scale state assessments: "We were having trouble keeping the CSAP out of the objective setting until we decided that we didn't want teachers using state assessments for objective setting. It was like the hand of God reached in and rescued us and led to a major breakthrough. We separated CSAP from objectives, which simplified everything."

Final Details: ProComp had no quotas or maximum numbers for who could benefit from particular components and uncapped annual and career earnings for teachers who met or exceeded expectations. In summarizing ProComp, Allen laughed:

> The new system is much less complex than it looks, while the old system is more complex than it looks. In compiling long-term cost projections, ProComp was easily modeled, but the single-salary schedule was nearly impossible since there are so many weird interactions in the data. Resistance to ProComp has been as much an issue of familiarity as complexity. After all, more than 50 years of propaganda support the single-salary schedule.

Ongoing Labor Relations

During Wartgow's tenure, relations with DCTA improved steadily until negotiations soured over budget cuts in 2003. The 2003–2004 settlement was reached using interest-based bargaining, a form of negotiating where parties seek common ground and attempt to satisfy mutual interests in contrast to the traditional focus on defending positions. Some of DCTA's members supported this new form of collaboration, while others accused DCTA leadership of being "in bed" with DPS management. The 2003–2004 settlement raised total compensation for teachers only 2.8%, which covered the increased cost of benefits, but it was not the pay raise members expected. When DPS pointed out that teachers had bargained for a greater raise than all other city employees, DCTA continued to refer to the settlement as a "salary freeze." DCTA President Wissink said that this dissension led to internal discussions about DCTA's role:

> We have been asking ourselves, "Is DCTA a union or an association?" As a union, we should be bargaining and handling grievances. But, as an association, our responsibility would be handling professional teaching and staff development. We also ask ourselves if we want a partnership or a relationship with DPS. We like collaboration, but some DCTA members get nervous if we seem to agree with DPS on everything. When there are tensions during lawsuits or negotiations, DPS does not like for us to disagree in public. Sometimes it seems like random acts of collaboration.

Tensions were heightened when DCTA remained neutral on a $310 million bond and $20 million mill-levy vote in November 2003 to support construction, systems, and programs for DPS. DCTA said it could not support any call for funds that did not include teachers' pay raises. On the other hand, DPS and the newly elected mayor, a strong Wartgow supporter, were concerned that voters could not be asked to increase taxes for teachers' salaries twice in two years, given the anticipated $25 million mill-levy override election for ProComp funds in November 2005.

Preparing for the Vote

In early December 2003, DCTA's leadership met to discuss the issues they felt needed to be addressed before ProComp could be accepted. A memo circulated at that meeting highlighted their six main objectives: that ProComp be fair,

affordable, sustainable, manageable, and attractive to teachers and that it contribute to improving student achievement (see the memo in Exhibit 10). DCTA's executive director said, "To me, the scary thought is not the merits of the proposal—because I think we can create something good—but where we will find the principals to implement it? No matter how good the tool is, if you put it in the hands of someone who can't use it, you still get a lousy product." Tensions were high around the district, and a DCTA poll conducted in January showed only 19% favored ProComp. Fifty-eight percent of members surveyed were opposed, with the balance undecided.

During the ensuing negotiations and debates, DPS and DCTA agreed on how issues not addressed during negotiations would be resolved, and in February 2004, DPS and DCTA reached a tentative agreement on ProComp after DCTA agreed to postpone talks regarding 2004–2005 salaries.

With a complete plan endorsed by DPS, DCTA, Denver's mayor, *The Denver Post,* as well as other local foundations and community groups, the JTF and the Design Team plunged into a promotional campaign. Detailed summaries of ProComp appeared in a February 2004 brochure (see Exhibit 9), as did hypothetical compensation profiles for new and experienced teachers (see Exhibit 11). The DPS/DCTA online salary calculator, used to compute figures in the hypothetical profiles, was reportedly very important in convincing teachers that they would benefit from the plan by allowing them to preview the effects of the new system on their pay. Communication also attempted to address confusion about the relationship between the Design Team, the PFP pilot, the JTF, and ProComp. A JTF flyer included the following teacher's quote:

> ProComp is NOT Pay for Performance. Pay for Performance is dead. ProComp is to PFP like

Velcro was to the space industry—an offshoot. This is a completely different product. We learned from the pilot that paying people more did not change their work ethic; teachers already work hard! What works is having teachers and principals set strategic teaching objectives based on district and union goals. It's about creating a common vision for a world class, urban school district—one that teachers will want to teach in because they'll make more money while working together to produce skilled, literate students.[8]

A DCTA poll conducted in early March showed that 38% of members approved of ProComp, while 39% were opposed. Twenty percent remained undecided. District and union officials visited all 136 schools and 15 work sites in 13 days. (Teachers at the 12 DPS charter schools were not eligible for collective bargaining.) Labor organizers, including retired union leaders, followed up by visiting one-on-one with hundreds of teachers around the district. The JTF and the Design Team worked with the Board and foundations to hire professional campaign promoters. This strategy worked in favor of ProComp, which was approved by 59% of the 2,718 DCTA members who voted on March 19, 2004. Pending the $25 million mill-levy vote planned for November 2005, ProComp was scheduled to be implemented in January 2006. Current DPS teachers would have seven years to opt in to ProComp, while DPS teachers hired after January 2006 would automatically be enrolled (Exhibit 4 summarizes key events).

Next Steps

As leaders across DPS and DCTA looked ahead, they saw a lot of work. "Hardly pausing to celebrate the go-ahead they got from teachers," wrote one reporter, "proponents of a plan to remake the educator's salary scale in Denver have fixed their eyes on persuading city voters to ap-

prove a tax increase to pay for it."[9] Wartgow added, "There are lots of details to work out, and the 41% 'no' vote signals a significant distrust factor that we need to address. We need to capitalize on this positive momentum, and a difficult 2004–2005 labor settlement could set us back. We are focused on putting together a budget that can be seen as fair and supportive." By the end of March 2004, Wissink was "cautiously optimistic" about reaching a settlement on 2004–2005 salaries before the end of the school year, although she was concerned about how DPS would handle an anticipated 2004–2005 budget shortfall and other ongoing issues.

Around the city, confusion about the details of ProComp mingled with excitement and concerns. A DPS/DCTA press release in late March 2004 proclaimed: "ProComp is not merit pay. A better term for the ProComp system is results-based pay. Teachers do not receive increases until they demonstrate results—of their classroom skills (through a new evaluation system that will have observable criteria), through obtaining certification . . . and for documenting measurable growth of their students." The DPS Board president commented:

> At first, some of us were disappointed to see our dream of a purely performance-based compensation system diluted so substantially. We wondered if we'd given away too much. But, I'm satisfied now that we've broken the mold as much as was possible. I'm confident that we will continue to work with teachers to connect their compensation to DPS goals. I'm increasingly convinced that *what* gets accomplished is just as important as *how* it gets done.

Another DPS Board member added:

> I'm concerned that we've created a system that's too cumbersome. Will the principals really take time to review the objectives? And, if they do, what are we willing to take off their plates?

How can we shift things? Evaluating teachers is a hard thing to do, and hurting morale with bad evaluations is sometimes just not worth it. There are many unknowns. I don't want to be cynical, because in theory, this new approach to compensating teachers is revolutionary. But, looking forward 10 to 20 years, I wonder if our vision will be carried out the way we are currently hoping it will.

As they looked ahead, Allen, Jupp, and Wartgow identified a number of key internal projects. In the short term, DPS and DCTA needed to create a functional leadership structure that could assign and supervise the ongoing work of the JTF and the Design Team (as the latter was still in place to support the JTF reforms after the PFP pilot concluded). With respect to the proposed plan itself, protocols were needed for the professional development units (PDUs), as was an evaluation system for determining satisfactory performance. Supports for the objective-setting process, which were well established in pilot schools, needed to be implemented across the system. Protocols for managing ProComp's unique fiscal governance structure also needed to be established.[10] With declining enrollment, an anticipated $25 million state budget cut, and a stagnant economy, observers across the district wondered about how cooperation between DPS and DCTA would fare.

Wartgow sat back and reflected on the progress of compensation reform thus far:

The pilot helped us build the hugely important data system and supports, but it's the change in culture that has really been a superintendent's dream. Having teachers calling me, demanding to know how their kids are doing, is a whole new ballgame. They don't want to wait for CSAP scores to come out in case they need to change their approach or their materials. What excites me about ProComp is that we are working toward a breakthrough in how teachers are rewarded for their hard work.

My colleagues in the business sector think I'm crazy to be excited about the chance to pay a bilingual special education teacher more than a secondary social studies teacher. They don't understand what a big change this is for us. What I like about ProComp is that it encourages good teachers to stay in the classroom by offering the opportunity for larger paychecks that used to be only available for administrators. Keeping good people working with our students is a big step toward improving student outcomes and closing the achievement gap.

I hope DPS will be up to the challenge of implementing ProComp.

Notes

1. All DPS/DCTA compensation agreements include classroom teachers, nurses, social workers, and other education specialists. For simplicity and clarity, subsequent references to "teachers" imply this entire bargaining unit.

2. Property taxes are calculated based on a rate of dollars per $100, or mills (.001). Changes to the tax rate, called mill-levy overrides, are decided by general elections. Figures cited from Bess Keller, "Next Pay-Plan Decision Up to Denver Voters," *Education Week,* March 31, 2004, p. 3.

3. A more detailed explanation of these approaches appears in CTAC's December 2001 report, *Pathway to Results: Pay for Performance in Denver.*

4. Quoted by CTAC in "Objectives: Linchpin of the Pilot," *Pathway to Results,* p. 29.

5. CTAC reported full results in *Catalyst for Change: Pay for Performance in Denver Final Report,* January 2004, published online at http://ctacusa.com/denver-vol3-final.pdf.

6. Teachers may apply to the national Board for Professional Teaching Standards for certification as an "accomplished teacher" in one of 24 areas of specialization. More information can be found online at www.nbpts.org/.

7. Distinguished-school status was based on 30 to 40

school-performance indicators being developed in the DPS Multiple Indicators Project, including student growth data, school climate, attendance, and graduation rates.

8. Christine LaHue of Morey Middle School, quoted in February 2004 ProComp brochure published by the Design Team.

9. Keller, "Next Pay-Plan Decision Up to Denver Voters," p. 3.

10. In response to concerns about fiscal management, the DPS/DCTA agreement established a ProComp "trust fund" and Board of Directors to oversee funds from the anticipated mill-levy override. This group had authority to approve annual plans, which could adjust the value of individual elements—both up and down—in order to keep the system in balance over time.

Exhibit 1
DPS Demographic Profile

Overview	2003–04
District Area Demographics	
Total Population[a]	544,636
Per Capita Income (in 1999)[b]	$24,101
Families below poverty level (in 1999)	10.6%
Median household effective buying income (income after taxes)[c]	$45,207
Percent of Denver community living below the poverty line (1999)[d]	12.1%
Percent of county residents holding college degrees	38.7%
Unemployment (2002)[e]	3.5%
Student Demographics	
Number of students (K-12)	72,489
Hispanic	57.0%
White	19.7%
African-American	18.9%
Other (including Native American and Asian)	4.3%
Eligible for free and reduced-price lunch	66.4%
Students with IEPs	11.4%
English language learners	20.3%
Graduation rate[f]	70.6%
Dropout rate[g]	4.0%
Schools and Staff	
Number of schools	148
Elementary	90
Middle	20
High	14
Alternative/Charter	24
Total Headcount	14,173
Teachers	4,076
Average teacher salary	$52,271
Student/teacher staffing ratio (Elem, Middle, High)	25:1

Source: District data unless cited otherwise.

[a] Census 2000 data published by National Center for Education Statistics Web site, http://www.nces.ed.gov/surveys/sdds/singledemoprofile.asp?county1=0803360 &state1=8, accessed February 9, 2004.

[b] Denver's income after taxes ranked 15.5% higher than the national average and ranked the region fifth among the 30 largest metro areas in total effective buying income. Historically, the Denver metro area had higher income than the national average, reflecting a high concentration of two-income households in the area.

[c] Median household income figure published by Metro Denver Economic Development Corporation Web site, http://denvernet.org/mdn/site/population.asp, accessed August 19, 2003.

[d] National Center for Education Statistics Web site, accessed August 5, 2003.

[e] Metro Denver Economic Development Corporation Web site, accessed August 19, 2003.

[f] Graduation rate is determined by following one group of students (a cohort) over a four-year period from grades 9–12.

[g] Dropout rate is a one-year snapshot of all students who drop out of school during one year. This rate considers all students in grades 7–12.

Exhibit 2

District (DPS) and State (CO) CSAP Achievement Data, 1996–97 to 2002–03

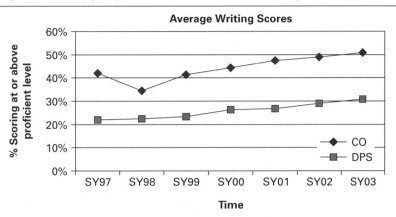

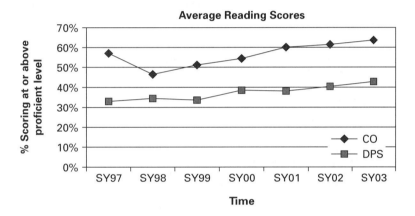

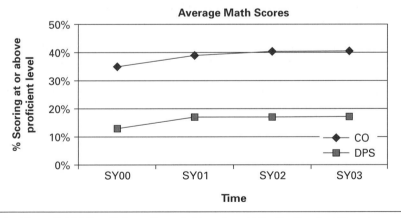

Source: Summarized from district files. Full results available online at http://testing.dpsk12.org/rescsap03b.htm. Reading and writing graphs include scores for Spanish language "Escritura/Lectura" exams. The CSAP system was upgraded and expanded in 2002. In 2001–02–2002–03, students in grades 3–10 took CSAP reading and writing exams, and students in grades 5–10 took CSAP mathematics exams. In prior years, fewer students in fewer grades were tested.

Exhibit 3

Negotiated 2003–04 Single-Salary Schedule[a]

| | Level | Six Lanes[b] | | | | | |
		B.A.	B.A.+30	B.A.+60/M.A.	M.A.+30	M.A.+60	Ph.D.
	TiR[d]	$31,320		$31,779			
	1	32,971	$33,213	33,454	$34,552	$36,853	$39,169
	2	33,073	33,386	33,697	36,077	38,482	40,903
	3	33,225	33,657	35,101	37,601	40,112	42,642
	4	33,480	33,927	36,503	39,124	41,745	44,377
Thirteen Steps[c]	5	33,785	35,335[e]	38,053	40,770	43,505	46,251
	6	33,988	36,837	39,671	42,494	45,341	48,219
	7	35,421	38,399	41,337	44,316	47,257	50,290
	8	36,912	39,993	43,087	46,197	49,274	52,449
	9	38,456	41,709	44,924	48,164	51,431	54,702
	10	40,092	43,481	46,860	50,247	53,620	57,057
	11	41,784	45,301	48,843	52,358	55,922	59,521
	12	43,566	47,237	50,944	54,657	58,334	62,082
	13[f]	45,546	49,408	53,401	57,131	61,012	64,919

Examples:
Any teacher new to DPS with no teaching experience and a B.A. degree would make $31,320.
A teacher with an M.A. and seven years' experience with DPS would make $41,337.
A teacher with a Ph.D. and 12 years' experience with DPS would make $64,919.

Source: DCTA website and interviews.

[a] This schedule does not include additional compensation for extra duties such as coaching or other extracurricular supervision.

[b] Six lanes based on an individual's accumulated education increments: B.A. = bachelor's degree; B.A. + 30 = bachelor's degree plus 30 hours of master's coursework; B.A. +60/M.A. = bachelor's degree plus 60 hours of master's coursework or a master's degree; M.A. + 30 = master's degree plus 30 hours additional coursework; M.A. + 60 = master's degree plus 60 hours additional coursework; Ph.D. = doctorate. Average salary increase from lane to lane is 7%.

[c] Thirteen steps based on years of teaching experience. Average salary increase from step to step is 4%.

[d] Teacher-in-residence level was for interns who had a B.A. but lacked education coursework necessary for Step 1 eligibility. Tuition for coursework was deducted from all TiR salaries, as they were required to be working toward an advanced degree.

[e] Shaded area represents results of DPS/DCTA negotiations in 1999, when the starting teacher's salary was bumped up to $30,000. Referred to by the negotiating team as the "squished upper left hand corner," these figures increase at unique rates.

[f] When teachers reach the "end" of the salary schedule after 13 years of service, their salary increases by $1,263 upon completion of 15, 20, 25, and 30 years of satisfactory service. For example, a teacher with an M.A. and 16 years with DPS would make $54,664 (Step 13 M.A. = $53,401 + 1 longevity $1,263). A teacher with a B.A. and 21 years at DPS would make $48,072 (Step 13 B.A. = $45,546 + 2 longevity $2,526).

Exhibit 4
Timeline of Key Events

Date	Event
Spring 1999	Superintendent Moskowitz first proposed abandoning single-salary schedule during negotiations.
August 1999	DPS/DCTA agreed to begin pay-for-performance (PFP) pilot after bargaining impasse
Fall 1999	CTAC hired, 12 pilot schools began objective setting.
March 2000	Rose Community Foundation gave $1 million; pilot extended to four years.
June 2000	First PFP compensation awarded
Summer/ Fall 2000	PFP training for pilot schools; second-year objectives due.
Spring 2001	OASIS launched.
June 2001	Wartgow appointed superintendent
September 2001	High schools joined pilot
November 2001	Joint Task Force on Teacher Compensation (JTF) convened
December 2001	CTAC published interim report on PFP pilot.
February 2002	JTF began seminar phase.
November 2002	JTF began design phase; Broad Foundation gave $1 million.
April 2003	JTF briefed principals and DCTA reps on first conceptual recommendation of ProComp.
June 2003	PFP pilot ended.
November 2003	Denver voters approved $310 million bond and $20 million mill levy for DPS
January 2004	CTAC published final report on PFP pilot.
February 2004	DPS Board ratified ProComp agreement; DCTA leadership recommended ProComp proposal to its members; ProComp presented to Denver community and organizers hired.
March 19, 2004	59% of DCTA members approved ProComp.
—	—
PROJECTED EVENTS	
Spring 2004	*Ongoing 2004–05 salary negotiations.*
June 2004	*ProComp transition team scheduled to begin implementing transition plan to oversee development of new compensation system.*
November 2005	*Denver voters to decide $25 million mill-levy override.*
January 1, 2006	*Partial implementation of ProComp scheduled to begin.*
Fall 2006	*Full implementation of ProComp scheduled to begin.*
November 1, 2009	*Third-party evaluation of ProComp report due.*
December 31, 2013	*ProComp contract expires unless renegotiated.*

Source: Created by the casewriter from internal documents and conversations. Italicized summary of ProComp agreement adapted from DPS/DCTA agreement posted at http://denverteachercompensation.org/Recommendations.html.

Exhibit 5

Three Exemplary Objectives

Position	Grade	Rationale	Population	Interval	Assessment	Expected Growth	Learning Content	Strategies
Reading	3	School Improvement Plan Literacy Objectives Closing the Gap—District Goal	26 third-grade ELA-S students	1 year	DRA/QRI	**Pretest scores** 10/26 students scored at DRA level 12 or lower 8/26 scored between DRA levels 12 and 24 8/26 scored above DRA level 24. 75% of all students will increase their DRA levels by 14 levels on the DRA.	Standard 1: Print-sound code Standard 2: Accuracy, fluency, self-correcting strategies; Comprehension Standard 3: Reading habits	• Daily English Language Development • Vocabulary Development; Shared Reading • Monitoring of English Language and Literacy Progress in the ELD block • Daily Independent Reading and mini-lessons • Discussing reading from Read Aloud, Shared Reading, and Independent Reading
Secondary	Connected Math	Supports the implementation of the Math Initiative	One eighth-grade team (110 students)	1 year	Extended response items from GLMA	**Baseline data** All students are partially proficient or below. **Expected growth** All students will improve one or more proficiency level.	Learn to use expository form to explain math concepts.	• Daily focus lessons to introduce problem-solving strategies and math vocabulary • Modeling and guided practice on writing math-framed paragraphs • Whole class shared writing activities • Small group discussions • Weekly math journal entries • Individual weekly conferences to analyze progress
Music	4	Supports the School Improvement Plan	26 fourth-grade students	1 semester	Teacher-made performance assessment and rubric	**Baseline data** All students scored less than 6. **Expected growth** 80% of the fourth-grade class will pass 6 out of 9 skill directives on the keyboard.	• Keyboard techniques and skills, rhythm, and meter • Including left and right hand with correct fingering and I,II,IV and V chord in the key of C major tunes from the written notation	• Model stage presence posture • Whole group instruction • Guided practice posture • Guided practice stage presence

Source: Selected and adapted by the casewriter from http://www.dpsteacherobjectives.org/DPS_Table_of_Contents.html, accessed April 5, 2004.

Exhibit 6

PFP Pilot Teachers' Objective-Setting Performance: Percentages by Rubric Level 1999–2003

Rubric Level	Levels of Performance for Teacher Objectives	Descriptors for Performance Levels	1999–00 (684)	2000–01 (788)	2001–02 (1280)	2002–03 (1260)
		n=				
4 Excellent	Meets all of the criteria.*	States clearly what the students will learn, expressing clearly and coherently all elements of the objective, including the assessment, and demonstrating high expectations for students. There is a strong sense of the whole.	.9	8.9	13.2	28.0
3 Acceptable	Meets basic criteria with some lack of completeness and/or cohesion.	Refers (i.e., from a skill section in a book or test or a program acronym) to what the student will learn but may lack thoroughness in addressing the elements or in making clear the relationship or unity among the elements. The student expectations may seem somewhat conditional or low.	24.1	22.6	34.1	44.2
2 Needs Improvement	Meets some of the criteria, but is inconsistent and/or lacks cohesive thought.	Attempts to address most of the elements of the objective but may not have stated the learning content, showing lack of understanding about what is expected or confusing the elements (stating the objective as an assessment goal rather than a learning goal). Expectations for students may be low.	61.3	54.1	51.7	26.9
1 Too Little to Evaluate	Does not meet the criteria; may show lack of understanding or effort.	Does not address the objective in a manner that shows either an understanding of the task at hand or an effort to complete the task as requested. Objectives may place too many conditions or exclude too many students to be reliably assessed.	7.6	13.5	.9	.3
		Unrated	6.1	1.0	.2	.6

* Four Traits or Criteria for Quality Education Objectives:

Trait One: Learning Content   Content is that which the teacher will teach and the student will learn. Quality learning content is significant to the subject or discipline, appropriate to the student level, and rigorous in thought and application. Content choices should reference agreed-upon standards for the subject and grade level.

Trait Two: Completeness   A complete expression of an educational objective includes the student population to be taught; the objective with learning content; the assessment; the strategy or strategies used by the teacher to address the content; the rationale for selecting the objective; baseline data that show prior knowledge and/or skills; and finally, the evidence that persuades the teacher that the objective has or has not been met.

Trait Three: Cohesion   Cohesion refers to the logic and unity among the elements and demonstrates that rigorous thought and careful planning have taken place in the development of the objective. It gives a sense of the whole over the parts.

Trait Four: Expectations   The complete learning objective demonstrates that the teacher understands both the student population and indi viduals to be addressed and holds high expectations for each student as well as for himself/herself.

Source: Rubric developed by CTAC and adapted by the casewriter from Chapter 4, *Catalyst for Change: Pay for Performance in Denver Final Report,* January 2004.

Exhibit 7

DPS/DCTA Joint Task Force (JTF) Membership (March 2004)

Task-Force Members

Richard Allen, JTF Co-Chair, DPS Assistant Superintendent, Budget and Finance

Gary Justus, JTF Co-Chair, Teacher, Abraham Lincoln High School

Jeff Buck, Teacher, South High School

Barbara Cooper, Principal, Hallett Elementary School

Diane Deschanel, School Nurse

Pete Hergenreter, Principal, Career Education Center

Jeanne Lyons, School Nurse

Barbara Nash, Retired Middle School Principal

André Pettigrew, DPS Assistant Superintendent, Administrative Services

Carmen Rhodes, Community representative (Political Director, Denver Area Labor Federation)

Jamie Rich, Teacher, Hamilton Middle School

Diane Waco, Teacher, Fallis Elementary School

Lee White, Community representative (Vice President, Geo. K. Baum, Inc.)

Technical Advisors to the Committee

Bruce Dickinson, DCTA Executive Director

Eric Hirsch, School Finance Consultant, Augenblick and Myers

Brad Jupp, Team Leader, PFP Design Team

John Myers, School Finance Consultant, Augenblick and Myers

Doug Rose, Independent Financial Analyst

Source: District documents.

Exhibit 8
JTF's Overall Goals for a Compensation System

Denver Public Schools/Denver Classroom Teacher's Association
Joint Task Force on Teacher Salary

Overall Goals for a Compensation System

The JTF established 4 overall goals that any new compensation system should achieve. Three of these goals related to the impact of the compensation on the overall efforts of the district while one related to characteristics of the compensation system itself.

These goals are:

1. **Motivational goals**—Any compensation system should motivate teachers to achieve specified goals by providing additional compensation for achievement of specified goals. These goals include but are not limited to setting high standards, enhancing the achievement of all students, closing the gap between lower performing and higher performing students, performing specified additional duties (e.g. coaching, committee work, special assignments) and participating in professional development. In order to accomplish this mission, specific measurement of goal achievement must be clearly defined and mutually agreed upon. In some cases (e.g. additional duties) this will be easily measured, while in other cases (e.g. student achievement), measurement is a significant issue in itself. Compensation systems should be positive rather than punitive.

2. **Career goals**—Any compensation system should provide appropriate compensation to attract, motivate and retain high quality teachers in all specialties over the course of a career. These goals would include economic and professional growth for teachers as they move through a career. In order to meet professional and monetary career needs, these goals will enhance and enable the transition between classroom teaching and jobs outside the classroom. Thus, any compensation system should establish effective competition with other employers (including non-educational employers).

3. **Professional goals**—Any compensation system should enhance the professional standing and dignity of teachers. It should allow a teacher the ability to take on additional professional responsibilities and be compensated. Risk taking and innovation in the pursuit of professional achievement should be encouraged and rewarded. Compensation systems should be positive rather than punitive.

4. **System goals**—Any compensation system should be affordable, manageable, equitable, sustainable, comprehensive, flexible and understandable by those who would be a part of it. The system should attempt to solve only those problems that could not be more effectively and appropriately addressed through other means.

Source: District files. A draft of these goals was circulated during 2001–02. This is the final version included in the DPS/DCTA March 2004 agreement regarding ProComp. The full text of the agreement is available online at http://denverteachercompensation.org/Recommendations.html.

Exhibit 9

ProComp Summary: The Four Components (February 2004)

Element	Knowledge and Skills			Professional Evaluation		Market Incentives		Student Growth		
	Professional Development Unit	Graduate Degree/NBPTS	Tuition Reimbursement	Unsatisfactory Performance	Satisfactory Performance	Hard-to-Staff Position	Hard-to-Serve School	Annual Objectives	CSAP	Distinguished School
Index[a] Multiplier	2% Index Salary	9% Index Salary	$1,000 Account	Delay of Satisfactory Increase	3% Index Salary every third year	3% Index Bonus	3% Index Bonus	1% Index Salary, 1% Index Bonus	3% Index Sustain... Increase	2% Index Bonus
Dollar Amount	$659	$2,967	$1,000		$989	$989	$989	$330	$989	$659
Decision Process	Protocol agreed to by DCTA and DPS	Protocol agreed to by DCTA and DPS	Protocol agreed to by DCTA and DPS	Current system remains in effect until DCTA and DPS agree on evaluation tool.	Current system remains in effect until DCTA and DPS agree on evaluation tool.	Method agreed to by DCTA and DPS	Method agreed to by DCTA and DPS	Teacher and Principal reach consensus	Method agreed to by DCTA and DPS	Method agreed to by DCTA and DPS
When the increase is applied	Upon submission proper document	Upon submission proper document	Upon submission proper document	July 1: delayed at least one year	July 1	In monthly installments, upon completion of service each month	In monthly installments, upon completion of service each month	In June, upon analysis of appropriate student data	In early fall, upon analysis of CSAP data	In early fall, upon completion of multiple measures of school performance
Does Increase Build Highest Salary Under PERA[b]?	Yes	Yes	No	Yes	Yes	No, but DCTA and DPS will seek to make this element build pension by the 2005–2006 school year.	Yes	Yes	Yes	
Year Implemented	2006–2007	2006–2007	2005–2006	2006–2007	2006–2007	2005–2006	2005–2006	2006–2007	2006–2007	2005–2006

[a] Index negotiated annually by DPS and DCTA. Current Index = $32,971.

[b] Public Employees' Retirement Association of Colorado.

Source: Compiled by the casewriter from DPS and DCTA documents, including ProComp overview posted online at http://denverteachercompensation.org/, accessed March 29, 2004.

Exhibit 10

DCTA Recommendation Concerns (December 2003 memo—adapted by the casewriter)

TO RECOMMEND OR NOT RECOMMEND

Is it fair?

—Will DCTA get credit from members as a forward-thinking union that is professionalizing teachers and structuring the appropriate rewards?

—Will non-CSAP teachers come to accept the CSAP bonus as being fair?

—Will this cause a divide between teachers on the new system and teachers on the old system, and how will this impact membership?

—Will the fact that teachers are paid differently erode our ability to unify our members?

—Will there be a perceived preference given to the new system in negotiations?

Is it affordable and sustainable?

—Will this in fact "break the mold" of how teachers are paid in a way that really increases teachers' salaries?

—Can a trust fund be set up to be foolproof and safe from raiding the funds for other purposes?

—In bad budget times for the general fund will the new system do OK because of the special funding and the current system not do OK, that is, will this be a protected funding source for only half our teachers?

—What will be the ramifications of negotiating two systems?

Is it manageable?

—Will this have the impact of making DPS function better while providing teachers with the information they need to make good instructional decisions?

—What will be the impact on our fellow associations?

—If the DPS systems cannot perform properly during implementation, will DCTA get the blame?

—Will there be more work for the DCTA staff because of complaints about fairness, especially with abusive principals?

—Will we have more teacher v. teacher disputes because of pay differences?

—Will there be the infrastructure to run the new compensation components, that is, evaluation, knowledge and skills, market incentives, and student growth?

Will it attract and retain teachers?

—Will the public give the credit to DCTA that it deserves for this project and support teachers more because of it?

—Will new teachers come to DPS (and join DCTA) if there is more risk involved in gaining annual increases than in other districts?

—Will teachers leave membership in DCTA if they feel cheated under the new system and then cannot get out of it?

—What will be the impact of the merger with PERA?

Will it improve student achievement?

—Will it actually improve student achievement or will it only contribute to increased test scores?

—Are we putting our stamp of approval on using student growth to evaluate teacher and school performance? How do we avoid that being the only criterion?

Source: Adapted by the casewriter from internal DCTA documents.

Exhibit 11
Hypothetical Compensation Profiles

Roy—Specialist, eighth year. Roy is a specialist who has worked at DPS for eight years. He has his master's degree but plans to earn another. After using the salary calculator, he determined that he can make more money at the moment under the current system because of the annual step increases. He chooses to wait to opt in to ProComp until 2009 when he is near the top of the step scale. After joining ProComp, he finishes his second master's and receives a $2,967 salary increase. Had he remained in the current salary system, he would not have been paid for that second degree. In addition, by completing professional developments units (PDUs) nearly every year, he receives $659 to continue his professional studies. For meeting the average of 88% of his student objectives, he earns $330 more in salary every time both annual objectives are met. By the time he ends his career 17 years from now, he will be making $7,000 more annually than he would have made if he stayed in the current system. Over the course of those years, he will have earned nearly $32,000 more under ProComp. More critically for him, as he nears retirement, his earnings continue to grow. Under the present system he would have received longevity increases totaling $2,500. Under the ProComp system, in those final 10 years, his salary increased nearly $8,000.

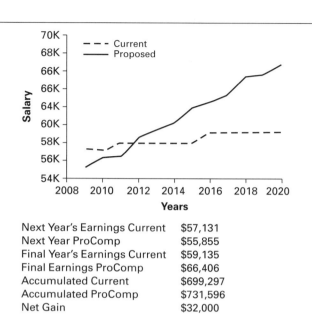

Next Year's Earnings Current	$57,131
Next Year ProComp	$55,855
Final Year's Earnings Current	$59,135
Final Earnings ProComp	$66,406
Accumulated Current	$699,297
Accumulated ProComp	$731,596
Net Gain	$32,000

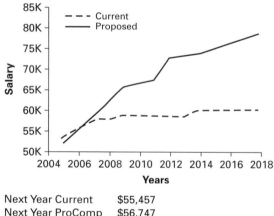

Next Year Current	$55,457
Next Year ProComp	$56,747
Final Year Current	$59,135
Final Year ProComp	$79,816
Total Earnings	$816,312
Total ProComp	$958,506
Net Gain	$142,194

Mary Ann—Middle School Teacher. Mary Ann is a middle school ELA-S teacher who has taught at DPS for 10 years. She has a master's degree and teaches in a school with a large number of students receiving free or reduced-price lunch. She also works in a position that typically is in high demand but short supply. By opting in to ProComp she can start being compensated for the hard work she does in an academically challenged environment. Her school is judged hard to serve by ProComp, which qualifies her for a $989 market incentive bonus every year she teaches at that school. Because her position is hard to staff, she qualifies for another $989 bonus every year she is in that position. Because of the special challenges in her school, she meets slightly less than the average number of her annual objectives, but she still earns $330 every time both objectives are met. She also receives compensation for PDUs—$659 every time she completes one—and when she chooses to get a second master's degree, she earns a $2,967 salary increase. Even though she only receives the market incentives for five years of her career, the amount adds up over time. By the time Mary Ann retires she is earning $79,816 under the ProComp system. Under the current system, she would be earning $59,135, a difference of more than $20,000 a year. During the final 15 years of her career, Mary Ann earns more than $140,000 more under ProComp than under the current system.

Exhibit 11 (continued)

Ginger—Early Career Teacher. A typical high school biology teacher, Ginger is hired into DPS with a B.A. degree. She begins the ProComp system in its initial year as a first-year teacher and plans to remain in the system for 25 years. She intends to get her master's degree in her seventh year and expects to complete a PDU nearly every year. A hard-working, but not exceptional, teacher, she expects to meet the average 88% of the student growth goals she sets over her career. Using those assumptions, this is how she fares.

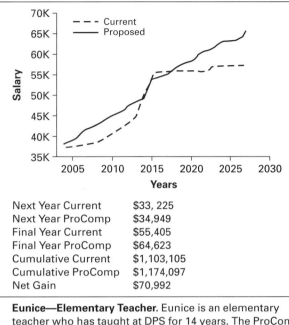

Next Year Current	$33, 225
Next Year ProComp	$34,949
Final Year Current	$55,405
Final Year ProComp	$64,623
Cumulative Current	$1,103,105
Cumulative ProComp	$1,174,097
Net Gain	$70,992

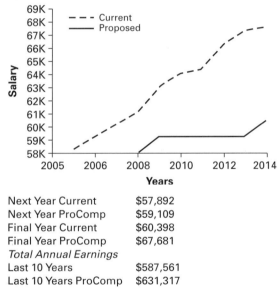

Next Year Current	$57,892
Next Year ProComp	$59,109
Final Year Current	$60,398
Final Year ProComp	$67,681
Total Annual Earnings	
Last 10 Years	$587,561
Last 10 Years ProComp	$631,317

Eunice—Elementary Teacher. Eunice is an elementary teacher who has taught at DPS for 14 years. The ProComp system can be of great benefit to her and other teachers who have gone past Step 13. This example shows how she can build income in the final years of her career simply by taking six PDUs in that time and meeting the average of 88% of her goals. For every PDU she completes, she earns $659, and for meeting objectives, she receives $330 in salary or a bonus. Should she wish to earn more, all she would have to do is to take more PDUs, or she could even get another advanced degree. She already has her master's, but should she choose to go after another, she would be compensated for it by ProComp. Under the current system she would not receive any extra pay for a second master's. From the moment she enters ProComp, Eunice would begin earning more—$1,200 in the first year. As a veteran teacher who has "topped out" on the 13-step salary schedule, she would receive a salary increase for longevity every five years under the current system. Under ProComp, she would get a $989 raise every three years for a satisfactory evaluation in addition to the PDU and student growth elements. When she retires in 10 years, Eunice will be making $7,000 a year more than she could have earned under the present system, building a significantly bigger base for her retirement. Over the course of those 10 years, she will have earned $43,000 more through ProComp.

Source: Compiled by the casewriter from February 2004 ProComp newsletter illustrating the impact of ProComp on four hypothetical teachers. All figures were computed using the DPS/DCTA salary calculator. They do not include cost-of- living adjustments, assuming those would be applied equally to both systems. A salary calculator was available to all at http:// www.teachercompensation.org.

DISCUSSION QUESTIONS

1. How would you describe the culture at LBUSD?

2. How well does the district achieve accountability at the school and district level?

3. In what ways are the key-results group and professional development important to district performance?

4. What other factors contribute to the district's performance?

James E. Austin ■ Allen S. Grossman ■ Robert B. Schwartz ■ Jennifer M. Suesse

Managing at Scale in the Long Beach Unified School District

Superintendent Holly Evans was worried. Six months after accepting the top post at a large urban public school district, Evans knew that the district's central office was not functioning at a high level. She knew that the district office could play a greater role in addressing the wide variation in student outcomes across the schools in her district. Evans wondered how to achieve high performance at all the sites despite differing capacities, governing structures (e.g., charter schools), and student demographics. She had discussed her plans to implement a substantial reorganization at the end of the school year with the governing school board and had won their support, but she had not yet identified a better solution. To help her with these difficult decisions, Evans decided to visit a few districts around the country to see how they were organized and managed. Her first stop was the third-largest school district in California: the Long Beach Unified School District.

District Structure

Students and Schools

Prior to leaving for Long Beach, Evans did her homework. She learned that in 2005–2006, the Long Beach Unified School District (LBUSD) served more than 92,000 students in the cities of Long Beach, Lakewood, Signal Hill, and Avalon on Catalina Island (see Exhibit 1 for district enrollment, 1996–2006). Within LBUSD, neighborhoods varied widely from the elegant homes along the ocean to the tightly packed downtown area. Typical of southern California, the student body represented diverse backgrounds and socioeconomic status. Fifty percent of students were Hispanic, 18% were African-American, 17% were white, 9% were Asian, and 6% were Filipino and Pacific Islander. Sixty-six percent of the students qualified for free or reduced-price meals, 26% were learning English, and 8% required special education services.

Some names and situations in this case are disguised, and Holly Evans is a fictitious character.

The district operated 91 schools including 61 elementary schools; 15 middle schools; six large, comprehensive high schools; three smaller high schools; a K–12 school; and five alternative sites. Parents were free to enroll their children in any school of their choice, although the student assignment formula did include a slight neighborhood preference.

LBUSD employed the equivalent of 4,431 full-time teaching staff in 2004–2005. The average teacher had spent 10.2 years in the district and 12.3 years teaching. New hires tended to balance retirements, and these averages had remained fairly consistent since 1998. In 2004–2005, new teachers accounted for 6.5% of the teaching staff, and 90.8% of the teaching staff had their full credentials. The average teacher's salary was $57,051, as compared with $57,294 statewide.[1]

The district's performance, as measured by California's Academic Performance Index (API), showed consistent growth. Although the means used to calculate API scores changed each year (making longitudinal comparisons difficult), the figure was designed to measure academic performance and growth of schools and was based on a variety of indicators.[2] API scores ranged from 200 to 1,000, and the statewide target was 800. LBUSD's base API score in 2005 was 713, which was the fourth highest in the state among the largest districts (see Exhibit 2 for a statewide demographic and API comparison chart). In 2005, 19 of the district's schools had not reached their state-target API scores, but 10 of those schools increased or maintained their performance from the previous year. In elementary schools, every school produced annual gains for five years in a row; in middle school, all but two of the 24 made annual gains and for high schools, all but five did so.

The California Department of Education also ranked schools in the state using an alternative process that compared one school with 100 others with similar demographic characteristics, levels, and predicted API scores. This "similar schools rank" was awarded by dividing this comparison group into 10 categories of equal size, called deciles, and ranking them from one (lowest) to 10 (highest). In 1999, 6% of LBUSD schools were ranked 1–3 (lowest), 34% were ranked 4–7 (average), and 60% were ranked 8–10 (highest). By 2005, 13% of LBUSD schools had 1–3 ranks, 32% ranked average, and 56% had the highest scores.

Evans saw that the district, like others across the nation, was wrestling with a persistent achievement gap between white and Asian students on one hand and Hispanic and African-American students on the other (see Exhibit 3 for an overview of the district's achievement gap).

Elementary and middle school sites were led by a single principal. At the high school level, LBUSD had employed coprincipals in its six large high schools since the mid-1990s. Contrary to the small-school trend taking hold in some large urban districts, LBUSD remained committed to these six comprehensive high schools, which had average enrollments of about 4,000 students each. Co-principals shared full responsibility for both operational and instructional leadership activities at their sites, and each pair decided themselves how to divide these tasks according to their individual strengths and preferences.

Discretion over staffing and budgets was the same for all 91 schools. Of every school's general fund budget, 85% went to personnel. Principals had discretion as to how to spend the additional 15% of their general fund allocation, as well as any categorical or grant funding awarded to their school. Each site could decide whether or not to allocate a portion of its school's budget for an assistant principal, and most did. In terms of staffing, principals could select their assistant principals from a district-approved list of candidates. Principals had the authority to hire teachers for any available slots following the district's transfer and assignment process required by collective bargaining agreements.

School administrators were commonly rotated across sites and levels. While elementary school principals did not always work at other levels, the majority of high school principals had worked at either the elementary or middle school level and had long tenures in the district. Principals also moved in and out of administrative roles in the central office. Although this "rotation policy" was unstated and informal, all principals expected that their assignments at a particular school would last only five to eight years.

At the elementary school level, the district used the state-mandated Open Court curriculum in literacy and Houghton Mifflin curriculum for math across all sites. A variety of curricula were designated for middle and high school academic programs. Sites were permitted to supplement with additional materials, and some of the comprehensive high schools had organized themselves into small learning communities (SLCs), where teachers selected curriculum based upon both state standards and SLC-related themes. There was wide variation across the high schools in themes and implementation of the SLCs, which was encouraged by district leadership. For example, some high schools had arts-related magnet programs, while others specialized in science or math. Also, due to federal funding grants and restrictions, schools with a greater percentage of English language learners or impoverished students received additional funding according to their individual student demographics.

District Organization and Focus

Upon Evans's arrival in Long Beach, she met the leadership team. Superintendent Christopher Steinhauser had led the district since 2002, having served as the deputy superintendent, an elementary school principal, teacher, and teacher's aide during his 24 years in the district. As did

those of many district administrators, both of Steinhauser's children attended LBUSD schools. Evans learned that prior to 1992 the district had been organized into three geographic areas and was fairly decentralized. In order to create a districtwide approach to education for each age group, LBUSD Superintendent Carl Cohn reorganized the district into levels, sought to establish a service mentality and structures for collaboration at the central office, and hired a mix of insiders and outsiders for key positions. The central office was divided into two units: instruction and support services. The instructional side was arranged by level: Deputy Superintendent Karen DeVries supervised elementary schools, Assistant Superintendent Gwen Mathews supervised middle schools and Head Start programs, and Assistant Superintendent Margaret "Maggie" Webster supervised high schools. Centralized support services, including finance, curriculum, human resources, research, and special education, were organized functionally. These departments worked to collaborate with each other and with the schools. Dr. Lynn Winters, assistant superintendent of Research, Planning and Evaluation, commented:

> Our primary function at the central office is to support the schools and focus on our students. The superintendent prior to Carl Cohn [who led the district from 1992 to 2002] pretty much dismantled the central office functions. Carl realized the importance of central office support and began rebuilding services to support instruction. He reinstituted curriculum and staff development and made it a cabinet-level position; he reconceptualized the role of research, taking all of the "accounting" functions from this office and allowing us to do real evaluation; and he hired a special education leader who was nationally recognized as a visionary. Today, the "old-school" central office structures and ways of working are replaced by a team approach to

serving schools. We work together with openness and mutual trust. Sometimes collaboration can be difficult, especially when resources are limited, but we know that we have to sort out our differences to ensure the best solutions for kids.

Centralized support and funding were allocated according to district priorities, although schools that were struggling (designated program improvement or state high-priority schools) received more state and federal resources than their more successful counterparts. These schools also received extra attention and coaching from district officials. However, no matter what the overall performance of a school, the central office attempted to respond to any specific requests or concerns. DeVries, Mathews, and Webster worked with the department heads to solve problems and allocate resources, and they would request support services for specific sites when needs that could not be addressed by the school's staff were identified.

High Schools

Under Cohn's leadership, the district focused much of its attention and resources on improving the educational quality of its K-8 offerings in order to better prepare students to succeed in high school. In 2002, LBUSD decided to address high school reform more explicitly. High school administrators developed a detailed "high school initiative" that sought to address four broad strands of reform:

- Increase achievement of all students in the academic content areas.

- Close the achievement gap by accelerating the learning of the lowest-performing students.

- Improve high school climate and culture among students and staff to support improved achievement.

- Build high school leadership capacity to de-

sign, implement, and sustain reform and improvement efforts.[3]

These goals were consistent with reform work taking place at all levels of the district and built on the work of the previous decade. The strategies for high school reform reflected widely held district beliefs about how to work for lasting change (see Exhibit 4 for a list of reform strategies). Each high school principal was given funds to engage teacher leadership in this reform work at their sites. Each site defined how they would implement these reforms and had the discretion to decide who would participate and in what ways.

In addition to high school reform, elementary, middle, and high schools had plans in place to help more struggling minority students achieve proficiency. District administrators acknowledged that their work in addressing the achievement gap was lagging, but they were determined to help all kids succeed.

When they were not responding to specific requests from the assistant superintendents, the district's support services were focused on the high school initiative. This meant that elementary and middle schools received less attention and support from the central office than they had in the preceding decade, although support and resources were still available on an as-needed basis.

Budget

Fiscally independent of the city of Long Beach, the district, on average, had received 13% of its revenue from local sources, 76% from the state of California, and 11% from federal grants and programs over the preceding 10 years. The district was currently experiencing the effects of a statewide fiscal crisis, which necessitated deep budget cuts for LBUSD. Declining enrollment also contributed to the district's financial pressure (see Exhibit 1). From 2002 to 2006, Steinhauser estimated that "between reductions and shifts we cut close to $50 million, including 24 central office positions." The district's total budget in 2005–2006 was a little more than $912 million from all sources (see Exhibit 5 for district financials). Each department was asked to take a 10% reduction for two years in a row. Steinhauser said:

> Cutting that much from the budget was very difficult, but we worked with all our stakeholders to underscore the importance of preserving classroom instruction. We believe that kids must come first, so their classrooms had priority as we faced tough decisions. Even though maintaining a low teacher-to-student ratio is very expensive, changing it was not on the table. We believe strongly that the 20–1 ratio in K-3 has been a huge benefit to the system, so we found other ways to fund it using some categorical money.

Assistant Superintendent Christine Dominguez, who supervised the Office of Curriculum, Instruction, and Professional Development, added:

> We wanted to avoid layoffs and protect the school sites. Chris brought in an advisory group and led discussions to get input from the community. He listened to the central office, even though we took huge cuts. Our goal is to just continue the improvement efforts. The worst-case scenario would be destroying the work we've done here. We had to keep finding ways to do more with less.

By freezing central office hires and consolidating positions, the central office shrank considerably, which resulted in heavy workloads and reduced staffing for the remaining leadership. Evans considered just how many central office positions could be consolidated before the leadership roles became unmanageable. She noted that DeVries and Winters planned to retire in August 2006, and the district anticipated a few high school principal retirements. Knowing the challenges of ensuring seamless succession, especially in such critical roles, Evans wondered if the next generation of district leadership was ready. Many of Steinhauser's recent hires to the district leadership team, especially in support positions, had strong elementary school backgrounds, and some secondary school administrators expressed concerns that there was a lack of understanding of the needs of older children and high schools in particular. Hiring in tight economic times was challenging, and Evans recognized that the district was facing hard choices. She wondered how the district would weather the continued financial strain presented by declining enrollments and the ongoing state budget debate in California.

Governance and Collective Bargaining

A five-member board of education governed LBUSD, set district policy, and approved the budget. Each member represented one of five regions of Long Beach. Although the regions had different characteristics and the poorest residents tended to be concentrated in the southwest section of the city, board practice encouraged members to act on behalf of "all kids," regardless of their neighborhood. After a decade of fairly stable board membership, there had been some turnover since 2002.

In speaking with district administrators, Evans learned that many were worried about the increase in unrest around the district promoted by the union. Long Beach had a history of cordial union-district relations, but confrontations with the current union leadership (many of whom were not native to LBUSD) had taken an uglier tone in the past few years, and the staff was unsettled. In the spring 2006 board elections, the Teacher's Association of Long Beach (TALB) endorsed three candidates to challenge the three incumbents up for reelection. One challenger won, one lost, and one was seated in the June runoff election.

Accountability System

Principal Perspectives

Evans spoke next with district leadership about their accountability system. She began by meeting with a focus group of principals from all levels, which included a mix of experienced and novice administrators serving at both high- and low-performing schools across the city. Evans asked the principals to discuss their assignments and the expectations placed on them by the district.

An experienced elementary school principal answered first. "This is a results-driven district," she said. "Everyone encourages us to have high standards, and the people who work here are friendly. Our supervisors are nurturing and also push us. They work right along with us." Evans saw nods all around the room. Principal Alejandro "Alex" Flores, who was in his fourth year at Wilson Classical High School, spoke next: "I came to Long Beach from another district, and immediately I saw that they have a totally different way of doing things. It is much more collaborative, and there is a real emphasis on instruction. Maggie holds us accountable. Some people may resent that, but I know it's not about her. It's about kids." "The pressure for results is felt everywhere," added a third principal. "The higher-achieving schools on our East Side have to figure out how to maintain high achievement. The schools downtown and on the West Side are expected to push the academic agenda forward. Nobody has an easy ride."

An elementary school principal chimed in, "With our rotation policy, we expect we could be asked to lead any school in the district, and we hear about the different challenges each site presents. Most of us have worked all over Long Beach." Another principal said, "There are different explanations for why they move us

around so much. I think they feel that once you get to a certain point in a school, you're prone to coast, so they move you again so you have to re-establish yourself and get out of your comfort zone." "My father, a former principal, used to say that the reason they moved principals around was so you couldn't create a fiefdom," a middle school principal added. "I think that it gets harder to demand improvement if you know the staff too well," commented an elementary school principal. "I mean, you know their strengths and their weaknesses . . . but they also know yours. I'm in my third school, and I like getting a clean slate every five years or so." A high school principal noted: "Principals don't always have much of a voice in deciding when or where they get to move, and that can cause some tension. Sometimes the district makes last-minute changes, and you find out that you have a new assignment right at the end of the summer. Then, there's no chance for goodbyes, for notification, and no time for closure with the old staff."

A middle school principal, whose school had recently been awarded the prestigious California Blue Ribbon, said, "I know I can be moved from my site at a moment's notice, so I travel light. I never have more than two boxes of personal items in my office—that's all I can carry." Another principal noted, "While the district does a decent job of placing people, they make mistakes. If someone is not working out, they don't usually last more than a year or two."

"During my first year at Edison, our API went down six points," said Mathilde "Matty" Zamora, the principal at Edison Elementary School. "Karen provided support by assigning a math coach who helped us with the application of math facts and the pacing of our instruction. He facilitated the implementation of a math facts program and an alternate math pacing program." Zamora and her team's efforts paid off. In 2005, the school's API score rose 88 points. In 2006, Edison was selected as a California Distinguished School, the state's top award. "We are recommending our approach to teaching math facts to others in the district," Zamora added. "It worked with our students, 100% of whom qualify for free or reduced lunch, and 76% are second-language learners. A number of my colleagues have already visited the school to see what they can take back to their sites."

"We meet with department heads, curriculum heads, and our coaching staff to determine the weak and strong areas," said one middle school principal. "We talk about what we need to do, and then I meet with the head of middle schools to learn about how this fits into the district's goals for the year. Our annual goal-setting is a collaborative process between the site and the central office which is revisited throughout the year." "Since we don't have departments, it's a little less complex at the elementary level," said a veteran elementary school principal. "I do more of the needs assessment on my own or in conversation with a few lead teachers. But, the basic structure is the same, and in my annual conversation with Karen we review my progress and goals."

"The expectation of continuous improvement is the same districtwide," added district veteran Rosalind "Roz" Morgan, who was a principal at Jordan High School. She continued: "There is a friendly competition among the high schools, and we know that all of the jobs are hard. We are all expected to be instructional leaders. This has been a major change in the last decade, and so we help each other out wherever we can. Sometimes I wake up in the middle of the night thinking about my data and how we're going to address the needs of all our kids."

Other principals echoed the importance of using data to inform site-based decision making. "We all live by the data," said an elementary school principal, "because that's how we know what's working." Flores added, "The data folks in Lynn's shop are great. She and her team work with us to provide the information and

analytic tools we need to analyze our student-achievement results."

The principals then recalled an incident the preceding year, when test scores at a high-performing school on the East Side fell: "As soon as the scores were published, that principal got a bunch of phone calls from other principals wanting to know what had happened and what they could do to help."

"We also rely heavily on the district curriculum staff to provide high-quality products," said a middle school principal. "Some of us struggle more with human resources," confessed one principal. "They aren't always as responsive as we'd wish." "We talk among ourselves," said a veteran principal. "We work together to make sure things happen." Another concluded:

> You have to have a certain personality to do this job, since it takes blood, sweat, and a lot of tears to succeed. The district works hard to ensure that there is a good fit between the leader and the school, and they work to support us, but we have the responsibility for our schools at the end of the day. It's our job to establish working relationships and trust with the teachers, the parents, and the students and to keep everyone focused on the kids.

District Management Philosophy for School Leadership

After meeting with the principals, Evans asked their supervisors—DeVries, Mathews, and Webster—more about their management philosophy and practices. She learned that all three leaders conducted both formative and summative evaluations of their administrators, and each had a system for annual planning with each site. Overall, it seemed that LBUSD encouraged a variety of management styles according to the strengths and weaknesses of different leaders as long as results were achieved. Evans met with each leader, then followed up with a group discussion. Evans, who was aware of her own challenge in diversifying her senior staff, noted that both Mathews and Webster were African-American and native to Long Beach, while DeVries had moved to California from Utah and was white. Evans began by asking DeVries, Mathews, and Webster to reflect on their individual roles, their expectations for principals and instructional staff, and how their philosophy of management had evolved over time.

Karen DeVries: Elementary Schools

I moved to Long Beach and joined LBUSD in 1980. I had a variety of teaching and leadership roles, mostly in elementary schools, before joining the supervisory team in 1996. Initially, I was responsible for supervising 23 schools. Then, budget cuts in 1999 necessitated a reorganization, at which point I assumed responsibility for all 52 LBUSD elementary schools. I became deputy in 2004, and I plan to retire in August 2006.

Everything starts with the data. I love the data, not because I'm a numbers freak, but because it's the way to talk about things. It's not emotional. It just speaks for itself. Because we all have access to it, the monitoring of student progress, especially for our lowest-performing kids, is available at all times. Visiting schools, walking into classrooms, yields more data. I also talk with principals and meet with teachers. Information is everywhere. If a school is struggling, we focus on interventions. Data doesn't matter unless you talk about how you're going to address the problems it reveals. The most important step in data analysis is making changes in instructional practice in the classroom. I work with principals who are as impatient as I am and have the expectation that we hold ourselves and our teaching staff accountable for results. Competence is expected; competent, meaning instructionally sound. If student achievement re-

sults aren't realized, additional attention is given to schools that are not making progress. If those efforts don't begin to have an effect, then I take more drastic steps. We all know when someone isn't doing their job. I think people respect that I won't tolerate lack of effort. I expect principals to do something about teachers who aren't doing their jobs, so I darn well better be doing something about principals who aren't doing their job. Sound instructional leadership and the ability to develop "followership" is critical. If you can't lead so that children have every opportunity to learn, there isn't a place for you in LBUSD.

Our district has a tremendous history with using an approach called "elements of effective instruction" [EEEI], which evolved from Madeline Hunter's lesson design [see Exhibit 6 for an outline of EEEI principles]. You have to know how to teach—how you're framing the learning, what process you'll use to explain it, how you'll motivate learners and give feedback. Our belief is that it doesn't matter what the teacher knows, it's what the kids learn. It is the teacher's responsibility to find out how their teaching impacts student learning. I expect that principals use EEEI in their evaluations of teachers, and I use it in my evaluations of them. Using data and implementing the EEEI pedagogy are paramount, even sacred. They are not up for discussion. In my mind, this is where the principals' work is most important. We need to keep asking, "Would I put my kid in that classroom?"

It's critical to establish trust and build the day-to-day relationships necessary to get the work done. Relationships are fragile. They are the hardest to build, and the first to go. In our annual reviews, I talk with principals about the importance of their relationships with their staff and community and also with each other. People don't trust easily, so I am careful to establish a culture where trustworthiness as well as instructionally competent principals can flourish.

I expect all schools to improve, no matter whether their level of achievement is high or low. However, no one person is out there by themselves. I can't stand it when there's no ownership by all of us for the issues that we all need to face to keep student achievement high. That has been tough during all of these budget cuts. Last year, as I started to get overloaded with the addition of the deputy superintendent role, I made up my mind that my contribution would be to keep things running as smoothly and as consistently through this hard time as I could. One way I began to share the load was by identifying 12 principal leaders, who started running our key-results meetings with other principals. I'd been working with them for six years, so they knew how those meetings should go. To watch them take on this additional responsibility was inspiring.

Gwen Mathews: Middle Schools, K-8 Schools, and Head Start Programs

I became an assistant superintendent in January 2005. Previously, I supervised the district's Head Start programs, and I am currently supervising the directors of both the Head Start and preschool programs as well as serving as assistant superintendent. Prior to joining the central office leadership team, I was a principal in three elementary schools, as well as a teacher, a specialist, and a facilitator. I also worked in the Integration Planning Department as a consultant earlier in my career.

When I got this job, I started by having conversations with my predecessor and doing research on the middle and K-8 schools. I invited several principals out to dinner and tried to get a feel for how they were thinking about what needed to be done to promote academic achievement in middle and K-8 schools. I engaged other principals in informal conversations as well. I knew many of them because I had worked in the district for 34 years, but I wanted to meet and get to know all of them.

I think they were pleased with the middle school reform movement, which began in the mid-1990s, and my goal was to take them to the next step—by examining effective practices, refining those practices in need of improvement, and identifying and implementing new concepts and practices. I actually shared ideas with Lynn Winters, who's a good sounding board and extremely knowledgeable about data. I basically asked questions so I could get a feel for where we were and where we needed to go.

I see my role as providing leadership and supporting the principals, who in turn provide leadership to their schools for raising the academic achievement levels of our students as measured by local, district, and state assessments. Before the year begins, I review the superintendent's goals and develop goals for middle and K-8 schools. I assist principals in establishing goals for their schools. I expect them all to learn, grow, and to meet the goals we set, which are basically in five areas:

- Data-driven instructional planning,

- Comprehensive, schoolwide literacy,

- Safe and orderly schools,

- Focused interventions to meet the needs of students at the far below- and below-basic levels and with low grade point averages, and

- Professional development.

I hold performance accountability conferences three times a year in addition to visiting schools. I think the principals understand that we will discuss issues as they arise, establish and identify areas to be improved, and share information. At the same time, principals know there are some major decisions made at the district level. When possible, we will seek to involve them before decisions are made. We also encourage site-based decision making and give schools a great deal of autonomy to do what they need to do to achieve results. Principals and their school-based site councils make decisions about how discretionary funds will be spent.[4]

Maggie Webster: High Schools

This is my 35th year in the district, and my fifth as an assistant superintendent. I began as a junior high school English teacher before moving into high schools. I worked on human relations strategies when the district experienced racial tensions in the 1970s and early 1980s before becoming a high school counselor, assistant principal, and then was part of the first shared principalship at Polytechnic High School in the early 1990s. Sharing responsibility for the instructional leadership at a campus with more than 4,000 students is the only way we can make the job manageable. It is tricky to pair people who can work together, but we believe it is worth it. Not only can coprincipals distribute leadership, but there is always an administrator on campus when the other is off-site.

We're in the fifth year of our current high school reform effort, which is focused on instruction. It places a high priority on student achievement. It implements a coherent, standards-based curriculum and instructional program; uses assessment data to improve instruction and achievement; provides available district instructional resources necessary to move student achievement forward; and is strongly based on professional development.

When I took this position five years ago, we sat down together, and I gave principals some brutal facts. Our high schools were not moving, we were not seeing success, and our students were not achieving as they should be. I said this was our fault, and we needed to do something. There weren't really models for success at big, urban, comprehensive high schools, so we started just looking at ourselves and talking about what it would mean to be an instructional leader at the high school. I asked them if they believed they were instructional leaders. I didn't want them to answer out loud, but I could see their answers as we looked around the room. I saw them thinking, "Yes, I'm an instructional leader because I'm supposed to be an instructional leader, but I'm not quite sure what that means and how I can demonstrate that." So, that's where we began.

And, five years later, I can tell you that 100% of LBUSD high school principals are instructional leaders, why they are, and how they arrived there. We work as a team to lead the learning of our students and teachers and departments. It looks different at each site, and each level uses different assessments. But student-assessment data is used by everyone to elevate instruction and to diagnose student learning. We keep asking, where is the learning problem? All the sites are trying to implement a continuous improvement instruction model to help us identify what needs to be done next.

I base principal evaluations on their instructional leadership and how they take responsibility for moving their schools from good to great, which is, in turn, based in their ability to demonstrate continuous improvement at their sites. It is important for me to see how they move their students into more rigorous and challenging curriculum. I want to see how they are growing their college-bound population and how they are decreasing dropout rates. I also look to see if they have the right people in the right seats and that they are working to either change the seats or the people.

We also have a very mobile population of students across schools, and our school community was feeling as though our reform efforts were always changing. So, now we are trying a consistent, steady approach, and we meet regularly to ensure that we are on the same page.

Right now, we are struggling with how to use instruction that is individually differentiated for each student. How do we know if it's working? How do we base our assessments in a department and in a curriculum to identify weak areas? How do we work with department chairs, curriculum leaders, and coaches to build an approach to particular learning needs? In response, we are trying to build professional learning communities within each school. Some are stronger than others. Some of our underperforming schools like Cabrillo and Jordan are making more progress because they have young staff who are eager to learn and have greater access to federal resources to fund external professional development. They try to share what they're learning with the other sites, but it is slow and challenging work.

Principal Rotation and Assignment

Following her individual conversations with DeVries, Mathews, and Webster, Evans talked with them about rotating principals. Mathews began:

This year, when I start to think about principal assignments, I will look at the strengths and talents of principals and try to create a match with

the staff and community in each school. The executive staff collaborates on assignments. In elementary and middle schools, we really share candidates depending on the needs of the school and where we think the candidate will be most successful. We work together as a team.

Webster added, "Matching coprincipals is delicate work, and we don't like to make too many changes at the high schools. Any change has the potential to affect the whole system." When reassignments occurred, the district sought to move them to other positions in the district where their strengths would be leveraged. DeVries commented:

My principals know that I know the job and that I will try to make the best decision for all of them. We try to identify the schools' needs, the leaders' strengths and developmental needs, and then find a match that suits everyone. Sometimes principals don't see why they've been assigned to a school, but they always rise to the challenge. It is our responsibility to know what our leaders can do—where they're succeeding, where they are struggling, and what they value—so we can help them continue to improve.

Key-Results Groups

As Evans talked with DeVries, Mathews, and Webster, she also noted that they each had mandatory monthly day-long "key-results" meetings with principals. The practice began with the middle school reform effort, where the middle school principals met to discuss their progress and challenges. The discussions were difficult at first, as external consultants "asked tough questions that we weren't used to answering," recalled one principal. As the meetings continued, they developed a focus on reviewing data and challenging issues facing the group.

When DeVries assumed responsibility for all elementary schools, she implemented a similar key-results practice for elementary schools. The principals met in small groups. For the first few years, DeVries had rotated membership in the key-results groups each year in an effort to "give people a chance to meet other principals." But, after receiving feedback that the rotation was too disruptive, DeVries established standing groups and selected principals to lead the monthly discussions aimed at sharing best practices. DeVries observed, "When we find a new idea that works, we want to know how and why it worked. Each site will then have the responsibility and option to see if that idea could work for their school. Demonstrating results is what matters to all of us."

Webster and the high school principals also used a key-results structure for meeting but adapted the model to suit their needs. Since the district sought to have one coprincipal on campus at all times, the high school principals were divided into two groups. For the first three years of their regular meetings, one focused on data and one focused on professional development. It was in these monthly working groups that the principals articulated their high school reform strategies work and shared the challenges in its implementation. The high school principals often invited district support staff to join these meetings so they could share information and challenges.

Professional Development

Before she left LBUSD, Evans summarized what she had learned about the district's approach to pedagogy and professional development. She learned that all incoming teachers received some training about the core EEEI philosophy, which was designed and mandated by the district. Principals also had some discretion regarding additional professional development offered at their site, according to their goals and priorities. The EEEI pedagogy was applied in conjunction with state-mandated curriculum and other materials.

District leadership also described their practice of "training the trainer," as there was a commitment to developing internal capacity for professional development, as well as an ongoing need to modify training to suit the district's specific needs.

"The district's commitment to professional development is long-standing," commented one principal. "If people leave us for another district, they are often surprised to see that our approach is not universal." "Of course," noted DeVries, "our focus on professional development is expensive and can be intense. But, we believe it is a cornerstone of our success." Mathews observed:

> We require all teachers—elementary, middle, and high—to learn and apply the essential elements of instruction. Some middle school teachers work with many different classes, so pacing schedules and changing classes can make it difficult to go back, reteach, and make sure the kids really learn their lessons. We are making sure that teachers and administrators go through refresher courses. The middle school principals just participated in a session on active participation. At the middle level, we see differentiation of instruction, active participation, monitoring of instruction, and guided practice as areas in which to focus.
>
> Our principals' meetings all focus on professional development including the essential elements. We meet at someone's school each month, and principals are responsible for identifying a critical question and something they want the other principals to look for while they're visiting. Last month, we talked about critical thinking skills and active participation, and then we walk through the school we're visiting and talk about what we see. Each principal was also required to conduct walkthroughs in their own school and have a discussion with their cohort group at the meeting.

Evans noted that there was a consistency in how things were done, which district employees called "the Long Beach way." She attended a few meetings during the course of her visit, and she noted that the language of the EEEI pedagogy seemed familiar to the majority of the staff. For example, when DeVries hosted a meeting for all the elementary school principals, Evans observed that even the meeting itself was interactive and focused and allowed principals time to talk among themselves as a group and to move around the room.

Challenges

As Evans flew home, she sat on the plane compiling her findings from the visit. While much of what she had learned in the district intrigued her, it was a lot of information to process. "Now I need to go back and apply some of this in my district," she mused. "So, what have I learned? Where should I begin? How many and which of these ideas will transfer to my district?"

Notes

1. Teacher demographics cited on the Education Data Partnership website: www.ed-data.k12.ca.us.

2. According to the California Department of Education, a school's score on the API is an indicator of a school's performance level. The statewide API performance target for all schools is 800. The baseline score summarizes the starting point of performance, and a school's growth is measured by how well it is moving toward or past that goal. A school's API base is subtracted from its API growth to determine how much the school improved in a year. The API score summarizes the results of various indicators from the state's Standardized Testing and Reporting (STAR) program including the California Standards Tests (CST) in subject areas, the norm-referenced California Achievement Test (CAT/6), and the California High School Exit Examination (CAHSEE). Statewide test results are incorporated into the API calculation according to the amount of weight, or emphasis, given to each test. Each school's content area weights are determined based on test weights established by the state and on the number of valid test scores in each content area and grade level at a school. API calculations result in content area weights that may be slightly different for each individual school. In addition, APIs are calculated for numerically significant student subgroups at a school to ascertain whether the school meets the "comparable improvement" criterion. For more detail, see http://www.cde.ca.gov/ta/ac/ap/apidescription.asp.

3. A full description of the high school initiative, "Every Student, Every Day: Responding to the Needs of All Learners," can be downloaded at http://www.lbusd.k12.ca.us/district/departments/high_school/initiative.asp.

4. All LBUSD schools have a school-site council that participates in site-based decision making. School-site councils, which include both district and community representatives, do not, however, hire or fire principals.

Exhibit 1
District Enrollment (1996–2006)

Year	Total	% White	% African-American	% Hispanic	% Asian, Pacific Islander, Filipino, Native American	% English Language Learners
1996	80,520	21	21	37	21	34.0
1997	83,038	20	21	39	20	35.1
1998	85,908	20	20	41	20	35.4
1999	89,214	19	20	42	19	35.0
2000	91,465	18	20	44	18	36.0
2001	93,694	18	20	45	17	36.4
2002	96,488	17	20	47	16	32.9
2003	97,212	17	19	48	16	32.3
2004	97,560	17	19	49	15	32.6
2005	96,319	17	18	49	15	29.5
2006	92,000	—	—	—	—	26.3

Source: District records.

Exhibit 2

Statewide Demographic and API Comparison Chart (2004–2005)

District Data	Los Angeles Unified	San Diego Unified	Long Beach Unified	Fresno Unified	Santa Ana Unified	San Francisco Unified	Garden Grove Unified	Sacramento Unified	Oakland Unified
Enrollment	741,367	134,709	96,319	80,760.00	61,693	57,144	50,030	51,420	49,214
Number of Schools	721	190	86	85	51	108	63	89	123
Student Demographics (Race)									
African-American	12	14	18	11	1	14	1	21	41
Native American or Alaskan Native	0	1	0	1	0	1	0	1	0
Asian	4	9	9	16	3	42	29	23	17
Filipino	2	7	4	0	0	6	1	1	1
Hispanic or Latino	73	43	49	54	93	22	52	30	33
Pacific Islander	0	1	2	0	0	1	1	1	1
White (not of Hispanic origin)	9	26	17	16	2	10	16	22	6
Student Demographics (Other)									
Participants in Free or Reduced-Price Lunch	78	54	61	82	78	54	61	63	71
English Learners	42	28	24	30	59	28	46	31	28
Participants in Gifted and Talented Program	9	21	7	11	7	16	5	6	9
Mobility, School Prior Year[a]	9	26	22	27	17	13	16	25	21
Average Parent Education Level[b]	2.24	2.85	2.57	2.32	1.53	2.61	2.52	2.67	2.4
API									
2002 API Base	595	677	648	579	570	683	680	644	568
2003 API Base	622	697	682	610	614	706	719	666	592
2004 API Base	633	710	694	623	628	724	722	679	601
2005 API Base	649	728	713	644	656	745	740	700	634
Growth in Prior Year (2004–2005)	16	18	19	21	28	21	18	21	33
Three-Year Growth (2002–2005)	54	51	65	65	86	62	60	56	66
Percent Decile 1–3 Schools (2005)[c]	51.0	28.4	21.1	69.4	66.7	35.2	20.9	41.0	67.7
Percent Decile 9–10 Schools (2005)	9.4	24.2	11.8	5.9	5.9	18.5	9.5	9.6	12.5

Source: California Department of Education, LBUSD Research Department, and casewriter analysis.

[a] Mobility represents the percentage of students who first attended the school in the current year. Students in the lowest grades are excluded.

[b] Average parent education level indicates average of all responses where "1" represents "Not a high school graduate" and "5" represents "graduate school."

[c] The California Department of Education ranks all the schools in the state from lowest to highest achieving. They then categorize the schools into 10 groups of equal size, called deciles. Each decile includes 10% of the schools in the state. The best 10% of schools receive a rank of 10, and the worst 10% receive a rank of 1. Percentage calculations in this table exclude small, charter, and alternative schools.

Exhibit 3

Achievement Gap Data (using CA standardized test scores and subject area API in English-language arts and math)

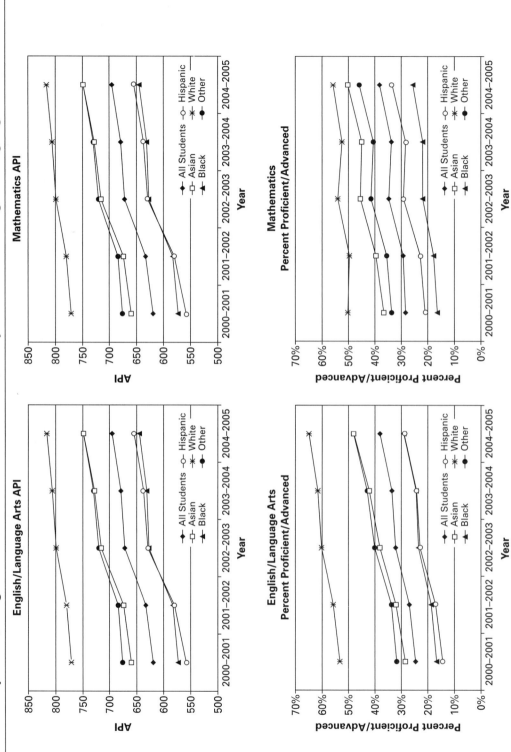

Exhibit 4
LBUSD High School Reform Strategies (2004)

"Every Student, Every Day" is based on the following proven strategies:

- Leadership development for high school principals

- School Level Professional Learning Communities

- Redesigning professional development

- Using data to drive instructional decision making

- Increasing parent engagement

The next phase of the high school reform will add the following key strategies:

- Extend and evolve the work of the Principal and Teacher professional learning communities

- Build distributed leadership by involving all teachers in instructional leadership

- Differentiate instruction

- Redesign the role of high school counselors to focus on student achievement

- Improve culture, climate and learning time

- Strengthen Seamless Education Partnership with local postsecondary education institutions, business and community leaders, to increase college access and success

- Bring business partners to the table to engage support and confirm alignment of expectations

- Provide tutors from postsecondary institutions to work with high school students.

Source: http://www.lbusd.k12.ca.us/district/departments/high_school/initiative.asp.

Exhibit 5

LBUSD Financial Information, 2002–2005 ($ million)

This statement includes revenues and expenditures from all LBUSD funds, including general, adult, preschool, insurance, cafeteria, and construction funds.

	SY04	SY05	SY06
Revenues by Source			
Local	$141.058	$146.841	$126.249
State	606.991	641.517	620.797
Federal Grants	104.562	123.655	137.148
Total Revenues	$852.611	$912.013	$884.194
Expenditures by Object			
Certificated Salaries	356.034	355.815	357.934
Classified Salaries	128.684	123.886	127.702
Benefits	123.559	144.533	159.790
Books and Supplies	51.832	39.062	39.527
Services and Other Operating Expenditures	130.152	136.875	185.358
Capital Outlay	58.844	51.135	34.124
Other Outgo[a]	15.819	21.102	21.530
Total Expenditures	$864.924	$872.408	$925.965
Operating Surplus/(Deficit)	($12.313)	$39.605	($41.771)

Source: Compiled by district financial office from LBUSD financial records (FINSYS).

[a] Object 7611-7619 was netted with local income 8911-8919.

Exhibit 6

Essential Elements of Effective Instruction

TEACH TO AN OBJECTIVE

Formulating an Objective		Teacher Actions	Taxonomy
• what the learner is to learn • what activity (behavior) the learner is to do • a statement of the condition • a statement of the performance level	**Concept of Congruency**	• provide information • ask questions • design activities • respond to learners	• knowledge • analysis • application • analysis • synthesis • evaluation

SELECTING OBJECTIVES AT THE CORRECT LEVEL OF DIFFICULTY

Task Analysis Process	The Diagnostic and Prescriptive Process	Monitor & Adjust

• state the objective
• clarify the learning
• list the essential learnings
  brainstorm
  impeach
• sequence the learnings
• restate as diagnostic questions
	• determine the topic
	• formulate/state the objective
	• write the task analysis
	• design the diagnostic survey
	• administer the test
	  interpret the survey
	• cluster the learners
	  write the prescription/plan the lesson
	• teach the lesson
	• evaluate – begin again
		• elicit overt behavior
		• check overt behavior
		• interpret overt behavior
		• act on interpretation

APPROPRIATE USE OF PRINCIPLES OF LEARNING

FOCUS	RATE & DEGREE	RETENTION	TRANSFER

Anticipatory Set
• related to similar past experience
• learner is actively involved
• congruent or relevant to the learning
 	
Motivation
• success
• level of concern
• interest
  novel/vivid
• knowledge of results
  specific immediate
• feeling tone
  pleasant
  unpleasant
  neutral
	Closure
	
	Active Participation
	• overt
	• covert
	• should be consistent not eventual
	
	Reinforcement
	• positive
	• negative
	• extinction
	  peaking
		Meaning
		• related to a similar past experience
		• translate into another form
		• of what use will this be to me?
		
		Modeling
		• correct demonstration presented to learners
		• criteria that make demonstration correct are known by the learners
		
		Practice
		• massed for a new learning
		• best when sessions are short and often
		• intermittent for a prior learning
		
		Mnemonic Devices
			Anticipatory Set
			• related to a similar past experience
			• learner is actively involved
			• congruent or relevant to the learning

Source: District files.

Managing Schools across Differences

The ultimate objective for an urban school district is to continuously improve overall student performance while eliminating the performance gaps among students. The variability in student performance that exists in every urban district in the United States is caused by some combination of differences in each school, including: the mix of students and their current skill levels, the instructional capacity of teachers, and the effectiveness of principals.

District leaders have attempted to recognize and address these variations as a key means of improving student performance. Their efforts to date have at best had limited success. One of the important elements missing from past and current efforts to manage schools across differences is an explicit managerial approach that district leaders could put into practice. We introduced and extended the concept of differentiation and integration to public education in response to the important questions created by this vacuum:[1] What exactly should the district office's role be within a high-performing system of schools, and what balance of oversight and support should the office provide to ensure that improvement takes place every day in every classroom in every

school? What should the relationship between individual schools and the district office look like, and how can the district office and schools work together to create and sustain their relationships? How can the relationships among groups of schools be strengthened and utilized to decrease their need for (and the district office's instinct toward) centralized approaches to their shared challenges? How can these relationships be developed to most effectively increase a school's self-reliance and schools' reliance on one another to create solutions to performance problems?

Used together as a managerial approach, differentiation and integration focus on the "how to" of implementing a districtwide improvement strategy across schools that are different from one another. This approach provides a framework for creating and sustaining an effective relationship between the district office and the schools. By effective relationship we mean one in which the district office provides the optimum support to enable schools with varying leadership capabilities, instructional capacity, and student mix to achieve continuous improvement in academic performance for all students. As part of this relationship, the district office must transform itself into a responsive force for building a coherent system of schools. Schools are accountable for raising the performance of all of their students, and for becoming productive members of a system by reciprocating the district office's efforts to build an effective relationship and by participating in knowledge-sharing and capacity-building activities with other schools.

Myriad districts have tried to define their district offices' relationships with schools through mandates or structural changes. We all know the limitations of district office efforts to impose a one-size-fits-all approach to managing schools. We also know that structural fixes implemented in isolation, such as decentralization or small schools, have not by themselves improved school performance on any meaningful scale. What distinguishes differentiation and integration from previous attempts at defining the relationships between the district office and schools and among groups of schools is that our approach works from the inside-out rather than from the outside-in, as it does with strategy development. Differentiation and integration assume that a district office cannot possibly know the correct mix of direction and support a school needs unless it knows the nature of its instructional problems. Once a district understands these problems, it can calibrate the type and intensity of support it provides from school to school—in other words, differentiate—according to the characteristics and needs of a particular school or groups of schools.

To achieve this objective, the district office must first take responsibility for creating an environment in which teachers, principals, and district administrators constantly try to uncover how and why instructional quality varies within and among schools, and to advance effective approaches for raising the level of teaching and learning in all schools. Only then will the district office be able to provide the kind of differentiated oversight, capacity-building, and outside assistance required to reduce performance vari-

ability across schools. The concept of differentiation is a familiar one in public education: Effective classroom instruction is differentiated—that is, tailored to the specific and often diverse needs of each student. A district's responsibility to provide differentiated support to schools is similar to a teacher's responsibility to provide differentiated instruction to her students.

In order for differentiation to achieve its full potential, it must be coupled with a way to knit a diverse set of schools and approaches into a system of schools. To accomplish this, the district office must, ideally in partnership with the schools, design and implement management mechanisms that create forces that pull schools together. These mechanisms should be implemented across all schools, regardless of their instructional model, capacity, or performance. If this integration is not done, the district risks its schools being fragmented into isolated units that are likely to continue producing variable performances. Differentiation and integration are not opposing forces; rather, they complement each other and work together to shape an environment that will lead to optimum performance for every school.[2] For example, a culture of high expectations and collaboration is necessary in order to produce continuous improvement in teaching and learning, regardless of the school's current performance, instructional capacity, or student mix. Therefore, a common culture can be a powerful integrating mechanism. A shared information system that provides accurate, timely performance data and facilitates the spread of effective practices among schools can also serve a critical integrating function.

We have grouped integrating mechanisms into four categories that align with the core purpose of integration—improved student performance. The first is *accountability,* which is the common understanding throughout a district of the expectations for performance in classrooms, schools, and groups of schools, and of the consequences of success or failure. The second category includes the activities critical to *organizational learning*—in other words, the concrete steps a district undertakes to ensure that staff members at all levels are improving their knowledge and skills, creating innovative solutions to performance problems, and spreading effective practices across classrooms and schools. The third category contains *strategic operating functions* that are cross-cutting in nature or that make sense for the district office to perform because of its size advantage. These functions include some aspects of the strategic use of human resources; information systems that collect, manage, and analyze performance data; and certain strategic tasks such as designing districtwide resource allocation systems. The fourth category is the *policy* that the district develops and requires schools to follow. This might include such things as a common curriculum, parameters for managing student discipline, or standards for community engagement that support the strategy

Relationship to the Coherence Framework

When designing a differentiating or integrating mechanism, a district must simultaneously undertake a broad range of activities that are coherent with one another and with the district's improvement strategy. The PELP Coherence Framework (PCF) is again useful as a tool to help leaders put differentiation and integration in place as a managerial approach to implementing a districtwide strategy for improvement. One example is that establishing and sustaining accountability for student outcomes across all schools—an integrating mechanism—requires district leaders to take action in each of the elements of the PCF. The culture, systems and structures, and resources and stakeholder relationships must all fit together and support one another if accountability is to take root in all corners of a school district. Similarly, professional development for teachers across classrooms,

schools, or groups of schools might be highly differentiated. A district leader must still consider how the organization's culture, systems and structures, resources and stakeholder relationships support the implementation of this differentiated approach.

Learning Objectives

The cases in Module IV address the management challenges of implementing differentiation and integration in order to attain high performance in all schools within a district when these schools have distinctive compositions of teachers and students and varying degrees of leadership capabilities. We suggest the following learning objectives for this module:

- Realize that every school has a unique set of needs when working to improve learning in the classroom, which requires differentiated responses from the district office in order to align with each school's unique characteristics

- Discover that despite each school's unique set of needs, there is still a requirement in some areas for consistency across all schools in order to integrate them into a high-performing school system

- Be able to use the PCF as a tool for the district office and its schools to develop and implement the required differentiating and integrating mechanisms

Cases

Module IV begins by introducing the management approach of differentiation and integration in a Portland, Oregon–based global nonprofit organization. "Mercy Corps: Positioning the Organization to Reach New Heights" presents the management challenges of an organization that has a variety of programs in forty-five countries, all of which must have consistently high-quality service and a positive impact. Each country has a unique set of clients, a range of program characteristics, and leaders and staff with varying capabilities and experience. "Managing the Chicago Public Schools" looks at managerial challenges that are strikingly similar to those of Mercy Corps. How does the district ensure and support high-quality teaching and learning across all of its 625 schools, each with its own unique needs, varying demographics, and a range of leadership capabilities?

The remaining cases zoom in on two districts that are attempting to use differentiation and integration as a concrete managerial approach to closing their achievement gaps between poor and minority students and their counterparts. In "The Star Schools Initiative at the San Francisco Unified School District," the district's leadership team faces a host of design questions and implementation challenges related to its strategy to dramatically improve the performance of its forty lowest-performing schools over the course of four years. In Module IV's final two cases, "Race, Accountability and the Achievement Gap" (parts A and B), the leaders of the Montgomery County Public Schools move through several phases of a strategy to eradicate the achievement gap, becoming increasingly reliant on differentiating and integrating mechanisms to implement their strategy successfully.

Discussion Questions

The following questions will serve as a guide to identifying the common ideas embedded in the case series in this module:

1. What are the main advantages of differentiation and integration as a managerial approach to attaining excellence across diverse operating units? What are its disadvantages?

2. How might a district office and schools decide which functions should be integrated across all schools, and which should be differentiated?

3. What are the key challenges of successfully implementing differentiation and integration? How should managers and leaders at all levels go about overcoming these challenges?

Notes

1. For more on this concept, see Paul R. Lawrence and Jay W. Lorsch, *Organization and Environment,* Boston: Harvard Business School Press, 1986.

2. In our model, the opposite of differentiation is standardization and the opposite of integration is fragmentation. Differentiation and integration are therefore complementary rather than opposing forces.

Allen S. Grossman ■ Caroline King

Mercy Corps: Positioning the Organization to Reach New Heights

Steve Zimmerman checked into the Kathmandu Hyatt for Mercy Corps' fourth biannual leadership conference in early November 2006 and smiled. He was soon greeting country director after country director (CD) with a hearty handshake. Zimmerman had left their ranks only two months prior to assume the newly created post of senior vice president for programs at the agency's headquarters (HQ) in Portland, Oregon. Zimmerman now managed Mercy Corps' international relief and development programs around the world.

The Nepal conference, entitled "Reaching New Heights," marked an inflection point in Mercy Corps' 25-year history. Buoyed by the agency's nimble and effective responses to recent humanitarian emergencies—notably the 2004 Indian Ocean tsunami that killed over 230,000 people in five countries; Hurricane Katrina's devastation of the U.S. Gulf Coast in 2005; and the destructive 2005 7.6 magnitude Pakistan earthquake—Mercy Corps' budget had nearly doubled from $106 million in FY02 to $197 million in FY06. Mercy Corps' opportunities to grow and serve an even larger number of beneficiaries were unprecedented.

Zimmerman's charge was to help the agency scale effectively and efficiently, while preserving Mercy Corps' entrepreneurial culture. Zimmerman confided, "A few big questions will be running through my mind during the conference. How do we organize and manage ourselves given our size, complexity, and growth potential? What support systems does the field need? How does HQ ensure that we don't get in the way of any CD's breakthrough idea? Who has the comparative advantage to perform specific functions—the field or HQ or a hybrid?"

The week-long Nepal conference, which brought together 125 Mercy Corps' senior HQ and field staff, board members, and strategic partners to reflect on the agency's accomplishments and opportunities, provided the perfect venue for Zimmerman to probe his questions.

Mercy Corps

Operating in 43 countries in FY06, Mercy Corps was the fifth largest international nongovernmental organization (INGO) in the international development industry (see map in Exhibit 1 and financial information in Exhibit 2). Mercy Corps was founded in 1981 to "alleviate suffering, poverty, and oppression by helping people build secure, productive, and just communities."[1] Mercy Corps worked in countries facing dire humanitarian crises, often precipitated by wars, natural disasters, or socioeconomic upheavals. The agency's programs fell into three broad categories: emergency relief services, sustainable economic development, and civil society initiatives.

Mercy Corps' approach to international relief and development was grounded in the principle of "social entrepreneurship." CEO Neal Keny-Guyer commented, "Our ability to innovate—to look at the same humanitarian challenge and respond in a creative and thoughtful way—is what sets Mercy Corps apart from other INGOs." Mercy Corps also prided itself on being a "field-driven" organization. President Nancy Lindborg noted, "We think our best ideas come from our field staff because they work in close partnership with the communities we serve, so we encourage the field to take risks and we follow their lead." Keny-Guyer frequently urged staff to "follow your passion" and "come up with bold, wild and crazy ideas!" Organization charts had been banned at the agency since his arrival as CEO in 1994. "Boxes move cargo, not organizations," explained Zimmerman.

Seventy-six percent of Mercy Corps' $219 million budget came from grants awarded by U.S. and foreign governments and multilateral organizations (e.g., United Nations). These revenues were *restricted;* the funds could only be used to pay for activities spelled out in the grants. Mercy Corps retained discretion over a certain percentage of each grant to cover administrative costs (known as "indirect cost recovery" or ICR). Giving from private corporations, foundations, and individuals represented 24% of the budget. Nine percent of private revenues were *unrestricted,* meaning Mercy Corps had total discretion over how to spend the funds. Mercy Corps used the unrestricted and ICR funds to pay for HQ staff and operations and to provide "core funds" for in-country activities that could not be supported by donor funding, such as assessing new program opportunities and opening new country programs. Of Mercy Corps' total annual budget, approximately 90% of resources directly funded programs.

Of Mercy Corps 3200 staff, approximately 3000 worked in the field and 200 worked in HQ offices based in Portland (the primary HQ), Washington, D.C., Boston, and Seattle, Edinburgh, Scotland, and Hong Kong. The agency had a flat organizational structure. Portland-based Keny-Guyer had four direct reports: chief financial officer, chief development officer, executive counselor, and a director-at-large. Washington, D.C.-based Lindborg's direct reports were Zimmerman, director of public affairs, director of the technical support unit, the head of the global emergency response team, a director-at-large, and the North Korea program staff. Mercy Corps was governed by a 19-member board of directors.

Envisioning Change

Throughout its 25-year history, Mercy Corps had refined its operating framework, known as the "vision for change" (see Exhibit 3). Lindborg explained how the vision for change guided the organization's activities and was thought to lead to mission accomplishment:

Mercy Corps' vision for change remains at the heart of who we are and what we do. Our theory and vision of change is that during times of turbulence, such as natural disasters, economic collapse, or social conflict, Mercy Corps is of greatest value by supporting community-led, positive change that seeks to catalyze the interaction of civil society, governments, and the private sector. By facilitating these relationships and helping communities become their own advocates, we contribute to the creation and sustainability of just, productive and secure communities.

Participants discussed five internal case studies that were prepared to illuminate how various country programs enacted the vision for change. The case studies featured Guatemala's land conflict resolution project, a child nutrition program in Indonesia, community-led economic development in Kyrgyzstan, a community capacity-building project in Kosovo, and a youth education program in Liberia. Reflecting on the programs' diversity, a senior manager noted, "The vision for change doesn't tell you what type of program to implement or how to do it—its more of a philosophy about catalyzing transformation. We leave it up to the CDs to figure out the *what* and the *how.*"

Lindborg invited participants to share how they used the vision for change in their day-to-day work. One CD commented, "We use it to orient new staff to Mercy Corps' mission, values, and approach." A manager of a group of CDs, known as a "regional program director," said, "The vision for change is a helpful diagnostic tool. I can sit with a CD and ask, Are you working across all three sectors—public, private, and civil society? If not, we're not going to make catalytic change and achieve our mission."

Managing the Field

New Structure: Regional Program Directors

In conjunction with Zimmerman's appointment as senior vice president, program on September 1, 2006, Mercy Corps announced a new program management and reporting structure for the field. The agency divided the world into six regions and named a regional program director (RPD) to lead each region (see RPD job description in Exhibit 4). Each RPD managed three to six CDs and all six RPDs reported to Zimmerman (see Exhibit 5 for Zimmerman's bio). Three country programs and a region lay outside the RPD structure. North Korea, a heavily policy-focused program, continued to report to Lindborg. Mongolia, China, and the Balkans reported to Zimmerman.

One RPD had been recently hired from Catholic Relief Services; the other five had been with Mercy Corps between one and eight years. The RPDs were encouraged to live in their respective regions; four moved to the field while two remained in Portland (see Exhibit 6 for RPD bios).

Prior to the RPD structure, four directors of program operations (DPOs) each managed around 10 countries from Portland and reported to Lindborg. Zimmerman, who reported to Lindborg, explained the rationale for the new RPD structure. "The DPOs were spread too thin. CDs also asked for a stronger, more connected presence in the field. My position was created to ensure that we can retain the right balance of decentralized and autonomous decision-making with a structure and operating style that prevents 'balkanization' into six little Mercy Corps. Getting the HQ-RPD-CD relationship right is my key challenge."

One of Zimmerman's first priorities was to figure out how to create a strong team out of the six RPDs. Zimmerman observed, "Each RPD brings his/her own management and leadership style. They are working in very different regional contexts and their CDs have diverse needs." Many countries of South and South East Asia were only recently recovering from civil conflicts and natural disasters, while the Middle East was frequently rocked by insurgencies. After more than 10 years, Mercy Corps' work in Central Asia and the Caucuses was winding down. Increasingly, the agency considered Africa a top priority given the continent's enormous humanitarian needs.

Expressing a widely held sentiment, RPD Diane Johnson said, "There are still a lot of unknowns about how the RPD structure will work, but I'm confident that Zimmerman's the right man for this job. He's a field man at heart and thinks strategically and operationally. Everyone—Neal, Nancy, and CDs—trusts and respects him."

Country Directors

The CD was the most senior management position for Mercy Corps in each country with program development, supervisory, and managerial responsibilities over all in-country personnel, programs, and policies. In addition to programmatic diversity, the 43 countries varied on a number of other dimensions. Some countries enjoyed stability; others experienced daily violence or periodic natural disasters. Annual FY07 country budgets ranged from $33 million to less than $500,000. Staff ranged from over 500 people scattered across the country to less than five in a single office.

Profile and Autonomy: Mercy Corps hired CDs with track records as social entrepreneurs and demonstrated management skills in international development or a related field (see CD job description in Exhibit 7). CDs often cited the agency's entrepreneurial spirit, non-bureaucratic and field-driven culture, and reputation for delivering high-quality, innovative programs around the world as their primary rea-

sons for joining Mercy Corps over other INGOs. "When I started as Mercy Corps' chief operating officer back in 1997, I knew all of the CDs," Zimmerman recalled. "Now that we've grown and hired more people from outside the agency, I'm meeting some CDs for the first time." Indeed, Mercy Corps had hired 37% of its CDs in the previous three years.

CDs enjoyed considerable autonomy in designing and managing their country programs and operations. As a result, programs across Mercy Corps' countries spanned a variety of sectors, including emergency relief, health, agriculture and food security, community and institutional capacity-building, sustainable economic development, and microfinance.

Zimmerman explained, "No two country programs look alike. We expect the CD to assess the key leverage points for building just, productive, and secure communities in his/her country, design innovative programs, and effectively manage implementation. I'm not sure that capability can be built; it's what we hire for." The CD, with support from HQ when needed, was responsible for generating all revenues to cover his/her country's programs by securing grants and other financial support. Thus, assessing funding opportunities, proposal writing, and managing donor relations took up a good deal of a CD's time.

Annual Plan and Accountability: The CD and his/her team developed an annual plan. The plan described Mercy Corps' goal in the country, the operating context, activities with objectives and impact indicators, and resource needs (see Exhibit 8). Zimmerman observed, "Some CDs submit a coherent country strategy, while others produce a summary of project activities. One challenge is helping CDs see that they can actually be more innovative—and make a greater impact—if they can define their respective programs in terms of desired quantitative results and if those programs are tightly integrated rather than pulling staff and resources in different directions."

CDs were held accountable for country objectives in two ways. First, country directors submitted quarterly reports describing progress towards planned objectives, any program modifications made, and support needed from HQ. RPDs then compared actual achievements against the annual plans and adjusted their support to CDs as necessary. Second, every Mercy Corps employee completed an individual operating plan (IOP) that outlined objectives, desired impact, activities, timeline, deliverables, and support/resources required. For CDs, the IOP correlated with the country annual plan, according to Zimmerman. An individual was evaluated annually against his/her IOP and received a salary increase based on the objectives achieved and his or her degree of compliance with the following performance expectations: (1) adapting culturally; (2) being a reliable team player; (3) being accountable for quality results; (4) representing Mercy Corps' mission; and (5) fostering innovation as a social entrepreneur. The RPDs evaluated the CDs in their respective regions.

At dinner that first evening in Nepal, Zimmerman talked with four CDs (see Exhibit 9 for the four country profiles).

Borys Chinchilla, Guatemala CD: A Guatemalan native, Chinchilla opened Mercy Corps' Guatemala office in 2002. Chinchilla had 20 years of international development experience, 15 of which he spent working for CARE. "I was attracted to Mercy Corps because the agency helps its CDs pursue new ideas," Chinchilla recalled.

Upon joining Mercy Corps, Chinchilla resurrected a project idea that he had floated (unsuccessfully) at CARE: partnering with a local NGO, the private sector, and governmental agencies to resolve the over 6,000 land disputes created in the wake of Guatemala's 36-year civil war. Mercy Corps HQ gave Chinchilla technical assistance to craft an unsolicited proposal to the U.S. Agency for International Development (USAID). USAID awarded Mercy Corps $1 million.

Between 2001 and 2006, the Mercy Corps' Guatemala program grew from $330,000 to $3 million, one to eight projects, and 8 to 75 staff. In FY06, in addition to the land conflict resolution project, other Guatemala programs included a community health project; disaster relief following Hurricane Stan in 2005; advocacy training for NGOs; and rural economic development.

Tom Ewert, Liberia CD: Ewert was one of the agency's first CDs. After three years as Kyrgyzstan's CD, Ewert headed up the agency's food security work for eight years, working five years out of Portland, and three in Washington, D.C. Ewert became the Liberia CD in January 2006.

"Liberia's community infrastructure program had gotten off to a slow start," recalled Ewert. "We had a two-year grant to help local communities design and implement 30 development projects by June 2006, but only five had even been started. We learned that the local contractors we had hired were corrupt and that our office did not have adequate staff capacity to manage the program."

By November 2006, Ewert had negotiated an additional six months with the program's donor and hired new contractors, a new program manager, and new finance officer. All 30 projects were underway or completed, and Ewert was working with staff to implement new operations and monitoring systems and assess new funding opportunities. The Liberia team also ran a community peace-building project and an effort to train young people with civic, health, and economic skills.

Patricia Kennedy, Tajikistan CD: A native New Yorker and former Peace Corps volunteer and manager, Kennedy was hired to manage Mercy Corps' conflict prevention program in the Tajikistan office in December 2005. After seven months on the job, the Tajikistan CD transferred to a new country office and Kennedy was offered the CD post. "The support I most need from my RPD is how best to navigate through the Mercy Corps system," she confided. "It is not always clear which decisions I can make on the ground and which decisions need HQ input."

After inheriting Tajikistan's seven programs, seven offices, and over 200 staff in August 2006, Kennedy got to work. She described her approach in Tajikistan, "Our systems and structures need to be strengthened so we can deliver the results we've already promised. Then, I hope to start designing innovative programs in the Mercy Corps way." The Tajikistan programs focused on stimulating economic development in the formerly conflict-ridden Tavildara valley, maternal-child health, creating microfinance institutions, and increasing food production and security.

Craig Redmond, Indonesia CD: Growing up on a farm in rural Indiana, Redmond served in the Peace Corps and worked to create microfinance institutions in Central Asia for the United Nations Development Programme and the U.N. Human Rights Commission from 1994–1998 before joining Mercy Corps in 1999. After managing a $45 million program with 12 NGO partners in Azerbaijan for the agency, Redmond served as the Eritrea CD for three years.

Three days after the Indian Ocean tsunami hit on December 26, 2004, Redmond who was already scheduled to take over as Indonesia's CD in June 2005, flew to Indonesia as part of an agency-wide disaster response team. "We were able to move fairly quickly out of relief and into long-term development," noted Redmond in Nepal. By FY07, the Indonesia annual budget had grown by two-thirds with an annual budget of $20 million; counting multi-year grants, the Indonesia programs totaled over $40 million. Projects included: economic development, health and nutrition, community infrastructure, microfinance, water/sanitation, disaster risk reduction, and emergency response.

During the Nepal conference, Redmond was awarded Mercy Corps' first biannual entrepreneurship and leadership award. The award recognized "the Mercy Corps team member whose work and character embodies the spirit and effects of our core values of entrepreneurial innovation and leadership." Several aspects of the Indonesia program under Redmond's leadership were highlighted, notably the creation of the country's first rating agency for microfinance institutions and the development of several partnerships with private companies, including Chevron Oil Company, Starbucks, ING, and Intel.

Organizing for Excellence

Lindborg kicked off the Nepal conference: "Mercy Corps is stronger than ever. We have unprecedented opportunities for growth and to serve many more people throughout the world," she said. "The central question of this conference is, 'Are we positioned to reach new heights?'"

Definitions: Leading a session about Mercy Corps' trajectory and performance, a board member asked, "Let's begin by defining a *high-performing organization*." Participants agreed on the following definition:

- Effectively and efficiently serves its target population

- Measures impact

- Systematically learns from its mistakes and successes

"We often say *social entrepreneurship* is Mercy Corps' key differentiator among INGOs. But what does it mean? Does it mean I can do anything I want?" he asked. Responses included:

- Spirit of risk-taking, seizing opportunities

- Innovative, flexible, adaptive, problem-solver

- Identifies an unmet need, designs and implements a new approach in line with the agency's mission and vision for change, gets results

Diagnostic: Shifting gears, the board member asked, "Describe Mercy Corps as an organization today." Communications Director Jeremy Barnicle opened up the discussion. "Mercy Corps is like a precocious adolescent. We're not afraid to try new things or take risks unlike some more mature organizations." Lebanon's deputy CD added, "Flexible responder. After Hezbollah started bombing our country this summer, it took us less than 24 hours to flip from long-term development work to emergency relief."

"If we want to achieve greater excellence, we need to put our collective weight behind a few key issues—like poverty alleviation—or we won't ever reach the tipping point," another participant commented. "We pride ourselves on being a flat, non-hierarchical organization, which is mostly a good thing," observed another participant. "It can be challenging though to figure out who to involve in making a decision and who ultimately has the responsibility to make the call."

"Mercy Corps is undergoing a lot of change," said someone else. "We've just created the new RPD structure; we've made a number of acquisitions like NetAid (global education programs for students) and the Film Connection (free online DVD movie rentals intended to raise global awareness). We're opening world action hunger centers in Portland and New York City and we're still relatively newcomers in some regions, particularly in Africa. It is a lot to digest. I'm also struggling to see how all this relates to my day-to-day work."

Recommendations: "Let's move into recommendations. What should Mercy Corps do to help us become a high-performing organization?" asked the board member. Suggestions included:

- "Take a chill pill." Wait two years before making any new acquisitions or strategic alliances,

or changing any organizational structures. Growth is okay, but it should be in our core areas: international relief and development.

- Further decentralize our program support operations (e.g., fundraising, technical support, human resources) by increasing our capacity and personnel at the regional level.

- Clarify decision-making authority and communication expectations.

As a long day came to a close, Keny-Guyer, Lindborg, and Zimmerman agreed to respond to the recommendations over the course of the coming year. The mood was jovial during the cocktail party with Nepali and other international dignitaries that followed. "One thing about Mercy Corps is that we're not afraid to look in the mirror and be self-critical. And, as you saw today, we're not afraid to say what we think!" quipped a participant.

Building Capaity

In January 2006, Mercy Corps hired Bill Farrell to manage its 30-person technical support unit (TSU). The TSU comprised six program areas—economic development, food security, civil society and conflict management, health, sustainable resource management, and new initiatives.

The TSU provided technical assistance to the country programs, such as conducting needs assessments, writing proposals, designing new programs, and supporting high-quality innovation in the technical fields. The TSU also represented Mercy Corps to major donors, such as USAID in Washington, D.C., and at professional conferences. Increasingly, TSU staff members were being asked to help the HQ-based resource development team craft concept papers to float in front of potential new donors, such as the Bill and Melinda Gates Foundation and Intel.

Mercy Corps had evolved its approach to providing technical support to the field. Originally, one director was hired per technical program area and reported to either then-COO Zimmerman or Lindborg. In 2004, the directors were gathered into one TSU and reported to Farrell's predecessor. Over the past few years, the TSU had grown substantially as additional staff were hired and subspecialty fields were added. Despite the growth, however, "demand for the TSU is far outstripping our capacity," assessed Farrell. "My people are getting burned out flying all around the world, and they are not able to get to know any one country well enough to provide specialized technical assistance. We've either got to keep growing TSU or find a new way of working," said Ferrell. This was the topic of Farrell's session in Nepal.

Farrell opened by sharing an example:

> Country X reaches out to the TSU for help with a health assessment that needs to be done within 30 days in order to submit a new grant proposal. We have one health person and she's in Niger for a week, then off to Pakistan and Guatemala. Country X cannot wait, so the mad dash begins with the CD sending out 100 emails asking for help from HQ, other countries, external consultants, etc. The CD has no idea who is going to be available or who has the right skill set to do the job. Sound familiar?

Heads nodded across the room. Farrell continued, "So, we have a choice. We can grow the TSU at HQ—but this is expensive. TSU salaries and benefits cost $2 million right now; 81% of which is paid for out of core funds. Or, we can devolve the TSU functions to the field." Lindborg added, "The challenge is how do we ensure that we have high-quality technical experts who are well-versed in the regional contexts and able to design innovative new programs—and how can we do so without adding one new core-funded technical support position in each of the six regions?

A New Model: Farrell proposed a two-stage transformation of the TSU. In the short-term, HQ and field staff would self-organize into "communities of practice" around specific areas of expertise, such as agricultural livelihoods or conflict management. As a result, an agricultural livelihoods program manager in any country would have a listserv of staff from around the world with related expertise to contact with questions about program design, evaluation, and management.

In the longer term, Farrell suggested that the agency leverage the expertise of the technical staff already working within the country offices. He described a potential model:

> Many of our countries already have a project manager and a technical expert working hand-in-hand, funded by the same grant. We could use our core funds to buy back one month of the technical person's time to send them as a consultant to another country. People love getting out of their silos, working in new country contexts, and meeting more colleagues. In this model, the individual wins, the countries win, and Mercy Corps wins.

Concurrently, Mercy Corps would maintain a small TSU team of five to seven HQ people who would report to Farrell. This core team, in conjunction with the respective communities of practice would play four roles: 1). provide technical assistance on new projects and proposals; 2). represent Mercy Corps to external audiences; 3). help field staff network and access external professional resources; and 4). maintain high-quality programming and further innovation. "This will be a paradigm shift for the agency, which is used to a large on-call TSU," noted Farrell. He added, "The real challenge will be in the sequencing and how fast we move. A decline in quality is not acceptable, but we'll need time to build capacity and make the transition."

Participants were generally receptive to the idea of forming communities of practice, but wondered who would be responsible for managing them. Devolving technical functions to the field was also widely embraced by the field. Senior management, however, had been reluctant to fully load each region with a full complement of technical specialists "in order to avoid heavy overhead costs and the creation of insular regional empires, while also ensuring we continue to innovate and share across the globe," explained Lindborg.

For example, some senior leaders had seen regional decentralization carried too far in other INGOs they had worked for, resulting in the creation of semi-autonomous regions that failed to share information, best practices and talent, which often led to uneven performance by region. Replication in functions performed by HQ and the field was another concern. On the other hand, Farrell noted, "We're so afraid of creating six fiefdoms, but we also run the risk of having 40+ principalities. Achieving consistent quality at the country level is challenging." Finally, some wondered who the field-based TSU staff would report to—TSU directors or the RPDs?

Measuring Impact

One day of the conference explored performance measurement and management. Afghanistan CD Nigel Pont was looking forward to the sessions. "Even though it is challenging to measure our impact, we are all trying to do a better job of specifying our expected results, tracking our progress, and learning which innovations can be scaled," he commented. "Without improving our ability to measure and quantify results, it will be very difficult to achieve our mission."

Looking Outside: Jumpstart

The board member returned to lead a case discussion about Jumpstart, a U.S.-based nonprofit that helped low-income preschoolers gain literacy skills. After discussing Jumpstart's performance management system and culture, the conversation shifted to Mercy Corps. "Without agency-wide performance metrics, how do we know and tell donors and beneficiaries that we are achieving our mission? How do we know if our vision for change works?" asked a participant.

RPD Matt Lovick countered, "But even Aaron Lieberman [Jumpstart's founder] says in the case that external funders don't ask for this information or even agree on which performance benchmarks are most important. If they're not asking for it, are we sure we should invest scarce resources to do it?" The issue was not only donor-dependent. Performance measurement was acknowledged as a widespread challenge in the international development industry, although efforts to develop standards and metrics for measuring impact within an agency and across agencies had been evolving over the past 5–10 years. Progress had been made in some technical areas, such as microfinance, health, and the delivery of humanitarian assistance. Other areas, such as community capacity-building, proved more challenging, and overall, the industry struggled to move from tracking outputs to measuring impact.

Looking Within: Monitoring and Evaluation at Mercy Corps

Following Jumpstart, Director of New Initiatives Myriam Khoury and Senior Program Officer Gretchen Shanks were on deck to facilitate a session about the agency's monitoring and evaluation (M&E) efforts. Khoury recalled, "Even two years ago, there was quite a bit of resistance about M&E; staff worried that it would hamper their ability to be creative. Now, CDs recognize that M&E is critical to their effectiveness, it can support creativity, and they want to know *how* to do it."

Khoury continued, "Some country programs have been able to develop very solid M&E systems, but others are struggling. We've developed some tools and frameworks at HQ, but it is difficult given our limited staffing, the high volume of support requests we get from the field, the diverse nature of our programs and the need to make sure that M&E systems are tailored to each country program." As the coffee break ended, she said, "We've got to use this session to have a conversation about how the field and HQ are going to work together to get more consistency in M&E at the country level."

Khoury opened by giving an overview of M&E at Mercy Corps. Design, monitoring, and evaluation (DM&E) was part of the TSU's new initiatives team. "Design" referred to support with program design and proposal development; M&E referred to efforts to track outcomes and impact. Two staff members worked on M&E at HQ. In the field, six countries had dedicated M&E staff onsite, although an increasing number of countries were working to create M&E positions. However, a debate arose within the agency over the most effective way to embed M&E in the organizational culture: Was it preferable to continue increasing the number of dedicated M&E staff or find ways to integrate M&E into every staff member's job responsibilities and expectations?

Referencing the slide below, Khoury presented Mercy Corps' approach to M&E. "The underlying principle is that M&E should live in the field. Thus, consistent and sound field-based M&E is the fundamental building block that must be in place before we start to pursue other uses of information, such as aggregation or comparison across country programs."

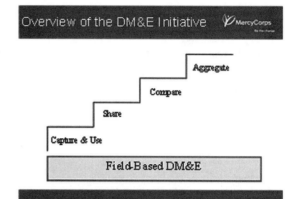

Source: Mercy Corps.

"M&E is starting to take hold at the project level, with people capturing and using the information to improve implementation and quality," continued Khoury. "Our primary goal is to support further strengthening of these efforts. Additionally, we are exploring options for sharing, comparing, and aggregating data within a country and across the agency."

Next, Shanks shared results of a survey conducted prior to the conference. Forty-three people responded to the survey: 60% were from the field, 37% were from HQ, and 3% were listed as other. When asked, "What keeps our programs from achieving excellence in M&E?" responses included: lack of strategic use of information (40%); poor data collection and management (25%); lack of technical skills (22%); lack of funding (12%); and lack of partner engagement (3%). When asked, "What are the main areas for improvement on M&E, participants said: time and attention during implementation (28%); technical knowledge support (27%); tools and systems (15%); budgeting (13%); clarity around good practices (10%); and incentives (7%).

Field Perspectives: Conference participants then broke up into small groups to discuss ideas about how to overcome each one of the barriers identified as an area for improvement on M&E. Chinchilla had asked for M&E training in Spanish from HQ for his Guatemala staff, and Kennedy said she was struggling to help her

Tajikistan staff recognize the importance of M&E. Ewert was working to strengthen the Liberia staff's capacity to design and implement strong M&E systems, and in the meantime, had brought in a volunteer graduate student to help conduct project evaluations. Farrell wondered, "Would we strengthen our agency if we had a full-time dedicated M&E staff person sitting in each region?"

At another table, Redmond shared Indonesia's approach to M&E. In 2005, Redmond's senior team started developing a country-wide M&E system and hired a senior manager to oversee the work full-time. The system, scheduled to be fully in place in 2007, would enable the Indonesia team to aggregate data from seven key performance indicators at the project level on up to show impact at the country level (see "impact indicators" in Exhibit 8). Redmond commented:

> Mercy Corps operates a large, diverse program in Indonesia—we have 30 multi-year grants totaling over $40 million for everything from tsunami recovery to child nutrition to community capacity-building. Previously, we only measured results at the project/program level and produced more output data than impact information. We needed a way to understand if we are making a difference in the communities in which we work and the magnitude of this change in order to improve our program design, quality, and impact.
>
> We also want to know how similar projects in different geographic areas contribute to our goals and objectives and help advance nationwide indicators. I love being innovative as much as anyone at Mercy Corps, but I'm even more interested in identifying which innovations we should scale. Indonesia has over 220 million people; a string of innovations that each serves 10,000 people is a drop in the bucket.

Another feature of the Indonesia M&E system was that it shared three performance indicators with Sri Lanka: % increase in sales and value of production; % increase in government resource allocation towards priority health, water, and sanitation, and financial needs; and % of staff with required set of core capacities/skills. Sri Lanka CD Josh DeWald explained:

> Craig and I worked together in Eritrea and we, with our colleague Mark Ferdig, agreed that M&E was the missing piece to being able to say, "Mercy Corps is accelerating long-term development" with the confidence that comes when you know your results. Now that we work in the same region again—we're both doing post-tsunami recovery work and strengthening M&E system development for our country programs—it seemed like the right time to test the use of cross-country indicators.

DeWald added, "M&E starts with having a strong country strategy. Otherwise, your performance indicators change from year to year depending on your projects and grants."

Operations Support

The goal of the operations functions (e.g., administration, finance, logistics, information technology, and security) was to support the effective and efficient delivery of program services. Zimmerman observed, "We're so integrated that our challenges are figuring out who has the core competency to perform the function (HQ, the field, or a hybrid), how to support the people performing the function, and how to ensure consistently high quality across the 43 countries."

Office in a Box

During Nepal, Mercy Corps unveiled Office in a Box (OIB), a comprehensive set of documents that described operations policies and offered best practice guidelines. OIB aimed to help a new field office start up its operations functions and strengthen operations management in existing field offices. OIB contained five manuals (finance, procurement, asset management, administration, and security) which detailed policies that field offices would be audited against on a biannual basis. Two guideline books (warehouse and fleet) described best practices gathered from field offices across the world; guidelines were not auditable.

"Previously, every CD invented their own operations systems, either from scratch or based on the systems from their prior country or agency," explained Procurement, Administration and Logistics Management (PALM) Director Laszlo Viranyi. "Some CDs developed strong systems, but others lacked the capacity to do it on their own. OIB sets minimum standards and ensures more consistent quality of our operations."

OIB was the brainchild of Viranyi and a few team members working together in Mercy Corps Afghanistan in 2002–2003. "Mercy Corps had been in the country over 10 years, but the payroll systems and procurement and logistics plans were very weak. I was hired to be a program manager, but I couldn't run my programs without effective operations support." Viranyi and his teammates redesigned Afghanistan's operations and started designing a set of operation systems and protocols.

The team informally shared some of their innovations, such as an electronic procurement system, with other country programs in the same region, including emergency start-up programs in Iraq and Iran. "Some of the team had worked in other Mercy Corps field offices and knew our challenges weren't unique," explained Viranyi. "After a few other countries embraced the electronic procurement system, I went to then-Regional Director Jim White and asked for some agency resources to design and share all of our protocols, which we called 'Office in a Box.' In true Mercy Corps fashion, White said, 'If you

have a passion for this, go forth and I'll see what I can do to help.'"

In late 2003, Viranyi became the agency's director of PALM, reporting to White, and assembled a small three-person team to develop OIB. "Mercy Corps likes to say it is 'manual averse' because we fiercely resist becoming a bureaucracy and constraining the field. But the field were the ones asking for some guidelines," explained White, now an RPD. Between 2004–2006, Viranyi's team created and field-tested OIB in six countries. Viranyi described the electronic procurement system as a "major selling point for OIB." "The system is so user-friendly and provides tangible benefits to program management and implementation that the field saw OIB as a collection of tools that makes their lives easier rather than centrally mandated bureaucratic procedures," he explained.

After Viranyi described OIB and responded to questions in Nepal, Zimbabwe CD Rob Maroni, who later in the week won an innovation award for entrepreneurial programming, thanked Viranyi and his colleagues. "This is exactly what I need. I want to be innovative when I design my programs. I don't want to waste time and energy reinventing the wheel on designing operations systems."

OIB was available to CDs on a disk or through the Mercy Corps' "digital library," an internal Web site designed to share best practices and tools across countries. OIB provided templates (e.g., job descriptions) and other tools (e.g., payroll system requirements) to help field staff with implementation of OIB. Following the Nepal conference, a PALM team member would be sent to assist with implementation in new country offices and offices that HQ had perceived as needing support to strengthen their operations systems.

Human Resources

Across the 43 countries, three recruiters were working to fill an average of 26 vacant field positions at any given time. The recruiters—two based in Portland and one in Scotland—managed the process of posting field-based job descriptions, screening applicants, and sending qualified resumes to CDs, who then managed the interview and hiring processes. The agency's HQ recruiting staff was considerably smaller than many of its colleague INGOs. The rationale, according to Lindborg, was based on Mercy Corps' belief that everyone was a recruiter and program team members who are the most familiar with the needs in the field should be closely involved in the hiring process.

Zimmerman elaborated, "Many of our successful hires came to us through a connection to a Mercy Corps staff person. When there is a vacancy, our CDs and RPDs call and email around for leads on potential candidates. Networking recruitment leads are critical." Some countries, typically the more developed and less conflict-ridden, experienced few challenges filling positions, while other countries struggled.

CDs often helped each other. For example, if an applicant resided in another Mercy Corps country, the hiring CD often called on the CD to conduct a face-to-face interview. Ewert explained, "We trust each other to screen for 'Mercy Corps fit' and the skills needed on-the-job. "As RPDs, we can help take on the challenge of filling positions in the hard-to-staff countries, like Sudan," added White. "Why shouldn't we share information about people in our region who are ready to move or take on new responsibilities and focus our collective effort recruiting talented staff for tough posts?"

Finance

From 2003–2006, CFO Steve Mitchell led an overhaul of Mercy Corps' accounting and finance systems. A team of 13 at HQ supported each country's finance manager and the staff who oversaw in-country finance and procurement activities. Mitchell, who left a 20-year career in the leveraged buyout banking industry to join Mercy Corps, recalled, "The quality of the staff capacity for finance varied a good bit across our countries."

In order to strengthen finance, Mitchell's team provided training, on-the-ground support and system-wide tools to the field. Six HQ-based regional finance officers (RFOs) traveled to the country offices and provided technical assistance to each country's finance manager. Training was provided through global and regional finance conferences and during RFOs' visits. Tools, such as finance and procurement manuals, were developed and eventually became part of OIB. Each country's finance manager was required to submit a monthly statement of revenues and expenses, as well as a quarterly reconciliation of balance sheets and income statement accounts to HQ. Starting in 2004, a more aggressive internal audit function was implemented, whereby all country offices were audited at least every two years.

HQ's finance support was differentiated based on a country's specific needs and context. Mitchell explained, "Some countries, like Iran, do not have any western banking conventions, such as checking accounts or credit cards, so we have to develop tailored systems. Some CDs are very skilled at managing finance operations; others have less capacity and are more likely to be hands-off unless there is a problem. Everything we're doing today—Office in a Box training, the messages from senior leadership, etc.—makes it clear that effective finance and operations management is just as much the responsibility of the CD as implementing entrepreneurial programs."

Program Operations Support

Thirty senior program officers, program officers, and assistant program officers, collectively known as the program operations team or "POps," supported RPDs, CDs, and field staff. POps provided "backstopping" support with proposal writing, recruiting, donor communications, liaison with other HQ departments, country staff logistics and, as needed, on-site field support. POps staff were assigned to a particular region and reported to their respective RPDs. Working out of HQ offices in Portland, Washington, D.C., and Scotland, POps staff were in frequent contact with CDs and other senior field staff via telephone and online. The POps team was under Zimmerman's management.

Managing the Field to Reach New Heights

As the Nepal conference drew to a close, Zimmerman articulated his challenges and critical tasks.

"Structuring effective relationships among HQ, the RPDs, and the CDs is essential for achieving our mission at the highest possible level," Zimmerman began. "Roles, responsibilities, decision-making authority, and lines of accountability and communication all had to be clarified in light of the new RPD structure. Direct lines used to connect HQ and CDs," he elaborated. "Anyone in HQ felt empowered to call the field, and vice versa. Now we've inserted the RPDs and we have to figure out how to ensure we continue to operate nimbly, entrepreneurially, and effectively."

Building a strong RPD team was another top priority. "My challenge is helping these six very different individuals see that by working together, the sum of six is greater than six," confided Zimmerman. He was working with the RPDs to figure out what level of communication and coordination was desirable among them. For now, the RPDs had agreed to meet three times per year in person and establish an online space to share documents and best practices. One such document was called the "Chess Board," a list of field staff who were ready to move or be promoted that RPDs would update and could consult as vacancies arose.

RPDs had been asking Zimmerman to help clarify their authority and accountability. For ex-

ample, RPDs only budget authority was over predetermined operational costs, such as travel. If a country wanted core funds to try a pilot project or hire a consultant to conduct an assessment, the RPD had to submit a request to the senior management team for core funds via Zimmerman. Zimmerman explained, "This process keeps us in the loop and helps us balance organizational priorities across the globe." Several RPDs suggested that each RPD be given a regional core funds budget from which the RPDs and CDs would set regional priorities and make resource allocation decisions. In terms of accountability, Zimmerman had set three expectations for the RPDs: 1). program growth; 2). effective program management and implementation; and 3). strong program monitoring and impact.

Enhancing strategy development represented another critical task. Zimmerman encouraged the RPDs to develop regional strategies. "Some regions, such as East Africa, are so interconnected—the borders are fluid, ethnic and clan lines cross political boundaries, and relief and development issues are truly regional in nature—that we cannot work in one country without being aware of the implications for 20 miles away," he explained. "If we're going to secure the funding needed for us to work at scale, we need to identify and address cross-cutting issues in more than one country. We have to leverage core competencies that we have already built into regional strategies, such as health services in South Asia and market-chain development in Central America." While the RPDs were on board with the idea, Zimmerman faced a formidable management challenge. He asked,

How do we avoid fiefdom-building by region and keep the RPDs connected to the "whole"? At the same time, how do we retain CDs' entrepreneurial spirit in the field, which we all view as the key to our success? No one wants cookie-cutter regions or country programs. That just wouldn't be Mercy Corps, and it wouldn't be effectively serving the needs of our beneficiaries.

We want to become a coherent organization where all of the pieces and people fit together. To do so, we have to strike the right balance between what we have now—letting 1,000 flowers bloom at the country level—and over-standardization.

The Nepal conference ended with a universal commitment to strengthening performance measurement and management at the agency. In Keny-Guyer's closing comments, he said, "We've heard the call from the field to further our investment in measuring our impact. We're going to take this on as an agency. When we are together again in two years, I know we will have piloted some additional metrics and will have lessons and practices to share and improve upon." Zimmerman's and Farrell's tasks were to figure out how to build M&E capacity in the field, how to capitalize on the M&E efforts already going on in the field (such as Indonesia and Sri Lanka's shared impact indicators), and how to design the performance metrics. Should standard agency-wide metrics be cascaded down to the region and country levels? How much flexibility, if any, should regions and countries have in developing their metrics?

Zimmerman had no time to waste. When he accepted the senior VP post, he told Lindborg and Keny-Guyer that he would stay in the position for two years. "By the time I move on, I hope we will have strengthened and institutionalized the HQ-RPD-country relationships to the point where we've built an even stronger foundation for Mercy Corps to reach new heights."

Exhibit 1
Mercy Corps: Headquarters and Country Offices

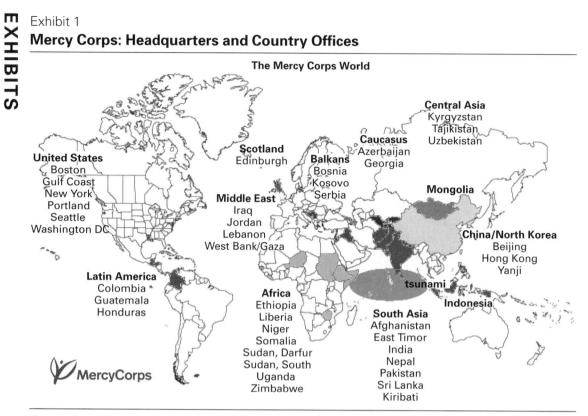

Source: Mercy Corps.

Exhibit 2

Mercy Corps Audited Financial Summary, FY02–FY06

	FY02	FY03	FY04	FY05	FY06 (unaudited)
Support & Revenue					
Government and Organization Support					
Government grants	62,660,683	84,535,704	86,832,551	77,125,488	85,297,653
International organization grants	2,562,159	1,878,838	7,793,232	2,848,232	3,095,440
Material aid	17,531,549	15,355,833	11,420,173	21,682,209	23,956,285
Subtotal	**82,754,391**	**101,770,375**	**106,045,956**	**101,655,929**	**112,349,378**
Private Support					
Contributions	7,566,822	7,305,522	6,922,117	22,189,581	37,828,132
Grants	4,200,494	2,584,596	4,007,137	10,926,807	9,801,196
Gifts in kind	10,435,595	5,098,010	22,052,014	30,505,681	33,316,107
Other	1,253,374	873,850	1,981,614	3,198,338	4,066,576
Subtotal	**23,456,285**	**15,861,978**	**34,962,882**	**66,820,407**	**85,012,011**
Total Support & Revenue	**106,210,676**	**117,632,353**	**141,008,838**	**168,476,336**	**197,361,389**
Expenditures					
Program					
Project expenditures	68,660,528	86,589,153	95,730,846	95,325,071	111,483,360
Material aid	27,967,144	20,453,843	33,472,187	52,187,890	57,272,392
Subtotal	**96,627,672**	**107,042,996**	**129,203,033**	**147,512,961**	**168,755,752**
Support Services					
General & administration	5,132,557	7,040,107	8,146,587	11,093,797	13,852,281
Resource development	2,900,946	3,323,317	3,718,933	7,250,100	8,860,273
Subtotal	**8,033,503**	**10,363,424**	**11,865,520**	**18,343,897**	**22,712,554**
Total Expenditures	**104,661,175**	**117,406,420**	**141,068,553**	**165,856,858**	**191,468,306**
Net	**1,549,501**	**225,933**	**(59,715)**	**2,619,478**	**5,893,083**

Notes: Figures do not include support, revenues and expenditures from Mercy Corps Scotland and Proyecto Aldea Global, a Honduran partner organization.

The support and revenue figures include only unrestricted net asset activity.

Source: Mercy Corps.

Exhibit 3
Mercy Corps Vision for Change

Source: Mercy Corps.

Exhibit 4

Regional Program Director (RPD) Job Description

The RPD is a senior agency leader and manager providing significant support and direction to the development and management of Mercy Corps' programs and initiatives. The RPD will ensure that Mercy Corps' country offices develop and deliver innovative, integrated, high impact programs. S/he will provide leadership, direction and accountability in managing and coordinating the agency's resources in support of vibrant and creative country programs. Working closely with the senior management team, the regional program director will ensure that country program operations are of the highest quality and standards.

ESSENTIAL JOB FUNCTIONS:

Strategy and Vision

- Support the CEO, president, CFO and senior vice president of program on matters pertaining to overall agency strategy, planning, budgeting, programming, and management.

- Support and oversee the management of country-level strategic planning, implementation, monitoring, and evaluation. Strategically position Mercy Corps for new opportunities in the region.

Program Operations and Management

- Support country leadership in developing and carrying out program and operations policies necessary for the fulfillment of Mercy Corps' mission, goals, and objectives and internal and donor policies.

- Ensure and oversee effective human, material, financial, and operational field support systems for all country programs, in cooperation with the senior vice president, CFO, and other senior staff.

- Ensure timely and targeted communication and information flow to all internal and external parties.

- Promote the development and implementation of internal program coordination and information sharing within and between regions, with Mercy Corps' support and oversight units and individuals between departments, and serve as a key representative on the senior management team.

Team Management

- Provide and encourage adequate mentoring, training, and staff development for country and deputy directors and their teams, helping to develop highly effective team performance with an eye towards helping to develop career paths and internal promotion.

- Participate in the recruitment, selection, orientation, and training of Mercy Corps' program teams.

Representation

- Build strong constituencies to include Mercy Corps' headquarters and regional office teams, international and local civil society leaders, government officials, donor community officials, diplomatic corps/military and embassies, vendors, media, and the general public.

Organizational Learning

- All team members are responsible for spending 5% of their work time in formal and/or non-formal professional-learning activities.

Exhibit 4 (continued)

ACCOUNTABILITY:

Reports Directly to Senior Vice President of Program

SUPERVISES: The Regional Program Director is responsible for the direct supervision of Country/Mission/Program Directors throughout Mercy Corps' global programs and a Program Support Team based in Portland, OR and/or Washington, DC and/or Scotland.

KNOWLEDGE AND EXPERIENCE:

- MA/S or equivalent in international development, political science, management, or other relevant field.
- 6–8 years' field experience in senior program management.
- 8–10 years' program operations experience including direct "hands-on" skills in program development, strategic planning, program implementation, and evaluation.
- 8–10 years' team management experience, i.e., staff supervision, mentoring, and development; training; finance and administration; donor relations; and inter-/intra-agency communications.
- Fluency in language(s) widely spoken and overseas experience in assigned region preferred.
- Demonstrated understanding of the critical development issues in the assigned region and significant experience with the challenges of operating programs in the region.
- Demonstrated proficiency and experience with public and private donors, government grant, and financial-management requirements.
- Exceptional program and project conceptualization and design skills.
- Successful and proven negotiation, communication, organization, and prioritization skills.

SUCCESS FACTORS:

- An entrepreneurial spirit that is both creative and flexible, while also accountable.
- Strong communication skills and a commitment to "inclusiveness" and consensus-building.
- Confident, creative, and participatory leadership skills and compassionate decisiveness.
- Ability to multi-task, prioritize, and problem solve.
- Ability to maintain attention to detail and strategic vision.
- Solid understanding of political, economic, social conditions, and historical context of region.
- Ability to obtain, analyze, and act on large amounts of security and program information from a diverse range of sources.

The successful Regional Program Director will conduct him/herself both professionally and personally in such a manner as to bring credit to Mercy Corps and in no way jeopardize the agency's humanitarian efforts. The most successful Mercy Corps staff members have a strong commitment to teamwork and accountability and make effective communication a priority in all situations.

The Regional Program Director will be expected to travel at least 35%.

Note: Abbreviated by casewriter.

Source: Mercy Corps.

Exhibit 5
Steve Zimmerman's Bio

Steve Zimmerman has more than 25 years of senior- and executive-level experience in the field of international development. An accountant and economist by training, he has a strong financial management background and has been instrumental in developing several Mercy Corps core program competencies, including its economic development portfolio.

Zimmerman joined Mercy Corps in 1997 as its first chief operating officer, dividing his time between the institutional development of Mercy Corps and the design and implementation of its worldwide programs. In 2003, he moved to Mongolia as country director, doubling the size of the program in less than one year and pioneering new development strategies focused on improving the rural economy. Two years later, in 2005, he assumed responsibility for Mercy Corps' China program as well. Zimmerman returned to Portland in September 2006 to assume his current post, in which he manages the agency's worldwide program operations.

Prior to joining Mercy Corps, Zimmerman was the chief financial officer for a large HIV–AIDS project in New York City. He has worked for a number of recognized international NGOs, including Save the Children, AFS Intercultural Programs, and Catholic Relief Services. He is a graduate of the University of Southern California.

Source: Mercy Corps.

Exhibit 6
Regional Program Director (RPD) Bios

Kathy Fry, Latin America RPD: Frye had over 20 years' experience in country and regional director positions, managing community development projects in the South Pacific. Fry joined Mercy Corps as senior program officer for Latin America in 2003. She lived and worked out of Portland, OR.

David Holdridge, Middle East RPD: Holdridge joined Mercy Corps in 2003. Holdridge had over 25 years' experience initiating and providing executive leadership in non-government humanitarian organizations in various countries in the Middle East, Africa, Central and Eastern Europe, Asia, and the U.S, including 20 years as a field manager and regional director with Catholic Relief Services. Holdridge lived between Amman, Jordan and Beirut, Lebanon.

Diane Johnson, South and South East Asia RPD: Johnson had been with Mercy Corps for four years. Within that time, she distinguished herself for leading the agency's successful efforts to support Afghanistan's democratic transition and in Bande Ache, Indonesia following the 2004 Indian Ocean Tsunami. She had been the DPO for South and South East Asia since June 2005. Johnson lived in Bangkok, Thailand.

Phil Oldham, West and Southern Africa RPD: Oldham joined Mercy Corps in August 2006. Prior, Oldham spent 15 years working for Catholic Relief Services in various HQ and field-management positions. Oldham was in the process of moving to Accra, Ghana.

Matt Lovick, East Africa RPD: After working 10 years as a CD for the international development contractor Cooperative Housing Foundation (CHF), Lovick came to Mercy Corps as a regional director for West Africa in 2005. Lovick lived in Nairobi, Kenya.

Jim White, Central Asia and the Caucuses RPD: White had been with Mercy Corps for nine years, serving as a CD in Kosovo and Tajikistan; a regional director for Pakistan, Afghanistan, and Iran; and a DPO. In addition to his RPD responsibilities, White also served as Zimmerman's deputy and oversaw Mercy Corps' procurement, administration, and logistics management (PALM) team. White worked out of Portland, OR.

Source: Casewriter interviews.

Exhibit 7
Country Director (CD) Job Description

PROGRAM/DEPARTMENT SUMMARY:

Mercy Corps has maintained a diverse, multi-sectoral relief and development program in Tajikistan since 1994. The current country strategy prioritizes microfinance, micro/small business development, community-based health interventions, HIV/AIDS, agricultural development, natural resources management, disaster preparedness, and conflict management as primary programmatic foci for future development. Mercy Corps Tajikistan implements programs through local partners to carry out interventions in specific regions and works closely with international and local NGO partners, local businesses, and local and national governments.

GENERAL POSITION SUMMARY:

The CD is the most senior management position for Mercy Corps in Tajikistan with program development, supervisory, and managerial responsibility over all in-country personnel, programs, and policies. The CD provides the vision and leadership in developing long-term strategies, conceptualizing new programs, mentoring and training senior expatriate and national staffs, ensuring effective program support and administration, monitoring overall program performance by tracking progress toward specified objectives.

ESSENTIAL JOB FUNCTIONS:

- Vision, leadership, and strategy
- Commitment to quality program development
- Commitment to staff development
- Capacity building of local partners
- Management and administration
- Finance, compliance management, and accountability
- Representation and diplomacy
- Reporting, monitoring, and evaluation
- Security
- Communications

REPORTS DIRECTLY TO: Regional Program Director

WORKS DIRECTLY WITH: Mercy Corps Tajikistan team and Mercy Corps offices in other countries in the region; HQ-based Program Operations, Finance, and Technical Support Units.

Exhibit 7 (continued)

KNOWLEDGE AND EXPERIENCE:

- MA/S or equivalent in the social sciences, economics, international development, or related discipline

- At least 10 years' experience working in international relief and development

- At least 5 years field-based experience in a senior leadership position building; developing, and managing programs and teams; developing organizational capacity; and providing financial oversight

- Experience with USAID-funded programs as well as protocols of one or more of the following donors: European Community, ECHO, private donors, and foundations

- Demonstrated ability to function as a social entrepreneur, sensitive to cultural context

- History of working effectively and respectfully with host country government, INGO, and NGO partners

- Commitment to the principles of participatory team management and community development

- Effective verbal and written communication, multi-tasking, organizational skills

- Russian or Tajik language skills and experience working in the NIS are highly preferred

SUCCESS FACTORS:

The successful CD will apply a strong combination of team leadership, program development, relationship-building, and communication abilities. As this position requires a significant amount of new program development to complement existing programs, the successful CD will have an outstanding ability to develop, manage, and integrate innovative programs within the current and future structure of Mercy Corps Tajikistan operations. The successful CD will have a strong commitment to teamwork and accountability.

Source: Mercy Corps.
Note: Abbreviated by casewriter.

Exhibit 8

Indonesia FY07 Country Plan (excerpt)

GOAL: Mercy Corps is in Indonesia to address the root causes of poverty, thereby improving the quality of life for disaster- and conflict-affected, urban, and coastal communities.

STRATEGIC OBJECTIVES	MAJOR STAFF ACTIVITIES	KEY OUTPUTS	IMPACT INDICATORS
1. Create productive relationships between citizens, government, civic- and private-sector partners that link communities to critical resources.	• Identify stakeholders • Identify stakeholder interests and activities • Identify barriers • Find mutual areas of interest and intervention • Define roles and responsibilities • Build trust and confidence • Build capacity of partners • Build connection between partners • Communicate and provide information • Generate models of productive partnership (in the context of objectives 2 and 3)	• Clear understanding of interests and motivations of stakeholders • Resource allocation according to community priorities • Community mobilized to access resources • Increased private sector involvement in communities • Ability of partners to make collective decisions and take action • Replicable models developed	1. % increase in government and private resources allocated to priority health, water and sanitation, and financial needs (including financial institutions)* 2. Capacity of communities to effectively secure and generate resources (Financial and Technical, Policies, Material) (Index)
2. Stimulate economic activity of target groups.	• Gain understanding of economic conditions and demands of community • Train and mentor local institutions to provide financial and non-financial services • Facilitate institutions' links to resources • Build community knowledge of services • Identify and provide incentives for changing behavior • Build staff capacity on economic principles and entrepreneurial behavior in programming	• Sustainable institutions actively lending and providing business (market linkages) services to poor people • Poor people accessing and utilizing loans and services for creating or expanding business activities • Expanded micro- and small-business activities employing workers	3. % increase in sales and value of production (yield)*

Exhibit 8 (continued)

3. Increase capacity of the community to improve health and address environmental, educational, and other needs.	• Conduct assessments Develop a participatory DM&E system • Develop models • Conduct training of staff and partners • Mentor and provide technical assistance • Create linkages	• Identified community needs and resources • Baseline conducted • Functioning DM&E system utilized by the communities • Model created • Specific sectoral knowledge increased and applied	4. % decrease in anemia (6–59.99 months; 6–14 years; pregnant and non-pregnant women only 15–40 years) 5. % increase in hand washing (adults) and % change in diarrheal rates for children under the age of 5
4. Increase organizational capacity to design, implement, administer, and learn from programs that improve the lives of our target communities in Indonesia.	• Recruit and select appropriate staff • Adopt flexible, enabling, responsive staff structure • Create performance-based staff-management system that challenges, inspires, rewards • Create training and learning opportunities • Develop DM&E system	• Staff skills assessment program • In-house mentoring and coaching resources • Training and learning programs • Regular participatory evaluations to extract lessons learned and to improve performance	6. % of staff with the required set of core capacities/skills* 7. % team having reached level x on the Program Quality & Learning Index

* Indicator was also tracked by Mercy Corps Sri Lanka.

Source: Mercy Corps Indonesia.

Exhibit 9
Selected Country Profiles

	Guatemala	Indonesia	Liberia	Tajikistan
Mercy Corps region	Latin America	South and South East Asia	East Africa	Central Asia/Caucuses
Total population	12.6 million	220.6 million	3.3 million	7 million
Gross national income per capita ($US)	$2,400	$1,280	$130	$330
Literacy rate	70.6%	87.9%	57.5%	99.4%
FY07 Mercy Corps budget	$3 million	$20.3 million	$2.1 million	$3.8 million
No. staff	75	511	80	120
No. offices	4	12	5	3
No. contracts/grants	14	30	4	4
No. beneficiaries	37,000	500,000	595,000	133,061
Program sectors	Emergency relief and recovery	Emergency relief and recovery/ Disaster risk reduction	Youth education	Agricultural livelihoods
	Civil society	Civil society	Civil society	Civil society
	Economic development	Economic development	Economic development	Economic development
	Health	Health & nutrition	Infrastructure	Health
		Microfinance		Microfinance
		Community infrastructure		Infrastructure
		Water and sanitation		

Sources: Mercy Corps data from Mercy Corps. Economic indicators (population, GNI) compiled from the World Development Indicators Database (http://*www.worldbank.org),* accessed December 22, 2006. Literacy rates compiled from The CIA World Fact Book (https://www.cia.gov/cia/publications/factbook/), accessed December 22, 2006.

DISCUSSION QUESTIONS

1. Why does Chicago have different categories of schools—e.g., contract, performance, and autonomous management and performance (AMPS)?

2. What are the key roles that the district should play across these schools? Why?

3. What is your assessment as to how well the district is filling its role in relation to the various categories of schools?

4. How important are the Area Instructional Officers (AIOs), and what are the key challenges to their effectiveness?

Richard F. Elmore ■ Allen S. Grossman ■ Caroline King

Managing the Chicago Public Schools

Each child who fails is our failure. . . . We can't ever accept that, because of poverty or social issues or family issues, our kids can't learn. They can learn. They've proven it. The question is, Can we do a better job of teaching? Not just in a few schools, but in every school?

—*Mayor Richard M. Daley*

With these words, Mayor Richard M. Daley opened the Chicago Public Schools' (CPS) kick-off retreat for the new school year on August 19, 2005. The district's senior managers and every principal were in attendance. While Daley's remarks acknowledged the district's progress under Chief Executive Officer Arne Duncan's administration, they also reflected a sense of urgency about sustaining and accelerating these gains at scale.

For the past four years, Duncan and his leadership team had been grappling with the challenge of managing for high performance in "every school." Scale, however, was not the only challenge. The city's 617 schools represented different types of schools, achievement levels, and capacities to improve teaching and learning. Duncan, a former professional basketball player,

noted: "There's no playbook for how to manage a complex district like CPS. We're trying to keep everyone's eye on the ball—producing better outcomes for every child."

Background

Serving over 426,000 students in 511 elementary and 106 high schools, CPS was the nation's third-largest school system in SY06.[1] The district employed 45,000 people and operated with a $4.1 billion budget. While the student body was diverse, historic economic and ethnic divisions among the city's neighborhoods created schools that largely reflected their surrounding communities. Fully 85% of students came from low-income families (see Exhibits 1 and 2 for CPS facts and figures).

CPS operated under a hybrid governance structure. The state legislature had turned the school system over to Daley in 1995. Daley appointed the district's seven-member board of education and chief executive officer, tapping Arne Duncan as CEO in 2001. Each school site had an elected local school council (LSC) consisting of staff, parents, and community members. LSCs hired, evaluated, and fired the principal and approved the budget and curricula. LSCs had been in place since 1988. The Chicago Teachers Union (CTU) represented the district's 27,000 teachers.

Duncan's Administration

Duncan was one of the longest-serving urban superintendents in the country. Dr. Barbara Eason-Watkins, a former principal credited with turning around one of the district's lowest-performing schools, served as chief education officer (CEdO). David Vitale, the former president and CEO of the Chicago Board of Trade, was chief administrative officer.

Reforms: Duncan's administration focused on three core strategies: advancing literacy, strengthening human capital, and providing additional learning opportunities for students. The Chicago Reading Initiative required all elementary students to receive two hours of balanced literacy instruction per day. While schools continued to choose their own reading programs—85 different programs had previously been in use across the district—CPS encouraged struggling schools to adopt one of five "district-recommended" reading programs. The district also identified two high-quality math curricula for K–5 and two for grades 6–8, as well as district-recommended curricula in math and science for high schools. District trainings were limited to these programs.

More targeted recruiting efforts now produced 10 applicants for every open teaching position, and 42% of teachers hired in SY06 held master's degrees. CPS had created a new Office of Principal Preparation and Development and had tightened principal eligibility. LSCs now hired principals from a pool of district-approved candidates who had demonstrated instructional leadership competencies. After-school, summer school, and kindergarten options had also proliferated across the city.

Area Structure: Duncan and Eason-Watkins had reorganized the district from six 100-school regions to 24 geographic "areas," which included 18 elementary (PK–8) and six high-school (9–12) areas. The number of schools in each area ranged from 18 to 44; areas with high schools and historically low-performing schools were smaller.

An area instructional officer (AIO) led each area. AIOs were charged with working with principals to improve instruction in schools and, along with LSCs, to evaluate principals. AIOs held one mandatory meeting for principals per month. As a group, AIOs met with Eason-Watkins and Chief Instructional Officer Domingo Trujillo during monthly "Area Coherence Meetings" to determine a citywide focus for the principals' meetings. Literacy, however, was a standing focus. Each AIO designed the format and activities for his or her principals' meetings, which ranged from two to six hours.

Each AIO was aided by a staff of three to six content coaches (e.g., literacy, mathematics), a school improvement planning coordinator, and a management support director. Coaches held area-wide trainings for teachers and worked directly in schools upon request by the AIO or principal. An AIO-led area team observed instruction in classrooms and monitored school improvement through quarterly school visits known as "walkthroughs."

Student Achievement: Student performance had steadily increased under Duncan. Between 2001–2005, the percentage of elementary students meeting or exceeding state standards on the Illinois Standards Achievement Test (ISAT) increased by nine percentage points in reading and 11 points in math (see Exhibit 3). By 2005, nearly 50% of elementary students met or exceeded standards, and the district's ISAT gains outpaced the state averages at every tested grade level. On the 11th-grade Prairie State Achievement Exam (PSAE)—which included reading, math, and science—31.4% of CPS students met or exceeded standards in 2005 compared with 27.2% in 2001. One-year high-school dropout rates steadily declined from 16.3% in 2001 to 10.2% in 2005.

Yet student performance levels and trends were highly variable across the district. Between 2003 and 2005, achievement on state tests rose in some areas, while it stayed flat or declined in others. Over 60% of students met or exceeded state standards in the two northernmost elementary areas in 2005; less than 40% of students met standards in seven other elementary areas.

The percentage of high-school students meeting or exceeding state standards by area ranged from 48.0% to 19.8%. Only 29 high schools had over 30% of students meeting PSAE standards. And only 12 high schools had 50% or more students earning an 18 or above on the ACT, the score needed to gain admissions to most four-year public colleges in Illinois.[2]

School Categories

The district's 617 public schools reflected diverse origins, characteristics, and management. Brief descriptions of major school categories follow[3] (see Exhibit 4a for a comparison; see Exhibits 4b and 4c for performance data).

Regular District Schools (280): Regular district schools were required to have elected LSCs report to an AIO and to hire certified, unionized employees. Budgets were "position-based," meaning that roughly 80% of a school's "general education funds" were allocated by the central office to positions based on staffing ratios (i.e., 28 students: 1 teacher and 1 engineer, per school). Principals controlled the remaining 20%, a discretionary budget of small line items for textbooks and other supplies. Total general education funds averaged $5,200 per elementary pupil and $6,500 per high-school pupil. Principals also controlled any state or federal compensatory funds (approximately $1,200 per pupil) based on the number of low-income students enrolled.

Autonomous Management and Performance Schools, AMPS (79): District schools granted 10 "autonomies" by CPS in SY06 based on high academic and operational performance. CPS identified the AMPS schools using 13 academic, operational, and compliance indicators and the chief education office's recommendation (see Exhibit 5). The district offered AMPS status to 85 schools; 79 participated (69 elementary and 10 high schools). AMPS mostly represented the district's highest-performing schools, although three schools that did not meet the academic criteria were also granted AMPS status. Eason-Watkins explained, "We had recruited some strong principals to challenging schools and we wanted to use AMPS as an incentive for them to stay." Of the 10 AMPS high schools, 6 were "selective enrollment" schools that used academic criteria to admit students.

CPS Probation Schools (226): "Probation" was the lowest school rating under the CPS accountability system. In probation schools, less than 40% of elementary students (or 30% in high schools) met state standards and performed at national norms on the Iowa Test of Basic Skills (ITBS), and the schools had failed to demonstrate "academic progress" as defined by the district (see Exhibit 6). The number of probation schools in an area ranged from 0 to 20.

NCLB Restructuring Schools (185): Schools designated as "restructuring" had failed to meet federal Adequate Yearly Progress targets in reading and math for five consecutive years. To comply with the No Child Left Behind Act (NCLB) of 2001, CPS would have to close or restructure the schools in SY07. One-hundred and thirty-seven of the restructuring schools were also on CPS probation.

Charter Schools (35): Charter schools were managed and governed by independent organizations and were exempt from all CPS policies and initiatives. They received and controlled 100% of district dollars based on the number of students enrolled ("per pupil budgets") and signed five-year performance contracts with the district. A 1996 state law permitted CPS to authorize up to 30 charters; 15 of the charters allowed multiple school sites. CPS had authorized 22 charters, and 35 sites were operating.

Performance Schools (3) and Contract Schools (1 to open SY07): Performance schools were district-run and hired CTU teachers, while contract schools were run by nonprofits and were free to hire non-unionized employees. Both types of schools received per-pupil budgets, had more flexibilities than regular district schools, and signed five-year performance agreements with the district.

The district created the performance and contract school categories in 2004. That year, Daley announced Renaissance 2010 ("Ren10"), a campaign to replace the district's lowest-performing schools with 100 new schools by 2010. Chief Officer for New Schools Hosanna Mahaley explained, "The Mayor wanted high-quality, innovative school options available in every part of the city and to offer more choice to parents. We were reaching our charter cap and the Mayor wanted to explore bold new options."

School design teams submitted proposals to open Ren10 schools through an annual competitive RFP process which called for charter, performance, or contract school proposals only. As of SY06, the board had closed 27 schools for "chronically poor performance" and had approved 37 Ren10 schools. By 2010, an estimated 71,000 students, nearly 18% of CPS enrollment, were expected to attend Ren10 schools.

Reflecting on the diversity of public schools, Duncan said, "We'd be missing the boat if all we do is create great new schools. We've got to learn lessons that help us improve the whole district."

A Strategy to Scale High Performance

Members of the CPS leadership team shared the mayor's concern about increasing the perfor-

mance of "every school." To that end, they had been refining the district's improvement strategy over the previous year. During the August 19, 2005 meeting, Eason-Watkins reaffirmed the district's commitment to its three core strategies (improving literacy, human capital, and student learning opportunities) and presented a "theory of change" intended to guide the district's work:

- Improved student learning requires improved instruction.

- Schools are the unit of change for instructional improvement, and principals are the leaders of that change.

- Area and central offices provide critical support for instructional improvement and differentiate that support based on school performance and need.

Eason-Watkins commented, "After four years of work, we still believed that improving instruction was the most powerful way to increase student achievement, but we wanted to clarify that there is no 'one-size-fits-all' model that works for 617 schools. Each principal must feel empowered to drive change and to receive the support that responds to the school's specific needs."

During SY06, the district took steps to enact its theory of change by setting clear expectations, providing effective and targeted support to schools, and making accountability more consistent.

Setting Clear Expectations

Five-Year District Student Outcome Goals

Based on focus groups with district leaders, school staff, students and their families, CPS established the "ultimate district goal" of "graduating all students prepared for success in post-secondary education and employment." Eason-Watkins announced the goal at the August 19, 2005 meeting, calling it "ambitious." Indeed, only 54% of CPS students even graduated from high school within five years. Historically, only six out of every 100 ninth graders earned a bachelor's degree within six years of starting college.[4]

To measure progress toward attaining the ultimate goal, CPS established five-year student outcome goals for 2006–2010. For each outcome goal, the district established the current performance in 2005 and the 2010 goal. At the elementary level, for example, the district aimed to increase the percentage of third graders who met or exceeded state reading standards from 42% in 2005 to 70% by 2010. In the upper grades, the district wanted 80% of high-school freshman to be considered "on track to graduate" by 2010, a jump from 54% in 2005. (See the 2010 outcome goals in Exhibit 7.)

Chief Planning Officer Larry Stanton noted, "We set district- and school-level student outcome goals because we needed to define success for the district and for schools. Everyone, particularly principals, needs to know what's expected of them so they can work toward achieving it. The goals were intended to be ambitious, but achievable."

School Annual Performance Targets and the SIPAAA

Annual School Targets: In fall 2005, CPS set annual school performance targets for 2006–2010. The targets represented each school's contribution to meeting the district's 2010 outcome goals. Elementary schools received annual targets for the percentage of students expected to meet

standards on the ISAT in grades 3, 6, and 8; and for schoolwide attendance. High schools received annual targets for the percentage of students expected to a). meet standards on the PSAE; b). be "on track to graduate"; c). graduate within five years; and d). complete high school as "college ready" (reflected in higher ACT scores).

The research, accountability, and evaluation department of CPS developed the annual targets based on a school's prior performance. School targets for the ISAT and PSAE were set equal to the "Safe Harbor" requirements under NCLB. To make Safe Harbor, an additional 10% of students who did not meet state standards the previous year (e.g., 2005) had to meet standards the following year (e.g., 2006). Table 1 shows ISAT targets for three elementary schools.

Chief Accountability Officer Dan Bugler noted, "We figured out that the district could achieve its 2010 outcome goals if every teacher helped two additional students meet or exceed state standards each year. This helped make the school targets and district outcome goals actually seem attainable."

For the other three high-school targets (the percentage of ninth graders on track to graduate, graduation rate, and college readiness), the district set school-level 2010 performance goals. The gap between a school's performance in 2005 and its 2010 goal represented the school's "performance gap." The annual targets were set so that a school was expected to close 10% of its performance gap in 2006; 20% in both 2007 and 2008; and 25% in both 2009 and 2010.

Table 1

Percentage of Students Meeting/Exceeding ISAT Standards in Three Elementary Schools with Different Levels of Performance

School	2005 Current	2006 Target	2007 Target	2008 Target	2009 Target	2010 Target
Elementary A	25%	32%	39%	45%	51%	55%
Elementary B	47%	52%	57%	61%	65%	68%
Elementary C	85%	87%	88%	89%	90%	91%

Source: CPS.

The actual size of a school's performance gap varied by current performance levels. Lower-performing schools had larger gaps to close by 2010. Table 2 shows five-year graduation targets for three high schools.

"The annual school targets will not be used for determining probation status but we're still considering other ways to use the targets as a performance management tool," explained Stanton. "We've gotten some push-back from schools on the targets because they do not track cohorts of students over time, which is a limitation of the current state testing system. The targets were developed to be aspirational, not to hold people's feet to the fire." CPS intended to refine the target-setting as "gains" data from the state test became available in future years.

School Improvement Plans: CPS introduced a new school improvement planning process for 2006–2008. The Illinois State Board of Education had required school improvement plans since 1993, and since 1998, had allowed CPS schools to use a uniform template entitled the "School Improvement Plan for Advancing Academic Achievement," or SIPAAA. According to Stanton, "Many of the plans were 200-page documents that did not set specific performance expectations. They mostly sat on a shelf collecting dust."

CPS streamlined the template for 2006–2008, which included annual school targets for the first time. In January 2006, every school in CPS, except charter schools, received a 20-page, 2006–2008 SIPAAA populated with its past performance and targets for SY07 and SY08. The SIPAAA outlined a process to help each school develop a plan to achieve its targets. Stanton explained, "We wanted to provide a structure to help schools design their own roadmaps for raising student achievement."

Each school first articulated a mission and vision. School leadership teams and stakeholders then assessed their school's strengths and weaknesses. In an "outcome analysis," the SIPAAA team reviewed four data sets: student outcomes, academic progress, student connection, and school characteristics.

In a "process analysis," schools used rubrics to self-evaluate five elements associated with school improvement referred to as the *Five Fundamentals of a Great School*. CPS had developed the *Five Fundamentals* by drawing upon research on reform efforts in Chicago, Boston, and other urban districts across the U.S. The Five Fundamentals comprised:

1. Instruction: The classroom activity that directly affects student learning. Includes the capacity of the teacher, the rigor of the content, and the engagement of students.

2. Instructional leadership: The school-level activity of principals and leadership teams, including scheduling, resource management, and curriculum planning.

3. Professional capacity: The school- or district-level activity that improves instruc-

Table 2

Percentage of Students Graduating in Five Years from Three High Schools with Different Levels of Performance

School	2005 Current	2006 Target	2007 Target	2008 Target	2009 Target	2010 Target
High School A	27%	30%	34%	38%	44%	49%
High School B	50%	52%	55%	58%	61%	65%
High School C	84%	85%	86%	86%	88%	89%

Source: CPS.

tional practices in the classroom. Includes professional development, coaching, and mentoring.

4. Learning climate: The school-level activity that promotes a safe and orderly environment.

5. Family and community involvement: The school-level activity that encourages interdependence with the community. This relationship promotes the growth, commitment, and sharing of student-learning resources.

Finally, each school defined priorities, designed curriculum and instruction interventions, and created a budget. Schools submitted SIPAAAs by April 7, 2006. AIOs approved SIPAAAs for the schools under their management. One elementary AIO commented, "This year produced the tightest alignment between schools' plans to improve student achievement and their allocation of resources that I've seen during my 20-plus years as an administrator with CPS."

Performance Contracts for All New Schools

CPS required all new charter, performance, and contract schools to sign consistent five-year performance contracts beginning in SY06. Before SY06, each new school had negotiated its own performance agreement with the district, although some schools never had an official agreement. Mahaley commented, "For the first time, we are holding all new schools accountable for the same things—improved student achievement, sound financial and operational management, and regulatory compliance—using the same metrics."

During the five-year contract period, the district conducted yearly performance reviews at new schools. At the end of the five years, the district could renew or terminate the contract. The district could close a charter, performance, or contract school at any time for poor academic

achievement or operational/fiscal mismanagement. The board had closed three charter schools between 1997–2006.

Eason-Watkins noted, "Over time, we hope to move more of our district schools to the performance contract model in order to facilitate a clear dialogue about expectations, accountability, and autonomy." The district was considering asking AMPS principals to sign performance contracts; it also wanted to use performance contracts to attract high-potential principals into low-performing schools.

Providing Effective and Targeted Support

Citing a desire to "provide effective, targeted support to schools," CPS implemented four initiatives during SY06: (1) differentiating treatment of schools; (2) clarifying the AIO role; (3) providing better student data; and (4) reorganizing the central office.

Differentiating Treatment of Schools

Duncan elaborated on the component of the district's theory of change that called on area and central offices to differentiate support to schools based on performance and need:

> Very simply, the approach is based on the reality that kids learn differently. You have to teach kids differently. And schools are no different. Schools are just one step larger than kids. Historically, though, we've had a communistic system. We treated all schools the same. And we treated too many, I argue, relatively poorly. You have to look at each child and each school individually and figure out what's best for them.

CPS differentiated support to three types of schools based on performance in SY06: (1) AMPS; (2) CPS probation schools; and (3) NCLB restructuring schools. Each of these categories included elementary and high schools. Concurrently, the district designed high-school interventions that cut across all performance levels.

1. Autonomous Management and Performance Schools (AMPS): In announcing AMPS, Duncan said, "We looked hard at all of the factors that go into creating a great school. These schools have obviously got it figured out and they have great principals. We have to build a culture of trust and give them the freedom to innovate. The best thing we can do is get out of their way."

The district granted the 79 AMPS schools the ability to exercise 10 "autonomies," such as opting out of the area structure or the district's new teacher-induction program. The principal could select as many of the 10 autonomies as desired (see Exhibit 8 for a list of AMPS autonomies and the schools' choices).

Fifty percent of AMPS schools opted out of the area structure. Out-of-area AMPS schools lost all access to the area staff, coaches, and professional development. These principals did not have to attend area principals' meetings, report to an AIO, or hold walkthroughs with the area team. AIOs no longer evaluated these principals; the district was in the process of identifying an alternate evaluator.

In-area AMPS schools still reported to and were evaluated by their AIO. These principals attended area principals' meetings and, depending on the AIO, held area walkthroughs. They were able to request support from AIOs and area coaches and to send teachers to area trainings.

Two AMPS principals reflected on their decisions:

> I relish autonomy, but I didn't want to jump out of the area this first year of AMPS. My AIO is very supportive and the professional development is valuable. As long as I can use the area supports to continue building the autonomy and capacity of my staff, I'll stay.

> I left the area because the AIO was controlling. And everything offered by the area was "one-size-fits-all"—the principals' meetings, the professional development for teachers, the walkthroughs. If differentiated instruction is our goal for students, why not do it with us?

Concurrently, CPS eliminated one elementary area and one traditional high-school area in SY06. As a result, some AIOs took in additional schools and watched their caseload grow, particularly when AMPS schools elected to remain in the area. For example, an area in which 100% of AMPS schools stayed and merged with a closed area grew from 22 to 34 elementary schools from SY05 to SY06. The AIO said, "I think the AMPS schools stayed because they get good support from all area staff, especially my coaches. But I have to be careful because the strong schools would snatch up all of my coaches' time if we let them!"

An AIO in which 86% of the area's AMPS schools opted out of the area commented:

> At first I was upset. It felt like we were rewarding the principals who had been the most resistant to anything from the central office or the area, because in terms of absolute test scores, they were at the high end of the district. But most of these schools had been making little to no gains; the schools' performance had flatlined. Maybe the AMPS schools will work harder this year to increase achievement because they cannot blame anyone else for holding them back.

Melissa Megliola, a former private sector consultant, managed AMPS with assistance from retired CPS principal Anthony (Tony) Jelinek. Megliola described her role: "My first goal is to make sure AMPS schools are kept in the loop. We have to ensure that life does not feel worse for them. My second goal is to advocate for AMPS schools within the central office so that they can exploit their autonomies in new and creative ways."

One elementary principal reflected on AMPS midway through SY06:

> The biggest difference under AMPS is that I don't have to hide anymore if I'm doing something "out-of-the-box" to better support my teachers and students. But some of the central offices still don't understand that as AMPS schools, we're allowed to do things differently. Fortunately, Melissa and Tony are there whenever we need someone to run interference.

All AMPS schools were given two years before their AMPS status would be reevaluated. Megliola explained, "We were asking schools to take new risks with us. We did not want anyone to fear being penalized if performance went down as a result." The criteria for admitting additional schools into AMPS were still being discussed, but Megliola imagined adding 5 to 15 schools per year.

The district intended to give AMPS schools more budgetary flexibility in SY07. Instead of receiving position allocations, AMPS schools would receive the dollars to cover the cost of an average district salary for each position previously budgeted to the school (known as "lump-sum budgeting"). The principal could then spend the dollars as he/she chose, as long as the school hired enough teachers to maintain class-size ratios as specified under the CTU contract.

2. CPS Probation Schools: Probation schools were treated differently in two respects. First, under board policy, CPS could assign an interim principal to any probation school if the previous principal had been removed due to poor performance.

Second, AIOs were given control over the probation schools' discretionary budgets in SY05. That year, the central office paid for a lead literacy teacher (LLT) in every probation school, and every school (depending on the amount of discretionary funds available) was required to pay for a second LLT, as well as reduced class size in grades 1–3, full-day kindergarten, and district-recommended curricula for literacy and math at specific grade levels. In the summer of 2005, Stanton's team held focus groups with AIOs and principals. Participants said that "uniform school improvement requirements were not effective" and stressed the need for flexibility to adapt strategies to local school conditions.[5]

In response, the curriculum offices designed Instructional Support Options (ISOs). ISOs were "packages" of interventions that individual schools could choose from in developing their 2006–2008 school improvement plans. Acting Math and Science Curriculum Officer Mike Lach explained, "ISOs are a menu of curriculum and instructional supports, such as materials, positions, and professional development. A school can choose a 'fully loaded' package or select items a-la-carte style. The idea is to help principals and AIOs select which interventions best fit a school's needs."

One elementary AIO explained the shift: "The budget approval process for probation schools was more of a negotiation this year. I sat with each principal and we assessed what was working and what was not. I did not completely throw out the guidelines from last year because in many cases they were effective, but each school was able to adapt and adjust rather than follow a set of rules."

3. NCLB Restructuring Schools: NCLB required districts to ensure that after a sixth year of missing Adequate Yearly Progress, a restructuring school enacted one of five plans:

- Reopen as a public charter school.

- Replace all or most of school staff who were relevant to the school's failure to make AYP.

- Contract a third party to operate the school.

- Turn the operation of the school over to the state.

- Implement any other major restructuring of the school's governance arrangement that makes fundamental reforms to improve academic achievement.

The Illinois State Board of Education ruled out state takeovers, and the district's charter cap limited that option. Given these constraints, CPS designed several options for its 185 restructuring schools.

Forty-four restructuring schools implemented one of the following "centrally directed initiatives":

- Close and reopen in the future under Ren10 (10 schools).

- Assign high-potential "turnaround" principals (2 schools).

- Share management responsibility with CTU for five years, with schools adopting comprehensive school reform models and piloting peer evaluation for teachers (8 schools).

- Partner with one of three external instructional improvement providers: America's Choice, Strategic Learning Initiatives, or Learning Point Associates (24 schools).

In the other 141 restructuring schools, AIOs were asked to work with principals during the SIPAAA process to identify interventions that would enhance student achievement and satisfy the law's requirements. AIOs were given responsibility for developing school-by-school plans that were then reviewed and approved by the CEdO. Plans had to be supported by data, both performance and qualitative data collected by the AIO through ongoing work in the schools. School plans called for staffing changes, new literacy programs, or changing the school's grade configuration, among other interventions.

4. High Schools: Two major efforts to improve support to high schools were underway:

Area 25 for small high schools: Between 2001 and 2003, the Bill and Melinda Gates Foundation and local Chicago foundations awarded CPS $25 million to open 32 small high schools by 2007. Five low-performing high schools would be converted into 20 autonomous small high schools, and 12 new start-up small high schools would be created. An intermediary, the Chicago High School Redesign Initiative (CHSRI), formed to channel the funding and help manage the effort.

Twenty-four small high schools (23 regular, 1 charter) had opened by SY06. These small schools enrolled fewer than 500 students and typically formed around a theme, such as medicine or the arts. Small schools received start-up funding and an additional $300 per pupil each year.

Also in SY06 CPS created a special area, Area 25, for the district's small high schools. Before that, small high schools had been interspersed across the six different high-school areas. Cynthia Barron, a high-school AIO since 2002, moved to head up Area 25. She commented:

> Small high-school principals are unique. They're very entrepreneurial, but they have a wide range of instructional knowledge and leadership skills. They also face unique challenges as they are each building a new school vision, staff, and structures. Area 25 was created to meet these unique needs. We want to provide the best support we can to these schools so that they are successful and [so] the larger system can learn from their innovations.

High-school transformation: In April 2006, CPS launched a $75–$100 million effort to strengthen high-school education, known as the "High-School Transformation" project. Some aspects applied to all high schools in the district (regular district, small, charter, probation, etc.), such as a new high-school scorecard. The scorecard reported school performance in four areas: student outcomes, academic progress, student connections, and school characteristics. In each area of measurement, schools also received a ranking against all other schools in the district. (See Exhibit 9 for a sample scorecard.) There were separate rankings for selective enrollment versus non-selective high schools.

Commenting on the new scorecard, Chief Officer for High Schools Dr. Donald Pittman said:

> We're sending a clear message about what high-school principals should be focused on. For the first time, we're recognizing the "value-add" of each school—student gains—in addition to absolute performance. And we've been able to identify some areas in which charter and other new schools are outperforming district schools. Too often in the past, we've launched new initiatives without a mechanism to evaluate [whether] they are any more effective than the old way of doing things.

Other aspects of the transformation project were designed with an opt-in implementation model. Over a three-year period, 50 of the district's high schools would be chosen to adopt the project's "instructional development systems." For each core subject (English, math, and science), participating schools would choose one of three "packages." Each package provided a standards-based college preparatory curriculum, materials, and assessments; professional development and coaching for teachers; and implementation support for principals. Through a RFP process, the district had selected external vendors to help build the packages.

Any high school, except charters, could apply to participate. CPS reported that 40 high schools applied for the first implementation year, known as "Wave 1." The district chose 14 schools based on leadership strength and teacher buy-in. These Wave 1 schools would begin implementing their selected packages in SY07, starting with 9th grade classrooms. The 14 schools ranged from high- to low-performing. Additional classrooms and new high schools would be added in SY08 and SY09.

Assistant Director for Planning and Development Angus Mairs explained, "We're not going to force this on high schools that feel better

off without the district's support. We hope that over time, if these approaches are as effective as we designed them to be, more and more high schools will voluntarily adopt them."

Clarifying the Area Instructional Officer's Role

Originally, AIOs were expected to spend 60% of their time improving instruction and 40% resolving schools' operational issues. Starting in SY06, AIOs were expected to spend 70% of their time working with principals to improve instructional leadership; 30% identifying, developing, and placing new principals; and 0% on school operations (see Exhibit 10). Six new business service centers (see p. 14) were being created to help pick up AIOs' operations responsibilities. Chief Instructional Officer Trujillo explained the rationale behind the AIO role clarification:

> We need AIOs to have the time to assist principals to obtain and align the resources that they say they need to be successful. Too often, AIOs find themselves taking on non-instructional issues because we at central office make too many demands of them. If the task is not an instructional one, we must find another mechanism for working with schools. And with 50% of our principals eligible to retire by 2010, we want and need AIOs to groom our next school leaders and advise LSCs on hiring.

An elementary AIO who had served in the position since its inception commented, "The clarification renewed my focus on instruction. I'm more likely to delegate non-instructional tasks or push back on the central office if they are asking me and my staff to spend time on something that would pull us away from our work in schools." She continued, "But, there's always challenges. Things always crop up—like parent concerns or an LSC that won't meet to approve a budget item."

The focus on the AIO role coincided with

the first significant wave of AIO retirements. Eighteen AIOs had occupied their positions since the area structure was created. Five AIOs would retire in June 2006. An additional five were expected to retire at the end of SY07.

Remarking on the retirements, Janet Knupp, director of a Chicago-based venture philanthropy that made investments to strengthen CPS leadership, observed, "The retirements give the district an opportunity to find the people who fit the newly clarified expectations. A deeper issue remains, however. Is an AIO's job doable? Is it really possible to effectively support more than 20 schools? If it's an impossible task, the system may only be setting the AIOs up to fail."

Providing Better Student Data

CPS took steps to strengthen the district's and schools' capacities to assess student performance over time in SY06. Previously, the district relied solely upon the Iowa Test of Basic Skills (ITBS) to measure individual student growth. However, the ITBS was not aligned with the Illinois state standards or the ISAT and PSAE state assessments. The district discontinued the ITBS in SY06.

Benchmark Assessments: CPS mandated two new commercial "benchmark" assessments in reading: the Dynamic Indicators of Basic Early Literacy Skills (DIBELS) and Learning First. DIBELS assessed first-graders' readiness to read and would be expanded to grades K–2 in probation schools. The Learning First assessment was administered three times per year (October, January, and May) in grades 3–8 and was aligned with the Illinois standards and the ISAT's format and content. The district provided each school with results by student, teacher, grade, and school within 10 days.

Eason-Watkins instituted new "Quarterly Progress Updates" with AIOs to track the results of district schools on the new benchmark assessments. She and Trujillo's team met with three to four neighboring AIOs at a time. AIOs discussed area performance trends and their efforts to help schools identify and target teachers' and students' weaknesses based on results. Commenting on the new meetings, one elementary AIO reflected, "These are problem-solving meetings. Barbara asks tough questions about how we are helping our principals use the data to design professional development for teachers or make curriculum changes based on the results."

All schools, except charters, had to administer DIBELS. In addition, all schools except charters and AMPS had to administer Learning First, although some charters and all 79 AMPS schools voluntarily signed up to use Learning First. Two areas piloted CPS math benchmark assessments, with districtwide adoption planned for SY07.

IMPACT: The district piloted a comprehensive Web-based technology solution, the Instructional Management Program and Communications Tool (IMPACT), in SY06. IMPACT was designed to replace the district's 30-plus year-old Legacy student information system; eliminate many paper-based, manual transactions; and provide a one-stop online curriculum and instruction planning resource for schools. IMPACT would allow the district to track the performance of individual or cohorts of students from year to year for the first time. Districtwide implementation of IMPACT would occur throughout SY07.

Reorganizing the Central Office

We're going to flip the pyramid in CPS this year. When I say flip the pyramid, I'm saying that the job of the central office is to support the schools, not manage them. Principals run schools and we're here to make their job easier and help them succeed in the only place that matters—in the classroom.

—Arne Duncan, August 19, 2005

Business Service Centers: In the fall of 2005, CPS piloted the first of three business service centers (BSCs). Each BSC would serve roughly 200 schools by providing training, monitoring, and support in budgeting, internal accounts, purchasing and contracts, facilities, security, and limited human resources support. Chief Administrative Officer Vitale commented, "I wanted a team out there that felt like they owned and were accountable for a set of schools. This cross-functional team provides one point of contact for schools—no more having to navigate the central office—and will know each school's needs."

Central-Office Reorganization: CPS unveiled a comprehensive reorganization in June 2006. Central-office departments would be oriented to serve five "school customers": early childhood, elementary schools, high schools, AMPS schools, and new/charter schools. Vitale explained the rationale for the reorganization. "It's simple. We wanted the organizational structure—and the way people work—to reflect our beliefs that schools are the unit of change and everyone else serves the schools. Identifying five types of schools reinforces our message that schools are unique and we cannot treat them like 'one-size-fits-all.'"

In fact, the reorganization worked Vitale out of a job by eliminating the chief administrative officer position. Vitale would phase out by the end of 2006. As a result, all departments would report to either Duncan or Eason-Watkins. The central office streamlining would save the district $25 million in administrative costs.

Creating Consistent Accountability Mechanisms

Consistent Performance Measures for All Schools

School Scorecards: The high-school scorecard represented the district's first attempt to rank all schools in Chicago on the same measures (see Exhibit 9). The scorecard was also the first CPS tool for sharing academic and non-academic school performance data with the public. "Parents really drove the design of the new high-school scorecard. It was such a user-friendly tool for promoting transparency around performance that we decided to create one for

elementary schools, too," explained Duncan. The district intended to unveil the elementary scorecard in SY07.

Accountability System to Probation Policy
More broadly, the district revamped its accountability system. Under the accountability system enacted in SY03, any non-charter district school open for more than three years received one of six labels—distinction, excellence, merit, opportunity, challenge, or probation—based on student performance (see Exhibit 6). The distribution of school ratings varied widely across the areas. Absolute performance and gains on the Illinois state tests (ISAT and PSAE) and the Iowa Test of Basic Skills (discontinued in SY06) largely determined a school's performance rating. Chief Accountability Officer Dan Bugler described the system:

> Absolute performance far outweighed gains. We had almost created a permanent underclass of schools that could never get out of probation even if they had been making impressive gains every year, but hadn't yet gotten above 40% of students meeting standards. And once a school had over 50% of students meeting standards, the labels became irrelevant—nothing really different happened if you were a school of merit, excellence, or distinction.

In March 2006, the Board of Education replaced the six-tiered accountability system with a new probation policy. All schools, except charters and Ren10 schools, would earn one of two ratings—probation or non-probation—based on performance and growth on four measures:

Elementary Schools	High Schools
> 40% meet ISAT reading standards	> 30% meet PSAE (composite score)
> 40% meet ISAT math standards	> 60% five-year graduation rate
> 40% meet ISAT science standards	> 35% of students make "gains" on college-ready tests
Student absentee rate < 15 days	Student absentee rate < 15 days

For each indicator, a school earned one point for absolute performance and one point for growth, resulting in a score between 0–8. Schools earning a 0–3 were automatically placed on probation; schools earning 6–8 received a non-probation rating. Schools obtaining a score of 4 or 5 received an initial probation rating, but were subject to an automatic review by the AIO.

Commenting on the new probation policy, Bugler said, "We wanted a consistent way to measure performance of all schools on a broader array of metrics than just test scores. We also wanted to incent progress for schools at all levels and to let AIOs 'make the call' more often as to whether a school really belonged on probation." Of the 226 schools currently on probation, only 150 would have automatically have been placed on probation under the new policy.[6]

Mahaley explained the exemption of charter and Ren10 schools from the new probation policy. "Their five-year performance agreements are rigorous and already provide opportunities for the district to address concerns if necessary, so we did not see the need to add an extra layer," she said.

Performance Evaluation

CPS was in the process of designing several new tools to strengthen performance evaluation at the end of SY06. These included:

- Central-office department evaluations based on annual department performance targets and principals' evaluations of support and service.

- AIO evaluations and bonuses based on area school progress.

- A new principal evaluation tool that included progress toward annual school performance targets as one of the evaluation criteria.

The Challenge Ahead: Putting the Pieces Together

As the school year came to a close in June 2006, Duncan and his leadership team reflected on their efforts to improve student performance. While the district's strategy was clear in their minds, they wondered how well people throughout the system's 617 schools and numerous central office departments understood the strategy. Did most people in CPS see a thread of coherence weaving together the various initiatives underway, or did they see a rush of random activities? The team acknowledged that unless it was able to effectively communicate and manage in a way that put all of the pieces together for everyone in CPS, the district would have a difficult time achieving its 2010 outcome goals.

Notes

1. SY is a PELP convention that denotes "school year." For example, SY06 refers to the 2005–2006 school year.

2. Melissa Roderick, Jenny Nagaoka, Elaine Allensworth, et al., *From High School to the Future,* Consortium on Chicago School Research, April 2006.

3. The number of schools in each category is for SY06 only. The total number of schools listed in this section exceeds 617 because a school could belong to more than one category. For example, Ames Elementary was on probation and in restructuring.

4. Consortium on Chicago School Research.

5. *CPS Instructional Support Options for Elementary and High Schools,* 2006, p. 4.

6. Elizabeth Duffrin, "New probation policy lets more schools off the hook," *Catalyst Chicago,* April 2006.

Exhibit 1

CPS Facts and Figures

CPS Overview

District Area Demographics (Census 2000)

Total population	2,896,016
Per capita income	$20,175
Households below poverty level	17.4%

Student Demographics

Number of students (PK–12)	426,812
African-American	49.8%
Latino	38.0%
White	8.8%
Asian/Pacific Islander	3.2%
Native American	0.2%
Low-income	85.2%
Limited English proficiency students	14.1%
Special education students	13.0%
Graduation rate	70.7%
One-year high-school dropout rate	10.2%
Mobility rate	24.0%

Schools and Staff (Largest district in IL)

Number of schools (including charters)	617
Elementary (PK–8 in various configurations)	511
High school (9–12)	106
Total staff	45,792
Teachers	26,719
Average teacher salary	$62,985
Teacher turnover	10.3%
Pupil/teacher ratios	
Elementary	22.7:1
High school	19.6:1

Sources: Census data available at http://nces.ed.gov/surveys/sdds/
singledemoprofile.asp?county1=1709930&state1=17, accessed May 1,
2006. District data from CPS files.

Exhibit 2

CPS Financial Statements, FY02–FY06

	FY 2002	FY 2003	FY 2004	FY 2005	FY 2006 (estimated)
REVENUES					
Property taxes	$1,479,968	$1,546,335	$1,571,065	$1,639,237	$1,678,328
Replacement taxes	$114,313	$105,960	$120,427	$145,724	$145,724
State aid	$1,467,914	$1,469,567	$1,481,448	$1,507,115	$1,618,678
Federal aid	$554,750	$608,693	$730,504	$762,955	$827,669
Interest and investment income	$68,050	$49,131	$39,501	$43,215	$38,034
Other	$89,505	$94,345	$149,253	$102,654	$123,752
Total Revenues	**$3,774,500**	**$3,874,061**	**$4,092,198**	**$4,200,900**	**$4,432,185**
EXPENDITURES					
Current:					
Instruction	$2,152,958	$2,214,781	$2,355,114	$2,429,014	$2,497,185
Pupil support services	$311,628	$320,380	$327,653	$323,225	$336,504
Administration support services	$148,297	$163,185	$168,563	$151,529	$163,528
Facilities support services	$302,007	$304,300	$291,900	$316,195	$389,533
Instructional support services	$299,807	$296,517	$310,166	$353,859	$431,265
Food services	$160,063	$170,238	$180,588	$173,872	$185,175
Community services	$47,523	$47,253	$49,933	$42,325	$47,144
Teacher's pension/retirement	$65,045	$65,045	$65,045	$65,045	$74,922
Capital outlay	$381,038	$443,873	$365,336	$389,450	$361,881
Debt service	$219,894	$255,239	$259,590	$315,809	$234,977
Other	$5,138	$12,322	$8,128	$5,912	$5,000
Total Expenditures	**$4,093,398**	**$4,293,133**	**$4,382,016**	**$4,566,235**	**$4,727,114**
REVENUES IN EXCESS OF/(LESS THAN) EXPENDITURES	**($318,898)**	**($419,072)**	**($289,818)**	**($365,335)**	**($294,929)**
OTHER FINANCING SOURCES(USES)					
Gross amounts from debt issuances	$232,693	$308,635	$765,995	$524,260	$325,000
Proceeds from notes	$0	$0	$0	$5,500	$0
Premiums	($9)	$8,803	$21,043	$43,450	$0
Payment to refunded bond escrow agent	$0	$0	($534,375)	($282,478)	$0
Transfers in/(out)	$0	$0	$0	$0	$0
Total other financing sources	**$232,684**	**$317,438**	**$252,663**	**$290,732**	**$325,000**
NET CHANGE IN FUND BALANCE	**($86,214)**	**($101,634)**	**($37,155)**	**($74,603)**	**$30,071**
Fund Balances, beginning of period	$1,345,272	$1,259,058	$1,157,424	$1,120,269	$1,045,666
Fund Balances, end of period	$1,259,058	$1,157,424	$1,120,269	$1,045,666	$1,075,737
COMPOSITION OF FUND BALANCE					
Reserved for Debt Service	$459,524	$437,711	$385,015	$294,700	$285,100
Reserved for Capital Projects	$434,400	$390,757	$427,748	$359,973	$354,792
Reserved for Other Purposes	$155,251	$120,597	$110,996	$142,447	$142,447
Unreserved	$209,883	$208,359	$196,510	$248,546	$293,398
Total	**$1,259,058**	**$1,157,424**	**$1,120,269**	**$1,045,666**	**$1,075,737**

Source: CPS Comprehensive Annual Financial Reports 2002–2005. Includes general operating, capital projects, and debt service funds.

Exhibit 3

Elementary Student Achievement Data

Percentage of Students Meeting or Exceeding Standards on the Illinois Standards Achievement Test (grades 3–8, all tests) 2000–2005

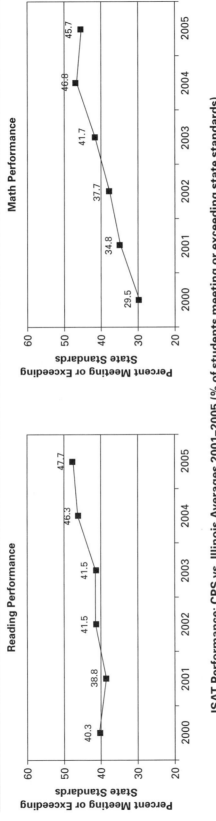

Reading Performance

Math Performance

ISAT Performance: CPS vs. Illinois Averages 2001–2005 (% of students meeting or exceeding state standards)

		Chicago Public Schools						Illinois					
Subject	Grade	2001	2002	2003	2004	2005	2005 to 2001 Change	2001	2002	2003	2004	2005	2005 to 2001 Change
Reading	**3rd**	36.0	35.0	35.8	41.3	42.1	**6.1**	62.0	63.0	62.0	65.0	66.6	**4.6**
	5th	34.0	37.0	38.8	42.7	43.4	**9.4**	59.0	59.0	60.4	60.9	62.8	**3.8**
	8th	48.0	55.0	50.5	54.6	59.4	**11.4**	66.0	68.0	63.7	67.1	72.7	**6.7**
Math	**3rd**	47.0	46.0	48.7	55.7	55.2	**8.2**	74.0	74.0	75.7	79.2	79.2	**5.2**
	5th	32.0	36.0	44.0	50.9	49.6	**17.6**	61.0	63.0	68.3	71.8	73.1	**12.1**
	8th	25.0	31.0	30.7	33.2	32.3	**7.3**	50.0	52.0	53.1	54.4	54.3	**4.3**
Science	**4th**	37.0	39.0	39.5	40.5	43.3	**6.3**	65.0	67.0	66.5	67.8	71.4	**6.4**
	7th	51.0	53.0	56.2	56.0	54.4	**3.4**	72.0	73.0	73.7	74.4	74.6	**2.6**

Source: CPS files.

Exhibit 4a

School Categories in Chicago, SY06

	Regular District	AMPS	CPS Probation	NCLB Restructuring	Charter	Performance	Contract
Number[a]	280	79	226	185	35	3	1 (SY07)
Authorizer	CPS	CPS 2005	CPS 2003	Federal law (NCLB) 2001	State law 1996	Mayor's Ren10 2004	Mayor's Ren10 2004
Operator	CPS	CPS	CPS	CPS or third party	Nonprofit	CPS	Nonprofit
Governance	LSC	LSC	LSC	LSC	Charter board	Board or LSC	Board or LSC
Student Assignment	Neighborhood unless selective	Neighborhood unless selective	Neighborhood unless selective	Neighborhood unless selective	Lottery	Lottery	Lottery
NCLB and IL Accountability	Yes	Yes	Yes	Yes	Yes	Yes	Yes
CPS Probation Policy	Yes	Yes	Yes	Yes	No	No	No
5-yr CPS Performance Plan and Annual Review	No	No	No	No	Yes	Yes	Yes
CPS Scorecard	Yes	Yes	Yes	Yes	Yes	Yes	Yes
CPS Annual Targets	Yes	Yes	Yes	Yes	No	Yes	Yes
CPS SIPAAA[b]	Yes	Yes	Yes	Yes	No	Yes	Yes
Report to AIO	Yes	Choice	Yes	Yes	No	Choice	Choice
Principal Eligibility	State Type 75, CPS Pool	State Type 75, CPS Pool	State Type 75, CPS Pool	State Type 75, CPS Pool	State Type 75	State Type 75, CPS Pool	State Type 75
Principal Hired by	LSC	LSC	LSC unless removed by CPS	LSC	Governing board	Governing board	Governing board

Exhibit 4a (continued)

	Regular District	AMPS	CPS Probation	NCLB Restructuring	Charter	Performance	Contract
Principal Evaluator	LSC, AIO	LSC, AIO if in-area	LSC, AIO	LSC, AIO	Governing board	Governing board	Governing board
CPS Curriculum Mandates Followed	Yes	Choice	Yes	Yes	No	Choice	Choice
CPS Benchmark Tests: Learning 1st, DIBELS	Yes	Yes	Yes	Yes	No	Yes	Yes
School Funding	Position-based	Position-based Lump-sum in SY07[c]	Position-based AIO controlled discretionary funds	Position-based	Per-pupil	Per-pupil	Per-pupil
CPS School Calendar and Hours	Yes	Choice	Yes	Yes	No	Choice	Choice
Teacher Certification Required	100%	100%	100%	100%	75% in schools established before 2003; 50% after	100%	100%
Teachers' Employer	CPS	CPS	CPS	CPS	Governing board	CPS	Governing board
CTU Teachers	Yes	Yes	Yes	Yes	No	Yes	Choice
CPS Salary Scale Required	Yes	Yes	Yes	Yes	No	Yes	No

Source: Casewriter analysis based on case interviews and CPS files.

a The number of schools in each category is for SY06 only. The total number of schools in this row will exceed 617 because a school could be in more than one category. For example, Marconi Community Academy was on CPS probation and slated for restructuring under NCLB.

b SIPAAA stands for School Improvement Plan for Advancing Academic Achievement. (SIPAAA is described on page 7.)

c "Lump-sum" budgeting is described on page 9.

Exhibit 4b

Performance Data by School Category: Elementary Schools

School Type	Total Enrollment 2005	Attendance Rate 2005	ISAT Reading % Meet/Exceed Standards			ISAT Math % Meet/Exceed Standards		
			2003	2004	2005	2003	2004	2005
All Elementary Schools								
High	1906	98.5	100.0	100.1	100.0	100.0	100.0	100.0
Median	602	94.2	38.7	44.6	46.6	39.4	47.3	46.7
Low	91	85.5	0.0	11.5	13.0	0.0	11.5	8.2
Regular District Schools								
High	1896	98.5	100.0	100.1	100.0	100.0	100.0	100.0
Median	595	95.2	51.1	55.0	57.3	55.4	59.7	58.3
Low	120	88.7	0.0	11.5	18.3	0.0	11.5	16.5
AMPS								
High	1796	97.7	96.9	100.0	97.8	99.0	100.0	100.0
Median	589	95.8	62.5	65.6	64.4	62.0	67.9	69.7
Low	186	93.7	26.8	35.4	42.1	30.1	43.3	44.2
CPS Probation								
High	1822	96.4	51.7	50.0	53.7	51.3	81.5	63.6
Median	613	92.1	29.3	32.4	32.7	28.8	29.7	28.3
Low	91	88.6	6.9	15.6	13.0	7.5	12.6	8.2
NCLB Restructuring								
High	1906	96.2	57.4	60.4	68.1	55.2	81.5	57.1
Median	598	92.2	28.2	32.2	33.2	28.0	29.8	28.6
Low	91	85.5	6.9	15.6	13.0	7.5	12.6	9.4
Charter								
High	n/a	n/a	59.7	66.7	81.0	62.0	68.2	93.3
Median	n/a	n/a	51.5	49.3	64.7	48.1	63.3	69.3
Low	n/a	n/a	33.3	36.3	40.4	36.2	22.2	29.2

Source: Casewriter analysis based on CPS files.

Notes: "All Elementary Schools" includes charter schools and other schools not eligible for probation, such as new and special education schools. Therefore, values may be lower than "probation" and different from any district reported data that excludes these schools. Some schools may be in more than one category (e.g., Marconi Community Academy was on CPS probation and slated for NCLB restructuring). Data not available for performance and contract schools.

Exhibit 4c
Performance Data by School Category: High Schools

School Type	Total Enrollment 2005	Attendance Rate 2005	% Freshmen On Track to Graduate 2005	5-year Graduation Rate 2005	1-year Dropout Rate 2005	PSAE Reading % Meet/Exceed Standards			PSAE Math % Meet/Exceed Standards		
						2003	2004	2005	2003	2004	2005
All High Schools											
High	4214	97.8	100.0	94.1	31.3	99.1	98.0	99.0	98.1	99.5	98.5
Median	1088	86.5	57.4	54.8	8.0	23.8	24.1	28.7	13.5	14.9	10.0
Low	66	68.6	2.9	4.8	0.0	6.5	4.1	10.8	0.0	1.8	0.0
Regular District Schools											
High	2152	97.8	100.0	75.2	31.3	58.1	77.5	70.8	50.5	64.7	64.3
Median	606	85.4	58.8	59.1	7.5	34.1	29.1	31.0	24.3	24.2	8.1
Low	66	68.6	2.9	4.8	0.0	6.5	4.1	10.8	0.0	3.1	1.3
AMPS											
High	4214	96.6	97.4	94.1	8.0	99.1	98.0	99.0	98.1	99.5	98.5
Median	859	93.3	83.9	80.6	2.8	76.1	82.7	84.0	67.6	71.8	66.4
Low	513	89.8	65.6	61.3	0.4	37.0	39.0	46.7	26.0	24.0	21.5
CPS Probation											
High	2735	91.2	77.5	71.0	22.8	40.2	37.5	48.3	33.6	32.9	29.6
Median	1375	85.2	51.1	50.9	11.6	18.2	18.8	23.9	8.8	9.7	7.9
Low	306	72.0	34.1	27.4	0.2	7.3	9.7	12.2	1.1	1.8	0.0
NCLB Restructuring											
High	2523	90.3	66.0	56.9	20.5	23.7	20.6	25.0	12.9	19.7	16.4
Median	1079	83.5	47.4	48.2	12.7	14.0	15.1	20.0	6.6	7.8	5.5
Low	514	72.0	34.1	27.4	7.4	8.8	9.7	15.2	1.1	1.8	0.5
Charter											
High	473	95.3 n/a		78.6	6.1	41.6	56.1	53.9	26.3	37.4	51.0
Median	328	94.6 n/a		76.1	3.8	23.8	24.1	30.4	14.3	14.9	10.0
Low	155	90.8 n/a		48.9	1.4	11.5	16.1	22.4	1.3	6.5	6.1

Source: Casewriter analysis based on CPS files.

Notes: "All High Schools" includes charter schools and other schools not eligible for probation, such as new and special education schools. Therefore, values may be lower than "probation" and different from any district reported data that excludes these schools. Some schools may be in more than one category (e.g., Crane Technical High was on CPS probation and slated for NCLB restructuring). Six of the 10 AMPS high schools used academic admissions criteria ("selective-enrollment"). Data not available for performance and contract schools.

Exhibit 5

AMPS Criteria

Autonomous Management and Performance Schools (AMPS)
2005–06 Year Eligibility Overview

Elementary Eligibility: Schools that have met most of the eligibility factors and have been recommended by the Chief Education Office are invited to participate in this program.

Indicator		Time Period	Rationale
Student Performance Indicators			
1.	Made AYP	2004 rating for 2004–05 school year	Schools making AYP are not subject to federal sanctions.
2.	Not in NCLB school improvement	2004 rating for 2004–05 school year	Schools not in NCLB School Improvement are not subject to federal sanctions.
3.	Schools of excellence, distinction, merit, and opportunity (see Exhibit 6 in this case)	2004 rating for 2004–05 school year	Schools have high or improving student performance indicators and are not subject to CPS Probation sanctions.
Asset Management Indicators			
4.	At least 97% of teachers are highly qualified by NCLB standards	Fall 2004 EQS audit	Shows schools with fully certified teachers who are teaching in their fields.
5.	"Excellent" or "adequate" custodial report	FY2004 and FY2003	Shows school has consistent record of maintaining clean, orderly buildings and grounds.
6.	Above average internal accounts ratings or no rating	Most recent data available	A rating of financial management.
7.	No major control violations	FY2004 and FY2005	A rating of financial management.
8.	Enrollment audit variance less than or equal to 10 students compared to enrollment reported on student information system	Fall 2004 Enrollment Audits	Indicator of school records management.
9.	Elementary daily attendance >= 95%	2003–04 school year	Indicates school does not need to spend extensive amount of time tracking student absences.
10.	Residing not attending <50% or utilization > 80%	2003–04 school year	Shows schools where children are choosing to attend or attending outside of their neighborhoods because the schools are at or above capacity.
Special Education Indicators			
11.	90% of students immunized	2004–05 school year	Standard set by State of Illinois.
12.	% LRE 3 <=30% or % LRE 3<= low incidence	2004–05 school year	Indicates school does not assign excessive number of students to self-contained special education classrooms.
13.	No major violation or citations from IL State Board of Education		

Exhibit 5 (continued)

CEdO Recommendation

Rationale: Data and indicators cannot capture all aspects of school climate and success. Representatives from the Chief Education Office work with schools on a daily basis and have greater insight into schools than what can be derived from the data points alone.

AMPS
High-School Eligibility

The same as above except:
- **Asset Management**
  - For Highly Qualified percent, using high-school average
  - 28-student variation for Enrollment Audit
- **School Climate**
  - Includes: Truancy <= high-school average
  - Includes: Dropout rate <=high-school average
  - Removes: Residing Not Attending as an indicator

Source: CPS files.

Exhibit 6

CPS Accountability System, 2003–March 2006

Accountability Ratings for Elementary Schools Based on Level of Achievement and Progress Level			
Overall level of achievement on the ITBS or ISAT:	**Progress Level**		
	Does Not Meet	**Meets**	**Exceeds**
Level I: Above 70% or more**	**Schools of Excellence**		**Schools of Distinction**
Level II: 50% - 69.9% **	**Schools of Merit**		
Level III: 40% - 49.9% **	**Schools of Opportunity**		
Overall level of achievement on the ITBS and ISAT:	**Less than 10 point Improvement**	**10 point Improvement**	
Level IV: Both Below 40%	**Schools on Probation**	**Schools of Challenge**	

**Does not apply for schools already on probation in 2003/2004 school year

Legend	
School of Excellence: A school in which 70 percent or more of its students score at or above the ITBS national norms in reading or meet or exceed the state standards on the ISAT composite (Achievement Level I school)and has either a meets or a does not meet progress rating based on its progress on four measures.	**School of Distinction:** A school that has at least 50 percent or more of its students scoring at or above the ITBS national norms in reading or meet or exceed standards on the ISAT composite and has earned an exceeds progress rating based on its progress on four measures
School of Merit: A school in which between 50 and less than 70 percent of its students score at or above the ITBS national norms in reading or meet or exceed the state standards on the ISAT composite (Achievement Level II school) and has either a meets or a does not meet progress rating based on its progress on four measures.	

School of Opportunity:
A school in which between 40 and less than 50 percent of its students score at or above the ITBS national norms in reading or meet or exceed the state standards on the ISAT composite.

School of Challenge:
A school that has a Level IV Achievement Level, but has made academic progress by:
a. Increasing the percent of students scoring at or above the national norm on the ITBS reading by a total of at least 10 percentage points over the last two years with positive improvement in each year, or
b. Increasing the percent of students meeting or exceeding state standards on the ISAT composite by a total of at least 10 percentage points over the last two years with positive improvement in each year, or
c. Increasing in any combination the percent of students scoring at or above the national norm on the ITBS reading and the percent of students meeting or exceeding state standards on the ISAT composite by a total of 10 percentage points in the last year with positive improvement on each test.

School on Probation:
A school that has a Level IV Achievement Level and has not made academic progress as defined under Schools of Challenge.

Source: CPS files.

Note: CPS used the same accountability ratings for high schools. The cut-points for student performance on the Prairie State Achievement Exam (PSAE) were: Level 1, Above 60%; Level II, 40%–59.9%; Level III, 30%–39.9%; and Level IV, Below 30%.

Exhibit 7
CPS 2010 Outcome Goals

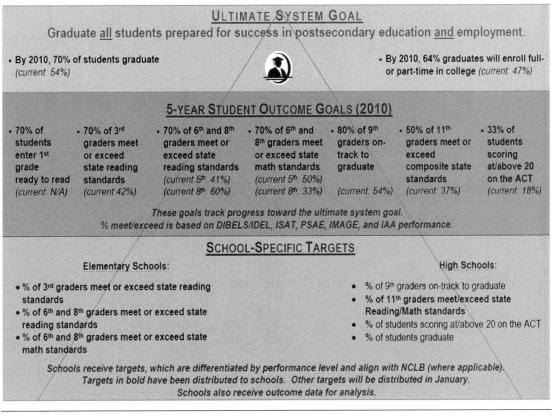

ULTIMATE SYSTEM GOAL
Graduate all students prepared for success in postsecondary education and employment.

- **By 2010, 70% of students graduate** *(current: 54%)*

- **By 2010, 64% graduates will enroll full- or part-time in college** *(current: 47%)*

5-YEAR STUDENT OUTCOME GOALS (2010)

- 70% of students enter 1st grade ready to read *(current: N/A)*
- 70% of 3rd graders meet or exceed state reading standards *(current 42%)*
- 70% of 6th and 8th graders meet or exceed state reading standards *(current 5th: 41%) (current 8th: 60%)*
- 70% of 6th and 8th graders meet or exceed state math standards *(current 5th: 50%) (current 8th: 33%)*
- 80% of 9th graders on-track to graduate *(current: 54%)*
- 50% of 11th graders meet or exceed composite state standards *(current: 37%)*
- 33% of students scoring at/above 20 on the ACT *(current: 18%)*

These goals track progress toward the ultimate system goal.
% meet/exceed is based on DIBELS/IDEL, ISAT, PSAE, IMAGE, and IAA performance.

SCHOOL-SPECIFIC TARGETS

Elementary Schools:

- **% of 3rd graders meet or exceed state reading standards**
- **% of 6th and 8th graders meet or exceed state reading standards**
- **% of 6th and 8th graders meet or exceed state math standards**

High Schools:

- % of 9th graders on-track to graduate
- % of 11th graders meet/exceed state Reading/Math standards
- % of students scoring at/above 20 on the ACT
- % of students graduate

Schools receive targets, which are differentiated by performance level and align with NCLB (where applicable).
Targets in bold have been distributed to schools. Other targets will be distributed in January.
Schools also receive outcome data for analysis.

Source: CPS files.

Exhibit 8

AMPS Autonomies and School Selections by Area

Area	No. of AMPS Schools	Restructured Day	New Teacher Induction	Curriculum	Autonomous School (out of area)	After School	Self-directed	Budget Transfers	Attendance Plan	School Calendar	SIPAAA
1	12	8%	83%	83%	33%	75%	50%	92%	92%	17%	83%
2	7	63%	38%	50%	63%	63%	63%	75%	75%	50%	88%
4	1	100%	0%	0%	0%	100%	0%	100%	0%	0%	100%
5	1	0%	0%	100%	0%	100%	100%	100%	100%	100%	100%
6	7	100%	57%	100%	0%	100%	57%	57%	86%	57%	100%
9	3	100%	67%	100%	33%	67%	100%	100%	100%	67%	100%
10	5	100%	20%	100%	100%	80%	100%	100%	100%	100%	100%
11	7	86%	100%	86%	86%	100%	43%	100%	100%	86%	86%
12	4	100%	100%	100%	100%	75%	50%	100%	100%	75%	100%
13	1	0%	0%	0%	0%	0%	100%	100%	0%	0%	0%
15	5	20%	60%	60%	0%	80%	40%	80%	60%	20%	100%
16	6	50%	50%	17%	50%	50%	50%	67%	67%	50%	67%
17	5	0%	20%	40%	100%	0%	0%	80%	0%	0%	0%
18	5	20%	60%	0%	0%	80%	80%	80%	80%	0%	0%
19	2	100%	100%	100%	100%	100%	50%	100%	100%	100%	100%
20	2	100%	50%	100%	100%	100%	100%	100%	100%	100%	100%
21	2	100%	50%	100%	100%	100%	100%	100%	100%	100%	100%
22	2	100%	50%	100%	0%	100%	50%	50%	100%	100%	100%
24	2	50%	50%	100%	0%	0%	100%	100%	100%	50%	100%
Total	**79**	**59%**	**60%**	**72%**	**50%**	**74%**	**60%**	**87%**	**82%**	**51%**	**81%**

1. **Restructured day:** Choose own dates for quarterly professional development days. Other district schools had to follow a set schedule of half-days, known as "restructured days."

2. **New teacher induction:** Opt out of district's program, receive $800 per new teacher, and design own program.

3. **Curriculum:** Opt out of districtwide curriculum initiatives (e.g., Reading 3-D progress monitoring tool for 1st grade).

4. **Autonomous school:** Opt out of the area (walkthroughs, principal meetings, access to area coaches).

5. **After school:** More flexibility in the hours, course content, and budget allocation for after-school program.

6. **Self-directed:** Assume responsibility for school operations and maintenance (e.g., contracting vendors directly instead of going through central office).

7. **Budget transfers:** Transfer money across line items without asking for area-level approval.

8. **Attendance plan:** Design own plan to increase attendance instead of following the district's plan.

9. **School calendar:** Set school year calendar, including breaks. (Most holidays are set by state law.)

10. **School improvement plan for advancing academic achievement (SIPAAA):** All IL schools are required by the state to submit a SIPAAA. AMPS schools were able to manage the planning process on their own without AIO oversight and thus were able to complete a shorter document.

Source: CPS files.

Note: There were no AMPS schools in Areas 3, 7, 8, 14, and 23.

Exhibit 9

High-School Scorecard for Kenwood Academy

Kenwood Academy
5015 South Blackstone Avenue · Chicago, IL 60615 · (773) 535-1350
SCHOOL SCORECARD

Data reflects 9-12 enrollment.
Total Membership: 1,684
% ELL Membership: 0.4
% Special Education: 10.3

	Score	CPS Rank	Trends & Benchmarks
STUDENT OUTCOMES			
Freshman Graduating in Five Years	64%	16 of 58	63 (2003) 67 (2004) 64 (2005)
Graduates Enrolled in College or Post-Secondary Education	55%	11 of 62	--
Employment Success (Under construction, available Fall 2006)	--	--	--
ACADEMIC PROGRESS			
Average ACT	18.6	6 of 69	Illinois Average - 19.9
Students Making Expected Gains	48%	6 of 70	--
Meet/Exceed PSAE State Standards	43%	6 of 69	37 (2003) 41 (2004) 43 (2005)
Students Enrolled in Advanced Placement Classes	8%	9 of 52	--
Students Scoring 3+ on Advanced Placement Exams	30%	15 of 27	--
Freshman On-Track to Graduate	65%	21 of 70	61 (2003) 62 (2004) 65 (2005)
Made NCLB Adequate Yearly Progress	No	--	--
STUDENT CONNECTION			
Average Days Absent per Student	20.2	32 of 81	--
Participation in Extracurricular Activities (Under construction, available Fall 2006)	--	--	--
Safe and Respectful School Climate (Under construction, available Fall 2006)	--	--	--
High Expectations and Support (Under construction, available Fall 2006)	--	--	--
SCHOOL CHARACTERISTICS			
Highly Qualified Teachers	84%	40 of 76	--
Average Days Absent per Teacher (Under construction, available Fall 2006)	--	--	--
School Cleanliness (Under construction, available Fall 2006)	--	--	--

Source: CPS files.

Exhibit 10

AIO Job Description, SY06

Principal Accountabilities for AIOs	Weight
1. Assist area principals to develop data-based school plans for improving instruction aligned with district goals and strategies. Help principals identify and utilize the support and resources necessary to successfully implement their school plans.	70%
2. Supervise and evaluate all area principals against established performance targets. Based on the evaluations, provide principals with opportunities for professional development that build on strengths and address weaknesses. When necessary, recommend principal removal to the chief executive officer. Facilitate conversations and collaboration among principals to address common challenges and share best practices.	
3. Assist area principals in planning, coordinating, and delivering school-based teacher professional development. Coordinate the delivery of district- and area-based professional development and other instructional support to area schools.	
4. Identify and support the development of potential candidates for the principalship in area schools. Lead principal succession planning, working with Local School Councils to help them identify and hire the best possible principals.	30%

Source: CPS files.

DISCUSSION QUESTIONS

1. What is the districtwide strategy in San Francisco? Assess the degree to which the STAR Schools Initiative is coherent with the districtwide strategy.

2. Evaluate the process the SFUSD team used to design and implement STAR. What worked well in the process? Why? What could have gone better?

3. What are the key elements of STAR that allow for differentiation between schools? Which elements are designed to achieve integration across schools? What are the strengths and limitations of the various elements of the intervention?

4. Has the program been successful so far? What is your evidence? What advice would you give the San Francisco team about STAR going forward? Be specific.

Stacey Childress ■ Jennifer M. Suesse

The STAR Schools Initiative at the San Francisco Unified School District

Early one morning in spring of 2006, Christine Hiroshima sat at her desk enjoying a rare moment of peace and quiet. As chief academic officer of the San Francisco Unified School District (SFUSD) since 2004, Hiroshima was responsible for the academic programs in the district's 107 schools, which served over 56,000 students (Exhibit 1). Hiroshima had one thing on her mind that day: how to continue improving student outcomes at the district's chronically underperforming schools.

The improvement of low-performing schools was the subject of national conversation and policy. State and federal accountability systems, including No Child Left Behind, imposed various sanctions on chronically failing schools. School leaders across the country were struggling to improve student outcomes in such schools. Observers could point to isolated school turnarounds but could find no example of an urban district achieving excellence across its entire system.

In San Francisco, underperforming schools had received close attention since a 1983 court ruling that SFUSD unconstitutionally "engaged in discriminatory practices and maintained a segregated school system."[1] In response, district leaders over the years had tried a variety of improvement strategies to address issues of achievement and equity across the city. Launched in fall of 2001, "Students and Teachers Achieving Results" (STAR) was the most recent effort and a critical piece of the district's "Excellence for All" strategy. STAR realigned district resources by providing struggling schools with a package of targeted services that included additional school personnel, central office support and oversight, and instructional resources that were often absent in low-income schools.

By 2005, the STAR program had generated promising results in many, but not all, of the 44 participating schools (Exhibit 2). Hiroshima knew her team needed a deeper understanding of the strengths and limitations of the intervention if they were to transform all of the district's chronically underperforming schools into beacons of excellence.

Developing a Coherent Strategy: "Excellence for All"[2]

In summer of 2000, the SFUSD Board of Education appointed Dr. Arlene Ackerman superintendent of schools following a nationwide search. With over 30 years of experience in public education as a teacher, principal, and deputy superintendent, Ackerman had most recently been the superintendent of the public school system in Washington, D.C. She articulated five core beliefs intended to guide the work of all stakeholders on behalf of SFUSD students: (1) children come first; (2) parents are our partners; (3) victory is in the classroom; (4) leadership and accountability are the keys to our success; and (5) it takes the entire community to ensure the success of all students.

Since 1983, SFUSD had operated under a consent decree, managed by a federal judge, that required the district to meet educational equity targets for all students. Upon her arrival, Ackerman appointed an educational equity committee to advise her on ways to respond more effectively to the requirements of the consent decree. The committee included members from SFUSD central and school staff, parents, board members, community leaders, and union leadership.

The committee found that the achievement gap between African-American and Latino students and their white and Chinese counterparts was widening. After controlling for student and school characteristics in 10 years of standardized test data, the committee demonstrated that African-American and Latino students as a group scored lower than other SFUSD ethnic groups, regardless of poverty or other factors. The educational equity committee reported that substantial numbers of SFUSD teachers and administra-

tors had lower expectations for African-American and Latino students and that some schools used a "dumbed-down" curriculum for these students. To address these findings, the committee put forth recommendations that were incorporated into a districtwide strategy for improvement. Ackerman and her team developed a five-year plan dubbed "Excellence for All" that included the input of over 3,000 teachers, parents, and other community members, who attended public input sessions and school meetings to discuss the plan.

The "Excellence for All" strategy focused on academic achievement for all students, the equitable allocation of district resources, and accountability for results. It included concrete actions to support the strategy, including giving parents a choice about where their children attended school, creating classrooms all over the city in which teachers had high expectations for all learners, and placing decisions about and accountability for instructional programs and the resources to support them in the hands of school communities. After obtaining unanimous board approval, Ackerman submitted the plan to the federal judge monitoring the consent decree in April 2001. The judge approved the 231-page document as SFUSD's plan to meet the mandates of the consent decree, and implementation of "Excellence for All" became a legal requirement (Exhibit 3).

To implement "Excellence for All" at the school level, SFUSD developed a weighted student formula (WSF) that attached a variable dollar amount to every student based on his or her learning needs. Each year principals received revenue based on their actual student enrollment and then conducted an academic planning process with their school-site councils (SSCs). Principals worked with SSCs to develop performance targets and an academic plan that was responsive to their students' achievement data from the prior year. Principals and SSCs then created budgets that allocated available resources to specific activities in their academic plans. All principals were evaluated annually on the achievement of their schools' performance targets and their management of staff, stakeholders, and financial resources.

A Star Is Born

One Friday afternoon in June 2001, Ackerman and then Chief Academic Officer Elois Brooks were discussing the persistent challenge of improving student achievement at the district's lowest-performing schools with an outside expert in grant funding, Dr. Mitzi Beach. Even though "Excellence for All" was a comprehensive strategy, Ackerman and Brooks believed that the district needed a specific intervention to adapt the strategy to the needs of chronically underperforming schools. Brooks was an experienced public educator who had arrived in San Francisco only a few months earlier when Ackerman persuaded her to join the SFUSD leadership team. Brooks explained: "I had never been a chief academic officer before, but I had been a principal. So, when I arrived in San Francisco, I asked myself, 'What would I want the Chief Academic Office to do if I were still a principal?' I didn't have any role models or firsthand examples, but I knew I wanted to focus on supporting schools, especially those that were struggling."

As the conversation continued on that Friday, Brooks walked around the third floor encouraging others to join their emerging analysis of root causes of poor performance in schools. She wanted to ensure that those with longer tenures in the district could contribute their "institutional knowledge" to the design of the intervention. "Dr. Beach's presence was also essential," Brooks recalled, "because she helped us figure out how to finance our plans from the moment they emerged. Arlene and I had worked with Mitzi in Washington, and she knew how to work with categorical and grant money." Ritu Khanna from the Data Planning and Research Department and Chief of School Operations Deborah Sims were among those who joined the conversation. Sims remembered:

> Elois marched right into Ritu and said, "Please get me the trend data on these schools we've identified. We've got to do something. There are just too many schools that are failing, or at least too many not making the accelerated gains that are needed. Let's go right now." We spent the rest of the day defining the elements of a successful school and the barriers that prevent success. We knew the most important element of a successful school is a principal who is a strong instructional leader—someone who understands how to really move a school forward academically. We assessed whether there were strong instructional leaders in each school. In places where there wasn't strong leadership, developing a strategy for filling that void became the most important element of the reform effort.

Ackerman added:

> I knew we could not approach each school separately, so we started to brainstorm about what issues these struggling schools had in common. I wanted us to talk not only about what the schools needed to change, but also what *we* needed to be doing differently at central office. I was looking for a systemic approach that would support rather than punish schools that were struggling to improve.

The discussion focused on core issues such as helping young and inexperienced teachers improve their practice, getting substitutes to travel to low-income neighborhoods, developing school leaders, and expanding access to extended learning opportunities. For Sims and Khanna, this was an opportunity to share what they had learned from prior efforts in low-performing schools in SFUSD.

Consent Decree: First, they discussed the legacy of the initial consent decree. The 1983 ruling demanded that SFUSD focus its attention on certain neighborhoods where discrimination and segregation appeared to be the worst. The consent decree included a four-phase implementation plan and named six schools ("Phase I schools") to be reconstituted immediately in the 1983–1984 school year. Reconstitution aimed at transforming the school environment by removing and replacing the existing school team (including administration, faculty, and staff). Plans for the Phase I schools were specific and well funded, while plans for an additional 19 schools to be included in the later phases, II–IV, were more vague. In 1992 a court-appointed "committee of experts" found, "Phase I schools had achieved statistically significant gains in student achievement for targeted students. Such gains were not consistently found in Phase II through IV schools."[3] In reviewing this analysis in June 2001, the team concluded that to be successful at scale the new intervention needed to be simultaneous, comprehensive, well organized, and coherent across multiple sites.

Comprehensive School Improvement Program (CSIP): The second intervention they discussed was CSIP, a court-ordered response to the 1992 committee's report that required "that 'low achieving targeted schools outside Phase I be reconstituted' and that the District 'annually reconstitute at least three schools every year till the task is completed.'"[4] To assist low-performing schools prior to reconstitution, CSIP included a one-year intervention that provided targeted schools with resources. If its year-end evaluation showed no improvement, a school could be reconstituted. Only a few schools were actually reconstituted in the mid-1990s, but CSIP was poorly received, and Sims and Khanna recalled that it was ineffective in improving performance. In contrast to reforms during Phase I of the consent decree, the term "reconstitution" took on negative connotations during CSIP.

From their review of CSIP, the team concluded that one-year interventions had little effect; therefore they needed a multiyear plan to support low-performing schools.

Immediate Intervention Underperforming Schools Program (II/USP): In 1999, the state of California began to involve itself in the challenge of low-performing schools through an initiative dubbed II/USP. SFUSD applied for state-funded planning grants of $50,000 per school under the program and received funding for 13 schools. As part of developing school improvement plans, the state required the district to collect feedback from schools regarding common obstacles to improvement, from which SFUSD identified five key barriers:

1. High percentage of inexperienced teachers at II/USP schools

2. Lack of implementation of standards-based instruction

3. Limitations on use/availability/management of state and federal funds

4. Disproportionate number of targeted students concentrated in the II/USP schools

5. Lack of coordination of instructional support programs, resources, operations, and services[5]

Khanna recalled:

> I assumed leadership of the Data Planning and Support Department only a few months before we joined the II/USP process. The exercise of developing plans informed by an analysis of the barriers—both on the district and school side—was a key factor in establishing our approach to low-performing schools. The state grant also provided money to hire an external evaluator, which gave us a way to create accountability for this work, and established a precedent of using research-based strategies for reform.

Dee Dee Desmond, a former principal at a Phase I consent decree school who worked with Khanna on the planning and implementation of II/USP and would subsequently take a lead role in implementing the STAR program, noted, "While staff was initially skeptical towards the CSIP programs because of reconstitution, the II/USP effort included resources for schools. We were able to begin working with a small group of low-performing schools to address both site and central office barriers to improvement."

Applying the Lessons of the Past

As the design team discussed these experiences, they concluded that they could design a program to draw on the things they had learned. They agreed that their new approach should avoid attaching a negative label to low-performing schools and should focus on deploying targeted resources to address specific barriers to performance at schools as well as the central office. The team named the program "Students and Teachers Achieving Results" to signal the focus on school-level supports and to attach a positive label to the new initiative. Brooks reminisced, "Most of the ideas of STAR emerged on that one day. I remember going home that evening feeling good about our work."

Over the next few weeks, the team sketched out the vision for the STAR program, drawing on their collective experiences as principals, administrators, parents, and teachers. They agreed on an overall goal "to increase student achievement at underperforming schools by providing targeted intervention at the school sites" and articulated four core beliefs as a foundation for the work:

- An underperforming school can become a school with high student achievement.

- Strong leadership at the school site is a key component to whole school change.

- Central office must position resources to support principals' development as instructional leaders.

- Underperforming schools commonly have similar issues and concerns. Likewise, successful schools share core elements that are linked to student achievement.

Selecting the STAR Schools

The STAR program had a broad set of criteria that qualified schools for entry. Rather than attempting to narrow the pool of candidates, Khanna explained, "We didn't just take the lowest-performing schools according to one measure but adopted a multiple-measures approach to the selection process." Thirty-nine elementary, middle, and high schools entered the program in fall of 2001 having met one or more of three eligibility criteria: participation in the II/USP program; an Academic Performance Index (API) score in the first, second, or third decile; and failure to meet no more than one of the performance targets in the annual principal evaluation process.

The team believed that no single intervention would be sufficient to address the myriad challenges facing underperforming schools. Based on school-level data and research about how to improve underperforming schools, the group defined three categories of interventions: additional school personnel, additional instructional resources, and additional district support. These interventions aimed to improve teaching and learning by increasing school, principal, parent, student, and teacher capacity simultaneously. Eventually, the design team's understanding of the chain of causality between each part of the intervention and improved outcomes was crystallized in a concept model for the program (Exhibit 4).

Additional School Personnel

After determining the total resources available, the design team decided to fund a total of five additional positions at each STAR school: an instructional reform facilitator, a long-term substitute, a parent liaison, an advisor in elementary and middle schools, and a learning support consultant. Some STAR roles would be part time and others full time, according to the demands of each role and funding limitations. The team articulated the performance barrier each role was designed to address, assigned school-site and district office responsibilities, and established successful school outcomes for each position. Although the program would be modified as implementation began, the purpose of each position and intervention was established from the outset. Desmond explained, "We believed that the school site was the critical place for change. Monies were designated to address certain common challenges that prevented low-performing schools from improving."

Instructional Reform Facilitators: Over the years, budget cuts had eliminated the traditional assistant principal positions in K–8 schools throughout the district, leaving principals with sole responsibility over school operations, student behavior management, and instructional leadership decisions. The team created the role of instructional reform facilitator to address challenges created by the overwhelming demands on principals' time that could distract from instructional improvement.

Affectionately known within SFUSD as "IRFs" (rhymes with "smurfs"), these individuals were responsible for facilitating all aspects of reform at the school site and for establishing a focus on curricular alignment and instructional improvement at the classroom level. Desmond said, "The role of the instructional reform facilitator was based on research that says in low-performing schools high faculty and administrator turnover leads to teachers that are underprepared to deliver instruction. So the IRF plays two key roles, both of which are outlined in their job description—instructional coach and change coach." Sims added:

> The IRF is an individual who is responsible on a daily basis for leading the instructional program, supporting and coaching teachers—a person

who has a deep knowledge base of pedagogy, instruction, and curriculum and therefore can support teacher growth by modeling effective instruction and facilitating meaningful professional development. Therefore, we were interested in IRF candidates with a minimum of five years of successful teaching experience, who understood teaching and learning and who were highly respected by their colleagues. The principal's role as the educational leader is to provide leadership by modeling, organizing, and creating the environment and conditions for rigorous learning and achievement to occur.

The district negotiated special status for IRFs (teachers on special assignment) with the teachers' union by clarifying that they would play no role in the formal evaluation of their peers. Principals were informed about the creation of the IRF role in July and asked to quickly recommend a candidate for the position from their staffs. Thirty-nine IRFs were hired by the district in August, most of whom had been recommended by their principals. Each IRF held appropriate state teaching credentials, at least five years of teaching experience, professional development and group facilitation experience, at least two years of leadership experience with school reform,[6] experience working with diverse populations, and the ability to communicate with multiple stakeholders.

Long-Term Substitutes: For some STAR schools, procuring substitutes was difficult because many teachers were reluctant to travel to neighborhoods in which these schools were located. To address this problem, the team assigned a long-term substitute to each STAR school. The goal was to minimize missed learning opportunities for students and provide continuity in the school community, since these teachers would be permanently staffed to individual sites.

Parent Liaisons: Under the supervision of their principal and the director of parent relations at central office, parent liaisons worked to increase parent, family, and community involvement on the assumption that parent involvement was an untapped resource in most low-performing schools. Their role was to raise parents' expectations about their child's potential for academic achievement, to educate parents to assist their children to be successful in school, to partner with parents to close the achievement gap, and to help schools provide better information for parents in order to encourage communication with parents and families.

Advisors: Because elementary and middle schools lacked staff who could focus exclusively on minimizing truancy and negative student behavior, STAR redefined school-based counselor roles that had previously focused on reactive discipline. Called an advisor, this more proactive role would assist with the development and implementation of activities to promote positive relationships among students, parents and families, community representatives, and school personnel.

Learning Support Consultants: The team considered staffing schools with tutors but chose instead to create a learning support consultant position. These individuals were tasked with helping to link school climates with assisting socially and emotionally challenged students with behavioral issues. Some learning support consultants were nurses, and they reported to the school health department.

Instructional Resources and District Support

Instructional Resources: STAR schools were also granted access to financial and material resources that were often missing from underperforming schools. These included test-preparation packets; an extra $150 for supplies for each teacher; additional resources to enhance school library collections and establish new parent centers at each school; music, art, and after-school programming; transportation services for after-school programs; and additional money for snacks.

District Support: STAR schools received extra support and oversight from the central office regarding the district core curriculum. Sandra Lam, director of curriculum, noted:

> With the STAR schools, we made it very clear that they had to focus on the core curriculum. We required them to have blocks of uninterrupted time for language arts and mathematics instruction which could not be interrupted with pullouts for other programs. This was a huge shift for teachers, because they'd never spent that much intensive time focused on reading. Some teachers were still teaching mathematics for less than half an hour each day, and the recommendation is for one hour daily. I think it took us at the central office a while to become clear about our expectations—that this was the requirement districtwide, but we would monitor the requirement in STAR schools.

STAR also provided principals with an academic plan review process, district content specialists (both special education and multilingual), leadership development workshops, and targeted professional development for their teachers and staff. As it did for additional staff, the STAR team articulated the barrier each support was designed to address, assigned school-site and district office responsibilities, and established successful school outcomes for each support.

All SFUSD principals reported to one of five assistant superintendents, and the STAR design team elected to work within this structure rather than creating a separate reporting relationship for low-performing schools. Each assistant superintendent was tasked with monitoring the implementation and effectiveness of STAR resources. A cornerstone of central office support was a series of visits to each STAR school.

These visits included "walkthroughs" of every classroom by a visiting central office team, followed by a conference in which school staff could discuss their progress and challenges with the central office visitors. STAR walkthroughs were intended as an opportunity for central and school staff to observe schoolwide teaching practices and work together to address challenges related to the school's academic goals. To conduct the walkthrough and conference process, each assistant superintendent assembled cross-functional teams with members from the Chief Academic Office, special education, multilingual programs, and specific content areas.

Funding STAR

Each STAR school participated in the annual academic planning process and received a lump-sum revenue allocation based on the weighted student formula calculation for its actual enrollment, as did all SFUSD schools. STAR schools also received an additional per student allocation, which by SY06 totaled $431 per pupil over and above the WSF funding. Total per pupil allocations at STAR schools ranged between approximately $4,000 and $5,000, depending on the effect the characteristics of the enrolled students had on the WSF. Additional expenses related to the STAR intervention were carried on the central office budget rather than on each school's budget.

The overall cost of the STAR intervention carried by the central office was approximately $9.5 million, most of which was invested in the additional staff positions (Exhibit 5). Approximately 70% of the total was paid for out-of-state categorical funds, with nearly $4.7 million coming from consent decree money and $1.9 million from a state initiative called economic impact aid. The remaining 30%, around $2.8 million, was funded through federal Title I dollars.

Implementing STAR

In order to roll out the new initiative by fall 2001, Ackerman asked Brooks to head up STAR

through the Chief Academic Office but to involve several central office departments and school leaders in the implementation. Brooks and the assistant superintendents supervised the hiring, training, and support of the initial IRFs. The Office of Parent Relations coordinated the training and support of parent liaisons, who were hired by principals. Other central office employees recruited volunteer tutors and developed an evaluation process for after-school and other supplemental programs. Principals were authorized to hire long-term substitutes for their sites. Schools were informed of the new role of advisors, who were then trained in their new duties.

Every school in SFUSD completed an annual academic plan based on prior-year performance data. Principals and their school-site councils developed a set of activities and programs in response to the data and then aligned their available financial resources to the plan. The STAR leadership team began the implementation year by conducting interviews with principals from each STAR school about their academic plans. The goal of the interviews was to help principals understand the connection between their students' academic data and their strategy for the year. Each principal received five questions as a guide for discussion:

1. Are the plan's objectives aligned with the data patterns?

2. Are explanations for the data patterns and strategic activities in your plan?

3. Does your plan include essential components of a successful school, that is, activities that address standards-based instruction, family and community involvement, and professional development?

4. How will your benchmarks help you achieve your objectives?

5. Are your activities aligned with your objectives?

Each interview proceeded as an open-ended discussion based on the questions, and the

STAR team recalled that principals exhibited a wide variation in their ability to answer these questions, signaling that some principals possessed a greater capacity for instructional leadership than others. In cases in which the team believed the principal needed development in instructional leadership, they counseled the principal to select a more experienced IRF to supplement his or her skills.

Following the principal interviews in early fall, the cross-functional teams began visiting schools for the first of the three walkthroughs each school would receive during the year. Brooks remarked:

> I knew we needed to come up with a system for accountability. Many aspects of the program were easy to implement because they matched what principals felt they needed to provide equity and increased achievement. However, finding a way to monitor schools was the most difficult part of the work and has required the most ongoing refinement. Principals and teachers were initially very skeptical of our plan to walk through their schools and didn't believe us when we said that the intention was not to evaluate individual teachers—but rather to evaluate the systems in schools to support instructional improvement.

The STAR design team did not mandate a specific protocol for assistant superintendents to implement in their walkthrough processes, and as a result there was wide variation in the quality and content of the feedback provided to school teams. In order to avoid appearing evaluative, the walkthrough teams attempted to give broad feedback about teaching practices they observed rather than singling out individual teachers for comment, but as a result principals reported that the feedback could be vague or confusing. Members of the various walkthrough teams informally shared their processes in an attempt to gain consistency across schools, but several par-

ticipants in the visits noted the lack of integration across assistant superintendents.

The cross-functional nature of the teams also exposed variation in expectations for schools across central office departments, and resolving these differences of opinion could be a slow process. Brooks felt that it took "at least until the third year" of STAR to reach consistency across the walkthrough teams.

Overall, the walkthrough process was highly valued by both school and central office staff. Deborah McKnight, executive director of special education, explained the worth of the process:

> I was able to use the process of instructional walkthroughs and academic planning to address core problems we were facing in my department. Too often, special educators were opting out of core curriculum training, and I would walk into certain classrooms and wonder just what kind of teaching could possibly take place in that environment. STAR forced the issue of incorporating teaching and learning and differentiation and good instruction—all the things special education needs to be—at the whole school level.

Lessons Learned

Over the course of the first year, the IRFs and long-term substitutes emerged as key elements of the STAR initiative. "For both principals and teachers," the district's year-end evaluation report stated, "additional school personnel proved to be the most powerful intervention . . . particularly Instructional Reform Facilitators and Long Term Substitutes." Evaluators reported the following "most successful" interventions (see Table A below).

The evaluation also showed that STAR schools wanted personnel better qualified to deal with crisis interventions (e.g., counselors, social workers, and nurses), as well as more common planning time in their schools and a clearer definition of the STAR roles (IRFs, parent liaisons, and substitutes). Modifications based on the

Table A

"Most Successful" Interventions as Reported by STAR School Administrators and Teachers

Administrators	Frequency	Teachers	Frequency
An Instructional Reform Facilitator	13	An Instructional Reform Facilitator	12
Long Term Substitutes	10	Long Term Substitutes	8
Instructional Walk-Throughs	9	Additional $150 for each teacher	6

Source: SFUSD *STAR* Schools Initiative 2001–2002 Formative Evaluation Findings.

evaluation's findings were implemented for the second year of STAR.

Ackerman acknowledged the need for adaptation and refinement after the first year: "Not everyone understood what we were trying to accomplish with STAR in the first year. I knew it would take time to get individual pieces to work properly, but this was a strong program, and I was confident it would get progressively better over time. I also had great confidence in Elois's ability to lead the implementation of this complex initiative."

Ackerman also recognized the limitations of the first-year rollout, explaining:

> It is a huge leap to get staff in central office to come out of their silos and see how all of the departments working together can better benefit schools. Furthermore, people who work in schools have no confidence that things can change in central office. Constant communication is key. It took a year for everyone to understand what we were trying to do. If I had to do it again, I would spend more time at the outset communicating our rationale for implementing the STAR program with staff at the school sites and central office. Communicating "why" and "how" the changes would improve student achievement might have made the initial year of implementation much smoother.

Clarifying the IRF Role and Adapting the Hiring Process

Although the IRF role was widely acknowledged as one of the most promising aspects of the STAR program in the first year, most of the

early feedback noted that "the fuzzy job descriptions were a real source of confusion, and resulted in multiple demands and duties being assigned to additional personnel."[7] This lack of clarity presented a number of challenges. As one IRF explained:

> When you are charged with instructional reform, some teachers are reluctant. When I first started, I had to help a teacher who wasn't very strong. He wanted to file a grievance because he felt I was going to evaluate him. Eventually we worked that out, and I learned from it. But it is not always easy to help a teacher realize they need to make changes and then to provide support and modeling for them. Sometimes I need more backing from the administrative team for holding teachers accountable. I can be a critical friend, but if the principal isn't making the case for why teachers need to work with me, then it can be hard.

Another recalled: "I remember walking into one of my first language arts meetings to present a central office direction that we would need to collaborate with each other and have a common curriculum at each grade level, and the entire team just walked out on me. I had a lot to learn about how to implement my responsibilities." To ensure greater consistency in implementation of the IRF role, as well as to clarify the hiring, training, and support of IRFs, Brooks and the STAR team charged Desmond, the executive director of school reform, with coordinating their efforts across the STAR school sites. IRFs still reported to their individual principals, but they met with Desmond biweekly. Desmond explained the challenge of allowing individual principals to recommend IRFs:

> IRFs did a variety of jobs their first year that ranged from lunch duty in the schoolyard to crunching numbers to coaching teachers. This new role of the IRF was being learned and implemented by the district and the schools. Many principals were gaining understanding of how they could use their IRFs and therefore demonstrated a wide range in ability to hire for this unique position.

In response, the central STAR team (assistant superintendents, Brooks, Khanna, and Desmond) modified the IRF selection process for the second year of STAR. They increased their efforts to screen and select centrally a qualified pool of candidates from which principals could select IRFs in an effort to achieve consistency in candidate quality and principals' understanding of the role. Principals could still recommend candidates, but the IRF role description and hiring guidelines were made more clear and strict. Desmond explained: "It was essential that the IRFs be hired at their school sites and view their principals as their line of authority, but we also needed them to have certain skills to ensure that they could do the complicated job we had outlined. Because I had no formal authority over the IRFs, the reporting structure required a delicate balance to be effective."

Additionally, Desmond identified a number of cores skills necessary for success as an IRF and created a centralized approach to developing them. She explained, "The IRFs needed a formalized professional development plan, so we developed a series of mandatory training sessions on topics such as using benchmark data and utilizing the other intervention supports that were part of STAR."

Even with a more coordinated hiring and training effort, IRF roles across the district remained varied. Some principals implemented

the intervention just as the design team had envisioned it. In these schools, IRFs took on specialized roles focused specifically on instructional improvement by coaching teachers and outlining plans for schoolwide professional development based on detailed analysis of student achievement data. At other sites, IRFs were also tasked with administrative duties such as discipline and schoolyard monitoring. One veteran IRF said, "If you had all of us in a room, you would get 44 different stories about what we do and why we're effective."

Principals echoed this wide range of opinions about the IRF's focus. One principal described her IRF as "my right-hand woman," explaining:

> I see my role as the link to the community, so I split my time between the community and the classroom. My IRF, on the other hand, spends 100% of her time focusing on instruction and helping teachers. It makes my job easier, because we both observe classrooms then confer and come up with strategies to help certain teachers or certain grade levels, whereas if I were alone making these decisions, I would have to bother another principal to brainstorm.

Another principal managed the IRF role in a different way:

> My IRF had a unique role in our school because she does a little bit of the administrative work, periodically attends to discipline—which is something we all do here because it is everyone's responsibility—and then she supports me as an instructional leader. We support each other in setting teachers up for success. Sometimes she'll go in and model a lesson, sometimes I will model.

Overall, IRFs, principals, and central staff agreed that the variation could be a challenge but that on balance it was valuable. As one IRF noted: "The flexibility in our role allows us to really lend support that might not be explicitly stated in our job descriptions. And that is a good thing. Even though our job description is two pages long and aims to encompass everything, the role of the IRF is to be able to go into a school and figure things out and lend support where it's needed."

By the third year of the program, 100% of STAR principals identified the role of the IRFs as one of three interventions critical to the continued success of the STAR program, with 88% citing IRFs as the first critical support.[8] As an unexpected consequence of STAR, the IRF role also created a new pipeline of potential school leaders. By spring 2006, 11 IRFs had become principals and seven had become assistant principals, often in STAR schools.

Managing Differences, Striving for Consistency

Finding the right balance between site authority and central control was an ongoing challenge, made all the more delicate by turnover among STAR principals. Some of the more skilled and experienced principals wanted more discretion over STAR programs and resources, while newer principals often needed more supervision and help with implementation. Some principals and IRFs felt that the central office was not equipped to offer varied levels of support according to individual school needs. An IRF elaborated:

> One of the most interesting aspects of STAR is the flexibility between central mandates and site needs. The STAR team at central office doesn't really know how to differentiate their support for us, but that's okay because we do know how onsite. My first year as an IRF, we worked with the bottom-quartile kids to pull their performance up and tried to establish some instructional continuity. But we're past that. Now we're focused on how to move midrange students to proficient

and above. We don't have to spend our time worrying about the same problems that we did our first year in STAR because we have flexibility at the site.

A principal described the give and take between the central office and her school:

> My IRF goes to a central office meeting every other week and comes back with ideas and then we hash it out and we say, "Does this make sense for us? Can we adapt that good central office idea to our site?" The STAR program wouldn't be as effective if it was wholly centralized, nor would it work if it was exclusively site based. Central office provides a map, but schools are able to adapt, and principals who know what they are doing make it work well.

As one IRF explained, being part of a larger community of practice was a key to achieving consistency: "The ability to meet together every other week is very helpful because we notice that there is commonality in our work. If we didn't meet together twice a month, we would probably be even more divergent than we are now."

Managing Complexity over Time

In addition to the IRF role, the STAR design team periodically reviewed the implementation of other parts of the intervention. The long-term substitutes were not working as they had planned. A lack of coordination with Human Resources meant that these individuals appeared at the top of the districtwide substitute list, which meant they were frequently called for duty at other sites. This prevented the consistency that the team had envisioned at some hard-to-staff schools.

Brooks also believed they should have approached the change in the advisor role differently: "Although we rewrote the job description for the advisors, we didn't ask people to reapply for their jobs. It was difficult to switch their mind-set from their prior focus—too many of them were used to just babysitting kids that principals didn't want sitting in their offices, and we didn't fully communicate our intention of the changes in the position."

The team also struggled to work out the balance between central- and site-based support for the parent liaisons. Deena Zacharin, who oversaw this element of STAR, explained:

> At first principals hired the parent liaisons. Sometimes they would hire an active parent, sometimes they would add hours to a long-term school employee. In 2004, the Office of Parent Relations began to hire and train the liaisons as central staff, and everyone had to reapply for their jobs. We brought in a lot of new people and since have been more successful implementing a consistent system and structure to increase parent involvement.

Some STAR schools did not respond sufficiently to the initial set of supports, and the team elected to increase the amount of attention and support they received, creating a category of schools called "Intensive STAR." In more troubled sites, they began to consider reconstitution.

In 2004, Brooks transitioned to the chief of staff role and was succeeded by Hiroshima, a former assistant superintendent. Brooks stayed connected to STAR and, almost five years after the original brainstorming meeting, she reflected: "I can't point to just one thing that STAR did for low-performing schools. Students at these sites need a variety of things. As I look back, I know that I learned that a central office must be a support for schools. If schools knew what to do to improve, they would do it. They need direction, but administrators need to respect schools for what they bring to the table."

Chief Development Officer Matthew Kelemen commented, "Overall, STAR is about help. There is increased monitoring, but it is primarily a support system. In a world of scarce resources, STAR schools get significant additional resources. When you talk to most people in these schools, they don't feel penalized for being in the program. Instead, they appreciate it. They appreciate the resources."

Myong Leigh, chief of policy and planning, highlighted the complexity of implementing a program like STAR as part of a larger strategy to improve performance:

It's important to remember that STAR was implemented about the same time as the site-based decision-making process, the weighted student formula, and a new principals' evaluation. STAR could have been in conflict with these other systems but in the end was not. Most of the key players at central office were involved in implementing all of these pieces, and we have managed to align them. When you step back from it, it's very cool.

New Challenges

In 2004, Ackerman determined that a number of Intensive STAR schools were not making sufficient progress and planned to reconstitute them over several years with support from the federal judge monitoring the consent decree. Once again, she asked Brooks to lead the effort. Called "Dream Schools," these sites were equipped with not only STAR resources but a prescribed school design. Additionally, all teachers and administrative staff had to resign and reapply for their positions. Almost none were rehired. The teachers' union had taken an increasingly oppositional stance under new leadership since 2003, and the Dream School plan and implementation accelerated the deterioration of its relationship with Ackerman. The union mobilized its membership and played a significant role in changing the makeup of the school board during the 2005 elections. The balance of power on the board shifted largely to opposition of management team recommendations regarding district policy and strategy.

Overall, SFUSD had improved student outcomes at all grade levels between 2001 and 2005 and had made progress in narrowing the achievement gap (Exhibit 6). In 2005, the district was named one of the top five urban school districts in the nation by the Broad Foundation and was recognized as the highest-performing urban district in California by the state department of education.

Nevertheless, political unrest culminated in Ackerman's resignation in early 2006. Brooks also elected to leave SFUSD. Concurrently, the judge monitoring the consent decree declined a request to renew the ruling and continue his oversight for another three-year term. Implementation of "Excellence for All" was no longer legally required, which concerned many administrators who relied on the judge to support the more contentious elements of the strategy.

On the financial front, expenses were projected to increase faster than revenues in SY07 due to declining enrollment and new union contracts negotiated in SY06 that committed the district to over $19 million in new annual spending. With an estimated shortfall of $5 million on its $450 million operating budget, district leaders explored options to significantly cut existing spending to balance the budget. Because the STAR program accounted for $9.5 million each year, the team began to consider reducing some of the supports to achieve their budget targets.

In response to the possibility of losing some STAR resources, one teacher said: "I have a problem with that. We accomplished the growth because of the extra money, because of the professional development, and the IRF position. If they take the resources away after we've progressed so much, it's almost like we're getting punished—these things helped us get where we are. If they take them away, it's like we're back at square one."

School leaders were concerned as well, as one elementary school principal explained:

Outside experts look at a program like STAR and think it's about reallocating and using resources differently. True, but it's also about *more* resources. STAR is designed well—I think having some things centrally designed and interconnected with schools is good, but I just want to go on the record and say that part of our performance problem in the past was too few resources. The STAR program brings extra resources to schools that need them most.

What Next?

From her perspective as chief academic officer, Hiroshima knew some tough decisions lay ahead. To reduce costs, she and the SFUSD leadership team had anticipated "graduating" successful schools from the STAR program. With this approach, schools that had improved would gradually lose STAR resources, which would reduce the program's cost but potentially jeopardize the gains schools had made. Hiroshima wondered if her team understood which elements of STAR were most effective and if they could design a scaled-back set of resources that would reduce overall costs but still provide ample support to schools and sustain their achievement gains.

Aside from the budget concerns, Hiroshima thought about the potential of the STAR approach for supporting improvement in schools that were not the lowest performing but still had a long way to go to achieve excellence. Assistant Superintendent Jeannie Pon believed non-STAR schools could benefit from STAR supports as well, saying, "STAR has been successful, and given experience working with my STAR schools, we are making ground and we want to continue the momentum. I wish my non-STAR schools had some of those STAR resources, too." In fact, if the team really understood which parts of STAR were most effective, was it possible to implement them in schools in the midrange of performance—those with API rankings of four—in order to accelerate their achievement gains? If some parts of STAR were discontinued universally, could some of the cost savings be re-allocated to implementing effective supports in a targeted number of non–STAR schools?

As she gathered her things for a school visit, Hiroshima was determined to carve out time to address these questions with her team.

Notes

1. 1983 Consent Decree written by the United States District Court for the Northern District of California, in the case *San Francisco NAACP, et al., vs. San Francisco Unified School District, et al.,* Civil No. C-78–1443 WHO.

2. This section is adapted from Stacey Childress and Robert Peterkin, "Pursuing Educational Equity at San Francisco Unified School District," PEL-005, The Public Education Leadership Project Case Series, Boston: Harvard Business School Publishing, 2004.

3. Report cited Ritu Khanna, John R. Flores, Bonnie Bergum, and Davida Desmond, "The History and Practice of Reconstitution in San Francisco," Department of Research, Planning and Evaluation, San Francisco Unified School District, presented at the annual meeting of the American Educational Research Association, April 19–23, 1999, p. 4.

4. Khanna, Flores, Bergum, and Desmond, "The History and Practice of Reconstitution in San Francisco," pp. 4–5.

5. Cited in district report, "Feedback from II/USP & CRSD site teams at the March 3, 2000 meeting on District Barriers I–V."

6. According to the posted job description, this included work with II/USP, Reading Recovery, the Bay Area Writing Project, the Bay Area School Reform Collaborative, the Bay Area Coalition for Equitable Schools, mentoring/coaching, resource/content specialist, restructuring, department chair, Urban Systemic Program, and other whole school change models.

7. SFUSD *STAR* Schools Initiative 2001–2002 Formative Evaluation Findings, p. 3.

8. Ingrid Roberson, SFUSD 2003–2004 STAR Evaluation Report, p. i.

Exhibit 1

SFUSD District Demographic and Organizational Data

District Area Demographics	SFUSD
Total Population	776,713
Per Capita Income (in 1999)	$34,556
Household Income in 1999 below Poverty Level	10.2%

Student Demographics	2005–2006
Number of Students (K-12)	56,236
Chinese	32%
Latino	22%
African-American	14%
Other Nonwhite	11%
White	9%
Filipino	6%
Decline to State	4%
American Indian	1%
Japanese	1%
Korean	1%
Free and Reduced Lunch	55.1%
Dropout Rate (2004–2005)	1.7%
Special Education	10.9%
Gifted & Talented	13.9%
English Language Learner	29.2%

Schools (6th-Largest District in CA)	2005–2006
Number of Schools	107
Elementary (K-5)	66
K-8	6
Middle (4–6, 5–7, 6–8, 7–9)	18
High	17

Staff Summary	2005–2006
Number of Certificated Staff	3,819
Administrators (District and School Site)	228
Average Salary of Staff	$57,022
Average Years of Service	11.1
Age Distribution of Staff	
35 Years and Below	30.9%
36 to 44 Years	20.2%
45 to 55 Years	27.4%
56 Years and Above	21.4%
Teacher Ethnicity (2002–2003)	
White	53.9%
Asian	20.1%
Hispanic	9.2%
Multiple/No Response	7%
African-American	6.2%
Filipino	3.1%
American Indian	0.5%

Source: District information drawn from Census 2000 data, downloaded on August 19, 2003 from http://www.nces.ed.gov/surveys/sdds/singledemoprofile.asp?county1=0634410&state1=6. Student and school information drawn from 2005–2006 SFUSD Accountability Report Card. Staff summary compiled from 2005–2006 SFUSD Summary, http://orb.sfusd/edu/profile/prfl-100.htm except for teacher ethnicity information, downloaded June 5, 2006 from http://www.ed-data.k12.ca.us/Navigation/fsTwoPanel.asp?bottom=%2Fprofile%2Easp%3Flevel%3D06%26reportNumber%3D16.

Exhibit 2a
STAR School Performance, Elementary Schools, 2001–2005

School	Grade Level	School Demographics	Star Status (B)	2001 (C)			2005 (C)			Change 2001–2005 (C)		
		AA & L / Low-income (A)		API Score	API Rank	SSI Rank	API Score	API Rank	SSI Rank	API Score	API Rank	SSI Rank
Bret Harte	K-5	75% / 67%	Continuing	546	2	3	648	2	3	102	0	0
Bryant	K-5	89% / 75%	Continuing	594	3	4	671	2	3	77	−1	−1
Carver	K-5	72% / 68%	Graduating	605	3	5	678	3	4	73	0	−1
Chavez	K-5	85% / 75%	Continuing	606	3	5	723	4	9	117	1	4
Cleveland	K-5	63% / 69%	Continuing	648	4	7	703	4	4	55	0	−3
Cobb	K-5	78% / 71%	Intensive	655	5	4	655	2	5	0	−3	1
Drew	K-3	82% / 65%	DREAM	532	2	1	614	1	1	82	−1	0
El Dorado	K-5	46% / 69%	Continuing	593	3	2	694	3	1	101	0	−1
Fairmount	K-5	70% / 61%	DREAM	532	2	1	626	1	1	94	−1	0
Flynn	K-5	80% / 79%	Continuing	515	1	1	636	1	2	121	0	1
Glen Park	K-5	60% / 71%	Graduating	596	3	3	755	6	7	159	3	4
Hillcrest	K-5	48% / 69%	Intensive	577	3	1	634	1	1	57	−2	0
Malcolm X	K-5	71% / 67%	Intensive	570	2	4	620	1	2	50	−1	−2
Marshall	K-5	86% / 85%	Intensive	539	2	2	633	1	1	94	−1	−1
McKinley	K-5	61% / 69%	Graduating	615	3	3	771	6	10	156	3	7
Milk	K-5	65% / 56%	Graduating	554	2	1	766	6	8	212	4	7
Monroe	K-5	46% / 71%	Intensive	612	3	2	714	4	2	102	1	0
Muir	K-5	87% / 72%	Continuing	520	1	3	636	1	1	116	0	−2
Parks	K-5	67% / 80%	Intensive	677	5	9	640	2	1	−37	−3	−8
Revere	K-6	74% / 68%	DREAM	509	1	1	639	2	1	130	1	0
Sanchez	K-5	86% / 70%	DREAM	516	1	2	648	2	3	132	1	1
Serra	K-5	69% / 85%	Graduating	583	3	3	702	4	4	119	1	1
Sheridan	K-5	52% / 76%	Graduating	640	4	4	785	7	10	145	3	6
Starr King	K-5	66% / 72%	Continuing	545	2	4	721	4	9	176	2	5
Swett	K-5	64% / 82%	Continuing	597	3	2	616	1	1	19	−2	−1
Treasure Island	K-5	64% / 70%	*CLOSING*	618	4	2	654	2	3	36	−2	1
Webster	K-5	66% / 87%	Continuing	604	3	5	704	4	4	100	1	−1
Willie Brown	K-6	76% / 74%	DREAM	599	3	2	526	1	1	−73	−2	−1

Source: District files, California Department of Education, and casewriter analysis.

Notes:
1. Percentages are combined representation of African-American and Latino students and combined free- and reduced-lunch students relative to total school enrollment.
2. Star status indicates differentiation among participating schools. Graduating schools are transitioning out of the program; continuing schools remain in STAR; intensive schools receive additional services due to slower improvement; DREAM schools were reconstituted in 2004 or 2005; closing schools will be shut down by the end of SY06.
3. California uses an Academic Performance Index (API) to measure school performance. The API score (200–1000) is calculated based on school performance on a variety of standardized tests, including the norm-referenced CAT-6 and the criterion-referenced California Standards Test. Each school's API score is then ranked against those of all other California schools and assigned to a decile (1–10), which translates into the API rank. In order to account for variations in school demographics, each school is also ranked against the 100 most similar schools in the state, which results in an additional decile score, the Similar Schools Index (SSI).

Exhibit 2b
Star School Performance, Middle and High Schools, 2001–2005

School	Grade Level	School Demographics	Star Status (B)	2001			2005			Change 2001–2005		
		AA & L / Low-income (A)		API Score	API Rank	SSI Rank	API Score	API Rank	SSI Rank	API Score	API Rank	SSI Rank
Burbank	6–8	59% / 66%	*CLOSING*	547	2	1	585	1	1	38	−1	0
Davis	7–9	75% / 52%	DREAM	430	1	1	519	1	1	89	0	0
Denman	6–8	44% / 66%	Graduating	609	4	1	690	5	4	81	1	3
Everett	6–8	85% / 70%	DREAM	497	1	1	563	1	1	66	0	0
King Jr.	6–8	44% / 64%	Graduating	655	5	7	695	5	6	40	0	−1
Lick	6–8	77% / 56%	Intensive	553	2	3	611	2	1	58	0	−2
Mann	6–8	87% / 63%	Intensive	579	3	2	586	1	1	7	−2	−1
Maxwell	6–8	70% / 70%	*CLOSING*	460	1	1	571	1	3	111	0	2
Vis Valley	6–8	38% / 78%	Graduating	579	3	4	667	4	6	88	1	2
Balboa	9–12	34% / 61%	Graduating	440	1	1	628	3	1	188	2	0
Burton	9–12	40% / 50%	Graduating	570	3	3	701	6	9	131	3	6
Galileo	9–12	22% / 54%	Graduating	547	3	3	744	8	9	197	5	6
ISA	9–12	62% / 54%	Intensive	543	3	6	603	2	5	60	−1	−1
Marshall	9–12	35% / 55%	Intensive	606	4	4	634	3	3	28	−1	−1
Mission	9–12	61% / 57%	Continuing	421	1	2	575	1	4	154	0	2
O'Connell	9–12	84% / 44%	DREAM	516	2	3	631	3	7	115	1	4

Source: District files, California Department of Education, and casewriter analysis.

Notes:
1. Percentages are combined representation of African-American and Latino students and combined free- and reduced-lunch students relative to total school enrollment.
2. Star status indicates differentiation among participating schools. Graduating schools are transitioning out of the program; continuing schools remain in STAR; intensive schools receive additional services due to slower improvement; DREAM schools were reconstituted in 2004 or 2005; closing schools will be shut down by the end of SY06.
3. California uses an Academic Performance Index (API) to measure school performance. The API score (200–1000) is calculated based on school performance on a variety of standardized tests, including the norm-referenced CAT-6 and the criterion-referenced California Standards Test. Each school's API score is then ranked against those of all other California schools and assigned to a decile (1–10), which translates into the API rank. In order to account for variations in school demographics, each school is also ranked against the 100 most similar schools in the state, which results in an additional decile score, the Similar Schools Index (SSI).

Exhibit 3
Excerpted Goals from "Excellence for All" Five-Year Plan

OVERVIEW OF EDUCATIONAL EQUITY GOALS

1. Increase the academic achievement of students of all races and ethnicities, and of English Language Learner and non-English Language Learner status, District-wide and for each school, and narrow the existing academic achievement gap between students of different races, ethnicities, and English Language Learner status, with this goal to be realized through the establishment of specific growth targets for improved academic achievement at each school, as measured by standardized tests and performance assessments.

2. Increase the enrollment and success of students of all races and ethnicities, and of English Language Learner and non-English Language Learner status, in honors courses, District-wide and for each school, at the middle and high school levels.

3. Increase the number and percentage of students of all races and ethnicities, and of English Language Learner and non-English Language Learner status, taking and completing Advanced Placement (AP) courses, District-wide and at each high school.

4. Increase the number and percentage of students of all races and ethnicities, and of English Language Learner and non-English Language Learner status, taking and earning a 3 or better on AP exams, District-wide and at each high school.

5. Decrease the overrepresentation of students from specific racial/ethnic groups and English Language Learner status in special education programs to the extent practicable by eliminating inappropriate referrals to and placements in such programs, District-wide and at each school.

6. Increase the exit rates for students of all races and ethnicities, and of English Language Learner and non-English Language Learner status, from special education programs, District-wide and at each school.

7. Increase the attendance rates for students of all races and ethnicities, and English Language Learner and non-English Language Learner status, District-wide and at each school, so that the attendance rate for students of each race, ethnicity, and English Language Learner status at every school is at least 98 percent.

8. Decrease the suspension rates for non-expulsionable offenses for students of all races and ethnicities, and of English Language Learner and non-English Language Learner status, District-wide and for each school.

9. Enhance early childhood education so that all children entering kindergarten in SFUSD, regardless of race or ethnicity or of English Language Learner or non-English Language Learner status, will possess the tools and skills necessary to be successful in school.

10. Increase the number and percentage of qualified, diverse teachers, District-wide and at each school, particularly at targeted schools. Targeted schools are those with a high number or percentage of low-performing students. A qualified, diverse teacher is defined as one who is credentialed and has:

- classroom experience (3–5 years);

- content-area expertise;

- pedagogical expertise; and

- cultural competencies.

Source: "Pursuing Educational Equity: Aligning Resources at San Francisco Unified School District," PEL-005.

Exhibit 4
STAR Concept Model

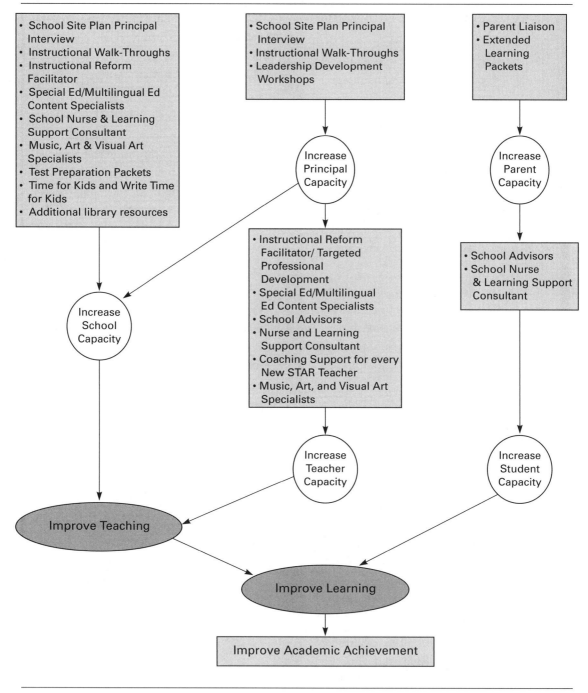

Source: District files.

Exhibit 5

Costs of STAR Intervention at Selected Schools, SY 2006

		STAR School			
		Glen Park **K–5**	**McKinley** **K–5**	**Sheridan** **K–5**	**Galileo** **9–12**
Total School-Level Budget		$1,433,405	$1,273,140	$1,057,743	$8,578,239
STAR Resource	**Avg Cost**				
Instructional Reform Facilitator	$74,217	$74,217	$74,217	$74,217	$74,217
Site Support Sub	$40,017	$40,017	$40,017	$40,017	$80,034
Parent Liaision (0.5 FTE)	$52,260	$26,130	$26,130	$26,130	$26,130
Elementary / Middle School Advisor	$55,118	$13,780	$13,780	$13,780	$0
Art/Music / Planning Time for 4th and 5th Grade	$74,217	$37,109	$37,109	$37,109	$0
Learning Support Consultant	$72,249	$43,349	$28,900	$36,125	$0
School Nurse	$86,166	$34,466	$17,233	$34,466	$0
Test Prep. Packets		$588	$552	$432	$10,010
Monthly Library Books		$935	$935	$935	$662
Home/School Learning Packets		$2,058	$1,932	$1,512	$10,800
Time for Kids ($5/student)	$5	$1,470	$1,380	$1,080	$0
Total STAR Resources carried at Central Office		**$274,119**	**$242,184**	**$265,802**	**$201,853**
Supporting Assumptions:					
Projected Enrollment		294	276	216	2,100
Site Support Sub FTE		1.00	1.00	1.00	2.00
Elementary / Middle school advisor FTE		0.25	0.25	0.25	0.00
Art/Music FTE		0.50	0.50	0.50	0.00
Learning Support FTE		0.60	0.40	0.50	0.00
Nurse FTE		0.40	0.20	0.40	0.00

Source: District analysis.

Exhibit 6

Change in SFUSD Performance on the California Standards Test, 2001–2005

	California Standards Test (CST) Change from 2001 to 2005 in Percent of Students at or above Basic							
	CST Language Arts 2001–2005				**CST Mathematics 2002–2005**[a]			
		STAR Only				**STAR Only**		
Grade Level	**District— All Students**	**AA**	**L**	**ELL**	**District— All Students**	**AA**	**L**	**ELL**
2	8%	7%	**17%**	**10%**	13%	**20%**	**17%**	**17%**
3	5%	7%	**14%**	**6%**	14%	**17%**	**27%**	**25%**
4	9%	**12%**	**19%**	**18%**	15%	**19%**	**23%**	**23%**
5	9%	**21%**	**17%**	**14%**	11%	6%	**17%**	**23%**
6	10%	9%	**14%**	5%	6%	0%	4%	5%
7	14%	**21%**	**19%**	**16%**	10%	4%	9%	**12%**
8	12%	9%	**15%**	**18%**	—	—	—	—
9	−1%	**15%**	**19%**	**15%**	—	—	—	—
10	1%	**3%**	**16%**	**8%**	—	—	—	—
11	7%	5%	**20%**	**17%**	—	—	—	—
Total	8%	**12%**	**17%**	**13%**	12%	**12%**	**16%**	**17%**

Source: District files and casewriter analysis.

[a] CST mathematics exams for grades 2–7 were administered for the first time in 2002. Students in Grades 8–11 are administered end-of-course mathematics tests based on their class enrollment.

Bold numbers indicate improvement rate higher than the comparable district rate.

AA: African-American; L: Latino; ELL: English language learner.

DISCUSSION QUESTIONS

1. Evaluate Montgomery County Public Schools' efforts to "raise the bar" and "close the gap" between 1999 and 2005.

   a. What has been their strategy?

   b. How successful have they been in making meaningful progress?

2. Based on the data in the case, should Frieda Lacey and Jerry Weast be alarmed and feel MCPS' efforts are inadequate to close the gap?

3. What are the most significant obstacles to accelerating their district's efforts to close the gap?

4. To what extent are race and racism significant issues in the case?

5. What is required for a district to effectively address the racial achievement gap?

6. Develop an action plan for Lacey, Weast and MCPS' executive team. Be as explicit as possible about what and how they should approach the problem.

Karen L. Mapp ■ David A. Thomas ■ Tonika Cheek Clayton

Race, Accountability, and the Achievement Gap (A)

During an off-site professional development retreat in July 2005, the senior leadership team of Maryland's Montgomery County Public Schools (MCPS) decided to take a hard look at the issue of race and the district's student achievement gap. Though the discrepancy in MCPS student performance between minority and white students had narrowed in some areas, African-American and Hispanic students continued to underperform white students across all grade levels. Realizing that MCPS's existing strategy might have some limitations, several team members expressed concerns that MCPS needed to seriously address issues of race and act deliberately to remove institutionalized barriers that inhibited or discouraged minorities from reaching their full potential. Upon returning from the week-long retreat, the leadership team moved swiftly to collaborate with other administrators on the topics discussed. Word spread fast that race and institutional barriers had become a high priority.

With a renewed focus on the achievement gap, African-American Deputy Superintendent Frieda Lacey perused fall 2004 10th-grade PSAT participation numbers, paying particular attention to African-Americans and Hispanics. She was disappointed to discover that the participation of some minority groups dipped below 70% in several high schools, although the district had communicated a 100% PSAT participation goal to principals since 2001 (see Exhibit 1 for PSAT participation figures). Lacey knew that staff had long documented and shared with principals the research that PSAT participation correlated with higher SAT scores. Knowing this, white Superintendent Jerry Weast aimed for 100% PSAT participation in 10th grade to maximize SAT scores and to identify high-performing students who had not enrolled in any advanced courses.

Lacey's concern for African-American and Hispanic students went well beyond the PSAT. If schools were not meeting participation targets, which were relatively easy to meet when compared to meeting test-performance targets, she wondered what other district efforts had been compromised, especially with regards to African-American and Hispanic students. Moreover, she considered how their mixed race leadership team could effectively tackle what some deemed to be highly sensitive issues that made many people uncomfortable when spoken about openly.

Historical Background

Montgomery County Demographics

Bordering the northwest side of Washington, D.C., Montgomery County was home to almost 1 million people of varied ethnicities by 2005.[1] As the total populace rose steadily over a 30-year period, the once mostly white suburban population gradually shifted from 95% to 65% white between 1970 and 2005.[2] As more African-American, Asian, and Hispanic families moved within county borders, neighborhoods generally became more racially integrated, although migration patterns showed that African-Americans and Hispanics tended to settle in geographical clusters close to the D.C. border.[3] Concurrently, the county's minority student population rose at an even higher rate because minority families averaged more children per household.[4] By the 2005–2006 school year, African-Americans and Hispanics comprised 43% of the student population and 25% of students were eligible to receive free and reduced meals.

Race Relations in MCPS

Often acknowledged as a county comprising affluent, progressive-minded people, Montgomery County had long wrestled with issues of race, particularly with the county's school system. In the early years before desegregation, Montgom-

ery County administered two separate school systems, one for African-American students and another for white students. Schools for African-Americans received less county funding relative to white schools and had to contend with inferior facilities, reading materials, and teacher compensation.[5] A former MCPS African-American student recalled his elementary school experience during segregation: "We had to be bused around on the back roads and go to an old school. . . . Our books had all been marked up, pages torn out, by kids who used the books first in the new school on the front roads."[6]

Just one month following the landmark U.S. Supreme Court *Brown v. Board of Education* decision in 1954, the MCPS Board of Education voted to appoint a committee of African-American and white school administrators to develop an integration implementation plan. By 1961, a slight majority of MCPS schools were desegregated using student transfer and busing tactics during a tumultuous period in which foes and supporters of integration publicly battled over the speed at which MCPS integrated its schools. The Montgomery County chapter of the National Association of the Advancement of Colored People (NAACP) repeatedly admonished the then MCPS Board and administration for deliberately moving slowly to perpetuate inequities between whites and blacks. At the same time, local white dissenters of integration protested the haste with which the district moved to integrate.

By 1980, the minority populations of African-Americans, Hispanics, and Asians had doubled over a decade of steady population growth. Newly elected board members who had campaigned to eliminate "forced busing" and "social engineering" successfully removed some busing plans, disbanded the board's minority relations committee, and abolished a mandatory course on black culture for MCPS teachers.[7,8] The board's subsequent controversial decision to close several largely integrated schools sparked a community debate and a challenge before the Maryland State Board of Education. Opponents successfully argued that the closings were "deliberate attempts to re-segregate the schools along the D.C. city line and protect certain high majority areas of the county from integration."[9] In response, the state intervened and ordered a stay on the board's contentious plans, which included redrawing enrollment boundary lines and removing special education programs from select integrated schools.[10] Subsequently, MCPS sought to integrate schools in other ways, including the use of race-based admissions and the creation of magnet programs in schools with large minority populations.

As the numbers of minority students increased, more discourse on the achievement gap and race emerged when high-profile issues surfaced. Magnet programs soon fell under criticism by minority leaders because while they served the purpose of drawing white students to schools with majority nonwhite populations, few African-Americans and Hispanics actually participated in the advanced academic programs. During the 1988 MCPS Board elections, each candidate was asked to describe the district's biggest deficiency in the education of multicultural students and how he or she would improve it. Incumbent board member Blair Ewing answered:

> The most serious problem the school system faces in the education of its multicultural student body is the lack of comprehensive and effective strategies for the successful education of minority students, in particular black and Hispanic students. Although progress has been made over the past five years, there is still no clearly identifiable set of strategies being systematically pursued throughout the school system, and no method for ensuring success for these students. What is needed is a set of approaches or strategies which can be applied, carefully tested and

replicated if measurement shows them effective. Smaller class sizes with teachers playing continuous supportive roles for children in the first four to six grades is a strategy I strongly support. Further research is needed into the causes and sources of minority student achievement problems. That has not been done and needs to be.[11]

The dialogue on race and district policy resurfaced in 1998 when disgruntled parents filed a federal lawsuit against MCPS upon learning that their child could not transfer schools because the transfer violated a school policy developed in 1980 to prevent racial segregation.[12] MCPS was later forced to abandon its practice of using race as a determining factor for school admissions after a federal court declared the practice unconstitutional.

Success for Every Student

Despite MCPS's struggles to address minority student performance, the district was still hailed as "one of the premiere school systems in the nation" when the board commissioned Yale University Professor Edmund Gordon to research the minority student achievement gap in 1990.[13] In his report titled "A Study of Minority Student Achievement in MCPS," Gordon noted that MCPS administrators and the community were concerned because "ethnic minority group students" were scoring approximately one standard deviation lower than "ethnic majority group students."[14] Specifically, the board wanted a comprehensive audit of the district's plan for addressing minority achievement, acknowledging that the existing plan had shown no evidence of progress.

In response to the board's request, Gordon's research team interviewed staff at all levels of MCPS, conducted classroom observations, administered surveys, and compiled quantitative data from a multitude of sources to deduce findings and develop recommendations. The findings indicated that the existing plan needed "several more elements for the improvement of minority student achievement and that those elements present were insufficiently comprehensive, insufficiently distributed, and inconsistently implemented."[15] Additionally, sub-studies conducted by the researchers found that minorities tended to be overrepresented in special education and underrepresented in higher-level courses.[16] Also, the report stated that "it was widely perceived that teachers and other school staff members tended to have low expectations of minority students and tended to invest less effort in the academic support and challenge of minority students" (see Exhibit 2 for summary of report findings and recommendations).[17]

The following year, newly appointed African-American Superintendent Paul Vance used Gordon's findings with his administration to develop "Success for Every Student (SFES): a plan to improve the achievement of low to average achieving students with special and critical emphasis on the needs of low to average achieving African American, American Indian, Asian American, and Hispanic students"[18] (see Exhibit 3 for SFES plan highlights). Early drafts of the SFES plan specifically singled out two groups with the subheading of the report ending, " . . . with special emphasis on the needs of low to average achieving African Americans and Hispanic students."[19] However, the board voted to remove the emphasis on African-Americans and Hispanics and broaden it to include all minority groups. Looking back on the board meeting in which the decision was made, one white administrator who was present remarked, "After the vote went through, the room felt as though the momentum to close the achievement gap died in that instant." Nevertheless, the board approved SFES, and Vance's administration implemented the plan's reform initiatives from spring of SY92 to the end of SY99 (see Exhibit 4 for select performance indicators for school years 1991, 1995, and 2000).[20]

Raise the Bar, Close the Gap

Almost 10 years after Gordon's report, a new MCPS Board of Education appointed Weast with a mandate for reform. By 1999, MCPS's white student population had shrunk from 62% in 1990 to 52%, while the overall student population grew by 21%.[21] Recognizing the growing trend of minority students, Weast sought to build a sense of urgency in the community to support district reform efforts to address the achievement gap.

To highlight the high correlation between low-performing schools and schools with largely minority populations, MCPS administrators created a map that geographically divided the district into two zones, red and green, based on socioeconomic indicators. Red represented "highly impacted" areas, and green represented affluent areas with relatively low demographic diversity (see Exhibit 5 for zone maps and figures).[22] The maps served as a starting point for communicating issues to stakeholders and for determining how the district should differentiate resources and management across schools. Using the maps and data to galvanize support from various community stakeholders, union leaders, and board members, the administration produced and widely distributed "A Call to Action: Raising the Bar, Closing the Gap" in November 1999, which expressed a new vision and plan for improving overall student achievement while striving to eliminate the achievement gap.

Weast decided to begin reforms at the elementary school level after reviewing an internal research report indicating that "the relationship between Grade 3 academic scores and high school honors course-taking was equally strong for all four major racial/ethnic groups in MCPS."[23] While instituting elementary school reforms, Weast directed high schools to focus on student outcomes on select targets, such as the

SAT and Advanced Placement (AP) exams, and to maximize the number of students who graduated ready to compete in college without remediation. Weast remarked on how setting high targets for high schools would create an internal demand for high-quality students within MCPS:

> People realized that schools needed to change how they identified and prepared students for higher-level courses. We broke that barrier in high school by opening up courses to student choice and using the PSAT to identify students who would have been overlooked, many of them African-American and Hispanic. It shined a light on students who were unprepared coming out of middle school.
>
> We knew that if we did this right, we could push the capacity for higher achievement, grade by grade, and shut down the argument that children would not be ready. We erased the perception right away when our first group of kindergarten students reached first grade already able to read. Someone termed them "Jerry's kids," and now these students are coming in waves toward middle school. Folks are rushing to fix things now before "Jerry's kids" come.[24]

In the first wave of reforms, administrators revamped specific components in all schools by changing the curriculum and hiring staff development teachers (see Exhibit 6 for a timeline of key reforms under Weast). Other initiatives, such as all-day kindergarten, reduced class sizes, and targeted professional development courses, started in the 60 most highly impacted elementary schools, called the "focus schools." Focus schools also gained access to additional financial and instructional resources depending upon the student population needs for differentiated instruction. Finally, initiatives like the Baldrige Initiative in Education started with the first group of schools volunteering to participate.[25] MCPS

planned to eventually roll out most reforms to all schools over a defined period of time.

Under Weast's leadership, MCPS also pushed to facilitate data-driven decision making for administrators and teachers. As a result, the percentage of MCPS staff that used technology to maintain student data rose from 10% in SY00 to 98% in SY02.[26] By 2005, MCPS had spent a significant portion of the budget modernizing its technological infrastructure under the Department of Shared Accountability with intentions to ensure that technological resources were updated and equitable across schools. To help teachers more efficiently use data to improve instruction and learning in classrooms, the department created a host of technological tools used to monitor students' mastery of curriculum. With the online Instructional Management System (IMS), MCPS documented a detailed account of each student's academic history, including test scores and academic interventions, to help teachers tailor instruction to the individual child. By the summer of 2005, all elementary and middle schools had access to IMS, and the system was set to roll out to high schools beginning in SY07. At that point, all MCPS students would have an online academic record that would follow them from school to school.

In 2005, after six years as superintendent, Weast generally garnered widespread support from most board members, union leaders, and community leaders. Under his leadership, the Montgomery County Council increased the MCPS budget by $100 million each year for six consecutive years, which reinforced his political power. However, tension between the MCPS administration and minority board leaders gradually increased as time wore on. Newly elected minority board members questioned the pace of reform implementation and the effectiveness of initiatives to help African-Americans and Hispanics achieve academically. While many stakeholders perceived the performance results from reform efforts under Weast to be tremendous progress, others felt as though not enough had changed for minority students since his arrival.

MCPS Leadership and Organizational Structure

Community Superintendents

In his first year as superintendent, Weast made a major organizational change by hiring six community superintendents to oversee principals, following a six-year period in which principals had minimal supervision (see Exhibit 7 for organizational structure and race of senior administrators). In the new role, community superintendents frequently visited schools and analyzed student achievement data to monitor school performance and evaluate principal performance. One white administrator described the previous structure:

> Before there were community superintendents, there were directors of school administration who had very little authority. Principals ran the district. And that was a by-product of a huge fight that began in the mid-1990s over budget cuts. Principals wanted to get rid of their overseers and the associate superintendents who ran areas with huge staffs. So as part of budget cutting, the previous superintendent cut them out. And for six years, schools had no supervision whatsoever with the exception of these directors of school administration.

Under the new model, each community superintendent managed a geographic region of approximately four clusters. A cluster included one high school and roughly all of the high school's feeder middle and elementary schools. Community superintendents participated in executive leadership meetings and played a significant role in implementing and monitoring strategic initiatives at the school level. They reported directly to white Chief Performance Officer Don Kress, who reported to Lacey. Understanding that each geographic region assigned to community superintendents presented different challenges, Kress gave community superintendents freedom to tailor their management of principals to their assigned region. For example, although all community superintendents led monthly meetings with their respective group of principals, the content of the meetings across community superintendents varied depending on what topics they deemed relevant to their schools' issues. At the end of SY05, five of the community superintendents were white and one was African-American (see Exhibit 8 for MCPS employee and student demographics).

Staff Development Teachers

Another structural change made under Weast's leadership was the addition of a staff development teacher in every school. To accompany the stream of reforms being pushed out to schools, MCPS leadership created the staff development role solely to provide professional development support to teachers. Although principals selected and hired staff development teachers, the central office provided training and monitored schools' use of the position to make sure that the original intent of the role was preserved. Additionally, the district assigned two instructional specialists to each community superintendent specifically to support staff development teachers.

Twice a year, staff development teachers received anonymous feedback from teachers, which was used by principals when evaluating their effectiveness. They supported as few as 30 teachers in some elementary schools to slightly over 200 teachers at some high schools. Feedback data showed that approximately 50% of teachers had never requested training options offered by the staff development teacher. Of the teachers who had, higher numbers of elementary school teachers reported satisfaction with their training when compared to middle school and high school teachers. The racial breakdown of staff development teachers was 82% white,

14% African-American, 2% Hispanic, and 2% Asian.

Targeting the Achievement Gap

The Data

By 2005, MCPS had amassed an extensive collection of demographic and performance data detailing student performance and the achievement gap. Demographic projections for the minority-dominated district showed the white student population shrinking to even lower percentages as the existing wave of elementary school students moved through the school system. To monitor student performance and the success of the district's reform efforts, MCPS collected and evaluated data disaggregated by minority subgroups over a wide variety of data indicators from grades K-12 (see Exhibit 4 to compare select SY05 results with those of previous years).

Weast's administration had realized the most progress in narrowing the achievement gap with student performance gains in elementary school reading- and math-proficiency levels, particularly in kindergarten. The latest data indicated that 81% of kindergarteners could read a level-three text with 90% or higher accuracy, up from 59% in SY02, the first year of Weast's kindergarten reforms.[27] Seventy-one percent of African-American and 69% of Hispanic kindergarteners could read at that level, up from 52% and 42%, respectively, in SY02. Additionally, the first cohort of students affected by Weast's initial kindergarten reforms had consistently scored higher each year on the Comprehensive Test of Basic Skills (CTBS) and Maryland State Assessment (MSA) standardized tests as they moved through the school system, with each subsequent cohort attaining mostly comparable achievement scores (see Exhibit 9 for elementary school performance data).

Nevertheless, the breakdown of test scores by ethnicity on the CTBS and MSA exams showed that African-American and Hispanic students still performed at substantially lower levels than their white and Asian counterparts. Standardized test scores within each subgroup had been improving incrementally over the years, similarly across green and red zones, although ethnic subgroups in the red zone appeared to be improving at a slightly faster rate than their green zone ethnic peers. Other areas of concern were the relatively low numbers of African-American and Hispanic students identified as gifted and talented (GT) and the high number of African-American males identified for special education (see Exhibit 10 for GT figures).

To assess the gap in middle and high schools, MCPS tracked an array of indicators, including MSA scores, enrollment in advanced courses, SAT and PSAT data, high school assessment exams, and suspension rates (see Exhibit 11 for select secondary performance figures). Although SAT participation numbers for African-Americans and Hispanics had increased since Weast's arrival, scores for those students remained flat even though the district's average SAT score steadily climbed to over 1100. Furthermore, African-American students were four times more likely to be suspended than white students. The graduation rate for Hispanic students had dropped by six percentage points to 82% since 2000, while the overall graduation rate for the county remained steady at 91%. Additionally, a disproportionate amount of African-American and Hispanic students attended two-year vocational/college prep junior colleges instead of matriculating into four-year colleges upon graduation.

Is Race an Issue?

Opinions on why the achievement gap existed and what MCPS should do about it varied within and across stakeholders. Another point of contention amongst many people in MCPS was whether or not race had anything to do with the achievement gap. White supervisor of MCPS diversity training Donna Graves commented on why MCPS needed to address issues of race:

> I think the central issue is that we don't want to talk about race. Most of us as white, mainstream Americans have been taught to be colorblind. So we assume that everybody's like us. And when we put interventions in place for a student of color based on our own white, middle-class perspectives, and the intervention doesn't work, we then unconsciously or sometimes consciously say, "Well see, we did this fabulous intervention and it didn't work. It must be the kids." It's not done in a malicious or intentional way, but it happens in classrooms every day.
>
> This is very difficult work because teachers tend to deny, defend, or shut down when you bring up issues of race. They've chosen this profession because they want to help children, but what is not understood is that despite our good intention, our teaching practices don't always have a positive impact on the student.

An African–American teacher commented on why there was an achievement gap in MCPS:

> I don't think it's a racial thing. It's a clash between inner-city thinking and suburban expectations. Most of our African-American students have left the inner cities and come to the suburbs because parents want to buy homes. They come to county schools where the environments are not predominantly black, and so they have to compete in a more rigid program. The expectations are higher, and they're not going to walk out of class, say what they want to say, disrupt the learning process, and get away with it. We would have parent conferences and do intervention programs with them. If that's not working, then we'd sit and have a serious conversation.
>
> We're also struggling because of the lack of parent support. We often call home. Phone numbers are disconnected. You try to send a letter home, the child intercepts the letter and the parent never receives it.

A white teacher commented on the connection between race and the achievement gap:

> I think there's a small achievement gap in terms of race, but I think it mostly comes from a student's incoming background knowledge. From what I see, there are definitely high- and low-performing kids across all races. And it's not necessarily tied to race but to socioeconomic status and how much support kids get at home.
>
> This school is so great because it's so diverse and there isn't a focus on the races. The focus is on each individual kid and just making sure that every kid gets the resources that they need in order to succeed. And it would kind of be unfair to say let's focus in on the African-Americans and make sure all the resources go to them.

A white principal commented on why MCPS needed to address issues of race openly:

> By not talking about it, we've ended up with *de facto* segregation. If you live in a community where parents want their kids to always achieve better than those other kids, and those other kids look African-American and Latino, then you have to talk about race. In some school systems where I've been we've fought about it. And actually that was better than not talking about it. Everybody had to move off their comfort zone and wrestle with things they were very uncomfortable with. So I choose to just be embarrassed about it and move with the embarrassment. If we don't talk about it, we'll never see other pieces that we think we know.

A white teacher remarked on the perception of racism in MCPS: "I think there is racism in disguise. I think we like to say that we're color-blind, but the reality is we're continually targeting these children. Why don't we just say we're trying to raise achievement? Why do we have to preface it with race? I want all my students to succeed. I don't just want the minority students to succeed."

Reexamining District Policies and Procedures

Over the years, the board and MCPS administration had revisited district policies and practices to evaluate effects on minority subgroups. By SY05, grading and reporting processes, advanced course enrollment, and GT identification had all been altered in some form to specifically address issues of equity or access.

Grading and Reporting Policy: In SY99, MCPS administrators discovered that grading scales varied widely across schools on countywide semester exams. For example, all algebra students took a countywide semester exam that accounted for 25% of the student's overall grade. Although the same test was administered to every student, individual schools determined the exam's grading scale. While a score of 66 earned an "A" on the exam at minority-dominated Albert Einstein High School, the same score earned a "D" at predominantly white Damascus High School.[28] Baffled administrators and board members publicly committed to equalizing grading and reporting activities across schools and started a collaborative effort to resolve the situation with parents, teachers, and administrators. Outraged by the different standards imposed on students, minority parents vocalized frustrations that schools like Einstein set low expectations for minority students and offered relatively low-quality instruction, thereby hurting minority students' readiness for college.[29] In SY00, MCPS implemented the first standardized grading scales for Algebra I and geometry final exams.

Managing teachers' interests to preserve judgment over student ability and parental concerns of inconsistency in grading across schools,

Weast formed a workgroup representing multiple stakeholders to examine grading practices and propose plans to make all grading systems equitable. Under the new policy approved by the board in March 2003, teachers had to grade students solely on how well the students met academic standards. Teachers would eventually be able to account for effort, participation, and extra credit separately in another mark.[30]

AP/Honors Course Enrollment:[31] In Weast's first year, his administration changed the AP and honors course enrollment procedures due to concerns that teachers were less likely to recommend qualified minority students for advanced courses. Under the new procedures, all students could self-select into any AP or honors course, although capacity constraints could limit enrollment numbers. Previously, students required a teacher's recommendation for consideration. A white principal commented on the revised procedure, "Removing the recommendation requirement was one of the biggest pieces making it possible to move more minorities into AP and honors courses. From my perspective, the teacher recommendation generally applied a downward pressure against students. Not in all cases, but probably more often than not."

While many people supported the shift to open enrollment, some teachers and students complained that advanced courses were becoming "watered down" and that teachers had to "dumb down" the curriculum for unqualified students. However, AP results from Bethesda Chevy-Chase High School (BCC) suggested that the policy did not affect the rigor or quality of AP instruction. At BCC, 91% of all students, 78% of African-Americans, and 79% of Hispanics took at least one AP or honors course. Although the total number of African-American and Hispanic students in AP courses jumped from 178 when the policy changed to 373 in SY05, AP exam scores still averaged the same. White BCC Principal Sean Bulson observed that their results confirmed that they were not diluting their curriculum and that "the students were rising to the challenge."

Gifted and Talented Identification (GT): In spring of 2005, MCPS revised the global screening process for identifying gifted and talented students in grade two with the intent of giving minority students more opportunities to demonstrate intellectual strengths. The new process increased the number of standard assessments used to identify students from one to two and realigned local norms used with the original standardized assessment. Under the new criteria, students could be identified as GT if they met the standard for one of the two standardized tests plus one other criterion. If neither assessment was met, the student could still be identified if standards were established in three of the following: parent nominations, MCPS staff nominations, teacher checklists, reading and mathematics instructional levels, or student performance data. Despite MCPS's efforts, the combined percentage of African-Americans and Hispanics identified as GT decreased slightly after the new global screening process was implemented in SY05 (see Exhibit 11).

Building Capability

To provide targeted professional development opportunities for administrators and school staff striving to close the achievement gap, Weast's administration created a Diversity Training and Development (DTD) department and a Professional Learning Communities Institute (PLCI).

Diversity Training and Development: The primary goal of DTD was to "develop, implement, and evaluate data-driven and research-based diversity training and development to school office and staff." White Associate Superintendent of the Office of Organizational Development (OOD) Darlene Merry commented on her decision to hire Donna Graves to spearhead DTD:

There were people who wondered why I did not select a minority candidate for this position, but I knew from the beginning that Donna was the right person to lead this effort. She has always demonstrated a deep passion for cultural competence, and she has inspired me to understand my own belief systems and how this affects the work that I do. Donna has a great deal of credibility with staff and the community, which she has earned over her 32 years working at MCPS. She is the one who has taught us to not be color-blind but instead to understand ourselves so that we can understand others. She has challenged us to talk about race so that we can understand it and build equitable classrooms for all students.

Early on, Graves operated alone without staff or a budget while researching other diversity training programs and reading literature to inform her knowledge of diversity development. In Graves's "Plan for Systemic Diversity Training and Development," she noted:

There is consensus in the research that staff development designed to ensure excellence and equity in education must be centered on teacher understanding of the powerful force culture exerts on teaching and learning. . . . First, staff must develop the awareness, knowledge, and understanding of their own culture and the beliefs, values, and assumptions that frame the educational practice of individuals and institutions. . . . Second, staff must increase their knowledge and understanding of the cultures of their students. . . . Third, educators must be able to use their knowledge and understanding of culture to create culturally sensitive learning environments and to deliver culturally responsive instruction.[32]

By the summer of 2005, DTD had grown to include three diversity specialists plus Graves and had begun work on three expressed key actions: to provide MCPS staff members with diversity awareness training, to build capacity of OOD staff, and to provide support and development for select schools and offices.

Process

To promote diversity awareness, DTD developed a website, coordinated multicultural courses, and produced technology-based awareness training. On the diversity training website, users could receive monthly e-mail tips for communicating high expectations for students. Also, the website offered up-to-date information from articles and research on teaching strategies for closing the achievement gap and facilitating diversity teamwork. DTD had also assumed responsibility for two long-standing district human relations courses, *Ethnic Groups in America* and *Education that Is Multicultural,* to satisfy the MCPS Board of Education requirement that all MCPS professional staff complete at least two courses on multiculturalism. Collaborating with MCPS's Instructional Television department, DTD endeavored to produce media-based training for all MCPS staff, with hopes of increasing awareness of bias and stereotyping observed in schools and the workplace.

External accountability? responsibility?

DTD aimed to build the capacity of all OOD staff members because OOD provided the majority of professional development training throughout the district, mainly to staff development teachers. By training all OOD staffers, DTD hoped to embed cultural competency into every training session—not just diversity training—offered to administrators, teachers, and other district staff. Also, DTD had the capability to provide ongoing support to a limited number of schools if the schools committed to diversity training for one year.

Despite the high "relevance" and "satisfaction with training" ratings given by participants of the group's diversity training sessions, DTD employees worried that they were "preaching to the choir." They believed in the effectiveness of the sessions' content, but they were concerned that staff development teachers, teachers, and principals who needed diversity training the most did not seek it out. One African-American administrator remarked:

> I don't think MCPS has truly committed to take some very serious steps to ensure that students of color, students of poverty, and students with disabilities get the support they need to be successful in schools. It's not consistent in the work that we do. There are some community superintendents who have taken diversity training seriously and have really done a good job in reaching their principals, but it doesn't go throughout. And only a few schools have made a commitment to work on diversity training.

perception

All participation in diversity training sessions by school-level staff was voluntary, and most sessions were restricted to staff development teachers who could bring along only one other person from their school. While some felt that portions of these diversity trainings should be mandatory for teachers, others warned that a top-down strategy could backfire. Merry noted that "in the past when the district required some school staff to take *The Skillful Teacher* training, teachers resisted, and the effectiveness of the training was compromised. Training has always been most effective when teachers and whole schools elected to participate on their own. Building commitment, not compliance, has become a hallmark of our work." A white staff development teacher commented on the district's diversity training offerings:

Research?

> I've attended pretty much all of them I can get my hands on. I find that the diversity team does a superb job with the materials they offer. One concern I have is that a lot of trainings are not open to teachers. I understand that there are limited resources and that we're supposed to

take the information back and share it with teachers. But it would be much better if there were other ways to more efficiently get the trainings out to all staff.

Professional Learning Communities Institute: Separately from DTD, MCPS administrators designed PLCI to help elementary schools develop high-performing teams that could effectively improve student achievement. In an effort to share effective practices from three high-performing MCPS elementary schools, two of which were highly impacted focus schools, an internal research team wrote case studies on Broad Acres, Ronald McNair, and Viers Mill elementary schools to be used as content for PLCI. Jamie Virga, principal of highly impacted Viers Mill Elementary, which went on to win a National Blue Ribbon School of Excellence Award from the U.S. Department of Education, was selected to lead the program.

Using the case study teaching method, PLCI convened participants from 11 elementary schools each year to study the processes, strategies, beliefs, practices, and tools that schools in the case studies used to increase and sustain student achievement. The institute then allowed participants time to reflect on their own school situation and apply their learning in developing a customized school plan. African-American Deputy Superintendent John Q. Porter remarked on the success of Broad Acres Elementary and why the district chose to highlight its success during PLCI:

> I think the greatest symbol and really the tipping point for us was what happened with Broad Acres. When your most impacted school, 99% minority and approximately 90% FARMS [free and reduced-price meals system], becomes one of your highest-performing schools, it's hard for any other school to say that minorities can't do well. So at that point, the conversation started to

change because we realized then that it was an issue of expectations, and if we didn't have high expectations then we had a problem.

School-Based Initiatives to Close the Gap

While district administrators and the MCPS Board worked to implement districtwide policies and practices that would lead to equitable outcomes, some principals and other school staff employed their own strategies to narrow the achievement gap. Using guidance from community superintendents and professional development opportunities from the district, school administrators sought different ways to make rigorous courses available for more minority students and to effectively support those students who elected to take more challenging courses. Catering to their unique student populations and challenges, MCPS schools varied widely in their attempts to help African-American and Hispanic students achieve at higher levels.

Broadening Access to Advanced Classes

In SY03, white Principal Ursula Hermann of Westland Middle School, an affluent green-zone school with a 64% white student population, moved all eighth graders into English GT classes and eliminated the eighth grade on-level English curriculum. She described the scenario that led to her decision:

> We were developing the master schedule, and our assistant principal said, "You know, we have 15 English sections, and 12 of them are for GT." Since we had been observing a rise in what we refer to as "*de facto* segregation" between on-level and GT classes, we looked at the demographics of on-level classes. What we discovered was that the composition of those classes was primarily our minority and special education

students. So we just took a deep breath and said, "We can't do this."

After reaching an agreement with Westland's cluster high school principal and the community superintendent, Hermann officially dissolved the on-level classes and reenrolled all students in GT English, which put approximately five reassigned students in each class. She also called parents and interviewed reassigned students to make them aware of the situation and to find out what the school could do to support them. Responding to remarks from students saying, "I'm not as smart as those kids, I can't read as fast, I can't keep up," the school provided access to additional classes and an after-school learning lab that could assist them with English and writing. Hermann noted, "We had no more failures than we did when kids were in on-level classes. The kids rose to the occasion." Still, school administrators and teachers received pushback from a few parents who felt that the GT English courses had become less challenging. In one reported incident, parents questioned the rigor of the class because of the increased number of minorities in their child's class. Hermann commented on parental resistance:

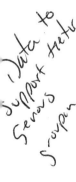

> We had a number of very heated parent meetings with a number of parents pretty adamant about going back to having discrete on-level and GT classes. It was clear—they believed that students who had not been tracked for accelerated classes in the past would have a negative effect on their children's learning. These concerns may have been fueled by stereotypical thinking or by a simple fear of change. They do want equity, but they also want to ensure their kids are challenged. I agree with them—we want all of our kids challenged.

> What I've done in eighth-grade English, I haven't done in grades six and seven or in math, because the issue is so big. If I want my whole

community to buy into it, I have to get them to truly understand that we are responsible for doing this with all students.

At Piney Branch Elementary School, a highly impacted grades three to five school comprising 42% African-American and 24% Hispanic students, the leadership team contemplated a different strategy to offer more minority students access to Math A (sixth-grade-level math). During the previous four years, the school's principal had directed third- and fourth-grade teachers to get more minority students ready for Math A by the fifth grade. In spring SY05, the leadership team evaluated students across seven fourth-grade sections, three of which were targeted for Math A. Teachers worried that a group of 17 minority students would not be ready enough to compete with other students. Instead of splitting the students up to join the other GT sections, the team considered creating a separate class that would meet longer and more frequently to adequately meet the needs of the students. To accommodate scheduling, the students would have to give up other parts of the fifth-grade curriculum, which would require parental consent. If all went as planned, the school would double the number of Math A sections from two to four, allowing 76 students, including 27 African-Americans and 12 Hispanics, to enroll in Math A or higher. A white school staff member described why Piney Branch pushed so hard for more minority students in higher-level math:

> We are two schools within one building—the majority school and the minority school. And in the last five years, we have been trying to build one community. I think it's more difficult for us because the kids don't arrive until third grade. Five years ago, the majority of white students would come from Takoma Park Elementary School coded GT, and most of the minority kids from Takoma Park or East Silver Spring Elemen-

tary had not qualified for GT. It took the right group of internal people with power who were ready to say, "There's something wrong with this picture." We had administrators who pushed hard for minority kids to go into advanced classes. And when you have that, things get moving.

Discussing Race Openly with Students

Under pressure to produce better student performance results on algebra high school assessments and MSA tests, the math team at Newport Mills Middle School began writing predictive assessment tests that they would administer three times a year (September, December, and February) to help them determine the areas in which students needed help. In an effort to motivate students to excel academically, the teachers explained the achievement gap to students in detail and developed a marketing strategy to encourage them to strive for higher test scores. Teachers Terri Bullock and Sally Moran described their strategy:

We put up a picture of George W. Bush and told our students, "NCLB is the national law. We have to prove nationally that you are performing at your age level. So this test is going to tell you, your parents, and us what we need to do to make this happen."

And we spoke openly with the kids about what groups they fell under, whether it was Latino, Hispanic, African-American, FARMS, ESOL, or another category. They understood and wanted to prove that just being a minority student did not mean they were stupid.

Categorizing by test results, the teachers placed students into three zones, red, yellow, or green. The red zone indicated that the student would not pass the state assessment exam if tested the next day, the yellow zone indicated that the student had a 50% chance of passing the exam, and the green zone indicated that the student would pass. In conjunction, the team developed the motto "Think Green" for the math department. Bullock commented on the success of the program:

Outside my room in the hallways, we posted the kids' names that were moving up, and the students in the green zone were so proud. I had a Latino student who acted tough, was in trouble with the law, but was very smart. After one test he moved from the red to yellow zone. And I said to him, "Look, you made it to the yellow zone." And he said, "That sucks, I wanted to be in green." Behind his back I wanted to scream, "Yes!" I was so excited that even he, like all of the kids, just totally bought into the program.

By the end of SY05, 38% of African-Americans and 46% of Hispanics in Newport Mills Middle School had completed algebra by eighth grade compared with the MCPS averages of 24% and 23%, respectively. Enrollment projections for SY06 indicated that 51% of African-American and 55% of Hispanic eighth graders would enroll in algebra at Newport Mills.

Special Programs Targeting Minority Students

Some schools had designed special programs specifically for minority students who needed additional academic support. At Bethesda Chevy-Chase High School, where the combined enrollment comprised just 30% of African-American and Hispanic students, the principal secured community funding to start a four-week summer program targeting minorities to help prepare low-performing eighth graders for ninth-grade English and algebra. Collaborating with middle school counselors and administrators, BCC leadership looked at student grade point averages, enrollment in lower math courses, and recipients of reading support to identify between 60 and 100 students for the program. In Forest Oak Middle School, an after-school program called Career Cadets enabled teachers to work with 20–30 at-risk students two days a week for two hours on academics or social issues. Teachers involved in the program observed a decrease in the number of student referrals and an increase in grades of the students who participated in the program.

Managing Expectations

Expectations of minority students were another issue that repeatedly surfaced going back to the early days of racial integration in MCPS. While Asian-Americans in MCPS worried about the effects of high academic expectations on Asian student performance in math and science, African-Americans and Hispanics were concerned about teachers and administrators whose behavior and practices revealed low academic expectations of their children.[33] Even though MCPS had put out a consistent message that all students could learn, many still believed that low expectations of minority students were pervasive among administrators and teachers of all races. A white staff development teacher commented on the beliefs of teachers: "Everyone knows that the politically correct thing to say in Montgomery County is 'every child can learn.' The difference is between those who know the party line and those who believe it. I would say that about one-third believe it in action, one-third isn't sure, and another third don't believe it."

An African-American principal described a significant challenge facing MCPS:

> As we become more and more diverse and as "Jerry's kids" move up, they're going to encounter environments that won't be as receptive. I'm not saying that we're there yet as a school, but we're aware of where the challenges are. We're always wondering how our school's environment influences or harms our students. We really care about academics and about making kids and parents feel good. But I often wonder how our students will be received when they move

on to other schools in the district. You can't change a school system until there are principals and people in place that have the same belief system and the right repertoire of skills. That's where we're stuck right now. The hard part is, how do you move people to the core beliefs that you want?

Next Steps

With two months to go before 10th graders took the fall 2005 PSAT in October, Lacey was determined to improve the participation numbers of African-Americans and Hispanics.

While figuring out the best way to mobilize PSAT participation efforts, Lacey reflected on the district's work to close the achievement gap. If it took this level of intervention to compel principals to push more students to take the PSAT, how much of an effort would it take from central office to ensure that other targeted achievement gap initiatives would be implemented at the school level? Did MCPS hold administrators, principals, and teachers accountable for the academic progress of minority students? Where should she begin looking to figure out how to dissect the situation surrounding the achievement gap? And most importantly, what should the executive team do to make a difference?

As she gathered her thoughts, she wondered what senior leadership needed to do to send administrators the right message to make this a priority.

Notes

1. "Montgomery County at a Glance," Montgomery County Department of Park and Planning—Research and Technology Center, February 2005.

2. "Montgomery County Population by Race and Ethnicity, 1970–2000," Montgomery County Park and Planning website, http://www.mc-mncppc.org/research/data_library/population/po8b.shtml, accessed May 11, 2006.

3. David Snyder, "Neighborhoods more integrated, study says," *The Washington Post,* July 4, 2002.

4. "Montgomery County Population by Race and Ethnicity, 1970–2000," Montgomery County Park and Planning website, http://www.mc-mncppc.org/research/data_library/population/po8b.shtm, accessed May 11, 2006.

5. Nina Clarke and Lillian Brown, *History of the Black Public Schools of Montgomery County, Maryland, 1872–1961,* New York: Vantage Press, 1978.

6. Sharon Moloney, "Growing up black," *The Cincinnati Post,* February 10, 1996.

7. Ben Franklin, "Minority Parents fight maryland school panel," the *New York Times,* March 1, 1982.

8. "Marian Greenblatt, ex-school official in Md., dies," Obituaries, *The Washington Post,* May 2, 1988.

9. Ben Franklin, "Minority parents fight Maryland school panel," the *New York Times,* March 1, 1982.

10. Ben Franklin, "Maryland orders stay of county school plan," the *New York Times,* August 7, 1982.

11. "Voters' Guide Weekly: Montgomery County Board of Education," *The Washington Post,* November 3, 1988.

12. Susan Ferrechio, "Schools appeal for return of race-based admissions," *The Washington Times,* November 3, 1999.

13. Edmund Gordon, "A Study of Minority Student Achievement in Montgomery County Public Schools," November 16, 1990.

14. Gordon, "A Study of Minority Student Achievement."

15. Gordon, "A Study of Minority Student Achievement."

16. Gordon, "A Study of Minority Student Achievement."

17. Gordon, "A Study of Minority Student Achievement."

18. "Success for Every Student," adopted by the board of education, January 6, 1992.

19. Copy of "Success for Every Student," draft, October 1991.

20. SY is a PELP convention that denotes "school year." For example, SY05 refers to the 2004–2005 school year.

21. "Annual Report on the Systemwide Outcome Measures, Success for Every Student Plan," MCPS, December 1995.

22. "Highly impacted" was an MCPS term used to define schools with significantly higher poverty, increased mobility, more students learning English as a second language, and disproportionately more African-Americans and Hispanics.

23. "Early Preparation and Supports in High School for Honors Course Participation," Honors/Advanced Placement Polices Practices and Enrollment, Appendix C4, Work Group Report, July 1999.

24. "Jerry's kids" labels the first cohort of kindergartners affected by reforms under the Weast administration. During SY05, Jerry's kids were in the fifth grade.

25. Baldrige in Education Initiative uses the Malcolm Baldrige Education Criteria for Performance Excellence, administered by the National Institute of Standards and Technology, as a framework for restructuring education and improving student performance.

26. MCPS website, http://www.mcps.k12.md.us/departments/technology/, accessed May 9, 2006.

27. The kindergarten benchmark is book level three or early emergent texts that typically have large print and spacing, a simple story line with familiar content, introduction of dialogue, and supportive illustrations. Children learn to read high-frequency site words while reading simple stories for meaning.

28. Manuel Perez-Rivas, "Montgomery math tests criticized as too variable," *The Washington Post,* April 11, 1999.

29. Manuel Perez-Rivas, "Latinos unidos in Montgomery: Immigrants speaking up over schools," *The Washington Post,* September 5, 1999.

30. Lori Aratani, "Montgomery Eases in new grading system: Teachers won't mark participation yet," *The Washington Post,* June 15, 2005.

31. Advanced placement (AP) courses are those for which a College Board Advanced Placement examination exists. A qualifying score on an AP exam may give the student college credit or advanced standing in a subject in many colleges. Honors courses provide expectations and opportunities for students to work independently at an accelerated pace, to engage in more rigorous and complex content and processes, and to develop authentic projects that reflect students' understanding of key concepts. Definitions provided by MCPS.

32. "MCPS Office of Staff Development Plan for Systemic Diversity Training and Development," draft, June 1, 2004.

33. Stephen Buckley, "Shrugging off the burden of a brainy image: Asian American students say stereotype of 'model minority' achievers is unfair," *The Washington Post,* June 17, 1991.

Exhibit 1
Fall 2004 MCPS PSAT Participation Results

Percentage of MCPS Grade 10 Students
Who Took the PSAT in Fall 2004 by School and Demographic Group (Excluding Students Who
Were Enrolled in ESOL[a] Levels 1 or 2, or a Life-skills or Community-based Special Education
Program at the Time of Testing)

High School	% Took PSAT—Fall 2004						
	Af.-Am.	**As.-Am.**	**Hispanic**	**White**	**FARMS**[b]	**SPED**[c]	**LEP**[d]
MCPS (district-wide)	**80**	**93**	**76**	**91**	**79**	**71**	**73**
Bethesda Chevy-Chase	87	92	91	95	89	88	100
Blair	84	90	86	93	87	78	48
Blake	93	96	89	93	94	82	83
Churchill	92	99	100	98	94	91	
Damascus	67	100	70	87	81	69	
Einstein	85	100	85	93	87	69	94
Gaithersburg	84	93	75	90	86	73	74
Kennedy	88	94	71	96	86	66	71
Magruder	70	91	68	89	68	64	80
Northwest	81	91	71	90	78	75	
Paint Branch	77	93	72	84	79	46	89
Poolesville	80	88	100	94		83	
Quincy Orchard	74	89	59	89	62	60	68
Richard Montgomery	75	95	81	92	82	78	72
Rockville	71	90	67	90	76	78	77
Seneca Valley	84	94	79	91	87	73	100
Sherwood	75	88	87	92	69	75	42
Springbrook	86	93	70	94	76	79	58
W. Johnson	65	89	77	93	72	82	67
Watkins Mill	82	94	79	90	77	72	83
Wheaton	80	86	68	72	78	55	71
Whitman	80	90	86	95	78	85	42
Wootton	97	97	82	96	92	93	100

Source: Montgomery County Public Schools.

[a] Students participating in English for speakers of other languages classes.

[b] The percentage of students participating in the free and reduced-price meals system.

[c] Students with disabilities.

[d] Students with limited English proficiency.

Exhibit 2
Findings and Recommendations Excerpts from Edmund W. Gordon, "A Study of Minority Student Achievement," 1990

FINDINGS

With respect to the specific charge as specified by the MCPS Board of Education, we find that:

1. the present Minority Student Achievement Plan includes several elements needed for the improvement of minority student achievement, but that those elements present are insufficiently comprehensive, insufficiently distributed, and inconsistently implemented;

2. the initiatives for each of the existing elements are unevenly planned, and in some instances, are unenthusiastically implemented and insufficiently communicated to staff and students;

3. the present measures of progress (e.g. accountability goals) are sophisticated and broadly accurate, but do not provide the character and quality of information concerning minority student achievement which are essential to inform program design and improvement; in addition, the present measures can contribute to a misleading picture of minority student achievement;

4. the organizational structure needed to support the Plan's implementation is not in place and functional; that it is widely perceived that there is no meaningful system of direction, support or accountability;

5. the entire organizational structure of the Minority Student Achievement Plan should enable active conceptual, moral and developmental leadership, on line resource and technical assistance and line authority for assessment and accountability;

6. the option to include recommendations has been exercised and they are included at the end of this report.

RECOMMENDATIONS

1. We recommend that priority attention be given to changes in some of the attitudes and behaviors of professional educators (administrators and teachers – majority and minority group member professionals) in regard to a) their expectations of minority students; b) their instructional behavior; and c) their support for the academic development of students;

2. We recommend that special attention be given to the need for changes in some of the characteristics and services of the schools and other educative institutions in regard to their functions, administrative management, component size, service delivery systems, students data management, resource availability, and resource deployment;

3. We recommend that attention be given to changes in attitudes, behaviors and conditions of the families and communities from which some minority group students come, since these attitudes, behaviors, and conditions relate to education and the support of academic achievement;

4. We recommend that attention be given to changing some of the attitudes and behaviors of minority students, themselves, in regard to academic learning and their participation in it;

5. We recommend that MCPS extend its concerns beyond the schools for which it is responsible and look at the community context in which these schools function in order to change some student perceptions of the expectations, models, opportunities, and rewards available in the larger community.

Source: Edmund W. Gordon, "A Study of Minority Achievement in Montgomery County Public Schools," Final Report, November 16, 1990.

Exhibit 3

Success for Every Student—Vision, Goals, and Outcomes in 1992

VISION

We, the people of Montgomery County, believe that a quality education is a fundamental right of every child. All children will receive the respect encouragement and opportunities they need to build the knowledge, skills and attitudes to be successful, contributing members of a changing global society.

GOAL 1—Ensure Success for Every Student

Provide the services and environment each student needs for intellectual challenge and social and emotional development. Each student will be able to communicate effectively, obtain and use information, solve problems, and engage in active, life-long learning.

GOAL 2—Provide an Effective Instructional Program

Teach all students a curriculum that describes what they should know and be able to do, includes the many perspectives of a pluralistic society, and establishes learning standards. Instruction must include a variety of teaching strategies and technologies, actively involve students, and result in their mastery of learning objectives.

GOAL 3—Strengthen Productive Partnerships for Education

Secure commitment of the entire community to maintain quality education in Montgomery County by building partnerships of families, community, business, and staff that promote and support initiatives to help all children succeed.

GOAL 4—Create a Positive Work Environment in a Self Renewing Organization

Develop a climate in which staff effectiveness and creativity are encouraged, respected, valued and supported to promote productivity and ownership for student success. Provide efficient and effective support and staff development for the instructional program.

OUTCOMES

A. Increase the percentage of students each year who meet the Maryland School Performance Program (MSPP state standards so that within four years all racial groups in the system will meet the standards.

B. Increase the percentage of students each year who meet the MSPP state standards so that within four years all racial groups in each school will meet the standards.

C. Increase the percentage of students each year who meet the MSPP local standards so that within four years all racial groups in the system will meet the standards.

D. Increase the percentage of students each year who meet the MSPP local standards so that within four years all racial groups in each school will meet the standards.

E. Increase completion by African American and Hispanic students of the PreK-8 algebra mathematics program that prepares students for successful completion of Algebra I in grade nine.

F. Increase participation of African American and Hispanic students in Honors and Advanced courses.

G. Increase participation and improve performance of African American and Hispanic students on PSATs and SATs.

Exhibit 3 (continued)

H. Eliminate disproportionate suspension rates of African American and Hispanic students in the system.

I. Eliminate disproportionate suspension rates of African American and Hispanic students in each school.

J. Eliminate disproportionate representation of African American students within special education programs.

Source: "Success for Every Student: a plan to improve the achievement of low to average achieving students, with special and critical emphasis on the needs of low to average achieving African American, American Indian, Asian American, and Hispanic students," adopted by the MCPS Board of Education, January 6, 1992.

Exhibit 4

Select MCPS Indicators: SY91, SY95, SY00, and SY05

	SY91	SY95	SY00	SY05
Total Enrollment	103,916	120,291	131,552	139,337
% African American	17%	19%	21%	23%
% Asian American	12%	13%	13%	14%
% Hispanic	9%	12%	15%	19%
% American Indian	0.3%	0.3%	0.3%	0.3%
% White	62%	57%	50%	43%
FARMS Enrollment	n/a	25,498	30,840	34,122
ESOL Enrollment	n/a	8,208	11,048	13,221
% Students Enrolled, Learning Disabled	4.4%	3.4%	4.5%	4.4%
% Af. Am. Males Enrolled	8.5%	7.1%	8.3%	7.8%
Graduation Rate	n/a	92%	92%	91%
African American	n/a	n/a	87%	89%
Hispanic	n/a	n/a	88%	82%
Suspension Rate	4.0%	5.4%	3.3%	4.6%
African American	9.5%	11.8%	6.5%	9.9%
Hispanic	5.2%	7.8%	3.7%	5.7%
SAT Number Tested	4,730	5,044	5,862	7,355
% African American	11%	14%	17%	19%
% Hispanic	5%	6%	7%	10%
Average SAT Score[a]	1080	1087	1093	1101
African American	909	940	915	917
Asian American	1107	1124	1125	1163
Hispanic	1024	996	960	942
White	1118	1137	1153	1174
AP/Honors Enrollment[b]	46%	53%	57%	66%
African American	25%	31%	35%	46%
Asian American	60%	68%	73%	82%
Hispanic	24%	28%	33%	45%
White	69%	60%	69%	79%
8th Grade Algebra 1 Completion[c]	n/a	n/a	43%	48%
African American	10%	11%	21%	24%
Asian American	43%	49%	61%	71%
Hispanic	10%	9%	16%	23%
White	32%	38%	55%	63%

Source: Montgomery County Public Schools.

[a] National average SAT score was 1028 in SY05—African American (864), Asian American (1091), Hispanic (922), White (1068).

[b] AP/Honors enrollment data under SY00 is actual enrollment data for spring semester SY01.

[c] National completion rate for Algebra 1 in Grade 8 was 25% in 2000, National Center for Educational Statistics, www.nces.ed.gov/nationsreportcard/mathematics, accessed June 16, 2006.

Exhibit 5

MCPS County Maps—Red/Green Zone Figures

Schools/Enrollment[a]	Red Zone	Green Zone	Total
Elementary	60	65	125
Middle			36
High			24
Special or Alternative			6
Career/Technology Center			1
Pre-K – 12 Enrollment			
African American	21,814	9,818	31,632
American Indian	201	189	402
Asian American	8,350	11,968	20,318
Hispanic	20,614	6,495	27,109
White	16,150	44,462	60,612
FARMS	26,547	7,348	33,895
ESOL	9,575	3,558	13,133

[a] MCPS does not use red/green zone categorization for middle and high schools because students residing in both zones overlap widely in secondary schools. Enrollment numbers represent students residing in these areas as of January 2005. Some students attend schools outside their area. FARMs and ESOL numbers are based on current enrollment in programs.

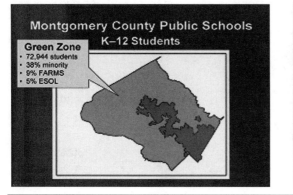 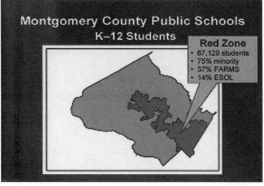

Source: Montgomery County Public Schools.

Exhibit 6

MCPS Reform Chronology under Superintendent Jerry Weast

1999	August	Weast hired as superintendent
1999	November	"Our Call to Action" report released to community
1999	November	Community superintendents hired
2000	January	Honors/AP Enrollment procedure changed
2000	January	Focus schools identified
2000	February	MCPS joins *Baldrige Initiative in Education*
2000	July	Kindergarten reform initiatives begin in focus schools
2000	July	Staff development teachers hired across all schools
2000	August	*Studying Skillful Teacher* course introduced
2001	July	Board institutes new curricular review policy
2002	February	Instructional Management System (IMS) launched at select elementary schools
2002	April	Graves hired to lead newly developed Diversity Training and Development group
2002	July	Math curricular limited to Harcourt and Everyday Mathematics district wide
2002	July	Daily reading and math requirements instituted across all schools in Grades 1–2
2003	March	Grading and reporting policy changed
2003	July	Daily reading and math requirements begin expansion to Grades 3–5
2004	July	Lacey promoted to Deputy Superintendent of Schools
2004	July	Diversity Training and Development Unit expanded
2004	September	A special focus is placed on recruiting and hiring minority candidates for leadership positions
2005	February	Gifted and Talented identification global screening process revised
2005	July	Professional Learning Communities Institute opens with 11 school teams
2005	July	Institutional barriers such as race identified as key area of focus for MCPS leadership

Source: Montgomery County Public Schools.

Exhibit 7

MCPS Organizational Chart (at end of SY05)

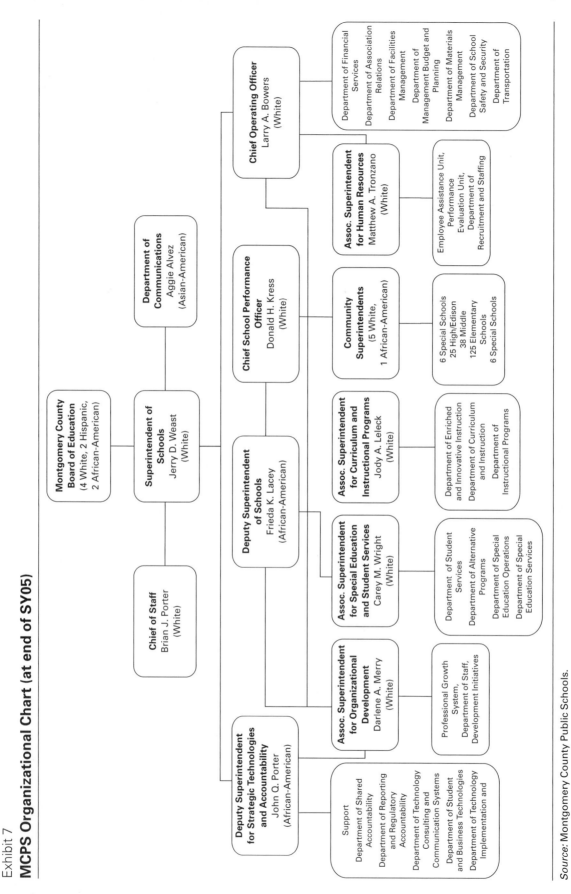

Source: Montgomery County Public Schools.

[a] Includes the African-American student member of the board of education. This yearly student-elected board position has some voting restrictions.

Exhibit 8
MCPS Student/Staff Demographic Figures

SY05 MCPS Overview

Student Demographics		*Teaching Staff*	
Number of students (K–12)	139,337	Number of teachers	11,632
White	43.3%	White	79.6%
African American	22.6%	African American	12.6%
Hispanic	19.4%	Hispanic	3.9%
Asian American	14.4%	Asian American	3.7%
American Indian	0.3%	American Indian	0.3%
Students receiving free and reduced-price meals (FARMS)	23.7%		
English-language learners (ESOL)	8.9%	Number of staff development teachers	206
Special education students (SPED)	11.9%	White	82.0%
		African American	13.6%
Administration and Staff		Hispanic	2.4%
Number of Administrators	685	Asian American	1.9%
White	63.9%	American Indian	0%
African American	29.6%		
Hispanic	3.9%		
Asian American	2.3%		
American Indian	0.3%		
Number of Principals	192		
White	66.0%		
African American	28.8%		
Hispanic	3.1%		
Asian American	1.6%		
American Indian	0.5%		
Total full-time employees (FTEs)	16,500		

Source: Montgomery County Public Schools.

Exhibit 9a

Comprehensive Test of Basic Skills (CTBS) Scores for Grade 2a

CTBS Scores for Grade 2 (Percent of Scores at or Above NP50)							
		Test Year					
		2000	2001	2002	2003	2004	2005
Red Zone 60 focus schools	Total	55.2%	53.1%	56.3%	60.4%	66.9%	68.6%
	American Indian	69.3%	56.2%	76.8%	51.8%	58.3%	62.9%
	Asian American	67.7%	67.2%	72.2%	75.7%	79.0%	80.3%
	African American	44.5%	43.4%	47.9%	50.8%	59.4%	62.6%
	White	72.0%	70.2%	73.1%	77.2%	81.7%	81.4%
	Hispanic	40.6%	38.8%	42.1%	50.6%	58.7%	61.0%
Green Zone	Total	73.3%	74.8%	77.2%	77.9%	82.0%	82.7%
	American Indian	75.4%	76.9%	81.5%	68.9%	62.7%	91.9%
	Asian American	83.6%	85.6%	85.6%	87.2%	89.5%	89.5%
	African American	46.6%	50.1%	49.8%	54.8%	62.6%	62.4%
	White	77.5%	79.8%	82.4%	82.2%	86.0%	87.8%
	Hispanic	54.2%	51.1%	56.9%	61.1%	67.5%	64.7%
County	Total	64.5%	64.0%	67.0%	69.6%	74.8%	76.0%
	American Indian	72.1%	64.9%	78.7%	60.6%	59.8%	76.1%
	Asian American	75.8%	76.6%	79.6%	82.5%	85.3%	85.8%
	African American	45.1%	45.4%	48.4%	52.0%	60.4%	62.6%
	White	75.9%	76.9%	79.8%	80.9%	84.9%	86.2%
	Hispanic	43.6%	41.1%	45.3%	52.8%	60.7%	61.9%

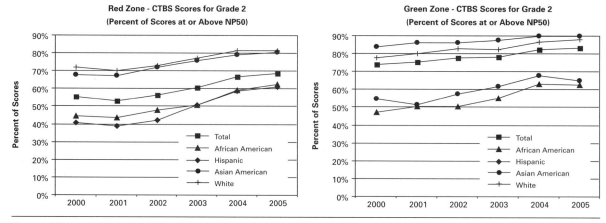

Source: Montgomery County Public Schools.

a The TerraNova CTBS measures basic reading, language, and mathematics skills and provides comparative information on the performance of students relative to the performance of students in the CTBS national norming samples. CTBS results are reported as national percentile ranks.

Exhibit 9b

Maryland State Assessments (MSAs)—MCPS Grade 3 Results by Race

Trends by Race—% of Students at Advanced and Proficient

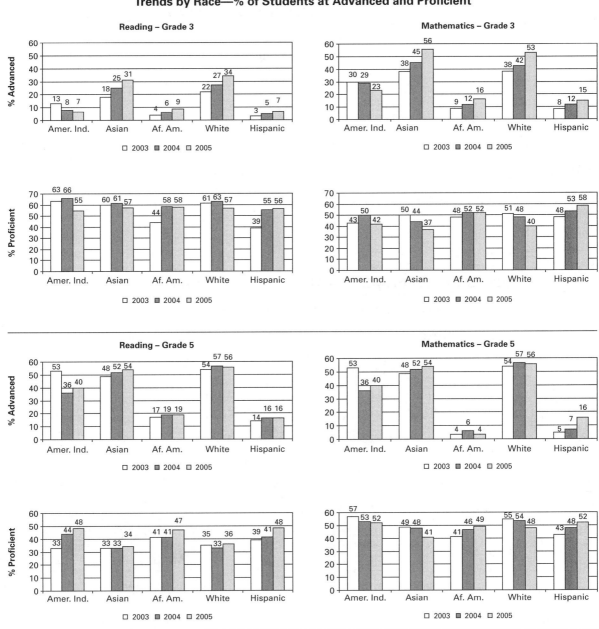

Source: http://mdreportcard.org.

Exhibit 10
MCPS Gifted and Talented (GT) Identification Figures

Number and Percentage of Grade 2 Students Screened and Identified in 2003–2004 and 2004–2005 by Race/Ethnicity

| | 2003–2004 | | | | 2004–2005 | | | |
| | Screened | | Identified | | Screened | | Identified | |
	N	%	n	%	N	%	n	%
All Students	10,118		4,503	44.5	9,875		3,333	33.8
African American	2,127	21	519	11.5	2,196	22.2	411	12.3
American Indian	26	0.2	7	0.2	37	0.3	18	0.5
Asian American	1,544	15.3	887	19.7	1,568	15.9	710	21.3
Hispanic	2,101	20.8	625	13.9	2,079	21.1	354	10.6
White	4,320	42.7	2,465	54.7	3,995	40.5	1,840	55.2

Source: Montgomery County Public Schools.

Exhibit 11a
Maryland State Assessments (MSAs)—MCPS Grade 8 Results

Grade 8 Trends by Race—% of Students at Advanced, Proficient or Basic

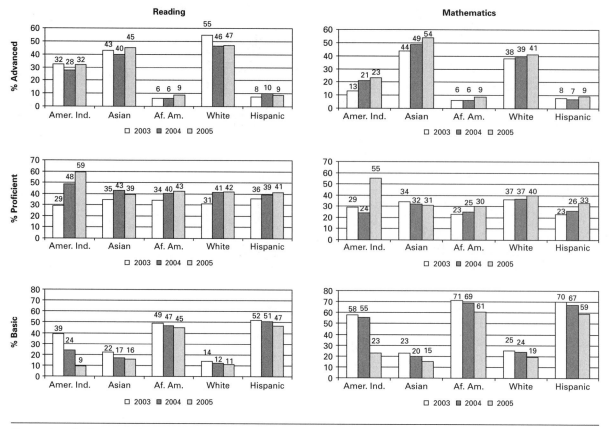

Source: http://mdreportcard.org.

Exhibit 11b
MCPS AP/Honors Enrollment Figures

Percent of Students Enrolled in at Least one Honors/AP Course and Total Enrollment (All Schools)

	Percent Enrolled (Spring Semester)				Total Enrollment			
	SY01	SY03	SY04	SY05	SY01	SY03	SY04	SY05
All Students	57	64	65	66	37,921	41,110	42,495	43,702
African American	35	43	44	46	7,770	8,584	9,259	9,802
American Indian	57	60	57	55	95	95	99	113
Asian American	73	80	81	82	5,454	6,051	6,209	6,336
Hispanic	33	40	42	45	5,226	6,199	6,817	7,311
White	69	76	78	79	19,376	20,181	20,111	20,140
LEP	17	23	25	32	2,318	2,643	2,793	3,171
FARMS	26	34	36	38	5,107	5,804	6,301	6,724
SPED	15	19	20	20	4,259	4,638	4,771	5,001

2001 and 2005 Senior Cohorts AP Participation and Performance: Grouping Based on Elementary School of Home Address

			Number in Cohort	Number Taking an AP Test	Percent Taking an AP Test	Number with at Least One 3	Percent of Cohort w/ at Least One 3
2001	**Red Zone**	African American	1,199	150	13%	85	7%
	60 focus	Asian American	591	242	41%	191	32%
		Hispanic	757	115	15%	88	12%
		White	1,423	584	41%	481	34%
		Total	3,970	1,091	27%	845	21%
	Green Zone	African American	493	110	22%	76	15%
		Asian American	651	404	62%	357	55%
		Hispanic	321	91	28%	81	25%
		White	2,917	1,486	51%	1,267	43%
		Total	4,382	2,091	48%	1,781	41%
	MCPS	African American	1,692	260	15%	161	10%
		Asian American	1,242	646	52%	548	44%
		Hispanic	1,078	206	19%	169	16%
		White	4,340	2,070	48%	1,748	40%
		Total	8,352	3,182	38%	2,626	31%
2005	**Red Zone**	African American	1,283	360	28%	203	16%
	60 focus	Asian American	586	360	61%	266	45%
		Hispanic	845	295	35%	248	29%
		White	1,217	702	58%	567	47%
		Total	3,931	1,717	44%	1,284	33%
	Green Zone	African American	604	191	32%	122	20%
		Asian American	843	655	78%	554	66%
		Hispanic	355	163	46%	146	41%
		White	3,272	2,116	65%	1,825	56%
		Total	5,074	3,125	62%	2,647	52%
	MCPS	African American	1,887	551	29%	325	17%
		Asian American	1,429	1,015	71%	820	57%
		Hispanic	1,200	458	38%	394	33%
		White	4,489	2,818	63%	2,392	53%
		Total	9,005	4,842	54%	3,931	44%

Source: Montgomery County Public Schools.

DISCUSSION QUESTIONS

1. How successful were the additional activities put in place after the July retreat? Evaluate the success of these efforts.

2. What is the underlying nature of the challenges and obstacles that district leaders faced in their attempts to create systemic change to close the achievement gap?

3. What skills and competencies are required to lead an initiative in which issues of race and class are at stake?

Karen L. Mapp ■ David A. Thomas ■ Tonika Cheek Clayton

Race, Accountability, and the Achievement Gap (B)

Several weeks after Maryland's Montgomery County Public Schools (MCPS) leadership team renewed their focus on race and the achievement gap, African-American Deputy Superintendent Frieda Lacey arrived at work early on September 29, 2005, to prepare for the morning executive leadership team meeting. In the meeting, her work would take center stage as she led discussions on PSAT participation and a new accountability system in development, called M-Stat. While organizing her remarks, she reflected on the leadership team's efforts to address the achievement gap since the team's return from the July retreat.

A Fresh Look at Enrollment Data

In early August 2005, the MCPS executive leadership team participated in a condensed simulation of the July retreat in which they continued discussions on race, access, and equity in the school district. Since MCPS's mathematics program had traditionally been viewed as having institutional barriers that impeded African-Americans and Hispanics, MCPS leadership decided to place a new emphasis on accelerating math instruction in elementary and middle

schools with the ultimate goal of all students completing Algebra 1 by eighth grade. Subsequently, white Superintendent Jerry Weast directed his administration to collect all advanced math enrollment figures disaggregated by race, starting with elementary schools. Since central office did not have much of this data on record, community superintendents had to go directly to schools for the information.

Already under pressure to implement school reforms, elementary school principals scrambled to submit the data, which revealed that at the beginning of the year just 23% of fifth-grade students enrolled in Math A (sixth-grade-level math) or above were African-American or Hispanic, even though they together made up 43% of the fifth-grade student population. Overall, 37% of MCPS fifth graders were enrolled in Math A or higher, ranging from 0% to 68% of the enrollment across elementary schools. Nevertheless, administrators were encouraged to see that the total number of all students enrolled in Math A or higher had increased substantially from 196 students in 2001 to 3,840 fifth graders in 2005. Also, a few red-zone schools stood above the average, like Piney Branch Elementary, which had 48% of its fifth graders enrolled in Math A or higher, 33% of whom were African-American and Hispanic students. By the end of the school year, the percentage of students enrolled in Math A who were African-American or Hispanic had risen to 39%.

At the middle school level, administrators took note of schools like Newport Mill Middle School, at which the math department had been successful in preparing 54% of the school's African-American and Hispanic eighth graders for enrollment in Algebra 1. Eager to learn their method and determine if it could be shared with other schools, Weast visited with the math department to get a better understanding of the school's strategy. Since staff at Newport Mill had heard rumors from central office that they had been accused of "teaching to the test" because of their relatively high achievement results, the math team was initially concerned when they learned that Weast planned to visit to understand how they achieved their results. Weast came away from his visit greatly impressed by what he saw and heard. "They get it," he said.

At the high school level, administrators began searching for underrepresented minority students who possessed the aptitude to excel in advanced courses but had not enrolled. Acting on the research suggesting that PSAT scores are good indicators for honors and AP course potential, the Department of Shared Accountability cross-referenced 11th-grade students' PSAT scores with AP and honors course enrollment lists.[1] The process identified any students with PSAT scores equal to or above 44 or 45 on the verbal and math sections, respectively, who were not enrolled in any honors or AP courses. High school principals received a list of all students flagged in addition to a separate list of just the African-American and Hispanic students identified, comprising 39% of the total number of students flagged. Each report listed the student's name, PSAT scores, grade point average, recent course grades, and whether or not they had ever enrolled in any AP or honors courses.

Noticing from the data that African-American and Hispanic students enrolled in higher-level courses scored significantly higher on the SAT, Weast believed that helping more minority students succeed in advanced courses was a critical component of closing the achievement gap. Subsequently, Weast's administration shifted its focus to communicating the district's new emphasis on helping more African-American and Hispanic students achieve in rigorous courses.

Framing the Discussion

In the early weeks following the retreat, senior administrators debated the appropriate language to use when discussing race issues within the district. While some preferred the description "removing institutional barriers," others favored the terms "institutionalized racism" because they believed that it most accurately described the real issue. A few administrators expressed concerns that using the word "racism" could potentially spark fear in some administrators and teachers who would misinterpret it to mean that they were racist. Weast distinguished between the two phrases, explaining that "institutionalized racism is the failure to act on removing institutional barriers that hold students of a particular race behind." MCPS administrators defined institutional barriers as those policies, procedures, and practices that do not serve all children equitably.

On September 14, 2005, Weast delivered an emotional speech to all MCPS administrators, including principals and senior leadership staff, to set the strategic focus for SY06. To frame his presentation on institutional racism, Weast referenced the aftermath of Hurricane Katrina to explain the connections between race, poverty, and access. Holding aloft a copy of a magazine that featured the face of a crying child from New

Orleans, Weast remarked that what happened to a largely African-American population during and after the hurricane was a metaphor for public education:

> That hurricane did something to me . . . you and I have talked about raise the bar and close the gap, and I've talked about who gets left behind if we don't have education. And I've actually been overemotional on this many times. But you know, the one thing that struck me was how people were sorted. It just really got to me. I know it got to you and other people. And I know that. . . . I can close my eyes and see the beautiful mountains when I feel troubled. Now when I close my eyes, I see those folks huddled in the Superdome with the roof coming off or in that facility in Houston. It's hard to say it's not about race, isn't it?

> . . .Now I am going to get right down into the race issue, and I am going to talk about Hispanics and African-Americans. And if it hurts, I'm sorry. I apologize respectfully, but I am going to talk about it. You need to talk about it. You need to have that [conversation] because we are going to [work] together to destroy institutional barriers that have sorted kids for way too long.

Closing out his reference to the aftermath of the hurricane, Weast made the connection one more time to the isolation of African-American and Hispanic students who are not given an opportunity to succeed academically. He stated, "We're not going to wake up one morning and find that our kids can't get out of town because they don't have enough money or any access [to public services]."

Weast said that a key component to overcoming the achievement gap included giving more African-American and Hispanic students access to high-level quality and equitable instruction. Referencing the advanced math enrollment data, he recognized the African-

American principal of Piney Branch Elementary because of the school's relatively high Math A enrollment figures. He then challenged the group to build the capacity to allow more minority students to participate in rigorous coursework, thereby creating a "continuous supply chain" of prepared students. Finally, he compared the merits of a "can-do belief system of courage, commitment, and productivity" to a "can't-do attitude of complacency, compliance, and inactivity."

Concerned about how principals might respond to Weast's observations of racism, senior administrators were later reassured by the overwhelmingly positive feedback he received. Lacey remarked: "The devastation of Hurricane Katrina and its aftermath really showed how issues of race, poverty, and access play out in our society. To have seen the images of Katrina on TV and then to have Jerry, a white man, stand up and show the parallels of Katrina with the school system was powerful and magnificent."

M-Stat

Impressed during the July retreat by a case discussion on the New York Police Department's Comstat data-driven accountability system, MCPS leadership sought to systemize a similar collaborative process that could be used by executive leadership staff, particularly the community superintendents. Spearheading the development of what the team called M-Stat, Lacey created an M-Stat framework by aligning elements from Comstat to a model already in use within MCPS, called Plan/Do/Study/Act (see Exhibit 1 for M-Stat framework). With M-Stat, leadership saw an opportunity to enable community superintendents to collectively look at data across schools and work together on crafting solutions to high-priority issues based on best practices and research.

Tailoring the focus of M-Stat to removing institutional barriers for African-Americans and

Hispanics, Lacey and her colleagues brainstormed all possible barriers that the district had in place that potentially hindered the success of minority students. The team agreed that the first few sessions of M-Stat should focus on PSAT participation and advanced course enrollment.

During the September 29th executive leadership team meeting, Lacey planned to further refine and test the M-Stat process beginning with a discussion on the upcoming fall 2005 PSAT that would be administered on October 12.

Executive Leadership Team Meeting— September 29, 2005

Lacey set aside two hours of the meeting to review M-Stat and the upcoming PSAT (see Exhibit 2 for regular meeting attendees). Starting with M-Stat, the team collaborated on changes to the framework before breaking into small groups to identify priority topics for M-Stat and discuss how to deal with issues of institutional racism as part of the process. Finally, each small group was asked to continue discussions beyond the meeting and submit summaries of their feedback to Lacey's team.

Moving on to PSAT participation, the room fell silent when Lacey asked community superintendents to explain the low participation numbers for African-American and Hispanic 10th graders on the fall 2004 PSAT. After what some described as a tense, uncomfortable pause, a few attendees questioned whether the 100% participation goal was realistic given the number of students enrolled in programs such as Fundamental Life Skills or levels one and two ESOL classes.[2] Lacey gave them one week to report back with specific plans from each high school to raise their minority PSAT participation numbers. At the same time, the participation target was recalibrated to exclude the aforementioned groups.

Noting the awkwardness in the room fol-lowing the moment she broached the PSAT participation data, Lacey thought carefully about how to foster a productive environment whereby everyone felt comfortable to be honest and open to new ideas while the district addressed tough issues relating to race. She wanted the community superintendents and others to feel both accountable for results and willing to openly discuss areas in which their schools were weak. With hopes of dissipating some of the embarrassment and tension from the first meeting, Lacey arranged to follow up on the PSAT participation work in the weekly meetings of the Office of School Performance, which included her, white Chief School Performance Officer Don Kress, and the community superintendents.

Fall 2005 PSAT and M-Stat Follow-Up

One week following the executive leadership team meeting, Lacey and Kress met with community superintendents to continue the M-Stat discussion with new information from principals regarding the strategies they would employ at each high school to improve PSAT participation. Lacey recalled:

> Our first efforts were not focused. There was a smorgasbord of strategies being put in place that addressed the total school population even though we had distributed the participation numbers by race and ethnicity. So I asked, "What are you doing specifically for African-American and Hispanic students at schools where the students are mostly white?" They were unable to provide me with specific answers, and I told them to bring the information back at the next meeting.

To boost participation numbers, schools used a combination of communication, incentive, and procedural tactics, including pancake breakfasts, threats to administer old PSAT exams to absent students, and sending letters home to parents in multiple languages. Specific strategies targeting African-American and Hispanic students included meeting with those students individually, meeting with related clubs or groups, and phoning minority-student parents. Ultimately, the community superintendents worked with their principals and one another to improve overall participation numbers of African-American and Hispanic students by two and eight percentage points, respectively (see Exhibit 3 for fall 2005 PSAT participation results). Thirteen out of the 24 high schools showed participation improvements from both minority groups. Some schools made substantial gains (5% or more) in the participation of African-American and Hispanic students.

As follow-up, Lacey's team compiled a list of best practices recommended by successful principals and planned to share them in a memo to all principals before SY07 began. Lacey's group also planned to recognize schools that increased overall, African-American, or Hispanic participation by five percentage points or more in the form of recognition requested by the principal. Schools with 95% participation or higher would also be recognized. The gains impressed Lacey, surpassing her expectations. "The community superintendents and principals responded to the challenge," she said.

Discovering and Removing Institutional Barriers

Honors/AP Potential Identification Tool (HAPIT)

Soon after Lacey's team completed the PSAT M-Stat exercise, the community superintendents went through another round of M-Stat to address the disproportionately low enrollment figures of African-American and Hispanic students in AP and honors courses. Lacey recalled:

> Again, we received pushback and lots of excuses like "the student didn't make a high enough grade in this course, or they didn't want

to move to a higher class," and so on. So we said to the community superintendents, "Have we provided them with the research showing that these students have the aptitude for more rigorous classes? And what have we done to let them know we're serious about this?" We then pulled together a work group of staff, principals, and guidance counselors to address the issue, and they came up with the tool HAPIT.

Building on the earlier work done to review PSAT scores and flag high-potential students who had not enrolled in any honors or AP courses, HAPIT allowed principals to easily compile a list of students who met certain criteria. The first version of HAPIT was a Microsoft Excel spreadsheet that allowed the user to filter down to a list of students based on a variety of factors, including ethnicity, PSAT scores, grades, course enrollments, and past performance on select MSA exams.

Hoping to get a better understanding of why some African-American and Hispanic students were on the flagged students list and had not enrolled in any AP or honors courses, Lacey decided in the fall of SY06 to meet with several minority students to learn their personal stories. Lacey described her conversations with students:

> First I met with a student who had a 4.0 GPA and PSAT scores higher than 44. She said, "I advocated for myself to be in an AP/honors course, but they told me that classes were full and that I should come back next year."

> Another student said, "Well, I'm a little ADD [attention deficit disordered] and a little lazy and I really don't want to do this," and I said, "But you made one of the highest PSAT math scores." Then I asked him, "What advanced math course would you be most interested in taking?" And he said, "Statistics." So I asked if he would go to the guidance counselor's office that day to enroll in that course during the fall, and he said,

"Yes." When the principal offered to take him, the student hesitated, so I offered to walk with him to the office. This is why it is so important that principals and teachers have relationships with the students. If there's already a relationship it can take as little as five minutes to encourage a student to challenge themselves to take more advanced courses. And I told *that* student I would be checking on his progress in the fall.

Relationship & Mentors

After scheduling the initial minority-student meetings at one high school, Lacey learned that many of the schools had begun moving the flagged students into higher-level courses. She commented:

> The good news was that by the time I showed up to the school, all but one of the students on the list had already been enrolled in an AP or honors course. Word had spread fast that we were developing the tool and visiting with students. By early spring, when I made plans to meet with more students, we only found four students who still met the initial criteria, all of whom had recently immigrated to the United States and were unfamiliar with how U.S. public school systems worked. I learned from them that the guidance counselors in their schools had automatically enrolled them in on-grade level courses even though the students had the capacity for higher-level courses. One student said to me, "I wish the counselor could have explained to me the different course levels or given me a test before putting me in those courses. I feel like I've wasted so much time." I knew we could fix that easily, so I'm determined to make it right.

Process & Procedures

By May 2006, all principals, guidance counselors, and resource teachers had been trained to use HAPIT, and the work group that developed the tool was investigating other potential applications. Since the initial identification of students in August 2005, 60 out of 80 minority students had been moved to enroll in at least one AP or honors course by spring 2006. This included 92% of identified African-American students and 63% of identified Hispanic students. Lacey was pleased. "The community superintendents acted quickly in demanding more from schools," she said.

Since the PSAT would be administered to both ninth and 10th graders in subsequent years, MCPS leadership planned to use HAPIT to identify students qualified for AP and honors enrollment even earlier. Plans also were underway to link the tool to MCPS's data warehouse so that the information could be updated in real time and be available online. The tool's progress was shared with the board of education on May 9, 2006. While pleased with the initial outcome, board members emphasized the importance of determining how the tool could be used to inform administrators and teachers about the other students who did not score above the PSAT threshold or meet other benchmarks.

Technology Drive Improvement

Mathematics Pathways

Beyond asking schools to build capacity for more students to take higher-level math courses, administrators were developing a "Mathematics Pathways" document to enable parents to see what math level their child would complete upon graduation if they continued on a given path of math instruction. Designed to make parents and students more aware of the academic path they were headed down, administrators were collaborating with union and parent leaders to design the document (see Exhibit 4 for draft Mathematics Pathways guide). Although board members and district administrators overwhelmingly supported Weast's push for more students to take algebra by the eighth grade and Math A by fifth grade, some teachers questioned whether or not most students were ready for Algebra 1 by eighth grade, while others did not

Sharing the Guide

understand the reasoning behind pushing so many students into advanced courses.

Shaping Expectations

Diversity Training and Development: Just as senior administrators returned from the July retreat, the Diversity Training and Development (DTD) department was finishing new online modules on *Courageous Conversations about Race* and *Communicating High Expectations to Students.*[3] The online multimedia, interactive modules were designed for staff development teachers and administrators to use in small or large groups of staff. Since DTD did not have the capacity to respond to all school requests for diversity training, the team planned to roll the modules out to all schools beginning in SY07 to facilitate diversity training at the school level.

Acknowledging the diversity training's value, a few community superintendents had taken the initiative to utilize DTD's offerings during their scheduled time with principals. For example, African-American Community Superintendent LaVerne Kimball, whose schools primarily served students residing in the green zone, had DTD specialists train her principals on the impact of "color-blindness" on teaching and learning (see Exhibit 5 for Kimball's follow-up e-mail and training study assignment).[4] White Community Superintendent Steve Bedford, who oversaw the geographic region with the highest degree of poverty and highest concentration of minority students, allocated a significant portion of time each month for diversity training specialists to work with his principals.

In some schools, there was evidence that the knowledge from the training had penetrated down to the teacher level by the terminology teachers used, such as "courageous conversations" and "color-blindness." However, administrators acknowledged that the majority of teachers had yet to experience any of the diversity training, particularly at the high school level. Additionally, specialists noted that participants

sometimes did not understand the point of the training. Nevertheless, the mostly positive feedback from many participants suggested that the training increased awareness of the role race played in education, compelled some to reconsider their position that they should be color-blind, and helped some to become more willing to introduce race into instructional conversations.

By the end of SY06, the department had set up a host of old and new diversity training sessions that would be offered on a first-come, first-served basis to school-based teams during the summer and the upcoming school year (see Exhibit 6 for a sample of summer diversity training offerings). Despite the department's efforts to address low expectations of African-American and Hispanic students, some MCPS employees still worried that the district was not doing enough. Since the professional development offerings related to race and the achievement gap were still voluntary, the decision for teachers and other school staff to take part in the training was usually made by a school's principal or staff development teacher.

Showcasing Minority Success Stories: In an attempt to address community expectations of African-American and Hispanic students, MCPS administration took the advice of African-American MCPS Board member Valerie Ervin, who wanted the district to showcase more high-achieving African-American and Hispanic students in the community. Worried about the constant negative associations of African-American and Hispanics resulting from discourse on the achievement gap, Ervin hoped that success stories would reinforce high expectations and positive images of African-Americans and Hispanics. Initially, the focus was on showcasing successful students and programs at board of education meetings.

Communicating Progress: While communicating race and achievement gap challenges, the administration also made a concerted effort to publicize minority student performance progress through the district's traditional channels: press conferences, newspapers, the MCPS website, and the MCPS cable television channel. In spring 2006, MCPS released news that African-American and Hispanic students had improved for the fourth consecutive year on the MCPS reading assessments and were steadily improving on the national CTBS test. Despite the growth in numbers of African-Americans and Hispanics taking AP exams, the February 2006 data showed that five times more African-American students in MCPS scored a 3 or higher when compared with African-American students nationwide. Also, two times as many MCPS Hispanic students scored a 3 or better on AP exams compared with Hispanic students nationwide. Furthermore, 20% of African-American and 22% of Hispanic seniors in the class of 2005 scored above 1100 on the SAT, compared with the national averages of 11% and 18%, respectively. Still, Asian-American and white students participated in AP courses and the SAT at much higher rates, and they significantly outperformed their African-American and Hispanic counterparts on SAT and AP exams.

Minority Leadership Recruitment

A year before the retreat, Weast directed administrators to meet with leaders of African-American, Asian-American, and Hispanic community groups and expand minority recruitment efforts for teachers and administrators. Recognizing the lack of minorities in the district's administration and teaching staff, Weast wanted administrators to recruit more minority candidates to the district and groom existing stellar candidates for leadership positions in central office and schools.

In November 2005, the newly formed Minority Leadership Recruitment Committee, comprising district administrators and minority community leaders, asked principals and community members to nominate outstanding mi-

norities for potential school leadership opportunities. The request brought their attention to 108 African-American, 18 Asian, 20 Hispanic, and 20 other ethnic candidates the district invited to participate in a Future Administrators Workshop. The committee hoped their efforts would ultimately lead to a racial composition of administrators that better reflected the student population. However, MCPS administrators expressed concerns that the district needed to expand its outreach much more than it had to really make an impact on administrative staff diversity.

Collaborative Action Process (CAP)

In response to the disproportionate number of minority students, particularly African-American males, MCPS leadership decided in early SY06 to make the Collaborative Action Process (CAP) mandatory for all schools. Piloted in several schools beginning in SY04, the CAP program allowed school-based teams to work with a CAP consultant to become trained in problem-solving approaches for students' learning or behavioral issues. The program helped schools to determine the appropriate academic or behavioral interventions to test or administer with individual students, student subsets, or grade levels. Preliminary results from the first wave of implementation in 30 schools showed a decrease in the number of student referrals to special education and in the number of students sent to the principal's office. The program was in various stages of implementation in 60 schools by the end of SY06.

Designing Accountability

School-Monitoring Calendars

In response to Weast's frustration that there was not enough consistency across the work of community superintendents, Lacey directed the community superintendents to create a school-monitoring calendar that would allow the community superintendents and principals to regularly work together on similar issues each month. The resultant calendar drafted in November 2005 focused on a specific set of data each month across all schools within a sublevel, elementary, middle, or high (see Exhibit 7 for an example of monthly data points and questions).

To determine the data indicators to be examined each month, community superintendents back-mapped from the desired performance results each school should expect to reach by the end of the school year. Therefore, each month the principals would ideally review data that could help them adjust, if needed, to meet end-of-year targets. The document went through several iterations to accommodate feedback from principals and other stakeholders. Beginning in July 2006, community superintendents planned to integrate the calendars into their monthly discussions with principals. Kress commented on principals' responses to the new monitoring system: "Most principals were happy because they could use the document to easily explain to their school staff what central office expected of them with regards to school performance. A few principals complained that the new system bordered on micromanaging." In addition to helping the district more carefully monitor school performance, administrators hoped the new system would enable them to better recognize strengths and weaknesses in individual schools and provide struggling principals with a framework to guide their own work.

Setting Improvement Targets

Another significant change related to district leadership's deliberate attempts to address the performance of minority subgroups was the development of specific school improvement targets broken down by race. Previous improvement targets communicated to principals were set system-wide and not tailored specifically to the past results of a school. Under the new system, schools had set targets for each ethnic sub-

group to meet each year until 2010 (see Exhibit 8 for an improvement target spreadsheet example). On each improvement target spreadsheet, the schools were disaggregated by community superintendent, making it clear which central office administrator would monitor and help principals reach the improvement goals. By the end of SY06, high school principals had received their targets, while middle school and elementary school principals were scheduled to receive targets in fall of SY07.

Forging Ahead

During subsequent administrative gatherings and MCPS Board of Education meetings, Weast continued the dialogue on institutional barriers and racism and defined what he called "The Path to Achievement," which concisely communicated his vision of what every student should achieve before graduating from MCPS (see Exhibit 9 for "The Path to Achievement" slide). When conveying his related strategy for closing the achievement gap in simplest terms, he used the formula "Access + Equity + Rigor = Achievement." Adding to Weast's equation, one community superintendent expanded on what needed to be done to improve minority–student achievement:

> We need to do three things to help our African-American and Hispanic students: (1) Give them access to the most rigorous and most comprehensive classes. (2) Provide them with an opportunity to be successful in those classes by offering adequate support systems. (3) And most important, we've got to invite the students to be in those classes. Many students or parents don't know the maneuverability of the system, and oftentimes they're counting on the system to do it for them.

Looking ahead, Lacey was pleased with the progress made thus far, but she was realistic about the challenges facing MCPS as leadership endeavored to close the achievement gap:

> We still have a tremendous amount of work to do. We have to do a better job at monitoring school data and reinforcing successful strategies for students who are struggling. When we get positive outcomes, we need to share that information. We need a formalized, systemic process that identifies and recognizes schools that are doing a great job. We need to package best practices to be shared with other schools. This means we must continue to disaggregate the data. And we need to strengthen the message that it's OK to have specific strategies in place for underperforming minority students.
>
> The biggest challenge is making sure that people have high expectations for all students. The one thing that I really think makes a difference in changing expectations is data. We have to keep showing performance results from successful schools to those individuals who just don't get it!

Notes

1. Clare Von Secker, "Using PSAT Scores to Identify Honors/AP Potential," Research Brief, Montgomery County Public Schools. She wrote, "Research conducted for the College Board shows that, in many AP courses, about one third of students with PSAT scores below the national averages have Honors/AP potential and are able to attain AP exam scores of 3 or higher (Camara, 1997, Camara & Millsap, 1998). The percentages of MCPS students with Honors/AP potential who score 3 or higher on AP exams exceed the percentages reported for national samples. As many as two thirds of MCPS AP test takers with PSAT verbal scores of 42 to 46 or math scores of 43 to 47 attain AP exam scores of 3 or higher on AP English, mathematics, science, and social studies examinations."

2. ESOL is an acronym for English for speakers of other languages. Students enrolled in ESOL are assigned a level according to their English proficiency. Levels one and two are the beginning levels. Fundamental Life Skills is a curriculum designed for students enrolled in special education programs who are non-diploma bound.

3. Based on the work of Glenn Singleton, MCPS defined "courageous conversations" as discussions to identify and break down racial/ethnic tensions, foster equality, and diminish conflict, including overt acts, misunderstandings, and miscommunications that lead to unequal treatment of individuals by race and ethnicity.

4. MCPS defined "color-blindness" as any policy, practice, or behavior that ignores race/ethnicity and skin color and treats these physical characteristics as inconsequential, deemphasizing their importance and focusing, instead, on providing all individuals with an equal chance to succeed in school, work, and life.

Exhibit 1
M-Stat Framework

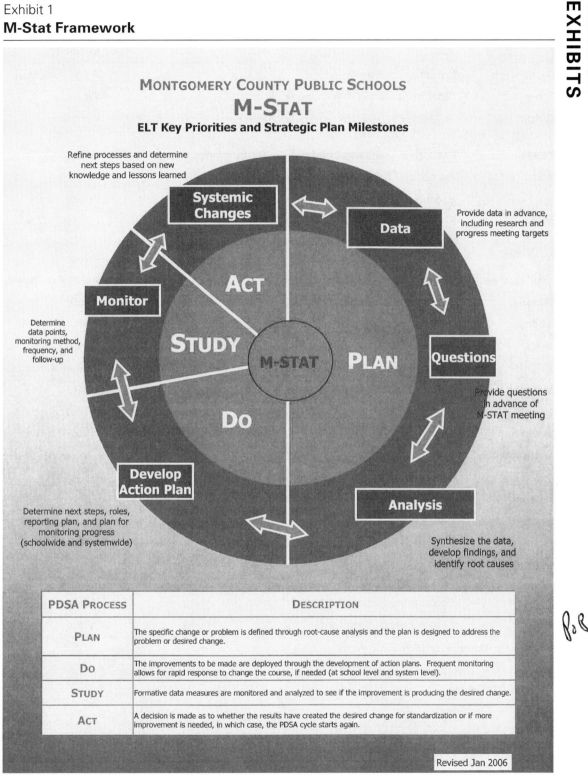

MONTGOMERY COUNTY PUBLIC SCHOOLS
M-STAT
ELT Key Priorities and Strategic Plan Milestones

Refine processes and determine
next steps based on new
knowledge and lessons learned

Systemic Changes

Data

Provide data in advance,
including research and
progress meeting targets

ACT

Monitor

Determine
data points,
monitoring method,
frequency, and
follow-up

STUDY

M-STAT

PLAN

Questions

Provide questions
in advance of
M-STAT meeting

DO

Develop Action Plan

Determine next steps, roles,
reporting plan, and plan for
monitoring progress
(schoolwide and systemwide)

Analysis

Synthesize the data,
develop findings, and
identify root causes

PDSA PROCESS	DESCRIPTION
PLAN	The specific change or problem is defined through root-cause analysis and the plan is designed to address the problem or desired change.
DO	The improvements to be made are deployed through the development of action plans. Frequent monitoring allows for rapid response to change the course, if needed (at school level and system level).
STUDY	Formative data measures are monitored and analyzed to see if the improvement is producing the desired change.
ACT	A decision is made as to whether the results have created the desired change for standardization or if more improvement is needed, in which case, the PDSA cycle starts again.

Revised Jan 2006

Source: Montgomery County Public Schools.

Exhibit 2

MCPS Executive Leadership Team, May 2006

Name	Title	Ethnicity
Aggie Alvez	Communications Director	Asian American
Brian Porter	Chief of Staff	White
Carey Wright	Associate Supt. for Special Education and Student Services	White
Cathy Pevey	Executive Assistant, Chief School Performance Officer	White
Darlene Merry	Associate Supt. for Organizational Development	White
David Hedges	Executive Assistant, Office of the Chief Operating Officer	White
Diane Mohr	Special Assistant, Office of the Deputy Supt. for Information and Organizational Systems	White
Don Kress	Chief School Performance Officer	White
Donna Hollingshead	Executive Director, Office of the Deputy Supt. of Schools	Asian American
Frank Stetson	Community Superintendent	White
Frieda Lacey	Deputy Superintendent of Schools	African American
Jody Leleck	Associate Supt. for Curriculum and Instructional Programs	White
John Q. Porter	Deputy Supt. for Information and Organizational Systems	African American
Kevin Maxwell	Community Superintendent	White
Larry Bowers	Chief Operating Officer	White
LaVerne Kimball	Community Superintendent	African American
Lori-Christina Webb	Executive Assistant, Office of the Deputy Supt. of Schools	African American
Mark Kelsch	Community Superintendent	White
Matt Tronzano	Associate Superintendent for Human Resources	White
Mike Perich	Coordinator, System-Wide Continuous Improvement	White
Robin Confino	Executive Assistant, Office of the Chief Operating Officer	White
Sherwin Collette	Executive Director, Office of the Deputy Supt. for Information and Organizational Systems	African American
Steve Bedford	Community Superintendent	White
Susan Marks	Community Superintendent	White

Source: Montgomery County Public Schools.

Exhibit 3
Fall 2005 PSAT Participation Results

	MCPS Grade 10 PSAT Participation Rates in Fall 2004 Compared with Fall 2005									
	Total		Af-Am		Asian		Hispanic		White	
School	2004	2005	2004	2005	2004	2005	2004	2005	2004	2005
MCPS	88	91	84	86	95	97	78	86	92	95
B-CC	94	95	88	92	92	100	92	95	96	94
Blair	90	90	87	88	91	98	89	82	93	98
Blake	94	91	94	85	96	92	88	88	95	96
Churchill	98	95	93	87	99	98	100	96	98	95
Damascus	85	92	75	90	100	92	71	84	86	94
Einstein	90	89	88	87	98	96	85	83	95	93
Gaithersburg	86	87	90	78	94	98	75	82	89	93
Kennedy	87	89	89	87	96	95	73	85	94	98
Magruder	83	90	69	85	92	99	68	84	89	92
Northwest	85	86	82	77	93	92	72	82	88	90
Northwood		95		96		94		94		95
Paint Branch	83	85	81	77	95	94	68	85	85	93
Poolesville	94	93	80	100	88	100	100	100	95	92
Quince Orchard	83	89	74	77	93	97	56	76	90	94
R. Montgomery	89	91	76	85	96	97	76	83	93	94
Rockville	82	91	70	92	92	100	73	88	89	90
Seneca Valley	88	95	82	94	98	100	81	94	92	94
Sherwood	90	94	79	80	89	100	89	93	93	96
Springbrook	88	87	91	85	93	95	71	79	92	95
W. Johnson	89	96	71	85	93	97	76	95	94	98
Watkins Mill	86	90	83	88	96	100	78	84	92	94
Wheaton	75	86	82	92	92	97	69	81	70	87
Whitman	94	98	80	100	92	97	93	92	96	98
Wootton	96	99	97	87	98	100	84	100	96	99

Source: Montgomery County Public Schools.

Exhibit 4
Draft Mathematics Pathways

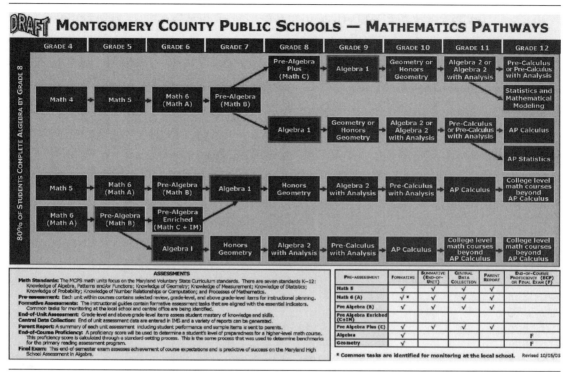

Source: Montgomery County Public Schools.

Exhibit 5a

E-mail Correspondence to Principals about Diversity Study Assignment

From:	Kimball, LaVerne
Sent:	Wednesday, October 12, 2005 5:40 PM
To:	Bishop, Richard ; Levine, Deena ; McEleney, Darlyne ; Poole, William ; Brubaker, Judy ; Bryant, Amy ; Edmundson, Gregory ; Evans Macfarlane, Eileen ; Joseph, Shawn ; Lange, Carol ; LeVine, Carol K; Morrison, Sylvia ; Queen, Dennis G; Sacco, Joseph M; Silverstein, Roni ; Chep, Lawrence ; Dardarian, Anne ; Riley, Jan ; Sample, Carole A; Schiavone Rupp, Kathryn; Shea, Daniel ; Vilkinofsky, Joan ; Wilson, Mary J; Carroll, Wanda ; Favret, Loretta; Gregory, William M; Johnson, Teri ; Kinsey-Barker, Pamela; Maxey, Suzanne ; Samm, AnnMarie
Cc:	Carroll, Joan; Shinn, Cathrine; Sagona, Donna M.; Nasser, Nora; Jones-Ewing, Kathryn
Subject:	Diversity Study Assignment

Dear Principals,

As you know, as a system, we have wholeheartedly embraced improving student achievement for underachieving subgroups. Glenn Singleton's point of view and research indicates that RACE really matters. To that end, we all recognize the importance of having courageous conversations around this issue. It is our hope that our quad cluster study of diversity will increase our comfort, knowledge, and skills in facilitating these discussions.

The assignment on "Colorblindness" may have been difficult for some, given the timeframe. For others, you may have already been engaging in discussions related to race, making the assignment, a continuation of your journey. While we realize the conversations you have been asked to engage staff in regarding "color blindness" may be challenging, we know you agree that they are important. As our professional learning community continues to study race and its impact on teaching and learning throughout the year, we are certain you will feel increasingly confident in your ability to facilitate these conversations.

A few people have reported that they have completed the assignment, and others have requested clarification. Attached is the original assignment with some minor clarifications in red, as well as questions that will guide our sharing at the October 19 meeting. If you have questions, do not hesitate to call Joan, Cathy, Donna, or myself.

LaVerne

Colorblindness9-28
assignmentv...

••

LaVerne Gray Kimball, Ed.D.
Office of School Performance
Community Superintendent for the
Northwest, Poolesville, Quince Orchard, Seneca Valley Quadcluster
301-315-7362

Expectations?

Source: Montgomery County Public Schools.

Exhibit 5b
Diversity Study Assignment—Color-Blindness

**Northwest/Quince Orchard/Seneca Valley/Poolesville Quad-Cluster
Follow-up Assignment from the 9-28-05 diversity session**

As an instructional leadership team, we need to take a closer look at how to begin addressing the issue of diversity, particularly with race and the achievement gap, to ensure that a culture of equitable practices, beliefs, behaviors, and attitudes, permeate within each school's environment, teaching and learning practices, leadership, etc.

Start thinking about:

- What does this mean to you and your work as a leader in your school?

- How you will take the understanding and information from the sessions back to your staff?

- Are there other key points addressed in the September 28, 2005 session on diversity, particularly race, and the achievement gap, that you will strive to incorporate within your school's culture?

Please select a group of staff members to engage in the following conversations. It is not necessary to engage all staff in the conversation at this time. You might wish to start with an administrative, leadership, departmental, or grade level team.

- Select a leadership group within your school to share Glenn Singleton's definition of colorblindness. Reflect on the implications of this definition for teaching and learning. How can teachers/leaders expand their lenses to ensure equitable teaching and learning practices?

- Throughout MCPS, disproportionate numbers of African American and Hispanic students are suspended? How does being "colorblind" exacerbate suspensions? Why is developing relationships with students a key strategy in establishing culturally sensitive learning environments that help students feel valued and connected?

Questions that will guide our sharing at the October 19 meeting:

In what ways was it difficult to discuss the concept of "color blindness" with your staff?

What would increase your level of comfort or ability to have these conversations with additional staff?

Source: Montgomery County Public Schools.

Exhibit 6

Sample of 2006 MCPS Diversity Training Summer Offerings

Title/Description	Audience	Capacity
Improving Latino Student Achievement – *Learn to capitalize on the cultural capital of Latino students to improve achievement. Discuss strategies for communicating effectively with Latino parents.*	Teachers, SDTs, Administrators	150
Equity, Race, and Achievement – *Engage in discussion and reflection that will support courageous conversations about race as you explore individual and institutional racism and their effects on student achievement.*	Teachers, SDTs, Administrators	100
Masks of Giftedness – *Analyze barriers that prevent recognition of giftedness in students. Examine curriculum and explore strategies that provide opportunities for students to demonstrate their gifts.*	Teachers, SDTs, Administrators	40
Understanding Islam – *Learn about Islamic culture and gain new understanding about Muslim students.*	Teachers, SDTs, Administrators	35
Developing Culturally Competent Schools – *In Day One, explore your cultural personal identity and learn about fundamental differences between mainstream culture and other cultures that impact teaching and learning. In Day Two, examine the patterns in traditional African American and Latino cultures that influence student achievement.*	Teachers, SDTs, Administrators	35
Communicating High Expectations to Students – *Learn to use the interactive online modules on teacher expectations to do small or large group training in your school. Engage your staff in a variety of interesting and innovative learning activities to reinforce mastery of new information through the use of interactive software.*	Teachers, SDTs, Administrators	30
Literacy Instruction for African American Adolescent Males – *Learn how the research on traditional African American culture intersects with the research on effective reading and writing instruction. Explore specific strategies for improving teaching and learning for African American adolescent males.*	Secondary Teachers, SDTs, Administrators	40
The Color of Disproportionality – *Examine policies, practices, and procedures that may result in the over-identification of African American students in special education programs and services. Explore culturally responsive practices to support the academic achievement of African American students.*	Teachers, SDTs, Administrators	35

Source: Montgomery County Public Schools.

Exhibit 7

December SY07—Example of Monitoring Calendar Items (High School) at MCPS

Performance Results/Data Points[1] *Aligned with the MCPS Strategic Plan and Bridges to Excellence*	**Questions to be Considered**
PSAT Results—Grades 10 and 11: # and % of students taking the test; student performance **Attendance:** # of students with high absenteeism **Suspensions:** # and % of students suspended; # of students with multiple suspensions **Completion of Geometry:** # and % of students not on target to complete geometry by the end of Gr. 10 **Results of the Nov. SAT:** # and % of students participating; student performance (>1100 combined verbal & math score) **Enrollment in Rigorous Courses:** # and % of students enrolled; identify student who can be moved to more rigorous instruction	1. How are the results of the PSAT used to support students in their preparation for the SAT, increase enrollment in Honors/AP/IB/Cambridge courses, and inform students and parents of the interpretation of the results, and for staff to inform instruction? 2. What strategies are being used to increase the enrollment and success of Af-Am and Hisp. students in the H/AP/IB/Cambridge/College level classes? 3. What analysis is being done in examining the interim grade reports? Subject, grade level, race groups, ESOL, and special education students? 4. How is the performance measured and monitored for students enrolled in grade 9 math classes including Algebra 1, Geometry, Honors Geometry, Algebra II and higher level mathematics? How does this compare to earlier results in the semester? 5. How is the performance of students taking the SAT monitored in order to advise students as to supports, addit. attempts on the SAT, and next steps? 6. What strategies are being used to support students to be successful in rigorous and above grade level instruction? 7. What procedures are in place to move students to higher level classes for the second semester? 8. What interventions are used to reduce absenteeism/suspensions and what evidence do you have that they are effective? 9. What analysis is occurring related to reducing suspensions: type, demographics, and interventions?

Other Areas Monitored

Quality Instructional Program	1. Have sufficient observations been completed to meet PGS requirements?

[1] All data points must be analyzed for all of the No Child Left Behind student groups.

Items Due to Office of School Performance – December	**Date Due**
• **Winter break plans** • Any local field trips - submit **MCPS form 210-4** for overnight and extended trips out of the Washington metropolitan area	12/8/06

Exhibit 7 (continued)

Monthly Reminders—December

General Management/Procedures/Events
- **Interim Progress Reports** – Send home interim progress reports.
- Prepare 2007-08 **school course bulletin**.

Student-Related
- Begin to evaluate student for **placement in higher level courses** as early as second semester.
- **SAT registration** for January testing is due - check about the students who are and are not registered.
- **New enrollment without immunization records:** 1. Accept the student only if he/she is homeless. 2. Parent/guardian must provide documentation of an appointment within 20 days of registering; if not provided within the time frame, a health related exclusion should occur.
- Complete **MCPS form 335-77C** – MSDE Education of Homeless Children and Youth, if there are homeless students enrolled.
- **Section 504 plans** – As students become eligible for Section 504 plans, enter data into OASIS.
- Submit the SEDS monthly report corrections (for students receiving more than 15 hours of special education).

Safety and Security
- **Fire Drills and Code Red/Blue Drill** – Complete the # of fire drills and Code Red/Blue drill due by the end of the month; **maintain a log of drills completed.** Remember to have at least 10 fire drills throughout the school year. Also review all school safety procedures with staff.
- **Telephone bomb threat card checklist** – Place by phones and review the instructions for use with staff.
- **Harassment and Intimidation (Bullying) Reporting Form** – Maintain binder with completed MCPS form 230-55.
- Inform OSP of any **sexual harassment** and **hate/violence** incidents.

Staff-Related
- **Log of Occupational Injuries/Illnesses** – Prepare MOSHA preprinted form.

Source: Montgomery County Public Schools.

Exhibit 8

Strategic Plan Improvement Targets for Graduating Cohort AP Participation and Performance*

| | AP Cohort Participation | | | | | | AP Cohort Performance: Percent of Cohort receiving a 3 or better on at least one AP test. | | | | | |
| | Most Recent (Actual) | % Participation (Expected) | | | | | Most Recent (Actual) | % Cohort Receiving at least one 3 (Expected) | | | | |
	2004	2006	2007	2008	2009	2010	2004	2006	2007	2008	2009	2010
District Average	**49.1**	**56.1**	**59.6**	**63**	**66.5**	**70**	**39.9**	**48.2**	**52.4**	**56.6**	**60.8**	**65**
% of Schools Achieving Expected	**8.7**	**50**	**62.5**	**75**	**87.5**	**100**	**8.7**	**50**	**62.5**	**75**	**87.5**	**100**
HISPANIC	*29.8*						*23.6*					
Bedford Blair	*16.1*					*70.0*	*15.4*					*65.0*
Einstein	*25.7*					*70.0*	*18.6*					*65.0*
Kennedy	*36.7*					*70.0*	*20.3*					*65.0*
Northwood	*n/a*					*70.0*	*n/a*					*65.0*
Kelsch Churchill	*76.9*					*70.0*	*73.1*					*65.0*
R. Montgomery	*39.1*					*70.0*	*34.4*					*65.0*
Rockville	*22.0*					*70.0*	*18.0*					*65.0*
Wootton	*77.3*					*70.0*	*50.0*					*65.0*
Kimball Northwest	*31.0*					*70.0*	*13.8*					*65.0*
Poolesville	*0.0*					*70.0*	*0.0*					*65.0*
Quince Orchard	*13.6*					*70.0*	*6.8*					*65.0*
Seneca Valley	*35.3*					*70.0*	*31.4*					*65.0*
Marks Blake	*40.6*					*70.0*	*25.0*					*65.0*
Paint Branch	*25.0*					*70.0*	*17.9*					*65.0*
Sherwood	*42.5*					*70.0*	*37.5*					*65.0*
Springbrook	*29.6*					*70.0*	*26.4*					*65.0*
Maxwell Damascus	*37.5*					*70.0*	*37.5*					*65.0*
Gaithersburg	*31.1*					*70.0*	*26.4*					*65.0*
Magruder	*22.2*					*70.0*	*20.8*					*65.0*
Watkins Mill	*18.8*					*70.0*	*15.0*					*65.0*
Stetson B-CC	*25.0*					*70.0*	*15.9*					*65.0*
W. Johnson	*30.0*					*70.0*	*30.0*					*65.0*
Wheaton	*34.3*					*70.0*	*28.6*					*65.0*
Whitman	*38.5*					*70.0*	*30.8*					*65.0*

Source: Montgomery County Public Schools.

*Does not include IB participation or performance.

Exhibit 9

The Path to Achievement—Presented by Superintendent Jerry Weast on January 8, 2006

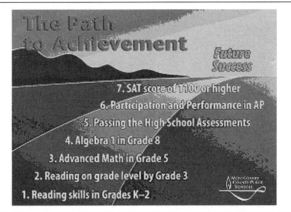

Sustaining High Performance over Time

The work of systemwide improvement is a continuous process, not an event. It takes time to develop an improvement strategy; it takes time to test that strategy against the realities of classrooms, schools, and communities; it takes time to discover the limits of a strategy and make necessary adjustments; and it takes time to adapt a strategy to the ever-changing context of accountability systems, demographic shifts, and new knowledge. The work of public education is inherently unstable: System leadership changes according to the demands of locally elected school boards, not according to the long-term demands of sustained instructional improvement. Accountability systems shift according to the demands of state and federal policy, not according to the limits of capacity in local schools and school systems. Student demographics change according to economic factors and migration patterns that are largely outside the control of local teachers and administrators. Creating, managing, and sustaining a systemwide improvement strategy under these conditions poses severe challenges.

In previous modules, we have examined how to form and implement a systemwide improvement strategy. The PELP Coherence Framework (PCF) provides guidance for identifying the major organizational elements of a district, for connecting them in a coherent way, and for organizing and managing the strategy's implementation. In each of the cases discussed thus far, we have focused primarily on what a powerful, focused improvement strategy looks like, not on how to sustain that strategy over time. Now we shift our attention to the problem of sustainability.

The very idea of sustainability runs counter to some very deeply rooted political and cultural forces in U.S. public education. From the late nineteenth century to the present, public school systems have been evaluated not on how well they sustain improvements in student performance over time, but on how responsive they are to the demands of competing internal and external constituencies. As we have noted in other places, the typical large urban school system's organizational chart is an accumulation of balkanized programs and managerial functions that have been crafted to meet the demands of competing constituencies, rather than to organize and manage a deliberate, coherent improvement process.[1] State and federal policymakers have aggravated this tendency by creating categorical programs and policies that require local education agencies to create separate functions within their organizations. Consequently, local school districts are traditionally very good at responding to external demands, and very bad at creating and sustaining improvements in the instructional core over time.[2]

Accountability systems demand sustained improvement, but school systems typically are not organized, managed, or governed in ways that are compatible with the demands of such improvement. Furthermore, state and federal policymakers, while they currently emphasize accountability for student performance, have not changed the previous policies that have caused fragmentation at the local level. So local school systems are left with the task of how to reconcile all the previous demands of competing constituencies and fragmented policies, while at the same time building a coherent strategy and organizational structure for managing sustained improvement in student performance over time. This work poses the most difficult challenges that local school systems have confronted in the history of U.S. education.

The work of sustained improvement in large school systems, then, is not simply a matter of organizing and managing in better and smarter ways. It is a matter of changing deeply rooted cultural beliefs and political constraints that work against sustained improvement. A simpler way of saying this is that school systems are not designed to do the work we are asking them to do.[3] Long-term success requires sustained attention to transforming the beliefs, practices, and political incentives that surround leadership in school systems, not just the organization and management of those systems.[4]

The cases in Module V also demonstrate that sustained improvement is a learning process—at the individual, organizational, and system levels. None of the examples of sustained improvement that we have found involve the simple linear process of framing and then implementing a strategy. They all involve serial, continuous learning that is informed by the experience of practice and by feedback from all levels of the organization about what works and what doesn't. Investment in learning is a critical part of all strategies for improvement.

Learning Objectives

The cases in Module V pose, more explicitly than earlier cases, the broader set of issues raised by sustained improvement in student performance by large school systems. These cases provide a deep look at two well-developed improvement strategies in districts that got an early start on the work. They raise the same questions as earlier cases about the formulation and implementation of an improvement strategy, but they move a stage beyond those cases and address the deeper issues involved in sustaining a strategy over time. The learning objectives for this module are:

- Use the PCF, and the knowledge developed in previous modules, to analyze the main components of the strategies in the cases and to draw conclusions about the relative success of those strategies, as well as their strengths and weaknesses

- Identify factors that enhance or impede the sustainability of an improvement strategy over time, and identify which of those factors can be built into the strategy and which are out of the control of system leaders

- Identify how school systems that have improvement strategies in place respond to changes in the social and political environment, and how those responses affect the sustainability of the strategy

- Build an understanding of how to use strategy to transform the culture of a system in a way that supports and sustains improvement over the long run

Cases

Module V opens with "Meeting New Challenges at the Aldine Independent School System," which shows a fully developed improvement strategy in the process of a substantial midcourse correction. This strategy was triggered by changes in state accountability policy and a reassessment of the district's past success in transforming its culture around a focus on improving student performance.

The module then revisits Long Beach, California. "Long Beach Unified School District (A): Change That Leads to Improvement (1992–2002)" traces the development of the Long Beach improvement strategy over the course of school superintendent Carl Cohn's tenure. The case provides a detailed look at the key components of the strategy and at the strategy's impact on performance, on the culture of the district, and on its political climate. "Long Beach Unified School District (B): Working to Sustain Improvement (2002–2004)" picks up at the end of Cohn's tenure and raises the question of what his successor, Chris Steinhauser, should do to sustain the system's improvement strategy in the face of changing conditions and a changing reform agenda.

Discussion Questions

The following questions will serve as a guide to identifying the common ideas embedded in the case series in this module:

1. What is distinctive about the design and implementation of the improvement strategies in these districts? Evaluate the strategies using the PCF and your own ideas about what makes an effective improvement strategy.

2. How would you evaluate the effectiveness of the senior leadership in the two districts in building and implementing an improvement strategy?

3. How well do the two strategies address the issues of building a supportive culture and changing the political climate for sustainability?

4. What factors threaten the sustainability of the improvement strategies; which ones are subject to influence by district leaders and which ones are not?

5. What would you advise the superintendents in Aldine and Long Beach (case B) to do in order to sustain and build the improvement strategies in their districts?

Notes

1. Stacey Childress, Richard Elmore, and Allen Grossman, "How to Manage Urban School Districts," *Harvard Business Review* 84, no. 11 (November 2006), pp. 55–68.

2. Frederick Hess, *Spinning Wheels: The Politics of Urban School Reform,* Washington, DC: Brookings Institution Press, 1999).

3. See Richard F. Elmore, "Bridging the Gap between Standards and Achievement" and "Building a New Structure for School Leadership," in *School Reform from the Inside Out: Policy, Practice, and Performance,* Cambridge, MA: Harvard Education Press, 2004, pp. 89–132, 41–88.

4. See Andy Hargreaves and Dean Fink, *Sustainable Leadership,* San Francisco: Jossey-Bass, 2006.

DISCUSSION QUESTIONS

1. How coherent are the elements—culture, systems, structures, resources, and stakeholders—of Aldine Independent School District?

2. Based on your analysis in question 1, what changes, if any, would you recommend to Kujawa as she faces new challenges?

3. What are the strengths and weaknesses of Kujawa's management approach to area superintendents and principals?

4. How effectively has Kujawa handled the fifth-grade reading problem? What should she have done differently and what should she do now?

Stacey Childress ■ Allen S. Grossman ■ Caroline King

Meeting New Challenges at the Aldine Independent School District

Aldine Independent School District (AISD) Superintendent Nadine Kujawa reviewed the district's 2005 Texas assessment results with mixed emotions. On one hand, AISD students had performed roughly at the same level as their counterparts statewide—a notable accomplishment for the largely minority and low-income school system. Seventy-one percent of AISD students met standards in mathematics as compared to 70% of students statewide, while 81% of pupils were reading on grade level in AISD, just slightly below the 83% state average. On the other hand, three of the district's 62 schools were rated *academically unacceptable* by the state for the first time since 1995.[1]

Kujawa had weathered difficult times before during her 41-year career in AISD. As the former deputy superintendent for curriculum and instruction, Kujawa was the chief architect of reforms that had moved AISD from the third lowest among Harris County's 54 school systems in 1994 to the state's largest consecutively

recognized school system in 2001, with approximately 90% of students passing state assessments. When Kujawa assumed the helm at AISD in the fall of 2001, she found herself driving a redoubling of efforts in anticipation of a considerably more challenging state assessment, which launched in 2003. Under the new test, student achievement dropped sharply, a sizeable achievement gap reemerged, and AISD lost its *recognized* status.

To date, Kujawa had followed closely in the footsteps of her revered predecessor, "Sonny" M. B. Donaldson (1986–2001), by keeping a laser-like focus on student achievement and refining the organizational and instructional changes introduced during his administration. Kujawa wondered what it would take to regain high levels of academic achievement in AISD—continuing to improve the longstanding practices that had brought the district success in the past or rethinking the district's managerial approach altogether?

Overview of Assessment and Accountability in Texas

The over 1,500 public school districts in Texas operated under an extensive standards-based accountability system, the result of a 25-year reform effort (see Exhibit 1 for a timeline of key events). State policies adopted throughout the 1990s and early twenty-first century, coupled with new federal regulations, ratcheted up expectations for districts and schools to raise student achievement.

In 1990, the Texas Education Agency (TEA) introduced the state's first criterion-referenced test, the Texas Assessment of Academic Skills (TAAS).[2] TAAS measured students' mastery of the state's reading, mathematics, and writing standards in grades 3–10; however, TAAS was largely perceived as a test of basic skills. With the introduction of TAAS, state, district, and school test results were disaggregated by race, socio-economic status, and other subgroups for the first time. In 1994, the TEA began publicly rating districts and schools based on TAAS results and other achievement indicators. From highest to lowest, the rating labels used were: *exemplary, recognized, academically acceptable,* and *academically unacceptable.*[3]

In 1997, the state implemented more challenging content standards, known as the Texas Essential Knowledge and Skills (TEKS), and began work on a new assessment aligned with the TEKS. Six years later, in 2003, the Texas Assessment of Knowledge and Skills (TAKS) replaced the TAAS. The TAKS tested students' mastery of the TEKS, and was widely considered a more rigorous assessment of students' conceptual and analytical skills. TAKS reading and mathematics tests were administered in grades 3–11. TAKS also tested writing, science, and social studies at designated grade levels.

The TEA phased-in the TAKS passing standards between 2003 and 2005, which made it more difficult for students to meet state standards by increasing the scale score each year.[4] Although students took the TAKS for the first time in 2003, districts and schools retained their TAAS-based 2002 accountability ratings that transition year. 2004 marked the first year that TAKS results were used to determine the rankings. High school students failing the TAKS exit exams were denied diplomas. Promotion requirements were adopted incrementally to follow a cohort of students. Starting in 2003, 3rdgraders had to meet TAKS reading standards to enter the 4th grade. Beginning in 2005, 5th graders were required to meet TAKS reading and mathematics standards for promotion, and 8th grade would be added in 2008.

AISD Background

Serving a working-class community of Houston, Texas, (AISD) was the 76th-largest school system in the U.S. and the eleventh largest in Texas. From 1990–2005, demographic shifts altered the district's student body from relatively middle class and ethnically balanced to increasingly low-income and minority. During this same period, student enrollment grew steadily by approximately 2.5% per year.

In SY05,[5] AISD enrolled 56,127 students in 62 schools and had a $429 million annual budget (see Exhibits 2, 3a, and 3b for district facts and figures). Hispanics comprised 58% of AISD students, African-Americans 33%, whites 6%, and Asians 2%. Slightly over three-quarters of students qualified for free or reduced-price meals and 25% were learning English for the first time. Schools belonged to one of five "verticals" and were organized as early childhood/pre-kindergarten centers, elementary schools (grades K–4), intermediate schools (grades 5–6), middle schools (grades 7–8), 9th grade centers, and senior high schools (grades 10–12). According to the district, the multiple structures enabled schools to more effectively meet students' academic and social needs. For example, 9th grade centers were created in 1999 to ease the high school transition and stem a growing dropout rate.

A seven member Board of Education (the "Board") served as the policymaking body in AISD. Trustees were elected at large to three-year terms, and the Board enjoyed relatively stable membership as four trustees had each served over 12 years in SY05. On the night before their regularly scheduled monthly meeting, the Board held a public study session to preview the agenda. If the Board could not reach consensus on an issue during the study session, it tabled the item until the following month in order to avoid acrimonious public debates. At the end of each quarter, the Board and superintendent reviewed the district's progress towards meeting targets outlined in the AISD strategic plan. As Board seats became vacant, current members encouraged people with strong ties to the district who shared the AISD student achievement agenda to run for office.

As Texas was a "right to work" state, AISD teachers had the choice whether or not to join and/or financially support the three local teachers' associations operating in the district. The associations offered members professional advice, development, and networking opportunities. In SY05, the three groups collectively counted about 1,000 of Aldine's 3,616 teachers as members.

Superintendent Nadine Kujawa and the AISD Journey

Kujawa's Background

Kujawa had attended district schools and graduated from Aldine Senior High School. Upon receiving her bachelor's degree in elementary education from Sam Houston State University, Kujawa returned to AISD as a second grade teacher. After five years in the classroom and earning a master's degree in education from the

University of Houston, Kujawa served as principal in three elementary schools, the district's personnel director, assistant superintendent of human resources, and deputy superintendent of curriculum and instruction.

A Shock to the System (1994–1995)

1994 marked a turning point for AISD and Kujawa's career. That year, the district received its first public accountability rating from the state. Kujawa recalled Aldine's "lackluster" SY94 *academically acceptable* rating as "the shock our system needed to wake up." Fifty percent of students failed the TAAS tests (see Exhibit 4). The results also revealed a substantial achievement gap between white and minority students. Whereas 85% of whites passed the TAAS reading exam, only 65% of African-American and 71% of Hispanics passed. On TAAS math, 72% of whites passed compared to 42% and 55% of their African-American and Hispanic counterparts, respectively.

In 1995, then Superintendent Donaldson promised the Board that AISD would achieve *recognized* status by 1996. Donaldson then offered Kujawa her "dream job"—deputy superintendent of curriculum and instruction—a position that had been vacant for three years. Kujawa recalled:

> Even though I had been in HR for 18 years, the instructional program in the classroom remained my first love and I was excited to focus my attention on teaching and learning again. We first visited other school systems starting to show dramatic gains on the TAAS, such as Brazosport Independent School District (BISD). While smaller in size, Brazosport served kids like ours. BISD proved that low-income and minority students could learn and pass the TAAS. We felt that if BISD could do it, so could we. To do it, though, we knew we needed to change.

The AISD Turnaround and Kujawa's Appointment (1996–2002)

From SY96–SY01, while Donaldson focused on reorienting the district's operations to support principals, Kujawa revamped curriculum and instruction. AISD earned its first *recognized* label in SY97, a status it upheld for six years (see Exhibit 5).

Following Donaldson's retirement in 2001, the Board voted unanimously to appoint Kujawa as AISD's first female superintendent. The Board president at the time commented on the deliberations:

> The board quickly arrived at a consensus around one stabilizing force: the local Aldine leadership team. Our attention was immediately focused on a key team player responsible for curriculum development and delivery, Deputy Superintendent Nadine Kujawa . . . The board made a deliberate decision to continue the current academic achievement initiative . . . [and] Mrs. Kujawa was selected because she possesses the skill-sets necessary to maintain focus on student achievement . . . The Texas Education Agency has raised the academic achievement bar and Aldine will be ready to respond.[6]

In SY02, the final year that the state administered the TAAS and Kujawa's first year as superintendent, approximately 90% of AISD students, including African-American, Hispanic, and low-income pupils, passed the state assessments (see Exhibit 4).

Kujawa Tackles TAKS (2003–2005)

Despite the district's apparent success under TAAS, Kujawa was not satisfied. She remembered:

> I knew that TAAS was a basic skills test and that we were entering a whole new world with TAKS. Even though we had attained high TAAS scores, the district's SAT and Iowa Test of Basic Skills (ITBS) scores had remained flat and well behind national and state averages (see Exhibit 6). I knew the district had to do more to prepare students for success in college or the workforce. At the same time, I felt that AISD had the right foundation in place to confront the TAKS challenge head on. Our key to continuous improvement has been to keep singing the song that everybody already knows while adding new verses.

The district's SY03 TAKS scores delivered a second "shock to the system." Only 49% of students met standards in science, 70% in mathematics, 78% in reading, 85% in writing, 86% in social studies. While Kujawa and her cabinet had expected AISD's results to decline under TAKS, they were surprised by the precipitous drop. They were also frustrated to see that an achievement gap, something they had worked so hard to eliminate over the past decade, had reemerged (see Exhibit 7).

While AISD students achieved incremental gains on the SY04 and SY05 TAKS, Kujawa's sights were set much higher. She expected AISD to educate all students to meet state standards, and she continued to drive the district towards achieving this goal. As she puzzled over her next steps, Kujawa reflected on the district's decade-long transformation in hopes of identifying key success factors as well as potential shortcomings.

Setting Objectives and Measuring Progress

Upon assuming the helm at AISD in SY02, Kujawa set out to clarify the district's mission and work. "We had taken a big step forward under TAAS in that we finally defined our 'business' as improving student achievement, but I was not yet convinced that everyone in the district—all 7,500 employees—understood their contribution," Kujawa recalled. After adopting the Baldrige Education Criteria for Performance Excellence (Baldrige), Kujawa led a strategic planning process involving principals and teachers from every school, senior and mid-level managers, clerical and operations staff, and external stakeholders.[7] The district articulated a new mission statement, "Produce the Nation's Best," and four objectives:

1. AISD will demonstrate sustained growth in student achievement;

2. AISD will recruit, employ, and retain a quality teaching, administrative, and support staff to attain excellence in student performance;

3. AISD will allocate resources to maximize excellence; and

4. AISD will increase and improve stakeholder partnerships and satisfaction.

A member of Kujawa's cabinet held ownership for each objective. Each "owner" developed an action plan, managed implementation, and monitored and reported on district progress towards meeting the objective each quarter using a "scorecard." The scorecard outlined all of the district activities that were underway to accomplish the specific objective. Quarterly performance data for each was measured against the district's one-, three-, and five-year targets; prior quarters from the same school year; and the previous school year's average. Assistant Superintendent of Curriculum and Instruction Wanda Bamberg, who was responsible for objective #1, described an example of how the cabinet used the scorecards. "One quarter, the scorecard showed that student attendance had dropped significantly. We brainstormed why it fell, discussed what were we going to do to increase it, and how we were going to evaluate the effectiveness of our actions next quarter. Before the scorecards, we would have been lucky to discover we had a problem before the end of the year."

Every central office department, vertical area, and school developed action plans and companion scorecards aligned with the district's four objectives. In schools, every department, such as language arts and mathematics, also had action plans. Following the lead of some innovative principals, Kujawa intended to extend the action plans and scorecards to individual teachers, students, and parents in the near future. In 2005, Kujawa reflected on AISD's experience with Baldrige and strategic planning:

> Baldrige is not magic, nor a silver bullet for managing change or improving performance. It is a system that forces you to look at the processes you are using to achieve results. Adopting Baldrige simply allowed our entire district to find a new way of planning, communicating, and working together. Once we diagnosed the key drivers of student performance, we were able to better focus the work of everyone in the district, measure our effectiveness, and strive for continuous improvement.

Organizing the Aldine Way

Pre-K–12 Vertical Areas

AISD Schools belonged to one of five "verticals." Each vertical was named after its senior high school and included the pre-K–9 feeder schools. Four verticals (Aldine, Eisenhower, MacArthur, and Nimitz) comprised neighborhood schools, while the fifth vertical, Carver, encompassed all magnet schools. Economically disadvantaged students represented between 73% and 83% of each vertical; other demographic indicators varied as a reflection of the communities served (see Exhibit 8).

An area superintendent (AS) managed each vertical. Prior to 1995, an assistant superintendent for elementary schools had managed over 30 early childhood and K–8 buildings while a counterpart supported a dozen secondary schools. Donaldson introduced the vertical structure in 1995 to increase pre-K–12 alignment and reduce the number of principals reporting to any one central office supervisor.

Area Superintendents: Area Superintendents (AS) convened vertical meetings with their principals every other week, often meeting in a different school. Area superintendents monitored principals' school action plans, conducted school "walkthroughs," and evaluated principals. The five ASs reported directly to Kujawa, with whom they met weekly to discuss trends and challenges across the district.

The area superintendents in place in SY05 had a long history together spanning various district roles. All five had spent the majority of their careers in AISD; each started out in the district as a classroom teacher, and four of the five had served as an assistant principal and principal. MacArthur AS Margarita Byrum and Eisenhower AS Wilbert Johnson had led their respective verticals since their inception in 1995; the other three had between three and five years experience in the position.

The five area superintendents scheduled meetings together as a group on an as-needed basis, and frequently shared information informally. Nimitz Area Superintendent Doris Delaney explained, "Since we have all worked together for quite a while in different capacities, it is very easy for us to have one-on-one conversations when we need advice or support. We also do our best to meet as a group as our schedules permit. But, if there is a crisis, we make sure that we all pull together."

Two area superintendents shared reflections on their role in 2005:

> My two most important jobs are hiring exceptional principals and playing a brokering role to help my principals find the resources and supports they need. They control their own funds, but they look to me for advice, for example, when they wanted to adopt a new program for English language learners vertical-wide. We want the Aldine vertical to be the best in the dis-

trict, not only because we have a healthy sense of competition, but because we don't want to be the vertical to hold the district back.

> —*Gloria Cavazos, Aldine Area Superintendent (1999–2005)*

> What is important to me is that my principals set reasonable targets, and then meet them. People need to believe and see that they can be successful. And the Eisenhower schools have been showing continuous improvement that way for 10 years. Sometimes you come out number one, and sometimes you come out number three. What is important is that my principals achieve their targets.

> —*Wilbert Johnson, Eisenhower Area Superintendent (1994–2005)*

Horizontal Resources

Horizontal Meetings: School leadership teams from across all five verticals and central office administrators participated in biweekly "horizontal" meetings. In 1995, district leadership changed the content of the horizontal meetings from administrative to instructional, with a focus on providing professional development for principals. Throughout the years, horizontal meetings emphasized three topics: analyzing achievement data, unveiling instructional strategies that would be rolled out to teachers, and celebrating results. School leadership teams and central office curriculum managers also spent part of the meetings in grade-level breakout groups. Discussions focused on diagnosing common challenges, sharing organizational and instructional practices, and grade-level initiatives.

Program Directors: A team of over 35 program directors (PD) shepherded curriculum design and content area professional development in AISD. Each content area (e.g., mathematics) had at least two PDs, one for elementary grades and one for secondary grades. Program directors resided at the central office and reported to Bamberg, with whom they met weekly. Program directors attended vertical meetings if requested by an area superintendent, and all horizontal meetings. A principal could invite a PD to work on their school at any time; however, PDs worked most closely with the lowest performing schools in their content area and grade level.

School Management and Support

Leadership Teams: Each school was managed by the principal and a leadership team, typically comprised of the vice principals, department and grade-level chairs, and teacher coaches known as "skills specialists." Leadership teams developed school action plans and budgets, made curricular and managerial decisions, designed professional development, and planned parent engagement activities. Principals held ultimate decision-making authority and were held accountable for student achievement results and fiscal responsibility by area superintendents. Reflecting on this relationship, MacArthur Area Superintendent Margarita Byrum said, "It is my job to know when a principal needs a pat or a push to get to the next level in optimizing educational services for the children."

School Budgets: Using staffing ratios based on student enrollment, the central office determined the minimum number of administrative and instructional positions required at each school. *Average* salary costs were used to enable principals to hire individuals without regard for their *actual* salary.[8] These personnel costs consumed approximately 80% of the school's budget. The remaining 20% included special revenues (e.g. state and federal compensatory funds or other grants) and the "principal's budget," which covered supplies and other operational expenses. Some schools raised additional money and in-kind contributions through fundraisers. Principals exercised complete control over their special revenue funds, principal's budget, and fundraising proceeds. If the principal purchased additional staff, such as a teacher, the principal had to pay the individual's *actual* salary cost. The only criteria that the finance office used to evaluate school budgets were that the proposed activities served an instructional purpose and supported improved student achievement. Assistant Superintendent for Finance Keith Clark explained:

Our philosophy is that the principal has the best understanding of what the teachers and students at his/her school need to accelerate academic achievement, and therefore, we should not tie the principal's hands behind their back. And if the principal believes something will raise academic achievement, then he or she will pay for it. But we make the principals stand by their decisions by holding them accountable for results.

Skills Specialists: Skills specialists (SS) were school-based veteran teachers that offered support in a core content area, such as English/language arts, mathematics, or science. Skill specialists analyzed student assessment data with teachers, modeled strategies to differentiate instruction, and worked with struggling students. Every elementary, middle, and intermediate school had at least one full-time SS; high schools had at least two. Many principals hired additional SS with their discretionary funds.

Curriculum and Instruction Reforms

During the mid- to late- 1990s, Kujawa established a new districtwide standards-based curriculum, known as the "benchmark targets," and revamped professional development in the district. "Under TAAS, we learned we could only make progress as a system if all of our teachers understood the concepts embedded in the state standards and how to teach them. Once kids mastered the standards, I knew the TAAS scores would take care of themselves, and they did," Kujawa recalled.

AISD Curriculum: The Benchmark Targets

Specifying Skills: Prior to the mid-1990s, each AISD school designed its own curriculum, often with little connection to the Texas state standards. Following the introduction of the TAAS, isolated schools began making headway on the test. The district's performance overall remained stagnant, however, as reflected by the district's *academically acceptable* ratings in SY94 and SY95.

In 1996, Kujawa spearheaded the creation of districtwide curriculum frameworks, which later became known as the "benchmark targets." The benchmark targets outlined the skills every student was expected to master in a given subject at each grade level, and were divided into six- or nine-week sequences (see Exhibit 9 for a sample). Each skill referenced a specific state standard and specified the cognitive level of instruction and student mastery expected for each skill based on Bloom's taxonomy of educational objectives.[9] The cognitive levels moved from basic actions, such as summarizing facts, to more advanced competencies, such as applying or creating concepts.

Kujawa reflected on how the benchmark targets impacted the district:

> We invested heavily in professional development for teachers and we started holding principals accountable for improving performance on state assessments. "The Aldine way" is simply letting people know what you expect of them and then giving them the resources, support, and flexibility to achieve results. By the time TAKS came around, we were fortunate to have the benchmark structure in place. We certainly had to tweak it, but we did not have to spend time and energy inventing something new.

Teachers also praised the benchmark targets. One Nimitz area elementary teacher who left the district to teach in another state commented, "Lesson planning felt like a 'free-for-all' without the benchmark targets and I lost confidence that I was effectively preparing students to take the state's standardized assessment," she said. "I knew if I came back to AISD, I could help my students succeed again."

Implementing the Benchmark Targets: While the district required every school to follow the benchmark targets, principals retained autonomy in choosing how to design and deliver the curriculum in their school. Working with the school leadership team, principals made choices about their school's educational program based on district and school action plans, student needs, previous assessment results, teacher capacity and input, and available resources. For example, elementary schools implemented a variety of reading programs, including direct instruction, balanced literacy, and guided reading.

Assessing Progress: Every school administered mandatory "benchmark assessments" in December and May to evaluate students' mastery of the benchmark targets. Benchmark assessments existed for every grade level and content area, and were revised each summer. Principals, area superintendents, and Kujawa used the benchmark test results to assess the effectiveness of instruction, teacher training, and resource allocation in schools.

Some schools instituted additional assessments. For example, at the MacArthur area Oleson Elementary School, every class started with a "warm up" exercise that teachers used to identify students' strengths and weaknesses and differentiate instruction as needed. Every class ended with an assessment of student learning (e.g., worksheet, collage, or verbal exercise). Teaching teams developed six-week "checkpoint" tests based on the benchmark targets to give more frequent measures of student learning. Fisackerly credited the school's approach to assessment with easing the TAAS–TAKS transition at Oleson. "While we had to make some adjustments, we felt confident that we had tools and a way of working together that would help our students meet, and even exceed, the new state standards," Fisackerly explained.

Indeed, while serving students from AISD's most academically at-risk populations, Oleson was one of only four AISD elementary schools to maintain its SY02 exemplary rating in SY04, the first year that the state used TAKS scores to determine district and school ratings. Kujawa formally encouraged every elementary principal to visit Oleson in SY05, but by Spring 2005, many principals had not found the time to do so. However, Oleson had hosted many visitors from other districts.

Some verticals adopted a common assessment. For example, Nimitz Area Superintendent Doris Delaney and her principals selected an external vendor to create three-week tests to complement the benchmark assessments.

Improving Instruction

Kujawa had also led the charge to revamp AISD's 10 professional development days. Prior to the mid-1990s, AISD offered professional development to teachers primarily though one-time workshops, which Kujawa described as "random selection." From SY96–SY00, Kujawa and her team designated 3-$\frac{1}{2}$ days for district-wide training, allowing schools to design their own staff development for the remaining 6-$\frac{1}{2}$ days.

Districtwide and School Professional Development: The district used its 3-$\frac{1}{2}$ professional development days to hold training before the start of school, in October, and January. The district's sessions emphasized understanding the state standards, the state assessments, and instructional strategies to help students develop higher-order thinking skills. At each school, the principal and leadership team designed and implemented the 6-$\frac{1}{2}$ days of school-based professional development, which was often tailored by grade level and subject.

In 2000, when over 85% of students passed the TAAS reading and mathematics tests at every

AISD school, the district handed control over all 10 staff development days to principals. With the advent of the TAKS, however, in SY03, Kujawa reclaimed the district's 3-$\frac{1}{2}$ days. Bamberg explained, "TAKS was a new reality for us, but we had already learned under TAAS how important it was to set the same standards and expectations for everyone from the beginning." Kujawa had planned to relinquish the district's control over professional development again in SY06, but the SY05 TAKS results made her wonder if schools needed more time to increase their capacity to effectively structure professional development on their own.

Vertical Professional Development: Some verticals also developed verticalwide professional development approaches. For example, between 1995 and 2005, all 10 MacArthur schools had pooled a portion of their school-based financial resources each year in order to work collectively with two external professional development providers. "One of my objectives is to create alignment from pre-K through 12th grade," explained MacArthur Area Superintendent Margarita Byrum. "As a result of the vertical professional development, the MacArthur area schools share a common language and set of expectations around curriculum and instruction and a belief system that every child can achieve."

Attracting Talent, Growing Leaders

In 2005, Kujawa explained AISD's approach to staffing:

> Everyone you see in a leadership position has a long history in the district and has moved as the district has moved. We start by bringing in the very best teachers we can find, and then tap those who are doing outstanding jobs for instructional leadership roles in schools. We are extremely selective about whom we hire as principals, and we encourage the best ones to take increasingly tougher assignments. And those

who express an interest in playing a larger role in the district, we move into central office management roles so that the classroom remains front and center in all that we do.

Teachers

Deputy Superintendent Archie Blanson described how the district's approach to recruiting teachers had evolved over time. "While we had always worked hard to recruit the best and brightest teachers, we stopped defining our competition as merely other school districts in the late 1990s," said Blanson. "Our competition is the job market, period. It's the top chemistry graduate who would rather work at Exxon than teach in AISD."

In SY05, district representatives attended over 200 job fairs around the world, cultivated numerous university partnerships, and promoted alternative certification programs to attract non-traditional candidates. At the Board's behest, AISD teacher salaries ranked within the top five among surrounding school districts. While AISD hired between 400–600 new teachers per year, nearly seven qualified applicants existed for every open position. While the district's annual teacher turnover rate was 12.4%, the experience of the AISD teaching corps had remained relatively consistent from 1994–2004 (see Exhibit 10).

Principals

People throughout the district reflected on how the state accountability environment had impacted the principalship in AISD. Blanson commented:

> Prior to TAAS, most of our principals were ex-football coaches, especially in the high schools. They had always seemed like fine principals, but the moment you started talking about curriculum, subgroups' performance on the TAAS, and providing differentiated instruction to every

child, it was difficult for some of them to make the transition. As student enrollment rose steadily during the 1990s, we built a lot of new schools and made sure we only hired people with instructional backgrounds into the principalship.

A senior high school principal in SY05 who had served as a principal in both the Aldine and Carver verticals since SY94 recalled, "No one wanted to be at the bottom of the barrel. Everyone wanted to be a *recognized* school and so, we did whatever it took to get our kids to pass the TAAS and get there. We're doing the same with TAKS."

In SY05, all 62 AISD principals had come up through the district's teacher-assistant principal ranks, and had an average of six years of experience in the principalship. First-year principals were usually placed in elementary schools. As vacancies arose at the middle and secondary levels, area superintendents often hired successful elementary principals from within the vertical. Area superintendents interviewed candidates for principal vacancies within their verticals and made hiring recommendations to Kujawa. Many area superintendents included all of their principals in the interview and selection process.

A second-year MacArthur area elementary school principal compared his relationships with vertical versus horizontal colleagues:

> Each vertical is like a clique with its own culture, as many of us have worked together as teachers and administrators for a long time. Within the vertical, we treat each other like family and share everything—what's working, what's not, and where we are stumped. As a new principal by AISD standards, I have not yet developed that same level of trust with principals outside my vertical. My school is rated *exemplary* and I feel a bit uncomfortable drawing attention to myself and what my school is doing.

Performance Incentives and Evaluation

In the late 1990s, AISD implemented an "accountability incentive award system" for all district employees. Staff were evaluated annually using a scorecard tied to district-, department-, or school- level objectives depending on the person's position. In SY05, Kujawa revised the award system to make the superintendent and senior cabinet ineligible for financial rewards.

The district capped contracts with principals and teachers at two-years with renewal subject to evaluation. Area superintendents evaluated principals based on objectives outlined on their school action plans related to student achievement, AYP status, student attendance, promotion and/or graduation rates, staff attendance and retention rates, and efficient use of resources. Principals evaluated teachers on their own attendance, student attendance, and student achievement. Principals had the ability to place struggling teachers on "growth plans" and dismiss teachers after two years.

Schools earning an *exemplary* or *recognized* rating received financial awards. AISD allocated the award to a school as a lump sum, and a school committee comprised of teachers and staff elected by their peers then decided how to disburse the funds. For example, one exemplary elementary school received a $50,000 incentive award in SY05. The committee debated whether to divide the money equally between all of the K–4 teachers, or to award a higher amount to the third and fourth grade teachers since only third and fourth graders took the TAKS tests. The school eventually decided to split the money evenly, with each K–4 teacher receiving approximately $1200.

When schools were not achieving results, the district intervened by placing principals on growth plans comprised of staff development and monitoring. Principals who failed to improve within three years could be released, although to date, senior leaders commented that no AISD principal had ever been dismissed

based on performance. Kujawa explained her approach:

> If we see that a principal is not meeting their student achievement objectives, I ask the principal to diagnose the root causes and design a plan of attack, and then my leadership team plays a heavy monitoring and support role. I give principals three years to demonstrate that they can produce results, but that doesn't mean I stand around the first two years. If achievement languishes, we may get increasingly more prescriptive if we need to, but never authoritative. We've never found success that way in AISD. But, if student performance has not improved at the level we agreed upon by the end of the three years, then the principal and I have a serious conversation about their ability to lead the school.

Kujawa Assesses AISD

As Kujawa studied the SY05 TAKS results, she found the fifth grade reading scores particularly troubling. For the third year in a row, the percentage of AISD fifth readers meeting reading standards lagged about 10 points below the statewide average. In keeping with "the Aldine way," Kujawa had tasked elementary principals in SY03, SY04, and SY05 with diagnosing the root causes of the fifth graders' low test scores and implementing interventions to improve performance in their respective schools. In addition, Kujawa charged Bamberg's curriculum and instruction team with supporting principals' efforts and the five area superintendents with monitoring results.

The stagnant SY05 fifth grade reading scores convinced Kujawa that she needed to radically change her approach. "When you hit crisis mode, it's the superintendent's job to take over the helm of the ship, point the direction, and steer the course," she explained. Furthermore, the unresolved issue illuminated three of

Kujawa's broader concerns: strengthening instruction, managing the verticals, and balancing autonomy and organizational learning. Kujawa believed that making progress in these three areas would be critical if the district was going to accelerate student performance at all grade levels in SY06.

Managing Instruction

Acknowledging the pressures caused by the high-stakes accountability environment, there was some debate over the extent to which AISD teachers were imparting test-taking strategies versus developing their students' cognitive and critical thinking skills. The principal of an elementary magnet school offered a concrete example of the tension experienced by teachers: "The reality is, if your third graders do not pass TAKS, they will not be promoted to the fourth grade, and that will be public knowledge. That puts a lot of pressure on teachers to emphasize test-taking skills, particularly for struggling students."

While acknowledging that the shift from TAAS to TAKS generated "total panic and chaos" among teachers, one elementary teacher from the Aldine vertical welcomed the challenge. "We're actually letting the kids think again," she remarked. "Under TAAS, we were teaching them how to take a test and how to 'trick the TAAS monster.' Kids have to be able to think at a much more conceptual level on the TAKS. It's actually the way I thought we were supposed to teach the whole time."

Sara Ptomey, the program director for secondary mathematics, also suggested that the district's instructional reforms had not deeply penetrated high school classrooms. "Since the 10th grade TAAS exit exam only tested seventh or eighth grade level competencies, many high school teachers could get away with peppering their class with some test-taking skills while their instruction stayed status quo lecture style, meaning 'I taught it, and if Johnny didn't learn it, it's his fault,'" Ptomey remarked.

Bamberg also suggested that the benchmark targets needed major revision, not just another "summer rewrite." "I think we may have written our benchmark targets so discretely that many teachers are unable to see or help their students understand the bigger conceptual links that are tested on TAKS," Bamberg explained. "We are also finding that teachers may have taught the appropriate skill of a benchmark target, but not at the right level, which means that our instruction is not aligned with our curriculum," she added.

Managing the Verticals

Uneven performance by vertical represented another major area of concern. Indeed, the student achievement data indicated that the MacArthur schools had consistently outperformed the other four verticals since SY97, and had weathered the TAKS transition with the least impact on student performance (see Exhibit 5). Further, the MacArthur vertical had achieved these results while serving the highest percentage of socioeconomically disadvantaged students (83%) and second highest percentage of English language learners (34%) as compared to the other four verticals. The vertical performance gaps were further illuminated by the 2005 accountability ratings and the reemergence of *academically unacceptable* schools in the district (see Exhibit 5).

As Kujawa hypothesized about the potential causes of the performance gaps that existed across the verticals, she also focused on the area superintendents' leadership. On one hand, she accepted the unique managerial styles and approaches of her five area superintendents. "I expect the area superintendents to deliver a consistent message about our performance expectations and then work with their principals to ensure that those results are achieved. However, I expect *how* the area superintendents do that to vary based on their individual strengths and weaknesses," Kujawa said.

On the other hand, she had observed some distinguishing characteristics among the verticals which appeared directly related to both the area superintendent's managerial style and student achievement. Kujawa identified three key practices:

1. The instructional and leadership capacity of the principals hired in the vertical;

2. An area superintendent's level of engagement with principals in developing and monitoring school action plans, problem solving, and brokering support versus spending time on administrative or operational issues; and

3. The degree to which an area superintendent fostered collaboration, trust, and shared expectations among their principals.

At the same time, Kujawa grappled with how to productively manage the spirit of competition that flourished across the verticals:

> Our area superintendents are all "top-flyers," and naturally, they are quite competitive and take pride in sharing their schools' successes. If we're not careful, though, each vertical can become like a kingdom of its own. I have to work extremely hard to ensure that each vertical sees itself as part of a larger whole, and that the whole is only as strong as the sum of its parts.

Balancing Autonomy and Organizational Learning

While area superintendents often observed innovations in their schools, the district was hesitant in taking the lead to translate individual school practices into districtwide mandates, including those that appeared to produce above average gains in student achievement. Kujawa explained:

> In AISD, we believe in setting expectations for results and then allowing leaders to use their creativity in determining how they will achieve those results. The expectations that student performance will continue to increase is clear, but *how* principals get there is up to them because

to truly move a school, the leader has to develop their own belief system. We can point and show them what is working well in another school, and if they think something will be effective in their school, they'll adopt it. Until a principal internalizes what they have seen and turned it into their own practice, it just won't work.

"Our senior high schools alone demonstrate that schools can develop multiple pathways to success," Kujawa continued. Indeed, all five of the district's senior high schools earned exemplary or *recognized* ratings during the final year of TAAS while employing very different approaches. For example, Aldine Senior followed a four-period 90 minute block schedule, implemented a computer-based skills program for students failing state assessments, and piloted small learning communities. Alternatively, MacArthur Senior High School had hired former elementary teachers as skills specialists and remediation teachers, invested heavily in professional development, and followed a seven period, 45-minute class schedule.

However, Kujawa recognized that the five senior high schools had responded quite differently to the arrival of TAKS. While MacArthur and Carver earned *recognized* labels in SY04, the other three senior high schools dropped to *academically acceptable*. Concurrently, while the district's results on the TAKS science tests (which were given in grades 5, 8, 10 and 11) were low overall, some schools and verticals were beginning to make faster progress on the TAKS than others. She considered the extent to which it was possible to extract "best practices" from the higher-performing schools and verticals, and if the district should play more of a leadership role in disseminating those practices.

In keeping with "the Aldine way," Kujawa was generally opposed to mandating that schools adopt specific implementation practices, although precedents did exist. Bamberg recalled an example from the late 1990s:

We found one middle school that was significantly outpacing the others on the 1995 state assessments. I talked to the principal and found out that she had brought teachers together over the summer to divide the benchmark targets into weekly instructional timelines. Other schools within the same vertical quickly adopted the timelines. By 1997, the schools using the timelines demonstrated consistently higher student achievement gains. After determining that the timelines were the only unique thing that these higher-performing schools were doing differently from other schools, we decided to take a leap of faith and mandate the timelines districtwide. Principals and teachers were hesitant at first, but for the most part, the timelines have helped teachers truly understand the scope and sequence of the curriculum and hold each other accountable for staying on track every week.

Looking Ahead

As Kujawa weighed her options, she grappled with the most serious challenge of her 41 year career with AISD. The educational and managerial approaches that had allowed the district to dramatically improve student achievement under TAAS were not producing the high levels of performance under TAKS that Kujawa desired. Reviewing the SY05 TAKS results, Kujawa was determined to lead the district to higher levels of success both quickly and deliberately. As Kujawa deliberated over her next steps, she reflected:

> I believe in "the Aldine way," meaning all of the systemic elements we put into place that enabled our students to excel over the past 10 years. However, as I look ahead, I suspect there are elements of the organization that need to be redefined in order to accelerate student performance again. My question is what to keep, tweak, or replace? And if I make changes, I think

it is important to anticipate the impact of those changes on the rest of the organization.

Notes

1. Under the Texas accountability system, districts and schools were rated *exemplary, recognized, academically acceptable, or academically unacceptable* based on student performance on state tests and other achievement indicators.

2. Criterion-referenced assessments compare an individual's performance to a specific performance standard and not to the performance of other students. In contrast, norm-referenced assessments rank a student's performance in relation to the performance of a larger "norm group." See http://www.cresst.org/resources/glossary_set.htm.

3. In 1996, the state replaced *accredited* with *academically acceptable* and *unaccredited* with *academically unacceptable.*

4. The only exception was in the 11th grade which followed a four-year phase-in process between 2003 and 2006. Thus, the 2005 TAKS performance standard was lower for the 11th grade as compared to grades 3–10.

5. SY is a PELP convention that denotes "school year." For example, SY05 refers to the 2004–2005 school year.

6. Spring 2001 issue of *Inside Aldine,* http://www.aldine.k12.tx.us/news/specific_article.cfm?ID=58.

7. Baldrige is a performance management tool utilized in Brazosport and at some other school systems nationwide.

8. For example, teachers earned between $38,000–$57,928 annually based on years of experience and education credentials.

9. In 1956, educational psychologist Benjamin Bloom developed a taxonomy of instructional objectives based on the six major types of cognitive learning: knowledge, comprehension, application, analysis, synthesis, and evaluation.

Exhibit 1
Timeline of Assessment, Standards, and Accountability in Texas

Year	Event
SY80	Texas Assessment of Basic Skills (TABS) introduced for reading, mathematics, and writing in grades 3, 5, and 9.
SY81	The Essential Elements, the first statewide K-12 content standards adopted.
SY84	Perot Commission issued recommendations, including annual state testing in all numbered grades, barring struggling students from athletics ("no pass, no play"), denying diplomas to students failing a high school exit exam, and mandating public accountability reports on student performance by district. Recommendations were enacted into law by House Bill 72.
SY86	Texas Education Assessment of Minimum Skills (TEAMS) replaced TABS in an effort to measure minimum rather than basic skills. TEAMS tested reading, math, and writing in grades 1, 3, 5, 7, 9 and 11. The 11th grade test was considered an exit exam and the Class of 1987 became the first cohort required to pass the exit exam in order to receive a diploma.
SY91	Texas Assessment of Academic Skills (TAAS), the state's first criterion-referenced test, introduced to measure student's mastery of the Essential Elements. TAAS tested reading, math, and writing in grades 3, 5, 7, 9, and 11. TAAS results were disaggregated and reported by school, district, and state.
SY93	TAAS extended to grades 3–8 in reading and math; writing in grades 4 and 8; and the exit level exam was moved from grade 11 to 10.
SY94	District and school performance-based accountability rating system implemented. Ratings primarily based on TAAS passing rates.
SY98	Texas Essential Knowledge and Skills (TEKS) K-12 content standards replaced the Essential Elements.
SY02	Final year district and school accountability ratings based on TAAS results.
SY03	Texas Assessment of Knowledge and Skills (TAKS) test replaced TAAS. TAKS was administered for reading, writing, math, social studies, and science in grades 3–11. Passing standards increased each year from SY03-SY05 for grades 3–10, and from SY03-SY06 for grade 11. Districts and schools retained SY02 accountability ratings.
SY04	District and school accountability ratings based on TAKS results for the first year.
SY05	TAKS passing standards phase-in completed for grades 3–10.
SY06	TAKS passing standards phase-in completed for grade 11.

Source: Timeline of Testing in Texas, Achieve Three Paths One Destination: Standards-based Reform in Maryland, Massachusetts, and Texas; *Texas Public Schools 150 Years Sesquicentennial Handbook 1854–2005.*

Exhibit 2

AISD Facts and Figures

SY05 AISD Overview

District Area Demographics (Census 2000)

Total Population	221,223
Median household income	$33,291
Families below poverty level	17.5%
Percent of county residents holding bachelor degree or higher	18.6%

Student Demographics

Number of students (Pre-K–12)	56,127
Hispanic	58.0%
African-American	33.1%
White	6.4%
Asian/Pacific Islander	2.4%
Native American	0.1%
Economically Disadvantaged	76.6%
Limited English Proficient	24.9%
Special education students	9.8%
Graduation rate (4-year)	76.8%
Dropout rate (4-year)	4.3%

Schools and Staff (11th-largest district in TX)

Number of schools	62
Early childhood/Pre-K centers	5
Elementary (K–4)	29
Middle or Intermediate (5–6, 7–8)	17
Ninth grade (9)	4
Senior high (10–12)	5
Alternative	2
Total staff	7,522
Teachers	48.1%
Auxiliary Support (custodians, etc.)	27.7%
Educational Aides	13.7%
Professional Support (clerical staff, etc.)	6.7%
School Administration	2.9%
Central Administration	0.9%
Average teacher salary	$44,492
Average years experience of teachers	11
Teacher turnover rate	12.4%
Pupil/Teacher ratios	
Pre-K–4	22:1
Gr. 5–6	28:1
Gr. 7–12	29:1

Source: Census 2000 data from http://www.nces.ed.gov/surveys/sdds/singledemoprofile.asp?county1=4807710&state1=48, accessed March 9, 2005. AISD data from *Texas Education Agency Academic Excellence Indicator System 2003–04 District Performance Report.* TEA Web site, http://www.tea.state.tx.us/cgi/sas/broker, accessed March 9, 2005. and *Aldine at a Glance, Information and Facts about the AISD in Houston, Texas.*

Exhibit 3a

AISD Annual Financial Statements, 1997–2004 (in $000)

	1997	1998	1999	2000	2001	2002	2003	2004
Revenue								
State	155,104	171,574	186,905	199,855	217,344	154,036	239,368	229,627
Local and intermediate	99,427	106,431	111,284	114,053	128,975	136,780	154,597	161,894
Federal	13,328	14,123	17,280	20,485	21,617	24,351	29,062	38,465
Total Revenues	267,859	292,128	315,469	334,393	367,936	315,167	423,027	429,986
Expenditures								
Current:								
Instruction and instructional related services	157,784	166,064	192,422	207,432	224,690	211,729	256,459	258,834
Instructional and school leadership	19,111	20,234	23,364	25,548	26,548	24,755	33,321	32,674
Support services—student based[a]	27,967	30,634	33,447	40,270	43,917	39,508	46,288	47,659
General administration	5,848	6,283	7,193	7,477	8,981	8,448	10,617	10,287
Support services—nonstudent based[b]	27,237	29,292	33,015	35,549	37,800	31,194	37,945	36,487
Ancillary services	80	78	176	240	413	376	438	465
Debt service	11,591	20,213	13,888	16,207	36,094	18,004	39,426	19,221
Capital outlay	22,607	54,986	50,497	6,745	10,525	24,291	45,670	20,535
Intergovernmental charges					267	286	280	182
Total Expenditures	272,225	327,784	354,002	339,468	389,235	358,591	470,469	426,344
Excess (deficiency) of revenues over (under) expenditures	(4,366)	(35,656)	(38,533)	(5,075)	(21,299)	(43,424)	(47,442)	3,642
Other financing sources and (uses):								
Other resources[c]	69046	34725	13,263	137	87,424	3112	78,446	219
Other uses[d]	(103364)	(756)	(1,785)	(1,173)	(2,905)	(4284)	(4,280)	(6,442)
Total other financing sources and (uses)	58,682	33,969	11,478	(1,036)	84,519	(1172)	74,166	(6,223)
Extradordinary item (use)								(241)
Fund balance—beginning	54,314	124,343	122,658	95,603	89,465	152,683	108,088	134,812
Fund balance—end	124,343	122,658	95,603	89,465	152,683	108,088	134,812	131,990

Source: District files.

Exhibit 3b

AISD Per Pupil Expenditures by Function, 1997–2004 ($)

	1997	1998	1999	2000	2001	2002	2003	2004
Instruction	3,004	3,146	3,444	3,664	3,885	4,108	4,297	4,521
School Leadership	301	320	355	383	403	450	445	488
Central Administration	138	146	151	150	173	198	193	191
Other Operating	1,505	1,558	1,755	1,827	1,913	2,029	2,058	2,117
Non Operating	380	409	542	463	448	571	480	976
Total	**5,328**	**5,579**	**6,247**	**6,487**	**6,822**	**7,356**	**7,473**	**8,293**

Source: Texas Education Agency Academic Excellence Indicator System District Reports, 1994–2004.

Exhibit 4
District TAAS Results, SY94–SY02

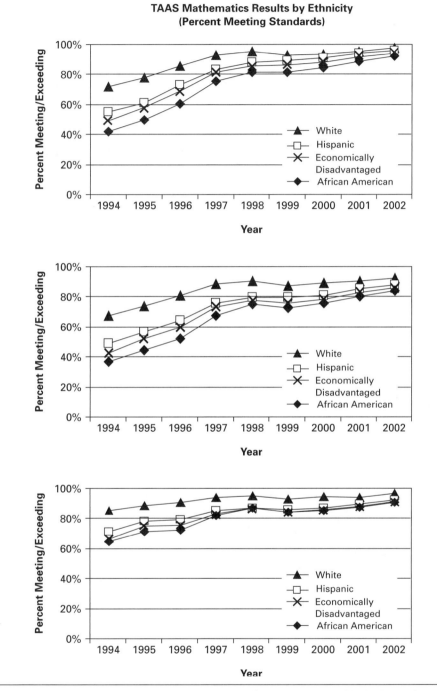

Source: Texas Education Agency, Academic Excellence Indicator System. Multi-year District Report for 1994–2002.

Exhibit 5

District and School Accountability Ratings by Vertical, SY94–SY04

| | TAAS | | | | | | | | | TAKS | |
District Rating	SY94 Acad. Acceptable	SY95 Acad. Acceptable	SY96 Acad. Acceptable	SY97 Recognized	SY98 Recognized	SY99 Recognized	SY00 Recognized	SY01 Recognized	SY02-SY03 Recognized	SY04 Acad. Acceptable	SY05 Acad. Acceptable
School Ratings (#):											
Exemplary	0	4	1	6	5	4	4	9	13	7	5
Recognized	0	15	9	20	20	19	32	31	31	28	16
Acad. Acceptable	42	20	34	19	20	25	15	11	7	20	31
Acad. Unaccept.	0	4	0	0	0	0	0	0	0	0	3
Not Rated-Other	2	2	2	2	2	2	2	2	2	2	2
Total	44	45	47	47	47	50	53	53	53	57	57
School Ratings (#) by Vertical:											
Aldine											
Exemplary	0	0	0	0	0	0	0	0	2	1	1
Recognized	0	3	1	6	3	4	5	8	6	5	4
Acad. Acceptable	7	3	6	1	4	4	3	0	0	3	4
Acad. Unacceptable	0	1	0	0	0	0	0	0	0	0	0
Not Rated-Other	0	0	0	0	0	0	0	0	0	0	0
Total	7	7	7	7	7	8	8	8	8	9	9
Carver											
Exemplary	0	0	0	0	0	1	1	3	2	1	1
Recognized	0	0	3	3	6	2	7	5	9	10	4
Acad. Acceptable	9	9	7	8	5	9	5	5	2	3	8
Acad. Unacceptable	0	1	0	0	0	0	0	0	0	0	1
Not Rated-Other	0	0	1	0	0	0	0	0	0	0	0
Total	9	10	11	11	11	12	13	13	13	14	14

Exhibit 5 (continued)

	TAAS									TAKS	
	SY94	SY95	SY96	SY97	SY98	SY99	SY00	SY01	SY02-SY03	SY04	SY05
Eisenhower											
Exemplary	0	2	0	1	0	0	0	0	1	0	0
Recognized	0	6	1	2	4	3	5	6	5	4	2
Acad. Acceptable	8	0	7	5	4	6	4	3	3	7	9
Acad. Unacceptable	0	0	0	0	0	0	0	0	0	0	0
Not Rated-Other	0	0	0	0	0	0	0	0	0	0	0
Total	8	8	8	8	8	9	9	9	9	11	11
MacArthur											
Exemplary	0	2	1	4	3	2	2	5	7	4	3
Recognized	0	2	2	4	3	4	7	4	3	4	3
Acad. Acceptable	9	4	6	1	3	3	1	1	0	2	4
Acad. Unacceptable	0	1	0	0	0	0	0	0	0	0	0
Not Rated-Other	0	0	0	0	0	0	0	0	0	0	0
Total	9	9	9	9	9	9	10	10	10	10	10
Nimitz											
Exemplary	0	0	0	1	2	1	1	1	1	1	0
Recognized	0	4	2	5	4	6	8	8	8	5	3
Acad. Acceptable	9	4	8	4	4	3	2	2	2	5	6
Acad. Unacceptable	0	1	0	0	0	0	0	0	0	0	0
Not Rated-Other	2	2	2	2	2	2	2	2	2	2	2
Total	11	11	12	12	12	12	13	13	13	13	13

Source: Texas Education Agency Academic Excellence Indicator System District Reports, 1994–2004.

Note: Does not include pre-Kindergarten/early childhood centers.

Exhibit 6

Comparative SAT and 5th Grade ITBS Results

Year	Average SAT Scores for the U.S., Texas, and AISD (SY94–SY04)		
	U.S.	*Texas*	*AISD*
SY94	1,003	884	823
SY95	1,010	885	799
SY96	1,013	891	808
SY97	1,016	993	921
SY98	1,017	992	911
SY99	1,016	992	890
SY00	1,019	989	865
SY01	1,020	990	871
SY02	1,020	987	869
SY03	1,026	986	875
SY04	1,026	989	874

Source: District and State SAT Scores from the Academic Excellence Indicator System District Performance Reports, SY94–SY05, Texas Education Agency Web site, http.//www.tea.state.tx.us, accessed March 9, 2005; and National SAT scores from 2005 College Bound Seniors, A Summary Report from the College Board, http://www.collegeboard.com/prod_downloads/about/news_info/cbsenior/yr2005/2005_CBSNR_total_group.pdf, accessed March 9, 2005.

Note: In SY97, the SAT introduced a new testing format.

	Iowa Test of Basic Skills Results: AISD 5th Grade, All students (SY01–SY05)				
	SY01	*SY02*	*SY03*	*SY04*	*SY05*
Avg. Standard Score	198.6	N/A	200.0	200.2	198.1
Grade Equivalent	4.7	N/A	4.7	4.7	4.6
National Percentile Rank	39	N/A	40	41	38
# Tested	3,586	N/A	3,875	3,885	3,954

Source: District files.

Note: Core results include reading, language, and mathematics.

Exhibit 7

AISD TAKS Results by Student Subgroup, SY03–SY05

	Percentage of All AISD Students (grades 3–11) Meeting Standards on TAKS Tests									
	All Students (State)	All Students (District)	African American	Hispanic	White	Native American	Asian/ Pacific Islander	Special Education	Economic Disadvan- taged.	Limited English Proficient
TAKS Test										
Reading/ELA										
2005	83%	81%								
2004	80%	77%	74%	77%	86%	92%	86%	53%	75%	62%
2003	72%	69%	64%	70%	80%	89%	78%	48%	67%	55%
Mathematics										
2005	70%	71%								
2004	66%	63%	53%	66%	76%	74%	84%	39%	62%	60%
2003	57%	56%	47%	59%	68%	74%	79%	34%	55%	52%
Writing										
2005	89%	89%								
2004	89%	88%	85%	90%	87%	> 99%	92%	70%	87%	84%
2003	78%	78%	73%	80%	88%	60%	90%	49%	77%	69%
Science										
2005	66%	57%								
2004	56%	46%	38%	47%	71%	89%	71%	26%	43%	18%
2003	42%	31%	23%	30%	55%	67%	59%	12%	27%	8%
Soc Studies										
2005	88%	88%								
2004	84%	86%	84%	85%	95%	> 99%	95%	68%	84%	50%
2003	76%	76%	73%	76%	89%	71%	86%	59%	75%	39%
All Tests										
2005										
2004	57%	52%	43%	55%	66%	70%	72%	30%	51%	47%
2003	47%	43%	35%	45%	58%	71%	64%	24%	41%	37%

Source: 2003–2004 data cited from Texas Education Agency Academic Excellence Indicator System District Report 2004. 2005 data cited from preliminary Texas Education Agency reports. See www.tea.state.tx.us.

Note: All results were calculated using the 2005 TAKS passing standard to allow for longitudinal analysis. In 2003 and 2004, the 2005 standard was referred to as the "Panel Recommendation." "All Tests" and student subgroup data were unavailable for 2005 at the time of case publication.

Exhibit 8

Demographic Data by Vertical, SY05

	Aldine	Carver	Eisenhower	MacArthur	Nimitz
Number of Students	10,078	11,417	11,639	10,183	13,047
White	4.3%	5.7%	3.4%	4.4%	9.9%
Hispanic	73.1%	52.8%	50%	82.3%	48.9%
Black	20.5%	39.3%	42.7%	12.7%	38.7%
Asian	2.0%	2.1%	3.9%	0.5%	2.3%
Indian	0.1%	0.1%	0.1%	—	0.2%
% Economically Disadvantaged	81.9%	76.7%	76.1%	82.9%	73.2%
% English Language Learners	36.9%	22.7%	21.6%	34.2%	19.9%
% Special Ed	9.1%	7.1%	10.2%	10.1%	12.4%

Source: District files.

Exhibit 9
Sample Benchmark Target: Third Grade Language Arts

ASSURANCES

By the end of third grade, the student will:

1. Write a narrative, informative and descriptive composition using story elements, correct sentence structure, punctuation, capitalization, and usage.

2. Identify nouns, verbs, adjectives, words with prefixes and suffixes, singular and plural possessives and contractions.

3. Develop and expand their vocabulary by analyzing alternative spellings for same sounds, silent consonants, syllabication and mastery of the Dolch and Fry Word List for third grade.

4. Spell a variety of words using rules/patterns and generalizations.

5. Read a lengthy literature selection fluently and be able to answer the following types of questions: identify the main idea, cause and effect, character feelings, sequential order, setting, predicting outcomes, summary, fact and details and be able to use context clues to identify unknown words.

6. Speak with fluency and understanding for different purposes and occasions using appropriate rate and volume.

LANGUAGE ARTS—FIRST SIX WEEKS:

Reading/comprehension. The student uses a variety of strategies to comprehend selections read aloud and selections read independently. (TEKS 3.9)

36. Use prior knowledge to anticipate meaning and make sense of texts. (TEKS 3.9A) *Develop, Master*

37. Establish purposes for reading and listening such as to be informed, to follow directions, and to be entertained. (TEKS 3.9B) *Develop, Master*

38. Retell or act out the order of events in stories. (TEKS 3.9C/TAKS Obj. #1, 3) *Develop, Master*

39. Act purposefully when comprehension breaks down using such strategies as re-reading, searching for clues, and asking for help. (TEKS 3.9D) *Develop, Master*

40. Make/explain inferences from texts to predict outcomes and determine important ideas, causes and effects, and drawing conclusions. (TEKS 3.9F/TAKS Obj. #4) *Develop, Master*

41. Produce summaries of a selection. (TEKS 3.9H/TAKS Obj. #1) *Develop, Master*

42. Represent text information in different ways, including story maps, graphs, and charts. (TEKS 3.9I/TAKS Obj. #3) *Develop, Master*

43. Distinguish fact from opinion. (TEKS 3.9J/TAKS Obj. #4) *Introduce, Develop, Master*

44. Practice different kinds of tasks and questions. (TEKS 3.9K) *Develop, Master*

Exhibit 10

AISD Teachers by Years of Experience, 1994–2004

	1994	2004
Number of Teachers	2,716	3,616
Years of Experience		
0–5	45.0%	37.5%
6–10	16.4%	20.4%
11–20	27.8%	24.1%
20+	10.7%	18.0%

Source: Texas Education Agency Academic Excellence Indicator System District Reports, 1994–2004.

James E. Austin ■ Allen S. Grossman ■ Robert B. Schwartz ■ Jennifer M. Suesse

Long Beach Unified School District (A): Change That Leads to Improvement (1992–2002)

In September 2002, 43-year-old Christopher Steinhauser became the 12th superintendent of the Long Beach Unified School District (LBUSD). Steinhauser succeeded Carl Cohn, a popular leader who led the district from 1992 to 2002. During Cohn's long tenure as superintendent, LBUSD implemented many new initiatives including the adoption of a mandatory K-8 school uniform policy, standards-based instructional reform, and the development of a partnership with local institutions of higher education. LBUSD also ended social promotion for the district's third, fifth, and eighth graders and required all students to be able to read by the end of third grade. Steinhauser knew it would be a challenge to follow in Cohn's footsteps, but he was dedicated to educating the children of Long Beach. A former LBUSD student himself, Steinhauser had also served the district as a teacher's aide, teacher, principal, area superintendent, central office director, and deputy superintendent prior to his promotion. As Steinhauser contemplated his predecessor's record and how

to build on it, he asked himself: "What has been critical to our success thus far?"

Long Beach in the Early 1990s

Economic Tailspin

Located in Southern California adjacent to Los Angeles, this heavily industrialized port city was the fifth-largest city in the state with nearly half a million residents. Due to immigration from Asia and Latin America, Long Beach was on its way toward becoming the most ethnically diverse city in the nation.[1] Ongoing population growth strained the local economy, which was reeling from the closure of a U.S. Navy base and the downsizing of operations at McDonnell Douglas, the city's largest employer.

Moreover, rising levels of gang activity threatened public safety. Residents were devastated on April 29, 1992, when riots raged across the city following the acquittal of four white police officers accused of assaulting African-American Rodney King. The damage caused by burning, looting, and violence was a terrible blow to this historically tight-knit community, once nicknamed "Iowa by the sea." One Long Beach native recalled:

> Long Beach felt like a war zone in the early 1990s. The state's economy was sinking. All major revenue-earning businesses downsized. We couldn't catch our footing. The civil unrest left entire blocks of residences and business burned to the ground. We were no longer a navy town, nor a shipyard, nor an aerospace town. As middle-class jobs disappeared, there was white flight, and some wondered if we would become a ghost town.

The Cohn Era Begins

In the midst of this community turmoil, Carl Cohn was appointed superintendent, the first African-American to hold that position. A Long Beach native, former Compton high school history teacher, and LBUSD high school counselor, Cohn earned his doctorate in urban educational policy and planning at UCLA and worked as an LBUSD administrator in a variety of assignments from 1977–1984 and 1988–1990. While away from Long Beach in the mid-1980s, Cohn taught courses in the politics of education at the University of Pittsburgh and California State University, Los Angeles. Cohn served as an LBUSD area superintendent for the two years prior to his promotion to superintendent in September 1992. His background was considered somewhat nontraditional for a Long Beach superintendent, since he had never been a principal.

Cohn took over California's third-largest school system, the 32nd-largest school district in the U.S. In response to the influx of immigrants, enrollment at LBUSD had grown steadily, from 57,467 in SY82[2] to 96,488 in SY02 (Exhibit 1 shows enrollment changes). The city's changing demographics were reflected in LBUSD's students, who spoke over 46 different languages at home. By the end of Cohn's tenure, more than one-third of LBUSD students were learning English, and more than two-thirds were poor. Population growth was uneven across the city, resulting in overcrowded classrooms and busing programs. LBUSD brought children from the central and western sections of the city into the more affluent east-side neighborhoods.[3]

In addition to the challenges of growth and diversity, LBUSD's financial picture was unpromising at the outset of Cohn's tenure. LBUSD was fiscally independent (not under city or county jurisdiction). Budget shortfalls caused by recessions at the state and national levels impacted the district's funding. The district cut its proposed budget by more than $5 million in SY92, $8 million in SY93, and $9 million in SY94. Total LBUSD revenues grew from $423 million in SY93 to $972 million in SY02 (Exhibit 2 profiles financial information from SY93–SY02).

A Call to Action

In early 1993, the mayor convened an influential and diverse set of leaders from the press, business, and education fields to address three critical areas facing Long Beach: economic development, education, and public safety. The Mayor's Task Force worked to define some shared goals for improving the community.

As they prepared to implement their ideas, members of the Mayor's Task Force reflected on the inefficacy of many past community public education initiatives and decided to create a unique vehicle to sustain their focus. In October 1993, they brought the three new leaders of Long Beach's educational institutions together to forge the Long Beach Educational Partnership.[4] In the first of many conversations, Cohn and his counterparts from Long Beach City College (LBCC) and California State University, Long Beach (CSULB), discussed the city's education system. Cohn reflected on the importance of the community's voice:

Meeting together with other leaders reinforced my sense that the issue of education had the community's attention and support. We worked hard to prevent a statewide voucher initiative in 1993, and when voters defeated the proposal, we felt that we had been given a second chance. It was important for us to prove our worthiness when voters asked us to "improve the existing system, not create a new one." They didn't want business as usual anymore in our public schools, and I felt we had been given a clear mandate for change.

Governance

Board Membership and History

A five-member Board of Education (henceforth referred to as the "Board") governed LBUSD and set district policy. Each Board member represented one of five regions of Long Beach. Although the poorest residents were concentrated in two regions in the southwest section of the city, all five members' regions included culturally and economically diverse neighborhoods, reflecting the city's integrated nature. Boundaries for these five regions were established in 1988, when, in an attempt to address the changing demographic profile of Long Beach, citizens voted to change Board election policies. Prior to the vote, Board members were elected by the city at-large. The redistricting led to the election of four new members, including the first Latino and African-American.

Following this membership turnover, the Board became more explicit in its efforts to, as one member explained, "work together to act in the best interest of all kids across the city." LBUSD had a history of stable Board membership, and residents, school district officials, and Board members alike spoke about the high quality and dedication of past and current members. According to local sources, officers rarely used Board membership as a stepping-stone to other public offices.

Giugni's Legacy

As Cohn and the Board surveyed the work ahead, they evaluated the legacy LBUSD inherited from Cohn's predecessor, Tom Giugni. Long Beach superintendents averaged eight years of service on the job, which more than doubled the three-year national average. Giugni, who led LBUSD from 1986 to 1992, was the first "outsider" hired as LBUSD superintendent in more than 50 years.

One Board member characterized Giugni's working relationships with individual Board members as a "divide and conquer strategy." Giugni labored to improve relations between LBUSD and the local teachers' union, the Teacher's Association of Long Beach (TALB). "Giugni and TALB's executive director," recalled the district's former director of employee relations, "slowly worked to switch LBUSD-TALB negotiations from bargaining over words to bargaining about concepts. TALB began discussing issues that came to our attention as problems to be solved rather than threats to their system."

In an effort to decentralize the entrenched central-office power structure, Giugni replaced the traditional elementary and high school assistant superintendents with five "area superintendents," each responsible for one section of the city. Giugni was careful to ensure that the new areas did not match Board members' regions, and he promoted Cohn to take charge of one area. Veteran administrators recalled that this change began to "topple the hierarchy and break down fiefdoms." In addition, schools received more responsibility for curriculum decisions, as Giugni eliminated the central curriculum department. Giugni retired in 1992. In reflecting on Giugni's tenure, Steinhauser said, "Superintendent Giugni had an 'everybody do your own thing' philosophy, and schools were disconnected from the central office. By creating the area structure, he encouraged a healthy competition, but expectations across the district were inconsistent."

A New Approach to Governance

During his tenure as an area superintendent, Cohn had been frustrated by the time and energy senior staff devoted to preparing for semimonthly Board meetings, which he felt distracted central office's focus on support for schools. So, he and the Board agreed to experiment with a new way of working. Both Cohn and the Board members believed that "strength would breed strength." They wanted neither a weak superintendent nor a weak Board and worked to establish a structure that would suit both parties.

They decided that the Board would hold quarterly retreats, rather than meeting with LBUSD senior staff in long, semimonthly meetings. By law, the Board conducted a superintendent's review in a closed session. Cohn asked that the Board initiate a "90-day superintendent review" as part of these full-day workshops, because he felt it was imperative to "get problems out on the table." Cohn felt this gave him a chance to talk with the Board "when everyone could really let their hair down and get into the issues."

As stipulated in California's Brown Act, the Board continued its practice of semimonthly open sessions, but these regular meetings were considerably shortened. Usually, public business was conducted in less than an hour. Five standing committees—providing oversight for LBUSD business, instruction, personnel, finance, and purchasing and contracts—also remained intact, and each Board member sat on two committees. As long as two Board members were present, committees could meet with LBUSD staff privately prior to each semimonthly meeting to prepare items for the agenda. Board member Karin Polacheck reflected on the experience:

> With Carl's predecessor, everything was very prescriptive. Giugni met with his staff to prepare three days in advance. Their reports were very polished, but there was little dialogue or listening. Carl felt that talking together without an agenda was critical. He really believed that we were community representatives, and he wanted a chance to hear our concerns. Our first quarterly retreat started with an evaluation of Carl. Together, we defined the six to eight things we wanted him to work on, and then said, "Okay, we'll talk about that in three months." This established our rapport and gave us a sense that we were working together as a team. We knew Carl cared about kids, and our conversations built an incredible sense of trust. I believe our retreat structure was our strength.

Board Initiatives

During their retreats, Cohn and the Board discussed the many challenges facing LBUSD and developed a shared vision for how the district could address some of the short and long-term community concerns regarding public safety, equal opportunity, and quality education. They agreed that the district should focus on *"raising standards in dress, behavior, and achievement."* This three-part goal was established in one of the early Board retreats and led to a sequence of what LBUSD called "Board initiatives." Board initiatives were long-term projects requiring the consistent focus and attention of the district's many stakeholders.

Over time, Cohn, the Board, and the LBUSD senior staff came to see the district staff as agents of implementation for Board policies. As superintendent, Cohn was designated the spokesperson for district policies. Cohn explained his philosophy of governance:

> Extraordinary teaming emerged from those retreats, because people really spent time together hashing out the issues. The fur flew when we disagreed, but then understandings would emerge and we could move forward and make decisions together. Even if we had to wait

an extra year to get consensus, I insisted upon unanimity around big issues. Split votes might have offered hope or a reason to avoid our initiatives to anyone who opposed our mandate for change, and we couldn't afford distractions or detractors. I was lucky that our Board members' political instincts were invariably excellent. They knew what mattered to this community, and I listened carefully to those views.

Getting to Work: Implementing Reforms

School Uniforms: Adopting the Nation's First Mandatory Policy

In January 1994, the Board adopted its first initiative mandating school uniforms for elementary and middle school students. While many districts around the country had experimented with voluntary uniform policies in attempts to curb gang-related violence, LBUSD was the first district in the nation to mandate uniforms.

The mandatory policy was implemented after LBUSD conducted some site-based experiments. Cohn had first explored the use of school uniforms when he led the district's anti-gang task force in the late 1980s. Cohn described a scene where a few dozen children, caught in the middle of a gang shootout, were forced to the floor of a school bus. "We needed to give safe passage for students through some very tricky terrain," he said. "We realized the way to make students identity apparent was with uniforms. We didn't think about all the other issues. It was safety, pure and simple."[5] In response to Cohn's prodding, LBSUD soon gave principals the option of adopting uniform requirements at their schools. The district discovered, "that for those schools that adopted uniforms, they soon found that their students were earning better grades, were better behaved and were less frequently absent."[6]

In light of these results, the district convened meetings with parents, teachers, and other stakeholders across the community to gauge interest in the idea of a system-wide mandatory uniform policy for K-8 students. LBUSD staff determined that the community favored the idea and felt this support was sufficient to withstand possible legal challenges regarding students' civil liberties. Following a vigorous debate at the next quarterly retreat, the Board unanimously approved the policy. This system of piloting and consultation became the standard approach for subsequent Board initiatives.

In the first year of mandatory uniform implementation (SY95), suspensions across the district dropped 32%, and one reporter wrote, "every category of infraction—from assaults to drug use to sex offenses—has fallen as well, sometimes precipitously. Teachers and administrators said they believe most students also perform better academically, though other initiatives begun at the same time make it difficult to single out the role of the uniforms."[7] Unsuccessful suits filed against LBUSD by the American Civil Liberties Union and others argued that the policy violated state law "by essentially intimidating parents through a cumbersome exemption process and by not providing sufficient uniforms or financial aid to those who can't afford the outfits,"[8] which prompted the state legislature to adopt provisions protecting uniform policies. LBUSD worked to advertise and streamline the exemption process and also to find creative solutions to the financial aid problem. By 1998, the district reported 99% compliance, with only 600–700 students officially requesting exemption.[9] Following the Long Beach example, schools in more than 35 states had mandatory uniform policies by 2000.[10]

Developing Standards for Academic Excellence

Many factors during the early 1990s led to changes in the area of instruction at LBUSD. Nationally, the movement toward standards-based instruction, which was popular by the decade's end, started slowly with individual school and teacher experiments. The National Council of Teachers of Mathematics developed and released the first set of national standards in 1989. These "guidelines for excellence" sparked a new chapter in the nation's enduring debate about what students should know and be able to do as a result of their schooling.

While political support for standards in California was uncertain following the governor's veto of the state's new learning assessment system in 1994, Cohn and other key administrators felt "academic standards were an inevitable and important lever for school improvement."[11] Locally, they encouraged the fledgling Long Beach Educational Partnership to foster dialogue among teachers, administrators, business leaders, university experts, and parents about the means for improving the city's educational offerings. Participants expected early partnership meetings to focus on the unacceptable number of LBUSD high school graduates who entered local colleges without adequate skills in literacy or math. However, as the groups talked together they discovered that two-thirds of LBUSD third graders were reading below grade level. These conversations led LBUSD to decide that rigorous grade-level standards were needed to ensure that all students would be prepared to learn at higher levels.

Calls for change were also being voiced internally. When Cohn became superintendent, curricular decisions were quite decentralized, as Giugni had disbanded the district's curriculum department. Christine Dominguez, who would eventually take responsibility for the Office of Curriculum, Instruction and Professional Development, commented:

> Carl believed that the purpose of the central office was to support schools in serving children. He made it clear that we were expected to spend time in schools and told us to find out what was needed by going out and just listening. This was a major shift.

> We decided to hold focus groups to find out what, if anything, people would want if we recreated a curriculum function in the central office. Teachers and principals said they wanted more consistent expectations and support. Parents complained that the lack of uniformity among classrooms and schools was confusing. So, our focus on standards evolved from trying to meet those needs.

LBUSD formed core academic committees in language arts, math, science, and history/social science. In SY95, these four groups began drafting content standards, the first of three core components of a standards-based system. These three components included:

- Content standards specifying what students should know in each subject area

- Performance standards clarifying the content standards with specifics about how students would demonstrate mastery, how students' performances would be judged and graded, and, implicitly, how teachers needed to teach

- Performance assessments measuring students' attainment of the performance standards, thus making all students, teachers, and schools accountable for reaching a common, verifiable level of achievement[12]

The committees spent months drafting content standards, and a large number of "critical friends" including foundation partners, parents, and local faculty from LBCC and CSULB were involved in the final review process. By June 1995, the first set of English/language arts content standards, designed as benchmarks for grades 2, 5, 8, and 12, were developed and approved by the Board. Implementation began in SY96. Content standards were soon completed in other areas and were in place for all grade levels by SY98. Under the leadership of the curriculum department, with support from the research department, initial performance standards and assessments were developed and piloted in SY98. When California began issuing state academic standards in 1998, LBUSD redrafted their standards to achieve full integration with the state's.

Reforming Instruction

While the standards work was getting underway, many district stakeholders were concerned that additional actions were needed to focus attention on improving students' performance, especially in the early grades. Board members agreed failing students could no longer be promoted, and they adopted a series of three initiatives over the next five years: elementary literacy (adopted in 1995), middle school reform (1996), and high school reform (1999). Partial funding for these projects came from a $63.7 million settlement awarded to LBUSD by the state in 1995 following resolution of a 13-year lawsuit, in which LBUSD sought reimbursement for costs incurred in implementing voluntary desegregation efforts during the 1980s.[13]

K-3 Literacy Initiative: In response to data that illustrated serious reading problems for the district's youngest students, the Board adopted its second initiative in 1995, which stated, *"every child would read before exiting the third grade."* Children who could not read were sent to summer school. Referred to as the "Third Grade Reading Initiative," this project was masterminded by Dominguez and Steinhauser, who was then director of special projects. They focused their efforts on developing standards and related assessments for each grade level, redirecting resources, and revamping professional development at all 56 elementary schools.[14] Resources were targeted at the schools that faced the biggest challenges, a philosophy that permeated LBUSD's approach to resource allocation. Benchmark books, aligned with district standards, were chosen to measure progress (Exhibit 3 details student performance on benchmark books).[15]

As instructional reform in the early grades unfolded, LBUSD encountered an unexpected hurdle when California abruptly passed class-size reduction legislation in 1996. By mandating a maximum of 20 students per classroom teacher in grades one through three, this law created an urgent need for qualified elementary teachers, who were already in short supply. Thus, in partnership with CSULB faculty, LBUSD created the Early Literacy Institute, which offered professional literacy training for all K-3 teachers district-wide. This mandatory 36-hour course integrated existing LBUSD pedagogy with strategies for standards-based literacy instruction. Sessions addressed language acquisition, applied phonics, and student assessment within the context of the Essential Elements of Effective Instruction, a pedagogical method for linking instructional objectives with student behaviors and outcomes developed by Madeline Hunter. The Institute received rave reviews from veteran and new teachers alike. Coaches were also provided for low-performing schools. Dominguez said:

> The reform process was hard and sometimes very emotional. We weren't used to constructive criticism, and suddenly outside evaluators were giving us critical feedback. Many people didn't know how to accept it, which led to a lot of hurt feelings. We had to learn how to act upon new ideas, instead of getting defensive. Recounting it now, it sounds like we knew what we were doing. But, it was messy. When we started, we didn't really know how all the pieces would fit together in the end. People kept asking us to describe what the district would look like when the reforms were complete, but we couldn't explain the whole picture because we were creating a system as we went along. When it got really rough, we could put on our parent hats, since many of us—including Carl, Chris, and myself—had kids in the system. Going home each night was a powerful reality check.

Between 1999 and 2002, the number of fifth graders reading at grade level increased from 6.7% to 53.5%. In SY02, 40% of third-grade students who attended summer school raised their reading achievement to grade level or above.

Middle School Reform: To address lagging academic performance in LBUSD middle schools, the Board adopted the "Eighth Grade Initiative" in 1996, which barred eighth graders who failed more than one class from enrolling in high school.[16] To improve student performance, efforts focused on implementing standards-based reforms and expanding professional development for teachers and principals. The middle school work built on more than a decade of change in the way LBUSD educated young adolescents. During the late 1980s, LBUSD followed the nationwide trend and converted its seventh- to eighth-grade junior high schools into sixth- to eighth-grade middle schools. Martha Keizer, a retired administrator who managed some of the transition process from junior high to middle schools, recalled:

> Necessary shifts in teacher and administrative attitudes appeared in every form from the ridiculous to the sublime. They had to figure out how to implement core classes, advisories, elective wheels, and many other brand new concepts. It was hard work, and some people made it more difficult than others. So, I insisted that LBUSD pay to chisel new names on each building. It sounds silly, but I believe that attending to small but important details can sometimes make the harder, more challenging things seem more manageable. Once "Middle School" was written in stone, people knew there was no going back.

Once middle schools were established, LBUSD concentrated on implementing standards-based reforms. At the urging of Clark Foundation program officer Hayes Mizell, an office of middle school reform was established in the early 1990s. Mizell commented:

> I wanted to be sure that this reform wouldn't fall into the lap of just one person, but that key people at different levels would sit down and talk together on a regular basis. Carl was clear that he wanted his team to build a system with the force and focus needed to drive change all the way to the classroom. We kept reinforcing this expectation of accountability in formal and informal ways. Some people found our approach to be a bit challenging, since on the one hand, we were offering financial and other support, and on the other, we were not shy of being critical or asking tough questions.

Cohn brought in a young teacher named Kristi Kahl to manage the middle school effort, following two long-established traditions at LBUSD: early promotion and rotation of leaders across the district. Unlike many other districts, in which principals and administrators followed isolated career paths, leaders in Long Beach were expected to rotate among assignments and switched not only among schools but between the central office and schools, as well as across departments. Principals rarely worked at one school for more than five years, and central administrators moved among departments. Those responsible for annual assignments took a system-wide view in placing people, especially principals, trying to find the "best fit" between an individual's skills, the local school community, and district needs.

Area superintendent Dorothy Harper worked in close collaboration with Dominguez and the curriculum department and Lynn Winters, who headed up the research department, to upgrade the district's professional development. Efforts focused on linking district offerings and expenditures to standards-based pedagogy. Slowly, many LBUSD one-day training modules were replaced with subject-matter workshops spanning the school year and supported at school sites by teacher coaches. George Perry, a consultant, who helped with this endeavor, observed:

> I used to think teachers would welcome the opportunity to take responsibility for their own professional development, but I've learned that teachers care about their students and what happens in their classrooms—period. Everything else falls to a distant second. Dorothy, Chris, and Lynn took responsibility to lead a systemic change and tried to figure out how that work could be implemented in individual schools and classrooms through developing clear expectations and systems of support. Their collaboration was wonderful, though that type of interaction didn't exist at other levels.

When a 1998 study showed that many principals were inadequately informed or involved in the reform, the district arranged seminars and literacy training for principals that mirrored the teachers' workshops.[17] The leadership team worked with others to integrate activities across their departments based on information that described student needs. Building the district's capacity for "data-driven decision making" was a key component in designing interventions and support systems that achieved results. The district leadership team collaborated with principals to establish an understanding of their new role as instructional leaders. Together, they implemented many new practices including curriculum mapping, student portfolios, coaching, mentoring, school and classroom walkthroughs, and open evaluation of student work. Principal evaluations were also redesigned. The challenge of establishing new middle school cultures led to turnover among LBUSD principals. Harper recalled: "I think the biggest barrier to change was that we had such pride in the way we were. This made it difficult to determine what was no longer needed. Some people were frightened

when Carl came up with these new ideas, ideas that challenged what had worked well for Long Beach in the past. It was hard to let things go."

In 1999, Cohn and his team decided to eliminate the area superintendencies and reorganize the central-office infrastructure by level. Harper took over the newly created middle school superintendent's office. This change helped to address some of the misalignment and confusion that resulted from the area structure. Kahl reflected on the struggles to advance a cohesive middle school reform agenda:

> Early efforts were very fragmented, because each area superintendent was responsible for a few middle schools, and they each had their own vision for what the reforms would look like. Once the standards work got under way, an understanding among the executive staff began to emerge. We discovered that our standards weren't really all that measurable and that aligned performance assessments were lacking. Slowly, we abandoned many of the earlier reforms—like advisories and heterogeneous groupings—because we couldn't find evidence that they were helping. We wanted teachers to be teaching in their areas of expertise. Now, structurally, many of our middle schools look much like the old junior highs, but the rationale and the instruction are very different.

High School Initiative: Reform at LBUSD's six comprehensive high schools was not the main focus of LBUSD's efforts during the 1990s. Cohn said: "We decided that the best path to high school reform was to bring better-prepared students to high school." This was a major departure for LBUSD, as high schools and high school leaders blazed the path for reform throughout the 1960s and 1970s. "Parents want safe elementary schools," Harper commented, "but a district is only as good as its high schools. Communities rally around high schools." Local residents, including many LBUSD staff, maintained strong ties based on their high school affiliations.

Despite the decision to focus attention on K-8 reform, LBUSD leaders did not ignore high schools. They encouraged sites to experiment. Cohn hired an outsider from Oklahoma to become a principal at Polytechnic High School, the district's flagship high school, who created the first co-principalship in district history.[18] LBUSD also acquired an abandoned naval base as the site for a new high school to serve the crowded western side of the city, which housed many of the city's poorest and newest residents. Harper recalled, "When LBUSD got the land for Cabrillo, people around Long Beach sat up and noticed Carl. They said, 'This guy makes things happen.'" Cabrillo High School opened in 1996. The Board also negotiated with TALB and converted one high school into a classical academy. Wilson Classical High School opened in 1997, the first high school to require a minimum GPA and school uniforms.

In 1999, the Board passed the "High School Initiative."[19] Ninth-grade students who read two or more levels below grade level were targeted for intervention, which included mandatory summer school and specialized classes.

Changing Role of the Central Office

As district officials and teachers reflected on Cohn's superintendency, they commented frequently on the quality of the central-office team. Cohn promoted insiders including Harper, Steinhauser, Dominguez, DeVries, and others to lead reform efforts. Dominguez was surprised at her promotion. She recalled, "Carl appointed me as the director of curriculum when he became superintendent. Initially, I did not apply for the position, because it wasn't something I wanted to do. But he encouraged others to push me to do it. He saw something in me that I didn't see in myself."

In addition, Cohn recruited two nationally recognized experts, Dr. Lynn Winters and Dr. Judy Elliott, to lead the research and special education departments, respectively. These appointments took place in a district where a majority of employees were born and raised in Long Beach.

Research Department

Winters left the National Center for Research on Evaluation, Standards, and Student Testing (CRESST) to join LBUSD in 1995. She was responsible for coordinating testing programs, implementing state accountability programs, and conducting research and evaluation studies. Under Winters's direction, LBUSD's capacity for data collection and interpretation expanded rapidly.

The 13 members of the research department worked closely with teachers, principals, and the curriculum department to implement district-developed end-of-course exams in key subjects and grade levels, which were correlated to state assessments. The department's motto was "serving schools." They wrote and reviewed test specifications for district assessments, built a distribution infrastructure, and scored and reported district and state test results. In addition to its data-processing role, the research office worked to help principals and teachers make sense of the rapidly escalating amount of available information. One middle school teacher observed, "Access to the data really drove the change process for our school. It cut through the emotion." Elementary Assistant Superintendent Karen DeVries added:

> Once Lynn and her team got to work, we could look at student and grade-level achievement data. Teachers started realizing that anybody at LBUSD could see their results. Around the schools, people started to ask tough questions like, "How come this 'regular' classroom is outscoring the 'gifted' classroom?" Suddenly, we

could compare progress and results from different teaching strategies for every child, grade level, and school. This really leveled the playing field and changed the conversation.

When asked to describe her position at LBUSD, Winters laughed, "I'm the sand in the oyster." Dominguez echoed many of her colleagues when she said, "Lynn is brilliant, caring, and can be viewed as abrasive. She came in with a whole new sense of how to generate data and kept asking hard questions. She was our own internal critical friend, always pushing us forward." In reflecting on Winters's role at LBUSD, Cohn added:

> She convinced our teachers that data could help them in their classrooms by explaining clearly the link between accountability and their mission of creating bright futures for kids. Many of them didn't want to believe her, but she won them over.

Special Education Department

In 1999, Elliott moved to Long Beach from the National Center of Educational Outcomes. Introduced to Cohn by Winters, she brought the district's philosophy of "education for ALL kids" to the office of special education. It was apparent to Elliott that the central office had too many traditional compliance-oriented staff with little or no curriculum expertise. By 2002, more than half of her special education staff were general educators. She also worked to integrate her department's operations with others around the district by creating four "co-appointment" positions. She established staffers in curriculum, research, bilingual education, and student support services who reported both to Elliott and the respective assistant superintendents of those departments. And, in an effort to foster "customer service and responsiveness to site needs," Elliott distributed cell phones to her administrators and gave their numbers to principals. She noted,

"Having someone on the other end of the phone helped to build trust and credibility, which was important since the tricky compliance issues in special education scare many people." Elliott reflected:

> When I came to this office, the district was fighting fires, running out to schools, responding constantly to crises. One drops important details when always in a crisis mode. I wanted people to stop panicking and realize that we as a district needed to move toward systematically addressing situations that were symptoms of bigger issues. It was apparent to me that folks had always supplied people at school sites with fish and had not taken time to teach them how to fish. Building that capacity takes time, energy, credibility, and education." I told my staff, "We're going to teach our schools to fish for themselves now." Coming here was inspiring, but very challenging. In this town where everyone seems to have gone to high school together, I am a total renegade. I think there are five outsiders in the central office."

Steinhauser reiterated the importance of working together to educate all the children of Long Beach: "When I worked with the team in the special projects and government programs office, we agreed that LBUSD would not worship at the altar of compliance. It was our obligation to make sure the rules did not get in our way of doing the right thing for kids." Elliott added, "As we approach the upcoming budget cuts, special education is not first on the chopping block. We're shoulder to shoulder with everyone else." District officials and Board members shared this philosophy.[20]

Cohn's Philosophy

"What's best for kids" was Cohn's favorite aphorism. He endeavored to create a culture in which, as one Board member stated, "Nobody cares who gets credit for good ideas."

Top Down and Bottom Up: As an area superintendent, Cohn was responsible for two low-performing LBUSD schools in a tough neighborhood. Cohn installed two promising principals, Steinhauser and Randy Ward and charged each with turning his school around. Within months, both schools were seeing dramatic improvements. Cohn commented: "Chris and Randy had very different styles, but both were knocking my socks off in two equally tough schools. I realized that I didn't need to impose one kind of reform; everybody doesn't need to do this work in the same way. By doing things differently, we could learn from each other."

As district superintendent, Cohn continued to seek a balance between "top-down mandates" and "bottom-up reforms." On the one hand, the district wanted to "let 1,000 flowers bloom" and encouraged site-level innovation. On the other hand, Dominguez admitted:

> The district was becoming more prescriptive about instruction. Certain things that the superintendent and district leadership felt were critical to our success were nonnegotiable. Nonnegotiable items included some specific training sessions, some materials, and the presence of coaches at low-performing schools. Some "nonnegotiables" were implemented across the district, while others only applied to low-performing schools.

Delegation and Risk Taking: One district leader said, "Carl operated in a nonhierarchical, very personal way. Far from a micromanager, he encouraged debate, was quick to delegate responsibilities, and held people accountable for failures." Cohn hosted a monthly "Cookies with Carl" meeting, which was open to anyone in the district. These drop-in gatherings were well attended, attracting staff from all levels since, as one teacher recalled, "You could really cut through red tape if necessary."

Fostering debate and accountability, however, was a challenge for LBUSD. Tomio Nishimura, a retired Air Force financial inspector who took charge of the district's business and financial operations in 1990, observed:

> Coming from the military, I was surprised at the amount of politics that were involved at LBUSD. In the Air Force, everything was cut and dried. As an officer, I was given tremendous authority, which included the responsibility for others' well-being. When I first arrived here, I found that many people were reluctant to make decisions for fear of offending someone. The common solution was, well, let's form a committee. I told my people that they should never be afraid to make a decision, even if it was the wrong one, because indecision was unacceptable. This avoidance of decision making—what some people call the culture of nice—is a problem in school districts.

Harper, a fellow African-American, met Cohn when both were called to assist with lunchtime supervision in the early 1970s during the district's period of racial integration. She recalled one decisive moment that captured his approach:

> I remember one middle school reform meeting, when a principal continued to pester Carl with the same question. Carl was friendly, but finally he stopped the meeting and said, "Let me tell you, people who cannot deal with ambiguity might as well put their keys on the table." The room was a hush; you could have heard a pin drop. But statements like that stuck with people.

Selecting Cohn's Successor

When Cohn announced his intention to retire, the Board decided against conducting a national search and selected Steinhauser as Cohn's successor. Board president Bobbie Smith described the selection process:

We knew we wanted continuity. The district was in a good place and moving in a good direction, and we did not want an outside person coming in feeling that they needed to make big changes. Chris was Carl's deputy and a product of Long Beach, and we could predict a very smooth transition. Though Chris lacks Carl's breadth of experience, we trust him, and he was our unanimous choice.

Reflections and Results

As they reflected on the change process, board member Polacheck observed:

We did not identify initiatives just for the sake of having initiatives. They emerged as we discussed our vision for what we wanted the district to become. We made progress as the community coalesced around a positive issue, and then we just got to work on the problems. The process just happened. Maintaining a positive, collaborative, high-energy direction focused on high standards and improved student achievement kept the district moving forward. We kept ourselves focused.

The district used many different measures to track its progress. The state accountability program, developed in 1999 by the California Department of Education, used an academic performance index (API) to rank school improvement. By SY02, 50 schools won the Governor's Performance Award for meeting or exceeding their growth targets. In total, 69% of LBUSD schools met their targets, which exceeded the 52% statewide total. API scores at six LBUSD schools (7% of the total) remained the same or declined.[21] Scores on the Stanford 9 (SAT9) exam, administered in all California public schools, increased overall, and the largest gains were concentrated in the earliest grades (see Exhibit 5). While SAT9 scores improved for students of all ethnic groups, a persistent gap in achievement remained between white and Asian students on the one hand, and African-American and Hispanic students on the other (see Exhibit 6).

From 1992 to 2002, dropout rates decreased by nearly two-thirds (see Exhibit 7), while the number of students taking advanced placement (AP) courses rose steadily. The 78% pass rate on AP exams at Polytechnic High, LBUSD's flagship school, was the highest rate of any urban high school in the country.[22] Attendance rates held steady, at around 95%.

Ongoing Relationships with Stakeholders

When Cohn reflected on his tenure, he cited labor relations as one of the most significant areas of personal learning:

After a pretty heated exchange one day early in my superintendency, TALB's president suggested that we visit schools together to resolve a discrepancy in what we were hearing from teachers about a number of issues. I worried that such a visit might escalate the negativity, but I went anyway. And, one high school visit turned out to be an experience that influenced the course of labor relations throughout the rest of my time at LBUSD. The truth is I had no idea how difficult a job it was being president of an urban teacher's union. I presumed that teachers and their association leadership were fairly monolithic in their views and disagreements between them would never be shared in front of me. But, I was wrong. After nearly two hours of discussion, I was feeling sorry for the union president because the faculty was beating up on him. Some felt TALB had not done enough to support retirement incentive programs.

I went back to my office and told Tomio to come up with a retirement incentive program that would capture all of the teachers at that high school that wanted to retire. We presented

TALB with this new benefit in a one-hour negotiating session, and the practice of my visiting schools with TALB's president became a regular practice. It served to dramatically improve labor relations by suggesting to the larger organization that listening to teachers in a collaborative manner was an important value that I held. And we never had a teachers' strike, and negotiations never lasted more than two days.

One LBUSD negotiator added:

Through shared decision making, TALB and LBUSD worked collaboratively, contributing to a productive climate and good morale throughout the district. Good relations with TALB extended our ability to focus resources on instruction and student achievement rather than contentious litigation.

Steinhauser Looks Ahead

Sitting at his desk in September 2002, Steinhauser looked back at the district's achievements during the Cohn era. He pondered which aspects of the change process would apply to the work ahead. With a looming state fiscal crisis and a slowing rate of enrollment growth, LBUSD faced many new challenges. A number of key LBUSD leaders—including two Board members, TALB's executive director, Harper, Winters, and Nishimura—were nearing retirement, and successors needed to be identified. California was also considering a mandatory new literacy program called Open Court, which threatened the district's commitment to allowing site-level innovation. One retired administrator commented:

Chris and Carl share a vision for improvement, and they both care passionately about children. Neither has a flashy style, and their partnership has been successful, partly because they have very different strengths. Carl cared about ideas,

not details. As a former counselor, he was a good listener and did a lot of work within the community. He delegated much of the responsibility for building capacity throughout the system to his team. Conversely, Chris is much more hands-on. He knows both instruction and finance and is more extroverted. National policy interests him less; he is focused on Long Beach. People have been working hard, and they are tired. I worry about burnout. And with our recent success, I worry about complacency. There is still so much work to be done.

As Steinhauser sat back in his chair, he glanced overhead and saw the large dollar sign that hung over his desk. "The buck stops here," he said. "I know we need to make the right decisions for the children of Long Beach."

Notes

1. Relative to the 65 most populous U.S. cities, cited by the City of Long Beach, http://www.ci.long-beach.ca.us/news/ displaynews.asp?News ID=313.

2. PELP cases use the convention "SY" to designate, in this instance, school year 1981–1982.

3. During the mid-1990s, Lakewood and Signal Hill, two distinct neighborhoods within LBUSD, petitioned to separate from the district. Cohn recalled, "These separatist movements were a major distraction. After nearly five years and countless county committee hearings, the state unanimously refused these requests."

4. J. W. Houck, K. C. Cohn, and C. A. Cohn, eds., *Partnering to Lead Educational Renewal: High-Quality Teachers, High-Quality Schools,* New York: Teachers Colle Press, 2004, documents a full history of the Long Beach Educational Partnership.

5. J. Sterngold, "Taking a new look at uniforms and their impact on schools," the *New York Times,* June 28, 2000.

6. "School uniforms growing in favor in California," National Desk, the *New York Times,* September 3, 1994.

7. A. Pertman, "California finds uniform success," *The Boston Globe,* January 13, 1996.

8. Pertman, "California finds uniform success."

9. K.C. Cohn and C.A. Cohn, "School Improvement Initiatives in Long Beach, California: The Quest for

Higher Student Achievement, Behavior and Dress Standards," *Education* 119, no. 2, (Winter 1998), p. 181.

10. Sterngold, "Taking a new look at uniforms."

11. Quoted from Anne Mackinnon's *Standards-Based Middle Grades Reform in Six Urban Districts, 1995–2001: A Report on the Program for Student Achievement of the Edna McConnell Clark Foundation,* 2003, http://www.emcf.org, p. 22. This report gives a full overview of the reform in LBUSD middle schools.

12. Adapted from Mackinnon, *Standards-Based Middle Grades Reform in Six Urban Districts, 1995–2001.*

13. See Peter Schmidt, "California agrees to pay district for desegregation expenses," *Education Week,* May 10, 1995.

14. A detailed explanation of this initiative is provided in K. DeVries, J. Seal, T. Bellmar, T. Suzuki, C. Dominguez, and C. Steinhauser, "Working Together to Improve Reading in the Early Grades," in Houck et al., *Partnering to Lead Educational Renewal: High-Quality Teachers, High-Quality Schools,* chap. 2.

15. The district sought a waiver from the state to supplement mandated textbooks with "little books" for guided reading.

16. LBUSD assigned low-performing eighth graders to the Long Beach Preparatory Academy. Long Beach Prep, which opened its doors in SY97, was considered a temporary measure by many district officials. While the number of failing eighth graders fell by more than half in its first two years of implementation, Long Beach Prep graduates experienced difficulty in rejoining their high school classmates. LBUSD closed the academy in June 2001.

17. A series of reports published at http://www.middleweb.com/Reformingschools.html including John Norton, "Standards-Based Reform: Now Comes the Hard Part," fall 1999, described the middle school reform work at LBUSD.

18. H.J. Green participated in the integration of the Tulsa schools, where he was the first white principal of the formerly all-black Booker T. Washington High School. Because he was the first "outsider" appointed to an LBUSD principalship, many district old-timers felt that "Had H.J. failed, no other outside staff would have been hired by the district."

19. Information about the High School Initiative is available at http://www.lbusd.k12.ca.us/high/high_school_initiative.htm.

20. One unique example of LBUSD leaders' commitment to all kids was captured in the creation of the Mary McLeod Bethune Transitional Center for homeless stu- dents. Established within a family homeless shelter in 1991, the Bethune school provided health, social, and academic services to the city's homeless children and was supervised by Guigni, Cohn, and Harper.

21. Cited from the California Department of Education Web site, http://data1.cde.ca.gov/dataquest/2002Grth_dst.asp.

22. Cited by Carl Cohn, "Turning education's rhetoric into reality," *Education Week,* February 20, 2002.

Exhibit 1
LBUSD Enrollment SY82–SY02

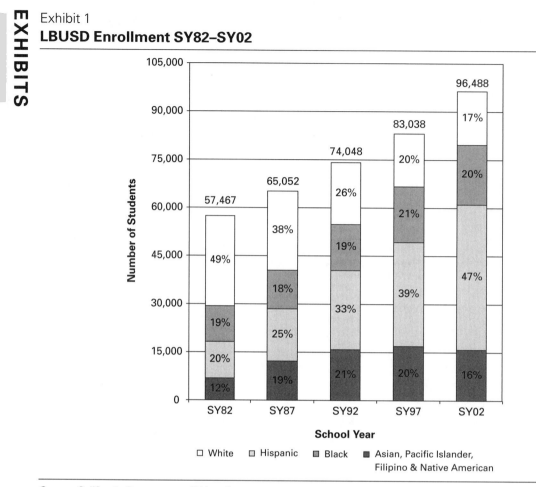

Source: California Department of Education.

Exhibit 2

LBUSD Financial Information SY93–SY02 ($ million)

This statement includes revenues and expenditures from 14 LBUSD funds, including general, adult, preschool, insurance, cafeteria, and construction funds.

	SY93	SY94	SY95[a]	SY96	SY97	SY98	SY99[b]	SY00	SY01	SY02
Revenues by Source										
Local[c]	$44.846	$31.012	$35.182	$40.132	$64.956	$76.535	$103.937	$86.489	$91.511	$174.010
State[d]	332.118	344.978	382.462	344.779	388.658	453.805	481.287	550.008	617.994	702.749
Federal Grants	45.775	49.569	55.875	57.169	57.292	64.707	72.122	76.825	86.028	95.496
Total Revenues	**$422.739**	**$425.559**	**$473.519**	**$442.080**	**$510.906**	**$595.047**	**$657.346**	**$713.322**	**$795.533**	**$972.255**
Expenditures by Use										
Direct Instruction[e]	$201.740	$211.068	$234.085	$245.318	$273.200	$303.451	$334.498	$377.795	$441.080	$466.163
Pupil Support & Site/Central Administration	69.630	69.879	76.581	81.065	89.847	93.277	104.600	112.450	134.727	140.038
Building Services, Upkeep & Construction	93.694	96.529	72.628	83.081	110.927	119.740	162.060	170.193	190.199	275.782
Other Expenses[f]	42.937	38.694	39.785	35.334	38.015	57.718	58.710	57.158	62.408	69.925
Net Transfers/Uses	(2.233)	(2.454)	(2.819)	(2.304)	(2.049)	(2.002)	(2.161)	(2.043)	(2.676)	(2.697)
Total General Expenditures	**$405.768**	**$413.716**	**$420.260**	**$442.494**	**$509.940**	**$572.184**	**$657.707**	**$715.553**	**$825.738**	**$949.211**
Operating Surplus/(Deficit)	16.971	11.843	53.259	(0.414)	0.966	22.863	(0.361)	(2.231)	(30.205)	23.044

Source: Compiled by district financial office from LBUSD financial records.

[a] State revenues in SY95 included $63.7 million desegregation claim settlement amount. A "Desegregation Funds Committee Recommendations" report, presented to the LBUSD Board on May 21, 1996, describes how these funds were used to fund maintenance and facilities, Cabrillo High School, K-8 literacy programs and materials, discretionary school funding (allocating $30/student to schools for four years), and an unrestricted endowment.

[b] Construction bond approved by local electorate in SY99.

[c] Local property taxes transferred to the state for distribution. This line includes mostly interest prior to SY99, when bond funds became available for distribution.

[d] Includes state (per pupil) appropriation plus categorical program funding.

[e] Ninety percent of LBUSD's general fund, used for K-12 direct instruction, is funded by the state.

[f] Includes books, supplies, contracts, and other operating expenses.

Exhibit 3
LBUSD Benchmark Book Assessments Summary

Benchmark Book Assessments test students' reading fiction and nonfiction at grade level. Percentages occasionally dropped from year to year due to internal realignment of the benchmark books with standardized test norms. Benchmark books were also aligned to norm-referenced tests. Data collected showed correlations ranging from .67–.73 for each grade level Benchmark Book Assessment and the spring 2001 Stanford Achievement Test 9 Reading NCE scores.

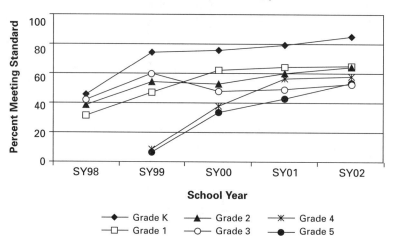

Benchmark Summary

| Grade | Met Standard (%) | | | | |
	SY98	SY99	SY00	SY01	SY02
0	45.7	74.0	75.4	79.1	84.7
1	31.2	47.4	61.8	64.2	65.2
2	38.8	54.3	52.7	59.7	64.4
3	42.5	60.2	48.1	49.1	53.1
4		8.9	38.0	56.4	58.1
5		6.7	33.6	42.8	53.3

Source: District files. An explanation of the development of LBUSD's Benchmark Assessment program is in "Working Together to Improve Reading in the Early Grades," by K. DeVries, J. Seal, T. Bellmar, T. Suzuki, C. Dominguez, and C. Steinhauser, Chapter 2 in *Partnering to Lead Educational Renewal: High-Quality Teachers, High-Quality Schools.*

Exhibit 4

SAT9 Reading and Mathematics Scores SY98–SY02 (percent scoring at or above the 50th national percentile rank)

Figures indicate the percentage of students who scored at or above the 50th national percentile rank (NPR), who are purported to have demonstrated achievement at or above grade level.

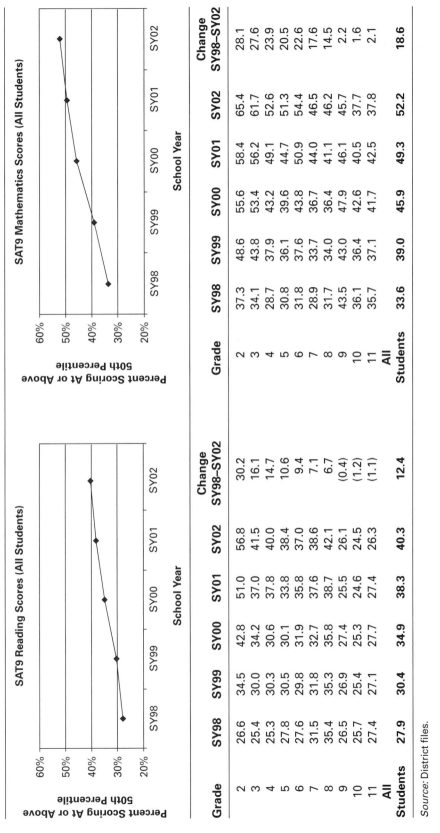

SAT9 Reading Scores (All Students)

Grade	SY98	SY99	SY00	SY01	SY02	Change SY98–SY02
2	26.6	34.5	42.8	51.0	56.8	30.2
3	25.4	30.0	34.2	37.0	41.5	16.1
4	25.3	30.3	30.6	37.8	40.0	14.7
5	27.8	30.5	30.1	33.8	38.4	10.6
6	27.6	29.8	31.9	35.8	37.0	9.4
7	31.5	31.8	32.7	37.6	38.6	7.1
8	35.4	35.3	35.8	38.7	42.1	6.7
9	26.5	26.9	27.4	25.5	26.1	(0.4)
10	25.7	25.4	25.3	24.6	24.5	(1.2)
11	27.4	27.1	27.7	27.4	26.3	(1.1)
All Students	**27.9**	**30.4**	**34.9**	**38.3**	**40.3**	**12.4**

SAT9 Mathematics Scores (All Students)

Grade	SY98	SY99	SY00	SY01	SY02	Change SY98–SY02
2	37.3	48.6	55.6	58.4	65.4	28.1
3	34.1	43.8	53.4	56.2	61.7	27.6
4	28.7	37.9	43.2	49.1	52.6	23.9
5	30.8	36.1	39.6	44.7	51.3	20.5
6	31.8	37.6	43.8	50.9	54.4	22.6
7	28.9	33.7	36.7	44.0	46.5	17.6
8	31.7	34.0	36.4	41.1	46.2	14.5
9	43.5	43.0	47.9	46.1	45.7	2.2
10	36.1	36.4	42.6	40.5	37.7	1.6
11	35.7	37.1	41.7	42.5	37.8	2.1
All Students	**33.6**	**39.0**	**45.9**	**49.3**	**52.2**	**18.6**

Source: District files.

Exhibit 5

SAT9 Reading and Mathematics Scores SY98–SY02 by Ethnicity (percent scoring at or above the 50th national percentile rank)

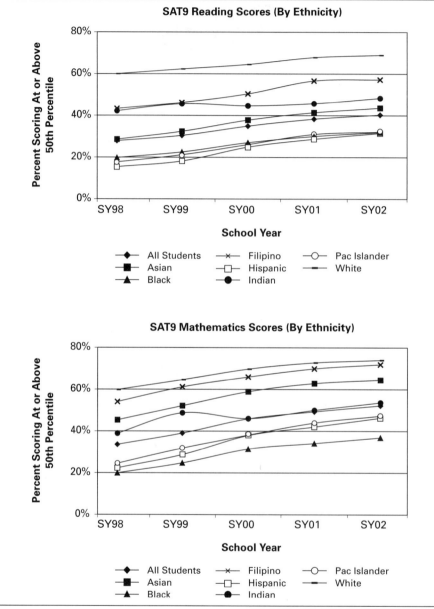

Source: District files.

Exhibit 6

LBUSD One-Year Dropout Rate for Students in Grades 9–12 (SY92–SY02)

The dropout rate is calculated by dividing the number of 9–12 grade
dropouts by the total 9–12 grade enrollment.

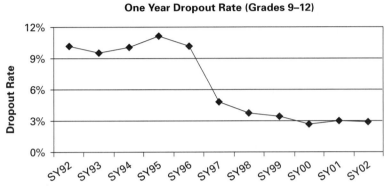

One Year Dropout Rate (Grades 9–12)

School Year	One-Year Dropout Rate	Number of Dropouts
SY92	10.20%	1,886
SY93	9.50%	1,807
SY94	10.10%	1,951
SY95	11.10%	2,194
SY96	10.20%	2,113
SY97	4.80%	1,037
SY98	3.80%	835
SY99	3.40%	799
SY00	2.70%	654
SY01	3.00%	771
SY02	2.90%	771

Source: California Department of Education, Educational Demographics Unit Web site, http://data1.cde.ca.gov/
dataquest/ASPGraph3.asp?Level= District&cName= LONG^BEACH^UNIFIED&cCode=1964725, accessed June 1,
2004.

James P. Honan ■ Robert B. Schwartz ■ Allen S. Grossman ■ Jennifer M. Suesse

Long Beach Unified School District (B): Sustaining Improvement during a Leadership Transition (2002–2004)

On June 17, 2004, Christopher Steinhauser returned to his office after visiting the third annual retreat for Long Beach Unified School District (LBUSD) high school principals. Steinhauser realized that his second year as superintendent of LBUSD was nearly complete. Though a statewide fiscal crisis had forced the district to make some tough choices during 2002–2004, Steinhauser commented:

> There is a lot of work ahead to do what's best for Long Beach's kids, but I believe that the pillars of our organization are stronger than ever. The work of the past decade evolved without a formal plan because we concentrated on the shared goals and objectives at the heart of each initiative. I have worked at LBUSD for my entire career, and we will continue to build on our strengths.

Building on a Decade of Reform (1992–2002)[1]

In September 2002, Steinhauser succeeded highly regarded Superintendent Carl Cohn,

who led LBUSD from 1992 to 2002. During Cohn's tenure, the district and city worked together to address many challenges including growing diversity, economic adversity, and threats to public safety. Cohn collaborated with the LBUSD Board of Education to foster a new type of governance relationship. Together, they developed a series of "board initiatives" designed to address the district's goal of "raising standards of dress, behavior, and achievement." Major initiatives included adopting a mandatory K-8 school uniform policy, implementing standards-based K-8 instructional reform, ending social promotion, laying a foundation for high school reform, and developing partnerships with local institutions of higher education.

Steinhauser served as Cohn's deputy for three years prior to Cohn's retirement. Together, they transformed the role of the central office by linking departments more closely with classroom instruction. Centralized instructional support functions were integrated into the elementary, middle, and high schools, as well as the research offices, and special education was redesigned to provide more direct services to sites. An office of curriculum and professional development, eliminated due to severe cutbacks in the early 1990s, was reestablished to foster high-quality professional development activities for principals and teachers to ensure that standards-based instruction was implemented consistently across the district. In 2003, LBUSD received the Broad Prize for Urban Education in recognition of its achievements.[2]

Steinhauser Takes Charge

After his unanimous selection as superintendent by the five-member board of education (henceforth referred to as the board), Steinhauser and LBUSD confronted changes in California's financial and educational environment. The state's rising deficit, caused by changes in the economy and the energy crisis, resulted in severe funding shortfalls for public schools. Financial pressures were exacerbated by the district's declining student enrollment. Relations with many key stakeholders also changed during Steinhauser's first two years on the job due to new board membership, new teacher's association leadership, and retirements from the central office. Steinhauser planned to use these challenges as an opportunity to streamline central office administrative functions and improve organizational communication. At the same time, LBUSD was working hard to maintain its momentum in improving student achievement at the elementary and middle school levels. However, Steinhauser's new priority was "fixing high schools." He considered high school reform to be the most difficult and important task facing urban districts across the nation and was determined that LBUSD take on this "last frontier."

Financial Pressures

Enrollment Changes: After more than 20 years of rapidly increasing growth, student enrollment at LBUSD began slowing in SY03.[3]

District records revealed that fewer new kindergarteners were entering LBUSD, while transfers into district high schools continued at a steady pace. In SY04, 97,560 students attended the district's 95 schools. Of these students, 49% were Hispanic/Latino, 18.6% were African-American, 16.9% were white (non-Hispanic), 9.7% were Asian, and 5.8% represented a wide range of other ethnic groups including Filipino and Pacific Islander. Thirty-three percent of the students were learning English as a second language, 65% received free or reduced-price lunch, and 8% were enrolled in special education.

State Budget Shortfalls: Ongoing state budget shortfalls were a major concern for LBUSD, since 90% of its general fund (accounting for 64% of the district's total revenues) was disbursed from the state (Exhibit 1 details SY99–SY03 district financial information). After three consecutive years of forced reductions totaling $42 million from its planned annual budget, cutting an additional $15 million in SY04 proved especially difficult. Under Steinhauser's leadership, LBUSD convened a committee of 52 stakeholders including administrators, teachers, and other community members to review the budget in a series of 10 meetings. The group set priorities, which included avoiding direct cuts to school sites and layoffs, while at the same time preserving class-size reductions at all levels. After California voters approved a statewide school bailout bond in March 2004, allowing schools to dodge the need for more drastic cutbacks, the budget committee presented its proposal to the board. The board accepted the committee's recommendations, with minor changes.

"Even though we've had to cut $57 million over the past four years," Steinhauser said, "nobody hangs their head around our offices. People are still working hard, and we have avoided layoffs." District administrators agreed. "But," one noted, "we're tired, we're burnt out, and everyone feels like they are on the chopping block." Chief Business and Financial Officer Tomio

Nishimura added that budget reductions since 2000 had "left funding for classrooms and related resources untouched, as the district had restricted cuts to school site support, instructional support, and general administrative support services." Nishimura explained LBUSD's approach: "If you were to view the district's organizational structure as a series of concentric circles, classrooms would be in the innermost circle. Should further cuts be required in SY05, we will move slowly inward. I would expect pupil support services [e.g., counselors, nurses, psychologists, librarians] to face careful scrutiny along with site support staff." Looking back at the process, Steinhauser remarked:

> We turned over every rock in the organization and looked carefully at any department whose budget grew out of proportion to changes in enrollment. The budget process took an inordinate amount of my time this year. There were some hard choices to make, and we found some places that had been ignored for too long. In the end, we met our goal, and the fiscal challenges did not take away our focus on doing what's best for kids.

Looking ahead, Nishimura predicted that the tough times were not over:

> While the voter's approval of revenue bonds and a gradual improving of the state economy have negated the need for draconian cuts, we are nonetheless receiving less from the state than we'd like to. We are holding on to the promise of a full recovery within the next few years. However, given California's reliance on personal income and sales taxes to fund education, I expect we'll be on a financial roller coaster for years to come.

Additionally, some stakeholders were worried because California was considering a new school-funding policy based on a weighted student formula.[4] LBUSD strongly opposed this approach. "Allocating resources to sites according to a weighted student formula would destroy Long Beach," said Steinhauser. "All our work has focused on equitable treatment for *all* of our kids. Since the state can't give us any more money, people would see this as robbing Peter to pay Paul. It would distract our principals and create huge problems in the community."

A Changing of the Guard: Evolving Stakeholder Relationships

Board Turnover: Following nearly a decade of consistent board leadership, major membership turnover ensued just as Steinhauser took charge.[5] A few months prior to board President Bobbie Smith's retirement, Smith received a standing ovation at a luncheon celebrating Long Beach's education system. Steinhauser told the assembled group, "Our achievements at LBUSD did not occur by accident. They happened because of visionary leadership by our board of education." While Steinhauser was sorry to lose Smith and her colleagues, he was delighted with the results of the April 2004 election when both candidates Smith endorsed were selected. "It is a seamless transition," he said. By the start of SY05, four of the five board members had less than four years' experience. This was a dramatic reversal for Long Beach where, only two years earlier, board members' average tenure had exceeded 10 years. While most LBUSD officials were optimistic about the new board members, some found the rapid turnover a bit unsettling.

Strained Relationship with Teacher's Association of Long Beach (TALB): Between SY02 and SY03, TALB's 5,500 members elected a new executive director and a new president and brought in a new assistant executive director from the California Teacher's Association (CTA). After nearly 10 years of mostly productive interactions between TALB and LBUSD, TALB's current leadership and the budget crisis created new tensions. In the fall of 2003, when

LBUSD opened annual salary negotiations for SY05, it could offer no raises and proposed modifications to the teachers' health benefits package. TALB rebuffed the district's offer, and negotiations stalled. During the impasse, one veteran teacher commented, "We are entering into a new age of distrust, where there is increased militancy. This is unheard of in our district." Despite this perspective, after two days of mediation in February 2004, the health-care issue was resolved.

Steinhauser reflected on the events:

In recent years, I think some rank and file members felt that TALB was too cozy with the district. So they chose leaders who had a philosophy not always based on the collaborative approach we've come to expect. During the impasse, a few teachers called me to ask if some of the negative things they were hearing were true. "Is it really that bad?" Throughout the process, I directed the staff to stick to the high road. No matter what, we will always treat people with respect and be open and honest in our communication.

"Our teachers work so hard," concluded one board member. "We were disappointed that we were at odds with TALB this year, but it was understandable given that tight financial times have prevented us from offering raises for teachers in the past three years. I think we must find a way to provide increases next year."

By the end of SY04, the new CTA representative left Long Beach, and TALB was reorganizing and hiring a new executive director and staff leadership. Uncertainty would prevail until the district had a chance to work with the new leaders.

Central-Office Changes and Retirements: At the central office, Steinhauser made relatively few changes to the organization in his first two years as superintendent. Among them, he asked

Dorothy Harper to become deputy superintendent. In addition to her new responsibilities, Harper would continue to supervise the K–8 and middle schools due to financial constraints. Steinhauser, who had worked with low-performing elementary schools prior to his promotion, added an administrator to the superintendent's office to oversee these sites. Assistant Superintendent Karen DeVries would be responsible for all 51 elementary schools, which included 16 year-round sites. The net result of the various retirements and reassignments was a reduction of 10 senior management slots.

Stakeholders from across the district described the transition from Cohn to Steinhauser as "smooth." But with Nishimura and Harper approaching retirement in SY04, there was still some unease. To address this, Steinhauser involved both TALB leadership and the two board budget committee members in interviewing external candidates for Nishimura's replacement. In addition to these retirements, Lynn Winters, who ran the LBUSD research department; the public information director; at least two high school principals; the chief financial officer; the special projects director; and the elementary school superintendent were nearing retirement, although none had announced specific departure plans.

Administrative Actions

Promotions: Throughout the spring of 2004, Steinhauser wrestled with reorganizing responsibilities among existing staff. Given the budget crunch, he knew he would "have to do more with less." His decision to promote DeVries to the deputy position, announced at a board meeting in early June, took some by surprise. Steinhauser and DeVries had been close colleagues for over a decade, working together to supervise elementary schools and in the special projects office. Steinhauser's choice to create an assistant superintendent of middle schools and Head Start was even more unexpected, since combining preschool programs with middle schools was unconventional. Nevertheless, his selection of Head Start Director Gwen Matthews for the role was well received. Harper would be assisted in her middle school and deputy superintendent responsibilities by DeVries, Matthews, and Steinhauser. Finally, Steinhauser promoted an internal candidate to become the assistant superintendent of human resource services. Administrators noted that all three of these newly promoted officials, like Steinhauser, had once been LBUSD elementary school principals. Additional promotions and reorganization announcements were expected throughout the summer. Steinhauser reflected on these personnel moves:

> One thing I learned from Carl is the importance of having each position backed up with a bench that is two and three people deep. Just like a football team. Your first- and second-string players could get hurt, and then what have you got? So, I keep a mental map of the checkerboard—where people are, where they're going. I kept my cards close to my chest as I thought about promotions. Looking ahead, I think the overall system will benefit from some realignment. Change is hard for some people, and I have to remind myself to be clear and not move too fast.

Implementing Baldrige: Leaders across the district also noted that Steinhauser had a more "operational focus" than his predecessor. For example, he was implementing the Baldrige System for Performance Excellence,[6] a district-wide process for continuous improvement. Based on feedback received through the Baldrige process in SY04, Steinhauser decided to decentralize some student support services ranging from attendance and expulsions to nurses and gang intervention specialists and reorganize the information services branch involving data systems from both the instruction and business sides of the house.

Opinions among the senior staff were divided regarding the Baldrige System. One administrator commented: "I like that Chris is trying to implement a more uniform system for collaborative planning. He places emphasis on training us to communicate in a systematic way. It is helpful for me to know what my colleagues' priorities are. This process forces us to model for sites what we are always asking them to do: give and receive feedback about organizational performance."

Other administrators were frustrated with the Baldrige process and "jargon." They pointed to the district's ongoing struggle to bring a service orientation to the information services, purchasing, and payroll departments and questioned the system's ability to yield genuine improvement. Some officials were skeptical about Baldrige as a solution to the "bigger issue" of weak communication systems throughout the organization.

In response to this debate, Steinhauser said, "I don't care what we call it, but I want there to be a process in place by which people set priorities according to what their clients want." Steinhauser would continue Cohn's practice of one midweek meeting for senior staff as a forum for discussion of these and other issues. He would also ensure that a small group of key leadership team members meet privately on a biweekly basis.

Ongoing Instructional Reform

Amidst this changing context and with fewer hands in the central office, Steinhauser and the LBUSD staff were committed to sustaining their focus on improving instruction and continuing the reform efforts started under Cohn, which had led to more schools meeting their state academic performance index (API) targets: 63% in

SY01, 69% in SY02, and 83% in SY03. In contrast, only 78% of schools statewide had similar success in SY03.

Sustaining K-8 Improvement

Elementary: Seeking Self-Sufficiency: Elementary school students had made slow but steady progress (Exhibit 3 includes California Standards Tests [CST] elementary school results). Then, in SY04, the California education code mandated that schools use a state-adopted literacy curriculum. For LBUSD, this meant that 59 schools had to implement a complex new curriculum called Open Court.[7] Deputy Superintendent DeVries remarked:

> Schools felt, rightly so, that this was a totally top-down mandate. Nevertheless, as everyone got to know Open Court, we discovered that this was actually an exceptionally strong curriculum which integrated many previously separate literacy components into a single package. But, the program was not particularly strong instructionally, which was frustrating for teachers. As a result, I told our principals and teachers: "Use this curriculum, but continue to make good instructional decisions in the Long Beach way." By the end of the year, principals reported that many of their best teachers were making the program work for their students and themselves and remained committed to improving instruction.

Due to a decline in elementary school enrollment, LBUSD wanted to implement a longstanding district goal of expanding the number of classrooms offering full-day kindergarten. After some tough negotiations, TALB and Steinhauser agreed to establish an automatic waiver process that would ensure that teachers could volunteer for all-day teaching duties. And, many did. In SY04, 85% of the teachers also participated in piloting the implementation of a volun-

tary district-wide, standards-based report card for elementary schools.

With these new projects in place and no reduction in DeVries's other responsibilities, DeVries rethought how she could get her work done. She decided to leverage her relationship with principals to help with "key-results walk-through" meetings. During these meetings, principals visited classrooms at one another's schools (some principals also included teachers in walk-throughs) and then reviewed "key-results" data highlighting student progress. DeVries selected 12 "lead principals" to manage key-results meetings with their peers. She commented: "Initially, I made this change in survival mode. These 12 principals were accountable to each other in these meetings, although lead principals do not evaluate their colleagues. By the end of the year, principals said that they wanted to keep this system in place. I guess it's not always bad to have scarce resources; it forced me to rethink things."

Middle Schools: Student performance on the CST in middle schools was mixed (see Exhibit 4). Harper responded by establishing a stronger focus on leadership and literacy, and she involved an outside consultant in designing her teachers' professional development. The middle schools also implemented principal walk-throughs to support the literacy focus in conjunction with monthly principals' meetings. Principals and department chairs were beginning to learn how to recognize and develop good instructional techniques for all classrooms.

With all the changes, there was some concern about the impending change in leadership at the middle school level. Bancroft Middle School's principal, Debbie Stark, stated:

> Dorothy Harper has so much wisdom and institutional knowledge, and she was a buffer for her principals. She protected us and encouraged us to take risks, which is an essential component of really moving schools forward. Looking at the

changes in the central office, I hope that the district will find ways to continue supporting principals' risk taking, especially when money is tight and accountability is strict.

Steinhauser's Mandate: A Focus on High Schools

Background: The district served over 26,000 ninth- through twelfth-grade students at six comprehensive and eight alternative high schools. Enrollment at each of the six comprehensive high schools exceeded 4,000 students, and each campus was under the collaborative leadership of two "co-principals." Every high school offered its own unique programming ranging from academic magnet programs to freshman academies to a classical high school. As in most districts across the nation, teachers were organized into departments and were trained and certified in a subject area (in contrast to the general elementary school certification, which often included coursework in teaching literacy).

In 1999, the board passed the High School Initiative, which focused on literacy and ended social promotion for ninth graders. When asked about the challenge of high school reform, former Superintendent Cohn responded, "Long Beach loves its high schools, and reforming them is a huge undertaking even in the best of times. I want to see Long Beach do it the Long Beach way."

Every Student, Every Day: Steinhauser wanted a reform strategy based on the standards-based, data-driven approach that had originated at the elementary and middle school levels. "From the beginning, we wanted the reforms to connect to all the K–8 work we'd done. High school reform was for *all* high schools and *all* kids." Webster stated:

In order to establish continuity from kindergarten through 12th grade, we were going to have to convince our high schools to make big changes. We were saying that subject expertise wasn't enough if the kids didn't learn.

Defining Goals: By the end of SY04, Webster and the high school principals had articulated four goals:

- Increasing achievement of all students in the core content areas
- Closing the achievement gap by accelerating the learning of the lowest-performing students
- Improving the high school climate and culture among students and staff to support improved achievement
- Building high school leadership capacity to design, implement, and sustain improvement efforts

The principals, with district support, also worked to develop a set of indicators to measure their progress. "The high schools are becoming data hogs," said Winters. "Now that they are learning how to use our data, they are keeping our department hopping with requests. Together, we are designing a way for them to evaluate their own work on a regular basis."

Early Results: While academic performance varied across the schools, all of the high schools met their statewide performance targets in SY03 and were eligible for the Governor's Performance Award as measured by their API scores (see Exhibit 5). A high school principal reflected on the progress of unfolding reforms:

Last year, there was a real emphasis on literacy district-wide, and it was very new, very different. It went against the traditional isolation and proprietary nature of high school cultures. One of the reasons I think that our high schools did well last year was because everyone was working together and there was focus.

LBUSD was progressing more rapidly than the state overall in decreasing the numbers of students whose scores on the California English/

Language Arts Standards Tests (CST) were below basic or far below basic. While the high schools had made progress, there was still an urgent need for improvement with only 35% of ninth graders, 28% of tenth graders, and 27% of eleventh graders scoring at proficient or advanced levels in SY03. LBUSD also saw a persistent gap in academic achievement between white and nonwhite students

To address this issue, LBUSD began steadily increasing the number of students taking advanced placement (AP) courses from SY01 to SY04 (see Exhibit 6). In SY05, the district planned to expand AP and honors course offerings by 20% and increase the enrollment of historically underrepresented Hispanic and African-American students. LBUSD was putting a number of supports in place to help those students succeed, including summer programs and AP teacher training. The district was also developing systems to identify students at risk of failing the statewide high school exit examination. by having all ninth and tenth graders take a practice exam in 2003.[8]

Reflections on Steinhauser's Leadership

District officials described Steinhauser as someone who "loved the details" of instruction and financial management. They characterized his leadership style as both "less questioning" and "more approachable" than Cohn's. Assistant Superintendent Christine Dominguez said:

> Like Carl, Chris spends a lot of time in the community and a lot of time in schools. But, he's much more hands-on. For example, last summer he taught a second-grade summer school class because he wanted to understand the new state-mandated Open Court literacy curriculum. Then, during this year's budget process, he demonstrated his mastery of federal categorical funding, as well as his ability to get input from

the community on tough issues. You don't often see a superintendent getting involved at that level. He really understands both the instructional and fiscal sides of the house.

While some officials commented quietly about how Steinhauser was not a "visionary like Carl," they also lauded him as one of the "most loved" leaders in the district. One administrator observed: "We have been fortunate to work with two extraordinary superintendents. Carl had never been a site administrator, so he made it clear that he needed us to do our jobs. Chris, on the other hand, knows every detail of site administration. He doesn't really need to rely on anyone, yet we know he has enough confidence to let us do our jobs."

One LBUSD veteran added, "Carl was a little more top-down than Chris, but they are both instructional leaders. Consequently, the transition felt seamless. The last thing managers needed was an abrupt shift in mission and practice. Once our course is set, people will adhere to it. Change is hard, and nobody wants to reinvent everything every year. We anticipate that Chris will be here for awhile." A principal added:

> In the past two years, our superintendent changed, our board changed, our union leadership changed, and some of our key leaders are retiring. I think that creates some fear in the organization. Everyone wonders, "What's the next big change around the corner?" We all know that we'll be fine, but nobody likes the uncertainty. Given the way things are, especially with the budget, I just feel a lot more in the dark than usual.

Winters reflected on the district's future. "Carl had a bold vision," she said. "How do we keep the vision alive during these times of change and financial retrenchment?"

Looking Ahead

Steinhauser continued to reflect on his first two years as superintendent:

> It's a risk, but I'm putting most of my eggs in the high school basket. We're hitting our high schools from the academic side of the house. I've kept everything that worked for Carl, and the board has been wonderfully supportive.
>
> But, I've been surprised by some of the politics. Even some of the best and brightest are afraid of change and constructive criticism. In a few instances, my faith in mankind has been tested. I've had to learn to pick my battles, and I am still learning how to avoid getting distracted from my main mission: student achievement. For me, the hardest part of the job is the loneliness because I can't share a lot of things with most people. Despite that, this has been enjoyable and rewarding.

Notes

1. See PEL-006, "Long Beach Unified School District (A): Change That Leads to Improvement (1992–2002)," for additional information about district reform efforts.

2. In 2002, the Broad Foundation began awarding this $1 million annual prize to one urban school district judged by education leaders and a review board to be making the greatest overall improvement in student achievement while at the same time reducing the performance gaps between income and ethnic groups. A report from the National Center for Educational Accountability documented Broad's evaluation of LBUSD. See http://www.broadfoundation.org for more information.

3. PELP cases use the convention "SY" to designate, in this instance, school year 2002–2003.

4. This proposal was based on William G. Ouchi, *Making Schools Work* (New York: Simon & Schuster, 2003). See PEL-005, "Pursuing Educational Equity: Aligning Resources at San Francisco Unified School District," for one example of the weighted student formula in use.

5. The changes in board membership began when board member Bonnie Lowenthal was elected to the Long Beach City Council in 2000. Her board seat remained vacant for nearly 10 months before residents elected Suja Lowenthal, her daughter-in-law and a government rela-

tions officer, to complete her unexpired term. Educator Karen Polacheck retired in 2002 after 14 years of board leadership, and her seat was filled by businessman James "Jim" Choura. Then, in early 2003, legendary Long Beach educator Ed Eveland died suddenly after more than 50 years of service to LBUSD, including nearly 11 on the board. In her published tribute to Eveland, board President Bobbie Smith wrote, "Ed had a grand vision for what school could be: school uniforms, the Classical High School, the end of social promotion, higher standards for all kids from all backgrounds." Eveland's supporters were relieved when retired LBUSD principal Jon Meyer assumed his seat in a special election. Finally, Smith, a popular and respected African-American board member, retired at the conclusion of SY04 following 16 years of board leadership. Smith's endorsee, fellow African-American and Dean of Long Beach City College Dr. Felton Williams, won easily in the April 2004 elections. Incumbent Meyer ran unopposed and was reelected. Of the old guard, only 14-year board veteran Mary Stanton, who represented the city's northern district, remained.

6. The Baldrige System aims to provide a systems perspective for understanding performance management. For more information, see the Baldrige National Quality Program Web site at http://www.quality.nist.gov.

7. Technically, schools could select from a state-approved list of curricula, but California's education code specified that schools receiving program improvement, immediate intervention underperforming, or Reading First funds use Open Court. This affected 51 K–5 and eight K–8 schools at LBUSD, though in keeping with past district practices, one high-performing school applied for and received a waiver.

8. Results showed that 68% of the classes of 2005 and 2006 passed the English/Language Arts portion, while 50%–65% passed the math portion (46.6% of the class of 2005 and 59% of the class of 2006 passed both).

Exhibit 1

LBUSD Financial Information, SY99–SY03 ($ million)

This statement includes revenues and expenditures from 14 LBUSD funds, including general, adult, preschool, insurance, cafeteria, and construction funds.

	SY99[a]	SY00	SY01	SY02	SY03
Revenues by Source					
Local[b]	$103.937	$86.489	$91.511	$174.010	$224.429
State[c]	481.287	550.008	617.994	702.749	602.280
Federal Grants	72.122	76.825	86.028	95.496	109.301
Total Revenues	**$657.346**	**$713.322**	**$795.533**	**$972.255**	**$936.010**
Expenditures by Use					
Direct Instruction[d]	$334.498	$377.795	$441.080	$466.163	$478.441
Pupil Support & Site/Central Administration	104.600	112.450	134.727	140.038	132.426
Building Services, Upkeep & Construction	162.060	170.193	190.199	275.782	263.486
Other Expenses[e]	58.710	57.158	62.408	69.925	72.760
Net Transfers/Uses	(2.161)	(2.043)	(2.676)	(2.697)	(2.946)
Total General Expenditures	**$657.707**	**$715.553**	**$825.738**	**$949.211**	**$944.167**
Operating Surplus/(Deficit)	(0.361)	(2.231)	(30.205)	23.044	(8.157)

Source: Compiled by district financial office from LBUSD financial records.

[a] Construction bond approved by local electorate in SY99.

[b] Local property taxes transferred to the state for distribution. This line includes mostly interest prior to SY99, when bond funds became available for distribution.

[c] Includes state (per pupil) appropriation plus categorical program funding.

[d] Ninety percent of LBUSD's general fund, used for K-12 direct instruction, is funded by the state.

[e] Includes books, supplies, contracts, and other operating expenses.

Exhibit 2

LBUSD SY04 Organizational Chart

District Organization 2003-2004

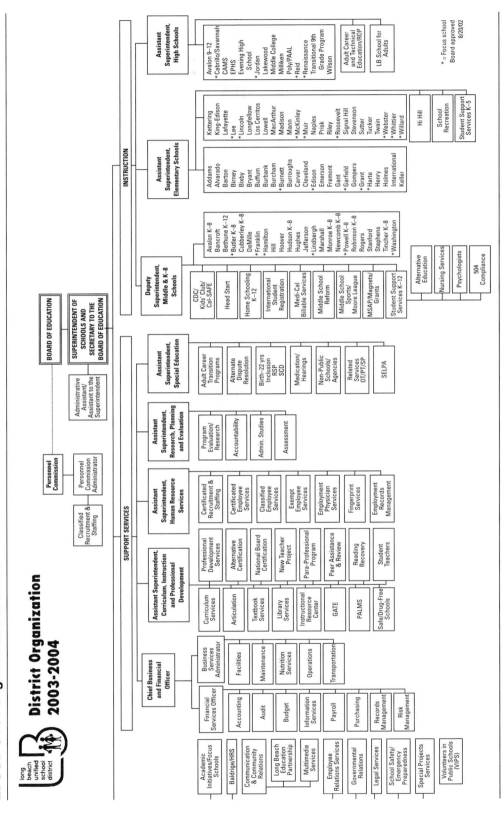

Source: District documents.

Exhibit 3

LBUSD Elementary School Performance on the California State Standards Tests

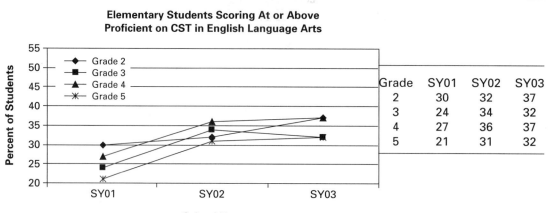

Grade	SY01	SY02	SY03
2	30	32	37
3	24	34	32
4	27	36	37
5	21	31	32

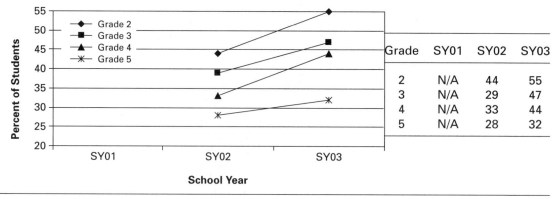

Grade	SY01	SY02	SY03
2	N/A	44	55
3	N/A	29	47
4	N/A	33	44
5	N/A	28	32

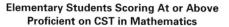

Source: California State Department of Education.

Exhibit 4

LBUSD Middle School Performance on the California State Standards Tests

**Middle School Students Scoring At or Above
Proficient in CST English Language Arts**

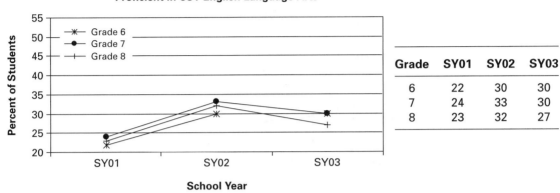

Grade	SY01	SY02	SY03
6	22	30	30
7	24	33	30
8	23	32	27

**Middle School Students Scoring At or Above
Proficient in CST Mathematics**

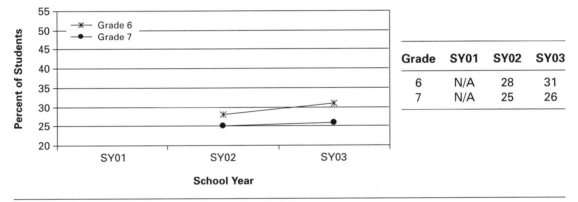

Grade	SY01	SY02	SY03
6	N/A	28	31
7	N/A	25	26

Source: California State Department of Education.

Exhibit 5

California State Academic Performance Index (API): Summary of Base Scores

The California Public Schools Accountability Act, adopted in 1999, required the Department of Education to calculate annual API scores summarizing school performance for public schools, including charter schools. Base scores ranged from 200 to 1,000, and the statewide performance target was 800. Scoring methodology was modified annually.

High Schools	SY04 Enrollment Grades 9–12	SY99	SY00	SY01	SY02	SY03[a]	Change SY99–SY03
Comprehensive							
Cabrillo	2,658	429	434	424	**465**[b]	**502**	73
Jordan	4,135	472	484	496	505	**528**	56
Lakewood	4,393	592	601[c]	609	622[d]	**664**	72
Millikan	4,180	586	595	606	607	**662**	76
Polytechnic	4,684	635	**661**	658	655[d]	**686**	51
Wilson Classical	4,309	582	**623**	629	629	**674**	92
Alternative							
Avalon	241	596	**626**	**654**	**660**	687	91
CAMS	610	909	**912**	904[c,d]	883[c,d]	**929**	20
Savannah Acad (Gr9)	478	468	**524**	531	**550**	639	171
Others[e]	2,184						
Total HS	27,872						

Source: Reported by the California Department of Education at http://api.cde.ca.gov/reports.asp.

[a] In SY03, base scores were calculated by aggregating individual student results from the California Achievement Test, 6th Ed. Survey (all content areas) as measured through national percentile rankings; the California State Standards Tests as measured through performance levels in English Language Arts (ELA), mathematics, history/social science, and science; the California Alternative Performance Assessment (for students with severe cognitive disabilities) as measured through performance levels in ELA and mathematics; and the California State High School Exit Exam as summarized on a pass/no-pass basis. Scores excluded mobile students (those not continually enrolled in the same district from October through the testing date).

[b] **Bold text** indicates eligibility for **Governor's Performance Award.** In SY03, qualifying schools (1) met annual growth targets, (2) demonstrated comparable improvement (as defined by the state) for all numerically significant ethnic and socioeconomically disadvantaged subgroups, (3) raised their overall API score a minimum of five points, (4) raised scores for all subgroups a minimum of four points, and (5) had at least 90% of students participate in STAR testing.

[c] All numerically significant subgroups at the school demonstrated comparable improvement.

[d] School met its schoolwide growth target.

[e] No API results reported for the Educational Partnership HS, Renaissance HS for the Arts, Will J. Reid HS, or the Evening HS. Enrollment calculated from district records.

Exhibit 6

Advanced Placement Enrollment, SY01–SY04

This illustrates the number of students as a percentage of total students enrolled in AP courses.

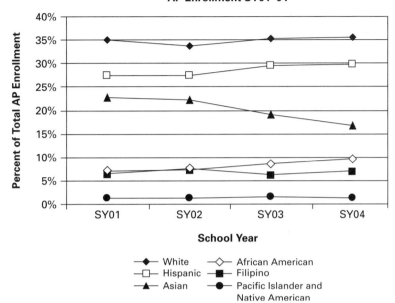

AP Enrollment SY01–04

Legend:
- ◆ White
- ◇ African American
- ☐ Hispanic
- ■ Filipino
- ▲ Asian
- ● Pacific Islander and Native American

Ethnicity	SY01	SY02	SY03	SY04	Percent of K-12 Enrollment SY04[a]
All Students[b]	n=2,291	n=2,443	n=2,556	n=2,715	n=97,560
White	35.1%	33.7%	35.3%	35.5%	16.9%
Hispanic	27.3%	27.5%	29.5%	29.9%	49.0%
Asian	22.9%	22.3%	19.1%	16.7%	9.7%
African-American	7.0%	7.4%	8.7%	9.6%	18.6%
Filipino	6.5%	7.5%	6.3%	7.0%	3.4%
Pacific Islander and Native American	1.2%	1.2%	1.4%	1.3%	2.3%

Source: Compiled from district files.

[a] Ethnicities as reported by the California Department of Education Educational Demographics Unit.

[b] The number of students enrolled in AP courses in each year.

Acknowledgments

Most of the material in this volume, which represents the collective efforts of dozens of people, was developed over a four-year period. It was written by professors and research associates in partnership with leaders and managers who are dealing with real challenges in complex organizations. As coeditors, we have had the privilege of collecting and synthesizing the insights and wisdom of these colleagues, and we want to acknowledge their many contributions.

Of the twenty cases in this collection, seventeen were written as part of the Public Education Leadership Project at Harvard University (PELP) by the four of us and a number of colleagues. Professors James Austin, Nancy Beaulieu, and David Thomas from Harvard Business School (HBS) and professors James Honan, Karen Mapp, Robert Peterkin, and Robert Schwartz of the Harvard Graduate School of Education (HGSE) all coauthored cases with us and with each other. In addition, HBS professor Lynda Applegate gave us permission to use her time-tested "Taco Bell: 1983–1994," and James Heskett, also of HBS, allowed us to use his classic "NYPD New." And from Stanford Graduate School of Business, professor Charles O'Reilly agreed to let us include his case, "Southwest Airlines: Using Human Resources for Competitive Advantage."

Nine urban public school districts participated as full partners in PELP, opening their doors and their stories to us and challenging and sharpening our thinking. These districts include Anne Arundel County and Montgomery County in Maryland; Boston, Massachusetts; Charleston, South Carolina; Chicago, Illinois; Harrisburg, Pennsylvania; Memphis, Tennessee; and San Diego and San Francisco, California. An additional six districts and a global nonprofit organization allowed us to write cases about their managerial challenges, and their willingness to commit many hours of organizational time to our development process was critical to our learning.

Because PELP included field work and teaching along with case development, a number of other faculty members from HBS and HGSE participated in the project, including Tiziana Casciaro, Amy Edmonson, Monica Higgins, Youngme Moon, and Rosabeth Moss Kanter from HBS, and Bob Kegan and Richard Murnane from HGSE. We also want to thank Tilman Freitag from HSGE for the terrific administrative support he provided to the team.

Two other HBS faculty colleagues deserve special mention. Michael Tushman was incredibly helpful to our early work to build a conceptual framework, and David Garvin, among other helpful advice, provided terrific insight into how to structure this volume.

Along with Harvard president Larry Summers, HBS dean Kim Clark and HGSE dean Ellen Lagemann supported the launch of PELP in 2003. Their successors, Jay Light at HBS and Kathleen McCartney at HGSE, provided continuity with their enthusiastic support. We also appreciate the generous support of the Harvard Business School Class of 1963. Under the leadership of Charley Ellis, the Class of 1963 made our work possible with a gift marking their 40th reunion.

The research directors and staff of the HBS Division of Research and Faculty Development provided unwavering support for this unusual cross-school interdisciplinary effort, and we appreciate their willingness to innovate. In particular we would like to thank senior associate deans Krishna Palepu and Debora Spar, as well as Angela Crispi, Rick Melnick, Ann Cichon, and Frank Urso.

Kelly Lawrence provided top-notch administrative support throughout the project, and especially on this book. And last but not least, we offer our deep thanks and admiration to the terrific team of research associates who worked with us on our research and case development efforts, as well as on the construction of this volume. Modupe Akinola, Jennifer Suesse, and Caroline King joined PELP at the beginning and helped us create the intellectual agenda, build relationships with our partner districts, and produce our first teaching cases. When Modupe left for a doctoral program, Tonika Cheek Clayton joined us, and in addition to working on the existing agenda she helped us sharpen our focus on managerial responses to the achievement gap. When Jen moved on, Tiffany Cheng joined just in time to immerse herself in the mountain of work necessary to produce this volume. Each of them had a dedication to the project's mission and an incredible capacity to manage multiple case sites and faculty styles—attributes critical to the quality of the content. Their intellectual contribution to the overall body of work is immeasurable.

Cambridge, Massachusetts
January 2007

About the Editors

Stacey Childress is a Lecturer at Harvard Business School, where she developed and teaches an MBA course called Entrepreneurship in Education. She is a cofounder of the Public Education Leadership Project, a joint initiative of Harvard's graduate schools of business and education. She has authored more than twenty case studies on education enterprises, and is a coauthor, with Richard F. Elmore and Allen S. Grossman, of the bestselling *Harvard Business Review* article, "How to Manage Urban Districts" (November 2006).

Richard F. Elmore is the Gregory R. Anrig Professor of Education Leadership at the Harvard Graduate School of Education. He is on the faculty of the Public Education Leadership Project, jointly run by Harvard's graduate schools of business and education. His most recent publications are *School Reform from the Inside Out: Policy, Practice, and Performance* (2004); *Building a New Structure for School Leadership* (2000); and *When Accountability Knocks, Will Anyone Answer?* (coauthored with C. Abelmann, 1999).

Allen S. Grossman, the MBA Class of 1957 Professor of Management Practice at Harvard Business School, is a faculty cochair of the Public Education Leadership Project, a joint project with the Harvard Graduate School of Education, whose mission is to enhance the quality of leadership and management in urban school districts. Grossman previously served as chief executive officer of Outward Bound USA, where he cofounded a comprehensive school reform model, Expeditionary Learning, implemented in over 130 public schools.

Susan Moore Johnson is the Pforzheimer Professor of Teaching and Learning at the Harvard Graduate School of Education, where she served as academic dean from 1993 to 1999. She studies and teaches about teacher policy, organizational change, and administrative practice. Johnson is a faculty cochair of the Public Education Leadership Project. She is also director of The Project on the Next Generation of Teachers, which examines how best to recruit, support, and retain a strong teaching force over the next decade. She is the author of *Finders and Keepers: Helping New Teachers Survive and Thrive in Our Schools* (2004).